C. VAN EATON

Studies in
Economic Development

STUDIES

IN ECONOMIC

DEVELOPMENT

Bernard Okun
PRINCETON UNIVERSITY

Richard W. Richardson
INTERNATIONAL MONETARY FUND

HOLT, RINEHART AND WINSTON
New York · Chicago · San Francisco · Toronto · London

Preface

This is a book of readings in the subject of economic development. It should be made clear at the outset that by economic development we refer not only to the problems of "underdeveloped countries," now struggling to extricate themselves from the toils of extreme poverty, but to the growth problems of the "advanced countries" as well. While the field is relatively "new"—though, perhaps paradoxically, it is also one of the oldest inquiries of systematic economic thought—interest in economic growth has been sufficiently contagious that since World War II the literature on this subject has reached flood proportions. Since the subject matter is so broad as not to lend itself too well to all-inclusive presentation in a single text, many teachers have preferred to assign to their students a number of specialized books and articles which represent prominent contributions in the field. Unfortunately, this has not been, in our own experience, an easy task, because many good and relevant articles are scattered throughout perhaps a score of journals. To ease this burden, this volume brings together selections on various topics which we consider to be useful and relevant for the student of economic development.

The volume is primarily addressed to an undergraduate audience studying economic development, either in courses exclusively oriented toward this subject or in the increasing number of other courses, in economics, sociology, and history, which are making room for this field in their syllabuses. It is also felt that graduate students may profit from the contents. The selections were made primarily with pedagogic criteria in mind, but happily enough the selections based on these criteria also represent in many cases original contributions by eminent writers in the field.

The plan of the volume is as follows. The introduction, Part One, consists of an essay by Professor Simon Kuznets; it explores some basic causes of the vast differences in levels of economic performance among the countries of the world. Part Two contains the major theories of economic growth spanning virtually the entire history of systematic thought, from Adam Smith to the present. Part Three is devoted to some approaches to the problems of the presently underdeveloped countries and encompasses some of the more controversial issues currently under discussion. Part Four considers some of the structural characteristics of both underdeveloped and advanced countries and changes in these characteristics that occur during the process of growth. In Part Five, a detailed discussion is presented on the meaning of and the problems of measurement inherent in some basic concepts and definitions employed in the field. The articles contained in Part Six consider the roles of the economic "factors of production"—land, labor, capital, and entrepreneurship—in the process of development. In Part Seven, the role of values and institutions in this process is delineated. The selections in Part Eight explore the nature, feasibility, and effectiveness of monetary, fiscal, and other policies, as well as the function of planning, for development. Finally, the concluding selection which comprises Part Nine, by Professor W. Arthur Lewis, poses in dramatic fashion some fundamental philosophical questions about the virtues and drawbacks of economic development.

Though our policy has generally been to minimize editorial interference with the work of the instructor, we have seen fit, in all parts except One, Five, and Nine, to include prefatory material intended to direct the attention of the student to aspects of the subject at hand which seem of particular interest, importance, or difficulty.

Princeton, N. J.   B. O.
January 22, 1961   R. W. R.

Contents

Contents

PART ONE

Introduction

SIMON KUZNETS

||||||||||||||||||||||||||||||||||||||||||||||||||||||||||||||||||||||||||||||||||||||||||||||||||||||||||||||||||||||||||||||||||||||||||||||||||||||||||||||||||||||||

International Differences
In Income Levels

Reflections on Their Causes

INTRODUCTION

Recent changes in the world scene have produced a feeling of greater involvement of all countries with each other, a keener interest in their diverse economic and social structures and functions. When events in a remote corner of the globe affect the lives and destinies of people thousands of miles away, we cannot easily retain the feelings of separateness and independence that may have characterized our thinking half a century ago. Concurrently, the closer linking of the world, in peace and in war, in international organization and in military conflict, has resulted in more information and in a greater effort to reduce the apparent qualitative differences in life around the globe to some comparable, measurable basis. The marked recent increase in quantitative data on population, health, food supply, industrial production, and income is in response to a natural urge to measure the similarities and differences in the social and economic structures of various nations; and to provide for national and international policy a more reliable basis than can be supplied by impressions of travelers, qualitative accounts of historians, or appraisals of geographers.

The increasing number of countries for which national income is estimated and the attention in recent years to international comparisons of income levels, are thus only one strand in the whole fabric of the study of the world framework of human society. This particular way of learning about mankind is still in its early stages. True, several international compilations and comparisons were made in the nineteenth century; and even, though on a much cruder basis, in the late seventeenth. But by current standards, the earlier compilations and comparisons have at most only suggestive value and are often misleading as indications of orders of magnitude. Even today, a critical examination reveals unreliability and inadequacy in a goodly portion of the current measures, which are so misleading in the impression of quantitative

From *Bolétin del Banco Central de Venezuela*, Nos. 65-66 (July-August 1950), pp. 20-36. Reprinted by permission of the publisher and the author. This article also appears in Simon Kuznets, *Economic Change* (New York, 1953), pp. 216-252.

3

precision that any figure suggests. Unless civilization suffers a serious relapse, the comparisons we draw today may look as crude to scholars fifty or a hundred years from now as the nineteenth-century comparisons look to us. We should bear this qualification in mind and not attribute too much significance to minor quantitative differences or draw unwarranted conclusions from the estimates. Even if we accept the qualifications, our interpretations may well prove superficial in the long run, chiefly because our accumulation of information concerning the various parts of world society is still in an almost embryonic stage.

Nevertheless, the data on income levels in various countries are already sufficient for at least a rough picture of the differences and of the associated social and economic characteristics. And there has been enough speculation and assertion about the causes of these differences to merit a review. The notes that follow are, as indicated by the subtitle, reflections on the theme— not results of a thorough analysis. But they may serve the useful purpose of stimulating further thinking on this important subject; and, possibly, of suggesting directions of further data collection and analysis that may prove fruitful.

A BRIEF STATISTICAL PICTURE

We begin our discussion with a brief statistical picture of international differences in income levels. More as a matter of convenience than because of the greater accuracy of the figures, I use here the compilation made by United States Department of State in laying the foundation for its Point Four program. These figures have several advantages: they refer to a prewar year (1939) relatively free of the disturbances and havoc of World War II; cover 53 countries which together account for about 85 percent of the world's population; and provide data not only on income but also on various other characteristics. I have used the figures in the State Department report as given, supplementing them only by approximations to the shares of nonagricultural sectors.

The income figures are in U.S. dollars, without correction for differences, in purchasing power and minor conceptual dissimilarities. Since for many of the 53 countries the statistical basis for estimates is exceedingly thin, minor differences can be attributed little significance and the specific ranking of the countries is also to be disregarded. Only the major contrasts among the groups of countries are important for the present purposes. They can be summarized as follows:

1. There are marked differences in per capita income levels among broad groups of countries. Even if the differences are exaggerated by peculiarities of income measurement,[1] and we should reduce the income ratio from over

---

[1] See the author's National Income and Industrial Structure, presented at the International Statistical Conferences in Washington, U.S.A., in September 1947.

10 to 1 (groups I to III) to perhaps 6 to 1, the range of differences is still substantial. These differences are not just a matter of a single year or two, but characterize the long-term income levels of the various countries.

2. The figures for the 53 countries in the table relate to only 85 percent of the world's population. The remainder (except the population of such countries as Spain, Portugal, and Turkey which might fall in group II) would probably fall in group III, since it is for the economically less developed countries of the world that statistics are lacking. The exceptional position of group I, with about one sixth of the world's population and over six tenths of the world's income, would be even more conspicuous were it possible to include the rest of the world. The position of group III, with almost seven tenths of the world's population but only about one fifth to one quarter of the world's income would be similarly accentuated.[2]

3. These differences measured by such a comprehensive *monetary* index as income per capita are corroborated by measures reflecting quantities of goods. The food supply per capita, especially if we deal with the more qualitatively select types, is, in group III, from one third to one fifth of that in group I; and the consumption of textiles per capita shows similar contrasts. Were data available on other consumer goods, more reflective of quality differences, the contrast would be even greater. In short, after allowances for roughness in measurement, real income levels per capita in group I (with one sixth of the world's population) and in group III (with almost two thirds of the world's population) must still be in the ratio of about 6 to 1.

4. These differences in real income level are associated with different patterns of population growth. The high-income-level countries have, on the whole, a low growth potential (low birth and death rates); whereas countries in group III have high growth potentials. An increase in per capita income levels in any country is contingent upon a rate of growth in total output exceeding that of population, unless the latter can be reduced by emigration. It will be thus seen that the problem of raising the low per capita income levels in group III countries is aggravated by its high growth pattern of population. Another correlate is the degree of literacy of population—high in group I and low in group III, with group II in the middle.

5. Differences in income level are also associated with differences in industrial structure, as revealed by the shares of nonagricultural industries in total income (line 9) and investment in industry per worker (line 11). Clearly the low income levels in countries in group III are connected with preponderance of agriculture in the economic structure, low levels of productivity in agriculture, low rates of industrial investment, low consumption of energy, and an undeveloped transportation system reflected in railroad mileage and freight carried. The opposites of these characteristics typify countries in group I. The list of characteristics of the national economies each viewed as

---

[2] Colin Clark's data for 1924-1935 in his *Conditions of Economic Progress* (London, 1940) yield similar results.

INTERNATIONAL DIFFERENCES IN PER CAPITA INCOME AND RELATED MEASURES, 53 COUNTRIES, 1939

	Groups of Countries by Per Capita Income				
	I	II	IIIa	IIIb	III
1. Per capita income (U.S.A. $)	461	154	86	31.5	41
2. Percent of total population	20	16	11	53	64
3. Percent of total income	64	18	6	12	18
4. Per capita income, index	100	33	19	7	9
5. Average population type	1.1	1.5	2.8	3.0	2.9
6. Expectation of life at birth (index)	100	82	..	..	63
7. Physicians per 1000 population (index)	100	73	..	..	16
8. Percent literate (index)	100	77	..	..	20
9. Percent of total income from nonagricultural industries	84	71	68	46	59
10. Average income of population dependent on agriculture (index)	100	39	..	..	8
11. Investment in industry per worker (index)	100	39	..	..	11
12. Energy consumed per day (Horsepower hours per capita, index)	100	24	..	..	5
13. Miles of railroads (per 1000 square miles of area, index)	100	72	..	..	32
14. Annual freight carried (ton miles per capita, index)	100	60	..	..	4
15. Daily per capita food supply (indexes)					
All foods (calories)	100	92	..	..	72
Animal proteins (oz.)	100	56	..	..	18
Fats (oz.)	100	57	..	..	32
16. Net annual consumption of textiles (lb. per capita, index)	100	40	..	..	26

Notes to Table

All entries, except for line 9, from *Point Four* (U. S. Department of State, publication 3719, released January 1950, Appendix C, pp. 103-124).

Groups of countries distinguished in the columns of the table are by size of per capita income. The following countries, arranged in declining order of per capita income, are included in each group:

   I (per capita income over $200): United States, Germany, United Kingdom, Switzerland, Sweden, Australia, New Zealand, Canada, Netherlands, Denmark, France, Norway, Belgium, Eire, Argentina.

  II (per capita income from $101 through $200): Union of South Africa, Finland, Chile, Austria, USSR, Italy, Greece, Czechoslovakia, Hungary, Bulgaria.

IIIa (per capita income from $51 through $100): Cuba, Yugoslavia, Poland, Japan, Venezuela, Egypt, Palestine, Costa Rica, Colombia, Peru, Panama, Ceylon, Mexico, Uruguay, Dominican Republic.

a productive framework could be expanded, but the few given in the table are sufficient to indicate the major differences.

ASSOCIATION AND CAUSATION

In considering the factors that determine international differences in income levels of the magnitude just revealed, it is a natural tendency to treat the associated characteristics as at least in part causative. If this tendency is carried to its fullest extent, it can be said that income levels in countries in group III are low *because* the population follows the pattern of high birth rates and high death rates; or because the population is illiterate; or because agriculture, which tends to be a low income industry, is preponderant, and secondary and tertiary industries (to use Colin Clark's terminology) are unimportant; or because industrial investment per worker is low; etc. It also follows from these statements that the way to get a higher level of income per capita is to change the population pattern; or shift working population from agriculture into nonagricultural sectors; or increase industrial investment per capita. Indeed, much of the discussion of industrialization of underdeveloped countries smacks of such identification of associated characteristics with causal factors.[3]

There is undoubtedly some truth in this interpretation. A population with high birth and death rates is handicapped as a body of economic pro-

---

[3] This is certainly the impression given by Colin Clark in *The Economics of 1960* (London, 1944) and by Louis Bean in International Industrialization and Per Capita Income, *Income and Wealth Studies,* Vol. 8 (New York, National Bureau of Economic Research, 1946)—to mention but two authors.

IIIb (per capita income from $22 through $50): Haiti, Nicaragua, Guatemala, Bolivia, Honduras, El Salvador, Brazil, Ecuador, Paraguay, India, Philippines, China, Indonesia.

All averages used in the table are, unless otherwise indicated, weighted arithmetic means. For entries other than income and population type data may be for fewer countries, especially in group III, than listed above.

Population types are identified as follows:

Type 1. Low growth potential. Birth rates below 25 per 1000. Low death rates. Small natural increase with prospect of relatively stationary population in the future.

Type 2. Transitional growth. Birth rates 25-35 per 1000. Both birth and death rates generally falling. Rapid population growth.

Type 3. High growth potential. Birth rates over 35 per 1000. Death rates (but not birth rates) generally declining. Rapid growth in absence of civil disturbance, famine, and epidemic.

The entries in line 5 are unweighted arithmetic means of entries for each country, given separately in the source.

Line 9 is based on data in *National Income Statistics, 1938-47,* and *National Income Statistics, 1938-48,* both published by the Statistical Office of the United Nations (in 1948 and 1950 respectively), supplemented for one or two countries by Colin Clark, *Conditions of Economic Progress* (London, 1940). In general, the ratios are for 1939 or the year closest to it, within a decade either way. The entries are unweighted arithmetic means for 13 countries in group I, 8 in group II, 6 in group IIIa, and 5 in group IIIb. Weighting by total income for each country would have produced even more striking differences.

ducers, if only because high mortality, particularly concentrated in the infant ages, means an exceedingly wasteful pattern of life—with energies of parents devoted to raising children of whom only a few reach productive ages. It is equally obvious that an illiterate population is more handicapped than a literate one in developing productive skills. Likewise a larger stock of productive capital is a prerequisite of high productivity. Somewhat less obvious is the relevance of industrial structure, i.e., the preponderance of nonagricultural industries. That agricultural industries per se are no less productive than nonagricultural ones is, of course, evident from a comparison of agricultural productivity in the United States or in New Zealand with say, the productivity of labor in manufacturing in India or China. But one can argue that greater industrial *diversification,* which implies a smaller share in the national economy of any single group of industries such as agriculture, is a factor making for higher over-all productivity since it permits a more balanced use of technical advances in a variety of industrial sectors.

But even if the above arguments are granted, the significance of these factors as *causes* of international income differentials is still to be considered. Taken in and of themselves, out of the full context of all aspects of social and economic life, differences in birth and death rates would scarcely have much effect on per capita productivity; and this may also be true of literacy, especially when one considers how superficial its level is even in the economically advanced countries of the world. And one certainly can ask whether the approach to industrial structure suggested above and implicit in many writings on industrialization of underdeveloped countries does not put the cart before the horse; income is not high *because* a smaller share of the nation's economy is accounted for by agriculture and is not low because of the preponderance of agriculture, but in certain countries agriculture accounts for a smaller share *because* income is high and in other countries agriculture predominates because over-all productivity is low. The reduction in the share of agriculture accompanying a rise in over-all productivity is due partly to the permissive factor of a higher level of productivity in agriculture itself; and partly to the inducive factor that when the standard of living rises, human tastes are such that the proportion of agricultural products wanted declines and that of products of other industries rises. Quantitative proof of the former statement is supplied by the table where the contrast in productivity of population dependent on agriculture between countries in groups I and III is even greater than the contrast in per capita total income (compare lines 10 and 4). The second proposition, decline in the proportion of agricultural products wanted with rise in per capita income above a certain level, is demonstrated in any cross-section analysis of consumer budgets at a given point of time, where the proportion of income spent on food and clothing (the former particularly being an agricultural product) declines sharply as we pass from the low to the upper income groups.

What was just said of the industrial structure of the economy as a *consequence* of reaching certain over-all productivity levels is also applicable to other characteristics. Literacy is perhaps as much, if not more, a consequence as it is a cause of high income levels; and the same is true of capital accumulation, industrial and otherwise. Population patterns with low birth rates and low death rates, too, are just as much consequences of a higher standard of living and higher income levels as their cause. Certainly in the historical development of countries during the last 150-200 years the rise in over-all productivity came first, followed by reduced death rates and then with a substantial delay, birth rates, increased literacy, capital accumulation, etc.

Because of this interaction of income level and other characteristics, the *statistical association* between them is no basis for assuming that these characteristics are causative factors. The increasing emphasis on quantitative measurement in international comparisons naturally makes it easy to translate close statistical association into significant causal relationships. In view of the continuous interplay of income levels and these associated characteristics, in which the former rather than the latter is often the determining variable, this simple translation is a logical trap that should be avoided lest it lead to intellectual sterility and to a dangerously mechanistic approach to policy implications.

Two conclusions can, I believe, be safely drawn from the discussion so far. (1) Factors such as population growth pattern, literacy, industrial structure, and capital investment are of *some* importance in determining international differences in levels of income. But their importance, per se, is much more limited than their close statistical association with per capita income suggests. Their *net* effect, if it could be measured, might account for but a small part of existing differences, and therefore leave much room for further search and explanation. (2) These characteristics are associated with income levels, both as causes and consequences, and together, with many others not specifically indicated in the table, form an interrelated complex. All policy measures to raise per capita income levels are implicitly steps in producing the whole complex into being, and should be so viewed. They must, therefore, be conceived as measures designed to raise income levels, *and* to change population patterns, *and* to increase levels of literacy, *and* to permit a different industrial structure of the economy, etc. The realization of the extent to which per capita income level is only a symbol of a whole socio-economic complex of conditions is important for any intelligent policy approach, as well as for analysis of causes.

"NATURAL" FACTORS

Since mankind is part and parcel of a physical world, a biological species living in conditions provided by nature, it seems reasonable to ask whether economic differences among human societies are not reducible to differences in either natural environment or biological characteristics. The temptation to look for such "natural" factors is great: if it were found that such factors beyond human control determine international differences in say income levels, the difficulty of disentangling the interrelated complex of economic and other social phenomena could be avoided. The finding of such "natural" factors would also provide solace to minds and hearts of men who are perturbed by many aspects of human society but are reluctant to face or despair of the painful task of amelioration: if these troubles could be charged to inexorable nature (as they used to be charged to inscrutable ways of Divine Providence), man could only bow to fate in the spirit of sadness and resignation.

Whatever the reasons, and some of them are warranted in the light of empirical observations, natural factors such as climate, topography, presumptive biological characteristics of particular groups of mankind (races, etc.) have appeared recurrently in attempts to explain international differences in political, social, and economic structures. On the surface, they also seem relevant to international differences in income levels. Without presuming to treat them adequately, we discuss them under two heads: (1) location-race factors; (2) irreproducible economic resources.

1. By location-race we mean factors represented by climatic-land aspects of the location of human societies, or by the presumptive biological characteristics of one human group as distinct from another. While differences in climatic and land conditions of various human societies are obvious and the so-called racial characteristics are subject to dispute and doubt, for purposes of discussion here, we take both for granted, and inquire whether they can be of significance in determining international differences in income levels.

The answer would seem to me largely in the negative, for two obvious but often neglected reasons. The first is the striking disparity in time between the location-race factors and their presumed consequences—international differences in economic performance. Climatic and land conditions at a given spot of the globe change exceedingly slowly on the scale of history of human society. Few significant changes in climate or state of the land have occurred within the five thousand years covered by the known historical stretch of human society (except those caused by man himself, in which case they are hardly "natural" factors). Yet economic performance in many parts of the globe has changed rapidly. Indeed, only a few portions of the globe have not been, at some time, at least quite high on the relative scale of economic performance, if not in the vanguard. Certainly, China and India, now classified among the lower of the countries in group III, were in this category; and the same is true of some of the predecessors of the present Latin American republics. As historical knowledge increases, we find more examples of outstanding economic and social performance in the past in places far outside the present orbit of economic leadership. Of course, there may be areas on the globe where climatic and land conditions are forbiddingly difficult, e.g., in the Arctic Circle. But the contribution of these factors to the explanation of current, or even of past, international differences in income levels is obviously small.

Exactly the same argument applies to presumptive racial characteristics and differences. Even if we accept for purposes of discussion the dubious proposition that innate, biological differences exist among various sectors of mankind, the time span of these differences—because they are assumed to be innate and biological—is exceedingly long on the scale of human history. Yet no matter what racial, etc. groups have been identified during the known historical stretch of human society, each has at some time or other been among the economically advanced societies: the Mongol race during China's leadership; the American Indians during the Mayan and Incan civilizations; the Negro races in some of the Ethiopian, Egyptian, and Berber kingdoms; the Semitic races through much of human history. I do not feel competent to pursue this subject in detail, nor is such detail needed here. The time spans between the location-race factors and interspatial or intergroup differences in economic and social performance are obviously too great for the former to play a significant part as a determinant of the latter.

But, granted this disparity, one may still contend that the location-race factors may be significant in that they effect genuine differences in natural conditions, thus limiting the adoption of methods by which high incomes are *currently* attained. To illustrate, assume that high levels are achieved only with the kind of exertion that is possible in temperate climates alone; or only by scientific endeavor, the capacity for which is claimed by some to be limited to the white races.

The speciousness of this argument is revealed by the second broad consideration that should lead us to deny much significance to location-race factors. Any historical distinctiveness in recent methods of attaining high income levels lies in the enormously increased power of man, developed by a diversified system of empirical science. Climatic and land conditions, as obstacles to human effort, are much less forbidding today than in the past; and the very growth of human technology means that location factors are less important today than they may have been in periods of more primitive technology. Likewise, the varieties of mental effort and capacity that go into the technology of today are much greater than they may have been in the past, so that it is even more doubtful today than it ever was, that some presumptive differences in innate, biological characteristics of different groups of mankind significantly affect the acceptance and use of the diversified corpus of modern economic practices.

Dismissing the race factor as an empirically unestablished element and confining our attention to the obvious location differences in climatic and other conditions, we reach two conclusions. (*a*) Location factors, in the current and recent past state of technology and human knowledge, could not, in and of themselves, have contributed materially to international differences in income levels. Whatever difficulties natural conditions presented could, for the most part, presumably have been overcome by concentration upon the problem of human ingenuity and science. (*b*) The natural conditions of many countries in group III are no more unfavorable to high income levels than those of many countries in group I. It would be difficult, for example, to demonstrate that nature per se is much less favorable in China than in Sweden or Australia; or that it is so much more favorable in England than in Mexico. At any rate, the burden of proof is upon the proponents of such theories; and no proof has been provided that takes full cognizance of the potentialities of human technology in dealing with even the most unfavorable aspects of land or climate.

2. The discussion above touched only implicitly upon a natural factor that is important in many analyses of international differences in economic performance—the supply of such irreproducible productive factors as cultivable land and minerals. Economic technology always, and modern economic technology is no exception, leans heavily upon extraction of certain irreproducible resources from the earth; and it has been claimed that a poor supply of such resources, *relative* to existing population, is a major factor in explaining low per capita income levels, and a rich supply relative to existing population, high income levels.

This claimed dependence of international differences in economic performance upon the relative supply of irreproducible resources cannot be examined in great detail here. The reflections that follow lead to a somewhat more critical view of this dependence than usually prevails, and suggest the limitations of the hypothesis adopted.

(*a*) "Economic resource" is a concept relative to a given state of technology. Until man learned to use coal for heating a steam engine or smelting iron ore, it was a domestic consumer good but hardly an important industrial fuel. When man learns to grow his food in trays of synthetic chemicals, the importance of land as a resource for the production of food will dwindle. Examples abound of many hitherto important economic resources that have lost almost all importance, and of many formerly unimportant or valueless parts of the earth that have recently become exceedingly valuable. Even more telling are cases of relative scarcity in the past of some irreproducible resource, strategic within the framework of an older technology, that have been overcome not by finding more of the scarce resource but by a change in technology and substitution of a new resource, more plentiful, and usually more effective. The conspicuous case, which in a sense laid the basis for modern economic technology, was the way the Industrial Revolution overcame the shortage of wood, as both fuel and industrial material, and of animal and wind power. More recent cases are the substitution of fixed nitrogen for natural guano and of synthetic for natural rubber. Hence, any emphasis on relative scarcity of irreproducible resources, as a factor in determining low levels of economic performance extending over a *long* period, must be countered with the question why no successful effort has been made by the victim of such scarcity to overcome it by changes in technology. To be retained, the hypothesis must, therefore, be rephrased: the have-not societies are poor because they have not succeeded in overcoming scarcity of natural resources by appropriate changes in technology, not because the scarcity of resources is an inexorable factor for which there is no remedy. And obviously human societies with low levels of economic performance are least able to overcome any scarcities of irreproducible resources by changes in technology; but this is a matter of social organization and not of bountifulness or niggardliness of nature.

(*b*) Our knowledge of the supply of irreproducible economic resources is inadequate. This is true even of resources that, because of their strategic importance, have been investigated and explored most intensively—as the continuous upward revisions of world supply of petroleum clearly indicate. It is even more true of minerals that have not been as intensively explored; and may also be true of the oldest resource available, viz., cultivable land, the knowledge of whose chemical and other properties is a recent addition to the stock of scientific information. This limitation of data on irreproducible resources, data that can be amassed only by considerable effort and by application of technical skill and knowledge—all scarce in the underdeveloped countries—is, unfortunately, greater for these countries, so that shortage biases are likely to be greatest for just the countries with low income levels. It follows that all our current estimates of the supply of irreproducible economic resources are slanted to minimize the supply in countries in groups II and III compared with the estimates for the developed countries in group I.

(*c*) The irreproducible economic resources that do exist in the countries with low income levels are not used as effectively as those in countries with higher income levels. Statistical support for this statement is readily available, ranging from measures of yield per acre of land for agricultural crops to comparisons of the rate of extraction of mineral resources with their estimated deposits. We cite one illustration, of interest because of its broad coverage. Recently, Professor A. P. Usher prepared estimates of world resources of mechanical energy (represented by reserves of oil, coal, and water power) as well as world output of such energy (extraction for minerals and production for water power).[4] From these estimates, largely for 1939, the proportionate shares of countries in groups I, II, and III were calculated, after allocating roughly to group III the countries not included in our table but covered by Professor Usher (except for Turkey, Spain, Portugal, and Rhodesia which were placed in group II). Countries in group I accounted for 44 percent of total world stock of mechanical energy resources; in group II for 19 percent; and in group III for 37 percent. The index of per capita stock of energy resources was, therefore, measured by about 2.5 in group I; 1.25 in group II; and 0.5 in group III. The contrast in relative supply between groups I and III is thus measured by a ratio of 5 to 1.

But the range in energy *consumed* per day per capita between groups I and III is much wider than that—about 20 to 1 (see table above, line 12). Moreover, Professor Usher's data indicate that in terms of production of mechanical energy resources (extraction, not use) group I accounts for 73 percent of the world total, group II for 12, and group III for only 15 percent. That production by countries in group I of 73 percent of the current supply, with a resources share of only 44 percent, indicates that their rate of extraction relative to stock is much greater than in the world at large. It would, of course, be theoretically just as possible for countries in group III to extract

---

[4] See his summary in "The Resource Requirements of an Industrial Economy," *The Tasks of Economic History,* 1947 Supplement to the *Journal of Economic History* (New York, 1948), pp. 35-46.

their irreproducible resources at a greater rate than the world at large, i.e., they could compensate for a smaller supply by drawing upon it at a faster rate. Yet their extraction rate is much lower—an indication that under existing circumstances and for some time to come an absolute shortage of irreproducible resources is *not* a limiting factor.[5]

(*d*) Finally, many industries and economic activities do not need irreproducible natural resources; and if they are needed, a country with a scarce supply can presumably secure them in trade, given a minimum network of international economic relations. England developed a flourishing cotton textile industry, without possessing the basic natural conditions for producing the raw material; and the same is true of the rubber product industries of the economically advanced countries of the world. To claim strategic significance for the relative supply of irreproducible resources is unwarranted, so long as many industries do not need them; and so long as international trading relations permit one country to compensate for shortage in irreproducible resources by specialization in other sectors of economic production.

All these arguments should not be interpreted as denying that under given conditions of technology, the possession of a large stock of natural resources by a country is an economic advantage; and the complete absence of such resources a disadvantage. They are intended to suggest only that, in explaining *long-term* international differences in levels of income, the relative supply of irreproducible resources is not a dominating factor; that our data on the presumptive relative scarcity of such resources in the underdeveloped countries are faulty to the point of being misleading; that in fact countries in group III fail, by a wide margin, to utilize the stock of resources which they do possess; and that, after full allowance for this factor is made, there is still a wide range of international differences in income levels to be explained.[6]

THE FACTOR OF SIZE

International comparisons are almost always in terms of the existing nation-states that differ widely in size, whether size is in terms of area, population, or some economic magnitude. Thus the list of 53 states distinguished

---

[5] It is somewhat misleading to deal with all countries in group III (or groups II and I) as a unit, since within each group, energy resources are unevenly distributed among the individual countries. But the general tenor of the argument would remain the same were we to deal with individual countries (e.g., China and India); and so long as the statements made in the text are not literally translated as applying to *every single* country in group III (or in the other groups), no harm is done.

[6] Specific figures in Professor Usher's tables suggest that the supply of irreproducible resources in many smaller countries in group III accounts for an income level *higher* than it would otherwise have been. In many, the fortunate existence of deposits of strategic raw materials (particularly petroleum) results in an active interest of firms from industrially advanced countries and in a higher level of national income than would otherwise be the case. Most common references to shortages of natural resources are to those of coal and iron. But a fairly high level of income can be attained without them, if only peaceful economic life is considered; and as a general rule, most of the large countries in group III have such resources but fail to utilize them at sufficiently high rates.

in the data underlying the table, includes huge units like India and China, each with over 350 million of population; and relatively small units like New Zealand and El Salvador, with less than 2 million each. Is the mere factor of size important in determining levels of economic performance per capita?

The question implies that even with international trade and other flows across boundaries, the existence of a separate state organization means at least partial isolation of the economic complex, barriers to an easy flow of goods and resources. Even if we assumed a world of free trade and free movement of capital and people, the several states, with their different languages and historical and cultural traditions, are societies that think of themselves as different and separate from each other; and economic flows among them, even in the absence of legal restrictions, would not be easy because of these barriers of language and different historical antecedents. If we add the realistic consideration of barriers to migration either of men or of capital and the various impediments in the way of a free flow of goods that are in fact created by a separatist state organization, we must conclude that the state structure does result in separate units, whose existence, because of the obstacles to free economic flow that they impose, may be an important factor in determining differences in over-all economic productivity.

This inference as to the possible importance of size of state in producing interstate differences in levels of economic performance is re-enforced by somewhat more specific arguments. First, some industries associated with modern technology require a minimum size of market to warrant the application of efficient methods of mass production. In such industries, e.g., iron and steel, aluminum, automobiles, shipbuilding, etc., the scale of units is quite large. For a country with a small population and a correspondingly small domestic market, such industries are feasible only if they can count, in the long run, on relatively free access to markets outside their country's boundaries. Under existing and even past conditions of the world, such access is precarious. It follows that countries below a certain minimum size cannot develop such industries (except sometimes at extra cost), and take advantage of some of the more advanced methods of economic production.

Second, some industries *must* locate within a country's boundaries, since no substitution for their products by imports is feasible. This is obviously true of the industry represented by the state itself and of industries rooted in the country's area and population (e.g., educational and other services, the construction industry, and the like). If we add the need for other domestically located industries induced by a desire to be independent of unreliable sources outside (particularly in case of disruption of normal channels of international intercourse), it is clear that a *minimum* complex of industries must be maintained within the state, and will be maintained regardless of size (excluding splinter units like Monaco or Luxemburg). But if the state has a small population, the need for a diverse industrial structure may well lead to an uneconomic scale of operation in many industries—even when the latter, unlike the giants of the type discussed in the preceding paragraph, have an absolutely low optimum scale of operation.

On the other hand, a small state may enjoy some advantages. It is easier for a small than for a large state to find a favorable position in the interstices of international economy. It is easier for a Norway, a Denmark, or a Switzerland, by taking advantage of some of its resources, to attain a high level of income per capita than it would be for a bigger state unit, say of the population dimensions of Italy, let alone a huge one like China. Also, it may be easier for a small state to achieve the degree of internal unity and cohesion of the population which so facilitates economic progress and prevents sharp internal conflicts from developing. On general grounds, one cannot assert that, given a relatively peaceful state of international relations, the balance of advantages is definitely against the small and in favor of the larger state unit. Such a negative conclusion would certainly be safe if we excluded the extreme ranges in size—the tiny units in which the basis for economic independence is almost completely absent and the huge units in which the problem of economic and social organization is of grave magnitude indeed.

In the light of this discussion, we can look at the figures and see what they suggest. For the 53 countries covered in the table the level of per capita income can be correlated with the size of the country as measured by its population. The coefficient of rank correlation (used to avoid the assumption of normality in the distribution of units by size or by per capita income),[7] calculated for all 53 countries is + 0.18, indicating some positive association between level of per capita income and population size; but not large enough to be significant. However, if we exclude India and China, where huge population masses are associated with very low per capita incomes, the coefficient rises to + 0.30, a value which for the 51 countries is statistically significant. If we could include more state units, the positive correlation might be even closer, because most of the additional units would be both small and characterized by low levels of per capita income.

There is thus some statistical evidence, for states below the line of huge population units, of a positive association between per capita income levels and size. In general, the larger the state, the higher its per capita income. But the association is far from close. Even as a purely statistical result, it may be shaky: there are altogether too many notable exceptions. While the factor of size in and of itself may contribute to international differences in income levels, at the present stage of our knowledge and analysis, no great weight can be attributed to it.

However, the importance of size as a factor may well be increasing. For the growing cleavage among states in the world today may mean that the disadvantages of small size may be sharply and catastrophically increasing. Indeed, within the orbit of the USSR these disadvantages are so great that small states as separate entities are fast disappearing. Where they remain, the restrictions on normal international economic intercourse may mean a serious deterioration in the relative position of small states, which may be only

---

[7] The formula used is 1—6 (Sum of d)^2/n (n^2—1), where d is the difference in ranks and n the number of pairs of items in the comparison.

partially counteracted by already observable efforts to merge them—for some purposes—into larger units.

A HISTORICAL VIEW

The limitations of the analysis developed so far, and the meagerness of its contribution to the explanation of international differences in income levels, may well be due to the author's ignorance or prejudice. But it may also result from the restriction of the analysis to *cross-section association* of income levels with other variables, and hence to its neglect of the historical antecedents of these levels. All the units whose economic performance we are comparing for a given year or decade are results of a long process of historical development; and our comparison is thus a cross-section in the stream of historical change, with divergent trends and different levels at whatever point we start tracing these trends. The question to which we seek the answer might be illuminated if we view the broad trends in historical development of which the current income levels are the outcome. Such a view, while necessarily superficial, may lead to certain broad conclusions that would provide at least a framework for a potentially more fruitful inquiry into the problem.

The suggestions yielded by such a broad historical view are stated *seriatim* without any effort at detailed documentation.

1. First, the range of international differences in income levels must be much wider today than it was say 150 to 200 years ago. This impression cannot be corroborated statistically, since our measures do not reach that far back; but its plausibility follows from the current figures. In countries in group III per capita income levels are close to minimum subsistence and it is clear that it would have been *physically* impossible for past income levels to be a fraction of the current levels in any country in group III. By contrast, per capita levels in countries in group I are far above any minimum subsistence and the more developed countries in the past (not necessarily those that are now in group I) could well have had income levels that are fractions of those now prevailing in group I. We know, in fact, that in the countries in group I the past century to a century and a half were marked by rapid growth in income per capita. And it is plausible to assume that the low per capita incomes in countries in group III are not due to an *absolute* decline of income levels during the last century or two; or that whatever secular decline in real per capita income occurred was relatively small. We can thus infer that the range in per capita income levels was much narrower about two centuries ago than it is today. To illustrate: if in countries in group III (allowing for the shift in identity) per capita levels two centuries ago were at the lowest say 50 percent of the present, about $20, and if in countries in group I (again allowing for shift in identity) per capita levels were say one seventh of the present, $65, the range narrows from over 10 to 1 to about

3 to 1. The narrowing of range in fact may well have been greater than in this illustration.

To put it differently, much of the current international spread in income levels is due to diversities among countries in the rate of growth of per capita income during the last 150-200 years: in some countries per capita income grew quite rapidly, in others very slowly if at all. Therefore, from a starting point of more equal levels, marked inequalities in per capita income have developed. Hence, current international differences in per capita income may be due in large part to diversities in the rate of growth of per capita income during the past two centuries. What factors induced and permitted some countries to attain a high rate of growth in per capita income, and why were the same or similar factors not operative in other countries?

2. The use of a span of one and a half to two centuries in the preceding section is not an accident: history suggests that the factors that operated in some countries and not in others are those associated with the "industrial system"—a concept used to designate a wide application of knowledge, based on empirical science, to the problem of economic and social technology. It is the adoption of the industrial system, combined with certain social and political concomitants, that is at the basis of the rapid growth of per capita income in some countries. And the industrial system dates from one and a half to two centuries ago.

It is important to emphasize here that, given an organization of the world into separate and competing states, there is *bound* to be inequality in the rate of spread of any new type of economic and social mode of life; and, consequently, inequality in levels of economic performance among countries. If a new economic system is ushered in, it certainly will not be "invented" and adopted simultaneously in all the countries of the world: such simultaneity could be attained only by some planned imposition of the change by a single world authority. The new type of economy, the secular innovation, will necessarily arise first in one or two countries in which historical antecedents and pressures combine to break through the crust of the existing economic and social habits toward a new and more productive mode of operation. Given this limitation of the origin of a secular innovation to one or a few countries, and its slow spread to others; given the significance of the secular innovation as a basis for a higher per capita income, it follows that its gradual spread across the face of the globe means *at any given time* differences in income levels among various countries—associated with the degree to which these countries have adopted the new and more productive mode of operation.

Economic history of the longer lived human societies provides several examples of this process of initial limited impact and then gradual, uneven spread of secular innovations. The successive effects of the discovery of the new world, as they filtered through first the pioneer explorer countries of Western Europe and then the others, is one conspicuous example. The spread of the system associated with the medieval town economy is another. In this sense, the originally limited impact of the industrial system (marked by "Industrial Revolution" in England) and its gradual and uneven spread to other countries is only another example of the introduction of a secular innovation in a world organized in competing states.

3. To repeat, the industrial system is the application of empirical science to basic and ever increasing areas of economic and social technology. That it is the basis of high levels of economic performance in countries in group I can be seen easily by comparing their industrial structure and mode of operation with those in countries in group III. In countries in group I many industries have developed whose basis is some recent scientific discovery (ranging from steam and steel to electricity, internal combustion engines, electronic communications, and atomic power as the most recent example), whereas in countries in group III they are, on the whole, either completely absent or present in minuscule amounts. Furthermore, the technical procedures used in the oldest industries, e.g., agriculture and construction, in the more advanced industrial countries utilize, to a much greater extent than in the countries in group III, the contributions of the empirical and rational approach that is the hallmark of modern science.

The feasibility of using the results of modern science and empirical knowledge in economic production is not merely a matter of availability of a stock of discoveries contributed by original workers or practical-minded adapters. Let us disregard for the moment the importance of social and economic organization as a precondition for adoption on a wide scale of the contributions of science to economic technology. A minimum of cultural adaptation is still required, regardless of the economic and political organization of society. Widespread use of scientific technology is impossible without a literate population, and in a society whose general outlook has not been sufficiently secularized to place a high value on rational calculation and material welfare. The very development of science, and the effective application of its results, requires a cultural milieu in which existing values do not impede an open-minded view on nature, a dispassionate consideration of empirical findings, and a strong desire to enhance the material welfare of man. It is hardly accidental that the growth and spread of science in the modern world was accompanied by and closely tied to broad secularization of those societies that led in the development; and that widespread application of science required and was accompanied by a shift in the general outlook of ever growing proportions of the population toward an acceptance of rational calculation, toward greater habituation to a life governed by the conventions of scientific measurement. Clearly, the development of science and widespread application of its results would have been impossible in the early Middle Ages in Western Europe, with an illiterate population, dominated by religious tenets and emphasis on the hereafter, completely unaccustomed to living by the clock and by rule, and reconciled to a status view of life where traditional patterns of economic procedure and behavior seemed hallowed by inviolable precepts of religious origin.

Whether under a system of private enterprise or communistic organization of the economy, of political democracy or authoritarian state, the adoption of an industrial system is thus not merely a matter of having a stock of scientific knowledge embodied in books or pamphlets; or even of the physical embodiment of such knowledge in machines and plants. Its effective use involves as a minimum an adaptation of the culture and mores of the population. Part of this adaptation we have already observed in discussing the relation between high income levels, literacy, and population type 1 (the latter reflecting a more rational approach to family life). But it has many more ramifications, most of which cannot be put into quantitative terms. Obviously, a change in cultural milieu, when needed for an effective adoption of the industrial system, may well be a slower and more painful process than the accumulation of savings and capital, or other material prerequisites of a higher level of economic performance.

4. The successful adoption of the industrial system, resulting in high levels of per capita income, has been limited, in fact, to countries that combined with it private enterprise as the main unit of economic organization and the democratic state as the dominating form of political organization. In all 15 countries in group I (except possibly Argentina, which is the lowest on the list, and even there the greatest development was under the aegis of private enterprise and political democracy), private enterprise was the main engine in introducing changes associated with the industrial system; and during the periods of rapid growth that brought them to high income levels, the state was a democratic organization. In fact, all of them are deep in the long-standing tradition of Western European development, part and parcel of the historical milieu out of which science and rational thinking, freedom of economic enterprise, and poltical democracy, grew. It is dangerous to assume that this association of rapid growth in income levels with free enterprise and political democracy was an historical accident.

Of course, the association is not hard and fast. Some countries in the same tradition and with the same antecedents, like Italy, Austria, and Czechoslovakia, failed to reach the levels of group I. And, more important, because such an association existed in the past, it does not necessarily follow that an effective adoption of the industrial system as a base of economic organization requires free enterprise and political democracy. At any rate, the Communist states of today proceed on a different premise: they assume that a more effective adoption of the industrial system is possible in combination with enterprise controlled by the state and an authoritarian structure of that state (I am disregarding the misuse of the term "democracy" in its application to states that have no free press, no free political parties, and none of the other basic characteristics of democracy). But history, while naturally subject to bias, leaves one with the distinct impression that a heavy burden of proof lies on those who think that an effective adoption of the industrial system is possible without free private enterprise and political democracy, granted the possible initial role of the state as aider and abettor. Certainly, the experience of those countries in the past that did introduce the industrial system with but an inadequate provision for freedom of enterprise and political democracy (Japan, and somewhat less so, Germany) is not encouraging. Their record, when viewed in the large, *necessarily* including the results of wars that could not be avoided precisely because of the failure to eradicate authoritarian and feudal elements from the past, is hardly indicative of a successful attainment of high income levels *in the long run*. However, we are on highly problematical grounds, and should perhaps only stress the connection in the past between effective adoption of the industrial system and freedom of private enterprise and political democracy; and ask whether this connection is indispensable, i.e., whether without it the use of the industrial system to raise the long term levels of per capita income would be much less effective.[8]

OBSTACLES TO THE SPREAD OF THE INDUSTRIAL SYSTEM

In so far as high income levels result from a rapid rate of growth in income per capita associated with the adoption of the industrial system, the range in current international differences is partly a function of the *slowness* with which the industrial system spread over the face of the globe. A rapid spread, say, in a decade or two, would bring a generally high level of income per capita and a much narrower range of differences in income level among countries. Because over some two centuries, the spread of the industrial system was limited to a small portion of mankind and because so many countries have as yet failed to take full advantage of it, the low income levels for most of the world and the high levels in countries in group I are in marked contrast. What are the obstacles to the adoption of the industrial system that may account for its slow spread, and thus partly account for the existing differences in per capita income levels among various countries?

1. One is tempted to think of the stock of technical knowledge as a free resource, fully available to all countries; of the contribution of science and empirical study as a universal possession of mankind. In a sense it is: most of it is overt and open to study and adoption by anyone. But this impression of universal availability of technical knowledge is partly an illusion. Scientific discoveries, and particularly their practical counterparts in inventions and technical improvements, are often the solution to a specific problem in a specific country adapted to the resources it possesses. The major technical changes at the core of the Industrial Revolution in England were partly colored by conditions in that country. The agricultural revolution of the eighteenth century, with its introduction of continuous crop rotation, scientific livestock breeding, and another wave of enclosures, represented adaptations of already known advanced practices to conditions of British agriculture. It is not clear that these technical changes would have been as valuable, or as

---

[8] Many aspects of the interrelation between an effective adoption of the industrial system and private enterprise-political democracy, argue for its indissolubility. The drive for profit and personal gain that animates economy under private enterprise; the supremacy of the consumer in a political democracy; the fostering of the spirit of inquiry and critical examination of evidence—are all powerful means of breaking resistance to change, encouraging extensive application of knowledge, and building industrial society on the lasting and solid base of a high standard of living of ultimate consumers. In contrast, the recent experiments in grafting the industrial system to a society deprived of personal freedom and with the ultimate consumers' needs forcefully subordinated to state imposed goals, seem much less effective—particularly as bases for peaceful economic growth for the long run.

relevant, to the type of intensive agriculture followed in China in the eighteenth and nineteenth centuries. The adaptation of coal in the Industrial Revolution in England to serve as the major fuel in iron smelting was a technical change eminently suited to British needs, with the country's abundant supply of coal. But it could not be directly useful to a country in which the main supply of energy is water power. And passing to less basic types of technical change, the series of inventions and improvements that went into organizing the United States methods of mass production (standardization, analysis of work tasks, continuous conveyor and assembly belts, plant organization, etc.) were obviously geared to large-scale plants well adapted to the huge domestic market—and not as easily adapted to smaller countries, even of the size of Great Britain.

Since inventions and technical changes bear the specific stamp of the originating country, their use by other countries is not a matter of taking over by direct imitation but of modification and adaptation. The magnitude of this modification may vary widely, from one type of technical change to another and from one country to another. But where it is required, sufficient will and talent are needed in the follower country, whenever such capacity and talent cannot be imported—and it cannot always be imported—from the originating leader country. The slow spread of the industrial system is thus, in part, due to difficulties involved in modifying the original technical change to fit different conditions.

The important implication of this observation is that the spread of modern industrial technology outward from its originating country most easily reaches such other countries as have either similar material conditions, or are closely associated by social and cultural antecedents. It is hardly an accident that so many of the countries in group I have close ties, blood or culture, with England, the leader of the industrial system. Australia, New Zealand, Eire, and Canada are certainly in this category; the United States bears a strong imprint of its original association with England; and a fair number of the European countries in group I are within the orbit of British economic influence (Denmark, and less so, other Scandinavian countries). In all these cases, connection with the originators of the industrial system was sufficient to provide, often on the spot, the talent necessary for the technical modification of the English industrial system.

2. Another reason for the slow spread of the industrial system may be the fact that in this competitive world, the pioneer countries use their economic superiority to impede growth elsewhere. The dynamics of economic and social growth in a world organized in competing states are such that success within a country often results in attempts to extend influence and dominate elsewhere. The aggressiveness of Western Europe through the centuries of its growth is an old story and need not be retold. It is clear that the advance of the industrial pioneering countries was accompanied by impacts upon the rest of the world that partly corroded and distorted the then current economic and social organization; and frequently resulted in political subjugation, hardly a favorable condition in the politically inferior countries for a rapid adoption of the industrial system. The story of imperialistic domi-

nation over countries in Asia, Africa, and Latin America is all in point. While such domination had some economic advantages, it certainly served to block the way to a concerted effort on the part of the dominated countries toward adoption of the industrial system. This is not to say that, free of foreign control, they would have seriously attempted to or succeeded in adopting the industrial system and laying the foundation for higher levels of economic performance. All that is meant here is that even if there were forces in these countries bent upon such attempts, necessary political independence had first to be acquired. And, in some cases, the very effort to secure political independence in turn strengthened forces in the country that in the long run were inimical to the effective adoption of the industrial system (*vide* the case of Japan).

3. But the most serious obstacle to the rapid spread of the industrial system is one that it shares with many major innovations: it means a marked break in established patterns of social and economic life; it destroys established interests; it requires a system of social values and a cultural milieu quite different from those that are the heritage of a long historical past in many countries. In short, it is a thoroughgoing revolution, in the full sense of the word. And revolutions are neither easily made nor successful without long preparation.

Industrialization and economic change in the major countries that went through it successfully engendered painful dislocations, and the long preparation of the cultural and social milieu (as well as some happy historical accidents) accounted in large part for a relatively successful solution of the difficulties. Especially in countries with a rich historical heritage, this impression of industrialization as a process of destruction, as well as of creation, is particularly strong. In England, in Germany, in other European countries adoption of the industrial system meant dislocation of the peasant off the land; the destruction of the artisan; the reduction in importance of the landed nobility; and a change in social values that was painful to many groups who lived by the old traditions. Only in the new, relatively "empty" areas to which European immigrants brought their training and skills, but not the full force of historical tradition and the rigidities of class structure, was the process less painful. But even here it meant the destruction of the aborigines; and in the United States, a civil war had to be fought before agreement was reached on the adoption of the industrial system with all its social and other concomitants.

The slowness of the spread of the industrial system is then the slowness with which, in old human societies with established traditions and social values and entrenched class interests, a new class is formed which views the industrial system as its ideal; which is willing to exercise pressure for the social changes requisite for the introduction of the system; and which becomes powerful enough to impose its interests, considered by it identical with the interests of society at large, upon the country. That this is far from an easy task, and that conditions favorable for the formation of such a class are not common, is evident after only a brief glance at the social structure and history of many of the countries now in groups III and II.

If, in addition, free enterprise and political democracy are considered prerequisites for and necessary accompaniments to the successful adoption of the industrial system, the obstacles imposed by historical heritage over the major parts of the globe become only the more obvious. Nor is it surprising that the countries with the oldest historical background, with the highest attainments in the past of economic and social performance within the *old* framework of technology and cultural values, are the ones in which the difficulties of a revolutionary transition to the new mode of life are the greatest. China and India are conspicuous illustrations, although other factors contribute to the extreme difficulty of adopting an industrial system evolved by and geared for countries of a size and material conditions so vastly different from these Asiatic agricultural empires.

4. The statements above do not mean that in countries in group III (or group II) avenues toward an increase in per capita income levels are few or completely barred. On the contrary, any country at any time, even the group I countries, can find various feasible ways to raise their income levels. For example, in China the rebuilding and extension of the inadequate railroad network; the reorganization of the property framework of agriculture; the establishment of an honest government administration; the application of relatively small amounts of technical skill and knowledge; and a vigorous campaign for limitation of family size—would go quite a way towards increasing per capita income. Similar observations, perhaps with different specific contents, could be made concerning most countries in group III. All that the arguments suggest is that the attainment by countries in group III of a per capita income level at all approaching those in group I is a process that requires a thoroughgoing revolutionary change in economic and social structure, in the cultural complex, and possibly a series of technological innovations so large as to be neither easily nor promptly securable.

One implication of these obstacles should be stressed. The spread of the industrial system is often assumed to be a process that will take its inexorable course in due time—like a slowly moving glacier whose course cannot be stopped or avoided. In the light of history such a picture is largely an illusion. True, *some* of the elements in the industrial system are likely to spread to all parts of the globe: e.g., the more important technological artifacts, like railroads, automobiles, electric power stations, etc. will find their way eventually, even if in moderate quantities, wherever there is room for them. But it is quite possible that for centuries to come these and other products of industrial civilization will be available in many countries in amounts far smaller relatively than they are now available in group I countries, and that the elements of the industrial system will constitute but small islands in the sea of a pre-industrial economy in many countries of the world. If by an industrial system we mean the full and effective utilization of the potentialities of empirical knowledge and science in economic production, even of the imperfect type now realized in countries in group I, its spread to all or even most countries of the globe is far from inevitable. For it is quite possible that many countries will not have the spearheading group, with sufficient power to break the crust of historical heritage and to evolve the forms of adaptation of the industrial system necessary for the relatively effective utilization of its potentials.

History provides several examples of secular innovations which have run their course *without* penetrating into or significantly affecting all countries, even those close to the origin of the innovation. The feudal system was a well nigh general institution in medieval Europe, and yet the Italian peninsula was not fully dominated by it. The idea of political democracy is over two centuries old at least, and its application in Western Europe over a century and a half old; but Spain and Portugal never had it to any significant extent, and never shifted to a system of social values free from the domination of religion. Yet these countries were geographically near the locus of the secular innovations in question. True, with the growth in power of transportation and communication, the world has become a smaller unit. But by the same token, the world as a whole is a more greatly diversified complex than just Western Europe, a complex whose parts bear the deep impress of different series of historical experiences and antecedents. That a universal spread of the industrial system, in a relatively efficient form, to all these historically different parts of the globe is an inevitable process, is highly problematical. The assumption that it is, just as the assumption of the inevitability of human progress, may well be a misconception that originated in the rationalistic theory of the 18th century and was reenforced in the 19th by the impressions made upon Western thinkers by the remarkable economic and social progress in countries directly within the field of their vision.

SOME IMPLICATIONS

The task of inference from the variety of historical experience is difficult at best; and it is particularly difficult and treacherous when attempted without detailed documentation and thorough data. The suggestions advanced here concerning the historical bases of international differences in income levels are but general impressions, which may well be, and probably are, colored by the author's personal judgments. They are, to repeat the warning made at the outset, merely reflections on the problem. But it is hoped that these reflections have some foundation in recorded data and facts; and that they will, therefore, at least provoke serious thought in directions that have heretofore been little emphasized in the statistical literature.

If these reflections are of some validity, they have a variety of implications, for both policy and further research. The implications for policy neither need nor can be discussed here in detail. We mention only the most obvious —that attempts at raising economic levels in countries that have so far failed to take advantage of the potentials of an industrial system are not merely a matter of adding a few plants (which without the necessary background are merely junkpiles of brick and steel), and not merely of importing a few technical experts who are more than likely to be ignorant of the history and institutional background of the country. It is more a matter of finding within the country whatever groups among its population are aware of the need for and the ways in which elements of the industrial system can be adopted; and of mobilizing support behind these groups in the difficult effort which they will necessarily face. Above all, policy action must be made in full cognizance of the social and cultural corollaries of higher levels of economic performance and of the implicit destruction of long-standing and entrenched interests and attitudes which the adoption of these corollaries threatens.

But I am not competent nor in a position to examine the policy implications adequately. My interest lies more in the suggestions for further study —which are, in a sense, the *raison d'être* of this whole discussion. The main lesson can be put briefly: instead of confining ourselves to mechanistic, cross-section comparisons of quantitative indexes, let us pay adequate attention to the historical trends which cumulate in the kind of international differences in income levels that we currently observe. All that has been said concerning these trends in explaining existing differences was a tentative summary of what little one can learn. It is more important as an indication of directions and questions around which further and more thorough inquiry into the processes of economic growth of nations can be built.

This inquiry into economic growth in various countries would utilize quantitative data on secular changes in population, national income and its structure, many of the components ordinarily distinguished in studies of national income and wealth, foreign trade and investment, and a host of other aspects of economic and social structure. But the inquiry cannot, and should not, be limited to quantitative data alone, even apart from the difficulties to be encountered in the scanty supply of such data for most countries. The historical heritage of the several countries as embodied in patterns and values dominating social behavior, their political structure, their attempts, successful and otherwise, to adapt the elements of the industrial system to conditions within their boundaries, would have to be examined. Much of the raw material for a systematic inquiry of this type lies in historical monographs and studies; much is still buried in the primary historical materials; and much may be lost beyond recovery. More significant, a proper analysis of data of this kind, in conjunction with quantitative data, would impose upon the scholar problems for which the tools of his particular discipline—whether it be economics, political science, sociology, anthropology, statistics—may not be adequate. And much of the effort spent in this direction may yield primitive and limited results, at least at first.

We cannot be too optimistic that this, or other similar, inquiries will establish some invariant pattern of economic growth of nations, or succeed in clearly distinguishing between the necessary and accidental conditions of the effective adoption of the industrial system. Indeed, one must beware of premature generalizations because of the temptation they create to disregard much of the variety and mutability of historical experience. But what alternatives are there, except an examination of the only raw material of experience that we have for studying human societies, their structure and activities as revealed in the past? One can hope that a better understanding of the latter, scanty as the resulting tested generalizations may be, would at least prevent us from placing too much confidence in a succession of theories that so often magnify partial and transient conditions into universal and immutable factors.

PART TWO

The Advanced
Countries:
Theories and Models
of Growth

Preoccupation WITH THE PROBLEM OF ECONOMIC development is not, as some may think, exclusively the domain of contemporary economic thought. Great economic thinkers of earlier eras were also profoundly concerned with the nature and causes of the growth of the "wealth of nations." In the history of economic thought, such figures as Adam Smith, David Ricardo, Thomas Robert Malthus, John Stuart Mill, and Karl Marx are prominently associated with theories of economic growth. With the passing of these figures, who, with the exception of Marx, belong to the "Classical School," interest in this area waned. But the importance of the subject is such that in the twentieth century it virtually underwent a rebirth in the hands of such economists as Joseph Schumpeter, Alvin Hansen, Roy Harrod, and Evsey Domar. This section traces the development of economic theory in this area from Adam Smith to the present.

A theory is designed to explain and perhaps to predict some process or phenomenon. It operates at a high level of abstraction, selecting only a few relevant variables from a multitude. The success of a theory, measured in terms of its explanatory or predictive power, then depends both on the logical rigor of its construction and upon the wisdom of the theorist in determining which variables are relevant.

Although it is the intention of this section to have most of the aforementioned economists speak for themselves, it may be helpful here, because of the importance of their contributions, to outline at some length a few of the more prominent elements that appear in their theories. Common to all of these is the emphasis placed, in greater or lesser degree, upon capital accumulation—the growth of the physical means of production—as the mainspring of economic growth. Because savings are clearly a prerequisite of investment in capital stock, all these writers assign a prominent place to savings in their theories. The precise role of savings in the growth process is, however, subject to varied interpretation. Smith, Ricardo, and Mill regard savings as virtuous almost without qualification; because they assume that all savings is translated by the "invisible hand" into investment, there is a clear and positive causal relation between savings and the rate of growth. Others, too, assign a broadly positive role to savings, but not in so unqualified a way. Malthus, for example, argued (well in advance of his time) that nations could have, with respect to savings, too much of a good thing. He emphasized that too much savings implies too little consumption, thus causing a tendency to "glut" and a consequent underutilization of capital—a condition inimical to sustained growth. Under the influence of Keynes, Hansen later propounded a somewhat similar theme, suggesting that investment opportunities may not be sufficient to absorb the savings potential of an advanced economy, a situation resulting in "secular stagnation." Savings as a potential embarrassment to the economy was later spelled out more precisely in the Keynesian-influenced models of Harrod and Domar (of which we here include the latter), where it is shown how a "wrong" amount of savings—either too much or too little in relation to investment demand—can derail the economy from a smooth path of growth.

All the economists in this section address themselves primarily to the problem of economic growth in countries already on the path of development. Despite the phenomenal progress in these countries that has occurred in the past one hundred fifty to two hundred years, it is perhaps surprising that many of these writers entertain the expectation, and develop theories that predict, that growth will be retarded and eventually stagnated. In view of the much longer history of negligible economic progress preceding this period (with which the economists were well acquainted), however, such theories may appear less startling.

Adam Smith was more optimistic in his outlook than some others. According to him, capital accumulation resulting from savings, together with the growth of a population imbued with the propensities to "truck, barter and exchange," lead to a division of labor, the introduction of machinery, and consequent increases in the productivity of labor. All of these combine to promote economic development. But Smith believed, for all this, that a "degree of opulence" will eventually be reached where the stock of capital is so large, in relation to other resources and to the "extent of the market" (effective consumer demand), that the rate of profit will fall, thus discouraging capital accumulation and further growth.

The theories of David Ricardo and John Stuart Mill also point to eventual stagnation, though their explanation for this outcome differs from Smith's. The law of diminishing returns in agriculture is the cornerstone of their analysis. To state the matter only cursorily, a positive rate of profit motivates savings and capital accumulation, thus raising income, the demand for labor, and ultimately, because of increased wage rates, the size of the population. A larger population generates an increased demand for food which, because of the operation of the law of diminishing returns and the scarcity of arable land, will be forthcoming only at higher prices. Although the population will ultimately return to a subsistence wage level, money wages must now be permanently higher because of the higher price of food. In this process, rent has also risen, "and . . . little consequently remains for the profits of stock." Capitalists are thus robbed of their motive for accumulation, and growth ceases. To this point, Mill and Ricardo are in substantial agreement, but it should be noted that Mill takes a complacent and Platonic view of the "stationary state." The advent of this stationary condition, though it means the cessation of capital accumulation and population growth, implies for him no cessation of human improvement or even, paradoxically enough, of technological progress. The latter, however, is devoted entirely to increased leisure rather than to any increase in output.

Whereas Karl Marx's prediction of the ultimate overthrow of capitalism is part of the broader fabric of his "dialectic materialism," his theory of economic growth under capitalism is built with the aid of analytic tools largely borrowed from the classical economists. Marx, like Ricardo, argued that capital accumulation would eventually reduce the rate of profit and thus the rate of economic growth. But where Ricardo built upon the concept of diminishing returns, Marx depends upon the phenomenon of the declining rate of "surplus value." This is the return to the capitalist that results from his exploitation of the working class: the wage payments that the capitalist must make to the laborer is something less than he derives from the laborer's output. Over time, however, the exigencies of competition induce capitalists to substitute machinery for labor. But machinery, unlike human beings, yields no surplus value, and thus the rate of profit (surplus value divided by "constant" plus "variable" capital) will fall, as the ratio of capital machinery to labor rises. In attempting to counteract the falling rate of profit, capitalists increase the hours of work and reduce the wages of labor, thus worsening the plight of an already exploited class.

Joseph Schumpeter's theory of economic development represents a departure from the previous theories we have mentioned in that it incorporates no prediction or implication of inevitable economic stagnation. In his system, the burden of economic growth is borne by the entrepreneur. The "entrepreneur" is defined by Schumpeter in a very precise way: he is an innovator, and his function is to "reform or revolutionize the pattern of production by exploiting an invention or, more generally, an untried technological possibility for producing a new commodity or producing an old one in a new way . . . and so on." The rate of economic growth in the capitalist system therefore depends in a critical way upon the size, quality, and activity of the enterpreneurial class. But entrepreneurs operate in fits and starts. Their innovations tend to appear in clusters, and therefore economic growth is not a smooth and steady affair: its path, in fact, can be traced only through the ebb and flow of the business cycle.

Nothing in Schumpeter's purely economic analysis bodes ill for future economic development under capitalism, but social and political forces growing out of the economic system are regarded by him as altogether another affair. He believed that it is in the very nature of successful capitalism to engender an atmosphere that is fundamentally hostile to the entrepreneurial class. On the one hand, the tendency to monopolistic "bigness" and to organizational routine tend to usurp the entrepreneurial function; on the other hand, the growing strength of labor unions and increased government intervention ("vexatious administration and irrational taxation" and so forth) tend to impede it. Ultimately, these and other social and poltical forces will, in Schumpeter's view, result in the dissolution of capitalism in its "traditional" form. But it should be made perfectly clear that this unfavorable prognosis for the capitalistic system does not necessarily imply any diminution of the rate of growth, for Schumpeter did not deny that growth may continue under a different economic system.

Schumpeter's extensive analysis of economic development stands out in bold relief in a period, roughly between 1870 and 1930, when there appears to have been a general flagging of interest in the problem. Throughout this period, the major part of theoretical endeavors were devoted to problems of a microeconomic character: broadly speaking, concern centered on achieving the efficient allocation of scarce resources. Thus, for example, Alfred Marshall, the leading economist of his time, devoted relatively little space to the question of growth, and what comments he makes are not cast in a formal theoretical framework. These comments, however, are sufficiently cogent and suggestive to warrant their inclusion in this section.

The catastrophic world depression of the 1930s prompted a rude awakening of interest in the growth problem. As the depression wore on to intolerable length, the belief arose among some economists that the advanced countries were in the grip, not merely of a cyclical disturbance, but of "secular stagnation." This view, of which Alvin Hansen was the foremost exponent, centers around the notion that advanced, "mature" economies eventually experience a permanent decline in investment opportunities. "The approaching cessation of population growth and the disappearance of new territories for settlement and exploitation" reduce the incentive for private investment, and these are not sufficiently compensated by the third major factor, technological change. Using an essentially Keynesian analysis, Hansen concludes that investment demand falls below the economy's savings potential, and that the actual growth of national income falls below the rate of which the economy is capable, with unemployment becoming a chronic condition. This concept of stagnation, it should be mentioned, is much less extreme than that of J. S. Mill and the Classical School in general. For the latter, it meant the complete cessation of growth of capital, output, and population; for Hansen, it is a matter of development at a decreasing rate, with general underemployment of resources.

With few exceptions, the formal theories we have discussed up to this point have embodied, either explicitly or implicitly, predictions about the long-run outcome of the process of economic development and, as we have seen, these predictions have been predominantly pessimistic. In contrast, the Domar "model" of economic growth cannot be termed pessimistic, if only because it makes no prediction of any kind. The model derives the conditions concerning savings, investment, and the rate of growth of income required for the stable growth of the economy—that is, growth with neither unemployment of resources nor inflation. It does not, however, specify whether we can expect these conditions actually to be realized. Thus, the Domar *model* differs from the previous *theories* in two fundamental respects: first, it contains no prediction concerning long-run growth trends; secondly, it is concerned less with explaining the forces that account for growth than with explaining why the *path* of growth is likely to be strewn with pitfalls.

ADAM SMITH

|||||||||||||||||||||||||||||||||||||||||||||||||||||||||||||||||||||||||||||||||||||||||||||||||||||||||||||||||||||||||||||||||||||||||||||||||||||||||||

The Wealth of Nations

OF THE DIVISION OF LABOUR

ITS ADVANTAGES

The greatest improvement in the productive powers of labour, and the greater part of the skill, dexterity, and judgment with which it is any where directed, or applied, seem to have been the effects of the division of labour.

The effects of the division of labour, in the general business of society, will be more easily understood, by considering in what manner it operates in some particular manufactures. . . .

To take an example . . . from a very trifling manufacture; but one in which the division of labour has been very often taken notice of, the trade of the pin-maker; a workman not educated to this business (which the division of labour has rendered a distinct trade), nor acquainted with the use of the machinery employed in it (to the invention of which the same division of labour has probably given occasion), could scarce, perhaps, with his utmost industry, make one pin in a day, and certainly could not make twenty. But in the way in which this business is now carried on, not only the whole work is a peculiar trade, but it is divided into a number of branches, of which the greater part are likewise peculiar trades. One man draws out the wire, another straights it, a third cuts it, a fourth points it, a fifth grinds it at the top for receiving the head; to make the head requires two or three distinct operations; to put it on, is a peculiar business, to whiten the pin is another; it is even a trade by itself to put them into the paper; and the important business of making a pin is, in this manner, divided into about eighteen distinct operations, which in some manufactories, are all performed by distinct hands, though in others the same man will sometimes perform two or three of them. I have seen a small manufactory of this kind where ten men only were employed, and where some of them consequently performed two or three distinct operations. But though they were very poor, and therefore but indifferently accommodated with the necessary machinery, they could, when they exerted themselves, make among them about twelve pounds of pins in a day. There are in a pound upwards of four thousand pins of a middling size. Those ten persons, therefore, could make among them upwards of forty-eight thousand pins in a day. Each person, therefore, making a tenth part of forty-eight

Reprinted from *The Wealth of Nations* (New York: The Modern Library, 1937), pp. 3-416, with omissions.

thousand pins, might be considered as making four thousand eight hundred pins in a day. But if they had all wrought separately and independently, and without any of them having been educated to this peculiar business, they certainly could not each of them have made twenty, perhaps not one pin in a day; that is, certainly, not the two hundred and fortieth, perhaps not the four thousand eight hundredth part of what they are at present capable of performing, in consequence of a proper division of labour and combination of their different operations. . . .

This great increase of the quantity of work, which, in consequence of the division of labour, the same number of people are capable of performing, is owing to three different circumstances; first, to the increase of dexterity in every particular workman; secondly, to the saving of the time which is commonly lost in passing from one species of work to another; and lastly, to the invention of a great number of machines which facilitate and abridge labour, and enable one man to do the work of many. . . .

It is the great multiplication of the productions of all the different arts, in consequence of the division of labour, which occasions, in a well-governed society, that universal opulence which extends itself to the lowest ranks of the people. Every workman has a great quantity of his own work to dispose of beyond what he himself has occasion for; and every other workman being exactly in the same situation, he is enabled to exchange a great quantity of his own goods for a great quantity, or, what comes to the same thing, for the price of a great quantity of theirs. He supplies them abundantly with what they have occasion for, and they accommodate him as amply with what he has occasion for, and a general plenty diffuses itself through all the different ranks of the society. . . .

THE PROPENSITY TO TRUCK, BARTER, AND EXCHANGE

This division of labour, from which so many advantages are derived, is not originally the effect of any human wisdom, which foresees and intends that general opulence to which it gives occasion. It is the necessary, though very slow and gradual, consequence of a certain propensity in human nature which has in view no such extensive utility; the propensity to truck, barter, and exchange one thing for another.

Whether this propensity be one of those original principles in human nature, of which no further account can be given; or whether, as seems more probable, it be the necessary consequence of the faculties of reason and speech, it belongs not to our present subject to enquire. It is common to all men, and to be found in no other race of animals, which seem to know neither this nor any other species of contracts. . . .

As it is by treaty, by barter, and by purchase, that we obtain from one another the greater part of those mutual good offices which we stand in need of, so it is the same trucking disposition which originally gives occasion to the division of labour. In a tribe of hunters or shepherds a particular person makes bows and arrows, for example, with more readiness and dexterity than any other. He frequently exchanges them for cattle or for venison with his companions; and he finds at last that he can in this manner get more cattle and venison, than if he himself went to the field to catch them. From a regard to his own interest, therefore, the making of bows and arrows grows to be his chief business, and he becomes a sort of armourer. Another excels in making the frames and covers of their little huts or moveable houses. He is accustomed to be of use in this way to his neighbors, who reward him in the same manner with cattle and with venison, till at last he finds it his interest to dedicate himself entirely to this employment, and to become a sort of house-carpenter. In the same manner a third becomes a smith or a brazier; a fourth a tanner or dresser of hides or skins, the principal part of the clothing of savages. And thus the certainty of being able to exchange all that surplus part of the produce of his own labour, which is over and above his own consumption, for such parts of the produce of other men's labour as he may have occasion for, encourages every man to apply himself to a particular occupation, and to cultivate and bring to perfection whatever talent or genius he may possess for that particular species of business. . . .

When the division of labour has been once thoroughly established, it is but a very small part of a man's wants which the produce of his own labour can supply. He supplies the far greater part of them by exchanging that surplus part of the produce of his own labour, which is over and above his own consumption, for such parts of the produce of other men's labour as he has occasion for. Every man thus lives by exchanging, or becomes in some measure a merchant, and the society itself grows to be what is properly a commercial society. . . .

THE DIVISION OF LABOUR AND THE EXTENT OF THE MARKET

As it is the power of exchanging that gives occasion to the division of labour, so the extent of this division must always be limited by the extent of that power, or, in other words, by the extent of the market. When the market is very small, no person can have any encouragement to dedicate himself entirely to one employment, for want of the power to exchange all that surplus part of the produce of his own labour, which is over and above his own consumption, for such parts of the produce of other men's labour as he has occasion for. . . .

The great commerce of every civilized society, is that carried on between the inhabitants of the town and those of the country. It consists in the exchange of rude for manufactured produce, either immediately, or by the intervention of money, or of some sort of paper which represents money. The country supplies the town with the means of subsistence, and the materials of manufacture. The town repays this supply by sending back a part of the manufactured produce to the inhabitants of the country. The town, in which there neither is nor can be any reproduction of substances, may very properly be said to gain its whole wealth and subsistence from the country. We must not, however, upon this account, imagine that the gain of the town is the loss of the country. The gains of both are mutual and reciprocal, and the division of labour is in this, as in all other cases, advantageous to all the different persons employed in the various occupations into which it is subdivided. The inhabitants of the country purchase of the town a greater quantity of manufactured goods, with the produce of a much smaller quantity of their own labour, than they must have employed had they attempted to prepare them themselves. The town affords a market for the surplus produce of the country, or what is over and above the maintenance of the cultivators, and it is there that the inhabitants of the country exchange it for something else which is in demand among them. The greater the number and revenue of the inhabitants of the town, the more extensive is the market which it affords to those of the country; and the more extensive that market, it is always the more advantageous to a great number. . . .

. . . Between whatever places foreign trade is carried on, they all of them derive two distinct benefits from it. It carries out that surplus part of the produce of their land and labour for which there is no demand among them, and brings back in return for it something else for which there is a demand. It gives a value to their superfluities, by exchanging them for something else, which may satisfy a part of their wants, and increase their enjoyments. By means of it, the narrowness of the home market does not hinder the division of labour in any particular branch of art or manufacture from being carried to the highest perfection. By opening a more extensive market for whatever part of the produce of their labour may exceed the home consumption, it encourages them to improve its productive powers, and to augment its annual produce to the utmost, and thereby to increase the real revenue and wealth of the society. These great and important services foreign trade is continually occupied in performing, to all the different countries between which it is carried on. They all derive great benefit from it, though that in which the merchant resides generally derives the greatest, as he is generally more employed in supplying the wants, and carrying out the superfluities of his own, than of any other particular country. . . .

It is not by the importation of gold and silver, that the discovery of America has enriched Europe. . . . By opening a new and inexhaustible market to all the commodities of Europe, it gave occasion to new divisions of labour and improvements of art, which, in the narrow circle of the ancient commerce, could never have taken place for want of a market to take off the greater part of their produce. The productive powers of labour were improved, and its produce increased in all the different countries of Europe, and together with it the real revenue and wealth of the inhabitants. The commodities of Europe were almost all new to America, and many of those of America were new to Europe. A new set of exchanges, therefore, began to take place which had never been thought of before, and which should naturally have proved as advantageous to the new, as it did to the old continent. . . .

THE ACCUMULATION OF CAPITAL

In that rude state of society in which there is no division of labour, in which exchanges are seldom made, and in which every man provides everything for himself, it is not necessary that any stock[1] should be accumulated

---

[1] Stock means capital.—EDS.

or stored up beforehand, in order to carry on the business of the society. Every man endeavors to supply by his own industry his own occasional wants as they occur. When he is hungry, he goes to the forest to hunt; when his coat is worn out, he clothes himself with the skin of the first large animal he kills; and when his hut begins to go to ruin, he repairs it, as well as he can, with the trees and the turf that are nearest it. . . .

As the accumulation of stock must, in the nature of things, be previous to the division of labour, so labour can be more and more subdivided in proportion only as stock is previously more and more accumulated. The quantity of materials which the same number of people can work up, increases in a great proportion as labour comes to be more and more subdivided; and as the operations of each workman are gradually reduced to a greater degree of simplicity, a variety of new machines come to be invented for facilitating and abridging those operations. As the division of labour advances, therefore, in order to give constant employment to an equal number of workmen, an equal stock of provisions, and a greater stock of materials and tools than what would have been necessary in a ruder state of things, must be accumulated beforehand. But the number of workmen in every branch of business generally increases with the division of labour in that branch, or rather it is the increase of their number which enables them to class and subdivide themselves in this manner.

As the accumulation of stock is previously necessary for carrying on this great improvement in the productive powers of labour, so that accumulation naturally leads to this improvement. The person who employs his stock in maintaining labour, necessarily wishes to employ it in such a manner as to produce as great a quantity of work as possible. He endeavors, therefore, both to make among his workmen the most proper distribution of employment, and to furnish them with the best machines which he can either invent or afford to purchase. His abilities in both these respects are generally in proportion to the extent of his stock, or to the number of people whom it can employ. The quantity of industry, therefore, not only increases in every country with the increase of the stock which employs it, but, in consequence of that increase, the same quantity of industry produces a much greater quantity of work.

Such are in general the effects of the increase of stock upon industry and its productive powers. . . .

. . . Every increase or diminution of capital, therefore, naturally tends to increase or diminish the real quantity of industry, the number of productive hands, and consequently the exchangeable value of the annual produce of the land and labour of the country, the real wealth and revenue of all its inhabitants.

PARSIMONY, SAVINGS, AND PRODIGALITY
Capitals are increased by parsimony, and diminished by prodigality and misconduct.

Whatever a person saves from his revenue he adds to his capital, and either employs it himself in maintaining an additional number of productive hands, or enables some other person to do so, by lending it to him for an interest, that is, for a share of the profits. As the capital of an individual can be increased only by what he saves from his annual revenue or his annual gains, so the capital of a society, which is the same with that of all the individuals who compose it, can be increased only in the same manner.

Parsimony, and not industry, is the immediate cause of the increase of capital. Industry, indeed, provides the subject which parsimony accumulates. But whatever industry might acquire, if parsimony did not save and store up, the capital would never be the greater.

Parsimony, by increasing the fund which is destined for the maintenance of productive hands, tends to increase the number of those hands whose labour adds to the value of the subject upon which it is bestowed. It tends therefore to increase the exchangeable value of the annual produce of the land and labour of the country. It puts into motion an additional quantity of industry, which gives an additional value to the annual produce. . . .

Great nations are never impoverished by private, though they sometimes are by public prodigality and misconduct. The whole, or almost the whole public revenue, is in most countries employed in maintaining unproductive hands. Such are the people who compose a numerous and splendid court, a great ecclesiastical establishment, great fleets and armies, who in time of peace produce nothing, and in time of war acquire nothing which can compensate the expence of maintaining them, even while the war lasts. Such people, as they themselves produce nothing, are all maintained by the produce of other men's labour. When multiplied, therefore, to an unnecessary number, they may in a particular year consume so great a share of this produce, as not to leave a sufficiency for maintaining the productive labourers, who should reproduce it next year. The next year's produce, therefore, will be less than that of the foregoing, and if the same disorder should continue, that of the third year will be still less than that of the second. Those unproductive hands, who should be maintained by a part only of the spare revenue of the people, may consume so great a share of their whole revenue, and therefore oblige so great a number to encroach upon their capitals, upon the funds destined for the maintenance of productive labour, that all the frugality and good conduct of individuals may not be able to compensate the waste and degradation of produce occasioned by this violent and forced encroachement. . . .

CAPITAL, LABOUR, AND NATIONAL OUTPUT

There is one sort of labour which adds to the value of the subject upon which it is bestowed: there is another which has no such effect. The former, as it produces a value, may be called productive; the latter, unproductive labour. Thus the labour of a manufacturer adds, generally, to the value of the materials which he works upon, that of his own maintenance, and of his master's profit. The labour of a menial servant, on the contrary, adds to the value of nothing. . . .

The labour of some of the most respectable orders in the society is, like that of menial servants, unproductive of any value, and does not fix or realize itself in any permanent subject, or vendable commodity, which endures after that labour is passed, and for which an equal quantity of labour could afterwards be procured. The sovereign, for example, with all the officers both of justice and war who serve under him, the whole army and navy, are unproductive labourers. They are the servants of the public, and are maintained by a part of the annual produce of the industry of other people. Their service, how honourable, how useful, or how necessary soever, produces nothing for which an equal quantity of service can afterwards be procured. . . . Like the declamation of the actor, the harangue of the orator, or the tune of the musician, the work of all of them perishes in the very instant of its production. . . .

The annual produce of the land and labour of any nation can be increased in its value by no other means, but by increasing either the number of its productive labourers, or the productive powers of those labourers who had before been employed. The number of its productive labourers, it is evident, can never be much increased, but in consequence of an increase of capital, or of the funds destined for maintaining them. The productive powers of the same number of labourers can not be increased, but in consequence either of some addition and improvement to those machines and instruments which facilitate and abridge labour; or of a more proper division and distribution of employment. In either case an additional capital is almost always required. It is by means of an additional capital only, that the undertaker of any work can either provide his workmen with better machinery, or make a more proper distribution of employment among them. When the work to be done consists of a number of parts, to keep every man constantly employed in one way, requires a much greater capital than where every man is occasionally employed in every different part of the work. When we compare, therefore, the state of a nation at two different periods, and find, that the annual produce of its land and labour is evidently greater at the latter than at the former, that its lands are better cultivated, its manufactures more numerous and more flourishing, and its trade more extensive, we may be assured that its capital must have increased during the interval between those two periods, and that more must have been added to it by the good conduct of some, than had been taken from it either by the private misconduct of others, or by the public extravagance of government. But we shall find this to have been the case of almost all nations, in all tolerably quiet and peaceful times, even of those who have not enjoyed the most prudent and parsimonious governments. . . .

THE LONG-RUN BEHAVIOR OF WAGES AND PROFITS

A man must always live by his work, and his wages must at least be sufficient to maintain him. They must even upon most occasions be somewhat more; otherwise it would be impossible for him to bring up a family, and the race of such workmen could not last beyond the first generation. . . .

There are certain circumstances, however, which sometimes give the labourers an advantage, and enable them to raise their wages considerably above this rate; evidently the lowest which is consistent with common humanity.

When in any country the demand for those who live by wages; labourers, journeymen, servants of every kind, is continually increasing; when every year furnishes employment for a greater number than have been employed the year before, the workmen have no occasion to combine in order to raise their wages. . . .

The demand for those who live by wages, therefore, necessarily increases with the increase of the revenue and stock of every country, and cannot possibly increase without it. The increase of revenue and stock is the increase of national wealth. The demand for those who live by wages, therefore, naturally increases with the increase of national wealth, and cannot possibly increase without it. . . .

The rise and fall in the profits of stock depend upon the same causes with the rise and fall in the wages of labour, the increasing or declining state of the wealth of the societies; but those causes affect the one and the other very differently.

The increase of stock, which raises wages, tends to lower profit. When the stocks of many rich merchants are turned into the same trade, their mutual competition naturally tends to lower its profit; and when there is a like increase of stock in all the different trades carried on in the same society, the same competition must produce the same effect in them all. . . .

. . . As capitals increase in any country, the profits which can be made by employing them necessarily diminish. It becomes gradually more and more difficult to find within the country a profitable method of employing any new capital. There arises in consequence a competition between different capitals, the owner of one endeavoring to get possession of that employment which is occupied by another. But upon most occasions he can hope to justle that other out of this employment, by no other means but by dealing upon more reasonable terms. He must not only sell what he deals in somewhat cheaper, but in order to get it to sell, he must sometimes too buy it dearer. The demand for productive labour, by the increase of the funds which are destined for maintaining it, grows every day greater and greater. Labourers easily find employment, but the owners of capital find it difficult to get labourers to employ. Their competition raises the wages of labour, and sinks the profits of stock. . . .

Since the time of Henry VIII, the wealth and revenue of the country have been continually advancing, and, in the course of their progress, their pace seems rather to have been gradually accelerated than retarded. They seem, not only to have been going on, but to have been going on faster and faster. The wages of labour have been continually increasing during the same period, and in the greater part of the different branches of trade and manufactures the profits of stock have been diminishing.

It generally requires a greater stock to carry on any sort of trade in a great town than in a country village. The great stocks employed in every branch of trade, and the number of rich competitors, generally reduce the rate of profit in the former below what it is in the latter. But the wages of labour are generally higher in a great town than in a country village. In a thriving town the people who have great stocks to employ, frequently cannot get the number of workmen they want, and therefore bid against one another in order to get as many as they can, which raises the wages of labour, and lowers the profits of stock. In the remote parts of the country there is frequently not stock sufficient to employ all the people, who therefore bid against one another in order to get employment, which lowers the wages of labour, and raises the profits of stock. . . .

In our North American and West Indian colonies, not only the wages of labour, but the interest of money, and consequently the profits of stock, are higher than in England. . . . A new colony must always for some time be more understocked in proportion to the extent of its territory, and more underpeopled in proportion to the extent of its stock, than the greater part of other countries. They have more land than they have stock to cultivate. . . . As the colony increases, the profits of stock gradually diminish. When the most fertile and best situated lands have been all occupied, less profit can be made by the cultivation of what is inferior both in soil and situation, and less interest can be afforded for the stock which is so employed. In the greater part of our colonies, accordingly, both the legal and the market rate of interest have been considerably reduced during the course of the present century. As riches, improvement, and population have increased, interest has declined. The wages of labour do not sink with the profits of stock. The demand for labour increases with the increase of stock whatever be its profits; and after these are diminished, stock may not only continue to increase, but to increase much faster than before. It is with industrious nations who are advancing in the acquisition of riches, as with industrious individuals. A great stock, though with small profits, generally increases faster than a small stock with great profits. . . .

The acquisition of new territory, or of new branches of trade, may sometimes raise the profits of stock, and with them the interest of money, even in a country which is fast advancing in the acquisition of riches. The stock of the country not being sufficient for the whole accession of business, which such acquisitions present to the different people among whom it is divided, is applied to those particular branches only which afford the greatest profit. Part of what had before been employed in other trades, is necessarily withdrawn from them, and turned into some of the new and more profitable ones. In all those old trades, therefore, the competition comes to be less than before. The market comes to be less fully supplied with many different sorts of goods. Their price necessarily rises more or less, and yields a greater profit to those who deal in them, who can, therefore, afford to borrow at a higher interest. For some time after the conclusion of the late war, not only private people of the best credit, but some of the greatest companies in London, commonly borrowed at five per cent. who before that had not been used to pay more than four, and four and a half per cent. The great accession both of territory and trade, by our acquisitions in North America and the West Indies, will sufficiently account for this, without supposing any diminution in the capital stock of the society. So great an accession of new business to be carried on by the old stock, must necessarily have diminished the quantity employed in a great number of particular branches, in which the competition being less, the profits must have been greater. . . .

In a country which had acquired that full complement of riches which the nature of its soil and climate, and its situation with respect to other countries, allowed it to acquire; which could, therefore, advance no further, and which was not going backwards, both the wages of labour and the profits of stock would probably be very low. In a country fully peopled in proportion to what either its territory could maintain or its stock employ, the competition for employment would necessarily be so great as to reduce the wages of labour to what was barely sufficient to keep up the number of labourers, and, the country being already fully peopled, that number could never be augmented. In a country fully stocked in proportion to all the business it had to transact, as great a quantity of stock would be employed in every particular branch as the nature and extent of the trade would admit. The competition, therefore, would everywhere be as great, and consequently the ordinary profit as low as possible.

But perhaps no country has ever yet arrived at this degree of opulence. . . .

DAVID RICARDO

||||||||||||||||||||||||||||||||||||||||||||||||||||||||||||||||||||||||||||||||||||||||||||||||||||||||||||||||||||||||||||||||||

On Economic Growth

ON RENT

It remains . . . to be considered, whether the appropriation of land, and the consequent creation of rent, will occasion any variation in the relative value of commodities, independently of the quantity of labour necessary to production. In order to understand this part of the subject, we must enquire into the nature of rent, and the laws by which its rise or fall is regulated.

Rent is that portion of the produce of the earth, which is paid to the landlord for the use of the original and indestructible powers of the soil. . . .

On the first settling of a country, in which there is an abundance of rich and fertile land, a very small proportion of which is required to be cultivated

Reprinted from *On the Principles of Political Economy and Taxation,* 3d ed., 1821, edited by P. Sraffa (Cambridge, Eng.: Cambridge University Press, 1951), pp. 67-291, with omissions.

for the support of the actual population, or indeed can be cultivated with the capital which the population can command, there will be no rent; for no one would pay for the use of land, when there was an abundant quantity not yet appropriated, and, therefore, at the disposal of whosoever might choose to cultivate it.

On the common principles of supply and demand, no rent could be paid for such land, for the reason stated why nothing is given for the use of air and water, or for any other of the gifts of nature which exist in boundless quantity. With a given quantity of materials, and with the assistance of the pressure of the atmosphere, and the elasticity of steam, engines may perform work, and abridge human labour to a very great extent; but no charge is made for the use of these natural aids, because they are inexhaustible, and at every man's disposal. In the same manner the brewer, the distiller, the dyer, make incessant use of the air and water for the production of their commodities; but as the supply is boundless, they bear no price. If all the land had the same properties if it were unlimited in quantity, and uniform in quality, no charge could be made for its use, unless where it possessed peculiar advantages of situation. It is only, then, because land is not unlimited in quantity and uniform in quality, and because in the progress of population, land of an inferior quality, or less advantageously situated, is called into cultivation, that rent is ever paid for the use of it. When in the progress of society, land of the second degree of fertility is taken into cultivation, rent immediately commences on that of the first quality, and the amount of that rent will depend on the difference in the quality of these two portions of land.

When land of the third quality is taken into cultivation, rent immediately commences on the second, and it is regulated as before, by the difference in their productive powers. At the same time, the rent of the first quality will rise, for that must always be above the rent of the second, by the difference between the produce which they yield with a given quantity of capital and labour. With every step in the progress of population, which shall oblige a country to have recourse to land of a worse quality, to enable it to raise its supply of food, rent, on all the more fertile land, will rise. . . .

It is often, and, indeed, commonly happens, that before No. 2, 3, 4, or 5, [lands numbered in order of decreasing quality] or the inferior lands are cultivated, capital can be employed more productively on those lands which are already in cultivation. It may perhaps be found, that by doubling the original capital employed on No. 1, though the produce will not be doubled, will not be increased by 100 quarters, it may be increased by eighty-five quarters, and that this quantity exceeds what could be obtained by employing the same capital, on land No. 3.

In such case, capital will be preferably employed on the old land, and will equally create a rent; for rent is always the difference between the produce obtained by the employment of two equal quantities of capital and labour. If, with a capital of 1000 £., a tenant obtained 100 quarters of wheat from his land, and by the employment of a second capital of 1000 £., he obtain a further return of eighty-five, his landlord would have the power at the expiration of his lease, of obliging him to pay fifteen quarters, or an equivalent value, for additional rent; for there cannot be two rates of profit. If he is satisfied with a diminution of fifteen quarters in the return for his second 1000 £., it is because no employment more profitable can be found for it. The common rate of profit would be in that proportion, and if the original tenant refused, some other person would be found willing to give all which exceeded that rate of profit to the owner of the land from which he derived it. . . .

If, then, good land existed in a quantity much more abundant than the production of food for an increasing population required, or if capital could be indefinitely employed without a diminished return on the old land, there could be no rise of rent; for rent invariably proceeds from the employment of an additional quantity of labour with a proportionally less return.

The most fertile, and most favourably situated, land will be first cultivated, and the exchangeable value of its produce will be adjusted in the same manner as the exchangeable value of all other commodities, by the total quantity of labour necessary in various forms, from first to last, to produce it, and bring it to market. When land of an inferior quality is taken into cultivation, the exchangeable value of raw produce will rise, because more labour is required to produce it.[1]

The exchangeable value of all commodities, whether they be manufactured, or the produce of the mines, or the produce of land, is always regulated, not by the less quantity of labour that will suffice for their production under circumstances highly favourable, and exclusively enjoyed by those who have peculiar facilities of production; but by the greater quantity of labour necessarily bestowed on their production by those who have no such facilities; by those who continue to produce them under the most unfavourable circumstances; meaning—by the most unfavourable circumstances, the most unfavourable under which the quantity of produce required, renders it necessary to carry on the production. . . .

The reason then, why raw produce rises in comparative value, is because more labour is employed in the production of the last portion obtained, and not because a rent is paid to the landlord. The value of corn is regulated by the quantity of labour bestowed on its production on that quality of land, or with that portion of capital, which pays no rent. Corn is not high because a rent is paid, but a rent is paid because corn is high; and it has been justly observed,[2] that no reduction would take place in the price of corn, although landlords should forego the whole of their rent. Such a measure would only enable some farmers to live like gentlemen, but would not diminish the quantity of labour necessary to raise raw produce on the least productive land in cultivation. . . .

The rise of rent is always the effect of the increasing wealth of the country, and of the difficulty of providing food for its augmented population. It is a symptom, but it is never a cause of wealth; for wealth often increases most rapidly while rent is either stationary, or even falling. Rent increases most rapidly, as the disposable land decreases in its productive powers.

---

[1] This conclusion follows from Ricardo's labor theory of value.—EDS.
[2] See Malthus's *Inquiry into the Nature and Progress of Rent* (1815), p. 57.

Wealth increases most rapidly in those countries where the disposable land is most fertile, where importation is least restricted, and where through agricultural improvements, productions can be multiplied without any increase in the proportional quantity of labour, and where consequently the progress of rent is slow.

If the high price of corn were the effect, and not the cause of rent, price would be proportionally influenced as rents were high or low, and rent would be a component part of price. But that corn which is produced by the greatest quantity of labor is the regulator of the price of corn; and rent does not and cannot enter in the least degree as a component part of its price.[3] Adam Smith, therefore, cannot be correct in supposing that the orginial rule which regulated the exchangeable value of commodities, namely, the comparative quantity of labour by which they were produced, can be at all altered by the appropriation of land and the payment of rent. Raw material enters into the composition of most commodities, but the value of that raw material, as well as corn, is regulated by the productiveness of the portion of capital last employed on the land, and paying no rent; and therefore rent is not a component part of the price of commodities.

We have been hitherto considering the effects of the natural progress of wealth and population on rent, in a country in which the land is of variously productive powers; and we have seen, that with every portion of additional capital which it becomes necessary to employ on the land with a less productive return, rent would rise. It follows from the same principles, that any circumstances in the society which should make it unnecessary to employ the same amount of capital on the land, and which should therefore make the portion last employed more productive, would lower rent. Any great reduction in the capital of a country, which should materially diminish the funds destined for the maintenance of labour, would naturally have this effect. Population regulates itself by the funds which are to employ it, and therefore always increases or diminishes with the increase or diminution of capital. Every reduction of capital is therefore necessarily followed by a less effective demand for corn, by a fall of price, and by diminished cultivation. In the reverse order to that in which the accumulation of capital raises rent, will the diminution of it lower rent. Land of a less unproductive quality will be in succession relinquished, the exchangeable value of produce will fall, and land of a superior quality will be the land last cultivated, and that which will then pay no rent. . . .

ON PROFITS

. . . it remains for us to consider what is the cause of the permanent variations in the rate of profit, and the consequent permanent alterations in the rate of interest.

---

[3] The clear understanding of this principle is, I am persuaded, of the utmost importance to the science of political economy.

We have seen that the price[4] of corn is regulated by the quantity of labour necessary to produce it, with that portion of capital which pays no rent. We have seen, too, that all manufactured commodities rise and fall in price, in proportion as more or less labour becomes necessary to their production. Neither the farmer who cultivates that quantity of land, which regulates price, nor the manufacturer, who manufactures goods, sacrifice any portion of the produce for rent. The whole value of their commodities is divided into two portions only: one constitutes the profits of stock, the other the wages of labour.

Supposing corn and manufactured goods always to sell at the same price, profits would be high or low in proportion as wages were low or high. But suppose corn to rise in price because more labour is necessary to produce it; that cause would not raise the price of manufactured goods in the production of which no additional quantity of labour is required. If, then, wages continue the same, the profits of manufacturers would remain the same; but if, as is absolutely certain, wages should rise with the rise of corn, then their profits would necessarily fall. . . .

Thus in every case, agricultural, as well as manufacturing profits are lowered by a rise in the price of raw produce, if it be accompanied by a rise of wages. If the farmer gets no additional value for the corn which remains to him after paying rent, if the manufacturer gets no additional value for the goods which he manufactures, and if both are obliged to pay a greater value in wages, can any point be more clearly established then that profits must fall, with a rise of wages? . . .

It may be said that I have taken it for granted, that money wages would rise with a rise in the price of raw produce, but that this is by no means a necessary consequence, as the labourer may be contented with fewer enjoyments. It is true that the wages of labour may previously have been at a high level, and that they may bear some reduction. If so, the fall of profits will be checked; but it is impossible to conceive that the money price of wages should fall, or remain stationary with a gradually increasing price of necessaries; and therefore it may be taken for granted that, under ordinary circumstances, no permanent rise takes place in the rise of necessaries, without occasioning, or having been preceded by a rise in wages.

The effects produced on profits would have been the same, or nearly the same, if there had been any rise in the price of those other necessaries, besides food, on which the wages of labour are expended. The necessity which the labourer would be under of paying an increased price for such necessaries, would oblige him to demand more wages; and whatever increases wages, necessarily reduces profits. But suppose the price of silks, velvets, furniture, and any other commodities, not required by the labourer, to rise in consequence of more labour being expended on them, would not that affect profits? Certainly not: for nothing can affect profits but a rise in wages; silks

---

[4] The reader is desired to bear in mind that, for the purpose of making the subject more clear, I consider money to be invariable in value, and therefore every variation of price to be referable to an alteration in the value of the commodity.

and velvets are not consumed by the labourer, and therefore cannot raise wages.

It is to be understood that I am speaking of profits generally. I have already remarked, that the market price of a commodity may exceed its natural or necessary price, as it may be produced in less abundance than the new demand for it requires. This, however, is but a temporary effect. The high profits on capital employed in producing that commodity, will naturally attract capital to that trade; and as soon as the requisite funds are supplied, and the quantity of the commodity is duly increased, its price will fall, and the profits of the trade will conform to the general level. A fall in the general rate of profits is by no means incompatible with a partial rise of profits in particular employments. It is through the inequality of profits, that capital is moved from one employment to another. Whilst then general profits are falling, and gradually settling at a lower level in consequence of the rise of wages, and the increasing difficulty of supplying the increasing population with necessaries, the profits of the farmer may, for an interval of some little duration, be above the former level. An extraordinary stimulus may be also given for a certain time, to a particular branch of foreign and colonial trade; but the admission of this fact by no means invalidates the theory, that profits depend on high or low wages, wages on the price of necessaries, and the price of necessaries chiefly on the price of food, because all other requisites may be increased almost without limit.

It should be recollected that prices always vary in the market, and in the first instance, through the comparative state of demand and supply. Although cloth could be furnished at 40s. per yard, and give the usual profits of stock, it may rise to 60 or 80s. from a general change of fashion, or from any other cause which should suddenly and unexpectedly increase the demand, or diminish the supply of it. The makers of cloth will for a time have unusual profits, but capital will naturally flow to that manufacture, till the supply and demand are again at their fair level, when the price of cloth will again sink to 40s., its natural or necessary price. In the same manner, with every increased demand for corn, it may rise so high as to afford more than the general profits to the farmer. If there be plenty of fertile land, the price of corn will again fall to its former standard, after the requisite quantity of capital has been employed in producing it, and profits will be as before; but if there be not plenty of fertile land, if, to produce this additional quantity, more than the usual quantity of capital and labour be required, corn will not fall to its former level. Its natural price will be raised, and the farmer, instead of obtaining permanently larger profits, will find himself obliged to be satisfied with the diminished rate which is the inevitable consequence of the rise in wages, produced by the rise of necessaries.

The natural tendency of profits then is to fall; for, in the progress of society and wealth, the additional quantity of food required is obtained by the sacrifice of more and more labour. This tendency, this gravitation as it were of profits, is happily checked at repeated intervals by the improvements in machinery, connected with the production of necessaries, as well as by discoveries in the science of agriculture which enable us to relinquish a portion of labour before required, and therefore to lower the price of the prime necessary of the labourer. The rise in the price of necessaries and in the wages of labour is however limited; for as soon as wages should . . . equal . . . the whole receipts of the farmer, there must be an end of accumulation; for no capital can then yield any profit whatever, and no additional labour can be demanded, and consequently population will have reached its highest point. Long indeed before this period, the very low rate of profits will have arrested all accumulation, and almost the whole produce of the country, after paying the labourers, will be the property of the owners of land and the receivers of tithes and taxes. . . .

I have already said, that long before this state of prices[5] was become permanent, there would be no motive for accumulation; for no one accumulates but with a view to make his accumulation productive, and it is only when so employed that it operates on profits. Without a motive there could be no accumulation, and consequently such a state of prices never could take place. The farmer and manufacturer can no more live without profit, than the labourer without wages. Their motive for accumulation will diminish with every diminution of profit, and will cease altogether when their profits are so low as not to afford them an adequate compensation for their trouble, and the risk which they must necessarily encounter in employing their capital productively. . . .

Thus we . . . arrive at the . . . conclusion . . . that in all countries, at all times, profits depend on the quantity of labour requisite to provide necessaries for the labourers, on that land or with that capital which yields no rent. The effects then of accumulation will be different in different countries, and will depend chiefly on the fertility of the land. However extensive a country may be where the land is of a poor quality, and where the importation of food is prohibited, the most moderate accumulations of capital will be attended with great reductions in the rate of profit, and a rapid rise in rent; and on the contrary a small but fertile country, particularly if it freely permits the importation of food, may accumulate a large stock of capital without any great diminution in the rate of profits, or any great increase in the rent of land. . . .

EFFECTS OF ACCUMULATION ON PROFITS AND INTEREST

From the account which has been given of the profits of stock, it will appear, that no accumulation of capital will permanently lower profits, unless there be some permanent cause for the rise of wages. If the funds for the maintenance of labour were doubled, trebled, or quadrupled, there would not long be any difficulty in procuring the requisite number of hands, to be

---

[5] The "state of price" refers to a price level so high that the resulting necessarily high wages will leave the rate of profit at zero.—EDS.

employed by those funds; but owing to the increasing difficulty of making constant additions to the food of the country, funds of the same value would probably not maintain the same quantity of labour. If the necessaries of the workman could be constantly increased with the same facility, there could be no permanent alteration in the rate of profits or wages, to whatever amount capital might be accumulated. Adam Smith, however, uniformly ascribes the fall of profits to accumulation of capital, and to the competition which will result from it, without ever adverting to the increasing difficulty of providing food for the additional number of labourers which the additional capital will employ. "The increase of stock," he says, "which raises wages, tends to lower profit. When the stocks of many rich merchants are turned into the same trade, their mutual competition naturally tends to lower its profit; and when there is a like increase of stock in all the different trades carried on in the same society, the same competition must produce the same effect in all." Adam Smith speaks here of a rise of wages, but it is of a temporary rise, proceeding from increased funds before the population is increased; and he does not appear to see, that at the same time that capital is increased, the work to be effected by capital, is increased in the same proportion. M. Say has, however, most satisfactorily shewn, that there is no amount of capital which may not be employed in a country, because demand is only limited by production. No man produces, but with a view to consume or sell, and he never sells, but with an intention to purchase some other commodity, which may be immediately useful to him, or which may contribute to future production. By producing, then, he necessarily becomes either the consumer of his own goods, or the purchaser and consumer of the goods of some other person. It is not to be supposed that he should, for any length of time, be ill-informed of the commodities which he can most advantageously produce, to attain the object which he has in view, namely, the possession of other goods; and, therefore, it is not probable that he will continually produce a commodity for which there is no demand.

There cannot, then, be accumulated in a country any amount of capital which cannot be employed productively, until wages rise so high in consequence of the rise of necessaries, and so little consequently remains for the profits of stock, that the motive for accumulation ceases. While the profits of stock are high, men will have a motive to accumulate. Whilst a man has any wished-for gratification unsupplied, he will have a demand for more commodities; and it will be an effectual demand while he has any new value to offer in exchange for them. . . .

Productions are always bought by productions, or by services; money is only the medium by which the exchange is effected. Too much of a particular commodity may be produced, of which there may be such a glut in the market, as not to repay the capital expended on it; but this cannot be the case with respect to all commodities; the demand for corn is limited by the mouths which are to eat it; for shoes and coats by the persons who are to wear them; but though a community, or a part of a community, may have as much corn, and as many hats and shoes, as it is able or may wish to consume, the same cannot be said of every commodity produced by nature or by art. Some would consume more wine, if they had the ability to procure it. Others having enough of wine, would wish to increase the quantity or improve the quality of their furniture. Others might wish to ornament their grounds, or to enlarge their houses. The wish to do all or some of these is implanted in every man's breast; nothing is required but the means, and nothing can afford the means, but an increase of production. If I had food and necessaries at my disposal, I should not be long in want of workmen who would put me in possession of some of the objects most useful or most desirable to me.

Whether these increased productions, and the consequent demand which they occasion, shall or shall not lower profits, depends solely on the rise of wages; and the rise of wages, excepting for a limited period, on the facility of producing the food and necessaries of the labourer. I say excepting for a limited period, because no point is better established, than that the supply of labourers will always ultimately be in proportion to the means of supporting them.

THOMAS ROBERT MALTHUS

‖‖‖

On the Progress of Wealth

STATEMENT OF THE PARTICULAR OBJECT OF INQUIRY

There is scarcely any inquiry more curious, or, from its importance, more worthy of attention, than that which traces the causes which practically check the progress of wealth in different countries, and stop it, or make it proceed very slowly, while the power of production remains comparatively undiminished, or at least would furnish the means of a great and abundant increase of produce and population.

In a former work[1] I endeavored to trace the causes which practically keep down the population of a country to the level of its actual supplies. It is now my object to shew what are the causes which chiefly influence these supplies, or call the powers of production forth into the shape of increasing wealth.

Among the primary and most important causes which influence the wealth of nations, must unquestionably be placed, those which come under

Reprinted from *Principles of Political Economy*, 2d ed. (London: William Pickering, 1836), pp. 309-413, with omissions.

---

[1] *Essay on the Principle of Population.*

the head of politics and morals. Security of property, without a certain degree of which, there can be no encouragement to individual industry, depends mainly upon the political constitution of a country, the excellence of its laws and the manner in which they are administered. And those habits which are the most favourable to regular exertions as well as to general rectitude of character, and are consequently most favourable to the production and maintenance of wealth, depend chiefly upon the same causes, combined with moral and religious instruction. It is not however my intention at present to enter fully into these causes, important and effective as they are; but to confine myself chiefly to the more immediate and proximate causes of increasing wealth, whether they may have their origin in these political and moral sources, or in any others more specifically and directly within the province of political economy.

It is obviously true that there are many countries, not essentially different either in the degree of security which they afford to property, or in the moral and religious instruction received by the people, which yet, with nearly equal natural capabilities, make a very different progress in wealth. It is the principal object of the present inquiry to explain this; and to furnish some solution of certain phenomena frequently obtruded upon our attention, whenever we take a view of the different states of Europe, or of the world; namely, countries with great powers of production comparatively poor, and countries with small powers of production comparatively rich.

. . . The practical question then for our consideration is, what are the most immediate and effective stimulants to the continued creation and progress of wealth.

POPULATION AS A STIMULUS TO THE INCREASE OF WEALTH

That a continued increase of population is a powerful and necessary element of increasing demand, will be most readily allowed; but that the increase of population alone, or, more properly speaking, the pressure of the population hard against the limits of subsistence, does not furnish an effective stimulus to the continued increase of wealth, is not only evident in theory, but is confirmed by universal experience. If want alone, or the desire of the labouring classes to possess the necessaries and conveniences of life, were a sufficient stimulus to production, there is no state in Europe, or in the world, which would have found any other practical limit to its wealth than its power to produce; and the earth would probably before this period have contained, at the very least, ten times as many inhabitants as are supported on its surface at present. . . .

It will be said perhaps that the increase of population will lower wages, and, by thus diminishing the costs of production, will increase the profits of the capitalists and the encouragement to produce. Some temporary effect of this kind may no doubt take place, but it is evidently very strictly limited. The fall of real wages cannot go on beyond a certain point without not only stopping the progress of the population but making it even retrograde; and before this point is reached, the increase of produce occasioned by the labour of the additional number of persons will have so lowered its value, and reduced profits, as to determine the capitalist to employ less labour. . . .

To suppose a great and continued increase of population is to beg the question. We may as well suppose at once an increase of wealth; because such an increase of population cannot take place without a proportionate or nearly proportionate increase of wealth. The question really is, whether encouragements to population, or even the natural tendency of population to increase beyond the funds destined for its maintenance, will, or will not, alone furnish an adequate stimulus to the increase of wealth. And this question, Spain, Portugal, Poland, Hungary, Turkey, and many other countries in Europe, together with nearly the whole of Asia and Africa, and the greatest part of America, distinctly answer in the negative.

THE STIMULI TO THE INCREASE OF WEALTH

ACCUMULATION, OR SAVINGS

The Nature of Effective Demand   Those who reject mere population as an adequate stimulus to the increase of wealth, are generally disposed to make everything depend upon accumulation. It is certainly true that no permanent and continued increase of wealth can take place without a continued increase of capital. . . .

But we have yet to enquire what is the state of things which generally disposes a nation to accumulate; and further, what is the state of things which tends to make that accumulation the most effective, and lead to a further and continued increase of capital and wealth.

. . . the consumption and demand occasioned by the workmen employed in productive labour can never *alone* furnish a motive to the accumulation and employment of capital; and with regard to the capitalists themselves, together with the landlords and other rich persons, they have, by the supposition, agreed to be parsimonious, and by depriving themselves of their usual conveniencies and luxuries to save from their revenue and add to their capital. Under these circumstances, it is impossible that the increased quantity of commodities, obtained by the increased number of productive labourers, should find purchasers, without such a fall of price as would probably sink their value below that of the outlay, or, at least, so reduce profits as very greatly to diminish both the power and the will to save.

It has been thought by some very able writers, that although there may easily be a glut of particular commodities, there cannot possibly be a glut of commodities in general; because, according to their view of the subject, commodities being always exchanged for commodities, one half will furnish a market for the other half, and production being thus the sole source of demand, an excess of the supply of one article merely proves a deficiency in the supply of some other, and a general excess is impossible. M. Say, in his distinguished work on political economy, has indeed gone so far as to state that the consumption of a commodity by taking it out of the market diminishes demand, and the production of a commodity proportionably increases it.

This doctrine, however, as generally applied, appears to me to be utterly unfounded, and completely to contradict the great principles which regulate supply and demand.

It is by no means true, as a matter of fact, that commodities are always exchanged for commodities. An immense mass of commodities is exchanged directly, either for productive labour, or personal services: and it is quite obvious, that this mass of commodities, compared with the labour with which it is to be exchanged, may fall in value from a glut just as any one commodity falls in value from an excess of supply, compared either with labour or money. . . .

M. Say, Mr. Mill, and Mr. Ricardo, the principal authors of these new doctrines, appear to me to have fallen into some fundamental errors in the view which they have taken of this subject.

In the first place, they have considered commodities as if they were so many mathematical figures, or arithmetical characters, the relations of which were to be compared, instead of articles of consumption, which must of course be referred to the numbers and wants of the consumers.

If commodities were only to be compared and exchanged with each other, then indeed it would be true that, if they were all increased in their proper proportions to any extent, they would continue to bear among themselves the same relative values; but, if we compare them, as we certainly ought to do, with the means of producing them, and with the numbers and wants of the consumers, then a great increase of produce with comparatively stationary numbers or with wants diminished by parsimony, must necessarily occasion a great fall of value estimated in labour, so that the same produce, though it might have *cost* the same quantity of labour as before, would no longer *command* the same quantity; and both the power of accumulation and the motive to accumulate would be strongly checked.[2]

It is asserted that effectual demand is nothing more than the offering of one commodity in exchange for another which has cost the same quantity of labour. But is this all that is necessary to effectual demand? Though each commodity may have cost the same quantity of labour in its production, and they may be exactly equivalent to each other in exchange, yet why may not both be so plentiful as not to command more labour, than they have cost, that is, to yield no profit, and in this case, would the demand for them be effectual? Would it be such as to encourage their continued production? Unquestionably not. Their relation to each other may not have changed; but their relation to the wants of the society, and their relation to labour, may have experienced a most important change. . . .

Another fundamental error into which the writers above-mentioned and

---

[2] In terms of modern value theory, "labour cost" is analogous to average cost, and "labour commanded" is analogous to market price; therefore, the difference between labour commanded and labour cost is unit profit.—EDS.

their followers appear to have fallen is, the not taking into consideration the influence of so general and important a principle in human nature, as indolence or love of ease.

. . . The effect of a preference of indolence to luxuries would evidently be to occasion a want of demand for the returns of the increased powers of production supposed, and to throw labourers out of employment. . . . That an efficient taste for luxuries and conveniences, that is, such a taste as will properly stimulate industry, instead of being ready to appear at the moment it is required, is a plant of slow growth, the history of human society sufficiently shows; and that it is a most important error to take for granted, that mankind will produce and consume all that they have the power to produce and consume, and will never prefer indolence to the rewards of industry, will sufficiently appear from the slight review of some of the nations with which we are acquainted. . . .

It has also been said, that there is never an indisposition to consume, that the indisposition is to produce. Yet, what is the disposition of those master manufacturers and merchants who produce very largely and consume sparingly? Is their will to purchase commodities for their consumption proportioned to their power? Does not the use which they make of their capital clearly show that their will is to produce, not to consume? And in fact, if there were not in every country some who were indisposed to consume to the value of what they produced, how could the national capital ever be increased?

A third very serious error of the writers above referred to, and practically the most important of the three, consists in supposing that accumulation ensures demand; or that the consumption of the labourers employed by those whose object is to save, will create, such an effectual demand for commodities as to encourage a continued increase of produce. . . .

Upon this principle it is supposed that if the richer portion of society were to forego their accustomed conveniences and luxuries with a view to accumulation, the only effect would be a direction of nearly the whole capital of the country to the production of necessaries, which would lead to a great increase of cultivation and population. . . . there would undoubtedly be more necessaries produced than would be sufficient for the existing demand. This state of things could not, however, continue; since, owing to the fall which would take place, cultivation would be checked, and accumulation be arrested in its progress.

It is therefore obvious that without an expenditure which will encourage commerce, manufactures, and personal services, the possessors of land would have no sufficient stimulus to cultivate well; and a country such as our own, which had been rich and populous, would, with too parsimonious habits, infallibly become poor and comparatively unpeopled. . . .

If, in the process of saving, all that was lost by the capitalist was gained by the labourer, the check to the progress of wealth would be but temporary, as stated by Mr. Ricardo; and the consequences need not be apprehended. But if the conversion of revenue into capital pushed beyond a certain point must, by diminishing the effectual demand for produce, throw the labouring classes out of employment, it is obvious that the adoption of parsimonious habits beyond a certain point, may be accompanied by the most distressing effects at first, and by a marked depression of wealth and population afterwards.

It is not, of course, meant to be stated that parsimony, or even a temporary diminution of consumption, is not often in the highest degree useful, and sometimes absolutely necessary to the progress of wealth. A state may certainly be ruined by extravagance; and a diminution of the actual expenditure may not only be necessary on this account, but when the capital of a country is deficient, compared with the demand for its products, a temporary economy of consumption is required, in order to provide that supply of capital which can alone furnish the means of an increased consumption in future. All that is contended for is, that no nation can *possibly* grow rich by an accumulation of capital, arising from a permanent diminution of consumption; because such accumulation being beyond what is wanted in order to supply the effectual demand for produce, a part of it would very soon lose both its use and its value, and cease to possess the character of wealth. . . .

Mr. Ricardo has very clearly shewn that the rate of profits must diminish, and the progress of accumulation be finally stopped, under the most favourable circumstances, by the increasing difficulty of procuring the food of the labourer. I, in like manner, endeavor to shew in my essay on *The Principle of Population* that, under certain circumstances the most favourable to cultivation which could possibly be supposed to operate in the actual state of the earth, the real wages of the labourer would gradually become more scanty, and the progress of population be finally stopped by the increasing difficulty of procuring the means of subsistence.

. . . Fully acknowledging that there is hardly a country in the four quarters of the globe where capital is not deficient, and in most of them very greatly deficient, compared with the territory and even the number of people; and fully allowing at the same time the extreme desirableness of an increase of capital, I should say that, where the state of the demand for commodities was such as to afford much less than ordinary profits to the producer, and the capitalists were at a loss where and how to employ their capitals to advantage, the saving from revenue to add still more to these capitals would only tend prematurely to diminish the motive to accumulation, and still further to distress the capitalists, with little increase of a wholesome and effective capital.

. . . The most powerful stimulants may, under peculiar circumstances, be resisted; yet still it will not cease to be true that the natural and legitimate encouragement to the increase of capital is that increase of the power and will to save which is held out by certain and steady profits; and under circumstances in any degree similar, such increase of power and will to save must almost always be accompanied by a proportionate increase of capital. . . .

Though it may be allowed therefore that the laws which regulate the increase of capital are not quite so distinct as those which regulate the increase of population, yet they are certainly just of the same kind; and it is equally vain, with the view to the permanent increase of wealth, to continue converting revenue into capital, when there is no adequate demand for the products of such capital, as to continue encouraging marriage and the birth of children without a demand for labour and an increase of the funds for its maintenance.

FERTILITY OF THE SOIL

In speaking of the fertility of the soil as not affording with certainty an adequate stimulus to the continued increase of wealth, it must always be recollected that a fertile soil gives at once the greatest natural capability of wealth that a country can possibly possess. When the deficient wealth of such a country is mentioned, it is not intended to speak positively, but comparatively, that is with reference to its natural capabilities; and so understood, the proposition will be liable to few or no exceptions. Perhaps, indeed, it may be said that no instance has occurred, in modern times, of a large and very fertile country having made full use of its natural resources; while there may have been many instances of small and unfertile states having accumulated within their narrow limits, by means of foreign commerce, an amount of wealth very greatly exceeding what could be expected from their physical capabilities. . . .

LABOUR-SAVING INVENTIONS

Inventions to save labour seldom take place to any considerable extent, except when there is a decided demand for them. They are the natural consequence of improvement and civilization, and, in their more perfect forms, generally come in aid of the failing powers of production on the land. The fertility of the soil, being a gift of nature, exists whether it is wanted or not; and must often therefore exceed for many hundred years the power of fully using it. Inventions, which substitute machinery for manual exertions, being the result of the ingenuity of man, and called forth by his wants, will, as might be expected, seldom exceed those wants.

But the same law applies to both. They both come under the head of facilities of production; and in both cases a full use cannot be made of this facility, unless the power of supply which it furnishes be accompanied by an adequate extension of the market.

When a machine is invented, which, by saving labour, will bring goods into the market at a much cheaper rate than before, the most usual effect is such an extension of the demand for the commodity, by its being brought within the power of a much greater number of purchasers, that the value of the whole mass of goods made by the new machinery greatly exceeds their former value; and, not withstanding the saving of labour, more hands, instead of fewer, are required in the manufacture. . . .

When however the commodity to which machinery is applied is not of such a nature that its consumption can extend with its cheapness, the increase of wealth derived from it is neither so great nor so certain. . . .

. . . it is known that facilities of production have the strongest tendency to open markets, both at home and abroad. In the actual state of things therefore, there are great advantages to be looked forward to, and little reason to apprehend any permanent evil from the increase of machinery. The presumption always is, that it will lead to a great extension both of wealth and value. But still we must allow that the pre-eminent advantages derived from the substitution of machinery for manual labour, depend upon the extension of the market for the commodities produced, and the increased stimulus given to consumption; and that, without this extension of market and increase of consumption, they must be in a considerable degree diminished. Like the fertility of land, the invention of good machinery confers a prodigious power of production. But neither of these great powers can be called fully into action, if the situation and circumstances, or the habits and tastes of the society prevent the opening of a sufficient market, and an adequate increase of consumption.

The three great causes most favourable to production are, accumulation of capital, fertility of soil, and inventions to save labour. They all act in the same direction; and as they all tend to facilitate supply, without reference to demand, it is not probable that they should either separately or conjointly afford an adequate stimulus to the continued increase of wealth. . . .

ADDITIONAL COMMENTS ON SAVINGS AND WEALTH

It has already been shown that the value of the whole produce cannot be maintained in the case of a rapid accumulation of capital occasioned by an actual and continued diminution in the expenditure and consumption of the higher classes of society in the form of revenue. Yet it will be most readily allowed that the saving from revenue to add to capital is an absolutely necessary step in the progress of wealth. How then is this saving to take place without producing the diminution of value apprehended?

It may take place, and practically almost always does take place, in consequence of a previous increase in the value of the national revenue, in which case a saving may be effected, not only without any diminution of demand and consumption, but under an actual increase of demand, consumption, and value during every part of the process. And it is in fact this previous increase in the value of the national revenue which both gives the great stimulus to accumulation, and makes that accumulation effective in the continued production of wealth. . . .

The fortune of a country, though necessarily made more slow, is made in the same way as the fortunes of individuals in trade are generally made—by *savings,* certainly; but by savings which are furnished from increased gains, and by no means involve a diminished expenditure on objects of luxury and enjoyment.

Many a merchant has made a large fortune although, during the acquisition of his fortune, there was perhaps hardly a single year in which he did not rather increase than diminish his expenditure in objects of luxury, enjoyment, and liberality. The amount of capital in this country is immense, and it certainly received very great additions during the last forty years; but on looking back, few traces are to be found of a diminished expenditure in the shape of revenue. If some such traces however are to be found, they will be found in exact conformity to the theory here laid down; they will be found during a period, when, from particular circumstances, the value of the national produce was not maintained, and there was in consequence a diminution of the power of expenditure, and the comparative check to the production of wealth. . . .

THE MEANS OF INCREASING THE VALUE OF OUTPUT

The causes most favourable to that increase of value which depends upon distribution are 1st, the division of landed property; 2dly, internal and external commerce; 3dly, the maintenance of an adequate proportion of the society employed in personal services, or otherwise entitled to make a demand for material products without contributing directly to their supply. . . .

THE DIVISION OF LANDED PROPERTY

. . . though it be true that the division of landed property, and the diffusion of manufacturing and mercantile capital to a certain extent, are of the utmost importance to the increase of wealth; yet it is equally true that, beyond a certain extent, they would impede the progress of wealth as much as they had before accelerated it. There is a certain elevation at which the projectile will go the farthest: but if it be directed either higher or lower, it will fall short. With a comparatively small proportion of rich proprietors, who would prefer menial servants, retainers, and territorial influence to an excessive quantity of manufactured and mercantile products, the power among capitalists of supplying the results of productive labour would be much greater than the will to consume them, and the progress of wealth would be checked by the want of effectual demand. With an excessive proportion of small proprietors both of land and of capital, all great improvements on the land, all great enterprizes in commerce and manufactures, and most of the wonders described by Adam Smith, as resulting from the division of labour, would be at an end; and the progress of wealth would be checked by a failure in the powers of supply.

It will be found, I believe, true that all the great results in political economy, respecting wealth, depend upon *proportions;* and it is from overlooking this most important truth, that so many errors have prevailed in the prediction of consequences; that nations have sometimes been enriched when it was expected that they would be impoverished, and impoverished when it was expected that they would be enriched; and that such contradictory opinions have occasionally prevailed respecting the most effective encouragements to the increase of wealth. But there is no part of the whole subject, where the efficacy of proportions in the production of wealth is so strikingly exemplified, as in the division of landed and other property; and where it is so very obvious that a division to a certain extent must be beneficial, and beyond a certain extent prejudicial to the increase of wealth. . . .

COMMERCE

The second main cause favorable to that increase of exchangeable value, which depends upon distribution, is internal and external commerce.

Every exchange which takes place in a country, effects a distribution of its produce better adapted to the wants of the society. It is with regard to both parties concerned, an exchange of what is wanted less for what it wanted more, and must therefore raise the value of both the products. . . .

. . . This is the simple and obvious [point] often adverted to as the foundation of every act of barter, whether foreign or domestic, namely, the increased value which results from exchanging what is wanted less for what is wanted more. After we had, by our exports of home commodities, obtained in return all the foreign articles above-mentioned, we might be very much puzzled to say whether we had increased or decreased the *quantity* of our commodities, but we should feel quite certain that the new distribution of produce which had taken place, by giving us commodities much better suited to our wants and tastes than those which had been sent away, had decidedly increased the exchangeable value of our possessions, our means of enjoyment, and our wealth. . . .

PERSONAL SERVICES AND UNPRODUCTIVE CONSUMERS

The third main cause which tends to keep up and increase the value of produce by favouring its distribution is the employment of individuals in personal services, or the maintenance of an adequate proportion of consumers not directly productive of material objects. . . .

Every society must have a body of persons engaged in personal services of various kinds; as every society, besides the menial servants required, must have statesmen to govern it, soldiers to defend it, judges and lawyers to administer justice and protect the rights of individuals, physicians and surgeons to cure diseases and heal wounds, and a body of clergy to instruct the ignorant, and administer the consolations of religion. No civilized state has ever been known to exist without a certain portion of all these classes of society in addition to those who are directly employed in production. To a certain extent therefore they appear to be absolutely necessary. But it is perhaps one of the most important practical questions that can possibly be brought under our view, whether, however necessary and desirable they may be, they must be considered as detracting so much from the material products of a country, and its power of supporting an extended population; or whether they furnish fresh motives to production, and tend to push the wealth of a country farther than it would go without them.

The solution of this question evidently depends, first, upon the solution of the main practical question, whether the capital of a country can or cannot be redundant; that is, whether the motive to accumulate may be checked or destroyed by the want of effective demand long before it is checked by the difficulty of procuring the subsistence of the labourer. And secondly, whether, allowing the *possibility* of such a redundance, there is sufficient reason to believe that, under the actual habits of mankind, it is a probable occurrence.

In the Chapter on Profits, but more particularly in the Third Section of the present Chapter, where I have considered the effect of accumulation as a stimulus to the increase of wealth, I trust that the first of these questions has been satisfactorily answered. And in the present Section it has been shewn that the actual habits and practice of the productive classes, in the most improved societies, do not lead them to consume as revenue so large a proportion of what they produce, even though assisted by the landlords, as to prevent their finding frequent difficulties in the employment of their capitals. We may conclude therefore, with little danger of error, that such a body of persons as I have described is not only necessary to the government, protection, health, and instruction of a country, but is also necessary to call forth those exertions which are required to give full play to its physical resources. . . .

What the proportion is between the productive labourers and those engaged in personal services, which affords the greatest encouragement to the continued increase of wealth, it has before been said that the resources of political economy are unequal to determine. It must depend upon a great variety of circumstances, particularly upon the fertility of the soil and the progress of invention in machinery. A fertile soil and an ingenious people cannot only support without injury a considerable proportion of consumers not directly productive of material wealth, but may absolutely require such a body of demanders, in order to give effect to the powers of production. While, with a poor soil and a people of little ingenuity, an attempt to support such a body would throw land out of cultivation, and lead infallibly to impoverishment and ruin. . . .

On the whole it may be observed, that the specific use of a body of unproductive consumers, is to give encouragement to wealth by maintaining such a balance between produce and consumption as will give the greatest exchangeable value to the results of the national industry. If such consumers were to predominate, the comparatively small quantity of material products brought to market would keep down the value of the whole produce, from the deficiency of quantity. If, on the other hand, the productive classes were in excess, the value of the whole produce would fall from excess of supply. There is therefore a certain proportion between the two which will yield the greatest value, and command for a continuance the greatest quantity of labour; and we may safely conclude that, among the causes necessary to that distribution, which tends to keep up and increase the exchangeable value of the whole produce, we must place the maintenance of a certain body of consumers who are not themselves engaged in the immediate production of material objects. This body, considered as a stimulus to wealth, should vary in different countries, and at different times, according to the powers of production; and the most favourable result evidently depends upon their numbers being best suited to the natural resources of the soil, and the skill, and acquired tastes of the people. . . .

JOHN STUART MILL

||||||||||||||||||||||||||||||||||||||||||||||||||||||||||||||||||||||||||||||||||||||||||||||||||||||||||||||||||||||||||||||||||||||||||||||||||

Economic Progress and the Stationary State

GENERAL CHARACTERISTICS OF A PROGRESSIVE STATE

. . . We have surveyed the field of economical facts, and have examined how they stand related to one another as causes and effects; what circumstances determine the amount of production, of employment for labor, of capital and population; what laws regulate rent, profits, and wages; under what conditions and in what proportions commodities are interchanged between individuals and between countries. We have thus obtained a collective view of the economical phenomena of society, considered as existing simultaneously. . . . All this, however, has only put us in possession of the economical laws of a stationary and unchanging society. We have still to consider the economical condition of mankind as liable to change, and indeed (in the more advanced portions of the race, and in all regions to which their influence reaches) as at all times undergoing progressive changes. We have to consider what these changes are, what are their laws, and what their ultimate tendencies; thereby adding a theory of motion to our theory of equilibrium—the Dynamics of political economy to the Statics.

In this inquiry, it is natural to commence by tracing the operation of known and acknowledged agencies. Whatever may be the other changes which the economy of society is destined to undergo, there is one actually in progress, concerning which there can be no dispute. In the leading countries of the world, and in all others as they come within the influence of those leading countries, there is at least one progressive movement which continues with little interruption from year to year and from generation to generation; a progress in wealth; an advancement in what is called material prosperity. All the nations which we are accustomed to call civilized, increase gradually in production and in population: and there is no reason to doubt, that not only these nations will for some time continue so to increase, but that most of the other nations of the world, including some not yet founded, will successively enter upon the same career. It will, therefore, be our first object to examine the nature and consequences of this progressive change; the elements which

Reprinted from *Principles of Political Economy*, 2d ed. (London: The Colonial Press, 1900), Vol. II, pp. 210-265, with omissions.

constitute it, and the effects it produces on the various economical facts of which we have been tracing the laws, and especially on wages, profits, rents, values, and prices.

Of the features which characterize this progressive economical movement of civilized nations, that which first excites attention, through its intimate connection with the phenomena of Production, is the perpetual, and so far as human foresight can extend, the unlimited, growth of man's power over nature. Our knowledge of the properties and laws of physical objects shows no sign of approaching its ultimate boundaries: it is advancing more rapidly, and in a greater number of directions at once, than in any previous age or generation, and affording such frequent glimpses of unexplored fields beyond, as to justify our belief that our acquaintance with nature is still almost in its infancy. This increasing physical knowledge is now, too, more rapidly than at any former period, converted by practical ingenuity, into physical power. The most marvellous of modern inventions, one which realizes the imaginary feats of the magician, not metaphorically but literally—the electromagnetic telegraph—sprang into existence but a few years after the establishment of the scientific theory which it realizes and exemplifies. Lastly, the manual part of these great scientific operations is now never wanting to the intellectual: there is no difficulty in finding or forming, in a sufficient number of the working hands of the community, the skill requisite for executing the most delicate processes of the application of science to practical uses. From this union of conditions, it is impossible not to look forward to a vast multiplication and long succession of contrivances for economizing labor and increasing its produce; and to an ever wider diffusion of the use and benefit of those contrivances.

Another change which has always hitherto characterized, and will assuredly continue to characterize, the progress of civilized society, is a continual increase of the security of person and property. The people of every country in Europe, the most backward as well as the most advanced, are, in every generation, better protected against the violence and rapacity of one another both by a more efficient judicature and police for the suppression of private crime, and by the decay and destruction of those mischievous privileges which enabled certain classes of the community to prey with impunity upon the rest. They are also, in every generation, better protected, either by institutions or by manners and opinion, against arbitrary exercise of the power of government. Even in semibarbarous Russia, acts of spoliation directed against individuals, who have not made themselves politically obnoxious, are not supposed to be now so frequent, as much to affect any person's feelings of security. Taxation, in all European countries, grows less arbitrary and oppressive, both in itself and in the manner of levying it. Wars, and the destruction they cause, are now usually confined, in almost every country, to those distant and outlying possessions at which it comes into contact with savages. Even the vicissitudes of fortune which arise from inevitable natural calamities, are more and more softened to those on whom they fall, by the continual extension of the salutary practice of insurance.

Of this increased security, one of the most unfailing effects is a great increase both of production and of accumulation. Industry and frugality cannot exist, where there is not a preponderant probability that those who labor and spare [save] will be permitted to enjoy. And the nearer this probability approaches to certainty, the more do industry and frugality become pervading qualities in a people. Experience has shown that a large proportion of the results of labor and abstinence may be taken away by fixed taxation, without impairing, and sometimes even with the effect of stimulating, the qualities from which a great production and an abundant capital take their rise. But those qualities are not proof against a high degree of uncertainty. The government may carry off a part; but there must be assurance that it will not interfere, nor suffer anyone to interfere, with the remainder.

One of the changes which most infallibly attend the progress of modern society, is an improvement in the business capacities of the general mass of mankind. I do not mean that the practical sagacity of an individual human being is greater than formerly. I am inclined to believe that economical progress has hitherto had even a contrary effect. A person of good natural endowments, in a rude state of society, can do a greater number of things tolerably well, has a greater power of adapting means to ends, is more capable of extricating himself and others from an unforeseen embarrassment, than ninety-nine in a hundred of those who have known only what is called the civilized form of life. How far these points of inferiority of faculties are compensated, and by what means they might be compensated still more completely, to the civilized man as an individual being, is a question belonging to a different inquiry from the present. But to civilized human beings collectively considered, the compensation is ample. What is lost in the separate efficiency of each is far more than made up by the greater capacity of united action. In proportion as they put off the qualities of the savage, they become amenable to discipline; capable of adhering to plans concerted beforehand, and about which they may not have been consulted; of subordinating their individual caprice to a preconceived determination, and performing severally the parts allotted to them in a combined undertaking. Works of all sorts, impracticable to the savage or the half-civilized, are daily accomplished by civilized nations, not by any greatness of faculties in the actual agents, but through the fact that each is able to rely with certainty on the others for the portion of the work which they respectively undertake. The peculiar characteristic, in short, of civilized beings, is the capacity of cooperation; and this, like other faculties, tends to improve by practice, and becomes capable of assuming a constantly wider sphere of action. . . .

The progress which is to be expected in the physical sciences and arts, combined with the greater security of property, and greater freedom in disposing of it . . . and with the more extensive and more skillful employment of the joint-stock principle, afford space and scope for an indefinite increase of capital and production, and for the increase of population which is its ordinary accompaniment. That the growth of population will overpass the increase of production, there is not much reason to apprehend; and that it should even keep pace with it, is inconsistent with the supposition of any real improvement in the poorest classes of the people. It is, however, quite possible that there might be a great progress in industrial improvement, and in the signs of what is commonly called national prosperity; a great increase of aggregate wealth, and even, in some respects, a better distribution of it; that not only the rich might grow richer, but many of the poor might grow rich, that the intermediate classes might become more numerous and powerful, and the means of enjoyable existence be more and more largely diffused, while yet the great class at the base of the whole might increase in numbers only, and not in comfort nor in cultivation. We must, therefore, in considering the effects of the progress of industry, admit as a supposition, however greatly we deprecate as a fact, an increase in population as long-continued, as indefinite, and possibly even as rapid, as the increase of production and accumulation. . . .

THE TENDENCY OF PROFITS TO A MINIMUM

Continuing the inquiry into the nature of the economical changes taking place in a society which is in a state of industrial progress, we shall next consider what is the effect of that progress on the distribution of the produce among the various classes who share in it. We may confine our attention to the system of distribution which is the most complex, and which virtually includes all others—that in which the produce of manufacturers is shared between two classes, laborers and capitalists, and the produce of agriculture among three, laborers, capitalists, and landlords.

The characteristic features of what is commonly meant by industrial progress, resolve themselves mainly into three—increase of capital, increase of population, and improvements in production. . . .

. . . we are prepared to take into consideration a mixed case, in which two elements of expansion are combined, both population and capital increasing. . . . Let us examine what will be the effect, on rent and profits, of this double progress.

Population having increased, without any falling off in the laborer's condition, there is of course a demand for more food. The arts of production being supposed stationary, this food must be produced at an increased cost. To compensate for this greater cost of the additional food, the price of agricultural produce must rise. The rise extending over the whole amount of food produced, though the increased expenses only apply to a part, there is a greatly increased extra profit, which, by competition, is transferred to the landlord. Rent will rise, both in quantity of produce and in cost; while wages, being supposed to be the same in quantity, will be greater in cost. The laborer obtaining the same amount of necessaries, money wages have risen; and as the rise is common to all branches of production, the capitalist cannot indemnify himself by changing his employment, and the loss must be borne by profits.

It appears, then, that the tendency of an increase of capital and population is to add to rent at the expense of profits: though rent does not gain all that profits lose, a part being absorbed in increased expenses of production, that is, in hiring or feeding a greater number of laborers to obtain a given amount of agricultural produce. By profits, must of course be understood the *rate* of profit; for a lower rate of profit on a larger capital may yield a larger gross profit, considered absolutely, though a smaller in proportion to the entire produce.

This tendency of profits to fall, is from time to time counteracted by improvements in production: whether arising from increase of knowledge, or from an increased use of the knowledge already possessed. . . .

. . . The economical progress of a society constituted of landlords, capitalists, and laborers, tends to the progressive enrichment of the landlord class; while the cost of the laborer's subsistence tends on the whole to increase, and profits to fall. Agricultural improvements are a counteracting force to the two last effects; but the first, though a case is conceivable in which it would be temporarily checked, is ultimately in a high degree promoted by those improvements; and the increase of population tends to transfer all the benefits derived from agricultural improvement to the landlords alone. . . .

We now arrive at the fundamental proposition. . . . When a country has long possessed a large production, and a large net income to make savings from, and when, therefore, the means have long existed of making a great annual addition to capital; (the country not having, like America, a large reserve of fertile land still unused), it is one of the characteristics of such a country, that the rate of profit is habitually within, as it were, a hand's breadth of the minimum, and the country therefore on the very verge of the stationary state. By this I do not mean that this state is likely, in any of the great countries of Europe, to be soon actually reached, or that capital does not still yield a profit considerably greater than what is barely sufficient to induce the people of those countries to save and accumulate. My meaning is, that it would require but a short time to reduce profits to the minimum, if capital continued to increase at its present rate, and no circumstances having a tendency to raise the rate of profit occurred in the mean time. . . .

RESTRAINTS ON THE FALLING RATE OF PROFIT

What, then, are these counteracting circumstances, which, in the existing state of things, maintain a tolerably equal struggle against the downward tendency of profits, and prevent the great annual savings which take place in this country, from depressing the rate of profit much nearer to that lowest point to which it is always tending, and which, left to itself, it would so promptly attain? The resisting agencies are of several kinds.

THE "WASTAGE OF CAPITAL"

First . . . is the waste of capital in periods of overtrading and rash speculation, and in the commercial revulsions by which such times are always followed. It is true that a great part of what is lost at such periods is not destroyed, but merely transferred, like a gambler's losses, to more successful speculators. But even of these mere transfers, a large portion is always to foreigners, by the hasty purchase of unusual quantities of foreign goods at advanced prices. And much is also absolutely wasted. Mines are opened, railways or bridges made, and many other works of uncertain profit commenced, and in these enterprises much capital is sunk which yields either no return, or none adequate to the outlay. Factories are built and machinery erected beyond what the market requires, or can keep in employment. Even if they are kept in employment, the capital is no less sunk; it has been converted from circulating into fixed capital, and has ceased to have any influence on wages or profits. Besides this, there is a great unproductive consumption of capital, during the stagnation which follows a period of general overtrading. Establishments are shut up, or kept working without any profit, hands are discharged, and numbers of persons in all ranks, being deprived of their income, and thrown for support on their savings, find themselves, after the crisis has passed away, in a condition of more or less impoverishment. Such are the effects of a commercial revulsion: and that such revulsions are almost periodical, is a consequence of the very tendency of profits which we are considering. By the time a few years have passed over without a crisis, so much additional capital has accumulated, that it is no longer possible to invest it at the accustomed profit: all public securities rise to a very high price, the rate of interest on the best mercantile security falls very low, and the complaint is general among persons in business that no money is to be made. Does not this demonstrate how speedily profit would be at the minimum, and the stationary condition of capital would be attained, if these accumulations went on without any counteracting principle? But the diminished scale of all safe gains inclines persons to give a ready ear to any projects which hold out, though at the risk of loss, the hope of a higher rate of profit; and speculations ensue, which, with the subsequent revulsions, destroy, or transfer to foreigners a considerable amount of capital, produce a temporary rise of interest and profit, make room for fresh accumulations, and the same round is recommenced.

This, doubtless, is one considerable cause which arrests profits in their descent to the minimum, by sweeping away from time to time a part of the accumulated mass by which they are forced down. But this is not, as might be inferred from the language of some writers, the principal cause. If it were, the capital of the country would not increase; but in England it does increase greatly and rapidly. This is shown by the increasing productiveness of almost all taxes, by the continual growth of all the signs of national wealth, and by the rapid increase of population, while the condition of the laborers is certainly not declining, but on the whole improving. These things prove that each commercial revulsion, however disastrous, is very far from destroying all the capital which has been added to the accumulations of the country since the last revulsion preceding it, and that, invariably, room is either found or made for the profitable employment of a perpetually increasing capital, consistently with not forcing down profits to a lower rate.

IMPROVEMENTS IN PRODUCTION

This brings us to the second of the counter-agencies, namely, improvements in production. These . . . enable a greater amount of capital to be accumulated and employed without depressing the rate of profit: provided always that they do not raise, to a proportional extent, the habits and requirements of the laborer. If the laboring class gain the full advantage of the increased cheapness, in other words, if money wages do not fall, profits are not raised, nor their fall retarded. But if the laborers people up to the improvement in their condition, and so relapse to their previous state, profits will rise. All inventions which cheapen any of the things consumed by the laborers, unless their requirements are raised in an equivalent degree, in time lower money wages: and by doing so, enable a greater capital to be accumulated and employed, before profits fall back to what they were previously.

Improvements which only affect things consumed exclusively by the richer classes do not operate precisely in the same manner. The cheapening of lace or velvet has no effect in diminishing the cost of labor; and no mode can be pointed out in which it can raise the rate of profit, so as to make room for a larger capital before the minimum is attained. It, however, produces an effect which is virtually equivalent; it lowers, or tends to lower, the minimum itself. In the first place, increased cheapness of articles of consumption promotes the inclination to save, by affording to all consumers a surplus which they may lay by, consistently with their accustomed manner of living; and unless they were previously suffering actual hardships, it will require little self-denial to save some part at least of this surplus. In the next place, whatever enable people to live equally well on a smaller income, inclines them to lay by capital for a lower rate of profit. . . . All improvements, therefore, in the production of almost any commodity, tend in some degree to widen the interval which has to be passed before arriving at the stationary state. . . .

FOREIGN TRADE

Equivalent in effect to improvements in production is the acquisition of any new power of obtaining cheap commodities from foreign countries. If necessaries are cheapened, whether they are so by improvements at home or importation from abroad, is exactly the same thing to wages and profits. Unless the laborer obtains, and by an improvement of his habitual standard, keeps, the whole benefit, the cost of labor is lowered, and the rate of profit raised. As long as food can continue to be imported for an increasing population without any diminution of cheapness, so long the declension of profits through the increase of population and capital is arrested, and accumulation may go on without making the rate of profit draw nearer to the minimum. . . .

THE EXPORTATION OF CAPITAL

This brings us to the last of the counter-forces which check the downward tendency of profits in a country whose capital increases faster than that of its neighbors, and whose profits are therefore nearer to the minimum. This is, the perpetual overflow of capital into colonies or foreign countries, to seek higher profits than can be obtained at home. I believe this to have been for many years one of the principal causes by which the decline of profits in England has been arrested. It has a twofold operation. In the first place, it does what a fire, or an inundation, or a commercial crisis would have done; it carries off a part of the increase of capital from which the reduction of profits proceeds. Secondly, the capital so carried off is not lost, but is chiefly employed either in founding colonies, which become large exporters of cheap agricultural produce, or in extending and perhaps improving agriculture of older communities. It is to the emigration of English capital, that we have chiefly to look for keeping up a supply of cheap food and cheap materials of clothing, proportional to the increase of our population: thus enabling an increasing capital to find employment in the country, without reduction of profit, in producing manufactured articles with which to pay for this supply of raw produce. Thus, the exportation of capital is an agent of great efficacy in extending the field of employment for that which remains: and it may be said truly that, up to a certain point, the more capital we send away, the more we shall possess and be able to retain at home.

. . . As long as there are old countries where capital increases very rapidly, and new countries where profit is still high, profits in the old countries will not sink to the rate which would put a stop to accumulation; the fall is stopped at the point which sends capital abroad. It is only, however, by improvements in production, and even in the production of things consumed by laborers, that the capital of a country like England is prevented from speedily reaching that degree of lowness of profit, which would cause all further savings to be sent to find employment in the colonies, or in foreign countries. . . .

THE STATIONARY STATE

. . . Toward what ultimate point is society tending by its industrial progress? When the progress ceases, in what condition are we to expect that it will leave mankind?

It must always have been seen, more or less distinctly, by political economists, that the increase of wealth is not boundless: that at the end of what they term the progressive state lies the stationary state, that all progress in wealth is but a postponement of this, and that each step in advance is an approach to it. We have now been led to recognize that this ultimate goal is at all times near enough to be fully in view; that we are always on the verge of it, and that if we have not reached it long ago, it is because the goal itself flies before us. The richest and most prosperous countries would very soon attain the stationary state, if no further improvements were made in the productive arts, and if there were a suspension of the overflow of capital from those countries into the uncultivated or ill-cultivated regions of the earth.

This impossibility of ultimately avoiding the stationary state—this irresistible necessity that the stream of human industry should finally spread itself out into an apparently stagnant sea—must have been, to the political economists of the last two generations, an unpleasing and discouraging prospect; for the tone and tendency of their speculations goes completely to identify all that is economically desirable with the progressive state, and with that alone. With Mr. M'Culloch, for example, prosperity does not mean a large production and a good distribution of wealth, but a rapid increase of it; his test of prosperity is high profits; and as the tendency of that very increase of wealth, which he calls prosperity, is towards low profits, economical progress, according to him, must tend to the extinction of prosperity. Adam Smith always assumes that the condition of the mass of the people, though it may not be positively distressed, must be pinched and stinted in a stationary condition of wealth, and can only be satisfactory in a progressive state. The doctrine that, to however distant a time incessant struggling may put off our doom, the progress of society must "end in shallows and in miseries," far from being, as many people still believe, a wicked invention of Mr. Malthus, was either expressly or tacitly affirmed by his most distinguished predecessors, and can only be successfully combated on his principles.

I cannot . . . regard the stationary state of capital and wealth with the unaffected aversion so generally manifested towards it by political economists of the old school. I am inclined to believe that it would be, on the whole, a very considerable improvement on our present condition. I confess I am not charmed with the ideal of life held out by those who think that the normal state of human beings is that of struggling to get on; that the trampling, crushing, elbowing, and treading on each other's heels, which form the existing type of social life, are the most desirable lot of human kind, or anything but the disagreeable symptoms of one of the phases of industrial progress. It may be a necessary stage in the progress of civilization, and those European nations which have hitherto been so fortunate as to be preserved from it may have it yet to undergo. It is an incident of growth, not a mark of decline, for it is not necessarily destructive of the higher aspirations and the heroic virtues. . . . But it is not a kind of social perfection which philanthropists to come will feel any very eager desire to assist in realizing. Most fitting, indeed, is it, that while riches are power, and to grow as rich as possible the universal object of ambition, the path to its attainment should be open to all, without favor or partiality. But the best state for human nature is that in which, while no one is poor, no one desires to be richer, nor has any reason to fear being thrust back, by the efforts of others to push themselves forward.

That the energies of mankind should be kept in employment by the struggle for riches, as they were formerly by the struggle of war, until the better minds succeed in educating the others into better things, is undoubtedly more desirable than that they should rust and stagnate. While minds are coarse, they require coarse stimuli, and let them have them. In the mean time, those who do not accept the present very early stage of human improvement as its ultimate type may be excused for being comparatively indifferent to the kind of economical progress which excites the congratulations of ordinary politicians; the mere increase of production and accumulation. For the safety of national independence it is essential that a country should not fall much behind its neighbors in these things. But in themselves they are of little importance, so long as either the increase of population or anything else prevents the mass of people from reaping any part of the benefit of them. I know not why it should be a matter of congratulation that persons who are already richer than anyone needs to be should have doubled their means of consuming things which give little or no pleasure except as representative of wealth; or that numbers of individuals should pass over, every year, from the middle classes into a richer class, or from the class of the occupied rich to that of the unoccupied. It is only in the backward countries of the world that increased production is still an important object: in those most advanced, what is economically needed is a better distribution, of which one indispensable means is a stricter restraint on population. Leveling institutions, either of a just or of an unjust kind, cannot alone accomplish it; they may lower the heights of society, but they cannot, of themselves, permanently raise the depths.

On the other hand, we may suppose this better distribution of property attained, by the joint effect of the prudence and frugality of individuals, and of a system of legislation favoring equality of fortunes, so far as is consistent with the just claim of the individual to the fruits, whether great or small, of his or her own industry. We may suppose, for instance, . . . a limitation of the sum which any one person may acquire by gift or inheritance, to the amount sufficient to constitute a moderate independence. Under this twofold influence, society would exhibit these leading features: a well-paid and affluent body of laborers; no enormous fortunes, except what were earned and accumulated during a single lifetime; but a much larger body of persons than at present, not only exempt from the coarser toils, but with sufficient leisure, both physical and mental, from mechanical details, to cultivate freely the graces of life, and afford examples of them to the classes less favorably circumstanced for their growth. This condition of society, so greatly preferable to the present, is not only perfectly compatible with the stationary state, but, it would seem, more naturally allied with that state than with any other. . . .

It is scarcely necessary to remark that a stationary condition of capital and population implies no stationary state of human improvement. There would be as much scope as ever for all kinds of mental culture, and moral and social progress; as much room for improving the Art of Living, and much more likelihood of its being improved, when minds cease to be engrossed by the art of getting on. Even the industrial arts might be as earnestly and as successfully cultivated, with this sole difference, that instead of serving no purpose but the increase of wealth, industrial improvements would produce their legitimate effect, that of abridging labor. Hitherto it is questionable if all the mechanical inventions yet made have lightened the day's toil of any human being. They have enabled a greater population to live the same life of drudgery and imprisonment, and an increased number of manufacturers and others to make fortunes. They have increased the comforts of the middle classes. But they have not yet begun to effect those great changes in human destiny, which it is in their nature and in their futurity to accomplish. Only when, in addition to just institutions, the increase of mankind shall be under the deliberate guidance of judicious foresight, can the conquests made from the powers of nature by the intellect and energy of scientific discoverers, become the common property of the species, and the means of improving and elevating the universal lot. . . .

KARL MARX

|||||||||||||||||||||||||||||||||||||||||||||||||||||||||||||||||||||||||||||||||||||||||||||||||||||||||||||||||||||||||||||||||||||||||||||||||||||

Capital

THE LABOUR-PROCESS AND THE PROCESS OF PRODUCING SURPLUS-VALUE [1]

The capitalist buys labour-power in order to use it; and labour power in use is labour itself. The purchaser of labour-power consumes it by setting the seller of it to work. By working, the latter becomes actually, what before he only was potentially, a labour-power in action, a labourer. In order that his labour may reappear in a commodity, he must, before all things, expend it on something useful, on something capable of satisfying a want of some sort. Hence, what the capitalist sets the labourer to produce, is a particular use-value, a specified article. The fact that the production of use-values, or goods, is carried on under the control of the capitalist and on his behalf, does not alter the general character of that production. . . .

The labour-process, turned into the process by which the capitalist consumes labour-power, exhibits two characteristic phenomena. First, the labourer works under the control of the capitalist to whom his labour belongs; the capitalist taking good care that the work is done in a proper manner, and that the means of production are used with intelligence, so that there is no unnecessary waste of raw material, and no wear and tear of the implements beyond what is necessarily caused by the work.

Secondly, the product is the property of the capitalist and not that of the labourer, its immediate producer. Suppose that a capitalist pays for a day's labour-power at its value; then the right to use that power for a day belongs to him, just as much as the right to use any other commodity, such as a horse

Reprinted from *Capital* (Chicago: Charles H. Kerr and Company, 1909), Vol I, pp. 197-693, and Vol. III, pp. 247-305, with omissions. Volume I is translated from the third German edition by Samuel Moore and Edward Aveling, and edited by Frederick Engels. Volume III is translated from the first German edition by Ernest Untermann and edited by Frederick Engels.

[1] From Volume I.

that he has hired for the day. To the purchaser of a commodity belongs its use, and the seller of labour-power, by giving his labour, does no more, in reality, than part with the use-value that he has sold. From the instant he steps into the workshop, the use-value of his labour-power, and therefore also its use, which is labour, belongs to the capitalist. By the purchase of labour-power, the capitalist incorporates labour, as a living ferment, with the lifeless constituents of the product. From his point of view, the labour-process is nothing more than the consumption of the commodity purchased, i.e., of labour-power; but this consumption cannot be effected except by supplying the labour-power with the means of production. The labour-process is a process between things that the capitalist has purchased, things that have become his property. The product of this process also belongs, therefore, to him, just as much as does the wine which is the product of a process of fermentation completed in his cellar.

The product appropriated by the capitalist is a use-value, as yarn, for example, or boots. But, although boots are, in one sense, the basis of all social progress, and our capitalist is a decided "progressist," yet he does not manufacture boots for their own sake. Use-value is, by no means, the thing *qu'on aime pour lui-même* in the production of commodities. Use-values are only produced by capitalists, because, and in so far as, they are the material substratum, the depositaries of exchange-value. Our capitalist has two objects in view: in the first place, he wants to produce a use-value that has a value in exchange, that is to say, an article destined to be sold, a commodity; and secondly, he desires to produce a commodity whose value shall be greater than the sum of the values of the commodities used in its production, that is, of the means of production and the labour-power, that he purchased with his good money in the open market. His aim is to produce not only a use-value, but a commodity also; not only use-value, but value; not only value, but at the same time surplus-value. . . .

The surplus-value generated in the process of production by C, the capital advanced, or in other words, the self-expansion of the value of the capital C, presents itself for our consideration, in the first place, as a surplus, as the amount by which the value of the product exceeds the value of its constituent elements.

The capital C is made up of two components, one, the sum of money c laid out upon the means of production, and the other, the sum of money v expended upon the labour-power; c represents the portion that has become constant capital, and v the portion that has become variable capital. At first then, $C = c + v$: for example, if £500 is the capital advanced, its components may be such that the £500 equals £410 const. plus £90 var. When the process of production is finished, we get a commodity whose value equals $(c + v) + s$, where s is the surplus-value; or taking our former figures, the value of this commodity may be (£410 const. + £90 var.) + £90 surpl. The original capital has now changed from C to C', from £500 to £590. The difference is s or a surplus value of £90. Since the value of the constituent elements of the product is equal to the value of the advanced capital, it is mere tautology to say, that the excess of the value of the product over the value of its constituent elements, is equal to the expansion of the capital advanced or to the surplus-value produced. . . .

. . . We know that the value of the constant capital is transferred to, and merely re-appears in the product. The new value actually created in the process, the value produced, or value-product, is therefore not the same as the value of the product; it is not, as it would at first sight appear $(c + v)$ $+ s$ or £410 const. + £90 var. + £90 surpl.; but $v + s$ or £90 var. + £90 surpl. not £590 but £180. If c equals 0, or in other words, if there were branches of industry in which the capitalist could dispense with all means of production made by previous labour, whether they be raw material, auxiliary material, or instruments of labour, employing only labour-power and material supplied by Nature, in that case, there would be no constant capital to transfer to the product. This component of the value of the product, i.e., the £410 in our example, would be eliminated, but the sum of £180, the amount of new value created, or the value produced, which contains £90 of surplus-value, would remain just as great as if c represented the highest value imaginable. We should have $C = (0 + v) = v$ or C' the expanded capital $=$ $v + s$ and therefore $C' - C = s$ as before. On the other hand, if $s = 0$, or in other words, if the labour-power, whose value is advanced in the form of variable capital, were to produce only its equivalent, we should have $C = c$ $+ v$ or C' the value of the product equals $(c + v) + 0$ or $C = C'$. The capital advanced would, in this case, not have expanded its value. . . .

In the first place then we equate the constant capital to zero. The capital advanced is consequently reduced from $c + v$ to v, and instead of the value of the product $(c + v) + s$ we have now the value produced $(v + s)$. Given the new value produced $=$ £180, which sum consequently represents the whole labour expended during the process, then subtracting from it £90, the value of the variable capital, we have remaining £90, the amount of the surplus-value. This sum of £90 or s represents the absolute quantity of surplus-value produced. The relative quantity produced, or the increase percent of the variable capital, is determined, it is plain, by the ratio of the surplus-value to the variable capital, or is expressed by $\frac{s}{v}$. In our example this ratio is $\frac{90}{90}$, which gives an increase of 100 percent. This relative increase in the value of the variable capital, or the relative magnitude of the surplus-value, I call, "the rate of surplus-value."

We have seen that the labourer, during one portion of the labour-process, produces only the value of his labour-power, that is, the value of his means of subsistence. Now since his work forms part of a system, based on the social division of labour, he does not directly produce the actual necessaries which he himself consumes; he produces instead a particular commodity, yarn for example, whose value is equal to the value of those necessaries or of the money with which they can be bought. The portion of his day's labour devoted to this propose, will be greater or less, in proportion to the value of the necessaries that he daily requires on an average, or, what amounts to the same thing, in proportion to the labour time required on an average to produce them. If the value of those necessaries represents on an average the expenditure of six hours' labour, the workman must on an average work for six hours to produce that value. If instead of working for the capitalist, he worked independently on his own account, he would, other things being equal, still be obliged to labour for the same number of hours, in order to produce the value of his labour-power, and thereby to gain the means of subsistence necessary for his conservation or continued reproduction. But as we have seen, during that portion of his day's labour in which he produces the value of his labour-power, say three shillings, he produces only an equivalent for the value of his labour-power already advanced by the capitalist; the new value created only replaces the variable capital advanced. It is owing to this fact that the production of the new value of three shillings takes the semblance of a mere reproduction. That portion of the working day, then, during which this reproduction takes place, I call *"necessary"* labour-time, and the labour expended during that time I call *"necessary"* labour. Necessary, as regards the labourer, because independent of the particular social form of his labour; necessary, as regards capital, and the world of capitalists, because on the continued existence of the labourer depends their existence also.

During the second period of the labour-process, that in which his labour is no longer necessary labour, the workman, it is true, labours, expends labour-power; but his labour, being no longer necessary labour, he creates no value for himself. He creates surplus-value which, for the capitalist, has all the charms of a creation out of nothing. This portion of the working day, I name surplus labour-time, and to the labour expended during that time, I give the name of surplus-labour. It is every bit as important, for a correct understanding of surplus-value, to conceive it as a mere congelation of surplus-labour-time as nothing but materialised surplus-labour, as it is, for a proper comprehension of value, to conceive it as a mere congelation of so many hours of labour, as nothing but materialised labour. The essential difference between the various economic forms of society, between, for instance, a society based on slave labour, and one based on wage labour, lies only in the mode in which this surplus-labour is in each case extracted from the actual producer, the labourer.

Since, on the one hand, the values of the variable capital and of the labour-power purchased by that capital are equal, and the value of this labour-power determines the necessary portion of the working day; and since, on the other hand, the surplus-value is determined by the surplus portion of the working day, it follows that surplus value bears the same ratio to variable capital, that surplus-labour does to necessary labour, or in other words, the rate of surplus value $\frac{s}{v}$ equals $\frac{\text{surplus labour}}{\text{necessary labour}}$. Both ratios, $\frac{s}{v}$ and $\frac{\text{surplus labour}}{\text{necessary labour}}$ express the same thing in different ways; in the one case by reference to materialised, incorporated labour, in the other by reference to living, fluent labour.

The rate of surplus-value is therefore an exact expression for the degree of exploitation of labour-power by capital, or of the labourer by the capitalist.[2]. . .

THE ACCUMULATION OF CAPITAL

Whatever the form of the process of production in a society, it must be a continuous process, must continue to go periodically through the same phases. A society can no more cease to produce than it can cease to consume. When viewed, therefore, as a connected whole, and as flowing on with incessant renewal, every social process of production is, at the same time, a process of reproduction.

The conditions of production are also those of reproduction. No society can go on producing, in other words, no society can reproduce, unless it constantly reconverts a part of its products into means of production, or elements of fresh products. All other circumstances remaining the same, the only mode by which it can reproduce its wealth, and maintain it at one level, is by replacing the means of production—i.e., the instruments of labour, the raw material, and the auxiliary substances consumed in the course of the year—by an equal quantity of the same kind of articles; these must be separated from the mass of the yearly product, and thrown afresh into the process of production. Hence, a definite portion of each year's product belongs to the domain of production. Destined for productive consumption from the very first, this portion exists, for the most part, in the shape of articles totally unfitted for individual consumption. . . .

It does not alter matters any, if simple reproduction is replaced by reproduction on an enlarged scale, by accumulation. In the first instance the capitalist consumes the entire surplus-value, in the second he demonstrates his civic virtue by consuming only a part of it and converting the remainder into money.

The surplus-value is his property, it has never belonged to anybody else. If he advances it to production, he makes advances from his own funds just as he did on the day when he first came on the market. . . .

Accumulate, accumulate! That is Moses and the prophets! "Industry furnishes the material which saving accumulates."[3] Therefore, save, save, i.e., reconvert the greatest possible portion of surplus-value, or surplus-product into capital! Accumulation for accumulation's sake, production for production's sake: by this formula classical economy expressed the historical mission

---

[2] Although the rate of surplus-value is an exact expression for the degree of exploitation of labour-power, it is, in no sense, an expression for the absolute amount of exploitation. For example, if the necessary labour equals 5 hours and the surplus-labour equals 5 hours, the degree of exploitation is 100 percent. The amount of exploitation is here measured by five hours. If, on the other hand, the necessary labour equals 6 hours, and the surplus-labour 6 hours, the degree of exploitation remains, as before, 100 percent, while the actual amount of exploitation has increased 20 percent, namely from five hours to six. . . .

[3] A. Smith, 1. c., Bk. III, Ch. 3.

of the *bourgeoisie,* and did not for a single instant deceive itself over the birth-throes of wealth. But what avails lamentation in the face of historical necessity? If to classical economy, the proletarian is but a machine for the production of surplus-value; on the other hand, the capitalist is in its eyes only a machine for the conversion of this surplus value into additional capital. Political economy takes the historical function of the capitalist in bitter earnest. In order to charm out of his bosom the awful conflict between the desire for enjoyment and the chase after riches, Malthus, about the year 1820, advocated a division of labour, which assigns to the capitalist actually engaged in production, the business of accumulating, and to the other sharers in surplus-value, to the landlords, the place-men, the beneficed clergy, &c., the business of spending. It is of the highest importance, he says, "to keep separate the passion for expenditure and the passion for accumlation."[4]. . .

The proportion in which surplus-value breaks up into capital and revenue[5] being given, the magnitude of the capital accumulated clearly depends on the absolute magnitude of the surplus-value. Suppose that 80 percent were capitalized and 20 percent eaten up, the accumulated capital will be £2,400 or £1,200, according as the total surplus-value has amounted to £3,000 or £1,500. Hence all the circumstances that determine the mass of surplus-value operate to determine the magnitude of the accumulation. We sum them up once again, but only in so far as they afford new points of view in regard to accumulation. . . .

THE GENERAL LAW OF CAPITALIST ACCUMULATION

The composition of capital is to be understood in a twofold sense. On the side of value, it is determined by the proportion in which it is divided into constant capital or value of the means of production, and variable capital or value of labour-power, the sum total of wages. On the side of material, as it functions in the process of production, all capital is divided into means of production and living labour-power. This latter composition is determined by the relation between the mass of the means of production employed, on the one hand, and the mass of labour necessary for their employment on the other. I call the former the *value-composition,* the latter the *technical composition of capital.* Between the two there is a strict correlation. To express this, I call the value-composition of capital, in so far as it is determined by its technical composition and mirrors the changes of the latter, the *organic composition* of capital.[6] Wherever I refer to the composition of capital, without further qualification, its organic composition is always understood. . . .

Growth of capital involves growth of its variable constituent or of the

---

[4] Malthus, 1. c., pp. 319, 320.
[5] Revenue is that portion of surplus-value used for consumption by the capitalist—i.e., the portion not reinvested.—EDS.
[6] The organic composition of capital has been defined either as $\frac{c}{v}$ or as $\frac{c}{c+v}$.—EDS.

part invested in labour-power. A part of the surplus-value turned into additional capital must always be retransformed into variable capital, or additional labour-fund. If we suppose that, all other circumstances remaining the same, the composition of capital also remains constant (i.e., that a definite mass of means of production constantly needs the same mass of labour-power to set in motion,) then the demand for labour and the subsistence-fund of the labourers clearly increase in the same proportion as the capital, and the more rapidly, the more rapidly the capital increases. . . .

According to the economists themselves, it is neither the actual extent of social wealth, nor the magnitude of the capital already functioning, that lead to a rise of wages, but only the constant growth of accumulation and the degree of rapidity of that growth. (Adam Smith, Book I, Chapter 8.) So far, we have only considered one special phase of this process, that in which the increase of capital occurs along with a constant technical composition of capital. But the process goes beyond this phase.

Once given the general basis of the capitalistic system, then, in the course of accumulation, a point is reached at which the development of the productivity of social labour becomes the most powerful lever of accumulation. "The same cause," says Adam Smith, "which raises the wages of labour, the increase of stock, tends to increase its productive powers, and to make a smaller quantity of labour produce a greater quantity of work."

Apart from natural conditions, such as fertility of the soil &c., and from the skill of independent and isolated producers (shown rather qualitatively in the goodness then quantitatively in the mass of their products), the degree of productivity of labour, in a given society, is expressed in the relative extent of the means of production that one labourer, during a given time, with the same tension of labour-power, turns into products. The mass of the means of production which he thus transforms, increases with the productiveness of his labour. But those means of production play a double part. The increase of some is a consequence, that of the others a condition of the increasing productivity of labour. E.g., with the division of labour in manufacture, and with the use of machinery, more raw material is worked up in the same time, and, therefore, a greater mass of raw material and auxiliary substances enter into the labour-process. That is the consequence of the increasing productivity of labour. On the other hand, the mass of machinery, beasts of burden, mineral manures, drainpipes, &c., is a condition of the increasing productivity of labour. So also is it with the means of production concentrated in buildings, furnaces, means of transport, &c. But whether condition or consequence, the growing extent of the means of production, as compared with the labour-power incorporated with them, is an expression of the growing productiveness of labour. The increase of the latter appears, therefore, in the diminution of the mass of labour in proportion to the mass of means of production moved by it, or in the diminution of the subjective factor of the labour process as compared with the objective factor.

This change in the technical composition of capital, this growth in the mass of means of production, as compared with the mass of the labour-power that vivifies them, is reflected again in its value-composition, by the increase of the constant constituent of capital at the expense of its variable constituent. There may be, e.g., originally 50 percent of a capital laid out in means of production, and 50 percent in the labour-power; later on, with the development of the productivity of labour, 80 percent in means of production, 20 percent in labour-power, and so on. This law of the progressive increase in constant capital, in proportion to the variable, is confirmed at every step (as already shown) by the comparative analysis of the prices of commodities, whether we compare different economic epochs or different nations in the same epoch. The relative magnitude of the element of price, which represents the value of the means of production only, or the constant part of capital consumed, is in direct, the relative magnitude of the other element of price that pays labour (the variable part of capital) is in inverse proportion to the advance of accumulation. . . .

THE CENTRALIZATION OF CAPITAL

. . . Capital grows in one place to a huge mass in a single hand, because it has in another place been lost by many. This is centralization proper, as distinct from accumulation and concentration.

The laws of this centralization of capitals, or of the attraction of capital by capital, cannot be developed here. A brief hint at a few facts must suffice. The battle of competition is fought by cheapening of commodities. The cheapness of commodities depends, *ceteris paribus,* on the productiveness of labour, and this again on the scale of production. Therefore, the larger capitals beat the smaller. It will further be remembered that, with the development of the capitalist mode of production, there is an increase in the minimum amount of individual capital necessary to carry on a business under its normal conditions. The smaller capitals, therefore, crowd into spheres of production which Modern Industry has only sporadically or incompletely got hold of. Here competition rages in direct proportion to the number, and in inverse proportion to the magnitudes, of the antagonistic capitals. It always ends in the ruin of many small capitalists, whose capitals partly pass into the hands of their conquerors, partly vanish. . . .

THE INDUSTRIAL RESERVE ARMY

The accumulation of capital, though originally appearing as its quantitative extension only, is effected, as we have seen, under a progressive qualitative change in its composition, under a constant increase of its constant, at the expense of its variable constituent.

. . . With the advance of accumulation, therefore, the proportion of constant to variable capital changes. If it was originally say 1:1, it now becomes successfully 2:1, 3:1, 4:1, 5:1, 7:1, &c., so that, as the capital increases, instead of $\frac{1}{2}$ of its total value, only $\frac{1}{3}$, $\frac{1}{4}$, $\frac{1}{5}$, $\frac{1}{6}$, $\frac{1}{8}$, &c., is transformed into labour-power, and, on the other hand, $\frac{2}{3}$ $\frac{3}{4}$, $\frac{4}{5}$, $\frac{5}{6}$, $\frac{7}{8}$ into means of production. Since the demand for labour is determined not by the amount of capital as a whole, but by its variable constituent alone, that demand falls progressively with the increase of the total capital, instead of, as previously assumed, rising in proportion to it. It falls relatively to the magnitude of the total capital, and at an accelerated rate, as this magnitude increases. With the growth of the total capital, its variable constituent or the labour incorporated in it, also does increase, but in a constantly diminishing proportion. The intermediate pauses are shortened, in which accumulation works as simple extension of production, on a given technical basis. It is not merely that an accelerated accumulation of total capital, accelerated in a constantly growing progression, is needed to absorb an additional number of labourers, or even, on account of the constant metamorphosis of old capital, to keep employed those already functioning. In its turn, this increasing accumulation and centralisation becomes a source of new changes in the composition of capital, of a more accelerated diminution of its variable, as compared with its constant constituent. This accelerated relative diminution of the variable constituent, that goes along with the accelerated increase of the total capital, and moves more rapidly than this increase, takes the inverse form, at the other pole, of an apparently absolute increase of the labouring population, an increase always moving more rapidly than that of the variable capital or the means of employment. But in fact, it is capitalistic accumulation itself that constantly produces, and produces in the direct ratio of its own energy and extent, a relatively redundant population of labourers, i.e., a population of greater extent than suffices for the average needs of the self-expansion of capital, and therefore a surplus-population. . . .

But if a surplus labouring population is a necessary product of accumulation or of the development of wealth on a capitalist basis, this surplus population becomes, conversely, the lever of capitalistic accumulation, nay, a condition of existence of the capitalist mode of production. It forms a disposable industrial reserve army, that belongs to capital quite as absolutely as if the latter had bred it at its own cost. Independently of the limits of the actual increase of population, it creates, for the changing needs of the self-expansion of capital, a mass of human material always ready for exploitation. . . .

THE LAW OF THE FALLING TENDENCY OF THE RATE OF PROFIT[7]

THE THEORY OF THE LAW

With a given wage and working day, a certain variable capital, for instance of one hundred, represents a certain number of employed labourers. It is the index of this number. For instance, let 100 p. st. be the wages of 100 labourers for one week. If these labourers perform the same amount of

---

[7] From Volume III.

necessary as of surplus-labour, in other words, if they work daily as much time for themselves as they do for the capitalist, or, in still other words, if they require as much time for the reproduction of their wages as they do for the production of surplus-value for the capitalist, then they would produce a total value of 200 p. st., and the surplus-value would amount to 100 p. st. The rate of surplus-value, $\frac{s}{v}$, would be 100 percent. But we have seen that this rate of surplus-value would express itself in considerably different rates of profit, according to the different volumes of constant capitals c and consequently of total capitals C. For the rate of profit is calculated by the formula $\frac{s}{C}$.

Take it that the rate of surplus-value is 100 percent. Now, if

$$c = 50, \text{ and } v = 100, \text{ then } p' = \frac{100}{150}, \text{ or } 66\frac{2}{3}\%.$$

$$c = 100, \text{ and } v = 100, \text{ then } p' = \frac{100}{200}, \text{ or } 50\%.$$

$$c = 200, \text{ and } v = 100, \text{ then } p' = \frac{100}{300}, \text{ or } 33\frac{1}{3}\%.$$

$$c = 300, \text{ and } v = 100, \text{ then } p' = \frac{100}{400}, \text{ or } 25\%.$$

$$c = 400, \text{ and } v = 100, \text{ then } p' = \frac{100}{500}, \text{ or } 20\%.$$

In this way, the same rate of surplus-value, with the same degree of labour exploitation, would express itself in a falling rate of profit, because the material growth of the constant capital, and consequently of the total capital, implies their growth in value, although not in the same proportion.

If it is furthermore assumed that this gradual change in the composition of capital is not confined to some individual spheres of production, but occurs more or less in all, or at least in the most important ones, so that they imply changes in the organic average composition of the total capital of a certain society, then the gradual and relative growth of the constant over the variable capital must necessarily lead to a *gradual fall of the average rate of profit,* so long as the rate of surplus-value, or the intensity of exploitation of labour by capital, remain the same. Now we have seen that it is one of the laws of capitalist production that its development carries with it a relative decrease of variable as compared with constant capital, and consequently as compared to the total capital, which it sets in motion. This is only another way of saying that the same number of labourers, the same quantity of labour-power set in motion by a variable capital of a given value, consume in production an ever increasing quantity of means of production, such as machinery and all sorts of fixed capital, raw and auxiliary materials, and consequently a constant capital of ever increasing value and volume, during the same period of time, owing to the peculiar methods of production developing within the capitalist system. This progressive relative decrease of the variable capital as compared to the constant, and consequently to the total, capital is identical with the progressive higher organic composition of the average social capital. It is.

in another way, but an expression of the progressive development of the productive powers of society, which is manifested by the fact that the same number of labourers, in the same time, convert an ever growing quantity of raw and auxiliary materials into products, thanks to the growing application of machinery and fixed capital in general, so that less labour is needed for the production of the same, or of more, commodities. This growing value and volume of constant capital corresponds to a progressive cheapening of products, although the increase in the value of the constant capital indicates but imperfectly the growth in the actual mass of use-values represented by the material of the constant capital. Every individual product, taken by itself, contains a smaller quantity of labour than the same product did on a lower scale of production, in which the capital invested in wages occupies a far greater space compared to the capital invested in means of production. The hypothetical series placed at the beginning of this chapter expresses, therefore, the actual tendency of capitalist production. . . .

We have seen that a certain stage of capitalist development, in which the organic composition of capital, $c:v$ shows the proportion of 50:100, expresses a rate of surplus-value of 100 percent by a rate of profit of $66\frac{2}{3}$ percent, and that a higher stage, in which $c:v$ shows the proportion of 400:100, expresses the same rate of surplus-value by a rate of profit of only 20 percent. What is true of different successive stages in the same country, is also true of different contemporaneous stages of development in different countries. In an undeveloped country, in which the first-named composition of capital is the rule, the average rate of profit would be $66\frac{2}{3}$ percent, while in a country with the other, higher, stage of development, the average rate of profit would be 20 percent. . . .

COUNTERACTING CAUSES

If we consider the enormous development of the productive powers of labour, even comparing but the last thirty years with all former periods; if we consider in particular the enormous mass of fixed capital, aside from machinery in the strict meaning of the term, passing into the process of social production as a whole, then the difficulty, which has hitherto troubled the vulgar economists, namely that of finding an explanation for the falling rate of profit, gives way to its opposite, namely to the question: How is it that this fall is not greater and more rapid? There must be some counteracting influences at work, which thwart and annul the effects of this general law, leaving to it merely the character of a tendency. For this reason we have referred to the fall of the average rate of profit as a tendency to fall. . . .

The rate at which labour is exploited, the appropriation of surplus-labour and surplus-value, is raised by a prolongation of the working day and an intensification of labour. . . .

Whatever tends to promote the production of relative surplus-value by mere improvements in methods, for instance in agriculture, without altering the magnitude of the invested capital, has the same effect. While the constant capital does not increase relatively to the variable in such cases, taking the variable capital as an index of the amount of labour-power employed, the mass of the product *does* increase in proportion to the labour-power employed. . . .

It might be asked, whether the causes checking the fall of the rate of profit, but always hastening it in the last analysis, include the temporary raise in surplus-value above the average level, which recur now in this, now in that line of production for the benefit of those individual capitalists, who make use of inventions, etc., before they are generally introduced. This question must be answered in the affirmative. . . .

CONSEQUENCES OF THE FALLING RATE OF PROFIT

A fall in the rate of profit and a hastening of accumulation are in so far only different expressions of the same process as both of them indicate the development of the productive power. Accumulation in its turn hastens the fall of the rate of profit, inasmuch as it implies the concentration of labour on a large scale and thereby a higher composition of capital. On the other hand, a fall in the rate of profit hastens the concentration of capital and its centralisation through the expropriation of the smaller capitalists, the expropriation of the last survivors of the direct producers who still have anything to give up. This accelerates on one hand the accumulation, so far as mass in concerned, although the rate of accumulation falls with the rate of profit.

On the other hand, so far as the rate of self-expansion of the total capital, the rate of profit, is the incentive of capitalist production (just as this self-expansion of capital is its only purpose), its fall checks the formation of new independent capitals and thus seems to threaten the development of the process of capitalist production. It promotes overproduction, speculation, crises, surplus-capital along with surplus-population. Those economists who, like Ricardo, regard the capitalist mode of production as absolute, feel nevertheless, that this mode of production creates its own limits, and therefore they attribute this limit, not to production, but to nature (in their theory of rent). But the main point in their horror over the falling rate of profit is the feeling that capitalist production meets in the development of productive forces a barrier which has nothing to do with the production of wealth as such; and this peculiar barrier testifies to the finiteness and the historical, merely transitory character of capitalist production. It demonstrates that this is not an absolute mode for the production of wealth, but rather comes in conflict with the further development of wealth at a certain stage. . . .

The creation of . . . surplus-value is the object of the direct process of production, and this process has no other limits but those mentioned above. As soon as the available quantity of surplus-value has been materialised in commodities, surplus-value has been produced. But this production of surplus-value is but the first act of the capitalist process of production, it merely terminates the act of direct production. Capital has absorbed so much unpaid labour. With the development of the process, which expresses itself through a falling tendency of the rate of profit, the mass of surplus-value thus produced is swelled to immense dimensions. Now comes the second act of the process. The entire mass of commodities, the total product, which contains a portion which is to reproduce the constant and variable capital as well as a portion representing surplus-value, must be sold. If this is not done, or only partly accomplished, or only at prices which are below the prices of production, the labourer has been nonetheless exploited, but his exploitation does not realize as much for the capitalist. It may yield no surplus-value at all for him, or only realize a portion of the produced surplus-value, or it may even mean a partial or complete loss of his capital. The conditions of direct exploitation and those of the realization of surplus-value are not identical. They are separated logically as well as by time and space. The first are only limited by the productive power of society, the last by the proportional relations of the various lines of production and by the consuming power of society. This last-named power is not determined either by the absolute productive power nor by the absolute consuming power, but by the consuming power based on antagonistic conditions of distribution, which reduces the consumption of the great mass of the population to a variable minimum within more or less narrow limits. The consuming power is furthermore restricted by the tendency to accumulate, the greed for an expansion of capital and a production of surplus-value on a large scale. This is a law of capitalist production imposed by incessant revolutions in the methods of production themselves, the resulting depreciation of existing capital, the general competitive struggle and the necessity of improving the product and expanding the scale of production, for the sake of self-preservation and on penalty of failure. . . .

The real barrier of capitalist production is capital itself. It is the fact that capital and its self-expansion appear as the starting and closing point, as the motive and aim of production; that production is merely production for *capital,* and not vice versa, the means of production mere means for an ever expanding system of the life process for the benefit of the *society* of producers. The barriers, within which the preservation and self-expansion of the value of capital resting on the expropriation and pauperization of the great mass of producers can alone move, these barriers come continually in collision with the methods of production, which capital must employ for its purposes, and which steer straight toward an unrestricted extension of production, toward production for its own self, toward an unconditional development of the productive forces of society. The means, this unconditional development of the productive forces of society, comes continually into conflict with the limited end, the self-expansion of the existing capital. Thus, while the capitalist mode of production is one of the historical means by which the material forces of production are developed and the world-market required for them created, it is at the same time in continual conflict with this historical task and the conditions of social production corresponding to it. . . .

. . . The rate of profit is the compelling power of capitalist production, and only such things are produced as yield a profit. Hence the fright of the English economists over the decline of the rate of profit. That the bare possibility of such a thing should worry Ricardo, shows his profound under-standing of the conditions of capitalist production. The reproach moved against him, that he has an eye only to the development of the productive forces regardless of "human beings," regardless of the sacrifices in human beings and capital *values* incurred, strikes precisely his strong point. The development of the productive forces of social labour is the historical task and privilege of capital. It is precisely in this way that it unconsciously cre-ates the material requirements of a higher mode of production. What worries Ricardo is the fact that the rate of profit, the stimulating principle of capital-ist production, the fundamental premise and driving force of accumulation, should be endangered by the development of production itself. And the quantitative proportion means everything here. There is indeed something deeper than this hidden at this point, which he vaguely feels. It is here demonstrated in a purely economic way, that is, from a bourgeois point of view, within the confines of capitalist understanding, from the standpoint of capitalist production itself, that it has a barrier, that it is relative, that it is not an absolute, but only a historical mode of production corresponding to a definite and limited epoch in the development of the material conditions of production. . . .

A. J. YOUNGSON

Marshall on Economic Growth

All of Marshall's books and many of his occasional writings contain something of his views on economic development as a historical process. None of them contains a complete or particularly elaborate statement, the fuller developments being found in *Industry and Trade* and in the first edition of the *Principles*. To attempt an exposition of Marshall's views on this sub-ject therefore requires the collation of a good deal of material, published over thirty-six years, and written, in all probability, over a still greater period of time. This does not seem to matter much, however, as the views expressed in *Money, Credit, and Commerce,* published in 1923, do not differ markedly from those to be found in the *Principles* or in the evidence given before the Gold and Silver Commission in 1887.

Marshall never produced a theory of economic growth, and there is no

From *Scottish Journal of Political Economy* (February 1956), pp. 1-18, with omissions. Reprinted by permission of the publisher and the author.

such thing as a "Marshallian system." To speak of Marshall's "determinants" of economic growth is therefore apt to be misleading unless the word is dissociated from the idea of some logically complete construct. What Marshall did was to outline the nature and operation of certain forces which he considered to be of prime importance in causing or facilitating economic development. For the sake of brevity we may call these forces determinants of economic growth; and taking the word in this slightly special sense, we may conveniently separate the Marshallian determinants into three classes. First, there are the long-run, fundamental determinants; secondly, there are those influences which seem to bulk large enough in Marshall's treatment to be called major, but which differ from the fundamental determinants in being of a more economic, man-made character; and thirdly, there are the minor influences. This classification is of course somewhat arbitrary, but it is a helpful one in summarising Marshall's ideas.

FUNDAMENTAL DETERMINANTS

Marshall lists four determinants which are long-run and fundamental in their working, although the fourth is of a somewhat different nature from the other three. Basic and unalterable, there are climate, and natural resources and advantages conveniently disposed. Where nature is ungenerous, there is no surplus out of which progress may begin to be derived. "And therefore, as Buckle has pointed out, all early civilisations have been in warm climates where the necessaries of life are small, and where Nature makes bountiful returns even to the rudest cultivation."[1] But progress here cannot be sustained; physical toil is too hard, intellectual dilettantism too easy, and therefore it is in the "invigorating atmosphere" of "colder climates,"[2] where, moreover, the sea provides man with the possibility of constant intercourse, "knowledge, freedom and the power of variation," that progress finally takes root and continues. And after these two, there is human character. Thus we learn that the "strength of character of the Romans fitted them for business"[3]; that the United States owes some of its prosperity to its being inhabited by "a mixture of races of great energy and alertness"[4]; that the English "from 1066 down to the present time . . . the same people"[5] after centuries of economic backwardness "at last . . . threw their own special characteristics into business affairs with such energy, and such quickness of adaptation to the ever-increasing massiveness of the economic problems of the Western World, that they became its chief pioneers of progress and trade."[6]

---

[1] Alfred Marshall, *Principles of Economics* (London, 1890), Bk. I, Ch. 2, sect. 1. All references to the *Principles* are to the first edition unless otherwise stated. Passages corresponding to those quoted are as a rule to be found in Appendix A of the later editions.

[2] *Principles*, Bk. I, Ch. 2, sect. 1. See also *Principles*, Bk. I, Ch. 3, sects. 1 and 3.

[3] *Ibid.*, Bk. I, Ch. 2, sect. 4.

[4] *Money, Credit, and Commerce* (London, 1923), p. 221.

[5] *Industry and Trade* (London, 1919), p. 35.

[6] *Ibid.*

The fourth fundamental determinant is not a "natural" but a political one: this is human freedom. Economic growth is depicted by Marshall, in fact, almost as the material counterpart of the growth of freedom, the second of the two great covariants of history. Thus we are reminded that primitive societies suffer from the rule of custom, probably "the most important of all the causes which have delayed the growth of the spirit of free enterprise among mankind"[7]; the cities of the Middle Ages, we are told, "led the way towards modern industrial civilization" and might have realised it had they retained "their first love of liberty and social equality"[8]; only an inferior development can be achieved by those who, whatever their "industrial virtues," are "more patient and more easily contented, more submissive and less full of initiative," more tolerant of "bureaucratic management,"[9] than the English and the Americans.

Next after this group, more precise and for the most part more specifically economic, come what we have called the major influences in Marshall's conception of economic growth. There are five of these, two of them evidently of greater importance than the others.

MAJOR INFLUENCES

First there stands a composite sort of influence which could be described as the willingness and ability to save. This is dealt with most fully in the *Principles,* away from the more general discussions of economic growth, but it is nowhere forgotten. The fundamental point here is simple: "with the growth of openings for the investment of capital there is a constant increase in that surplus of production over the necessaries of life, which gives the power to save."[10] And with the growth of this power there may well go a growth of inclination, a strengthening of "habits of forethought and the willingness to incur present exertion in the expectation of a remote benefit."[11]

This idea is elaborated in three different directions. First, there must be security for savings: "The thriftlessness of early times was in a great measure due to the want of security that those who made provision for the future would enjoy it."[12] Secondly, there is the part played by the institution of money: "The growth of a money-economy and of modern habits of business does indeed hinder the accumulation of wealth by putting new temptations in the way of those who are inclined to live extravagantly. . . . But . . . a money-economy increases the variety of the uses between which a person can distribute his future expenditure. . . . And, what has had a far greater effect on the growth of wealth, it has rendered it far easier for a man to provide a

---

[7] *Principles,* Bk. I, Ch. 2, sect. 2.
[8] *Ibid.,* Bk. I, Ch. 2, sect. 7.
[9] *Memorials of Alfred Marshall,* edited by A. C. Pigou (London, 1925), p. 275.
[10] *Principles* (8th ed.), Bk. IV, Ch. 7, sect. 2.
[11] *Industry and Trade,* p. 143.
[12] *Principles* (8th ed.), Bk. IV, Ch. 7, sect. 4.

secure income for his wife and children after his death; for, after all, family affection is the main motive for saving."[13]

Lastly, there is the question of the distribution of income; and here Marshall seems to have been of two minds. In the chapter of the *Principles* from which we have been quoting, the matter is put in this way: "The power to save depends on an excess of income over necessary expenditure; and this is greatest among the wealthy. But . . . the older economists took too little account of the fact that human faculties are as important a means of production as any other kind of capital; and we may conclude, in opposition to them, that any change in the distribution of wealth which gives more to the wage receivers and less to the capitalists is likely, other things being equal, to hasten the increase of material production, and that it will not perceptibly retard the storing up of material wealth."[14] To this Marshall adds that such redistribution may even, given time, contribute to the growth of accumulated physical capital. This view is repeated in *The Economics of Industry* (1892).[15] But in *Industry and Trade* (1919) the argument seems to be, on the whole, that the existence of large gains by large capitalists in risky undertakings, leading to "an exceptionally large aggregate of new income in the hands of the commercial classes,"[16] is, at least in the case of the United States in the second half of the nineteenth century, of benefit to economic growth. And there seems to be an implication that this view could be generalised.

The second major influence of seemingly outstanding importance in Marshall's thought is also a composite one, usually to be found under the heading of improved transport or "massive production." In Marshall's thought improved transport, external economies, and the law of increasing return are intimately and inseparably bound up with one another; and in the well-known passage in Book V of the *Principles*,[17] in which Marshall hovers on the verge of a discussion of imperfect competition, it is the cost of transport which is called in to preserve the existence of the small manufacturer working in a sphere of production subject to the law of increasing return; and that preservation is not of a very sure kind, for "time is on the side of the more economic methods of production," *i.e.,* the costs of distribution are apt to diminish with time. This type of argument appears again and again when Marshall is discussing economic expansion. In *Industry and Trade*[18] the "slowness of the growth of foreign trade" between 1660 and 1760 is ascribed to the fact that "the new markets beyond the seas were really very narrow," due to the uncertainty and high cost incurred in the carriage of merchandise. This is the prelude to a brief account of transport improvements in England in the eighteenth century, and the section ends: "Each victory [over difficulties] tended to increase the area over which the goods could be marketed,

---

[13] *Ibid.,* Bk. IV, Ch. 7, sect. 5.
[14] *Ibid.,* Bk. IV, Ch. 7, sect. 7.
[15] P. 135.
[16] Pp. 154-155.
[17] *Principles* (8th ed.), Bk. V, Ch. 7, sect. 2.
[18] *Op. cit.,* p. 37.

and therefore the scale of production; and therefore in many industries at least the economy of production; and therefore again the area over which the goods could be marketed; and so on in ever widening circles."[19] An identical argument helps to explain what Marshall held to have been the "exceptionally great changes" in industry in the decade or two prior to 1887; "the changes are, I think, chiefly due to the great fall, the unparalleled fall, in the cost of transport, which renders it worth while to do a great many things that it was not worth while to do before."[20]

The three remaining "major influences" may be dealt with more briefly. Chief among them perhaps, and closely connected with the second, is the conjuncture of Petty's "great rule" that "each country flourisheth in the manufacture of its own native commodities,"[21] with the fact of one of these native commodities being "so uniform in substance and in shape as to give large scope for play of the economies" of specialisation.[22] This is exemplified by wool and iron in England, and shipbuilding in Holland in the seventeenth and eighteenth centuries. Next there is the importance of a country's having had experience of capitalistic forms of organisation before embarking upon large-scale production. Thus it is argued that entrepreneurs in England gained invaluable experience in organising the cottage industries long before the advent of the factories. Lastly, and mentioned only once in Marshall's writings although clearly of great consequence, there is the "temporary suspension of the pressure of the Law of Diminishing Return from land."

> The Law of Diminishing Return [to national effort?] is almost inoperative in Britain just now [1907], but after a generation or two it may again be a powerful influence here and nearly all over the world. Wages in Britain are now but very little affected by the rate of growth of population and the pressure on the means of subsistence. . . . But the world is really a very small place, and there is not room in it for the opening up of rich new resources during many decades at as rapid a rate as has prevailed during the last three or four. When new countries begin to need most of their own food and other raw produce, improvements in transport will count for little. From that time onward the pressure of the Law of Diminishing Return can be opposed only by further improvements in production; and improvements in production must themselves gradually show a diminishing return.[23]

MINOR INFLUENCES

We now come to those influences which seem least important in Marshall's structure of ideas, and which we have classified as minor influences.

---

[19] *Industry and Trade,* p. 41.
[20] Evidence before the Gold and Silver Commission, Q. 9831.
[21] *Industry and Trade,* p. 33.
[22] *Ibid.,* p. 55.
[23] *Memorials of Alfred Marshall,* p. 326.

Four of them are worth mentioning. First of all, alluded to in nearly every one of Marshall's works, there is the importance to a nation of having a "middle class." Thus we are told that in seventeenth-century England "the middle class and some parts of the working class adopted a severe view of life" and promoted industrial development by concentrating upon the production of articles "with a solid and lasting utility"[24]; by contrast, in eighteenth-century France the "luxury of the rich and the poverty of the poor combined to make France a bad market for substantial simple goods, which are not choice enough for the rich, nor cheap enough for the common people."[25] A middle class, in short, provides a market for goods well adapted to "massive production," while the "fusion of different ranks"[26] in society breeds that business enterprise which can take advantage of such a market. Secondly, the importance of efficient and reasonably incorruptible government is stressed. Education also receives a brief mention and, lastly, there is an almost equally brief reference to the role of prices. It seems beyond question that as far as economic growth was concerned Marshall attached little importance to changes in the price level—at any rate to changes such as had been known in the nineteenth century. In *Industry and Trade* there is a mild suggestion on page 87 that rising prices retard economic growth, and on page 88 an equally mild suggestion that they help it. In the evidence before the Gold and Silver Commission the argument is, on the whole, in favour of falling prices because manufacturers are then obliged "to exert themselves to the utmost" and lenders to be "much more careful about their loans."[27] But not much importance seems to be attached to the argument.[28]

To sum up, Marshall insists chiefly on the importance of climate, of the national character (which he admits is in part determined by natural and institutional factors), of the capacity to save, and of "massive production." The great secret of economic growth is to achieve this last, but it is a complex idea. If the first two are right—and much stress is laid on the second—then what chiefly matters is the possession of *home* resources, which may readily be utilised to increase the capacity to save and to achieve massive production, and the existence of extensive markets. Help is also given if men and ideas are mobile and can readily be got together—this tells in favour of the United States and Great Britain and against France—if there are institutional arrangements which encourage the trading of present for future benefits, and if there is a middle class to demand "solid wares" in quantity; it is also helpful if there is social mobility. Honest government, education, the distribution of income and the behaviour of prices—all of these are worth a mention but scarcely more. Everywhere the importance of improved transport is insisted upon. . . .

---

[24] *Principles,* Bk. I, Ch. 3, sect. 3.
[25] *Industry and Trade,* pp. 110-111.
[26] *Principles,* Bk. I, Ch. 3, sect. 1.
[27] Evidence before the Gold and Silver Commission, Q. 9816.
[28] A general statement of Marshall's position on this point is to be found in *Official Papers by Alfred Marshall,* pp. 7-10.

JOSEPH A. SCHUMPETER

||||||||||||||||||||||||||||||||||||||||||||||||||||||||||||||||||||||||||||||||||||||||||||||||||||||||||||||||||||||||||

On the Theory of Economic Development

THE FUNDAMENTAL PHENOMENON OF ECONOMIC DEVELOPMENT

Our problem is as follows. The theory of the first chapter describes economic life from the standpoint of a "circular flow," running on in channels essentially the same year after year—similar to the circulation of the blood in an animal organism. Now this circular flow and its channels do alter in time, and here we abandon the analogy with the circulation of the blood. For although the latter also changes in the course of the growth and decline of the organism, yet it only does so continuously, that is by steps which one can choose smaller than any assignable quantity, however small, and always within the same framework. Economic life experiences such changes too, but it also experiences others which do not appear continuously and which change the framework, the traditional course itself. They cannot be understood by means of any analysis of the circular flow, although they are purely economic and although their explanation is obviously among the tasks of pure theory. Now such changes and the phenomena which appear in their train are the object of our investigation. But we do not ask: what changes of this sort have actually made the modern economic system what it is? nor: what are the conditions of such changes? We only ask, and indeed in the same sense as theory always asks: how do such changes take place, and to what economic phenomena do they give rise?

The same thing may be put somewhat differently. The theory of the first chapter describes economic life from the standpoint of the economic system's tendency toward an equilibrium position, which tendency gives us the means of determining prices and quantities of goods, and may be described as an adaptation to data existing at any time.[1] In contrast to the conditions of the circular flow this does not mean in itself that year after

Reprinted by permission of the publishers from Joseph A. Schumpeter, *The Theory of Economic Development,* trans. by Redvers Opie (Cambridge, Mass., Harvard University Press, 1934), pp. 61-90, with omissions. Copyright 1934 by The President and Fellows of Harvard College.

---

[1] By "data," Schumpeter means circumstances, events, or facts given and assumed for the purpose of the analysis.—Eds.

year "the same" things happen; for it only means that we conceive the several processes in the economic system as partial phenomena of the tendency toward an equilibrium position, but not necessarily toward the same one. The position of the ideal state of equilibrium in the economic system, never attained, continually "striven after" (of course not consciously), changes, because the data change. And theory is not weaponless in the face of these changes in data. It is constructed so as to be able to deal with the consequences of such changes; it has special instruments for the purpose (for example the instrument called quasi-rent). If the change occurs in the non-social data (natural conditions) or in noneconomic social data (here belong the effects of war, changes in commercial, social, or economic policy), or in consumers' tastes, then to this extent no fundamental overhaul of the theoretical tools seems to be required. These tools only fail—and here this argument joins the preceding—where economic life itself changes its own data by fits and starts. The building of a railway may serve as an example. Continuous changes, which may in time, by continual adaptation through innumerable small steps, make a great department store out of a small retail business, come under the "static" analysis. But "static" analysis is not only unable to predict the consequences of discontinuous changes in the traditional way of doing things; it can neither explain the occurrence of such productive revolutions nor the phenomena which accompany them. It can only investigate the new equilibrium position after the changes have occurred. It is just this occurrence of the "revolutionary" change that is our problem, the problem of economic development in a very narrow and formal sense. The reason why we so state the problem and turn aside from traditional theory lies not so much in the fact that economic changes, especially, if not solely, in the capitalist epoch, have actually occurred thus and not by continuous adaptation, but more in their fruitfulness.

By "development," therefore, we shall understand only such changes in economic life as are not forced upon it from without but arise by its own initiative, from within. . . .

Nor will the mere growth of the economy, as shown by the growth of population and wealth, be designated here as a process of development. For it calls forth no qualitatively new phenomena, but only processes of adaptation of the same kind as the changes in the natural data. Since we wish to direct our attention to other phenomena, we shall regard such increases as changes in data. . . .

. . . Development in our sense is a distinct phenomenon, entirely foreign to what may be observed in the circular flow or in the tendency toward equilibrium. It is spontaneous and discontinuous change in the channels of the flow, disturbance of equilibrium, which forever alters and displaces the equilibrium state previously existing. Our theory of development is nothing but a treatment of this phenomenon and the processes incident to it.

These spontaneous and discontinuous changes in the channel of the circular flow and these disturbances of the center of equilibrium appear in the sphere of industrial and commercial life, not in the sphere of the wants of the consumers of final products. Where spontaneous and discontinuous changes in consumers' tastes appear, it is a question of a sudden change in data with which the business man must cope, hence possibly a question of *motive* or an opportunity for other than gradual adaptations of his conduct, but not of such other conduct itself. Therefore this case does not offer any other problems than a change in natural data or require any new method of treatment; wherefore we shall neglect any spontaneity of consumers' needs that may actually exist, and assume tastes as "given." This is made easy for us by the fact that the spontaneity of wants is in general small. To be sure, we must always start from the satisfaction of wants, since they are the end of all production, and the given economic situation at any time must be understood from this aspect. Yet innovations in the economic system do not as a rule take place in such a way that first new wants arise spontaneously in consumers and then the productive apparatus swings round through their pressure. We do not deny the presence of this nexus. It is, however, the producer who as a rule initiates economic change, and consumers are educated by him if necessary; they are, as it were, taught to want new things, or things which differ in some respect or other from those which they have been in the habit of using. Therefore, while it is permissible and even necessary to consider consumers' wants as an independent and indeed the fundamental force in the theory of the circular flow, we must take a different attitude as soon as we analyze *change*.

To produce means to combine materials and forces within our reach. To produce other things, or the same things by a different method, means to combine these materials and forces differently. In so far as the "new combination" may in time grow out of the old by continuous adjustment in small steps, there is certainly change, possibly growth, but neither a new phenomenon nor development in our sense. In so far as this is not the case, and the new combinations appear discontinuously, then the phenomenon characterizing development emerges. For reasons of expository convenience, henceforth, we shall only mean the latter case when we speak of new combinations of productive means. Development in our sense is then defined by the carrying out of new combinations.

This concept covers the following five cases: (1) the introduction of a new good—that is one with which consumers are not yet familiar—or of a new quality of a good. (2) The introduction of a new method of production, that is one not yet tested by experience in the branch of manufacture concerned, which need by no means be founded upon a discovery scientifically new, and can also exist in a new way of handling a commodity commercially. (3) The opening of a new market, that is a market into which the particular branch of manufacture of the country in question has not previously entered, whether or not this market has existed before. (4) The conquest of a new source of supply of raw materials or half-manufactured goods, again irrespective of whether this source already exists or whether it has first to be created.

(5) The carrying out of the new organization of any industry, like the creation of a monopoly position (for example through trustification) or the breaking up of a monopoly position. . . .

. . . The carrying out of new combinations means . . . simply the different employment of the economic system's existing supplies of productive means—which might provide a second definition of development in our sense. That rudiment of a pure economic theory of development which is implied in the traditional doctrine of the formation of capital always refers merely to saving and to the investment of the small yearly increase attributable to it. In this it asserts nothing false, but it entirely overlooks much more essential things. The slow and continuous increase in time of the national supply of productive means and of savings is obviously an important factor in explaining the course of economic history through the centuries, but it is completely overshadowed by the fact that development consists primarily in employing existing resources in a different way, in doing new things with them, irrespective of whether these resources increase of not. In the treatment of shorter epochs, moreover, this is even true in a more tangible sense. Different methods of employment, and not saving and increases in the available quantity of labor, have changed the face of the economic world in the last fifty years. The increase of population especially, but also of the sources from which savings can be made, was first made possible in large measure through the different employment of the then existing means.

The next step in our argument is also self-evident: command over means of production is necessary to the carrying out of new combinations. Procuring the means of production is one distinct problem for the established firms which work within the circular flow. For they *have* them already procured or else can procure them currently with the proceeds of previous production. . . . There is no fundamental gap here between receipts and dispersements, which, on the contrary, necessarily correspond to one another just as both correspond to the means of production offered and to the products demanded. Once set in motion, this mechanism works automatically. Furthermore, the problem does not exist in a non-exchange economy even if new combinations are carried out in it; for the directing organ, for example a socialist economic ministry, is in a position to direct the productive resources of the society to new uses exactly as it can direct them to their previous employments. The new employment may, under certain circumstances, impose temporary sacrifices, privations, or increased efforts upon the members of the community; it may presuppose the solution of difficult problems, for example the question from which of the old combinations the necessary productive means should be withdrawn; but there is no question of procuring means of production not already at the disposal of the economic ministry. Finally, the problem also does not exist in a competitive economy in the case of the carrying out of new combinations, if those who carry them out have the necessary productive means or can get them in exchange for others which they have or for any other property which they may possess. This is not the privilege of the possession of property per se, but only the privilege of the possession of disposable property, that is such as is employable either immediately for carrying out the new combination or in exchange for the necessary goods and services. In the contrary case—and this is the rule as it is the fundamentally interesting case—the possessor of wealth, even if it is the greatest combine, must resort to credit if he wishes to carry out a new combination, which cannot like an established business be financed by returns from previous production. To provide this credit is clearly the function of that category of individuals which we call "capitalists." It is obvious that this is the characteristic method of the capitalist type of society—and important enough to serve as its *differentia specifica*—for forcing the economic system into new channels, for putting its means at the service of new ends, in contrast to the method of a non-exchange economy of the kind which simply consists in exercising the directing organs power to command.

It does not appear to me possible to dispute in any way the foregoing statement. Emphasis upon the significance of credit is to be found in every textbook. That the structure of modern industry could not have been erected without it, that it makes the individual to a certain extent independent of inherited possessions, that talent in economic life "rides to success on its debts," even the most conservative orthodoxy of the theorists cannot well deny. Nor is the connection established here between credit and the carrying out of innovations, a connection which will be worked out later, anything to take offense at. For it is as clear a priori as it is established historically that credit is primarily necessary to new combinations. . . .

. . . Whence come the sums needed to purchase the means of production necessary for the new combinations if the individual concern does not happen to have them? The conventional answer is simple: out of the annual growth of social savings plus that part of resources which may annually become free. Now the first quantity was indeed important enough before the war—it may perhaps be estimated as one fifth of total private incomes in Europe and North America—so that together with the latter sum, which it is difficult to obtain statistically, it does not immediately give the lie quantitatively to this answer. At the same time a figure representing the range of all the business operations involved in carrying out new combinations is also not available at present. But we may not even start from total "savings." For its magnitude is explicable only by the results of previous development. By far the greater part of it does not come from thrift in the strict sense, that is from abstaining from the consumption of part of one's regular income, but it consists of funds which are themselves the result of successful innovation and in which we shall later recognize entrepreneurial profit. . . .

Even though the conventional answer to our question is not obviously absurd, yet there is another method of obtaining money for this purpose, which claims our attention, because it, unlike the one referred to, does not presuppose the existence of accumulated results of previous development, and hence may be considered as the only one which is available in strict logic. This method of obtaining money is the creation of purchasing power by banks. The form it takes is immaterial. The issue of bank notes not fully covered by specie withdrawn from circulation is an obvious instance, but methods of deposit banking render the same service, where they increase the sum total of possible expenditure. Or we may think of bank acceptances in so far as they serve as money to make payments in wholesale trade. It is always a question, not of transforming purchasing power which already exists in someone's possession, but of the creation of new purchasing power out of nothing—out of nothing even if the credit contract by which the new purchasing power was created is supported by securities which are not themselves circulating media—which is added to the existing circulation. And this is the source from which new combinations *are* often financed, and from which they would have to be financed *always,* if results of previous development did not actually exist at any moment. . . .

We now come to the third of the elements with which our analysis works, namely the "new combination of means of production," and credit. Although all three elements form a whole, the third may be described as the fundamental phenomenon of economic development. The carrying out of new combinations we call "enterprise"; the individuals whose function it is to carry them out we call "entrepreneurs." These concepts are at once broader and narrower than the usual. Broader, because in the first place we call entrepreneurs not only those "independent" businessmen in an exchange economy who are usually so designated, but all who actually fulfill the function by which we define the concept, even if they are, as is becoming the rule, "dependent" employees of a company, like managers, members of boards of directors, and so forth, or even if their actual power to perform the entrepreneurial function has any other foundations, such as the control of a majority of shares. As it is the carrying out of new combinations that constitutes the entrepreneur, it is not necessary that he should be permanently connected with an individual firm; many "financiers," "promoters," and so forth are not, and still they may be entrepreneurs in our sense. On the other hand, our concept is narrower than the traditional one in that it does not include all heads of firms or managers or industrialists who merely may operate an established business, but only those who actually perform that function. Nevertheless I maintain that the above definition does no more than formulate with greater precision what the traditional doctrine really means to convey. In the first place our definition agrees with the usual one on the fundamental point of distinguishing between "entrepreneurs" and "capitalists" —irrespective of whether the latter are regarded as owners of money, claims to money, or material goods. This distinction is common property today and has been so for a considerable time. It also settles the question whether the ordinary shareholder as such is an entrepreneur, and disposes of the conception of the entrepreneur as risk bearer. Furthermore, the ordinary characterization of the entrepreneur type by such expressions as "initiative," "authority," or "foresight" points entirely in our direction. For there is little scope for such qualities within the routine of the circular flow, and if this had been sharply separated from the occurrence of changes in this routine itself, the emphasis in the definition of the function of entrepreneurs would have been shifted automatically to the latter. . . .

The entrepreneurial kind of leadership, as distinguished from other kinds of economic leadership such as we should expect to find in a primitive tribe or communist society, is of course colored by the conditions peculiar to it. It has none of that glamour which characterizes other kinds of leadership. It consists in fulfilling a very special task which only in rare cases appeals to the imagination of the public. For its success, keenness and vigor are not more essential than a certain narrowness which seizes the immediate chance and *nothing else*. "Personal weight" is, to be sure, not without importance. Yet the personality of the capitalistic entrepreneur need not, and generally does not, answer to the idea most of us have of what a "leader" looks like, so much so that there is some difficulty in realizing that he comes within the sociological category of leader at all. He "leads" the means of production into new channels. But this he does, not by convincing people of the desirability of carrying out his plan or by creating confidence in his leading in the manner of a political leader—the only man he has to convince or to impress is the banker who is to finance him—but by buying them or their services, and then using them as he sees fit. He also leads in the sense that he draws other producers in his branch after him. But as they are his competitors, who first reduce and then annihilate his profit, this is, as it were, leadership against one's own will. Finally, he renders a service, the full appreciation of which takes a specialist's knowledge of the case. It is not so easily understood by the public at large as a politician's successful speech or a general's victory in the field, not to insist on the fact that he seems to act—and often harshly—in his individual interest alone. We shall understand, therefore, that we do not observe, in this case, the emergence of all those affective values which are the glory of all other kinds of social leadership. Add to this the precariousness of the economic position both of the individual entrepreneur and of entrepreneurs as a group, and the fact that when his economic success raises him socially he has no cultural tradition or attitude to fall back upon, but moves about in society as an upstart, whose ways are readily laughed at, and we shall understand why this type has never been popular, and why even scientific critique often makes short work of it. . . .

The Contours of Economic Evolution

It will be useful to assemble the analytic tools so far described and to display the resulting skeleton—a sort of chassis of our model. Experience teaches that there is danger in doing this, and another appeal to the reader is in order, to reserve judgment and to grant provisionally all simplifications, in particular, the assumptions of perfect competition (with the possible exception of isolated monopoly positions) and of a state of perfect equilibrium from which to start. There is no saving, population is constant, and everything else is as we assume it to be in a state that conforms to the idea of the Theoretical Norm. We know (this, however, is no assumption) that, in the institutional pattern of capitalist society, there will always be possibilities of New Combinations (in the absence of all others, there would be those due to the steady increase of knowledge), and always some people able and willing to carry them out; and we know the reasons why this is so. To repeat again a point which has often been misunderstood, these people are by no means looked upon as particularly rare birds. All we postulate is that that ability is distributed as unequally as others are and all we hold is that this fact has an important influence on the mechanism of economic change—a statement which is no bolder and, if anything, more realistic than any of the set of assumptions familiar to every theorist. Motivation is supplied by the prospect of profit in our sense (mixed as the reader pleases with other stimuli) *which does not, be it remembered, presuppose either an actual or an expected rise in prices and expenditure.* What follows implies, besides institutional and technological assumptions that are essential, others of merely expository significance. In order to make the principle stand out clearly, we wish in particular to assume, in the first instance, absence of certain elements which in reality are very important—notably, errors in diagnosis or prognosis and other mistakes.

Some people, then, can see and work out with varying promptness plans for innovations associated with varying (and ideally correct) anticipations of profits, and set about struggling with the obstacles incident to doing a new and unfamiliar thing. . . . We look upon ability to take the lead as a part of the entrepreneurial aptitude, and this enables us, for our present purpose, to identify one man (as we could identify the tallest individual in a population) who is the first, for example, to decide on the production of a new consumers' goods. . . . Conforming to previous considerations, we suppose that he founds a new firm, constructs a new plant, and orders new equipment from existing firms. The requisite funds—his entrance ticket to the social store of means of production—he borrows from a bank. On the balance acquired by so doing he draws, either in order to hand the checks to other people who furnish him with goods and services, or in order to get currency with which to pay for these supplies. Under our assumptions he withdraws, by his bids for producers' goods, the quantities of them he needs from the uses which they served before.

Then other entrepreneurs follow, after them still others in increasing number, in the path of innovation, which becomes progressively smoothed for successors by accumulating experience and vanishing obstacles. We know the reasons why this is likely to happen in the same field or in—technologically, as well as economically—related fields: although in some respects a successful innovation will make other innovations easier to carry out in any field, it primarily facilitates them in the lines in which it may be directly copied as a whole or in part or for which it opens up new opportunities. Consequences begin to make themselves felt all over the system in perfectly logical concatenation. They are almost too obvious to describe. We will merely note, first, that our entrepreneurs may, under the circumstances envisaged, be relied on to spend their deposits promptly, excepting a minimum reserve. . . .

Second, there being no unemployed resources to start with, prices of factors of production will rise, and so will money incomes and the rate of interest (or, as the writer thinks it would be more correct to say, a positive rate of interest will emerge). Costs will rise against "old" firms as well as against entrepreneurs. But third, their receipts will also rise correspondingly to the expenditures of entrepreneurs on producers' goods, of the workmen and so on, now employed by them at higher wages, and of the recipients of all those increased payments. How individual firms or industries or sectors of the industrial organism will fare in this process depends on the shifts in demand that will occur in consequence. It is easy to see that there will be both gains and losses. In spite of the losses in some industries which must, under such circumstances, be expected to be a feature of the situation, all old firms taken together will, of course, show a net surplus. . . .

This is all that happens, under our present assumptions, until the first entrepreneur's plant gets into working order. Then the scene begins to change and a new business situation emerges, characteristically differing from the one we glanced at, but not less easy to understand. The new commodities—let us say, new consumers' goods—flow into the market. They are, since everything turns out according to expectation, readily taken up at exactly those prices at which the entrepreneur expected to sell them. We will also assume that from that moment onward the new firm will go on pouring out an unchanging stream of consumers' goods without any further change in its production function. . . .

These new commodities intrude into the economic world that existed before at a rate which will . . . be too great for smooth absorption. They intrude, nevertheless, gradually: the first entrepreneur's supply will not, in general, cause visible disturbance or be sufficient to alter the complexion of the business situation as a whole, although those firms may be immediately affected with the products of which the new commodities or the commodities produced by new methods are directly competitive. But, as the process gathers momentum, these effects steadily gain in importance, and disequilibrium, enforcing a process of adaptation, begins to show. It is important that the reader should master the mechanism before we go on to insert any further elements into it.

The nature of the effects on the "old" firms is easy to understand. It superimposes itself on the disequilibrium caused by the setting up of the new plant and equipment and the expenditure incident thereto. But while the effects of this were, even in those cases in which they spelled net losses, softened by the flow of that expenditure, the new disequilibrium enforces much more obviously difficult adaptations. They proceed not exclusively under the stimulus of loss. For some of the "old" firms new opportunities for expansion open up: the new methods or commodities create New Economic Space. But for others the emergence of the new methods means economic death; for still others, contraction and drifting into the background. Finally, there are firms and industries which are forced to undergo a difficult and painful process of modernization, rationalization, and reconstruction. It should be observed that these vital parts of the mechanism of economic evolution, which are readily seen to dominate many business situations and to produce results of fundamental importance, can never be revealed statistically by measuring variation in an index of production, or analyzed theoretically in terms of total output. Such an index would display nothing except increase. But mere increase in total output would not produce those effects. It is disharmonious or one-sided increase and shifts *within* the aggregative quantity which matter. Aggregative analysis, here, as elsewhere, not only does not tell the whole tale but necessarily obliterates the main (and the only interesting) point of the tale.

As long, however, as new enterprises continue to emerge and to pour their stream of expenditure into the system, all those effects may be over-compensated. The "turn" *need* not come, i.e., the situation described before *need* not give way to the situation we are trying to characterize now, until entrepreneurial activity slackens and eventually stops. Hence, it is essential to visualize clearly the reasons why entrepreneurial activity in fact slackens and stops at a point which can be theoretically determined. In actual life so many accidents and incidents combine to produce this result that we are never lacking plausible reasons with which to explain that stoppage in any given case. But this obscures the question of principle with which we are now concerned—whether the mechanism described would in the absence of such incidents and accidents run on forever (on a "prosperity plateau") or come to a stop from reasons inherent in it and by virtue of its own effects and of the business situations it creates.

First, since entrepreneurial activity characteristically starts off in a definite direction and does not distribute itself equally all over the industrial field —since it aims typically at production of a given commodity or group of commodities—its possibilities are, in every instance and in any given state of the economic body, definitely limited. The results of innovation act directly on certain individual prices, and therefore set definite limits on further advance in that direction or related directions. . . .

But second, since entrepreneurial activity upsets the equilibrium of the system and since the release of the new products, in particular, brings disequilibration to a head, a revision of values of all the elements of the system becomes necessary and this, for a period of time, means fluctuations and successive attempts at adaptation to changing temporary situations. This, in turn, means the impossibility of calculating costs and receipts in a satisfactory way, even if necessary margins are not altogether absent while that goes on. Hence, the difficulty of planning new things and the risk of failure are greatly increased. In order to carry out additional innovations, it is as necessary to wait until things settle down as it was in the beginning to wait for an equilibrium to be established before embarking upon the innovations the effects of which we are now discussing. Therefore, along with new products streaming into markets, and with repayments increasing in quantitative importance, entrepreneurial activity tends to slacken, until finally it ceases entirely.

. . . Two things only call for notice. First, the outstanding conductor that spreads effects all over the system (although its causal importance can easily be exaggerated and although its way of functioning is still more open to misinterpretation) is entrepreneurs' expenditure, and this expenditure is now being reduced. This proposition is not quite symmetrical to the analogous one in the case of the situation characteristic of the period of gestation since there, the element of "crowding out the old" being absent, all effects reached the system through that one channel. But as far as it may be allowed to pass muster, it should be observed that while mere stoppage of additional borrowing (remember that so far nobody borrows but entrepreneurs) would be sufficient under the circumstances to bring discomfiture to many firms and, in particular, to depress the price level, yet this is not all that happens. Repayment of bank loans by entrepreneurs, annihilating balances, comes in to accentuate effects. . . . It occurs without any initiative on the part of banks and would occur even if nobody ever went bankrupt or restricted operations, and if no bank ever called or refused a loan. We are not concerned with the questions whether a different and less passive reaction of the monetary mechanism would either intensify or soften the phenomena under consideration, and what monetary policy "should" be followed under the circumstances. All we are interested in at the moment is that money and credit do react in a definite way, that their behavior is nothing but adaptation to an underlying economic process by which that behavior, as well as the behavior of *all* aggregative quantities, is explained, while the reverse is not true.

Second, the sum total of the phenomena we are surveying forms a connected whole which has a definite meaning and, if such teleology is permissible, may be said to have a definite function. It constitutes the response by the system to the results of entrepreneurial activity—adaptation to the new things created, including the elimination of what is incapable of adaptation, resorbtion of the results of innovation into the system, reorganization of economic life so as to make it conform to the data as altered by enterprise, remodeling of the system of values, liquidation of indebtedness. It is readily seen that, under our assumptions and with but minor qualifications, that sequence of phenomena leads up to a new neighborhood of equilibrium, in which enterprise will start again. This new neighborhood of equilibrium is characterized, as compared to the one that preceded it, by a "greater" social product of a different pattern, new production functions, equal sum total of money incomes, a minimum (strictly zero) rate of interest, zero profits, zero loans, a different system of prices, and a lower level of prices, the fundamental expression of the fact that all the lasting achievements of the particular spurt of innovation have been handed to consumers in the shape of increased real incomes. Thus, as soon as the entrepreneurial impulse ceases to act which propelled it away from its previous neighborhood, the system embarks upon a struggle toward a new one, under the influence of forces which should now be perfectly clear and which are sure, barring occurrence of external disturbances, to land it there eventually. The process takes time and may display oscillations and relapses. But it is at the bottom of all those apparently irregular movements during which losses seem to be strewn at random over the whole of economic life, and under present assumptions cannot cease until, through however many rearrangements that are disavowed by the next day, it has accomplished the task. . . .

. . . it is by no means farfetched or paradoxical to say that "progress" unstabilizes the economic world, or that it is by virtue of its mechanism a *cyclical process*. A theory of economic fluctuations running in terms of external factors plus innovations might be considered self-evident and only another way of stating that there would be no cycles in an undisturbed stationary, or growing, flow. The reader should keep this in mind in the midst of the complications which must inevitably follow and in the face of the fact that theory as well as public opinion have steadfastly refused to take that common-sense view of the matter and persisted in tacitly assuming that "progress" is one thing (and naturally smooth) while fluctuations are another thing, differing from it, perhaps inimical to it. It is, after all, only common sense to realize that, but for the fact that economic life is in a process of incessant *internal* change, the business cycle, as we know it, would not exist. Hence, it is just as well to try to link so obviously important an element systematically to any explanation of the capitalist economy in general and of business cycles in particular. . . .

ALVIN H. HANSEN

||||||||||||||||||||||||||||||||||||||||||||||||||||||||||||||||||||||||||||||||||||||||||||||||||||||||||||||||||||||||||||||||||||||||

Economic Progress and Declining Population Growth

. . . Throughout the modern era, ceaseless change has been the law of economic life. Every period is in some sense a period of transition. The swift stream of events in the last quarter century offers, however, overwhelm-

Presidential address delivered to the American Economic Association, December 28, 1938. Reprinted from *American Economic Review* (March 1939), pp. 1-15, with omissions. Reprinted by permission of the American Economic Association and the author.

ing testimony in support of the thesis that the economic order of the western world is undergoing in this generation a structural change no less basic and profound in character than that transformation of economic life and institutions which we are wont to designate loosely by the phrase "the Industrial Revolution." We are passing, so to speak, over a divide which separates the great era of growth and expansion of the nineteenth century from an era which no man, unwilling to embark on pure conjecture, can as yet characterize with clarity or precision. We are moving swiftly out of the order in which those of our generation were brought up, into no one knows what. . . .

Schooled in the traditions of the Malthusian theory, economists, thinking in terms of static economics, have typically placed an optimistic interpretation upon the cessation of population growth. . . . In a fundamental sense this conclusion is, I think, thoroughly sound; for it can scarcely be questioned that a continued growth of population at the rate experienced in the nineteenth century would rapidly present insoluble problems. But it would be an unwarranted optimism to deny that there are implicit in the current drastic shift from rapid expansion to cessation of population growth, serious structural maladjustments which can be avoided or mitigated only if economic policies, appropriate to the changed situation, are applied. Indeed, in this shift must be sought a basic cause of not a few of the developments in our changing economy.

Adam Smith regarded growth of population as at once a consequence and a cause of economic progress. Increasing division of labor would, he argued, bring about greater productivity, and this would furnish an enlarged revenue and stock, from which would flow an enlarged wages fund, an increased demand for labor, higher wages, and so economic conditions favorable for population growth. Now a growing population, by widening the market and by fostering inventiveness, in turn facilitated, he thought, division of labor and so the production of wealth. Thus he arrived at an optimistic conclusion. Population growth, he held, stimulated progress and this in turn stimulated further growth and expansion. In contrast, the pessimistic analyses of Malthus and Ricardo stressed the limitation of natural resources and the danger of an increasing population's pressing down the margin of cultivation to a point at which real income would be reduced to a bare subsistence level. In this static analysis the more dynamic approach of Adam Smith was quite forgotten. If we wish to get a clear insight into the economic consequences of the current decline in population growth, it is necessary to return to the suggestion of Adam Smith and to explore more fully the causal interconnection between economic progress, capital formation, and population growth.

Economic analysis from the earliest development of our science has been concerned with the role played by economic progress. Various writers have included under this caption different things; but for our purpose we may say that the constituent elements of economic progress are (*a*) inventions, (*b*) the discovery and development of new territory and new resources, and (*c*) the growth of population. Each of these in turn, severally and in combination, has opened investment outlets and caused a rapid growth of capital formation. . . .

The expanding economy of the last century called forth a prodigious growth of capital formation. So much was this the case that this era in history has by common consent been called the capitalistic period. No one disputes the thesis that without this vast accumulation of capital we should never have witnessed the great rise in the standard of living achieved since the beginning of the Industrial Revolution. But it is not the effect of capital formation upon real income to which I wish especially to direct attention. What I wish to stress in this paper is rather the role played by the process of capital formation in securing at each point in this ascending income scale fairly full employment of the productive resources and therefore the maximum income possible under the then prevailing level of technological development. For it is an indisputable fact that the prevailing economic system has never been able to reach reasonably full employment or the attainment of its currently realizable real income without making large investment expenditures. The basis for this imperious economic necessity has been thoroughly explored in the last half century in the great literature beginning with Tougan-Baranowsky and Wicksell on saving and investment. I shall not attempt any summary statement of this analysis. Nor is this necessary; for I take it that it is accepted by all schools of current economic thought that full employment and the maximum currently attainable income level cannot be reached in the modern free enterprise economy without a volume of investment expenditures adequate to fill the gap between consumption expenditures and that level of income which could be achieved were all the factors employed. In this somewhat truistic statement I hope I have succeeded in escaping a hornets' nest of economic controversy.

Thus we may postulate a consensus on the thesis that in the absence of a positive program designed to stimulate consumption, full employment of the productive resources is essentially a function of the vigor of investment activity. Less agreement can be claimed for the role played by the rate of interest on the volume of investment. Yet few there are who believe that in a period of investment stagnation an abundance of loanable funds at low rates of interest is alone adequate to produce a vigorous flow of real investment. I am increasingly impressed with the analysis made by Wicksell who stressed the prospective rate of profit on new investment as the active, dominant, and controlling factor, and who viewed the rate of interest as a passive factor, lagging behind the profit rate. This view is moreover in accord with competent business judgment.[1] It is true that it is necessary to look beyond the mere *cost* of interest charges to the indirect effect of the interest rate structure upon business expectations. Yet all in all, I venture to assert

---

[1] *Cf.* J. E. Meade and P. W. S. Andrews, "Summary of Replies to Questions on Effects of Interest Rates," *Oxford Econ. Papers,* No. 1; also J. Franklin Ebersole, "The Influence of Interest Rates upon Entrepreneurial Decisions in Business—A Case Study," *Harvard Bus. Rev.,* Vol. xvii, pp. 35-39. The indirect effect on valuation is perhaps overlooked.

that the role of the rate of interest as a determinant of investment has occupied a place larger than it deserves in our thinking. If this be granted, we are forced to regard the factors which underlie economic progress as the dominant determinants of investment and employment.

A growth in real investment may take the form either of a deepening of capital or of a widening of capital, as Hawtrey has aptly put it. The deepening process means that more capital is used per unit of output, while the widening process means that capital formation grows *pari passu* with the increase in the output of final goods. If the ratio of real capital to real income remains constant, there is no deepening of capital; but if this ratio is constant and real income rises, then there is a widening of capital. . . .

. . . Considering the economy as a whole, including fields of economic activity other than manufacturing, there is no good evidence that the advance of technique has resulted in recent decades, certainly not in any significant measure, in any deepening of capital. Apparently, once the machine technique has been developed in any field, further mechanization is likely to result in an increase in output at least proportional to and often in excess of the net additions to real capital. Though the deepening process is all the while going on in certain areas, elsewhere capital-saving inventions are reducing the ratio of capital to output.

In order to get some insight into the effect of population growth upon capital formation, it is necessary to consider the role it plays in conjunction with other factors in the widening and deepening process. The widening of capital is a function of an increase in final output, which in turn is due partly to an increase in population and partly to an increase in per capita productivity, arising from causes other than a larger use of capital per unit of output. On the other hand, the deepening of capital results partly from cost-reducing changes in technique, partly (though this is probably a much less significant factor) from a reduction in the rate of interest, and partly from changes in the character of the output as a whole, with special reference to the amount of capital required to produce it.

Now the rate of population growth must necessarily play an important role in determining the character of the output; in other words, the composition of the flow of final goods. Thus a rapidly growing population will demand a much larger per capita volume of new residential building construction than will a stationary population. A stationary population with its larger proportion of old people may perhaps demand more personal services; and the composition of consumer demand will have an important influence on the quantity of capital required. The demand for housing calls for large capital outlays, while the demand for personal services can be met without making large investment expenditures. It is therefore not unlikely that a shift from a rapidly growing population to a stationary or declining one may so alter the composition of the final flow of consumption goods that the ratio of capital to output as a whole will tend to decline.

In the beginning stages of modern capitalism both the deepening and the widening processes of capital formation were developing side by side. But in its later stages the deepening process, taking the economy as a whole, rapidly diminished. And now with the rapid cessation of population growth, even the widening process may slow down. Moreover it is possible that capital-saving inventions may cause capital formation in many industries to lag behind the increase in output.

An interesting problem for statistical research would be to determine the proportion of investment in the nineteenth century which could be attributed (*a*) to population growth, (*b*) to the opening up of new territory and the discovery of new resources, and (*c*) to technical innovations. Such an analysis it has not been possible for me to make, and I shall venture only a few rough estimates together with some qualitative judgments. With respect to population growth some insight into the problem may perhaps be gained by considering first the role of population growth in the rise of aggregate real income. The various estimates agree that the annual rate of growth of physical output up to World War I was roughly 3 percent in Western Europe and nearly 4 percent in the United States. Of this average annual increase something less than half of the 3-percent increase in Western Europe can be attributed to population growth, while something more than half of the annual increase in the United States can be assigned to the increase in the labor supply. Thus it appears that per capita output has increased both in Western Europe and in the United States at approximately 1½ percent per annum. This increase can be attributed mainly to changes in technique and to the exploitation of new natural resources.

We have already noted that capital formation has progressed at about the same rate as the rise in aggregate output. Thus, as a first approximation, we may say that the growth of population in the last half of the nineteenth century was responsible for about 40 percent of the total volume of capital formation in Western Europe and about 60 percent of the capital formation in the United States. If this is even approximately correct, it will be seen what an important outlet for investment is being closed by reason of the current rapid decline in population growth. . . .

An interesting excursus would lead us into a consideration of the problem how far an increase in population itself contributed to a more efficient technique and so was in part responsible for the rise in per capita real income. According to the older Malthusian view, the growth of population would act counter to the effect of technological progress upon per capita productivity, and would thus slow down the rise in per capita real income. If this were correct, population growth considered by itself alone would tend to check the rise in per capita consumption, and this in turn, via the so-called *Relation,* would affect the volume of capital formation. According to the optimum population theory, however, it may not infrequently be the case, and indeed probably was during the greater part of the nineteenth century, that population growth itself facilitated mass production methods and accelerated the progress of technique. If this be correct, population growth was itself responsible for a part of the rise in per capita real income, and this, *via* the influence of a rising consumption upon investment, stimulated capital formation. Thus it is quite possible that population growth may have acted both directly and indirectly to stimulate the volume of capital formation.

It is not possible, I think, to make even an approximate estimate of the proportion of the new capital created in the nineteenth century which was a direct consequence of the opening up of new territory. The development of new countries was indeed so closely intertwined with the growth of population that it would be difficult to avoid double counting. What proportion of new capital formation in the United States went each year into the western frontier we do not know, but it must have been very considerable. Apparently about one-fourth of the total capital accumulations of England were invested abroad by 1914, and one-seventh of those of France.

These figures, while only suggestive, point unmistakably to the conclusion that the opening of new territory and the growth of population were together responsible for a very large fraction—possibly somewhere near one-half—of the total volume of new capital formation in the nineteenth century. These outlets for new investment are rapidly being closed. The report on *Limits of Land Settlement* by Professor Isaiah Bowman and others may be regarded as conclusive in its findings that there are no important areas left for exploitation and settlement. So far as population is concerned, that of Western Europe has already virtually reached a standstill; but that in Eastern Europe, notably in Russia, is still growing, and so also is that in the Orient. And much of this area will probably experience a considerable industrialization. But it is not yet clear how far the mature industrial countries will participate in this development through capital export. Russia still has a long way to go before she becomes completely industrialized; but foreign capital is not likely to play any significant role in this process. India will offer some opportunity for British investment, but the total is likely to be small relative to the volume of British foreign investments in the nineteenth century. China and the Orient generally offer, in view of the present and prospective turmoil in that area, relatively meager investment opportunities. At all events, no one is likely to challenge the statement that foreign investment will in the next fifty years play an incomparably smaller role than was the case in the nineteenth century.

Thus the outlets for new investment are rapidly narrowing down to those created by the progress of technology. To be sure, the progress of technology itself played in the nineteenth century a decisive role in the opening of new territory and as a stimulus to population growth. But while technology can facilitate the opening of new territory, it cannot create a new world or make the old one bigger than it is. And while the advance of science, by reducing the death rate, was a major cause of the vast nineteenth-century increase in population, no important further gains in this direction can possibly offset the prevailing low birth rate. Thus the further progress of science can operate to open investment outlets only through its direct influence on the technique of production.

We are thus rapidly entering a world in which we must fall back upon a more rapid advance of technology than in the past if we are to find private investment opportunities adequate to maintain full employment. Should we accept the advice of those who would declare a moratorium on invention and technical progress, this one remaining avenue for private investment would also be closed. There can be no greater error in the analysis of the economic trends of our times than that which finds in the advance of technology, broadly conceived, a major cause of unemployment. It is true that we cannot discount the problem of technological unemployment, a problem which may be intensified by the apparently growing importance of capital-saving inventions. But, on the other side, we cannot afford to neglect that type of innovation which creates new industries and which thereby opens new outlets for real investment. The problem of our generation is, above all, the problem of inadequate private-investment outlets. What we need is not a slowing down in the progress of science and technology, but rather an acceleration of that rate.

Of first-rate importance is the development of new industries. There is certainly no basis for the assumption that these are a thing of the past. But there is equally no basis for the assumption that we can take for granted the rapid emergence of new industries as rich in investment opportunities as the railroad, or more recently the automobile, together with all the related developments, including the construction of public roads, to which it gave rise. Nor is there any basis, either in history or in theory, for the assumption that the rise of new industries proceeds inevitably at a uniform pace. The growth of modern industry has not come in terms of millions of small increments of change giving rise to a smooth and even development. Characteristically it has come by gigantic leaps and bounds. Very often the change can best be described as discontinuous, lumpy, and jerky, as indeed D. H. Robertson has so vividly done. And when a revolutionary new industry like the railroad or the automobile, after having initiated in its youth a powerful upward surge of investment activity, reaches maturity and ceases to grow, as all industries finally must, the whole economy must experience a profound stagnation, unless indeed new developments take its place. It is not enough that a mature industry continues its activity at a high level on a horizontal plane. The fact that new railroad mileage continued to be built at about the same rate through the seventies, eighties, and nineties was not sufficient. It is the *cessation of growth* which is disastrous. It is in connection with the growth, maturity and decline of great industries that the principle of acceleration operates with peculiar force. And when giant new industries have spent their force, it *may* take a long time before something else of equal magnitude emerges. In fact nothing has emerged in the decade in which we are now living. This basic fact, together with the virtual cessation of public investment by state and local governmental bodies, as indicated by a decline of $2,000,000,000 in their net public debt since 1932, explains in large measure the necessary rise in federal expenditures.

Spiethoff was quite right when he argued that a vigorous recovery is not just spontaneously born from the womb of the preceding depression. Some

small recovery must indeed arise sooner or later merely because of the growing need for capital replacement. But a full-fledged recovery calls for something more than the mere expenditure of depreciation allowances. It requires
a large outlay on new investment, and this awaits the development of great
new industries and new techniques. But such new developments are not currently available in adequate volume. It is my growing conviction that the
combined effect of the decline in population growth, together with the failure
of any really important innovations of a magnitude sufficient to absorb large
capital outlays, weighs very heavily as an explanation for the failure of the
recent recovery to reach full employment. Other factors are certainly significant and important, particularly our failure to control the cost structure and
to grapple effectively with specific situations, such as those presented by the
railroads and by building construction.

We have noted that the approaching cessation of population growth and
the disappearance of new territory for settlement and exploitation may cut off
a half or more of the investment outlets which we were wont to make in the
past. We are thus compelled to fall back upon that measure of capital formation which is associated with the advance of technique and the rise in per
capita output. But current institutional developments are restricting even this
outlet. The growing power of trade unions and trade associations, the development of monopolistic competition, of rivalry for the market through expensive persuasion and advertising instead of through price competition, are
factors which have rightly of late commanded much attention among economists. There is, moreover, the tendency to block the advance of technical
progress by the shelving of patents.

Under vigorous price competition, new cost-reducing techniques were
compulsorily introduced even though the scrapping of obsolete but undepreciated machinery entailed a capital loss. But under the monopoly principle of
obsolescence new machines will not be introduced until the undepreciated
value of the old machine will at least be covered by the economies of the new
technique. Thus progress is slowed down, and outlets for new capital formation, available under a more ruthless competitive society, are cut off. Capital
losses which could not be avoided under rigorous price competition can be
and are avoided under an economic system more closely integrated by inter-
corporate association and imperfect competition. If we are to save the one
remaining outlet for private capital formation, deliberate action of a far bolder
character than hitherto envisaged must be undertaken in order to make the
price system and free enterprise sufficiently responsive to permit at least that
measure of capital formation to which the rate of technological progress had
accustomed us in the past.

Yet even though this much were achieved, it is necessary to recognize
that such a rate of progress would not provide sufficient investment outlets
to give us full employment of our resources. With a stationary population we
could maintain as rapid a rise in per capita real income as that experienced in
the past by making annually only half the volume of new investment to which

we have been accustomed. A volume of investment adequate to provide full employment could give us an annual percentage increase in per capita output greatly in excess of any hitherto attained.

Various measures have been offered to maintain full employment in the absence of an adequate rate of technological progress and of the development of new industries. Consumption may be strengthened by the relief from taxes which drain off a stream of income which otherwise would flow into consumption channels. Public investment may usefully be made in human and natural resources and in consumers' capital goods of a collective character designed to serve the physical, recreational and cultural needs of the community as a whole. But we cannot afford to be blind to the unmistakable fact that a solution along these lines raises serious problems of economic workability and political administration.

How far such a program, whether financed by taxation or by borrowing, can be carried out without adversely affecting the system of free enterprise is a problem with which economists, I predict, will have to wrestle in the future far more intensely than in the past. Can a rising public debt owned internally be serviced by a scheme of taxation which will not adversely affect the marginal return on new investment or the marginal cost of borrowing? Can any tax system, designed to increase the propensity to consume by means of a drastic change in income distribution, be devised which will not progressively encroach on private investment?[2]

As so often in economic life, we are confronted by a dilemma. Continued unemployment on a vast scale, resulting from inadequate private-investment outlets, could be expected sooner or later to lead straight into an all-round regimented economy. But so also, by an indirect route and a slower process, might a greatly extended program of public expenditures. And from the standpoint of economic workability the question needs to be raised how far such a program can be carried out in a democratic society without raising the cost structure to a level which prevents full employment. Thus a challenge is presented to all those countries which have not as yet submitted to the yoke of political dictatorship. In one of our round tables we are discussing divergencies in the success of governmental spending in democratic countries and in totalitarian states. Totalitarian states have the great advantage that they can rigorously check the advance of costs, including wage rates, while engaging in an expansionist program of public investment. Democratic countries cannot in modern times escape from the influence exerted by organized groups upon the operation of the price system. From the standpoint of the workability of the system of free enterprise, there emerges the problem of sovereignty in democratic countries confronted in their internal economies with powerful groups—entrepreneurial and wage-earning—which have robbed the price system of that impersonal and nonpolitical character idealized in the doctrine of *laissez faire*. It remains still to be seen whether political democracy can in the end survive the disappearance of the automatic price system.

Thus we are confronted with various alternatives. On the one side, there

---

[2] Joseph J. Spengler, "Population Movements, Employment, and Income," *Southern Econ. Jour.* (October 1938).

is the proposal to risk a negative governmental policy in the expectation that the recuperative forces to which we have long been accustomed will, in the absence of political interference, reassert themselves. On the other side, there is the proposal to go forward under full steam with unrestrained governmental expansion until full employment has been reached. Those who have no doubts whatever about the correctness of their economic analyses will not hesitate to make a bold choice of policy. But others, impressed with the stubborn economic realities of a rapidly changing world, on the one side, and the frailties of human nature in its power to make the appropriate adaptation to change, on the other, will not be so sure, and may prefer to take a course that risks neither a negative policy nor a breakdown of collective management. . . .

There are no easy answers to the problems that confront us. And because this is true, economists will not perform their function if they fail to illuminate the rapidly shifting course of economic development, and through such neglect unwittingly contribute to a dangerous lag in adjustments to change. Equally they will not perform their function if they fail to disclose the possible dangers which lurk in the wake of vastly enlarged governmental activities. Choices indeed must be made, and scientific analysis and painstaking research can aid by exploring the probable consequences of alternative choices. The problems which I have raised offer a challenge to our profession. The great transition, incident to a rapid decline in population growth and its impact upon capital formation and the workability of a system of free enterprise, calls for high scientific adventure along all the fronts represented by the social science disciplines.

EVSEY D. DOMAR

Expansion and Employment

"A slow sort of a country," said the Queen. "Now, *here,* you see, it takes all the running *you* can do, to keep in the same place. If you want to get somewhere else, you must run at least twice as fast as that."

Lewis Carroll, *Through the Looking Glass*

Our comfortable belief in the efficacy of Say's Law has been badly shaken in the last fifteen years. Both events and discussions have shown that supply does not automatically create its own demand. A part of income

From *American Economic Review* (March 1947), pp. 34-55, with omissions. Reprinted by permission of the American Economic Association and the author. Reprinted in Evsey D. Domar, *Essays in the Theory of Economic Growth* (New York: Oxford University Press, 1957), pp. 83-108.

generated by the productive process may not be returned to it; this part may be saved and hoarded. As Keynes put it, "Unemployment develops . . . because people want the moon; men cannot be employed when the object of desire (*i.e.,* money) is something which cannot be produced. . . . "[1] The core of the problem then is the public's desire to hoard. If no hoarding takes place, employment can presumably be maintained.

This sounds perfectly straight and simple; and yet it leaves something unexplained. Granted that absence of hoarding is a *necessary* condition for the maintenance of full employment, is it also a *sufficient* condition? Is the absence of hoarding *all* that is necessary for the avoidance of unemployment? This is the impression *The General Theory* gives. And yet, on a different plane, we have some notions about an increasing productive capacity which must somehow be utilized if unemployment is to be avoided. Will a mere absence of hoarding assure such a utilization? Will not a continuous increase in expenditures (and possibly in the money supply) be necessary in order to achieve this goal?

The present paper deals with this problem. It attempts to find the conditions needed for the maintenance of full employment over a period of time, or more exactly, *the rate of growth of national income* which the maintenance of full employment requires. . . .

As in many papers of this kind, a number of simplifying assumptions are made. Most of them will become apparent during the discussion. Two may be noted at the outset. First, events take place simultaneously, without any lags. Second, income, investment, and saving are defined in the *net* sense, *i.e.,* over and above depreciation. The latter is understood to refer to the cost of replacement of the depreciated asset by another one of *equal* productive capacity. These assumptions are not entirely essential to the argument. The discussion could be carried out with lags, and, if desired, in gross terms or with a different concept of depreciation. . . .

THE RATE OF GROWTH

It is perfectly clear that the requirement that income paid out should be returned to the productive process, or that savings be equal to investment, or other expressions of the same idea, are simply formulas for the retention of the income *status quo*. If underemployment was present yesterday, it would still remain here today. If yesterday's income was at a full-employment level, that *income level* would be retained today. It may no longer, however, correspond to full employment.

Let yesterday's full-employment income equal an annual rate of 150 billion dollars, and let the average propensity to save equal, say, 10 percent. If now 15 billions are annually invested, one might expect full employment to

---

[1] John M. Keynes, *The General Theory of Employment Interest and Money* (New York, 1936), p. 235.

be maintained. But during this process, capital equipment of the economy will have increased by an annual rate of 15 billions—for after all, investment *is* the formation of capital.[2] Therefore, the productive capacity of the economy has also increased.

The effects of this increase on employment will depend on whether or not *real income* has also increased. Since money income has remained, as assumed, at the 150-billion annual level, and increase in real income can be brought about only by a corresponding fall in the general price level. This indeed has been the traditional approach to problems of this kind, an approach which we shall have to reject here for the following reasons:

1. The presence of considerable monopolistic elements (in industry and labor) in our economy makes unrealistic the assumption that a falling *general* price level could be achieved without interfering with full employment. This of course, does not exclude *relative* changes among prices. As a matter of fact, if industries subject to a faster-than-average technological progress do not reduce their prices to some extent, a constant general price level cannot be maintained.

2. For an economy saddled with a large public debt and potentially faced (in peacetime) with serious employment problems, a falling price level is in itself undesirable.

3. A falling price level can bring about a larger real income only in the special case when prices of consumers' goods fall more rapidly than those of investment goods. For otherwise (with a constant propensity to save) money income will be falling as fast or faster than the price level, and real income will be falling as well. To prevent money income from falling so rapidly, the volume of real investment would have to keep rising—a conclusion which will be presently reached in the more general case.

4. Finally, the assumption of a falling general price level would obscure —and I believe quite unnecessarily—the main subject we are concerned with here.

For these reasons, a *constant general price level* is assumed throughout this paper. But, from a theoretical point of view, this is a convenience rather than a necessity. The discussion could be carried on with a falling or a rising price level as well.

To come back to the increase in capacity. If both money and real national income thus remain fixed at the 150-billion annual level, the creation of the new capital equipment will have one or more of the following effects: (1) The new capital remains unused; (2) The new capital is used at the

---

[2] The identification of investment with capital formation is reasonably safe in a private economy where only a small part of resources is disposed of by the government. When this part becomes substantial, complications arise. This question will be taken up again in Section II. Meanwhile, we shall disregard it and divide total national income, irrespective of source, into investment (*i.e.,* capital formation) and consumption.

The term "national income" is understood here in a broad sense, as total output minus depreciation, and does not touch on current controversies regarding the inclusion or exclusion of certain items. Perhaps "net national product" would be more appropriate for our purposes.

expense of previously constructed capital, whose labor and/or markets the new capital has taken away; (3) The new capital is substituted for labor (and possibly for other factors).

The first case represents a waste of resources. That capital need not have been constructed in the first place. The second case—the substitution of new capital for existing capital (before the latter is worn out, since investment is defined here in the net sense)—takes place all the time and, in reasonable magnitudes, is both unavoidable and desirable in a free dynamic society. It is when this substitution proceeds on a rather large scale that it can become socially wasteful; also, losses sustained or expected by capital owners will make them oppose new investment—a serious danger for an economy with considerable monopolistic elements.

Finally, capital may be substituted for labor. If this substitution results in a *voluntary* reduction in the labor force or in the length of the work week, no objections can be raised. Such a process has of course been going on for many years. But in our economy it is very likely that at least a part of this substitution—if carried on at an extensive scale—will be involuntary, so that the result will be unemployment.

The tools used in this paper do not allow us to distinguish between these three effects of capital formation, though, as will appear later, our concepts are so defined that a voluntary reduction in the number of man-hours worked is excluded. In general, it is not unreasonable to assume that in most cases all three effects will be present (though not in constant proportions), and that capital formation not accompanied by an increase in income will result in unemployed capital and labor.

The above problems do not arise in the standard Keynesian system because of its explicit assumption that employment is a function of national income, an assumption which admittedly can be justified only over short periods of time. Clearly, a full-employment income of 1941 would cause considerable unemployment today. While Keynes' approach—the treatment of employment as a function of income—is a reasonable first approximation, we shall go a step further and assume instead that *the percentage of labor force employed is a function of the ratio between national income and productive capacity.* This should be an improvement, but we must admit the difficulties of determining productive capacity, both conceptually and statistically. These are obvious and need not be elaborated. We shall mean by productive capacity the total output of the economy at what is usually called full employment (with due allowance for frictional and seasonal unemployment), such factors as consumers' preferences, price and wage structures, intensity of competition, and so on being given.

The answer to the problem of unemployment lies of course in a growing income. If after capital equipment has increased by (an annual rate of) 15 billions, an income of 150 billions leaves some capacity unused, then a higher magnitude of income can be found—say 155 or 160 billions—which will do the job. There is nothing novel or startling about this conclusion. The idea that a capitalist economy needs growth goes back, in one form or another, at least to Marx. The trouble really is that the idea of growth is so widely accepted that people rarely bother about it. It is always treated as an afterthought, to be added to one's speech or article if requested, but very seldom incorporated in its body. Even then it is regarded as a function of some abstract technological progress which somehow results in increasing productivity per man-hour, and which takes place quite independently of capital formation. And yet, our help in the industrialization of undeveloped countries will take the form not only of supplying technical advice and textbooks, but also of actual machinery and goods. Certainly the 80-odd billion dollars of net capital formation created in the United States in the period 1919-1929 had a considerable effect on our productive capacity.[3]

A change in productive capacity of a country is a function of changes in its natural resources (discovery of new ones or depletion of others), in its labor force (more correctly, man-hours available), capital and the state of technique.[4] Since changes in natural resources and technique are very difficult concepts, we can express changes in total capacity via changes in the quantity and productivity of labor or of capital. The traditional approach builds around labor. The several studies of the magnitude of total output corresponding to full employment, made in the last few years, consisted in multiplying the expected labor force (subdivided into several classes) by its expected average productivity.[5] This procedure did not imply that the other three factors (natural resources, technology, and capital) remained constant; rather that their variations were all reflected in the changes in productivity of labor.

It is also possible to put capital in the center of the stage and to estimate variations in total capacity by measuring the changes in the quantity of capital and in its productivity, the latter reflecting changes currently taking place in natural resources, technology, and the labor force. From a practical point of view, the labor approach has obvious advantages, at least in some problems, because labor is a more homogeneous and easily measurable factor. But from a theoretical point of view, the capital approach is more promising and for this reason: the appearance of an extra workman or his decision to work longer hours *only* increases productive capacity without, however, generating any income to make use of this increase. But the construction of a new factory has a *dual* effect: *it increases productive capacity and it generates income.*

The emphasis on this dual character of the investment process is the essence of this paper's approach to the problem of employment. If investment increases productive capacity and also creates income, what should be the magnitude of investment, or at what rate should it grow, in order to make

---

[3] This figure, in 1929 prices, is taken from Simon Kuznets, *National Income and Its Composition,* Vol. I (New York, 1941), p. 268. The actual figure was 79.1 billion dollars.

[4] Taking other conditions listed on p. 112 as given.

[5] See for instance E. E. Hagen and N. B. Kirkpatrick, "The National Output at Full Employment in 1950," *Amer. Econ. Rev.,* Vol. XXXIV, No. 4 (September 1944), pp. 472-500.

the increase in income equal to that of productive capacity?[6] Couldn't an equation be set up one side of which would represent the increase (or the rate of increase) of productive capacity, and the other—that of income, and the solution of which would yield the required *rate of growth?*

We shall attempt to set up such an equation. It will be first expressed in symbolic form, and later illustrated by a numerical example.

Let investment proceed at an annual rate of I, and let annual productive capacity (net value added) per dollar of newly created capital be equal on the average to s. Thus if it requires, say, 3 dollars of capital to produce (in terms of annual net value added) one dollar of output, s will equal one third or 33.3 percent per year. It is not meant that s is the same in all firms or industries. It depends of course on the nature of capital constructed and on many other factors. Its treatment here as a given magnitude is a simplification which can be readily dispensed with.

The productive capacity of I dollars invested will thus be Is dollars per year. But it is possible that the operation of new capital will take place, at least to some extent, at the expense of previously constructed plants, with which the new capital will compete both for markets and for factors of production (mainly labor). If as a result, the output of existing plants must be curtailed, it would be useless to assert that the productive capacity of the *whole economy* has increased by Is dollars per year.[7] It has actually increased by a smaller amount which will be indicated by $I\sigma$.[8] σ may be called the *potential social average productivity of investment.* Such a long name calls for an explanation.

1. As stated above, σ is concerned with the increase in productive capacity of the whole society and not with the productive capacity per dollar invested in the new plants taken by themselves, that is with s. A difference between s and σ indicates a certain misdirection of investment, or—more important—that investment proceeds at too rapid a rate as compared with the growth of labor and technological progress. . . .

2. σ should not be confused with other related concepts, such as the traditional marginal productivity of capital. These concepts are usually based on a *caeteris paribus* assumption regarding the quantity of other factors and the state of technique. It should be emphasized that the use of σ does not imply in the least that labor, natural resources and technology remain fixed. It would be more correct therefore to say that σ indicates the increase in productive capacity which *accompanies* rather than which is caused by each dollar invested.

3. For our purposes, the most important property of σ is its *potential character*. It deals not with an increase in national income but with that of

---

[6] This statement of the problem presupposes that full employment has already been reached and must only be maintained. With a small extra effort we could begin with a situation where some unemployment originally existed.

[7] These comparisons must of course be made at a full employment level of national income. . . .

[8] We are disregarding here external economies obtained by existing plants from the newly constructed ones.

the *productive potential* of the economy. A high σ indicates that the economy *is capable* of increasing its output relatively fast. But whether this increased capacity will actually result in greater output or greater unemployment, depends on the behavior of money income.

The expression $I\sigma$ is the supply side of our system; it is the increase in output which the economy *can* produce. On the demand side we have the multiplier theory, too familiar to need any elaboration, except for the emphasis on the obvious but often forgotten fact that, with any given marginal propensity to save, to be indicated by α, an increase in national income is not a function of investment, but of the *increment* in investment. If investment today, however large, is equal to that of yesterday, national income of today will be just equal and not any larger than that of yesterday. All this is obvious, and is stressed here to underline the lack of symmetry between the effects of investment on productive capacity and on national income.

Let investment increase at an absolute annual rate of ΔI (e.g., by two billion per year), and let the corresponding absolute annual increase in income be indicated by ΔY. We have then

(1) $$\Delta Y = \Delta I \frac{1}{\alpha} ,$$

where $\frac{1}{\alpha}$ is of course the multiplier.

Let us now assume that the economy is in a position of a full-employment equilibrium, so that its national income equals its productive capacity.[9] To retain this position, income and capacity should increase at the same rate. The annual increase in potential capacity equals $I\sigma$. The annual increase in actual income is expressed by $\Delta I(1/\alpha)$. Our objective is to make them equal. This gives us the fundamental equation

(2) $$\Delta I \frac{1}{\alpha} = I\sigma.$$

To solve this equation, we multiply both sides by α and divide by I, obtaining

(3) $$\frac{\Delta I}{I} = \alpha\sigma.$$

The left side of expression (3) is the absolute annual increase (or the absolute rate of growth) in investment—ΔI—divided by the volume of investment itself; or in other words, it is the relative increase in investment, or the annual percentage rate of growth of investment. Thus the maintenance of full employment requires that investment grow at the annual percentage rate $\alpha\sigma$.

So much for investment. Since the marginal propensity to save—α—is assumed to be constant, an increase in income is a constant multiple of an increase in investment (see expression [1]). But in order to remain such a constant multiple of investment, income must also grow at the same annual percentage rate, that is at $\alpha\sigma$.

---

[9] See note 6.

To summarize, the maintenance of a continuous state of full employment requires that *investment and income grow at a constant annual percentage (or compound interest) rate* equal to the product of the marginal propensity to save and the average (to put it briefly) productivity of investment.[10]. . .

These results were obtained on the assumption that α, the marginal propensity to save, and σ, the average productivity of investment, remain constant. The reader can see that this assmuption is not necessary for the argument, and that the whole problem can be easily reworked with variable α and σ. . . .

The expression (3) indicates (in a very simplified manner) conditions needed for the maintenance of full employment over a period of time. It shows that it is not sufficient, in Keynesian terms, that savings of yesterday be invested today, or, as it is often expressed, that investment offset saving. Investment of today must always exceed savings of yesterday. A mere absence of hoarding will not do. An injection of new money (or dishoarding) must take place every day. Moreover, this injection must proceed, in absolute terms, at an accelerated rate. The economy must continuously expand.[11]. . .

THE DUAL NATURE OF THE INVESTMENT PROCESS

We shall continue the discussion of growth by returning to expression (2) on page 115.

$$\Delta I\, \frac{1}{\alpha} = I\sigma,$$

which is fundamental to our whole analysis. As a matter of fact, the statement of the problem in this form (2) appears to me at least as important as its actual solution expressed in (3). To repeat, the left part of the equation shows the annual increment in national income and is the demand side, while the right part represents the annual increase in productive capacity and is the supply side. Alternatively, the left part may be called the "multiplier side," and the right part the "σ side."

What is most important for our purposes is the fact that investment appears on both sides of the equation; that is, it has a *dual effect*: on the left side it generates income via the multiplier effect; and on the right side it increases productive capacity—the σ effect. The explicit recognition of this dual character of investment could undoubtedly save much argument and

[10] The careful reader may be disturbed by the lack of clear distinction between increments and rates of growth here and elsewhere in the text. If some confusion exists, it is due to my attempt to express these concepts in nonmathematical form. Actually they all should be stated in terms of rates of growth (derivatives in respect to time). For a more serious treatment of this point, as well as for a more complete statement of the logic of the paper, see my article "Capital Expansion, Rate of Growth, and Employment," *Econometrica, Vol. XIV* (April 1946), pp. 137-147.

[11] After this paper was sent to the printer, I happened to stumble on an article by R. F. Harrod, published in 1939, which contained a number of ideas similar to those presented here. See "An Essay in Dynamic Theory," *Econ. Jour.,* Vol. XLIX (April 1939), pp. 14-33.

confusion. Unless some special assumptions are made, the discussion of the effects of investment on profits, income, employment, etc., cannot be legitimately confined to one side only. For the generation of income and the enlargement of productive capacity often have diametrically opposed effects, and the outcome in each particular case depends on the special circumstances involved.[12]

Analyzing expression (2) further, we notice that even though investment is present on both its sides, it does not take the same form: for on the σ side we have the *amount* of investment as such; but on the multiplier side we have not the amount of investment but its annual increment, or its absolute *rate of increase*.

The amount of investment (always in the net sense) may remain constant, or it may go up or down, but so long as it remains positive (and except for the rare case when $\sigma \leqq 0$) productive capacity increases. But if income is to rise as well, it is not enough that just any amount be invested: *an increase in income is not a function of the amount invested; it is the function of the increment of investment.* Thus the whole body of investment, so to speak, increases productive capacity, but only its very top—the increment—increases national income.

In this probably lies the explanation why inflations have been so rare in our economy in peacetime, and why even in relatively prosperous periods a certain degree of underemployment has usually been present. Indeed, it is difficult enough to keep investment at some reasonably high level year after year, but the requirement that it always be rising is not likely to be met for any considerable length of time.

Now, if investment and therefore income do not grow at the required rate, unused capacity develops. Capital and labor become idle. It may not be apparent why investment by increasing productive capacity creates unemployment of labor. Indeed, . . . this need not always be the case. Suppose national income remains constant or rises very slowly while new houses are being built. It is possible that new houses will be rented out at the expense of older buildings and that no larger rents will be paid than before; or that the new houses will stand wholly or partly vacant with the same result regarding the rents.[13] But it is also possible, and indeed very probable, that the complete or partial utilization of the new buildings which are usually better than the old ones, will require the payment of larger rents, with the result that less income will be left for the purchase of, say clothing; thus causing unemployment in the clothing trades. So the substitution of capital for labor need not

---

[12] The effects of labor-saving machinery on employment of labor is a good case in point. Some economists, particularly those connected with the labor movement, insist that such machines displace labor and create unemployment. Their opponents are equally sure that the introduction of labor-saving devices reduces costs and generates income, thus increasing employment. Both sides cite ample empirical evidence to prove their contentions, and neither side is wrong. But both of them present an incomplete picture from which no definite conclusion can be derived.

[13] It is worth noticing that in both cases the construction of the new houses represents a misdirection of resources, at least to some extent. But a complete avoidance of such misdirection is perfectly impossible and even undesirable.

take the obvious form of labor-saving machinery; it may be equally effective in a more circuitous way.

The unemployment of men is considered harmful for obvious reasons. But idle buildings and machinery, though not arousing our humanitarian instincts, can be harmful because their presence inhibits new investment. Why build a new factory when existing ones are working at half capacity? It is certainly not necessary to be dogmatic and assert that no plant or house should ever be allowed to stand idle, and that as soon as unused capacity develops the economy plunges into a depression. There is no need, nor is it possible or desirable, to guarantee that every piece of capital ever constructed will be fully utilized until it is worn out. When population moves from Oklahoma to California, some buildings in Oklahoma will stand idle; or when plastics replace leather in women's handbags, the leather industry may suffer. Such changes form the very life of a free dynamic society, and should not be interfered with. The point is that there be no vacant houses while prospective tenants are present but cannot afford to live in them because they are unemployed. And they are unemployed because income and investment do not grow sufficiently fast.

The extent to which unused capacity, present or expected, inhibits new investment greatly depends on the structure of industry and the character of the economy in general. The more atomistic it is, the stronger is competition, the more susceptible it is to territorial, technological, and other changes, the smaller is the effect of unused capacity on new investment. One firm may have an idle plant, while another in the same industry builds a new one; steel may be depressed while plastics are expanding. It is when an industry is more or less monopolized, or when several industries are financially connected, that unused capacity presents a particularly serious threat to new investment.

Strictly speaking, our discussion so far, including equation (2), was based on the assumption that α remained constant. If α varies within the time period concerned, the relation between investment and income becomes more involved. What the left side of the equation (2) requires is that *income* increase; and investment must grow only in so far as its growth is necessary for the growth of income. So if α declines sufficiently fast, a growing income can be achieved with a constant or even falling investment. But years of declining α have evidently been offset by others of rising α, because whatever information is available would indicate that over the last seventy years or so prior to this war the percentage of income saved was reasonably constant, possibly with a slight downward trend.[14] Therefore, in the absence of direct government interference, it would seem better not to count too much on a falling α, at least for the time being.

In general, a high α presents a serious danger to the maintenance of full employment, because investment may fail to grow at the required high rate,

---

[14] See Simon Kuznets, *National Product since 1869,* National Bureau of Economic Research (mimeo., 1945), pp. II-89. I do not mean that we must always assume a constant α: rather that we lack sufficient proof to rely on a falling one.

or will be physically unable to do so without creating a substantial difference between s and σ. This difference indicates that large numbers of capital assets become unprofitable and their owners suffer losses or at least disappointments. Space does not permit me to develop this idea at greater length here.[15] But it must be emphasized that what matters is not the magnitude of α taken by itself, but its relation to the growth of labor, natural resources, and technology. Thus a country with new resources, a rapidly growing population, and developing technology is able to digest, so to speak, a relatively large α, while absence or at least a very slow growth of these factors makes a high α a most serious obstacle to full employment.[16] But the problem can be attacked not only by lowering α, but also by speeding up the rate of technological progress, the latter solution being much more to my taste. It must be remembered, however, that technological progress makes it *possible* for the economy to grow, without guaranteeing that this growth will be realized.

In a private capitalist society where α cannot be readily changed, a higher level of income and employment at any given time can be achieved only through increased investment. But investment, as an employment creating instrument, is a mixed blessing because of its σ effect. The economy finds itself in a serious dilemma: if sufficient investment is not forthcoming today, unemployment will be here today. But if enough is invested today, still more will be needed tomorrow.

It is a remarkable characteristic of a capitalist economy that while, on the whole, unemployment is a function of the difference between its actual income and its productive capacity, most of the measures (*i.e.,* investment) directed toward raising national income also enlarge productive capacity. It is very likely that the increase in national income will be greater than that of capacity, but the whole problem is that the increase in income is temporary and presently peters out (the usual multiplier effect), while capacity has been increased for good. So that as far as unemployment is concerned, investment is at the same time a cure for the disease and the cause of even greater ills in the future.[17]. . .

CONCLUDING REMARKS

A traveler who sat in the economic councils of the United States and of the Soviet Union would be much impressed with the emphasis placed on investment and technological progress in both countries. He would happily

---

[15] See my paper, *Econometrica,* Vol. XIV, particularly pp. 142-145.

[16] *Cf.* Alvin H. Hansen, *Fiscal Policy and the Business Cycle* (New York, 1941), particularly Part IV.

[17] That income generating effects of investment are temporary and that new and larger amounts must be spent to maintain full employment has been mentioned in economic and popular literature a number of times. Particular use has been made of this fact by opponents of the so-called deficit financing, who treat government expenditures as a "shot in the arm" which must be administered at an ever increasing dose. What they fail to realize is that exactly the same holds true for private investment.

conclude that the differences between the economic problems of a relatively undeveloped socialist economy and a highly developed capitalist economy are really not as great as they are often made to appear. Both countries want investment and technological progress. But if he continued to listen to the debates, he would presently begin to wonder. For in the Soviet Union investment and technology are wanted in order to enlarge the country's productive capacity. They are wanted essentially as labor-saving devices which would allow a given task to be performed with less labor, thus releasing men for other tasks. In short, they are wanted for their σ effects.

In the United States, on the other hand, little is said about enlarging productive capacity. Technological progress is wanted as the creator of investment opportunities, and investment is wanted because it generates income and creates employment. It is wanted for its multiplier effect.

Both views are correct and both are incomplete. The multiplier is not just another capitalist invention. It can live in a socialist state just as well and it has been responsible for the inflationary pressure which has plagued the Soviet economy all these years, since the first five-year plan. And similarly, σ is just as much at home in one country as in another, and its effect—the enlarged productive capacity brought about by accumulation of capital—has undoubtedly had much to do with our peacetime unemployment.

But what is the solution? Shall we reduce σ to zero and also abolish technological progress, thus escaping from unemployment into the "nirvana" of a stationary state? This would indeed be a defeatist solution. It is largely due to technology and savings that humanity has made the remarkable advance of the last two hundred years, and now when our technological future seems so bright, there is less reason to abandon it than ever before.

It is possible that α has been or will be too high as compared with the growth of our labor force, the utilization of new resources, and the development of technology. Unfortunately, we have hardly any empirical data to prove or disprove this supposition. The fact that private investment did not absorb available savings in the past does not prove that they could not be utilized in other ways (*e.g.,* by government), or even that had private business invested them these investments would have been unprofitable; the investing process itself might have created sufficient income to justify the investments. What is needed is a study of the magnitudes of s, of the difference between s and σ which can develop without much harm and then of the value of α which the economy can digest at its full-employment rate of growth.

Even if the resulting magnitude of α is found to be considerably below the existing one, a reduction of α is only one of the two solutions, the speeding up of technological progress being the other. But it must be remembered that neither technology, nor of course saving, guarantee a rise in income. What they do is to place in our hands the *power* and the ability of achieving a growing income. And just as, depending upon the use made of it, any power can become a blessing or a curse, so can saving and technological progress, depending on our economic policies, result in frustration and unemployment or in an ever-expanding economy.

PART THREE

||||||||||||||||||||||||||||||||||||||||||||||||||||||||||||||||||||||||||||||||||||||||||||||||||||||||||||||||||

The Underdeveloped
Countries:
Modern Approaches
to Development

For all the obstacles to continued growth foreseen by the theorists of the previous section, they were at least spared one problem that plagues many economists today: how, in the first place, does an economy reach such a blissful state of development that one can afford the luxury of speculation about "advanced opulence" and stagnation? This section presents some approaches to the problem of underdeveloped countries that have been taken by some contemporary economists.

One of the most interesting and controversial issues raised in the contemporary literature on the underdeveloped countries concerns the relative contribution to economic growth made by different sectors of the economy. As we have seen, the classical economists, in their analysis of growth, drew a sharp distinction between the agricultural and nonagricultural sectors of the economy. Because they assumed the operation of the law of diminishing returns in agriculture but not in other sectors (constant or increasing returns to scale were regarded as characteristic of manufacturing), they tended to view agriculture as the ultimate restraint on economic (as well as population) growth.

Though contemporary writers no longer recognize the classical distinction with respect to diminishing returns, they have for different reasons continued to use the same dichotomy of economic sectors. A close negative correlation has been found to exist between levels of per capita income and the share of national output originating in agriculture. While causality cannot be adduced from statistical association alone, there are many who believe that industrialization of the presently underdeveloped and predominantly agricultural countries is the key to rapid economic growth and high levels of per capita income. There are also those, however, who point to such prominent examples as New Zealand and Denmark where high levels of economic performance were attained primarily through emphasis on agricultural development (see the selection by Jacob Viner).

The issue of agricultural versus nonagricultural development is discussed in at least two different contexts. There is, first, the question of the role of industrialization in the *historical* process of growth. Secondly, the vital question now confronting underdeveloped countries is the relative emphasis to be assigned by development *policy* and investment programs to agricultural development on the one hand and industrialization on the other.

Economic specialization, as suggested by the law of comparative advantage, is at the root of the view that some countries, by virtue of their particular endowment of resources, would do best to focus their energies on further development of their agricultural sectors. As efficient exporters of agricultural products, they would be in a position to satisfy their needs for manufactures by importing them from other countries that enjoy a comparative advantage in the production of such goods. The opposing view, however, is that agricultural economies will fare badly in international trade, because of long-run deterioration in the terms of trade—the terms on which agricultural goods exchange for manufactures (see Hans W. Singer's article). This view is, incidentally, in direct opposition to the classical view that the long-run terms of trade would move in favor of agriculture—a view stemming from the assumption of diminishing returns in agriculture but not in manufacturing. The statistical evidence on the historical course of the terms of trade is not clear-cut, and has been the subject of hot dispute. Even more uncertain—and more pertinent for development policy—is the *future* course of the terms of trade.

But the issue of agricultural specialization is not confined to expected adverse trends in the terms of trade. It is frequently argued that dependence on primary production—agriculture and mining—leaves some underdeveloped countries vulnerable in another respect. The primary commodity exports of these countries loom large in their national income, and such commodities tend on the average to fluctuate in world price and volume considerably more than do manufactured goods, when disturbances of a seasonal, cyclical, or random nature arise. These underdeveloped countries therefore experience more severe instability of national income than do the advanced countries, particularly when exports are limited to only a few commodities. This greater vulnerability of national income to disturbances most frequently originating in the advanced economies reinforces the conviction of many that broad-gauged industrialization, in reducing the dependence of the underdeveloped economies upon primary production and foreign trade, would be a good thing.

As a matter of economic policy, there appears to be something resembling consensus among the governments of the underdeveloped countries in favor of industrialization, though in the heavily populated countries with chronic food problems, such as India, there is clear awareness of the strategic role that agriculture must play in economic development.

Somewhat related to the theoretical controversy over agriculture versus industry is the discussion, prominent in the current literature, of the concept of *balanced growth*. The poor countries, struggling with the problem of raising their levels of living, find themselves caught up in what has been termed a "vicious circle of poverty." According to this conception, the low income of these countries is attributable to the low productivity of labor, which is in part a function of an inadequate supply of physical capital. But the shortage of capital results partly from the persistently low levels of saving —caused, in turn, by low income, thus completing the circle (see the selection by Ragnar Nurkse).

"Balanced growth" has been proposed (see the selections by P. N. Rosenstein-Rodan and by Nurkse) as a means of breaking this vicious circle and stimulating economic development. Because low incomes and a consequent lack of demand generally spell failure for any heavily concentrated investment in a single consumer-goods industry, it is suggested that investment be diversified over a broad range of such industries. Each industry, it is argued, will then generate, through its factor payments, a demand for the goods of the other industries sufficient to keep all of them viable. Investment projects that might be individually unprofitable would, taken collectively, be profitable.

This doctrine has not received undivided support. One of the strongest critiques (that of Marcus Fleming) accuses the theory of overemphasis on the demand side of the problem, to the neglect of the equally important supply side. Inadequate supplies of factors of production in underdeveloped countries—particularly capital and skilled labor—may make diversified and simultaneous investment projects unfeasible by sharply increasing the costs of production of all industries as they compete for the limited supply of factors.

P. N. ROSENSTEIN-RODAN

Problems of Industrialization of Eastern and South-Eastern Europe

"I should like to buy an egg, please," she said timidly. "How do you sell them?" "Fivepence farthing for one—twopence for two," the Sheep replied. "Then two are cheaper than one?" Alice said in a surprised tone, taking out her purse. "Only you *must* eat them both, if you buy two," said the Sheep. "Then I'll have *one,* please," said Alice as she put the money down on the counter. For she thought to herself, "They mightn't be at all nice you know."

Lewis Carroll, *Through the Looking Glass*

It is generally agreed that industrialization[1] of "international depressed areas" like Eastern and South-Eastern Europe (or the Far East) is in the general interest not only of those countries, but of the world as a whole. It is *the* way of achieving a more equal distribution of income between different areas of the world by raising incomes in depressed areas at a higher rate than in the rich areas. The assumptions in the case under discussion are: that there exists an "agrarian excess population" in Eastern and South-Eastern Europe amounting to 20-25 million people out of the total population of 100-110 million, *i.e.,* that about 25 percent of the population is either totally or partially ("disguised unemployment") unemployed. The waste of labor is by no means confined to rich industrial countries. It is considerably greater in poor agrarian countries. If the principles of international division of labor

From *Economic Journal* (June-September 1943), pp. 202-211. Reprinted by permission of the Royal Economic Society and the author.

[1] One might consider the industrialization of these countries as one chapter of agrarian reconstruction, or one might treat the improvement of agrarian production as one chapter of industrialization. What matters is to remember that the two tasks are interconnected parts of one problem.

are to be applied, labor must either be transported toward capital (emigration), or capital must be transported toward labor (industrialization). From the point of view of maximizing the world income, the difference between these two ways is one of transport costs only, and may be assumed to be negligible. Emigration and resettlement would, however, present so many difficulties in immigration areas (and in emigration areas) that it cannot be considered feasible on a large scale. A very considerable part of the task will have to be solved by industrialization.

In order to reach an "optimum size" of the industrial enterprises, the area of industrialization must be sufficiently large. This fact, as well as the possibility of lowering the marginal risk of investment make it imperative to aim at an economic unit comprising the whole area between Germany, Russia and Italy. Though large in terms of square miles or population, it is not large in terms of output. The total national income of this economic unit amounts to £2,000 million—*i.e.,* 40 percent of the income of Great Britain.

There are two fundamentally different ways of industrialization of that area:

(i) That Eastern and South-Eastern Europe should industrialize on its own, on the "Russian model" (by which we do *not* mean communism), aiming at self-sufficiency, without international investment. That would imply the construction of all stages of industry, heavy industry, machine industry, as well as light industry, with the final result of a national economy built like a vertical industrial concern. This way presents several grave disadvantages: (*a*) It can only proceed slowly because capital must be supplied internally at the expense of a standard of life and consumption which are already at a very low level. It implies, therefore, a heavy and, in our opinion, unnecessary sacrifice. (*b*) It will lead finally, since there are appropriate natural resources in the area, to an independent unit in the world economy implying a reduction in the international division of labor; *i.e.,* the output of the world as a whole would be less than it might be, the world would be poorer in material goods. (*c*) The difference in world economic structure is most clearly seen in the case of heavy industries. Building up heavy industries in Eastern and South-Eastern Europe at a great sacrifice would only add to the world excess capacity of heavy industry, and would constitute from the world's point of view largely a waste of resources.

(ii) The alternative way of industrialization would fit Eastern and South-Eastern Europe into the world economy, which would preserve the advantages of an international division of labor, and would therefore in the end produce more wealth for everybody. It would be based on substantial international investment or capital lending. This way presents several advantages: (*a*) It could proceed more quickly and at a small sacrifice of consumption of this area. From the point of view of international political stability there may be all the difference in the world if 50 percent of the agrarian excess population in Eastern and South-Eastern Europe were profitably employed within ten years after the war instead of, say, 20 percent. (*b*) The sound principles of international division of labor postulate labor-intensive—*i.e.,* light industries in overpopulated areas. (*c*) Even for the purposes of an expanding world economy, the existing heavy industries in the U.S.A., Great Britain, Germany, France, and Switzerland could certainly supply all the needs of the international depressed areas.

Clearly this way of industrialization is preferable to the autarkic one. It is a tremendous task, almost without historical precedent. There is no analogy to the process of industrialization in the early nineteenth century for a number of reasons which may be mentioned briefly before being examined in more detail. (*a*) International investment in the nineteenth century was largely self-liquidating, based on exchange of agrarian and industrial products. Nowadays liquidation can no longer be assumed to be "automatic," although the problem can be solved if it is properly planned. (*b*) Existing institutions of international investment (floating of shares and loans) are inappropriate to the task of industrialization of a whole area. They deal with too small units and do not take advantage of external economies. Capital mostly goes to individual enterprises. There has never been a scheme of planned industrialization comprising a simultaneous planning of several complementary industries, which is part of our plan for Eastern and South-Eastern Europe (see pp. 127-128). (*c*) Technical progress was the main driving-force in the nineteenth century. Industrialization in international depressed areas, on the other hand, implies the application of *given* technical knowledge. (*d*) The increase in overhead costs and fixed capital since the nineteenth century has raised the risk of loss of capital and lowered the mobility of resources and the flexibility of the economic system. It has vastly increased the average size of the firm. (*e*) Political risks of international investment are very much greater today than in the nineteenth century, when it was assumed that certain things were "not done." State supervision and guarantees can, therefore, substantially lower risks, and for that reason constitute the *conditio sine qua non* of international investment on a large enough scale. Active participation of the State in economic life is a new factor which must be taken into account as a new datum. (*f*) People (even Eastern Europeans!) are not as tough today as they used to be. Social conscience would not stand for as much misery in peacetime as was taken for granted in the Darwinist nineteenth century. Milder methods must be used.

An institutional framework different from the present one is clearly necessary for the successful carrying out of industrialization in international depressed areas. In what follows arguments are submitted tending to show why the whole of the industry to be created is to be treated and planned like one huge firm or trust.

The first task of industrialization is to provide for training and "skilling" of labor which is to transform Eastern European peasants into full-time or part-time industrial workers. The automatism of *laissez faire* never worked properly in that field. It broke down because it is not profitable for a private entrepreneur to invest in training labor. There are no mortgages on workers —an entrepreneur who invests in training workers may lose capital if these workers contract with another firm. Although not a good investment for a

private firm, it is the best investment for the State. It is also a good investment for the bulk of industries to be created when taken as a whole, although
it may represent irrecoverable costs for a smaller unit. It constitutes an
important instance of the Pigovian divergence between "private and social
marginal net product" where the latter is greater than the former. Training
facilities (including transport and housing) of one million workers per annum
would involve costs of certainly more than £100 million per annum—a sum
which may be too great to be borne by the State (or the Eastern European
national economy) if taken *apart* from the costs of the 50-percent participation in its own "Eastern European Industrial Trust"[2] that we shall propose.
It should be counted as capital investment in the Eastern European Industrial
Trust (E.E.I.T.).

That is not, however, the most important reason in favor of such a large
investment unit.

Complementarity of different industries provides the most important
set of arguments in favor of a large-scale planned industrialization. In order
to illustrate the issues involved, let us adopt the somewhat roundabout method
of analyzing two examples. Let us assume that 20,000 unemployed workers in
Eastern and South-Eastern Europe are taken from the land and put into a
large shoe factory. They receive wages substantially higher than their previous meager income *in natura*. It would be impossible to put them into
industry at their previous income standard, because they need more foodstuffs than they had in their agrarian semi-unemployed existence, because
these foodstuffs have to be transported to towns, and because the workers
have to pay for housing accommodation. If these workers spent all their
wages on shoes, a market for the products of their enterprise would arise
representing an expansion which does not disturb the pre-existing market, and
90 percent of the problem (assuming 10-percent profit) would be solved.
The trouble is that the workers will not spend all their wages on shoes. If,
instead, one million unemployed workers were taken from the land and put,
not into one industry, but into a whole series of industries which produce the
bulk of the goods on which the workers would spend their wages, what was
not true in the case of one shoe factory would become true in the case of a
whole system of industries: it would create its own additional market, thus
realizing an expansion of world output with the minimum disturbance of the
world markets. The industries producing the bulk of the wage goods can
therefore be said to be complementary. The planned creation of such a
complementary system reduces the risk of not being able to sell, and, since
risk can be considered as cost, it reduces costs. It is in this sense a special
case of "external economies."

It may be added that, while in the highly developed and rich countries
with their more variegated needs it is difficult to assess the prospective demand of the population, it is not as difficult to foresee on what the formerly

---

[2] The name is provisional for want of a better one. It will have to be changed
because of the unpleasant associations connected with the term "trust." Eastern European Industrial Corporation, Board—or Holding Company might be considered.

unemployed workers would spend their wages in regions where a low standard of living obtains.

Two other types of "external economies" will arise when a system of different industries is created. First, the strictly Marshallian economies external to a firm within a growing industry. The same applies, however (secondly), to economies external to one industry due to the growth of other industries. It is usually tacitly assumed that the divergence between the "private and social marginal net product" is not very considerable. This assumption may be too optimistic even in the case of a crystallized mature competitive economy. It is certainly not true in the case of fundamental structural changes in the international depressed areas. External economies may there be of the same order of magnitude as profits which appear on the profit and loss account of the enterprise.

The existing institutions of international and national investment do not take advantage of external economies. There is no incentive within their framework for many investments which are profitable in terms of "social marginal net product," but do not appear profitable in terms of "private marginal net product." The main driving-force of investment is the profit expectation of an individual entrepreneur which is based on experience of the past. Experience of the past is partly irrelevant however where the whole economic structure of a region is to be changed. An individual entrepreneur's knowledge of the market is bound to be insufficient in this case because he cannot have all the data that would be available to the planning board of an E.E.I.T. His subjective risk estimate is bound to be considerably higher than the objective risk. If the industrialization of international depressed areas were to rely entirely on the normal incentive of private entrepreneurs, the process would not only be very much slower, the rate of investment smaller and (consequently) the national income lower, but the whole economic structure of the region would be different. Investment would be distributed in different proportions between different industries, the final equilibrium would be below the optimum which a large E.E.I.T. could achieve. In the international capital market the existing institutions are mostly used to invest in, or to grant credit to, single enterprises. It might easily happen that any one enterprise would not be profitable enough to guarantee payment of sufficient interest or dividend out of its own profits. But the creation of such an enterprise, *e.g.,* production of electric power, may create new investment opportunities and profits elsewhere, *e.g.,* in an electrical equipment industry. If we create a sufficiently large investment unit by including all the new industries of the region, external economies will become internal profits out of which dividends may be paid easily.

Professor Allyn Young's celebrated example elucidates our problem. He assumed that a Tube line was to be built in a district and that an accurate estimate was made of costs and receipts. It was found that the rate of profit would be below the usual rate of yield on investments obtainable elsewhere. The project was found not profitable and was abandoned. Another enterprising company bought up the land and houses along the proposed Tube line and was then able to build the line. Although the receipts from the passenger traffic would not pay a sufficient rate of profit, the capital appreciation on the houses and land more than made up the deficiency. Thus the project was realized, the Tube line was built. The problem is: Is it desirable—*i.e.,* does it lend to an optimum allocation of resources and maximization of national income—that this form of capital gain (external economy) be included as an item in the calculus of profitability, or is it not? Allyn Young hints that it is not desirable because the capital appreciation of houses and land along the Tube line due to an influx of people from other districts has an uncompensated counterpart in a capital depreciation of houses and land in districts out of which people moved into the Tube-line district. Agricultural land in Eastern and South-Eastern Europe will, however, not depreciate when the agrarian excess of population moves out. In this case external economies should be included in the calculus of profitability.

External economies are often invoked as an argument in favor of a different program of industrialization. National and international investment should concentrate at the start on building of "basic industries" and public utilities which give rise to new investment opportunities. "Let us build railways, roads, canals, hydro-electric power-stations, the rest will follow automatically." Where the lack of transport facilities is a flagrant obstacle to economic progress, as, for instance, in China and parts of Latin America, that may indeed be the best start of development investment. The situation is different, however, in Eastern and South-Eastern Europe. There is no comparable deficiency in railroads there. Rail mileage per £ million of national income is very much higher than in the Far East. A general vision of the future economic structure is necessary in order to know where to build communications, how much of them, and what for. The quality of "basic" industries is not confined, moreover, to some public utilities. We have seen how complementarity makes to some extent all industries "basic."

If sufficient capital (national and international) is available for investment in "basic industries" the normal multiplier effect will "naturally" lead to further industrialization according to the advocates of this program. The argument assumes, however, a smooth working of the equilibrium mechanism of balance of payments and capital movements which is not likely to obtain in the structural disequilibrium situation after the war. Industrialization of international depressed areas, once it is accomplished, may create an equilibrium, from which onwards normal private incentives may operate successfully. But it seems hopeless to rely on them before that point is reached.

> Most of the countries of the world are undertaking national development or will undertake it after the war on the basis of imported capital equipment —locomotives, steel, tractors, steam shovels, cement mixers, turbines. In some instances they have foreign assets which can be used to purchase this equipment. In the majority of cases, however, they will be able to acquire it only by cutting down imports of consumer goods and pushing exports, to develop an export surplus, or by borrowing. Private investors . . . after the experience of the last twenty years, will probably not be willing to lend

monies in sufficiently large amounts or low rates of interest to enable national development in debtor areas to get off to a good start. The alternative
is for governments in creditor countries to guarantee the loans, or to lend
the funds themselves. . . . The availability of foreign funds, foreign technical
assistance and foreign machinery, however, will transform the process of
national development from one which would threaten to disrupt international
economic relations and trade into one which can make a key contribution to
the expansion of world income and the reorganisation of world trade.[3]

Governments in creditor countries will not guarantee the loans or
shares unless they see how interest or dividend service is assured. If they
have sufficient control on the board of E.E.I.T., they will be able to give the
guarantee at no cost or risk to themselves, since the real risks of the whole
enterprise are very much lower than the risks relating to parts of the whole
would be. But while the investment "pays" in Eastern and South-Eastern
Europe, it is not necessarily self-liquidating. Liquidation will have to be
planned—*i.e.,* one part of the industries created in Eastern and South-Eastern
Europe will have to be export industries. The flow of their exports will have
to be sold in creditor countries. These exports will represent the main part of
the rich countries' share in the world expansion. The placing of these exports
has to be foreseen and planned in such a way as to minimize the burden of
necessary adjustment of economic resources in the creditor countries. Eastern
and South-Eastern Europe will most probably cease to be an exporter of
cereals. It will export processed foods and light industrial articles.

International trade in the nineteenth century functioned more or less
smoothly because all countries had a high income elasticity of demand for
imports. On the higher standard of living in the rich countries of the twentieth
century the income elasticity of demand for imports may be lower. There
may be only one good for which the income elasticity of demand is high:
leisure which does not require imports of material goods. Accordingly, the
rich countries may have to accept a part of their share in economic expansion
in the form of more leisure. They may have a 40- or 35-hour week, while
Eastern Europe maintains a 48-hour week.

Attention is confined here to what ought to be done rather than how
it is to be done. The institutional implementation of this program must
be left over to another occasion. Its main outlines are: At least 50 percent of
the capital required must be supplied internally. "Creditor" and "debtor"
countries acquire each 50-percent shares of a trust formed of all the industries
to be created in the region. They will plan and proceed as business partners
with Government representatives on the board. The creditors acquire shares
in the trust which are redeemable after twenty years at 10 percent above
parity if an average dividend service of $4\frac{1}{2}$ percent at least has been maintained in the past. An *average* dividend service of 3 percent is guaranteed by
Governments on the shares subscribed in their countries. Private investments
in Eastern and South-Eastern Europe requiring foreign credits are licensed.

---

[3] *International Development Loans,* Planning Pamphlets, National Planning Association, No. 15 (New York, 1942), p. 14.

Shares may be acquired by contributions *in natura:* for instance, the establishment of branch factories. Guarantees of nondiscrimination in the internal taxation policy will be obtained from Eastern European authorities.

The aim of industrialization in international depressed areas is to produce a structural equilibrium in the world economy by creating productive employment for the agrarian excess population. It may be assumed that creditor countries will not be willing to enter into commitments for more than ten years. How much can be achieved in that period, and what is the rough order of magnitude of the capital required?

Industrial employment has to be found for (*a*) 20 million of the agrarian excess population + (*b*) 7-8 million = 40-50 percent of the increase in population during the next decade (assuming that 50-60 percent will be absorbed by agriculture) = 28 million people = 9 million active men and 3 million active women = 12 million workers. Up to 2 million workers can be employed in idle capacity. Capital has to be found for 10 million workers. Since the available capital is scarce, labor-intensive—*i.e.,* light industries—will prevail. According to such statistics as are available, the following classification of industries is proposed: (1) light industries—capital equipment per head £100–£400; (2) medium industries—capital equipment per head £400–£800; (3) heavy industries—capital equipment per head £800–£1,500. Since some heavy industries cannot be avoided, let us assume that £300–£350 per head will re required, including housing, communications and public utilities. That amounts to £3,000 million, to which has to be added £1,800 million on maintenance of old and new capital in ten years, giving a total of £4,800 million. Eastern Europe would have to supply at least 50 percent—*i.e.,* £2,400 million. Another £1,200 million of capital will be necessary for the improvement of agriculture, of which we assume that the bulk would have to be provided internally,[4] so that Eastern and South-Eastern Europe would have to supply £3,600 million capital internally between, say, 1946 and 1956.[5] Since its total income is £2,000 million per annum, that would represent a rate of investment of 18 percent (equal to that of Russia). Even if we take account of the gradually rising national income, rates of savings beginning with 8 percent and leading at the end of a ten-year period to 15 percent would seem to represent the maximum one can plan for. Assuming a national income rising annually by 4 percent, and an average rate of investment of 12 percent, the internal capital supply would only amount to $3,000 million. It appears, therefore, that even a bold and rather optimistic program of industrialization cannot abolish the whole of the surplus population in the next decade. At best 70-80 percent of the unemployed workers could be employed. It follows that emigration will still have to supplement industrialization. Besides that, however, German reparations in the

---

[4] A small part of it may be borrowed from abroad, but in this case in the form of bond credit.

[5] The immediate transition period of the first two years after the war is not included in these calculations, so that *de facto* it is a twelve-years plan, not a ten-years plan.

form of capital equipment might provide one part of the capital of the E.E.I.T. Reparations in money to the rich Western countries created a problem of the last war. There is no difficulty with reparations *in natura* to poor countries. Germany can increase her consumption above the wartime standard, and transfer reparations *in natura* representing 25-50 percent of what she used to spend on armaments.

RAGNAR NURKSE

||||||||||||||||||||||||||||||||||||||||||||||||||||||||||||||||||||||||||||||||||||||||||||||||||||||||||||||||||||||||||||||||||||||||||||||||||

Some International Aspects of the Problem of Economic Development

"A country is poor because it is poor." This seems a trite proposition, but it does express the circular relationships that afflict both the demand and the supply side of the problem of capital formation in economically backward areas. This paper will discuss some international aspects of the difficulties on both sides. It will take up only a few points and cannot even attempt to give anything like a balanced picture.

I

The inducement to invest is limited by the size of the market. That is essentially what Allyn Young[1] brought out in his reinterpretation of Adam Smith's famous thesis. What determines the size of the market? Not simply money demand, nor mere numbers of people, nor physical area. Transport facilities, which Adam Smith singled out for special emphasis, are important; reductions in transport costs (artificial as well as natural) do enlarge the market in the economic as well as the geographical sense. But reductions in any cost of production tend to have that effect. So the size of the market is determined by the general level of productivity. Capacity to buy means capacity to produce. In its turn, the level of productivity depends—not entirely by any means, but largely—on the use of capital in production. But the use of capital is inhibited, to start with, by the small size of the market.

Where is the way out of this circle? How can the market be enlarged?

From *American Economic Review* (May 1952), pp. 571-583. Reprinted by permission of the American Economic Association.

[1] "Increasing Returns and Economic Progress," *Economic Journal* (December 1928).

Although in backward areas Say's Law may be valid in the sense that there is generally no deflationary gap, it never is valid in the sense that the output of any single industry, newly set up with capital equipment, can create its own demand. Human wants being various, the people engaged in the new industry will not wish to spend all their income on their own products.[2] Suppose it is a shoe industry. If in the rest of the economy nothing happens to increase productivity and hence buying power, the market for the new shoe output is likely to prove deficient. People in the rest of the economy will not give up other things in order to buy, say, a pair of shoes every year, if they do not have enough food, clothing, and shelter. They cannot let go the little they have of these elementary necessities. If they were willing to give up some of their present consumption in exchange for an annual pair of new shoes, these things would be available for the shoe workers to make up the balance in their own consumption needs. As it is, the new industry is likely to be a failure.

The difficulty is not due fundamentally to discontinuities in the technical forms of capital equipment, though these may accentuate it. It is due above all to the inevitable inelasticity of demands at low real-income levels. It is in this way that lack of buying power cramps the inducement to invest in any individual industry.

The difficulty is not present, however, in the case of a more or less synchronized application of capital to a wide range of different industries. Here the result is an over-all enlargement of the market and hence an escape from the deadlock. People working with more and better tools in a number of complementary projects become each other's customers. Most industries catering for mass consumption are complementary in the sense that they provide a market for, and thus support, each other. This basic complementarity stems, of course, from the diversity of human wants. The case for "balanced growth" rests ultimately on the need for a "balanced diet."

The notion of balance is inherent in Say's Law. Take Mill's formulation of it: "Every increase of production, if distributed without miscalculation among all kinds of produce in the proportion which private interest would dictate, creates, or rather constitutes, its own demand."[3] Here, in a nutshell, is the case for balanced growth. An increase in the production of shoes alone does not create its own demand. An increase in production over a wide range of consumables, so balanced as to correspond with the pattern of consumers' preferences, does create its own demand.

How do we get balanced growth? Ordinary price incentives may bring it about by small degrees, though here the technical discontinuities can be a serious hindrance; besides, slow growth is just not good enough where population pressure exists. In the evolution of Western industrial capitalism, rapid growth was achieved, in Schumpeter's view, through the action of creative entrepreneurs producing spurts of industrial progress. Even though innova-

---

[2] See Paul N. Rosenstein-Rodan, pp. 127-128 in this book.—EDS.

[3] J. S. Mill, *Essays in Some Unsettled Questions of Political Economy* (London School of Economics reprint, 1948), p. 73.

tions originated each time in a particular industry, the monetary effects and other circumstances were such as to promote each time a wave of new applications of capital over a whole range of industries. It is easy to see how a frontal attack of this sort can succeed while yet any sizable investment in any particular industry may be discouraged by the limits of the existing market.

Other types of society may feel a need for some degree of central direction to produce the desired effect—at any rate initially. But whether balanced growth is enforced by government planning or achieved spontaneously by private enterprise is, in a sense, a question of method. Whichever method is adopted, the nature of the solution aimed at may be the same, though the "miscalculation" Mill warned against seems hard to avoid in either case.

II

On the international plane, these general considerations apply first of all to the problem of international investment. Why is it that private business investment abroad has tended in the past—in the last few years as well as in the nineteenth century—to shy away from industries working for the domestic market in underdeveloped areas and to concentrate instead on primary production for export to the advanced industrial centers? The facts do not support the view that the so-called "colonial" type of investment—in mines and plantations producing for export to the industrial creditor countries—was typical of nineteenth century foreign investment as a whole. They do suggest, however, that it was, and still is, fairly typical of private business investment in backward areas. American direct investments abroad definitely conform to this pattern. In underdeveloped countries, they work mostly in extractive industries—oil fields, mines, and plantations—producing for export markets; only in advanced areas (Canada and Western Europe) do they, significantly, show any great interest in manufacturing for local consumption.[4]

The reluctance of private business capital to go to work for domestic markets in underdeveloped countries, in contrast with its eagerness in the past to work there for export to the industrial nations, reflects no sinister conspiracy or deliberate policy. There is the obvious economic explanation: on the one hand, the poverty of the local consumers in the backward countries; on the other, the large and, in the nineteenth century, vigorously expanding markets for primary products in the world's industrial centers. In these circumstances it was natural for foreign business investment to form mere outposts of the industrial creditor countries, to whose needs these outposts catered.

Incidentally, the weakness of the market incentive for private investment in the domestic economy of a low-income area can affect domestic as well as foreign capital. It may help in some degree to account for the common observation that such domestic saving as does take place in underdeveloped countries tends to be used unproductively: hoarded, exported, or put into real estate.

---

[4] See H. J. Dernburg, "Prospects for Long-Term Foreign Investment," *Harvard Business Review* (July 1950), p. 42.

Private investment generally is governed by the pull of market demand, and private international investment is no exception to this. A particular instance of the relation between investment incentives and market demand appears in our old friend the acceleration principle. The relation holds, albeit in a different way, in space as well as in the time dimension. The conventional theory of factor proportions and capital movements is that in countries where there is little capital in relation to land and labor, the marginal productivity and hence the yield of capital will be high, and that, if it were not for extraneous impediments, capital would move to these countries from the areas where it is relatively abundant. This view is subject to the qualification that the high potential yield of capital in capital-poor areas may be capable of realization only through investment undertaken simultaneously in a number of complementary industries (or in public overhead facilities that serve to raise productivity in a number of different lines). A balanced increase in production generates external economies by enlarging the size of the market for each firm or industry. There is on this account as well as for other possible reasons, a discrepancy between the private and the social marginal productivity of capital. Even if we abstract from political and other risk factors, there is no guarantee that the motives that animate individual businessmen will automatically induce a flow of funds from the rich to the poor countries. The marginal productivity of capital in the latter compared with the former may be high indeed, but not necessarily in private business terms.

While the doctrine of balanced growth leaves plenty of room for international investment, it does reveal limits to the role of direct business investment. An individual foreign investor may not have the power, even if he had the will, to break the deadlock caused by low productivity, lack of real buying power, and deficient investment incentives in the domestic economy of a backward area. Even in the heyday of private foreign investment, however, capital outlays carried on by public authorities by means of private foreign loans were an important form of international investment. Loans to governments accounted for 30 percent of Britain's total overseas investments outstanding in 1914, with another 40 percent in railway securities and 5 percent in public utilities.[5] Clearly this does not leave any major proportion for the strictly colonial type of investments—in mines and plantations producing for the creditor countries.

Investment by public authorities financed from private—or public— foreign funds is a form of "autonomous" investment, since it does not depend closely, if at all, on the current state of market demand. By contrast, direct business investment must be classed as a form of "induced" investment since it generally has to be induced by tangible market demand, already existing or visibly coming into existence. Thus the general distinction between autonomous and induced investment is applicable in a certain sense to international investment as well.

International investment on private business account is attracted by markets, and for the poorer countries the big markets in the past were the

[5] H. Feis, *Europe, The World's Banker, 1870-1914* (New Haven, Conn.: Yale University Press, 1930), p. 27.

markets for export to the great industrial centers. Investment was induced by the investing countries' own demand. Foreign investment in extractive industries working for export is not to be despised, since it usually carries with it various direct and indirect benefits to the country where it is made. Why is even this type of investment now flowing out in only a small trickle? Aside, again, from the obvious political impediments, perhaps the answer is that the export markets for primary commodities have not been enjoying anything like the same rate of secular expansion as that which came about in the nineteenth century from the extraordinary growth of population as well as productivity in the Western industrial countries, and also from Britain's willingness to sacrifice her own agriculture to the requirements of international specialization. In recent decades, synthetic substitutes have affected unfavorably the demand for a number of staple products. The present raw-material boom is widely regarded as being due to special circumstances which may not last. In any case, it may take more than a boom—it may take something like a secular expansion of demand—to induce private foreign investment in underdeveloped areas for the production of primary commodities for export.

Reliance on direct business investment for the capital needed for economic development is therefore liable to a double disappointment. Not only is there little or no incentive for private business capital to go to work for the expansion of the domestic economies of low-income countries; even for the expansion of raw-material supplies for export, private business funds may not want to move out in any steady or sizable flow. But this, I repeat, applies to induced investment. It does not, or need not, affect international investment of the autonomous sort.

III

The case which the underdeveloped countries advance in favor of their "balanced growth" and "diversification" is not always well received. Does it not mean turning away from the principle of comparative advantage? Why do these countries not push their exports of primary products according to the rules of international specialization, and import the goods they need for a balanced diet? The answer is: because the notion of balance applies on the global scale as well. For fairly obvious reasons, expansion of primary production for export is apt to encounter adverse price conditions on the world market, unless the industrial countries' demand is steadily expanding, as it was in the nineteenth century. To push exports in the face of an inelastic and more or less stationary demand would not be a promising line of development. If it is reasonable to assume a generally less than unitary price elasticity of demand for crude foodstuffs and materials, it seems reasonable also to contend that, under the conditions indicated before, economic growth in underdeveloped countries must largely take the form of an increase in production for the domestic market.

These are some of the considerations that explain the desire for balanced growth and provide some economic justification for it. They do not constitute a case for autarky. As productivity increases and the domestic market expands, while the composition of imports and exports is bound to change, the volume of external trade is more likely to rise than to fall. But even if it remains the same there is not necessarily any harm in balanced growth on the domestic front. Take a country like Venezuela: petroleum accounts for about 90 percent of its exports but employs only about 2 percent of its labor force; the majority of the people work in the interior for a precarious subsistence in agriculture. If through the application of capital and increased productivity the domestic economy were to grow so that people working formerly on the land alone would now supply each other with clothing, footwear, houses and house furnishings as well as food products, while all the time petroleum exports remained the same and imports likewise constant in total volume, nothing but gain would result to the inhabitants without any loss to the outside world. No doubt there would be a fall in the proportion of foreign trade to national income. But could it not be that this proportion, in the many peripheral countries of this type, has been kept unduly high in the past simply by the poverty of the domestic economy? World income is a more basic criterion of world prosperity than the volume of international trade.

The characteristically important role which international trade played in the world economy of the nineteenth century was partly due to the fact that there was a periphery—and a vacuum beyond. The trade pattern of the nineteenth century was not merely a device for the optimum allocation of a given volume of resources; it was, as D. H. Robertson put it, "above all an engine of growth."[6] but of growth originating in and radiating from the early industrial centers. Even in this country we have been so accustomed to regard the early nineteenth century pattern as normal that we seldom stop to notice that the economic development of the United States itself has been a spectacular departure from it.

With the spread of industrialization, we have, however, noticed that the major currents of international trade pass by the economically backward areas and flow rather among the advanced industrial countries. Balanced growth is a good foundation for international trade, as well as a way of filling the vacuum at the periphery.

IV

Let us turn now to the supply side of the problem of capital formation for economic development. Here the circular relationship runs from the low-income level to the small capacity to save, hence to a lack of capital, and so to low productivity. It seems to be a common view that the capacity for domestic saving in underdeveloped countries depends on an initial increase in productivity and real income, because the existing level is too low to permit any significant margin of saving, and that some form of outside help—say,

---

[6] "The Future of International Trade," *Economic Journal* (March 1938), p. 5.

foreign investment—is required to bring about this initial improvement and so break the vicious circle.

This theory begins to look a bit shaky as soon as we realize that it is not only the absolute but also the relative level of real income that determines the capacity to save. Although the absolute level of even the poorest countries has risen, it is doubtful whether saving has become any easier; on the contrary, it may have become more difficult for them, because there has occurred at the same time a decline in their relative income levels in comparison with those of the economically advanced countries. The hypothesis seems to me plausible and, at any rate, worth considering. The great and growing gaps between the income levels of different countries, combined with increasing awareness of these gaps, may tend to push up the general propensity to consume of the poorer nations, reduce their capacity to save, and incidentally strain their balance of payments.

As we have seen from J. S. Duesenberry's recent book, *Income, Saving and the Theory of Consumer Behavior,* the hypothesis that individuals' consumption functions are interrelated rather than independent helps to account for certain facts that have seemed puzzling. The interdependence of consumers' preferences can affect, in particular, the choice between consumption and saving. The reason, for instance, why 75 percent of families in the United States save virtually nothing[7] is not necessarily that they are too poor to save or do not want to save; the main reason is that they live in an environment that makes them want new consumption goods even more. The reason is largely what Duesenberry calls the "demonstration effect"[8] of the consumption standards kept up by the top 25 percent of the people. When individuals come into contact with superior goods or spending patterns, they are apt to feel a certain tension and restlessness: their propensity to consume is increased.

These forces, it seems to me, affect human behavior to a certain extent in international relations as well. The consumption functions of different countries are in some degree interrelated in a similar way. On the international plane, also, knowledge of or contact with superior consumption patterns extends the imagination and creates new wants.

The leading instance of this effect is at present the widespread imitation of American consumption patterns. The American standard of living enjoys considerable prestige in the world. And it is always easier to adopt superior consumption habits than improved production methods. True, American production methods are also widely imitated; sometimes, indeed, too closely. But generally this requires investible funds. The temptation to copy American consumption patterns tends to limit the supply of investible funds.

The intensity of the attraction exercised by the consumption standards of the economically advanced countries depends on two factors. One is the size of the gaps in real income and consumption levels. The other is the extent of people's awareness of them. Even though the poorer countries have probably

---

[7] See Duesenberry, p. 39.
[8] *Ibid.,* p. 27.

all increased their per capita income over the last hundred years, the gaps have tended to widen. The position we have now reached is that two-thirds of the world's income goes to less than a fifth of the world's population in the most advanced countries, while at the bottom of the scale two-thirds of the world's population receives less than a sixth of the world's income; and that the average per capita income of the former group is about seventeen times as high as that of the latter.[9] The estimates on which these calculations are based are in many cases extremely crude, but probably not grossly misleading. They do not, of course, take account of voluntary leisure, which is one way in which the advanced nations have taken out their gains.

The gaps are great, but equally important is the fact that contact and communication are closer than ever before, so that knowledge of these gaps has increased. Think of such recent inventions as the radio, aviation, and the American movies. Communication in the modern world—in the free world at any rate—is close, and so the attraction of advanced consumption standards can exert itself fairly widely, although unevenly, in the poorer parts of the world.

This attraction is a handicap for the latecomers in economic development. It affects not only voluntary personal saving but also makes it politically more difficult to use taxation as a means of compulsory saving and to resist demands for government spending on current account. Some of the backward countries have large masses of disguised unemployment on the land, which could be mobilized for real capital formation, but not without strict curbs on any immediate rise in consumption. Others may hope to introduce improvements in agricultural techniques so as to release labor from primitive subsistence farming and make it available for capital works, but again not without restraints to prevent the increment from being immediately consumed. The use of potential domestic sources of capital can be seriously hampered by the dissatisfaction and impatience which the demonstration effect tends to produce.

The traditional view of international economic relations generally implies that a high level of productivity and real income in one country cannot hurt other countries and that, on the contrary, prosperity tends to spread. Of course there are many ways in which a country's prosperity will help its neighbors. But the particular effect now discussed is unfavorable. It puts an extra pressure on countries with a relatively low income to spend a high proportion of it. (This is quite apart from and in addition to the fact that some nations suffer from a cultural aversion to saving, due to the presence of traditional forms of conspicuous consumption. However, the "demonstration effect" imposes no additional strain on saving capacity when it leads merely to a switch from native to imported forms of consumption.)

A very poor society might find it extremely hard to do any saving even if it knew nothing about higher living standards in the outside world. The vicious circle that tends to keep down the volume of saving in low-income

---

[9] *National and Per Capita Incomes in 70 Countries, 1949* (Statistical Office of the United Nations, 1950).

countries is bad enough by itself. The point is that it is made even worse by the stresses that arise from relative as distinct from absolute poverty.

V

The poorer nations, in contact with the richer, feel continually impelled to keep their money incomes and outlays above what is warranted by their own capacity to produce. The result is an inflationary bias at home and a persistent tendency toward disequilibrium in the balance of payments. The doctrine of comparative advantage is, in my opinion, an effective answer to the simpler forms of the productivity theory of the dollar shortage. Yet here we seem to have reached, by the back door as it were, a theory of balance-of-payments disequilibrium based similarly upon differences in general levels of productivity. However, the comparative cost principle is fully respected. Disequilibrium results, not because productivity determines a country's export costs and competitive strength in the world market, not because the most productive country necessarily undersells all the others in all lines; disequilibrium results because a country's productivity determines its real income and consumption level and because differences in levels of living, when they are very large and widely known, exert an upward pressure on the consumption propensity of the poorer countries. In the classical view, a lack of balance in international trade can persist only because some countries try to "live beyond their means." We have now a simple explanation of why some countries do, in fact, persist in trying to live beyond their means.

The inflationary pressures and balance-of-payments difficulties are not, as such, the basic trouble. They could conceivably come from increased capital outlays and not from consumer spending. The trouble is that the demonstration effect leads directly to increased consumption, or attempts at increasing consumption, rather than investment. At least it makes an increase in saving peculiarly difficult as and when incomes and investment increase. It is for this reason that international income disparities may have to be treated not merely as a source of strain in the balance of payments but actually as an impediment to capital formation in the poorer countries.

VI

The almost universal countermove of the underdeveloped countries both to suppress the disequilibrium in their balance of payments and, what is more important, to offset the attraction of superior consumption patterns is the restriction of imports and especially of imports of a so-called "luxury" or "semiluxury" character. There is a widespread notion that a country, by cutting down imports of consumption goods through direct controls or prohibitive duties, can make more real capital available for its economic development in the form of imports of capital goods. Governments seem convinced that they are promoting the formation of capital whenever, in their commercial policy, they banish consumable imports in favor of imports of machinery and equipment

This simple idea that more capital can be got merely by pinching and twisting the foreign-trade sector of the economy seems to me to be an instance of the fallacy of misplaced concreteness. The foreign-trade sector of the economy enters into the circular flow of income. Every piece of capital equipment imported represents an act of investment which, in the absence of external financing, presupposes and necessitates a corresponding act of saving at home. If this act of saving is not forthcoming, the capital equipment imported may be offset by reduced investment or by disinvestment in the domestic economy, if the expenditure of money previously spent on consumable imports now draws away domestic factors from capital construction or maintenance. Only if this money is left unspent is the requisite saving generated quasi-automatically; this is possible but quite improbable. It is more likely that any net investment that may result from the increased imports of capital goods will be financed by the forced saving of inflation, as long as inflation has not yet passed the point where it ceases to be effective as an instrument of forced saving. It is possible, therefore, although not certain, that "luxury import restrictions" will lead to some increase in the rate of capital formation in an underdeveloped country.

Besides the quantity of investment, however, there is also a question of quality. Import restrictions unaccompanied by corresponding domestic restrictions will set up a special inducement to invest in domestic industries producing the goods—or substitutes for the goods—that can no longer be imported. If the domestic market is considered at all sufficient to warrant the establishment of such industries, the inducement may prove effective. But since it applies to the luxury and semiluxury type of goods, whose imports are restricted, the result will be that the country's capital supplies, scarce as they are, and painfully brought into existence, will be sucked into relatively unessential uses.

The luxury import restrictions of the underdeveloped countries in the world today seem to represent, in the last analysis, a desperate effort to offset the handicap which the demonstration effect imposes on the poorer nations—an effort to isolate the local consumption pattern from that of the advanced countries and so to make possible more domestic saving and capital formation. This effort deserves our sympathy. But it attacks only the surface of the problem. It attacks only that part of the propensity to consume which directly involves expenditure on imported goods. The demonstration effect tends, however, to operate through an upward shift in the general consumption function and not in the import consumption function alone. Luxury import restrictionism does not stop this pervasive indirect influence of international discrepancies in consumption levels. A more basic attack would be compulsory saving through public finance, although this is precisely one of the things that is made politically more difficult in the poorer countries by the great discrepancies in living standards.

Far more radical forms of isolation than luxury import restrictions have played a part in the development of two important countries. It is well known that Japan, in the early course of her industrialization, imitated the Western world in everything except consumption patterns. She had kept herself in a state of isolation for centuries, and it was comparatively easy for her to maintain this isolation in regard to consumption patterns. There is no doubt that this was part of the secret of her success in domestic capital formation.

The other instance of radical isolation is Soviet Russia's iron curtain (which of course is not merely a result of the present tension but was well established before World War II). While it certainly has other reasons for its existence, I am inclined to attach significance also to its economic function; that is, to the possible "materialist interpretation" of the iron curtain. Anyway, it illustrates the possibility that isolation may help to solve the economic problem of capital formation, in a world of great discrepancies in national living standards, by severing contact and communication among nations. Without communication, the discrepancies, however great, may become of little or no consequence and the "demonstration effect" may lose at least some of its potency.

That this might be a possible and perhaps a necessary solution is a disquieting thought, and one naturally turns in search of an alternative.

VII

Could it be that the alternative lies in unilateral income transfers or, in plain English, gifts from rich to poor countries? The foreign aid programs of the United States have certainly departed from traditional practices, and it may be that we have seen the beginnings of a system of international income transfers, comparable to the transfers that take place within a country as an automatic result of taxation proportional to income or, still more, of progressive taxation. A system of international grants-in-aid does not stem from any economic mechanism of the market place; nor does the principle of progressive taxation. Both are based on political value judgments, and both arise from pressures having to do with the coexistence and increasingly close association of people at widely different levels of material welfare.

Suppose we have a model, then, where on the one hand international income disparities open up gaps in the balance of payments and on the other unilateral income transfers come in to fill these gaps. Is this a sufficient and satisfactory solution to the problem of capital formation in the poorer countries? Clearly it is not. If nature is left to take its course, the income transfers coming in will be used in these countries for the satisfaction of the higher propensity to consume that is brought about by the disparity in real-income levels. No permanent basis will be created within the country for higher living standards in the future. It is nearly always possible to some extent to substitute foreign aid for domestic saving so that consumption is increased and no net contribution is made to the rate of total capital formation. It can happen even if the foreign resources are tied to specific productive projects. The point is not, of course, that this is bad, but that it fails to contribute to the foundations of economic development. The attraction of advanced living standards can thus interfere, not only with the harnessing of domestic saving potentials, but also with the effective use of external resources for economic development. It makes it more than ever necessary for an underdeveloped country to keep a tight rein on the national propensity to consume.

This applies obviously to autonomous international investment and, perhaps less obviously, also to improvements in the terms of trade. An improvement in the terms of trade puts at the country's disposal additional outside resources that can be used to promote economic development. By itself, however, it means simply an increment in the country's current income, derived from foreign trade. Without the corresponding domestic saving, this increment cannot lead to any net increase in the rate of investment. Here again the real task is not to extract more capital goods from foreign trade but to extract more saving from the national income.

The upshot is that external resources, even if they become available in the most desirable forms, are not enough. They do not automatically provide a solution to the problem of capital accumulation in underdeveloped areas. No solution is possible without strenuous domestic efforts, particularly in the field of public finance.

MARCUS FLEMING

||||||||||||||||||||||||||||||||||||||||||||||||||||||||||||||||||||||||||||||||||||||||||||||||||||||||||||||||||||||||||||||||||||||||||||||||||||||

External Economics and the Doctrine of Balanced Growth

The object of this paper is to examine an argument advanced by some of the most distinguished writers on the theory of economic development, to consider to what extent and under what conditions it is valid, and to point to some of its implications.

The argument in question runs roughly as follows. In underdeveloped countries there is little incentive to invest capital in the introduction of modern efficient methods of large-scale production in individual industries producing goods for domestic consumption because the markets for the respective industries are too small. Since, however, the adoption of such methods in any one such industry would increase the demand for the products of the other industries, the incentive would be much greater if investments in a wide range of consumer-goods industries were undertaken, or at least considered, in conjunction. The adoption of investment projects which, though unprofitable individually, would be profitable collectively would, it is implied, be a good thing. This argument is frequently referred to as the "doctrine of balanced growth."

From *Economic Journal* (June 1955), pp. 241-256, with omissions. Reprinted, with the author's revisions, by permission of the Royal Economic Society and the author.

Certain elements in the doctrine are adumbrated in Allyn Young's celebrated article on "Increasing Returns and Economic Progress."[1] The doctrine
itself is set forth briefly in Professor Rosenstein-Rodan's "Problems of Indus-
trialisation of Eastern and South-Eastern Europe"[2] and more fully in Chapter 1 of Professor R. Nurkse's *Problems of Capital Formation in Underdeveloped Countries.* The argument as presented in the present paper, however, does not purport to reproduce exactly the views of any of these writers,
who, incidentally, differ to some extent among themselves. What has been
attempted below is to set forth the doctrine in a somewhat extreme but precise form with the help of which it should be possible to assess the validity
of the particular variants suggested by Rosenstein-Rodan and Nurkse.

We must now attempt to analyse the argument under discussion into its
explicit and implicit elements. These are as follows:

(*a*) The installation in any one of a wide range of home-market
industries in an underdeveloped country or region of a new plant capable
of operating at a unit cost lower than that of existing production in the
industry might be financially unprofitable because of the smallness and
inelasticity of the market for the industry within the country or region in
question[3];

(*b*) if demand for the product of such an industry were increased
the installation of the new plant would become more profitable or less
unprofitable;

(*c*) any increase in output, involving a reduction in unit cost of
production, in a typical consumer-goods industry will tend to increase
real income and hence real demand for the products of most other
consumer-goods industries and thus to increase the profitability of installing more efficient plants in the latter provided, however, that interest
rates do not rise too much;[4,5,6]

---

[1] *Economic Journal* (December 1928).

[2] *Ibid.* (June-September 1943). [See pp. 124-132 in this volume.—EDS.]

[3] " . . . the small size of a country's market can discourage or even prohibit the
profitable application of modern capital equipment by any individual entrepreneur in
any particular industry." R. Nurkse, *Problems of Capital Formation in Underdeveloped
Countries* (Oxford: Basil Blackwell, 1957), p. 7.

[4] "Although the initial displacement may be considerable and the repercussions
upon particular industries unfavorable, the enlarging of the market for any one commodity produced under conditions of increasing returns generally has the net effect . . .
of enlarging the market for other commodities" (Allyn Young, *op. cit.,* p. 537). "The
industries producing wage goods can thus be said to be complementary" (Rosenstein-
Rodan, *op. cit.,* p. 206).

[5] "Where any single enterprise might appear quite inauspicious and impracticable
a wide range of projects in different industries may succeed because they will all support each other in the sense that the people engaged in each project now working with
more real capital per head and with greater efficiency in terms of output per man-hour
will provide an enlarged market for the products of the new enterprise in the other
industries" (Nurkse, *op. cit.,* p. 13).

[6] Our authors would not confine the scope of this interaction to consumer-goods
industries. They do, however, emphasise its applicability as between such industries,
and it is on this, as we shall see, particularly vulnerable application that I wish to focus
my criticism.

(*d*) it follows that the installation of more efficient plants of the type described in each of a wide range of consumer-goods industries, though unprofitable if undertaken separately, might be profitable if undertaken jointly.[5]

Moreover:

(*e*) The joint installation of such plants, if profitable, would be desirable (*i.e.,* would tend to increase real national income); and

(*f*) because of its effects on the incentive to install efficient new plants in other industries the installation of a single plant, though unprofitable, might tend to raise real national income.

The rather odd-sounding proviso about interest rates at the end of step (*c*) in the argument has to be introduced into my scheme to take account of the fact that Rosenstein-Rodan and Nurkse usually describe the interindustry relationships dealt with under (*c*) and (*d*) above as affecting not the profitability—net of interest—of installing efficient new plants but the "inducement to invest" or "marginal efficiency of investment," *i.e.,* the return on the capital invested in such new plants, including interest as well as profits. Now any thing which enhances the rate of return on a new plant will enhance its profitability also, provided that the relevant interest rate does not rise "too much," *i.e.,* provided that the supply of capital is not "too inelastic."

Let us now consider various steps in the argument in greater detail. Step (*a*) is clearly valid. In a country of low *per capita* income and/or scattered population and/or poor communications the demand in a given region for the output of even a generally consumed manufactured product may be so small that the output (at minimum unit cost) of a single modern plant whose installation is under consideration would exceed the total previous output of the product in that region. The particular demand curve for the output of the projected new plant, though elastic over the range of output for which it is displacing previous production, might be highly inelastic and steeply downward sloping for higher outputs. The unit-cost curve of the new plant, even though it lies, for larger outputs, below the unit cost of pre-existing production, may lie, for smaller outputs, above that unit cost, and for all outputs may lie above the demand curve for the plant. Under these conditions it would not be profitable to install the new plant.

Step (*b*) in the argument is likewise a valid one. If the particular demand curve for such a plant as has been described should be raised, *while cost conditions remain unchanged,* the effect would obviously be to reduce the loss associated with its operation, possibly to turn the loss into a profit.

The qualification is, however, all important. If the raising of the demand curve were to be accompanied by a raising of the unit-cost curve, the outcome might well be different. For a rise in the cost curve, taken by itself, would tend to reduce the profits, or increase the losses, of operating the plant, would reduce the scale of the plant's output if it were in operation, and might make it unprofitable to install the plant at all.

We come now to the central question, with which step (*c*) in the argument is concerned, as to the circumstances in which the installation of a low unit-cost plant in one industry will increase the profitability of a similar installation in another industry.

In a closed economy any increase in the supply of any consumer good A, the supply of other such goods remaining unchanged, will tend to increase the prices of each of the latter products relative to that of A, though in the case of close substitutes the increase will be small. The increase in real income associated with the expansion in output of A will normally lead to some increases in the demand for non-A commodities as well as for A, and, in order that the increase in demand should be confined to A, the price of non-A commodities must rise relative to that of A, i.e., there will be an increase in the real price of the average non-A commodity.*

This increase in the real price of non-A commodities, provided that it is associated with no change in real factor prices, will tend to cause the output of non-A commodities, taken as a group, to expand even under existing methods of production, and may make it profitable to install new large-scale plants. The extent to which this will occur will be greater: (a) the lower the income elasticity of demand for A, (b) the less the elasticity of substitution between A and non-A, and (c) the greater the elasticity of supply in non-A. But there will always be *some* positive reaction so long as the income elasticity of demand for A is less than unity, and the elasticity of substitution between A and B less than infinite, and so long as there is a positive elasticity of supply for non-A.

Step (d) in the argument follows directly from the previous steps.

Steps (e) and (f) are of a different character from the others in that they entail welfare-economic considerations. . . .

With respect to point (e) in the argument, the introduction of large-scale plants in a variety of increasing return industries will tend to reduce product prices (without reducing factor prices) in those industries, and will therefore confer transfer benefits on the rest of the community. If the net profit of the new plants is positive, therefore, the increment in direct net product resulting from their introduction will be still more positive. Unless, as is improbable, the new plants reduce aggregate factor supplies, bring about a deterioration in terms of trade or otherwise give rise to diseconomies outside the industries in question, their introduction is bound to enhance national real income.

As regards point (f), for reasons analogous to those just discussed, not only any introduction of new plants but also any increased output in existing plants which is profitable under imperfect competition is likely to have a positive direct net product and make a positive contribution to national income. Consequently, if expansion in industry A renders profitable the expansion of imperfectly competitive industry B, the total contribution to national income of the former expansion will include, not only the transfer benefits which it itself confers, but also the economies to which it gives rise in industry B.

---

* *I.e.,* an increase in the average price of non-A commodities relative to the average price of all commodities including A.

Even if the expansion at A is unprofitable, its total contribution may be positive, thanks to these transfer benefits and external economies.

A further point, which our authors might have made, but did not, is that the expansion of demand for an industry will increase not only the profit but also the direct net product involved in introducing a new plant there. Consequently, if conditions are such that the joint introduction of plants in a variety of industries may be profitable though the plants are individually unprofitable they will also be such that the plants would jointly yield a positive net product, even though individually none of them would do so.

As we have seen, the validity of step (c) depends on the assumption that real factor prices will not be affected when the supply of A is increased and that of non-A goods remains unchanged. This, however, could happen only in a limiting case. Normally real factor prices will be raised or lowered, or some raised and others lowered. There is, therefore, a possibility that the real prices of the factors entering into the operation of modern plants in non-A industries may rise to such an extent as to outweigh the rise in the real prices of non-A products, and thus to induce a contraction rather than an expansion in output and investment in non-A industries.

In what follows, we shall assume, in conformity with what appears to be the intention of the balanced-growth doctrine, that the influence exercised by an increase in the supply of A on the real demand for other products is randomly distributed among non-A industries with respect to the possibilities for obtaining economies from increased output and investment in such industries. In other words those industries which are of a critical size in this respect are not, on the average, either specially complementary to or specially competitive with, industry A.

Suppose, now, there is only one stage of production and only one homogeneous factor of production, "labor," which is available in fixed supply. Under these conditions the installation of the new plant[7] at A will increase the incentive to install efficient new plants in non-A industries provided that the wage rate does not rise so far as to prevent an expansion of output in the average non-A industry. And output in the average non-A industry will expand only if labor-input in non-A industries as a whole expands. Since the supply of labor is fixed, this can happen only if the input of labor at A contracts, *i.e.,* if the employment of labor at the new plant is less than the amount of labor released from the other production units in the industry.

Clearly the employment of labor at A cannot contract if A is a completely new industry at which there has been no previous production. Even, however, if there has been some previous production, it is probable in an underdeveloped country that this will be carried on in small units under conditions of constant (long-term) real unit cost. In this case if the new plant is unprofitable it is impossible that the employment of labor in the industry should decline.

---

[7] A "plant," in this model, may be conceived as a group of workers cooperating in some process that requires a minimum number of workers to achieve any output at all.

For since the pre-existing production units operate at constant labor cost, the price of the product in terms of wage units will remain constant so long as any of the pre-existing units continue to operate. Aggregate demand for the product will also remain constant, so that the output of the new plant will at first merely replace output of pre-existing units. If, at the point at which the new plant is itself producing practically the entire previous output of the industry it is still not profitable, though the product price in terms of wage units is almost at the level which made pre-existing production units profitable, the aggregate labor-cost—and employment—of the new plant must be higher than that of the entire industry prior to its installation. If the output of the new plant is further increased, though its *average* labor cost may fall, its *aggregate* employment of labor must be still further increased.

It would appear therefore that where there is a single factor of production in fixed supply the installation of an unprofitable new plant in industry A, even though its unit cost, at the least unprofitable output, is below that of pre-existing production, is likely[8] to induce contraction rather than expansion in other consumer-goods industries, to yield external *dis*economies rather than external economies. The installation, over a wide range of such industries, of a set of unprofitable large-scale plants would render them not less but more unprofitable than if they had been installed singly. It would, moreover, tend to reduce the real national product. At first sight, this might appear to be contrary to common sense, since the new plants were described as being more efficient and working at lower unit cost than pre-existing production in their respective industries. But this is only true of plants which are installed singly. If all the plants are installed together the rise in wages will force the typical new plant to operate at a level which keeps the labor requirement of its industry approximately what it was under pre-existing methods of production, and at this level, as we have seen, the unit costs of the new plants will be greater than those of pre-existing production.

The situation might be roughly expressed by saying that, whereas the balanced-growth doctrine assumes that the relationship between industries is for the most part complementary, the limitation of factor supply ensures that that relationship is for the most part competitive.

Taking account of the multiplicity of factors of production introduces certain complications and qualifications into the argument without greatly altering its conclusions. Each industry and method of production is likely to have factors which are more or less specific to it. Thus when the new plant is introduced at A there is likely to be some fall in the price of factors specific to the old-fashioned methods of production in the industry. As output in the old sector of the industry is curtailed there will be a decline in product price, and a corresponding decline in marginal cost in the form of nonspecific factors released to other industries, so that the aggregate receipts of the new

---

[8] This conclusion would be certain but for the possibility that this output from pre-existing production units might operate under conditions of diminishing returns. This, however, is more likely to occur where several factors of production exist, and is considered below.

plant will fall short of the value of factors released from the older sector of the industry and the plant may be unprofitable even though it employs fewer resources than those released from the older sector. This creates a possibility, though by no means a certainty, that an unprofitable plant, with a positive direct net product, may effect a net release of factors from the industry and thus create external economies.[9]

Another probable consequence of the multiplicity of factors of production is that the weighting or "mix" of factors used in running the new modern plant at A may resemble more closely the factor mix employed in running actual or potential modern plants in other industries than the combination of factors employed in production outside A taken as a whole. In this case it is possible that even if the plant installation at A on balance increases the supply of factors to non-A industries, it will so raise the prices of those factors which are particularly in demand for the running of modern plants that the net effect on the installation of such plants will be discouraging.

It would appear therefore that, so long as factors of production are in fixed supply, the introduction of large-scale production units in consumer industries is likely to give rise not to economies but to diseconomies in other industries competing for the consumer market, unless the former industries are already big enough for the introduction of the new plant to make possible a net reduction in the resources employed there: that this is unlikely to occur where the new unit is unprofitable, and cannot occur unless it passes the Dupuit test of the desirability of a "large" investment, *i.e.,* unless it has a positive direct net product.

It is noteworthy that the introduction of more efficient production methods in a large competitive industry such as agriculture is not only certain to be profitable but likely to release factors to other industries so long as the elasticity of demand for the industry as a whole is less than unity. This suggests that if underdeveloped countries were to press ahead with improvements of a financially profitable character in agriculture, they might do more to make profitable large-scale efficient production in other industries, such as manufacturing, which are in a phase of increasing returns, than by trying to develop simultaneously a wide range of such manufacturing industries.

Thus far we have assumed a closed economy. The introduction of foreign trade makes little difference to the argument. Indirectly, through the various mechanisms whereby external equilibrium is maintained, the demand for exports varies with the demand for imports. If the scope for economies of scale is equal in export and in home-market industries, it makes no difference which gains at the expense of the other. It will still be true that the expansion

---

[9] If the direct net product is negative, the new plant cannot possibly create external economies. For the direct net product of the new plant is measured by its price integral *less* its marginal-cost integral. And the net release of resources from the industry is measured by that part of its output which is curtailed, less the marginal cost integral of the new plant. And the price integral of the new plant cannot possibly fall short of the marginal-cost integral on the curtailed output of the older sector of the industry. So that the direct net product of the new plant must always exceed the net release of resources from the industry.

of industry A will create a balance of economies or diseconomies elsewhere, according as A absorbs less or more factors than before. It is, however, sometimes argued that in underdeveloped countries the export trades sell on more perfect markets than do the domestic trades, so that fewer unexploited opportunities for economies of scale remain in the former. If so, the expansion at A will be more likely to generate external economies of scale than the previous argument would imply if, as is often the case, the industry A happens to be one which is more competitive in product markets with imports, and/or more competitive in factor markets with exports, than it is, in the respective markets, with purely domestic industries.

In order really to salvage the doctrine of external economies under examination, however, it is necessary to drop the assumption that the supply of factors of production is fixed in favor of the assumption that the supply varies positively with real factor prices. For then, in order that an expansion in A should increase the profitability of additional output and the installation of new plants in industries producing other consumer goods, thus generating economies, it is no longer necessary that the employment of factors in A should actually decline as output increases, but merely that factor employment there should not rise more than the increased factor supply evoked by the rise in real factor prices. As we have seen, of our authors, only Rosenstein-Rodan explicitly assumes an elastic supply of labor in his illustration of the doctrine, though Nurkse, in arguing in terms of the inducement to invest, is in effect assuming some elasticity in the supply of capital.

It should be noted that the possibility of expanding the supply of labor at a given money wage by increasing the level of money demand would not constitute factor elasticity in the sense relevant here, since the whole argument is concerned with "real" demand, and full employment is assumed from the start. There are, however, a number of *prima facie* reasons why the supply of factors in an underdeveloped country or region may show a measure of elasticity of a sort relevant to the present argument. Not all of them, however, are very conclusive. For example:

(1) The supply of labor from individual workers may increase when real wages increase, because the workers are better able and more willing to work. But the opposite result is at least as likely to happen because the worker wishes to take out part of his real income in leisure, and "absenteeism."

(2) Higher real wages may attract workers on the margin of the labor force into employment, and higher rents may make it profitable to bring poorer qualities of land into cultivation. On the other hand, higher family incomes may lead to a withdrawal of marginal women, children, and older workers from the labor force.

(3) Higher real rewards may tempt workers and capitalists to migrate into the country or region in question, thus increasing the supply of factors there. Economies facilitated by this means in the area of immigration, however, may be balanced by diseconomies in the area of emigration.

(4) Higher real wages in a country at an early stage of demographic development may bring about an expansion of population which will entail an expansion in the labor force a couple of decades later. At a later stage of demographic evolution, however, higher real wages may have a zero or a negative effect on population growth.

For the purpose in hand the main potential sources of elasticity in the supply of factors of production are the three listed below, which will be discussed at greater length.

(5) In so far as factors of production are themselves products of an earlier stage of production—and here we depart from the assumption that there is only one stage of production—an increase in the real prices of those product-factors may bring about an increase in their supply and in the aggregate amount of factors supplied to subsequent stages of production.

(6) A rise in the demand for factory labor may attract workers from employments, such as agriculture, where their productivity is very low, and thus give rise to a virtual increase in the supply of labor or at least an increase in its supply to that sector of industry in which economies of large-scale operation are to be obtained.

(7) Higher interest rates may increase the supply of capital, especially from abroad.

First, let us take account of the "vertical disintegration" of production—the fact that industries buy the products of other industries, as well as original factors of production, and that some industries are predominantly suppliers of other industries rather than of final consumers. Thus far we have considered industries as acting on each other "horizontally," through the interrelated markets which they serve or the interrelated factors which they buy. But industries also affect each other in greater or lesser degree in a more direct manner, i.e., "vertically" as suppliers or customers. We are concerned with the effect of this "vertical" connection on the "horizontal" one, to which the balanced-growth doctrine, as expounded by Rosenstein-Rodan and Nurkse, primarily refers.

The introduction, in industries serving final consumers, of more efficient large-scale methods of production may encourage increased output in factor-producing industries if it tends to raise the prices of produced factors (intermediate products) more, or reduce them less, than the prices of the original factors of production used by the latter group of industries. Now, as a matter of fact, the type of technical changes associated with the substitution of large-scale for smaller-scale production not only tend to raise the demand for capital relative to labor but also to raise the demand for intermediate products as compared with original factors as a whole.

We may assume that, in an underdeveloped country, the industries producing factors of production—especially those producing power, transportation, minerals and capital goods—will, like the consumer-goods industries, frequently operate under conditions of imperfect competition, where efficient production is hampered by the smallness of the market. The stimulus given by the installation of large-scale production in consumer-goods industries to profitability, production, and investment in the supplying industries will therefore give rise to an increase in the net product of the latter. This means that the increased use, if any, of original factors in expanding the factor-producing industries will permit a more than equivalent increase in the supply of produced factors, so that the industries producing for final consumption will secure a net increase in the supply of the two sorts of factors taken together. It follows from this that the installation of modern large-scale production in one consumer-goods industry, even though it involves an increased use of factors of production—in both kinds—may nevertheless, in the manner described, leave other consumer-goods industries better supplied with factors than before, thus giving rise to economies there.

It is noteworthy that the chances that the introduction of more efficient large-scale operation in one consumer-goods industry will generate economies in another such industry are here increased only by reason of economies generated at an earlier stage of production. The latter, or "vertical," type of external economies will, of course, enhance real national income just as surely as the former or "horizontal" type, and in magnitude are likely to be the more important of the two. Moreover, the "vertical" generation of economies operates not only from later to earlier stages of production, but also with even greater probability, from earlier to later stages. Thus the expansion of output in a producer-goods industry, provided that it involves an increase in net product, will tend to increase the profitability of other industries in general, and will encourage economies in such of those industries as are operating under increasing returns.

There can be little doubt but that the conditions for a "vertical" transmission of external economies—whether forward from supplying industry to using industry, or backward from using industry to supplying industry—are much more favorable than for a "horizontal" transmission between industries at the same stage. There is, therefore, a much stronger case for joint planning of the development of industries at earlier and later stages of the same "line" of production than of industries at the final stage of different "lines." The fact that our authors, other than Allyn Young, seem to lay more emphasis on the "horizontal" rather than the "vertical" variant of the balanced-growth doctrine is probably due to the fact that the external economies underlying the former are less frequently discussed in the literature than those underlying the latter. But the "horizontal" transmission of economies may have been neglected by Marshall and his commentators precisely because, where it exists at all, it is relatively unimportant.

Let us now turn to the possibility, listed at (6) above, that the enhanced real demand for labor arising in various branches of secondary industry as a result of the expansion and modernization of one such industry may be satisfied by drawing labor away from an overcrowded agriculture where its marginal productivity is negligible or relatively low. As already mentioned, Rosenstein-Rodan, in expounding his version of the "horizontal" variant of the balanced-growth doctrine, explicitly assumes that the labor supply for industrial expansion is drawn from agriculture where it would otherwise be underemployed.

There can be no doubt of the fact, attested by many observers, that underemployment, in the sense specified above, exists in the agriculture of many underdeveloped countries. There can also be little doubt but that an expansion in the real demand for labor in any particular industrial branch would attract some of the underemployed agricultural labor to secondary industry, and to that extent would improve the prospect of reaping economies of scale in the industrial sector as a whole. The crucial question, however, so far as the creation of external economies is concerned, is whether the expansion of industrial branch A would lead to a transference of labor from agriculture to industry sufficient to permit an expansion of branches of industry *other than A*.

It is by no means clear how this question should be answered. Much will depend on the reasons for the prior existence of the agricultural underemployment. It is assumed that this is no mere case of inadequacy of monetary demand combined with rigidity of money wages in secondary industry. There remain two possible lines of explanation. One is that the underemployment is voluntary in the sense that real rewards for unskilled labor in industry are insufficiently in excess of those in agriculture to attract sufficient labor to equalize marginal productivity in the two sectors. Even though the marginal product of labor in agriculture be far below that in industry, labor may stay on the land partly because of a family system under which the individual worker is paid according to the *average* product of peasant labor rather than its *marginal product,* and partly because of inertia, and lack of enterprise.

In this event, however, it seems unlikely that more workers would be attracted from agriculture than are absorbed by the initial expansion in industry A. For expansion in A, output remaining constant elsewhere, is likely to increase the demand-price for food at least as much as for the products of other secondary industries. In so far as this expansion entails an increase in real income, it will no doubt tend to raised demand for manufactures in higher proportion than for food; but the increased output of A is likely to be more competitive with other manufactures than with food, and the probable transference of income from taxpayers—or whoever bears the losses of the expansion at A—to peasants and workers will tend to raise demand for food rather than manufactures. For these and other reasons[10] the real demand-schedule for labor in secondary production outside A appears more likely to fall than to rise relative to the schedule of real *per capita* income in agriculture. If the demand for labor A is sufficiently strong to draw labor from agriculture, it will be sufficiently strong to draw it from other secondary indus-

---

[10] Though any influences transmitted "vertically" to basic industries, or any repercussions on other industries of the economies generated in basic industries, are more likely to favor secondary production than agriculture, on the other hand, the latter is less likely to be affected by scarcity of capital or intermediate products resulting from the initial expansion at A.

tries also. The availability of underemployed agricultural labor may enable A's labor force to expand without that of other secondary industries having to contract as much as it otherwise would: it will not permit the latter to expand as well.

A second line of explanation for the initial state of underemployment in agriculture is that workers, while desirous of moving from agriculture to secondary industry, are unable to obtain employment there owing to the artificially high level of industrial wages maintained by labor unions, etc. In this event much depends on how these wages are determined. It is assumed that as the demand for labor expands in industry A, industrial money wages will rise at least as fast as prices in general: otherwise the agricultural unemployment would be of a type curable by mere monetary expansion—a hypothesis which we have excluded. If, as might well happen, the unions were to take advantage of the increased demand for labor in industry A to prevent any whittling away of the original disparity between industrial wages and agricultural incomes, this would entail a decline in secondary industries other than A unless the prices of non-A manufactures were to rise faster than those of agricultural products, which, as we have seen, is unlikely. Even if the unions were to confine themselves to preventing a decline in industrial real wages, it is quite possible, for the reasons discussed in the foregoing paragraph, that the rise in agricultural prices would so far outstrip the rise in prices of non-A manufactures as to entail a decline in the real demand-schedule for the latter, and hence a decline rather than an expansion of employment in non-A industries.

In all probability some tendency for industrial wages to be artificially maintained in relation to agricultural incomes is fairly general in underdeveloped countries. It is obvious that real wages are not in practice raised so fast in response to a rise in the real demand for industrial labor as to prevent all movement from country to town. This, however, does not prove that wages do not rise fast enough to nullify the benefits which the several industries would otherwise derive from *each other's* expansion.

Even if secondary industries other than A do not succeed in adding to or retaining their labor force, they may still expand if other factors of production become more plentiful. But the mere fact that agricultural labor is seriously underemployed provides no guarantee that an expansion in A which absorbs more factors than are created by associated economies in basic industries will draw sufficient labor out of agriculture to permit an increase in output, profits, and net product in secondary industries other than A.

Let us now turn to the third main possibility of factor elasticity, mentioned at (7) above, namely that the supply of capital is to some extent elastic with respect to the rate of interest. This assumption, as we have seen, has from the start been, in effect, woven into the balanced-growth doctrine by Rosenstein-Rodan and by Nurkse in so far as they express that doctrine in terms of the inducement to invest (see p. 145) above.

An elastic supply of capital would undoubtedly facilitate the creation of external economies of scale. If capital were in infinitely elastic supply, so that additional capital requirements in any industry had no effect on the cost or availability of capital for the use of other industries, and if all requirements could be met from domestic saving, then any expansion in industry A which did not involve an increased use of factors of production *other than capital* would be fairly certain to generate expansion, and the economies associated therewith, in other industries.

A distinction must be drawn, however, between capital obtained from foreign and from domestic sources respectively. When development is financed by foreign capital additional interest or dividends will have to be paid to capitalists resident abroad. In order to transfer these sums the country in which the development occurs will have to generate an export surplus partly by reducing imports and partly by increasing exports. So long as export industries offer the same sort of opportunities for economies of scale as those producing for the domestic market, the increase in exports will have no ill effect. If, on the other hand, no economies of scale are possible in export industries, only that part of the addition to the national factor supply which accrues to home-market industries will generate such economies.[11]

How elastic is the supply of capital in fact likely to be in an under-developed country or region? This is a question which cannot be satisfactorily answered, or even formulated, in terms of the comparative static analysis used in this paper—at least so far as capital of domestic origin is concerned. Any increase in real income associated with the expansion of capital and output at A would tend to raise the domestic supply of *saving* and gradually and cumulatively the domestic supply of *capital*. In the very long run the expansion at A might evoke an additional supply of domestic capital large enough to meet its own requirements and leave some over for other industries. Within the sort of time period which is of interest for the purposes of economic policy, however, capital-expansion in one industry is likely to be at the expense of capital-expansion in other industries, unless additional capital is available from abroad in highly elastic supply.

The transfer of capital from abroad, unlike the increase in supply from home saving, is responsive to the increase of interest rates or profit opportunities rather than to that of real income in the developing country. Though the two types of responsiveness in capital supply resemble each other in operating only over time, the bulk of any additional supply forthcoming from foreign sources in response to the higher interest rates, etc., is likely to appear much sooner than the bulk of any additional supply accumulated from new domestic savings.

It is impossible to generalize about the elasticity of supply of capital from abroad. In certain cases the supply curve may even be downward-sloping, as when the fact that *some* foreign capital is willing to venture into an underdeveloped country encourages additional supplies at even lower

---

[11] The net addition, if any, to the factor supply of home-market industries will be the larger the greater the share of import saving in the aggregate improvement in the real trade balance, and the smaller the proportion of that improvement which is required to offset deterioration in the terms of trade.

interest rates and lower profit expectations. Or the curve may be highly elastic for moderate amounts and inelastic for large amounts (if the capital is drawn from somewhat restricted circles of investors abroad). Or it may be elastic for some industries and inelastic for others. (Frequently the industries for which foreign capital supply is inelastic will be precisely the home-market industries where the economies of scale are most to be expected.) Or, in the case of countries having forfeited the confidence of investors, the supply of foreign capital may be highly inelastic all round.

Inelasticity in the supply of capital from abroad tends to render the doctrine of balanced growth not so much invalid as inapplicable. Even where a diversified investment program would yield a higher return on capital invested than would the projects taken individually, the higher cost of capital might make the large-scale progam as unprofitable as the piecemeal approach. More fundamental is the criticism already noted that even where capital is available in elastic supply the mere fact that it is obtained from abroad reduces the extent to which it can be used to exploit economies of scale in home-market industries and reduces the chances that the combined investment program will in fact yield a higher return to capital than would the projects taken one by one.

CONCLUSION

This paper has examined the basic assumptions underlying a modern variant of the balanced-growth doctrine, namely that the introduction of lower (unit) cost methods of production involving expansion in the output of an industry even if itself unprofitable, will enhance the profitability of other industries not specially related to it as customers or suppliers, and, if these industries are operating under imperfect competition, will promote economies of larger-scale production there.

We have concluded that the argument, as usually presented overemphasizes the repercussions on the demand for, and ignores repercussions on the costs of, the other industries, and that, in an economy where factors of production are in fixed supply, the introduction of unprofitable though efficient large-scale production in one industry is more likely to reduce than to increase the profitability of other industries.

We have seen, however, that the chances are much better for a "vertical" propagation of external economies, from customer industry to supplying industry, and especially from supplying industry to customer industry, and that developments in industries at different stages in the same "line" of production are more likely to afford each other mutual support than those in different lines of production.

Moreover, the chances that expansion in one industry will generate economies in other industries not "vertically" related to it will be increased if economies are generated "vertically" in factor-producing industries. This has the effect of introducing a measure of elasticity into the supply of factors of production which is in general favorable to the creation of external economies.

Conditions of elastic supply of labor or capital likewise tend to favor the applicability of the balanced-growth doctrine. The over-all elasticity of the labor supply is, however, likely to be low, and the ease with which labor can be transferred from agriculture to nonagricultural industry, where the opportunities for economies of scale are greater, has frequently been exaggerated.

As to capital, the domestic supply is likely to be practically inelastic within any short period of years. Access to imported capital, on the other hand, varies very much from country to country and from time to time; and, in any case, foreign capital is less effective than domestic capital in widening the market and promoting economies of scale.

The chances that diversified development in a variety of industries will play a mutually supporting, mutually validating role, as required by the balanced-growth doctrine, are greatest when the necessary additional capital is obtainable on easy terms, when unions can be prevented from pushing up real wages in industry, when reserves of underemployed agricultural labor are eagerly waiting to obtain industrial employment, when there are opportunities for economies of scale in the basic, factor-producing industries, and when, taken singly, the investments in question are only just not profitable. When too many of these conditions are absent the combined installation over a variety of industries of unprofitable though efficient undertakings may have the effect of rendering each of these undertakings still more unprofitable than if it had been set up by itself.

JACOB VINER

Gains from Foreign Trade

According to classical theory, the gain to a country or region from foreign trade consists in getting indirectly in exchange for those products in which a country has comparative advantage in production (or less comparative disadvantage) more goods, or better goods, than could be produced at home with the same quantity of productive resources, it being understood that the possible gain may be used to obtain increased leisure as well as more or better commodities. Foreign trade thus involves some degree of specialization, or of "international division of labor." Specialization, however,

From Jacob Viner, *International Trade and Economic Development* (Glencoe, Ill.: The Free Press, 1952), pp. 50-73, with omissions. Reprinted by permission of the publisher and the author.

is not a good in itself, but is good only so far as it increases real income, or yields a national net gain.

In the classical theory, it is assumed that production is normally carried on under conditions of diminishing marginal value productivity, and that this results from the combined operation of the law of diminishing returns and the law of diminishing utility. With natural resources taken as given in quantity, as more labor and capital are applied to these natural resources the output per unit of input of labor and/or capital after an early point diminishes. As the output of some commodities is increased relative to total production, the exchange-value per unit of these commodities falls, that is, their commodity or net barter terms of trade for other commodities decrease.

If all commodities were produced under conditions of increasing cost, each country would tend to produce some of every commodity (except those commodities whose money costs of production even for a very small output would exceed the prices at which they could be obtained from abroad) and "specialization" would be only partial, that is, would consist in some products being produced to an amount insufficient to supply domestic consumption while other products would be produced in quantities sufficient both to meet the domestic demand and to provide a surplus for export.

The classical school believed that manufactures were produced under conditions either of constant or of decreasing costs. To the extent that this was true, the only check to complete specialization would be the decline in value per unit of the products as output was increased, or in other words, the deterioration in the commodity terms of trade. There is no difference in kind, however, in the behavior of the long-run cost functions of primary products and manufactures, though there is probably a difference in degree. There is one universal long-run law of costs, namely, increasing real costs per unit of output as the output of a particular product is increased relative to the total output of a region or country.[1] I will henceforth assume that all production everywhere is carried on under conditions of long-run increasing cost, given the usual abstraction from dynamic factors such as new inventions, technological progress, and interregional migration of factors of production.

Even for the classical economists, this doctrine of the national profitability of partial specialization leads logically to free trade subject only to certain assumptions and qualifications.

In the first place, it is assumed that markets are free and competitive, so that market prices reflect, approximately at least, relative costs and the relative attractiveness of commodities at the margins of output and of purchase. The market is not postulated to be a perfect appraiser of real values, but it is held to make superior appraisals than would result from random fixing of prices, or from political or bureaucratic fixing of prices without regard to costs to producers or to preferences of buyers.

---

[1] For the argument by which I would support this concededly unusual position, I refer the reader to my "Supplement" of January 1950 to the reprint of my 1932 article on "Cost Curves and Supply Curves," in Richard V. Clemence (ed.), *Readings in Economic Analysis* (Cambridge, Mass.: Addison-Wesley, 1950), Vol. II, pp. 31-35.

In the second place, the whole analysis is based on long-run considerations. Possible short-run exceptions are abstracted from, or policy concessions to them are deliberately rejected as involving barriers to the attainment of greater long-run benefits.

In the third place, the classical free-trade argument takes for granted full employment (in the long run at least) and postulates better-quality employment rather than more employment as resulting from free trade.

In the fourth place, the classical argument must be interpreted as abstracting from the effect of free trade on the distribution of national income (as distinguished from the amount of income available for distribution) or as assuming that the distribution under free trade will be as "good" as or "better" than under protection. For the early English classical economists, the latter was the predominant assumption, and for nineteenth century England it was an appropriate one. English protection benefited directly mostly agriculture. Assuming perfect capital and labor mobility between agriculture and other industries, protection benefited mostly the landowning class, who were on the average distinctly the richest class, while free trade meant cheap food and other working-class commodities, and would benefit most obviously the workers. Even for English conditions, however, the assumption that free trade would not impair the distribution of the national income was valid only if it be accepted that a relative redistribution in favor of the workers, and even an absolute transfer of income from landlords to workers (and to owners of nonlanded property) was desirable.

Free trade operates to make some commodities relatively cheaper and other commodities relatively dearer. It operates, therefore, relatively to reduce the income of factors heavily employed in the protected industries and relatively to increase the income of factors heavily employed in the export industries. For the same reason, it operates relatively to reduce the real income of those classes of consumers who are heavy purchasers of export commodities and relatively to increase the real income of those classes of consumers who are heavy purchasers of hitherto protected commodities. All of these *relative* increases and decreases *may* also be absolute increases and decreases, and cases are conceivable where free trade, if unaccompanied by other measures, would not only make the relative distribution of income less equal, however degree of inequality of distribution was defined, but would absolutely decrease the income of the poorest sections of the population.

This, of course, is at least equally true of protection, however. Moreover, if it is granted that free trade will increase (or even not decrease) the national income, then it will always be theoretically possible by taxation, subsidy, or other measures so to redistribute the national income: (*a*) as to prevent any class from receiving a smaller share of the total national income; (*b*) as to prevent any individual or class of individuals from suffering an absolute decrease in income as the result of the adoption of free trade.[2]

In the fifth place, it was always an assumption of the classical economists

[2] See my *Studies in the Theory of International Trade* (New York: Harper & Brothers, 1937), p. 534.

that there was effectual occupational mobility of the factors in response to differences in real returns. This was actually more of a concession than they needed to make. All that they needed to assume was that the prices of the factors were determined in free, competitive markets, and this they had taken care of by their general assumption of competition. Given the flexibility of factor prices in response to relative conditions of supply and demand, there is no need for the free trader to make any mobility assumption except the assumption that there is not perverse mobility or an established tendency of owners of factors to choose employments where their factors will receive low returns. If all factors were permanently frozen to their original occupations, free trade would alter the price structure and the relative distribution of income, but it would make no change in the allocation of resources (except as below certain minimum rates of return some factors would be kept idle by their owners in preference to employment). The greater the degree of occupational mobility (up to the stage of "effective mobility," defined as the degree of mobility which would equalize the marginal rate of real income of any homogeneous class of factors whatever the occupation it was employed in), the greater the degree in which the potential benefits of free trade would be realized. But however short of this actual mobility might be, free trade could not fail to increase the aggregate national income. Even if mobility were zero, and the volume and structure of national production were therefore unaffected by free trade, there would still be gain from the wider range of choice available to purchasers of what to buy with their income.

So far, therefore, no qualifications of consequence have been conceded to the validity of the free-trade case if its assumptions of ample time for adjustment and of competitive markets are granted, and if allowance is made for the possibility of compensatory action by government if free trade otherwise would cause an undesired alteration in the distribution of national income.

I come now, however, to a logical flaw of considerable importance in the free-trade case as it was expounded by the majority of its advocates and as it has so far been expounded here. Free trade, they contended, was beneficial not only for the world as a whole, but for each country adopting it, even if it adopted it alone. There was often implicit in their argument the assumption that the only choice available to countries was between completely free trade and complete abstention from trade, an assumption which made their argument logically valid but unrealistic. Or, alternatively, they fell back upon another assumption, logically an invalid one, that the movement from protection to free trade would not alter the "commodity terms of trade," or the relative prices at which exports exchanged for imports.

There was here a rift in the ranks of the free-traders. A few of them, notably Torrens, John Stuart Mill, Marshall, Edgeworth, Taussig, conceded from the start that the unilateral substitution by a country of free trade for protection would move the terms of trade against that country. Most free traders, however, either ignored the issue, or dogmatically denied that there was a genuine issue, or blinded themselves to the validity of the argument. . . .

Taussig had conceded that if a country adopted free trade the terms of trade would move adversely to it, but he contended that the gains from a better allocation of resources would more than offset the loss from the impairment of the terms of trade. This is, however, only a possibility or perhaps a probability, and the theoretical possibility that it will not be true can be rigorously demonstrated. . . .

The terms-of-trade argument is unquestionably a theoretically valid argument from a nationalistic point of view for protection. What weight should be given to it in practice, however, is a reasonably debatable matter. To justify resort to protection as a long-run policy by any country, it would be necessary: (1) that the "reciprocal demand" of the outside world as a whole vis-à-vis that country has a low elasticity; (2) that its own "reciprocal demand" vis-à-vis the outside world has a high elasticity; (3) that if that country adopts protection it will not result in retaliatory or defensive or imitative action by countries with whom it has important trade relations; and (4) that if that country adopts protection, it will be administered with a high degree of skill and integrity. These conditions are sufficiently restrictive in combination to guarantee, I am convinced, that the scope for nationally profitable long-run protection is in practice very narrowly limited. From the cosmopolitan point of view, moreover, the free-trade case remains intact: long-run protection may injure all who practice it, and can benefit none except at the cost of greater injury to others. The only exception that has to be made to this conclusion, from a cosmopolitan point of view, is that if there is a poor country which benefits from its adoption of protection, and if the countries which are injured thereby are rich countries, the improvement in the international distribution of income which results may be an adequate offset to the reduction in aggregate world income.

Finally, although it is logically a short-run argument, and has so far in my discussion consequently been abstracted from, I must consider the "young country," or "infant industry," or "development" argument for protection. This is one of the oldest arguments for protection, even the term "infant industry" going back to at least the seventeenth century. It first received elaborate and enthusiastic exposition, however, by Friedrich List, early in the nineteenth century, and all modern expositions of it are, consciously or unconsciously, under the influence of the Listian doctrine.

No economist of consequence has ever challenged the theoretical validity of the argument for protection on "infant industry" grounds, the argument that temporary protection can speed the establishment and development of potentially profitable industries. When the argument has nevertheless been rejected, it has been on historical and practical grounds: (1) the selection of industries to be protected has often been arbitrary or irrational; (2) once protection is granted on any grounds, it opens the door to promiscuous protection; (3) protection to a particular industry is as likely to stifle or delay its genuine progress toward economic independence as to stimulate it, since it provides to those engaged in the industry a shelter against the normal consequences of inertia, inefficiency, or restrictive monopoly; (4) in past experience, the protection has generally tended to become permanent, instead of being removed either as the industry no longer needs it or as the industry has revealed permanent incapacity to operate without artificial support; and (5) the prospect of eventual ability of an industry to operate successfully without protection is not a sufficient claim for even temporary protection, for while the protection is being extended, it entails costs for the nation as a whole, including other industries which have to operate without the benefit of special aid. These seem to me all to be weighty objections persuasive on their face and supported by more than a century of corroborative experience. Moreover, even when a new industry promises, once it has been firmly established, to become a highly profitable part of the national economy, it will often be advisable to aid it during its immaturity by subsidy rather than by protection. The cost of the aid then becomes more obvious and calculable. The burden of support can then be placed where it rationally belongs, or where it is desired that it shall fall, instead of falling fortuitously on those who happen to be users of the industry's product. The market for the product in question is then left free to grow to the extent of its natural potentialities, instead of being artificially restricted by the high price which in the absence of a direct subsidy the high costs make necessary and the tariff makes possible. High import duties on products whose domestic production the duties were intended to stimulate have often had the reverse effect. By making the commodities in question too expensive except for a restricted clientele, they have made the industry seem unattractive to enterprisers because of the apparent limitations of the potential market.

Until quite recently, I had supposed that all or nearly all that I have been saying so far in this lecture was substantially noncontroversial, at least among professional economists, and I would have felt, perhaps, that I would be imposing upon your patience and goodwill in presenting such trite matter to you.

I have become aware, however, that there has been flowing from distinguished sources, and especially from the technical staff of the United Nations, new (or partially new) light on these matters, especially as they bear on "underdeveloped" countries. The doctrine that international division of labor in accordance with comparative costs is beneficial does not hold true, we are told, as far at least as concerns the trade relations between "developed" and "underdeveloped" countries. The relation of productivity to prices is such in "underdeveloped" countries that the exchange by such countries of primary products for the manufactures of developed countries, while especially profitable for the latter, is positively injurious to the former.

From none of this literature that I have seen have I been able to discover just what is an "underdeveloped" country, and why, if the export of primary products in exchange for manufactures is bad for the exporting countries, the sympathy of the world should not go out to Denmark as an exporter of butter and bacon; to New Zealand as an exporter of mutton, butter, and wool; to Australia as an exporter of wool and wheat; to California, Iowa, and Nebraska, and so on.

There has very recently been brought to my attention, as a place where

I could get needed enlightenment on these matters, a United Nations document, *The Economic Development of Latin America and its Principal Problems,* 1949, by Professor Raul Prebisch. I learn from this document that the doctrine of the mutual profitability of international division of labor is an obsolete dogma.

> In Latin America reality is undermining the outdated schema of the international division of labor, which, after acquiring great importance in the nineteenth century, continued to exert considerable academic influence until very recently.
>
> Within this framework, the specific task which fell to Latin America, as part of the periphery of the world economic system, was that of producing food and raw materials for the great industrial centres.
>
> There was no place in this schema for the industrialization of the new countries.

Anyone who has the slightest acquaintance with the actual writings of the English classical school knows that intellectually and temperamentally its members were incapable of staking out claims to particular industries for particular countries except on the one criterion that countries should so allocate their resources as to get the maximum economic return. Whatever may have been their forecasts, they would not have denied to Latin America, or to any other region, full right and justification to establish any kind of industry which gave genuine prospects of becoming an economically healthy industry. There was no place in their schema for the settling of economic issues by the invocation of territorial jealousies, by giving exercise to national superiority complexes, or by making concessions to national inferiority complexes.

All that I find in Prebisch's study and in the other literature along similar lines emanating from the United Nations and elsewhere is the dogmatic identification of agriculture with poverty, and the explanation of agricultural poverty by inherent natural historical laws by virtue of which agricultural products tend to exchange on ever-deteriorating terms for manufactures, technological progress tends to confine its blessings to manufacturing industry, and agricultural populations do not get the benefit of technological progress in manufactures even as purchasers, because the prices of manufactured products do not fall with the decline in their real costs. These natural laws seem to me for the most part mischievous fantasies, or conjectural or distorted history, or, at the best, mere hypotheses relating to specific periods and calling for sober and objective testing.

I readily concede that there is such a phenomenon as "underdeveloped countries" in some significant sense of the term, and that "underdevelopment" presents special problems. . . . At this point, however, I want to examine the truth, and if true, to consider the possible explanations, of the causal association of agriculture with poverty and industrialization with prosperity which the literature of "economic development" insists upon.

That agriculture is not necessarily associated with poverty becomes obvious when one considers Australia, New Zealand, Denmark, or Iowa and

Nebraska. That industrialization is not necessarily associated with prosperity becomes obvious when one considers Italy or Spain. It is undoubtedly true, however, that most of the poorest countries have largely rural populations, and that in most countries the per capita money incomes of the rural population are lower than those of the urban population. This must be conceded, but little else, to the already vast and rapidly growing literature which presents industrialization as the sure-cure for poverty.

Let me search for additional scraps of argument in the literature. In a 1946 article,[3] an American statistician and economist, Louis H. Bean, presented statistics for a wide range of countries purporting to show that the higher the proportion of the population in secondary (manufacturing) and tertiary (services and professions) industry, the higher the per capita incomes. The over-all positive correlation without manipulation was not strikingly high, but by grouping the countries in a substantially arbitrary fashion Bean succeeded in showing that within each group there was a high negative correlation between the ratio of agricultural to total population and (unadjusted monetary) per capita incomes. Without the slightest venture into supporting argument, Bean accepted this correlation as a demonstration that the high ratio of agricultural to total population was the *cause* of the low per capita incomes, and that industrialization was a certain cure for poverty. With no evidence presented other than the statistics of per capita incomes and the percentages of agricultural to total population in different countries, Bean was able to reach such striking conclusions as that "were it possible to industrialize China to the point where the agricultural population was 50 instead of 75 percent, its per capita income would rise from $50 to about $150," or threefold.

While I do not pretend to have investigated the matter, I feel confident that if the data were available it could be demonstrated that the positive correlation between the percentages of the national populations who were dentists or hairdressers and the national per capita incomes was even higher than Bean's correlations. If we followed his logic, we would take this as a demonstration that the way to cure poverty is to increase the number of dentists and beauty-parlors. This article is an extreme case, perhaps, but it is extreme in the frankness and clarity of its exposure of the method by which its conclusions were reached, not in the basic character of its logical method.

The earlier argument of a Rumanian economist, Mihaïl Manoïlesco, with whom I had a mutually unsatisfactory debate many years ago,[4] belongs to the same school of thought. Manoïlesco contends that because in all coun-

---

[3] "International Industrialization and Per Capita Income," *Studies in Income and Wealth* (New York: National Bureau of Economic Research, 1946), Vol. viii, pp. 119-144.

[4] See Manoïlesco, *The Theory of Protection and International Trade* (London 1931); my review of this book in *The Journal of Political Economy*, XI (1932), pp. 121-125; and Manoïlesco, *Die nationalen Produktivkrafte und der Aussenhandel* (Berlin, 1937), pp. 227-230, 275.

tries per capita incomes are higher in manufactures than in agriculture, pre-dominantly agricultural countries will raise their per capita incomes if by establishing tariff protection for manufactures they increase the proportion of the labor force engaged in manufactures.

Whatever the causal relationship of agriculture to poverty may be, of one thing we can be sure: it is not a simple one. I have already cited the fact that there are countries which are predominantly agricultural but which nevertheless are prosperous. This is a real difficulty for the doctrine that agriculture means poverty, and it needs explaining away. There are also great differences in the prosperity of different agricultural regions within the same country. In the early 1940s an American investigation showed that the income per farm family in the highest-income county in Iowa was thirty-nine times the income per farm family in the lowest-income county in Kentucky. It is clear that it could not have been agriculture alone which was responsible for the poverty in Kentucky and that agriculture was not a barrier to prosperity in Iowa. As Professor Theodore Schultz of the University of Chicago has pointed out, this 1:39 ratio is exactly the same as that found (I would say "alleged") by Colin Clark to exist between the per capita incomes of China and the United States.

Let us assume for the time being, however, that in every region and without exception money incomes are higher per capita in manufactures than in agriculture, and that the higher the ratio of nonagricultural population the higher is the per capita income. Let us also assume that the rural population is able to obtain employment in manufactures on equal terms with the urban population and that there are no biological or cultural or other differences in quality between rural and urban population. What possible explanations could then be offered for the differences between rural and urban per capita incomes?

One possible explanatory factor would be that agricultural families were larger than urban ones; that is, that either farm children survived to maturity in larger proportion than urban children or that farm parents chose to have more children (or had greater fertility) than did urban parents.

Another possible factor would be that the money-income data were mis-leading as measures of real income. There is concealed rural income in occupancy of owned houses, or in low rentals, in self-produced food and fuel, and in many services which are produced within the farm household but which in the cities have to be paid for in cash. In an urban family there may be several earners of money incomes and in the rural family only one recog-nized as such, but the household services which the farm-wife and children render are needed also in the city household but are there often bought with cash. It is not only a question of laundry and cooking and tailoring and dressmaking, but also of water supply and of grading and selecting and storing and packaging of food. A United States Department of Agriculture study in 1941 found that the money incomes of low-income American farmers had to be raised by two-thirds to obtain a true measure of income comparable with urban money incomes. The correction on this score is therefore a major one, at least in the United States.

There is also a concealed urban "negative income" as compared to rural incomes. This is aside from higher money costs in the cities for the same commodities and services as are available to rural dwellers. It consists (or *may* consist; I do not pretend to be an expert on these matters, and I know of no serious study of this matter) of extra needs which the urban dweller encounters, and whose cost is not deducted from his cash income in ordinary calculations. Such would be: the extra clothing requirements which are imposed by urban convention or employment conditions; the cost of technical education; trade union fees; the transportation cost of getting to and coming from the place of employment; the shorter working life; and probably other items that I know nothing of. This also is, or may be, an important possible explanation of the differences between recorded rural and urban per capita incomes. The literature which bases economic policy recommendations on differences in recorded money incomes between rural and urban life apparently sees no need for making allowance for the differences as between rural and urban areas in the economic and general welfare significance of recorded money incomes of given amounts.

There is still another source of statistical fallacy in the ordinary comparisons between agricultural and urban per capita incomes, when, as is often the case, "value of product added by manufacturing per worker" is used as the basis of measuring per capita urban output in order to compare it with rural per capita output. The fact is often overlooked or disregarded that when the "value of product added" data are divided by the number of workers to obtain the output per worker, important items of expense or input other than labor are left out of account: interest on capital used and depreciation and obsolescence of capital; taxes or fees for special services such as water, sewage, lighting, maintenance, cleaning and repair of streets, police protection, and so forth.

Finally, it being remembered that the hypothesis under consideration is one where rural population of equal quality and free to move into urban employments on equal terms with urban workers nevertheless remains on the land, the possibility should not be overlooked that the rural workers deliberately choose the rural life despite its lower material income because they prefer it, and that such preference should not be arbitrarily disregarded.

Let us now take at their face value all recorded money incomes, and concede that it is true for all regions that the higher the ratio of agricultural to total population the lower is the per capita income. It does not follow that within any region per capita agricultural incomes, given families of the same size, are lower than nonagricultural incomes, or that the high per capita incomes are the consequence of the low ratio of agricultural to total population.

Let us suppose that in a particular region, Iowa, for example, farmers are prosperous. Because they have high incomes, they will produce fewer services for themselves and buy more in shops, and hire more specialized consumers' services. Their incomes are also likely to be high, at least in part, because they engage in specialized agriculture. They will therefore buy more equipment, supplies, feed, specialized producers' services, power, and so forth. They will keep their children longer in schools, and buy more professional entertainment. To distribute all these goods and supply all these services the ratio of nonfarm to farm population will rise. Surely it is obvious that it would be absurd then to say that the high per capita income of the region was the consequence of the high ratio of nonfarm to total population. On the contrary, it would be the high per capita earnings of the farmers which would be the cause and explanation of the high ratio of nonfarm to farm population. Where farmers are poor, nonfarm population serving the farming community will be small, and probably also poor. Where farmers are prosperous, non-farm population employed in the tertiary industries will be large, and probably also prosperous. Agricultural poverty is here the cause, not the consequence, of the high proportion of the population engaged in agriculture.

Let us now assume: that farm workers have much lower real incomes on the average than workers in manufacturing industries; that there is no significant qualitative difference between farm and industrial workers, whether as the result of selective migration, of differences in racial origins, or from any other cause; and that average real incomes could be raised if farm population could be drawn into industry. Why should not this situation correct itself through the spontaneous migration of rural workers to the industrial areas until real incomes become equal in country and city?

It is not a sufficient answer to say that employment opportunities will in the absence of special measures be lacking in the cities, since if there is a competitive labor market, the rural workers will be able to get jobs by offering their services at lower than the prevailing urban rates, and real income rates will move toward equality as between city and country. To explain a chronic situation such as this, therefore, it is necessary to appeal to obstacles to movement of farm workers into industry which operate either in the rural areas themselves, or in the urban areas, or in both.

It is not difficult to find such obstacles. There may be inertia on the part even of the young in the rural areas, or they may not have available to them the education and the technical training necessary for their acceptability as factory workers, or they may not know of the opportunities open to them in the cities, although these would only partially explain why industries do not move into the rural areas in search of cheap labor supplies. The remedy here would not be the artificial stimulation of industry, but rather the appropriate education of rural children. There may also be closed labor unions in the towns, which make entrance into industrial occupations difficult and set conditions of entry which, purposefully or not, are harder for rural than for urban youths to meet. The appropriate remedy here would be to suppress such labor monopolies.

Let us now suppose that *real* incomes are lower in agriculture than in industry, and that by tariff protection or subsidies industry can be made to expand and to draw workers from the country into the cities. Is this sound economic policy?

The correct answer depends on why per capita real incomes are lower in agriculture than in manufacturing. There may be urban exploitation of agriculture, through monopolistic pricing by industrial employers, or through labor monopolies in the factories which by forcing wages up force up also the prices which the agricultural population has to pay for urban products and services—including government services. The tariff, supported as providing better employment opportunities for the agricultural population, may itself be a major instrument whereby agricultural real incomes are depressed. Government may also operate to depress agricultural real incomes by imposing its taxes, mainly or largely, directly or indirectly, on agriculture, and directing its expenditures mainly to the benefit of the urban population. Even though the rural population may have lower per capita incomes than the urban, it may nevertheless be the only economically healthy part of the population, the only part which gives good value to the community in exchange for what it gets from the community. Where the situation is one—as it often is—of urban exploitation of the rural population, to propose as a remedy the further subsidization of urban industry as a means of drawing rural workers to the city is equivalent to proposing to remedy the exploitation of worker bees by the drones by transforming the worker bees also to drones. It is obvious that it can work at all only as long as there still remain worker bees in the fields to be exploited.

The refutation of bad argument does not necessarily refute the conclusions reached by such argument. It is not my position that the path to economic progress is not, for many countries and even for most countries, by way of industrialization and urbanization. I have in fact conceded that as any country or any region becomes more prosperous it will normally tend to increase the ratio of its population which is nonagricultural. My position is a different one, and I will now state it frankly and positively for the first time. The real problem in poor countries is not agriculture as such, or the absence of manufactures as such, but poverty and backwardness, poor agriculture, or poor agriculture and poor manufacturing. The remedy is to remove the basic causes of the poverty and backwardness. This is as true in principle, and probably nearly as true in practice, for industrialized countries as for predominantly agricultural countries.

Misallocation of resources as between agriculture and manufactures is probably rarely a major cause of poverty and backwardness, except where government, through tariffs, discriminatory taxation and expenditure policies, and failure to provide on a regionally nondiscriminatory pattern facilities for education, health promotion, and technical training, is itself responsible for this misallocation. Where there is such government-induced misallocation, it is today more likely to consist of the diversion of agrarian-produced resources to the support of parasitic cities than of overinvestment of resources in primary industries and in workers in such industries.

Economic improvement may call for greater industrialization, but this should be a natural growth, appropriately facilitated by government but not maintained under hothouse conditions. In many countries, the most promising field for rapid economic development lies in agriculture, and the measures needed are primarily such as will promote health, general education, technical training, better transportation facilities, and cheap rural credit for productive use. There are no inherent advantages of manufacturing over agriculture, or, for that matter, of agriculture over manufacturing. It is only arbitrarily in fact that the line separating the two can be drawn. The choice between expansion of agriculture and expansion of manufactures can for the most part be left to the free decisions of capitalists, entrepreneurs, and workers. To the extent that there is need for government decision, it should be made on rational grounds, in the light of considerations of costs and of comparative returns from alternative allocations of scarce national resources, human and material. If direction is accepted from maxims and arbitrary dogmas and prejudices, from unsubstantiated and incredible natural laws of the inherent inferiority of one type of industry over another, then it is highly probable that the result will be the squandering of resources so scanty in supply that they need to be carefully husbanded, and the sore disappointment of the wishes of the great masses of population crying to be relieved of their crushing poverty.

In industrialized countries there tends to be a romantic idealization of agriculture and of the countryside. In nonindustrialized countries smoking chimneys and crowded factory towns become the irrational ideal. Let me cite you an example from an early visitor to Brazil, Louis Agassiz, the Swiss natural scientist, writing of Brazil in 1865, and finding in Brazil the basis for a romantic preference of agriculture over manufactures:

> When I remember the poor people I have seen in the watch-making and lace-making villages of Switzerland, hardly lifting their eyes off their work from break of day till night, and even then earning barely enough to keep them above actual want; and think how easily everything grows here, on land to be had for almost nothing, it seems a pity that some parts of the world should be so overstocked that there is not nourishment for all, and others so empty that there are none to gather the harvest. We long to see a vigorous emigration pour into this region so favored by Nature, so bare of inhabitants. But things go slowly in Brazil.

Romantic attitudes on the part of the general public, whether towards agriculture, as in some countries, or towards industrialization, as in others, are probably inevitable, and there is not much that can be done about them. But economists have a professional responsibility to do their professional thinking without corruption by romance, and to make their recommendations as to economic policy on the basis of the economic merits, as objective economic analysis and disciplined scrutiny of all the available and relevant facts indicate them to be. Their basic principle must be to insist that scarce resources shall be allocated to their socially most productive use, and wasting resources on romantic dreams is not such a use.

H. W. SINGER

||||||||||||||||||||||||||||||||||||||||||||||||||||||||||||||||||||||||||||||||||||||||||||||||||||||||||||||||||||||||||||||||||||||||

The Distribution of Gains between Investing and Borrowing Countries

International trade is of very considerable importance to underdeveloped countries, and the benefits which they derive from trade and any variations in their trade affect their national incomes very deeply. The opposite view, which is frequent among economists, namely, that trade is less important to the underdeveloped countries than it is to industrialized countries, may be said to derive from a logical confusion—very easy to slip into—between the absolute amount of foreign trade which is known to be an increasing function of national income and the ratio of foreign trade to national income. Foreign trade tends to be proportionately most important when incomes are lowest. Secondly, fluctuations in the volume and value of foreign trade tend to be proportionately more violent in that of underdeveloped countries and therefore *a fortiori* also more important in relation to national income. Thirdly, and *a fortissimo*, fluctuations in foreign trade tend to be immensely more important for underdeveloped countries in relation to that small margin of income over subsistence needs which forms the source of capital formation, for which they often depend on export surpluses over consumption goods required from abroad.

In addition to the logical confusion mentioned above, the great importance of foreign trade to underdeveloped countries may also have been obscured by a second factor; namely, by the great discrepancy in the productivity of labor in the underdeveloped countries as between the industries and occupations catering for export and those catering for domestic production. The export industries in underdeveloped countries, whether they be metal mines, plantations, etc., are often highly capital-intensive industries supported by a great deal of imported foreign technology. By contrast, production for domestic use, specially of food and clothing, is often of a very primitive subsistence nature. Thus the economy of the underdeveloped countries often presents the spectacle of a dualistic economic structure: a high productivity sector producing for export coexisting with a low productivity sector producing for the domestic market. Hence employment statistics in underdeveloped countries do not adequately reflect the importance of foreign trade,

From *American Economic Review* (May 1950), pp. 473-485. Reprinted by permission of the American Economic Association and the author.

since the productivity of each person employed in the export sector tends to be a multiple of that of each person employed in the domestic sector. Since, however, employment statistics for underdeveloped countries are notoriously easier to compile than national income statistics, it is again easy to slip, from the fact that the proportion of persons employed in export trade is often lower in underdeveloped countries than in industrialized countries, to the conclusion that foreign trade is less important to them. This conclusion is fallacious, since it implicitly assumes rough equivalence of productivity in the export and domestic sectors. This equivalence may be safely assumed in the industrialized countries but not in the underdeveloped countries.

A third factor which has contributed to the view that foreign trade is unimportant in underdeveloped countries is the indisputable fact that in many underdeveloped countries there are large self-contained groups which are outside the monetary economy altogether and are therefore not affected by any changes in foreign trade. In industrialized countries, by contrast, it is true that repercussions from changes in foreign trade are more widely spread; but they are also more thinly spread.[1]

The previously mentioned fact, namely, the higher productivity of the foreign-trade sector in underdeveloped countries, might, at first sight, be considered as a cogent argument in favor of the view that foreign trade has been particularly beneficial to underdeveloped countries in raising their general standards of productivity, changing their economies in the direction of a monetary economy, and spreading knowledge of more capital-intensive methods of production and modern technology. That, however, is much less clearly established than might be thought. The question of ownership as well as of opportunity costs enters at this point. The productive facilities for producing export goods in underdeveloped countries are often foreign owned as a result of previous investment in these countries. Again we must beware of hasty conclusions. Our first reaction would be to argue that this fact further enhances the importance and benefits of trade to underdeveloped countries since trade has also led to foreign investment in those countries and has promoted capital formation with its cumulative and multiplier effects. This is also how the matter is looked at in the economic textbooks—certainly those written by nonsocialist economists of the industrialized countries. That view, however, has never been really accepted by the more articulate economists in the underdeveloped countries themselves, not to mention popular opinion in those countries; and it seems to the present writer that there is much more in their view than is allowed for by the economic textbooks.

Can it be possible that we economists have become slaves to the geographers? Could it not be that in many cases the productive facilities for export from underdeveloped countries, which were so largely a result of

---

[1] A more statistical factor might be mentioned. Some underdeveloped countries—Iran would be an illustration—exclude important parts of their exports and imports from their foreign-trade statistics in so far as the transactions of foreign companies operating in the underdeveloped country are concerned. This is a tangible recognition of the fact that these pieces of foreign investments and their doings are not an integral part of the underdeveloped economy.

foreign investment, never became a part of the internal economic structure of those underdeveloped countries themselves, except in the purely geographical and physical sense? Economically speaking, they were really an outpost of the economies of the more developed investing countries. The main secondary multiplier effects, which the textbooks tell us to expect from investment, took place not where the investment was physically or geographically located but (to the extent that the results of these investments returned directly home) they took place where the investment came from.[2] I would suggest that if the proper economic test of investment is the multiplier effect in the form of cumulative additions to income, employment, capital, technical knowledge, and growth of external economies, then a good deal of the investment in underdeveloped countries which we used to consider as "foreign" should in fact be considered as domestic investment on the part of the industrialized countries.

Where the purpose and effect of the investments was to open up new sources of food for the people and for the machines of industrialized countries, we have strictly domestic investment in the relevant economic sense, although for reasons of physical geography, climate, etc., it had to be made overseas. Thus the fact that the opening up of underdeveloped countries for trade has led to or been made possible by foreign investment in those countries does not seem a generally valid proof that this combination has been of particular benefit to those countries. The very differential in productivity between the export sectors and the domestic sectors of the underdeveloped countries, which was previously mentioned as an indication of the importance of foreign trade to underdeveloped countries, is also itself an indication that the more productive export sectors—often foreign owned—have not become a real part of the economies of underdeveloped countries.

We may go even further. If we apply the principle of opportunity costs to the development of nations, the import of capital into underdeveloped countries for the purpose of making them into providers of food and raw materials for the industrialized countries may have been not only rather ineffective in giving them the normal benefits of investment and trade but may have been positively harmful. The tea plantations of Ceylon, the oil wells of Iran, the copper mines of Chile, and the cocoa industry of the Gold Coast may all be more productive than domestic agriculture in these countries; but they may well be less productive than domestic industries in those countries which might have developed if those countries had not become specialized to the degree in which they now are to the export of food and raw materials, thus providing the means of producing manufactured goods elsewhere with superior efficiency. Admittedly, it is a matter of speculation whether in the absence of such highly specialized "export" development, any other kind of development would have taken its place. But the possibility cannot be assumed away. Could it be that the export development has

---

[2] Often underdeveloped countries had the chance, by the judicious use of royalties or other income from foreign investment, to use them for the transformation of their internal economic structure—a chance more often missed than caught by the forelock!

absorbed what little entrepreneurial initiative and domestic investment there was, and even tempted domestic savings abroad? We must compare, not what is with what was, but what is with what would have been otherwise—a tantalizingly inconclusive business. All we can say is that the process of traditional investment taken by itself seems to have been insufficient to initiate domestic development, unless it appeared in the form of migration of persons.

The principle of specialization along the lines of static comparative advantages has never been generally accepted in the underdeveloped countries, and not even generally intellectually accepted in the industrialized countries themselves. Again it is difficult not to feel that there is more to be said on the subject than most of the textbooks will admit. In the economic life of a country and in its economic history, a most important element is the mechanism by which "one thing leads to another," and the most important contribution of an industry is not its immediate product (as is perforce assumed by economists and statisticians) and not even its effects on other industries and immediate social benefits (thus far economists have been led by Marshall and Pigou to go) but perhaps even further its effect on the general level of education, skill, way of life, inventiveness, habits, store of technology, creation of new demand, etc. And this is perhaps precisely the reason why manufacturing industries are so universally desired by underdeveloped countries; namely, that they provide the growing points for increased technical knowledge, urban education, the dynamism and resilience that goes with urban civilization, as well as the direct Marshallian external economies. No doubt under different circumstances commerce, farming, and plantation agriculture have proved capable of being such "growing points," but manufacturing industry is unmatched in our present age.

By specializing on exports of food and raw materials and thus making the underdeveloped countries further contribute to the concentration of industry in the already industrialized countries, foreign trade and the foreign investment which went with it may have spread present static benefits fairly over both. It may have had very different effects if we think of it not from the point of view of static comparative advantages but of the flow of history of a country. Of this latter school of thought the "infant" argument for protection is but a sickly and often illegitimate offspring.

To summarize, then, the position reached thus far, the specialization of underdeveloped countries on export of food and raw materials to industrialized countries, largely as a result of investment by the latter, has been unfortunate for the underdeveloped countries for two reasons: (*a*) because it removed most of the secondary and cumulative effects of investment from the country in which the investment took place to the investing country; and (*b*) because it diverted the underdeveloped countries into types of activity offering less scope for technical progress, internal and external economies taken by themselves, and withheld from the course of their economic history a central factor of dynamic radiation which has revolutionized society in the industrialized countries. But there is a third factor of perhaps even greater importance which has reduced the benefits to underdeveloped countries of foreign trade-*cum*-investment based on export specialization on food and raw materials. This third factor relates to terms of trade.

It is a matter of historical fact that ever since the seventies the trend of prices has been heavily against sellers of food and raw materials and in favor of the sellers of manufactured articles. The statistics are open to doubt and to objection in detail, but the general story which they tell is unmistakable.[3] What is the meaning of these changing price relations?

The possibility that these changing price relations simply reflect relative changes in the real costs of the manufactured exports of the industrialized countries to those of the food and primary materials of the underdeveloped countries can be dismissed. All the evidence is that productivity has increased if anything less fast in the production of food and raw materials, even in the industrialized countries[4] but most certainly in the underdeveloped countries, than has productivity in the manufacturing industries of the industrialized countries. The possibility that changing price relations could merely reflect relative trends in productivity may be considered as disposed of by the very fact that standards of living in industrialized countries (largely governed by productivity in manufacturing industries) have risen demonstrably faster than standards of living in underdeveloped countries (generally governed by productivity in agriculture and primary production) over the last sixty or seventy years. However important foreign trade may be to underdeveloped countries, if deteriorated terms of trade (from the point of view of the underdeveloped countries) reflected relative trends of productivity, this could most assuredly not have failed to show in relative levels of internal real incomes as well.

Dismissing, then, changes in productivity as a governing factor in changing terms of trade, the following explanation presents itself: the fruits of technical progress may be distributed either to producers (in the form of rising incomes) or to consumers (in the form of lower prices). In the case of manufactured commodities produced in more developed countries, the former method, *i.e.*, distribution to producers through higher incomes, was much more important relatively to the second method, while the second method prevailed more in the case of food and raw material production in the underdeveloped countries. Generalizing, we may say that technical progress in manufacturing industries showed in a rise in incomes while technical progress in the production of food and raw materials in underdeveloped countries showed in a fall in prices. Now, in the general case, there is no reason why

---

[3] Reference may be made here to the publication by the Economic Affairs Department of the United Nations on "Relative Prices of Exports and Imports of Underdeveloped Countries."

[4] According to U.S. data of the WPA research project, output per wage earner in a sample of 54 manufacturing industries increased by 57 percent during the twenty years, 1919-1939; over the same period, agriculture increased only by 23 percent, anthracite coal mining by 15 percent, and bituminous coal mining by 35 percent. In the various fields of mineral mining, however, progress was as fast as in manufacturing. According to data of the National Bureau of Economic Research, the rate of increase in output per worker was 1.8 percent p.a. in manufacturing industries (1899-1939) but only 1.6 percent in agriculture (1890-1940) and in mining, excluding petroleum (1902-1939). In petroleum production, however, it was faster than in manufacturing.

one or the other method should be generally preferable. There may, indeed, be different employment, monetary, or distributive effects of the two methods; but this is not a matter which concerns us in the present argument where we are not concerned with internal income distribution. In a closed economy the general body of producers and the general body of consumers can be considered as identical, and the two methods of distributing the fruits of technical progress appear merely as two formally different ways of increasing real incomes.

When we consider foreign trade, however, the position is fundamentally changed. The producers and the consumers can no longer be considered as the same body of people. The producers are at home; the consumers are abroad. Rising incomes of home producers to the extent that they are in excess of increased productivity are an absolute burden on the foreign consumer. Even if the rise in the income of home producers is offset by increases in productivity so that prices remain constant or even fall by less than the gain in productivity, this is still a relative burden on foreign consumers, in the sense that they lose part or all of the potential fruits of technical progress in the form of lower prices. On the other hand, where the fruits of technical progress are passed on by reduced prices, the foreign consumer benefits alongside with the home consumer. Nor can it be said, in view of the notorious inelasticity of demand for primary commodities, that the fall in their relative prices has been compensated by its total revenue effects.

Other factors have also contributed to the falling long-term trend of prices of primary products in terms of manufactures, apart from the absence of pressure of producers for higher incomes. Technical progress, while it operates unequivocally in favor of manufactures—since the rise in real incomes generates a more than proportionate increase in the demand for manufactures—has not the same effect on the demand for food and raw materials. In the case of food, demand is not very sensitive to rises in real income, and in the case of raw materials, technical progress in manufacturing actually largely consists of a reduction in the amount of raw materials used per unit of output, which may compensate or even overcompensate the increase in the volume of manufacturing output. This lack of an automatic multiplication in demand, coupled with the low price elasticity of demand for both raw materials and food, results in large price falls, not only cyclical but also structural.

Thus it may be said that foreign investment of the traditional type which sought its repayment in the direct stimulation of exports of primary commodities either to the investing country directly or indirectly through multilateral relations, had not only its beneficial cumulative effects in the investing country, but the people of the latter, in their capacity as consumers, also enjoyed the fruits of technical progress in the manufacture of primary commodities thus stimulated, and at the same time in their capacity as producers also enjoyed the fruits of technical progress in the production of manufactured commodities. The industrialized countries have had the best of both worlds, both as consumers of primary commodities and as producers of manufactured articles, whereas the underdeveloped countries had the worst of both worlds, as consumers of manufactures and as producers of raw materials. This perhaps is the legitimate germ of truth in the charge that foreign investment of the traditional type formed part of a system of "economic imperialism" and of "exploitation."

Even if we disregard the theory of deliberately sinister machinations, there may be legitimate grounds in the arguments set out above on which it could be maintained that the benefits of foreign trade and investment have not been equally shared between the two groups of countries. The capital-exporting countries have received their repayment many times over in the following five forms: (*a*) possibility of building up exports of manufactures and thus transferring their population from low-productivity occupations to high-productivity occupations; (*b*) enjoyment of the internal economies of expanded manufacturing industries; (*c*) enjoyment of the general dynamic impulse radiating from industries in a progressive society; (*d*) enjoyment of the fruits of technical progress in primary production as main consumers of primary commodities; (*e*) enjoyment of a contribution from foreign consumers of manufactured articles, representing as it were their contribution to the rising incomes of the producers of manufactured articles.

By contrast, what the underdeveloped countries have to show cannot compare with this formidable list of benefits derived by the industrialized countries from the traditional trading-*cum*-investment system. Perhaps the widespread though inarticulate feeling in the underdeveloped countries that the dice have been loaded against them was not so devoid of foundation after all as the pure theory of exchange might have led one to believe.

It is, of course, true that there are transfer difficulties on the part of the underdeveloped countries which are avoided by production for export directly to the investing countries, but the above analysis may perhaps make a contribution to understanding why this traditional investment system broke down so rapidly and so irreparably in 1929 and 1930. The industrialized countries had already received real repayment from their foreign investments in the five forms described above, and in these ways they may have collected a pretty good return on their investments. When on top of the returns received in those five forms they also tried to "get their money back," they may perhaps have been asking (in the economic, though not in the legal, sense) for double payment; they may have been trying to get a quart out of a pint bottle.

There is a fairly widespread impression that this traditional trend toward deteriorating price relations for primary producers has been sharply reversed since prewar days, although this impression is not as strong now as it was in the middle of 1948. Even if we take that point of time, which represents the peak of postwar primary commodity prices up till now, a detailed analysis does not bear out the impression that terms of trade have significantly improved in favor of the underdeveloped countries since prewar days.[5]

It may be suggested that the impression that price relations have sharply improved for primary producers can be attributed partly to the abnormal

---

[5] For details see the above mentioned study of "Relative Prices of Exports and Imports of Under-developed Countries" (Economic Affairs Department of the United Nations).

composition of primary commodity imports into the U.S. where coffee plays a predominating part (coffee prices have increased particularly heavily in the immediate postwar period), and also specially to the widespread idea that foreign trade between underdeveloped countries and industrialized countries is an exchange of the primary commodities of the former for the capital goods of the latter. In fact, among the imports of the underdeveloped countries capital goods do not generally form the largest category, mainly because the import of capital goods from abroad requires a great deal of complementary domestic investment in those countries for which the domestic finance does not exist or is not mobilized.

The major proportion of the imports of the underdeveloped countries is in fact made up of manufactured food (especially in overpopulated underdeveloped countries), textile manufactures, and manufactured consumer goods. The prices of the type of food imported by the underdeveloped countries, and particularly the prices of textile manufactures, have risen so heavily in the immediate postwar period that any advantage which the underdeveloped countries might have enjoyed in the postwar period from favorable prices realized on primary commodities and low prices of capital goods has been wiped out.

A further factor which has contributed to the impression that relative price trends have turned sharply in favor of primary producers since the war is the deterioration in British terms of trade and the publicity which this deterioration has received because of the strategic importance of the British balance of payments in the network of world trade. It should, however, not be forgotten that the changes in British postwar terms of trade do not merely represent *ceteris paribus* price changes but reflect considerable quantum changes; namely, an increase in the quantity exported and a decrease in the quantity imported. It may be suggested, perhaps, that these quantum changes rather than underlying price changes account for the adverse trend before devaluation of British terms of trade. Unless it is to be assumed that the elasticity of demand for British exports is infinite, it is obvious that an expansion in the volume of total exports of manufactured goods by almost 100 percent will be reflected in lower unit prices for British exports; conversely, the reduction in the quantity of British imports is also reflected in higher prices paid than would otherwise have been the case, partly as a reflection of the diminishing bargaining strength of Britain in consequence of lower imports and partly as a necessary political concession to primary producers to enable them to maintain their incomes in the face of lower quantities sold. The supposition that the changed quantity relations in British trade (as well as deliberate colonial development policies) are largely responsible for the adverse trend in British terms of trade rather than price changes in world markets is greatly strengthened by the fact that other Western European exporters of manufactured goods did not only fail to experience any deterioration in their terms of trade, but on the contrary showed improved terms of trade.[6] The effect of quantum changes on British terms of trade is of course difficult to

---

[6] *Economic Survey of Europe in 1948* (United Nations, Department of Economic Affairs), pp. 93-106, especially 97, 98, and 99.

disentangle statistically. It is more in the nature of a gain missed through inability of exploiting the postwar sellers' market pricewise to the full. It is surely a remarkable fact that in a world hungry for capital goods, and with her two most important direct industrial competitors eliminated, England should have experienced adverse terms of trade in the years 1945 to 1948.

At this point it might be worth noting the curious ambivalence which price relations in foreign trade play for the underdeveloped countries. Good prices for their primary commodities, specially if coupled with a rise in quantities sold, as they are in a boom, give to the underdeveloped countries the necessary means for importing capital goods and financing their own industrial development; yet at the same time they take away the incentive to do so, and investment, both foreign and domestic, is directed into an expansion of primary commodity production, thus leaving no room for the domestic investment which is the required complement of any import of capital goods. Conversely, when the prices and sales of primary commodities fall off, the desire for industrialization is suddenly sharpened. Yet, at the same time, the means for carrying it out are sharply reduced. Here again it seems that the underdeveloped countries are in danger of falling between two stools: failing to industrialize in a boom because things are as good as they are and failing to industrialize in a slump because things are as bad as they are.[7] It is no doubt true that failure to utilize high boom export proceeds more determinedly for capital formation because of purely temporary price relations shows a deplorable lack of foresight, but this is hardly very apposite criticism of those underdeveloped countries which rely mainly on private development. All private activity tends to be governed by the price relations of the day.

If our view is accepted (namely, that the traditional type of foreign investment as it was known prior to 1929 was "foreign" only in the geographical sense and not in the relevant economic sense), does it then follow that foreign investment has failed to fulfill one of the functions traditionally ascribed to it (and hoped for from it for the future): *i.e.,* to spread industrialization more widely and more evenly throughout the world? It would be premature to jump to this conclusion. What has been maintained in the preceding part of this argument is that past foreign investment, and the type of foreign trade which went with it, failed to spread industrialization to the countries in which the investment took place. It may be, however, that for a full understanding of the process we have to consider not merely the investing and the invested countries but a third group of countries as well.

It is an interesting speculation that European investment overseas was the instrument by which industrialization was brought to North America. Roughly speaking, the supplies of food and raw materials pouring into Europe as the result of the investment-*cum*-trade system and the favorable terms of trade engendered by this system enabled Europe to feed, clothe, educate,

---

[7] This ambivalence of changing terms of trade has also been stressed in a different context by Professor Lloyd Metzler in his important article on "Tariffs, Terms of Trade and Distribution of National Income," in the *Journal of Political Economy* (February 1949).

train, and equip large numbers of emigrants sent overseas, principally to the United States and Canada. Thus the benefits to the investing countries of Europe arising out of the system described above were in turn passed on to the United States—the converse of the Marshall Plan—and were the main foundation of the enormous capital formation the result of which is now to be observed in North America. This "macroeconomic" analysis is, of course, in no way contradicted by the fact that the individual migrant was motivated by the prospect of raising his standards of living by the transfer.

Attention may be drawn to the interesting statistical computation of Corrado Gini that even the enormous capital-stock characteristic of the United States economy is not more than the equivalent of the burden in consumption goods and in such services as health, education, and other provision for the immigrants—a burden which the United States was enabled to save by shifting it to the European mother countries of the immigrants. Perhaps in the final result it may be said that the ultimate benefits of the traditional investment-*cum*-trade system were not with the investing countries of Europe but with the new industrial countries of North America.[8]

If this analysis is correct, the industrialization of North America was made possible by the combination of migration and the opening up of under-developed overseas countries through European investment and trade. To that extent, Point Four and technical assistance on the part of the United States would be a gesture of historical justice and return of benefits received in the past.

It may be useful, rather than end on a wild historical speculation, to summarize the type of economic measures and economic policies which would result from the analysis presented in this paper. The first conclusion would be that in the interest of the underdeveloped countries, of world national income, and perhaps ultimately of the industrialized countries themselves, the purposes of foreign investment and foreign trade ought perhaps to be re-defined as producing gradual changes in the structure of comparative advantages and of the comparative endowment of the different countries rather than to develop a world trading system based on existing comparative advantages and existing distribution of endowments. This perhaps is the real significance of the present movement toward giving technical assistance to underdeveloped countries not necessarily linked with actual trade or investment. The emphasis on technical assistance may be interpreted as a recognition that the present structure of comparative advantages and endowments is not such that it should be considered as a permanent basis for a future international division of labor.

In so far as the underdeveloped countries continue to be the source of food and primary materials and in so far as trade, investment, and technical

---

[8] In more recent years, specially since 1924, U.S. capital accumulation had of course become quite independent from the original stimulus supplied by immigration, and proceeded without any visible check in spite of a heavy reduction in immigration. The argument put forward here is meant as a historical explanation rather than an analysis of the present sources of capital investment.

assistance are working in that direction by expanding primary production, the main requirement of underdeveloped countries would seem to be to provide for some method of income absorption to ensure that the results of technical progress are retained in the underdeveloped countries in a manner analogous to what occurs in the industrialized countries. Perhaps the most important measure required in this field is the reinvestment of profits in the under-developed countries themselves, or else the absorption of profits by fiscal measures and their utilization for the finance of economic development, and the absorption of rising productivity in primary production in rising real wages and other real incomes, provided that the increment is utilized for an increase in domestic savings and the growth of markets of a kind suitable for the development of domestic industries. Perhaps this last argument, namely, the necessity of some form of domestic absorption of the fruits of technical progress in primary production, provides the rationale for the concern which the underdeveloped countries show for the introduction of progressive social legislation. Higher standards of wages and social welfare, however, are not a highly commendable cure for bad terms of trade, except where the increment leads to domestic savings and investment. Where higher wages and social services are prematurely introduced and indiscriminately applied to export and domestic industries, they may in the end turn out a retarding factor in economic development and undermine the international bargaining strength of the primary producers. Absorption of the fruits of technical progress in primary production is not enough; what is wanted is absorption for reinvestment.

Finally, the argument put forward in this paper would point the lesson that a flow of international investment into the underdeveloped countries will contribute to their economic development only if it is absorbed into their economic system; *i.e.,* if a good deal of complementary domestic investment is generated and the requisite domestic resources are found.

PART FOUR

Characteristics
of Growing
Economies

Whereas the preceding two sections are primarily concerned with the causes of economic growth and backwardness, this section deals with some structural characteristics of underdeveloped countries and the changes in those characteristics which occur during, and to a large extent are the result of, the process of growth. The selections here do not offer a catalog of such characteristics; rather, they describe and analyze some salient features in terms of how they change over time.

The study by W. W. Rostow is the broadest in scope of the three selections. Using an essentially historical methodology, Rostow attempts to develop a broad picture of the development process from the earliest, "traditional" society to the most advanced, "high mass-consumption" economy. He postulates and describes five distinct "stages" of economic development, and attempts to account for the forces inherent in each stage that provide for the transition to the next.

There are several difficulties inherent in Rostow's approach. Aside from the notorious problem of accurate historical dating of the stages, a more cogent problem is that of explaining why any particular transition occurred precisely when it did and not at some other time. For example, Rostow suggests that in England the "take-off into self-sustained growth" (a concept that has gained wide currency) occurred in 1783, as the result of the establishment of "preconditions for take-off" that had been developing for more than one hundred years. Even if we accept without quarrel the year 1783 as the take-off date, we are still confronted with some serious problems. First, *why* are the preconditions specified precisely the ones *necessary* for the take-off? Moreover, the generality of the preconditions (for example, the proper "area of social latitude") suggests that the achievement of the right combination of preconditions cannot be precisely dated, but can reasonably be assumed to have existed prior to 1783. Therefore, a second broad question concerns the fact that we have no *sufficient* explanation for why the take-off occurred precisely when it did and not earlier or later. Despite these difficulties, Rostow's approach merits attention because it provides a useful and highly suggestive descriptive framework for historical research.

In view of the economic, social, and political interest that attaches to trends in personal-income distribution in the process of economic growth, it is surprising how little information is available and how little research has been undertaken on this subject. The article by Simon Kuznets represents a pioneering effort to deal with this topic in a systematic way. This is not to suggest, of course, that the subject of income distribution has been ignored in discussions of economic growth. As we have seen in an earlier section, Karl Marx was much concerned with what he regarded as the tendency of growth under capitalism to generate widening inequality. Indeed, it is to the growing misery of the working class and to the increasing concentration of wealth among the few that Marx ascribes the eventual political demise of capitalism.

Kuznets suggests that income inequality may well have been widening in England between 1780 and 1850, and this helps to explain Marx's view, as well as to provide the *raison d'être* of utopian socialist movements of the time. But Kuznets points out that this trend of widening inequality has more recently been reversed in the advanced countries, thus refuting Marx's prognosis. Much of his article is devoted to explaining the reasons for this newer trend of narrowing inequality. But in the underdeveloped countries, the picture is bleak indeed. In these countries, great income inequality is coupled with very low per-capita income. In view of this, Kuznets raises the grave question of whether the political framework of these countries will be able to survive the further widening of income inequality that he suggests may accompany the initial stages of economic development.

The article by P. T. Bauer and B. S. Yamey deals with changes in occupational distribution of the labor force among primary (mainly agricultural), secondary (mainly mining,[1] manufacturing, and construction), and tertiary (mainly commerce, transportation, and services) sectors that occur during the process of economic development. This topic has aroused considerable interest and controversy, particularly in connection with that part of the hypothesis advanced by Colin Clark suggesting that growth is accompanied by a relative increase in the percentage of the labor force engaged in tertiary activities. The authors present an interesting analytical discussion, supported by empirical evidence, which disputes this hypothesis.

It may be that other occupational breakdowns—such as the continuum from unskilled labor to high-level professional manpower—have greater *functional* significance for the analysis of economic growth. But the issue discussed by Bauer and Yamey is whether or not trends in the relative growth of the tertiary sector are even *symptoms* of economic development.

W. W. ROSTOW

|||||||||||||||||||||||||||||||||||||||||||||||||||||||||||||||||||||||||||||||||||||||||||||||||||||||||||||||||||||||||||||||||||||||||||||

The Stages of Economic Growth

This article summarizes a way of generalizing the sweep of modern economic history. The form of this generalization is a set of stages of growth, which can be designated as follows: the traditional society; the preconditions for take-off; the take-off; the drive to maturity; the age of high mass consumption. Beyond the age of high mass consumption lie the problems which are

From *The Economic History Review* (August 1959), pp. 1-15, with omissions. Reprinted by permission of the publisher and the author.

---

[1] Mining is here classified as a secondary activity, although in other contexts it is classified as primary.

beginning to arise in a few societies, and which may arise generally when diminishing relative marginal utility sets in for real income itself.

These descriptive categories are rooted in certain dynamic propositions about supply, demand, and the pattern of production; and before indicating the historical content of the categories I shall briefly state the underlying propositions.

A DYNAMIC THEORY OF PRODUCTION

The classical theory of production is formulated under essentially static assumptions which freeze—or permit only onceover change—in the variables most relevant to the process of economic growth. As modern economists have sought to merge classical production theory with Keynesian income analysis, they have introduced the dynamic variables: population, technology, entrepreneurship, etc. But they have tended to do so in forms so rigid and general that their models cannot grip the essential phenomena of growth, as they appear to an economic historian. We require a dynamic theory of production which isolates not only the distribution of income between consumption, saving, and investment (and the balance of production between consumers and capital goods) but which focuses directly and in some detail on the composition of investment and on developments within particular sectors of the economy. The argument that follows is based on such a flexible, disaggregated theory of production.

When the conventional limits on the theory of production are widened, it is possible to define theoretical equilibrium positions not only for output, investment, and consumption as a whole, but for each sector of the economy.[1] Within the framework set by forces determining the total level of output, sectoral optimum positions are determined, on the side of demand, by the levels of income and of population, and by the character of tastes; on the side of supply, by the state of technology and the quality of entrepreneurship, as the latter determines the proportion of technically available and potentially profitable innovations actually incorporated in the capital stock.[2] In addition, one must introduce an extremely significant empirical hypothesis; namely, that deceleration is the normal optimum path of a sector, due to a variety of factors operating on it, from the side of both supply and demand.[3] The equilibria which emerge from the application of these criteria are a set of sectoral paths, from which flows, as first derivatives, a sequence of optimum patterns of investment.

Historical patterns of investment did not, of course, exactly follow these

---

[1] W. W. Rostow, *The Process of Economic Growth* (Oxford, 1953), especially Ch. IV. Also "Trends in the Allocation of Resources in Secular Growth," Ch. 15 in *Economic Progress,* ed. Leon H. Dupriez, with the assistance of Douglas C. Hague (Louvain, 1955); also, "The Take-off into Self-Sustained Growth," *Economic Journal* (March 1956).

[2] In a closed model, a dynamic theory of production must account for changing stocks of basic and applied science, as sectoral aspects of investment, which is done in *The Process of Economic Growth, op. cit.,* especially pp. 22-25.

[3] *Ibid.,* pp. 96-103.

optimum patterns. They were distorted by imperfections in the private investment process; by the policies of governments; and by the impact of wars. Wars temporarily altered the profitable directions of investment by setting up arbitrary demands and by changing the conditions of supply; they destroyed capital; and, occasionally, they accelerated the development of new technology relevant to the peacetime economy and shifted the political and social framework in ways conducive to peacetime growth.[4] The historical sequence of business cycles and trend periods results from these deviations of actual from optimal patterns; and such fluctuations, along with the impact of wars, yield historical paths of growth which differ from those which the optima, calculated before the event, would have yielded. Nevertheless, the economic history of growing societies takes a part of its rude shape from the effort of societies to approximate the optimum sectoral paths.

At any period of time, the rate of growth in the sectors will vary greatly; and it is possible to isolate empirically certain leading sectors at early stages of their evolution, whose rapid rate of expansion plays an essential direct and indirect role in maintaining the over-all momentum of the economy.[5] For some purposes it is useful to characterize an economy in terms of its leading sectors; and a part of the technical basis for the stages of growth lies in the changing sequence of leading sectors. In essence it is the fact that sectors tend to have a rapid growth phase, early in their life, that makes it possible and useful to regard economic history as a sequence of stages rather than merely as a continuum, within which nature never makes a jump.

The stages of growth also require, however, that elasticities of demand be taken into account, and that this familiar concept be widened; for these rapid growth phases in the sectors derive not merely from the discontinuity of production functions but also from high price or income elasticities of demand. Leading sectors are determined not merely by the changing flow of technology and the changing willingness of entrepreneurs to accept available innovations: they are also partially determined by those types of demand which have exhibited high elasticity with respect to price, income, or both.

The demand for resources has resulted, however, not merely from demands set up by private taste and choice, but also from social decisions and from the policies of governments—whether democratically responsive or not. It is necessary, therefore, to look at the choices made by societies in the disposition of their resources in terms which transcend conventional market processes. It is necessary to look at their welfare functions, in the widest sense, including the noneconomic processes which determined them.

The course of birth rates, for example, represents one form of welfare choice made by societies, as income has changed; and population curves reflect (in addition to changing death rates) how the calculus about family size was made in the various stages; from the usual (but not universal) decline in birth rates, during or soon after the take-off, as urbanization took

---

[4] *Ibid.*, Ch. VII, especially pp. 164-167.
[5] For a discussion of the leading sectors, their direct and indirect consequences, and the diverse routes of their impact, see "Trends in the Allocation of Resources in Secular Growth," *op. cit.*

hold and progress became a palpable possibility, to the recent rise, as Americans (and others in societies marked by high mass consumption) have appeared to seek in larger families, values beyond those afforded by economic security and by an ample supply of durable consumers goods and services.

And there are other decisions as well that societies have made as the choices open to them have been altered by the unfolding process of economic growth; and these broad collective decisions, determined by many factors—deep in history, culture, and the active political process—outside the market place, have interplayed with the dynamics of market demand, risk-taking, technology, and entrepreneurship to determine the specific content of the stages of growth for each society.

How, for example, should the traditional society react to the intrusion of a more advanced power: with cohesion, promptness, and vigor, like the Japanese; by making a virtue of fecklessness, like the oppressed Irish of the eighteenth century; by slowly and reluctantly altering the traditional society like the Chinese? When independent modern nationhood was achieved, how should the national energies be disposed: in external aggression, to right old wrongs or to exploit newly created or perceived possibilities for enlarged national power; in completing and refining the political victory of the new national government over old regional interests; or in modernizing the economy?

Once growth is under way, with the take-off, to what extent should the requirements of diffusing modern technology and maximizing the rate of growth be moderated by the desire to increase consumption per capita and to increase welfare?

When technological maturity is reached, and the nation has at its command a modernized and differentiated industrial machine, to what ends should it be put, and in what proportions: to increase social security, through the welfare state; to expand mass consumption into the range of durable consumers goods and services; to increase the nation's stature and power on the world scene; or to increase leisure? And then the further question, where history offers us only fragments: what to do when the increase in real income itself loses its charm? Babies; boredom; three-day week ends; the moon; or the creation of new inner, human frontiers in substitution for the imperatives of scarcity?

In surveying now the broad contours of each stage of growth, we are examining, then, not merely the sectoral structure of economies, as they transformed themselves for growth, and grew; we are also examining a succession of strategic choices made by various societies concerning the disposition of their resources, which include but transcend the income and price elasticities of demand.

THE TRADITIONAL SOCIETY

The central economic fact about traditional societies is that they evolved within limited production functions. Both in the more distant past and in recent times the story of traditional societies is a story of endless change, reflected in the scale and patterns of trade, the level of agricultural output and productivity, the scale of manufactures, fluctuations in population and real income. But limitations of technology decreed a ceiling beyond which they could not penetrate. They did not lack inventiveness and innovations, some of high productivity. But they did lack a systematic understanding of their physical environment capable of making invention a more or less regular current flow, rather than a stock of *ad hoc* achievements inherited from the past. They lacked, in short, the tools and the outlook toward the physical world of the post-Newtonian era.

It followed from this productivity ceiling that food production absorbed 75 percent or more of the working force and that a high proportion of income above minimum consumption levels was spent in nonproductive or low productivity outlays: religious and other monuments; wars; high living for those who controlled land rents; and for poorer folk, there was a beggar-thy-neighbor struggle for land or the dissipation of the occasional surplus in an expensive wedding or funeral. Social values were geared to the limited horizons which men could perceive to be open to them; and social structures tended to hierarchy, although the traditional societies never wholly lacked paths for vertical mobility. The center of gravity of political power tended to reside in the regions, with the landowners, despite a fluctuating tension with those who—along with their soldiers and civil servants—exercised a degree of central authority.

THE PRECONDITIONS FOR TAKE-OFF

The initial preconditions for take-off were created in Western Europe out of two characteristics of the post-medieval world which interacted and reinforced each other: the gradual evolution of modern science and the modern scientific attitude; and the lateral innovation that came with the discovery of new lands and the rediscovery of old, converging with the impulse to create new technology at certain strategic points. The widening of the market—both within Europe and overseas—brought not only trade, but increased specialization of production, increased interregional and international dependence, enlarged institutions of finance, and increased market incentives to create new production functions. The whole process was heightened by the extension to trade and colonies of the old dynastic competition for control over European territories, inherited from the world of traditional societies.[6]

Britain was the first of the European nations to move from the stage of preconditions into take-off, a fact capable of various explanations but cer-

---

[6] This analysis shares with Schumpeter's the view that the ultimate causes of war were inherited from traditional societies, and were not a consequence of the more or less rational pursuit of direct economic interests. But, whereas Schumpeter tends to emphasize the persistence of irrational and romantic nationalist attitudes, this analysis would underline the structural fact that, once national sovereignty was accepted as a rule of the world arena, nations found themselves gripped in an almost inescapable oligopolistic struggle for power, which did have elements of noneconomic rationality.

tainly influenced by these circumstances: its achievement of a political and religious settlement by 1688; the area of social latitude and the limited but powerful incentives offered to noncomformists, who played a remarkable role in the process of industrial innovation; its naval and, thus, trading advantages, partly determined by a greater freedom from commitments to land warfare than the French; an endowment in industrial raw materials superior to the Dutch.

The existence of the British take-off from, say, 1783, set in motion a series of positive and negative demonstration effects which progressively unhinged other traditional societies or accelerated the creation of the pre-conditions for take-off, where the preconditions process was already under way.[7] Before examining the manner in which these demonstration effects were communicated, however, the structural characteristics of the precondi-tions period should be defined.

Technically, the preconditions for sustained industrialization have gen-erally required radical change in three nonindustrial sectors. First, a build-up of social overhead capital, notably in transport. This build-up was necessary not merely to permit an economical national market to be created and to allow natural resources to be productively exploited, but also to permit the national government effectively to rule. Second, a technological revolution in agriculture. The processes at work during the preconditions generally yielded both a general rise in population and a disproportionate rise in urban popula-tions. Increased productivity in agriculture has been generally a necessary condition for preventing the process of modernization from being throttled. Third, an expansion in imports financed by the more efficient production and marketing of some natural resources plus, where possible, capital imports. Such increased access to foreign exchange was required to permit the less advanced region or nation to increase the supply of the equipment and indus-trial raw materials it could not then itself supply, as well as to preserve the level of real income while social overhead capital of long gestation period was being created. Framed by these three forms of sectoral development, yielding both new markets and new inputs for industry, the initially small enclaves of modern industrial activity could begin to expand, and then sustain expansion, mainly by the plow-back of profits.

These technical developments required, in turn, prior or concurrent changes in the noneconomic dimensions of the traditional society: a willing-ness of the agricultural community to accept new techniques and to respond to the possibilities of the widened commercial markets; the existence and freedom to operate of a new group of industrial entrepreneurs; and, above all, a national government capable not only of providing a setting of peaceful order which encouraged the new modernizing activities but also capable and

---

[7] This article will not examine the preconditions process in the nations which, in Louis Hartz's phrase, were "born free" of traditional societies, mainly deriving from a British society already well advanced in the preconditions process or in regular growth. I refer to the United States, Canada, New Zealand, Australia, etc.

willing to take a degree of direct responsibility for the build-up of social over-head capital (including its finance); for an appropriate trade policy; and often, as well, for the diffusion of new agricultural and industrial techniques.

The political dimension of the preconditions deserves a further word, due to the peculiar mixture of positive and negative ways the demonstration effects of industrialization were transmitted from more advanced societies. In part the transmission consisted in making men in less advanced societies perceive that new positive choices were open to them: longer life for themselves and their children; new ranges of consumption; new devices of productivity; higher levels of welfare. At least equally powerful, however, was the negative demonstration that more advanced societies could impose their will on the less advanced, through the exercise of military force. A reactive nationalist sentiment—rooted in a perception of the link between industrialization and effective power in the world arena—came to be an extremely important factor in leading men to take the steps necessary to unhinge and transform the traditional society in such ways as to permit growth to become its normal condition. Without the affront to human and national dignity caused by the intrusion of more advanced powers, the rate of modernization of traditional societies over the past century and a half would have been much slower than, in fact, it has been.

Thus, it was not merely the German merchants but the German nationalists that led the way after 1848; not merely the Japanese merchants but the samurai after 1868; not merely the Russian middle class but a political, military, and civil service elite, smarting from the harsh lesson of the Crimean War and from a widening perception of the national costs of Russian backwardness; not merely the Chinese merchants but the intellectuals and the younger soldiers who sought effective modernization, by various routes in the whole long, turbulent sweep from the Opium War and the Taiping Rebellion forward.[8] Ataturk's role in Turkey—and his motivation—constitute a more typical case of the preconditions process than, let us say, the role and motivation of the innovating British nonconformists of the eighteenth century. The

---

[8] An element of reactive nationalism is not wholly lacking from earlier cases as well, apparently more purely economic in their motivation. The more rapid evolution in Britain than on the Continent of the preconditions for take-off can be viewed in part, as the product of a series of nationalist reactions to intrusion from more powerful or advanced neighbours: the Spanish in the sixteenth century; the Dutch in the seventeenth; the French in the eighteenth. These threats and national struggles may have yielded a sentiment which softened the rigidities of the traditional society, accelerated a new national settlement and permitted Britain to get on with the tasks of economic growth more effectively than others in the eighteenth century. And in the United States, too, the acceptance of the Constitution—reluctant at best—may have been made possible by a convergence of the desire of men of property to avoid the anarchy of a fragmented market and a certain casualness towards property rights, with the widespread perception in the mid-1780s that the United States might not be able to cope with more powerful nation states, intruding on the Confederation in one way or another, unless an effective central government existed. Hamilton's nationalism, and his conviction that American industrialization was necessary, transcended motives of private economic advantage.

evolution of colonial areas is also a version of the general case. There the positive and negative demonstration effects intermingled, under colonial rule; but they yielded, in the end, a local elite which accorded to political independence an overriding and urgent priority.

While a reactive nationalism has been a powerful engine of modernization it also posed problems for economic development; for it did not immediately and directly prepare men to face and handle the homely economic tasks of the preconditions and the take-off. On the contrary, when a new national government was achieved—in the face of the colonial power, the traditional society, or both in combination—its leaders were tempted to go on with the familiar game of politics and power rather than to turn promptly to the domestic tasks of modernization. There were real or believed external wrongs and humiliations to be righted; there were still rear-guard actions from elements in the traditional society to be dealt with; and much energy and resource could be allocated to the political—and sometimes military—problem of consolidating the power of the center over the old regional forces.

In short, some time often had to pass before men emerged in authority willing to accept the fact that the larger objectives of resurgent nationalism could not be achieved without turning wholeheartedly to the technical tasks of economic growth.[9] Both in the more distant past and in the contemporary world it is possible and useful to view societies in the stage of preconditions in terms of the changing balances struck among these three possible expressions of reactive nationalism. Until a definitive political transformation occurs—which harnesses national energies, talents, and resources around the concrete tasks of economic growth—the take-off is likely to be postponed: negatively, because the thin layer of modern technical and administrative talent in the society (as well as the society's margin of savings) is likely to be dissipated in activities of low or negative productivity; positively, because the government is unlikely to play its role effectively in the three sectoral developments—in social overhead capital, agriculture, and trade—necessary to create the matrix for sustained industrial growth.

THE TAKE-OFF

As I have suggested in an earlier article,[10] the take-off consists, in essence, of the achievement of rapid growth in a limited group of sectors,

---

[9] In his forthcoming study of the preconditions process in Japan, Turkey, and India, Mr. Lawrence Barss of MIT advances the hypothesis that it may be useful to distinguish two political stages, which he designates as the Transition and the Transformation. In the Transition, political life is dominated by men who want for their nations the benefits of modern independent status, but they are inhibited by many factors, including attitudes and ties of interest to the traditional society, from doing what must be done for economic growth. In the Transformation, a political leadership takes hold that, at last, means business.

[10] "The Take-off into Self-Sustained Growth," *op. cit.*

where modern industrial techniques are applied. Historically, the leading sectors in take-off have ranged from cotton textiles (Britain and New England); to railroads (The United States, France, Germany, Canada, Russia); to modern timber cutting and railroads (Sweden). In addition, agricultural processing, oil, import substitution industries, shipbuilding, and rapid expansions in military output have helped to provide the initial industrial surge.

The take-off is distinguished from earlier industrial surges by the fact that prior and concurrent developments make the application of modern industrial techniques a self-sustained rather than an abortive process. Not only must the momentum in the three key sectors of the preconditions be maintained but the corps of entrepreneurs and technicians must be enlarged, and the sources of capital must be institutionalized in such a way as to permit the economy to suffer structural shocks; to redispose its investment resources; and to resume growth. It is the requirement that the economy exhibit this resilience that justifies defining the take-off as embracing an interval of about two decades.

A result—and one key manifestation—of take-off is the ability of the society to sustain an annual rate of net investment of the order of, at least, 10 percent. This familiar (but essentially tautological) way of defining the take-off should not conceal the full range of transformations required before growth becomes a built-in feature of a society's habits and institutions.

In noneconomic terms, the take-off usually witnesses a definitive social, political, and cultural victory of those who would modernize the economy over those who would either cling to the traditional society or seek other goals; but—because nationalism can be a social solvent as well as a diversionary force—the victory can assume forms of mutual accommodation, rather than the destruction of the traditional groups by the more modern; see, for example, the role of the Junkers in nascent industrial Germany, the persistence of much of traditional Japan beyond 1880. By and large, the maintenance of momentum for a generation persuades the society to persist and to concentrate its efforts on extending the tricks of modern technology out beyond the sectors modernized during take-off.

THE DRIVE TO MATURITY

After take-off there follows, then, what might be called the drive to maturity. There are a variety of ways a stage of economic maturity might be defined; but for these purposes it is defined as the period when a society has effectively applied the range of (then) modern technology to the bulk of its resources.

During the drive to maturity the industrial process is differentiated, with new leading sectors gathering momentum to supplant the older leading sectors of the take-off, where deceleration has increasingly slowed the pace of expansion. After the railway take-offs of the third quarter of the nineteenth century—with coal, iron, and heavy engineering at the center of the growth process—it is steel, the new ships, chemicals, electricity, and the products of the modern machine tool that come to dominate the economy and sustain the over-all rate of growth. This is also, essentially, the case with the later Russian drive to maturity, after 1929. But in Sweden after 1890 it was the evolution from timber to wood pulp and paper; from ore to high-grade steel and finely machined metal products. The leading sectors in the drive to maturity will be determined, then, not merely by the pool of technology but by the nature of resource endowments; and it may be shaped to a degree, as well, by the policies of governments. Although much further detailed analysis would be required to apply this definition rigorously, I would offer the following sample as rough symbolic dates for technological maturity.[11]

Great Britain	1850
United States	1900
Germany	1910
France	1910
Sweden	1930
Japan	1940
Russia	1950
Canada	1950

The meaning of this technological definition of maturity—and its limits—may be better perceived by considering briefly a few specific problems posed by these particular dates.

Is France for example, on the eve of World War I, to be regarded as technologically mature, despite its large, comfortable, but technologically backward peasantry and its tendency to export large amounts of capital, despite certain technologically lagging industrial sectors? The case can, of course, be argued either way; but it does dramatize the need to allow, within the present definition, for regions of a nation or sectors of the economy to resist—for whatever reason—the full application of the range of modern technology. And this turns out to be generally true of nations which, by and large, one would judge mature. The United States of 1900 contained, after all, the South, whose takeoff can only be dated from the 1930s; and contemporary mature Canada contains the still lagging province of Quebec. The

---

[11] An oddity is to be noted. These dates, independently derived, come more or less sixty years after the dates established, on quite different criteria, for the beginning of take-off. There is no body of argument or evidence I can now offer to make rational such a uniformity. But it may be that when we explore the implications of some six decades of compound interest applied to the capital stock, in combination with three generations of men living under an environment of growth, elements of rationality will emerge.

technological definition of maturity must, then, be an approximation, when applied to a whole national society.

Japan as of 1940 poses a somewhat different problem. Can one rate as mature an economy with so labor-intensive an agricultural sector? The answer is affirmative only if one is prepared to take as a given—outside the definition of maturity—a society's decision about its population size. Within the Japanese population resource balance, its agriculture, with extraordinary refinement in the use of both water and chemical fertilizers, does indeed reflect a high form of modern technological achievement, even if modern farm machinery, designed to save labor, is capable of only limited use.

What about contemporary Russia, with more than 40 per cent of the working force still in agriculture and much modern technology still unapplied in consumer-goods industries? Here again, the present definition of maturity would not predetermine how a society chooses to allocate its technological capabilities. By and large contemporary Russia is to be judged a mature economy despite the fact that its leaders have chosen for political reasons to bear the costs of a low productivity agriculture and have chosen to concentrate capital and technology in sectors other than manufactured consumption goods. Put another way, the obstacles to full modernization of the Russian economic structure do not lie in the supply of capital, entrepreneurial administrators, or technicians.

Finally, there is the case of Britain, mature on this definition as early, say, as the Crystal Palace Exhibition. How is one to deal with the long interval between the stage of its maturity, in terms of the effective application of mid-nineteenth-century technology, and the next stage of growth: the age of high mass consumption, when the radical improvements in housing and durable consumers goods and services become the economy's leading sectors? The reasons for the gap in the British sequence lie in the nature of this next stage. The age of high mass consumption represents a direction of development a society may choose when it has achieved both technological maturity and a certain level of real income per head. Although income per head—and usually consumption per head—will rise in the drive to maturity, it is evident that there is no fixed connexion between technological maturity and any particular level of real consumption per head. The course of these variables after take-off will depend primarily on the society's population-resource balance and on its income-distribution policy. The process of growth, by definition, raises income per head, but it does not necessarily lead to uniformity of per capita income among nations or, even, among regions within nations. There are—and there are likely to be—technologically mature societies that are, so to speak, both rich and poor. When historical data on national income are developed to permit systematic comparison, we are likely to find that incomes per head, at maturity, vary over a considerable range. Mid-century Britain would, presumably, stand low in that range. The improvements in real income and consumption per head that occurred in the second half of the nineteenth century took the form of improvements in diet, housing, and urban overhead capital which, while substantial, did not create within Britain new leading industrial sectors—at least down to the bicycle boom of the 1890s.[12]

And so Britain, after Crystal Palace, moved onward in growth at a modest pace, using its capital and entrepreneurship substantially to help acquire resources with which it was not sufficiently endowed, and to help build the preconditions and assist the take-offs of other societies, suffering along the way some of the cost of having led in the process of industrialization, to enter the new century with most of its initial lead gone.[13] Put another way, the achievement of maturity by Western Europe and the United States early in the twentieth century, at the then existing level of technology, found Britain in a roughly equivalent position: while the newer nations had moved from take-off to maturity in the sixty years before World War I, Britain had moved, in terms of income levels, from being a relatively poor mature society to being a relatively rich, mature society.

As societies move to technological maturity, the structure and quality of the working force change. The proportion of the population in agriculture and rural life decreases; and within the urban population the proportion of semiskilled and white-collar workers increases.[14] This emergent working force is not only likely to organize itself with increasing effectiveness in the labor

---

[12] In a different perspective, it is possible to dismiss the gap between mid-nineteenth-century British technological maturity and twentieth-century high mass consumption as a simple product of technological history; that is, the technology of modern transportation, suburban housing, and household gadgetry did not exist in, say, the third quarter of the nineteenth century. And for many purposes that is a quite satisfactory way to look at the matter.

On the other hand, three considerations argue that it is worth regarding the British sequence in the second half of the nineteenth century as involving a gap. First, technology itself is, in its widest sense, not an independent variable (*Process of Economic Growth*, especially pp. 83-86). If the level of British incomes and consumption had been high enough, incentives might have existed which would have yielded a quite different evolution of technology. Second, the phenomenon of a gap in time between the attainment of technological maturity and the age of high mass consumption—the existence of relatively poor as well as rich mature societies—is more general than the British case. And a view of Britain in the second half of the nineteenth century as in the process of closing the gap may, for certain purposes, be linked suggestively to similar transitions in other societies. Third, much in British social, political (and, even, entrepreneurial) history in the second half of the nineteenth century is typical of transformations in attitude and policy which have occurred in other societies after technological maturity has been attained: the beginnings of serious welfare legislation, with the Ten Hours Bill; the pressures and reflections which lead the society to accept the Second and Third Reform Bills; the emergence of political coalitions which damped the power of industrial interests; the mounting intellectual attention and public sentiment focused on problems of social reform, laying the bases for the pre-1914 Liberal measures and the emergence of the Labor party. In short, even narrowly examined, much in British history in the period 1850-1900 is illuminated by the notion that this was a society which took its technological virtuosity as a given and, at a decorous rate, proceeded to seek, at the margin, welfare objectives beyond.

[13] The forces which relatively damped the rate of increase in British income and permitted its technological lead to be dissipated are, evidently, more complex than this sentence can suggest; but it would be inappropriate to this exposition to examine them at greater length here.

[14] Although Colin Clark's categories—of primary, secondary, and tertiary activity—do not fit precisely this analysis, his pioneer compilations suggest that considerable uniformities in the structure of the working force of mature economies exist.

markets, but also to perceive that the industrial civilization of which it is a part can offer levels and types of consumption not previously regarded as a realistic possibility on a mass basis. And the rise in real income per head is likely to make these new tastes effective. Further, the new working force, increasingly born to the city rather than transferred from the lower margins of rural life, is likely to perceive that it can bring its weight to bear on the political process in such ways as to make the government increasingly provide measures of social and economic security. Moreover, the character of leadership in industry begins to change as well. The take-off is usually managed by relatively modest, creative men with an insight as to how output in their sector can be radically expanded: the Boultons' and Lowells'. In the drive to maturity men take over with more grandiose visions, with a more acute sense of scale and of power: although there are vast differences between post-Civil War United States and Stalin's Russia, there is, nevertheless, a distant family resemblance between some of the great entrepreneurs of the American drive to maturity and the men who administered the Five Year Plans between, say, 1929 and 1953. At maturity, however, the professional managers become more important: the nameless comfortable, cautious committeemen who inherit and manage large sectors of the economy, while the society begins to seek objectives which include but transcend the application of modern technology to resources.

These sea-changes in the outlook and objectives of the working force and industrial management are likely to be accompanied by wider shifts in the society's mood, which the intellectuals and politicians articulate. They react against the harshness and social costs of the drive to maturity. The extension of industrialization ceases to be acceptable as an overriding goal: in an extension of the law of diminishing relative marginal utility, men appear to place a lowered valuation on further increments to what they have in abundance, and, at the margin, to seek new satisfactions. In the pre-1914 drive to maturity of Western Europe and the United States one can find, in each nation, reflections of this mood gradually gathering strength, centered about the question: how shall the mature industrial machine, with compound interest built firmly into its structure, be used? In the 1930s it was faced by Japan; and in the 1950s it confronts Russia.

THE AGE OF HIGH MASS CONSUMPTION

There have been, essentially, three directions in which the mature economy could be turned once the society ceased to accept the extension of modern technology as a primary, if not overriding objective: to offer, by public measures, increased security, welfare, and, perhaps, leisure to the working force; to provide enlarged private consumption—including single family homes and durable consumers goods and services—on a mass basis; to seek enlarged power for the mature nation on the world scene. A good deal of the history of the first half of the twentieth century can be told in terms of the pattern and succession of choices made by various mature societies as among these three alternatives.

After a brief and superficial flirtation with the attractions of world power at the turn of the century and after imposing a set of mild measures of social reform, during the Progressive period, the United States opted wholeheartedly in the 1920s for the second choice.[15] The boom of that decade was built squarely on the migration to suburbia, the mass extension of the automobile, and the household gadgetry which modern industry could provide. And these decisions to relocate the population and provide it with mobility, brought in their train not only new leading sectors—housing, automobiles, petroleum, rubber, electric-powered household devices, etc.—but also vast commitments to build new social overhead capital and commercial centers.

Down to 1914 Britain and Western Europe opted more substantially for public measures of social security, influenced perhaps by the higher proportions of urban population and by the greater power of socialist thought and political influence than in the United States. In addition, Germany was more seriously tempted than the United States to translate industrial maturity into enlarged world power; and in the inherently oligopolistic circumstances of the European arena of power, this decision led to a greater relative enlargement of military expenditures in Europe as a whole than in pre-1914 United States.

During the 1920s Britain, in effect, took its favorable terms of trade in the form of chronic unemployment in the export industries. Only in the 1930s did a pervasive recovery occur. This phase did begin to exhibit a shift into the age of high mass consumption: suburban housing, automobiles, and durable consumers goods began to assert themselves more strongly as leading sectors. But rearmament and war postponed the immediate fruition of this trend.

Although the post-1920 terms of trade problem struck the Continent with less force than Britain, there too the return to relative prosperity, of 1925-1929, did not move the economies far beyond pre-1914 patterns. France, on the whole, continued to stagnate down to World War II, and German recovery, while reflecting certain symptoms of the new phase, was dominated by rearmament.

Svennilson presents calculations of motor-vehicle production (private and commercial) which suggest the relative movements of the United States and Western Europe between the wars. In 1929 the four major European nations (Great Britain, Germany, France, and Italy) produced 702,000 vehicles; the United States, 5.4 million. After a decade of protracted depression in the United States (marked by a compensatory turn to the welfare state), and a

---

[15] The time lag in the United States between the achievement of technological maturity in, say, 1900, and the high mass consumption boom of the 1920s is to be accounted for in part by the relative stagnation of industrial real wages in the pre-1914 trend period, due to rising living costs (*Process of Economic Growth*, Ch. VI). The more protracted lag of Western Europe is partly a consequence of the economic impact of World War I and of the public policies and dominant social attitudes of the interwar years.

considerably greater degree of European recovery, the European figure was 1.1 million in 1938; the American, 2.5 million.[16]

In the decade 1946-1956 the United States resumed a pattern of recovery and growth markedly similar to that of the 1920s: the migration to suburbia, and the extension of the automobile and the standard mix of durable consumers household gadgets to 75 percent or more of American families. And, after an interval of postwar reconstruction, Western Europe resumed with force the similar but more laggard development of the 1930s. By the late 1950s Western European growth was based on the fact that this region had at last fully entered the age of durable consumers goods and services, experiencing a version of the American 1920s. The patterns of consumption, as among the various European countries, emerge as largely explicable in terms of income and price elasticities of demand.[17] And in Russia, as well, the inexorable attraction of the sewing machine, washing machine, refrigerator, and television was beginning to assert itself; and the first satellite town was under construction.[18] It was evident, however, from the pattern of future plans that the Soviet government was not yet prepared to give the vast hostages to fortune that follow a society's commitment to the mass automobile.

BEYOND CONSUMPTION

While Western Europe (and to a degree, also, Japan) were entering the era of high mass consumption and the Soviet Union was dallying on its fringes, an important new element entered the world economic system in the form of a quite unexpected tendency of birth rates to rise in rich societies.[19] Although the tendency can be observed in a number of countries, it is most marked in the United States. During the years of World War II the American birth rate rose from 18 to about 22 per 1000. This was judged at the time,

---

[16] Ingvar Svennilson, *Growth and Stagnation in the European Economy* (Geneva: United Nations, 1954), pp. 144-152. I am inclined to believe that the length of the American depression and its intractibility in the 1930s stems from the character of leading sectors in the age of high mass consumption. The diffusion of single-family housing, the automobile, etc. requires expanding levels of private income and, in effect, full employment. Moreover, until the diffusion process is actively under way certain major forms of investment are likely to be slack, because of idle capacity. Full employment is needed, in a sense, to maintain full employment when the leading sectors are consumption sectors. This was not true before 1914 when, even with unemployment high and incomes low, it might well pay to press on with railroadization, steel ships, etc. where the high expected rate of return over costs derived primarily from lowered costs. Put another way, in the age of high mass consumption a higher proportion of investment becomes endogenous, rather than exogenous, when the latter term is used to embrace investment stimulated by new technological possibilities.

[17] See, notably, Milton Gilbert and associates, *Comparative National Products and Price Levels* (Paris: OEEC, 1958).

[18] *Economic Survey of Europe in 1957* (Geneva: United Nations, 1958), pp. 14 and 22n.

[19] There have also been remarkable declines in birth rates in Japan and Italy in the 1950s, as new horizons of economic progress have opened up for large segments of the population.

and to a large degree it certainly was, a phenomenon of resumed full employment and early wartime marriages. In the postwar years, however, it moved up and has stayed at about 25 per 1000. An official forecast in 1946 estimated that the American population would reach 165 million in 1990; an official forecast of 1958 estimated that the figure might be of the order of 240 million by 1980.

The human motivations and social processes which have yielded this extraordinary result are not yet well understood; but Americans have behaved as if diminishing relative marginal utility set in to the expansion of real income along the old paths. They have opted at the margin for larger families; and this trend may be related to the high rate of expansion in family trips to national parks, motorboats, do-it-yourself implements, and, even, to a widely noted tendency to turn away from the pursuit of income and authority within the large-scale bureaucratic establishments where a high proportion of the population do their work.[20]

Whatever the motivation, however, an expansion of population on this scale will set up requirements for the lateral extension of the society's resources, including its requirements of social overhead capital. These requirements in any case had been enlarged by the consequences of the previous phase of extension in automobile ownership and suburban housing.[21] There is a vast American backlog of investment to be carried out in roads and in the reconstruction of old depopulated urban centers. Finally, a quite significant change in the dependency ratio is under way. After falling for about a century, the number of persons under 20 and over 65 in the American population supported by each 100 members of the working force had reached 74 in 1935; by 1955 the figure was 81; and if present population patterns persist it is estimated that the figure will rise to 98 by 1975.[22]

The pattern of American economic growth over the next several decades is likely to differ, then, from that of either the 1920s or the 1946-1956 decade; and it is likely to be based on somewhat different leading sectors. In any case, it is clear that American society, by its quiet collective decision about birth rates, has postponed the problems of a time of true affluence, when the full utilization of resources would not much matter.

The somewhat strenuous choice made by Americans as they pushed high mass consumption to a kind of logical conclusion, in the first decade after World War II, need not prove to be universal: the income elasticity of demand for children may vary. It is evident, however, that the march of compound interest is bringing some societies close to the point where the pursuit of food, shelter, clothing, as well as durable consumers goods and public and

---

[20] See, notably, Clyde Kluckhohn, "Have There Been Discernible Shifts in American Values in the Past Generation?" in *The American Style,* ed. by E. E. Morison (New York, 1958).

[21] See, notably, the calculations on social overhead requirements in *The Challenge to America: its Economic and Social Aspects,* Special Studies Project Report IV, Rockefeller Brothers Fund (New York, 1958).

[22] C. and I. B. Taeuber, *The Changing Population of the United States* (New York and London, 1958), p. 325.

private services, may no longer dominate their lives. A new and revolutionary set of choices is being confronted, or is a mere generation or so over the horizon.

This is not to say that the richer societies are without challenge. There is the problem of escaping from a treacherous nuclear-arms race. And there is the equal problem of organizing the planet, as the whole southern half of the globe and China move through the preconditions, into take-off and regular growth. But the era when the problem and human agenda imposed by the fact of scarcity is coming towards an end: the day when, in Marx's phrase, labor "has of itself become the prime necessity of life" is not all that far off, if nuclear destruction and the grosser forms of international disorder can be avoided. . . .

SIMON KUZNETS

Economic Growth and Income Inequality

The central theme of this paper is the character and causes of long-term changes in the personal distribution of income. Does inequality in the distribution of income increase or decrease in the course of a country's economic growth? What factors determine the secular level and trends of income inequalities?

These are broad questions in a field of study that has been plagued by looseness in definitions, unusual scarcity of data, and pressures of strongly held opinions. While we cannot completely avoid the resulting difficulties, it may help to specify the characteristics of the size-of-income distributions that we want to examine and the movements of which we want to explain.

Five specifications may be listed. First, the units for which incomes are recorded and grouped should be family-expenditure units, properly adjusted for the number of persons in each—rather than income recipients for whom the relations between receipt and use of income can be widely diverse. Second, the distribution should be complete, *i.e.,* should cover all units in a country rather than a segment either at the upper or lower tail. Third, if possible we should segregate the units whose main income earners are either still in the learning or already in the retired stages of their life cycle—to

Presidential address delivered to the American Economic Association, December 29, 1954. From *American Economic Review* (March 1955), pp. 1-28, with omissions. Reprinted by permission of the American Economic Association and the author.

avoid complicating the picture by including incomes *not* associated with full-time, full-fledged participation in economic activity. Fourth, income should be defined as it is now for national income in this country, *i.e.*, received by individuals, including income in kind, before and after direct taxes, excluding capital gains. Fifth, the units should be grouped by *secular* levels of income, free of cyclical and other transient disturbances.

For such a distribution of mature expenditure units by secular levels of income per capita, we should measure shares of some fixed ordinal groups—percentiles, deciles, quintiles, etc. In the underlying array the units should be classified by average income levels for a sufficiently long span so that they form income-status groups—say a generation or about 25 years. Within such a period, even when classified by secular income levels, units may shift from one ordinal group to another. It would, therefore, be necessary and useful to study separately the relative share of units that, throughout the generation period of reference, were continuously within a specific ordinal group, and the share of the units that moved into that specific group; and this should be done for the shares of "residents" and "migrants" within all ordinal groups. Without such a long period of reference and the resulting separation between "resident" and "migrant" units at different relative income levels, the very distinction between "low" and "high" income classes loses its meaning, particularly in a study of long-term changes in shares and in inequalities in the distribution. To say, for example, that the "lower" income classes gained or lost during the last twenty years in that their share of total income increased or decreased has meaning only if the units have been classified as members of the "lower" classes throughout those 20 years—and for those who have moved into or out of those classes recently such a statement has no significance.

Furthermore, if one may add a final touch to what is beginning to look like a statistical economist's pipe dream, we should be able to trace secular income levels not only through a single generation but at least through two—connecting the incomes of a given generation with those of its immediate descendants. We could then distinguish units that, throughout a given generation, remain within one ordinal group and whose children—through *their* generation—are also within that group, from units that remain within a group through their generation but whose children move up or down on the relative economic scale in their time. The number of possible combinations and permutations becomes large; but it should not obscure the main design of the income structure called for—the classification by long-term income status of a given generation and of its immediate descendants. If living members of society—as producers, consumers, savers, decision-makers on secular problems—react to long-term changes in income levels and shares, data on such an income structure are essential. An economic society can then be judged by the secular level of the income share that it provides for a given generation and for its children. The important corollary is that the study of long-term changes in the income distribution must distinguish between changes in the shares of resident groups—resident within either one or two generations—

and changes in the income shares of groups that, judged by their secular levels, migrate upward or downward on the income scale.

Even if we had data to approximate the income structure just outlined, the broad question posed at the start—how income inequality changes in the process of a country's economic growth—could be answered only for growth under defined economic and social conditions. And, in fact, we shall deal with this question in terms of the experience of the now developed countries which grew under the aegis of the business enterprise. But even with this limitation, there are no statistics that can be used directly for the purpose of measuring the *secular* income structure. Indeed, I have difficulty in visualizing how such information could practicably be collected—a difficulty that may be due to lack of familiarity with the studies of our colleagues in demography and sociology who have concerned themselves with problems of generation or intergeneration mobility and status. But although we now lack data directly relevant to the secular income structure, the setting up of reasonably clear and yet difficult specifications is not merely an exercise in perfectionism. For if these specifications do approximate, and I trust that they do, the real core of our interest when we talk about shares of economic classes or long-term changes in these shares, then proper disclosure of our meaning and intentions is vitally useful. It forces us to examine and evaluate critically the data that are available; it prevents us from jumping to conclusions based on these inadequate data; it reduces the loss and waste of time involved in mechanical manipulations of the type represented by Pareto-curve-fitting to groups of data whose meaning, in terms of income concept, unit of observation, and proportion of the total universe covered, remains distressingly vague; and most important of all, it propels us toward a deliberate construction of testable bridges between the available data and the income structure that is the real focus of our interest.

TRENDS IN INCOME INEQUALITY

Forewarned of the difficulties, we turn now to the available data. These data, even when relating to complete populations, invariably classify units by income for a given year. From our standpoint, this is their major limitation. Because the data often do not permit many size-groupings, and because the difference between annual income incidence and longer-term income status has less effect if the number of classes is small and the limits of each class are wide, we use a few wide classes. This does not resolve the difficulty; and there are others due to the scantiness of data for long periods, inadequacy of the unit used—which is, at best, a family and very often a reporting unit—errors in the data, and so on through a long list. Consequently, the trends in the income structure can be discerned but dimly, and the results considered as preliminary informed guesses.

The data are for the United States, England, and Germany—a scant sample, but at least a starting point for some inferences concerning long-term changes in the presently developed countries. The general conclusion suggested is that the relative distribution of income, as measured by annual income incidence in rather broad classes, has been moving toward equality—with these trends particularly noticeable since the 1920s but beginning perhaps in the period before World War I.

Let me cite some figures, all for income before direct taxes, in support of this impression. In the United States, in the distribution of income among families (excluding single individuals), the shares of the two lowest quintiles rise from 13½ percent in 1929 to 18 percent in the years after World War II (average of 1944, 1946, 1947, and 1950); whereas the share of the top quintile declines from 55 to 44 percent, and that of the top 5 percent from 31 to 20 percent. In the United Kingdom, the share of the top 5 percent of units declines from 46 percent in 1880 to 43 percent in 1910 or 1913, to 33 percent in 1929, to 31 percent in 1938, and to 24 percent in 1947; the share of the lower 85 percent remains fairly constant between 1880 and 1913, between 41 and 43 percent, but then rises to 46 percent in 1929 and 55 percent in 1947. In Prussia income inequality increases slightly between 1875 and 1913—the shares of the top quintile rising from 48 to 50 percent, of the top 5 percent from 26 to 30 percent; the share of the lower 60 percent, however, remains about the same. In Saxony, the change between 1880 and 1913 is minor: the share of the two lowest quintiles declines from 15 to 14½ percent; that of the third quintile rises from 12 to 13 percent, of the fourth quintile from 16½ to about 18 percent; that of the top quintile declines from 56½ to 54½ percent, and of the top 5 percent from 34 to 33 percent. In Germany as a whole, relative income inequality drops fairly sharply from 1913 to the 1920s, apparently due to decimation of large fortunes and property incomes during the war and inflation; but then begins to return to prewar levels during the depression of the 1930s.[1]

Even for what they are assumed to represent, let alone as approximations to shares in distributions by secular income levels, the data are such that differences of two or three percentage points cannot be assigned significance. One must judge by the general weight and consensus of the evidence—which

---

[1] The following sources were used in calculating the figures cited:

United States. For recent years we used *Income Distribution by Size, 1944-1950* (Washington, D. C., 1953) and Selma Goldsmith and others, "Size Distribution of Income Since the Mid-Thirties," *Review of Economic Statistics* (February 1954), XXXVI, pp. 1-32; for 1929, the Brookings Institution data as adjusted in Simon Kuznets, *Shares of Upper Groups in Income and Savings* (New York, 1953), p. 220.

United Kingdom. For 1938 and 1947, Dudley Seers, The *Levelling of Income Since 1938* (Oxford, 1951) p. 39; for 1929, Colin Clark, *National Income and Outlay* (London, 1937), Table 47, p. 109; for 1880, 1910, and 1913, A. Bowley, *The Change in the Distribution of the National Income, 1880-1913* (Oxford, 1920).

Germany. For the constituent areas (Prussia, Saxony and others) for years before World War I, based on S. Prokopovich, *National Income of Western European Countries* (published in Moscow in the 1920s). Some summary results are given in Prokopovich, "The Distribution of National Income," *Economic Journal* (March 1926), XXXVI, pp. 69-82. See also "Das Deutsche Volkseinkommen vor und nach dem Kriege," *Einzelschrift zur Stat. des Deutschen Reichs,* no. 24 (Berlin, 1932), and W. S. and E. S. Woytinsky, *World Population and Production* (New York, 1953), Table 192, p. 709.

unfortunately is limited to a few countries. It justifies a tentative impression of constancy in the relative distribution of income before taxes, followed by some narrowing of relative income inequality after World War I—or earlier.

Three aspects of this finding should be stressed. First, the data are for income before direct taxes and exclude contributions by government (*e.g.,* relief and free assistance). It is fair to argue that both the proportion and progressivity of direct taxes and the proportion of total income of individuals accounted for by government assistance to the less privileged economic groups have grown during recent decades. This is certainly true of the United States and the United Kingdom, but in the case of Germany is subject to further examination. It follows that the distribution of income after direct taxes and including free contributions by government would show an even greater narrowing of inequality in developed countries with size distributions of pretax, ex-government-benefits income similar to those for the United States and the United Kingdom.

Second, such stability or reduction in the inequality of the percentage shares was accompanied by significant rises in real income per capita. The countries now classified as developed have enjoyed rising per capita incomes except during catastrophic periods such as years of active world conflict. Hence, if the shares of groups classified by their annual income position can be viewed as approximations to shares of groups classified by their secular income levels, a constant percentage share of a given group means that its per capita real income is rising at the same rate as the average for all units in the country; and a reduction in inequality of the shares means that the per capita income of the lower-income groups is rising at a more rapid rate than the per capita income of the upper-income groups.

The third point can be put in the form of a question. Do the distributions by annual incomes properly reflect trends in distribution by secular incomes? As technology and economic performance rise to higher levels, incomes are less subject to transient disturbances, not necessarily of the cyclical order that can be recognized and allowed for by reference to business cycle chronology, but of a more irregular type. If in the earlier years the economic fortunes of units were subject to greater vicissitudes—poor crops for some farmers, natural calamity losses for some nonfarm business units— if the over-all proportion of individual entrepreneurs whose incomes were subject to such calamities, more yesterday but some even today, was larger in earlier decades, these earlier distributions of income would be more affected by transient disturbances. In these earlier distributions the temporarily unfortunate might crowd the lower quintiles and depress their shares unduly, and the temporarily fortunate might dominate the top quintile and raise its share unduly—proportionately more than in the distributions for later years. If so, distributions by longer-term average incomes might show less reduction in inequality than do the distributions by annual incomes; they might even show an opposite trend.

One may doubt whether this qualification would upset a narrowing of inequality as marked as that for the United States, and in as short a period as twenty-five years. Nor is it likely to affect the persistent downward drift in the spread of the distributions in the United Kingdom. But I must admit a strong element of judgment in deciding how far this qualification modifies the finding of long-term stability followed by reduction in income inequality in the few developed countries for which it is observed or is likely to be revealed by existing data. The important point is that the qualification is relevant; it suggests need for further study if we are to learn much from the available data concerning the secular income structure; and such study is likely to yield results of interest in themselves in their bearing upon the problem of trends in temporal instability of income flows to individual units or to economically significant groups of units in different sectors of the national economy.

AN ATTEMPT AT EXPLANATION

If the above summary of trends in the secular income structure of developed countries comes perilously close to pure guesswork, an attempt to explain these dimly discernible trends may surely seem foolhardy. Yet it is necessary to do so if only to bring to the surface some factors that may have been at play; induce a search for data bearing upon these factors; and thus confirm or revise our impressions of the trends themselves. Such preliminary speculations are useful provided it is recognized that we are at a relatively early stage in a long process of interplay among tentative summaries of evidence, preliminary hypotheses, and search for additional evidence that might lead to reformulation and revisions—as bases for new analysis and further search.

The present installment of initial speculation may be introduced by saying that a long-term constancy, let alone reduction, of inequality in the secular income structure is a puzzle. For there are at least two groups of forces in the long-term operation of developed countries that make for *increasing* inequality in the distribution of income before taxes and excluding contributions by governments. The first group relates to the concentration of savings in the upper-income brackets. According to all recent studies of the apportionment of income between consumption and savings, only the upper-income groups save; the total savings of groups below the top decile are fairly close to zero. For example, the top 5 percent of units in the United States appear to account for almost two thirds of individuals' savings; and the top decile comes close to accounting for all of it. What is particularly important is that the inequality in distribution of savings is greater than that in the distribution of property incomes, and hence of assets.[2] Granted that this finding is based on distribution of annual income, and that a distribution by secular levels would show less inequality in income and correspondingly less concentration of savings, the inequality in savings would still remain fairly sharp, perhaps more so than in holdings of assets. Other conditions

---

[2] See Kuznets, *op. cit.,* particularly Chs. 2 and 6.

being equal, the cumulative effect of such inequality in savings would be the concentration of an *increasing* proportion of income-yielding assets in the hands of the upper groups—a basis for larger income shares of these groups and their descendants.

The second source of the puzzle lies in the industrial structure of the income distribution. An invariable accompaniment of growth in developed countries is the shift away from agriculture, a process usually referred to as industrialization and urbanization. The income distribution of the total population, in the simplest model, may therefore be viewed as a combination of the income distributions of the rural and of the urban populations. What little we know of the structures of these two component income distributions reveals that: (*a*) the average per capita income of the rural population is usually lower than that of the urban; (*b*) inequality in the percentage shares within the distribution for the rural population is somewhat narrower than in that for the urban population—even when based on annual income; and this difference would probably be wider for distributions by secular income levels. Operating with this simple model, what conclusions do we reach? First, all other conditions being equal, the increasing weight of urban population means an increasing share for the more unequal of the two component distributions. Second, the relative difference in per capita income between the rural and urban populations does not necessarily drift downward in the process of economic growth: indeed, there is some evidence to suggest that it is stable at best, and tends to widen because per capita productivity in urban pursuits increases more rapidly than in agriculture. If this is so, inequality in the total income distribution should increase.

Two questions then arise: First, why does the share of the top-income groups show no rise over time if the concentration of savings has a cumulative effect? Second, why does income inequality decline and particularly why does the share of the lower-income groups rise if both the weight of the more unequal urban income distribution and the relative difference between per capita urban and per capita rural incomes increase? . . .

FACTORS COUNTERACTING THE CONCENTRATION OF SAVING

One group of factors counteracting the cumulative effect of concentration of savings upon upper-income shares is legislative interference and "political" decisions. These may be aimed at limiting the cumulation of property directly through inheritance taxes and other explicit capital levies. They may produce similar effects indirectly, *e.g.,* by government-permitted or -induced inflation which reduces the economic value of accumulated wealth stored in fixed-price securities or other properties not fully responsive to price changes; or by legal restriction of the *yield* on accumulated property, as happened recently in the form of rent controls or of artificially low long-term interest rates maintained by the government to protect the market for its own bonds.

To discuss this complex of processes is beyond the competence of this paper, but its existence and possible wide effect should be noted and one point emphasized. All these interventions, even when not directly aimed at limiting the effects of accumulation of past savings in the hands of the few, do reflect the view of society on the long-term utility of wide income inequalities. This view is a vital force that would operate in democratic societies even if there were no other counteracting factors. This should be borne in mind in connection with *changes* in this view even in developed countries, which result from the process of growth and constitute a re-evaluation of the need for income inequalities as a source of savings for economic growth. The result of such changes would be an increasing pressure of legal and political decisions on upper-income shares—increasing as a country moves to higher economic levels.

We turn to three other, less obvious groups of factors countervailing the cumulative effects of concentration of savings. The first is demographic. In the presently developed countries there have been differential rates of increase between the rich and the poor—family control having first spread to the former. Hence, even disregarding migration, one can argue that the top 5 percent of 1870 and its descendants would account for a significantly smaller percentage of the population in 1920. This is even more likely in a country like the United States with its substantial immigration—usually entering the income distribution at the lower-income levels; and may be less likely in a country from which the poor have emigrated. The top 5 percent of population in 1920 is, therefore, comprised only partly of the descendants of the top 5 percent of 1870; perhaps half or a larger fraction must have originated in the lower-income brackets of 1870. This means that the period during which effects of concentration of savings can be assumed to have cumulated to raise the income share of any given fixed ordinal group (whether it be the top 1, 5, or 10 percent of the population) is much shorter than the fifty years in the span; and hence these effects are much weaker than they would have been if the top 5 percent of 1870 had, through their descendants, filled completely the ranks of the top 5 percent of the population of 1920. Although the cumulative effect of savings may be to raise the relative income of a *progressively diminishing* top proportion of total population, their effect on the relative share of a *fixed* top proportion of the population is much reduced.

The second group of forces resides in the very nature of a dynamic economy with relative freedom of individual opportunity. In such a society technological changes is rampant and property assets that originated in older industries almost inevitably have a diminishing proportional weight in the total because of the more rapid growth of younger industries. Unless the descendants of a high-income group manage to shift their accumulating assets into new fields and participate with new entrepreneurs in the growing share of the new and more profitable industries, the long-range returns on their property holdings are likely to be significantly lower than those of the more recent entrants into the class of substantial asset holders. "From shirt sleeves to shirt sleeves in three generations" probably exaggerates the effects of this dynamism of a growing economy: there are, among the upper-income groups of today, many descendants of the upper-income groups of more than three or even four generations ago. But the adage is realistic in the sense that a *long unbroken* sequence of connection with rising industries and hence with major sources of continued large property incomes is exceedingly rare; that the successful great entrepreneurs of today are rarely sons of the great and successful entrepreneurs of yesterday.

The third group of factors is suggested by the importance, even in the upper-income brackets, of service income. At any given time, only a limited part of the income differential of a top group is accounted for by the concentration of property yields: much of it comes from the high level of service income (professional and entrepreneurial earnings and the like). The secular rise in the upper incomes due to this source is likely to be less marked than in the service incomes of lower brackets, and for two somewhat different reasons. First, in so far as high levels of service incomes of given upper units are due to individual excellence (as is true of many professional and entrepreneurial pursuits), there is much less incentive for and possibility of keeping such incomes at continued high relative levels. Hence, the service incomes of the descendants of an *initially high*-level unit are not likely to show as strong an upward trend as the incomes for the large body of population at lower-income levels. Second, a substantial part of the rising trend in per capita income is due to interindustry shift, *i.e.,* a shift of workers from lower-income to higher-income industries. The possibilities of rise due to such interindustry shifts in the service incomes of the initially high-income groups are much more limited than for the population as a whole: they are already in high-income occupations and industries and the range for them toward higher-paid occupations is more narrowly circumscribed.

These three groups of factors, even disregarding such legislative and political intervention as is indicated above, are all characteristics of a dynamic growing economy. The differentials in rate of natural increase between the upper- and the lower-income groups are true only of a rapidly growing population—with or without immigration—but accompanied by declining death rates and declining birth rates, a demographic pattern associated in the past only with the growing Western economies. The impact of new industries on obsolescence of already established wealth as a source of property income is clearly a function of rapid growth, and the more rapid the growth the greater the impact will be. The effect of interindustry shifts on the rise of per capita income, particularly of lower-income groups, is also a function of growth since only in a growing economy is there much shift in the relative importance of the several industrial sectors. One can then say, in general, that the basic factor militating against the rise in upper-income shares that would be produced by the cumulative effects of concentration of savings, is the dynamism of a growing and free economic society.

Yet while the discussion answers the original question, it yields no determinate answer as to whether the trend in income shares of upper groups is upward, downward, or constant. Even for the specific question discussed, a determinate answer depends upon the relative balance of factors—continuous concentration of savings making for an increasing share and the offsetting forces tending to cancel this effect. To tell what the trend of upper-income shares is likely to be, we need to know much more about the weights of these conflicting pressures. Moreover, the discussion has brought to the surface factors that, in and of themselves, may cause either an upward or a downward trend in the share of upper-income groups and hence in income inequality—in distributions of annual or of secular income. For example, the new entrants into the upper groups—the upward "migrants"—who rise either because of exceptional ability or attachment to new industries or for a variety of other reasons—may be entering the fixed upper group of say the top 5 percent with an income differential—either annual or long-term—that may be relatively *greater* than that of entrants in the preceding generation. Nothing in the argument so far excludes this possibility—which would mean a rise in the share of upper-income groups, even if the share of the old "resident" part remains constant or even declines. Even disregarding other factors that will be noted in the next section, no firm conclusion as to trends of upper-income shares can be derived from the bare model discussed. Search for further data might yield evidence that would permit a reasonably rough but determinate conclusion; but I have no such evidence at hand.

THE SHIFT FROM AGRICULTURAL TO
NONAGRICULTURAL SECTORS

What about the trend toward greater inequality due to the shift from the agricultural to the nonagricultural sectors? In view of the importance of industrialization and urbanization in the process of economic growth, their implications for trends in the income distribution should be explored—even though we have neither the necessary data nor a reasonably complete theoretical model. . . .

. . . It seems most plausible to assume that in earlier periods of industrialization, even when the nonagricultural population was still relatively small in the total, its income distribution was more unequal than that of the agricultural population. This would be particularly so during the periods when industrialization and urbanization were proceeding apace and the urban population was being swelled, and fairly rapidly, by immigrants—either from the country's agricultural areas or from abroad. Under these conditions, the urban population would run the full gamut from low-income positions of recent entrants to the economic peaks of the established top-income groups. The urban income inequalities might be assumed to be far wider than those for the agricultural population which was organized in relatively small individual enterprises (large-scale units were rarer then than now).

If we grant the assumption of wider inequality of distribution in sector B,[3] the shares of the lower-income brackets should have shown a downward trend. Yet the earlier summary of empirical evidence indicates that during the last 50 to 75 years there has been no widening in income inequality in the

---

[3] The two sectors discussed are agriculture (A) and all others (B).—EDS.

developed countries but, on the contrary, some narrowing within the last two to four decades. It follows that the intrasector distribution—either for sector A or for sector B—must have shown sufficient narrowing of inequality to offset the increase called for by the factors discussed. Specifically, the shares of the *lower* income groups in sectors A and/or B must have increased sufficiently to offset the decline that would otherwise have been produced by a . . . [shift from sector A to sector B.—Eds.]

This narrowing in inequality, the offsetting rise in the shares of the lower brackets, most likely occurred in the income distribution for the urban groups, in sector B. While it may also have been present in sector A, it would have had a more limited effect on the inequality in the countrywide income distribution because of the rapidly diminishing weight of sector A in the total. Nor was such a narrowing of income inequality in agriculture likely: with industrialization, a higher level of technology permitted larger-scale units and, in the United States for example, sharpened the contrast between the large and successful business farmers and the subsistence sharecroppers of the South. Furthermore, since we accept the assumption of *initially* narrower inequality in the internal distribution of income in sector A than in sector B, any significant reduction in inequality in the former is less likely than in the latter.

Hence we may conclude that the major offset to the widening of income inequality associated with the shift from agriculture and the countryside to industry and the city must have been a rise in the income share of the lower groups within the nonagricultural sector of the population. This provides a lead for exploration in what seems to me a most promising direction: consideration of the pace and character of the economic growth of the urban population, with particular reference to the relative position of lower-income groups. Much is to be said for the notion that once the early turbulent phases of industrialization and urbanization had passed, a variety of forces converged to bolster the economic position of the lower-income groups within the urban population. The very fact that after a while, an increasing proportion of the urban population was "native," *i.e.,* born in cities rather than in the rural areas, and hence more able to take advantage of the possibilities of city life in preparation for the economic struggle, meant a better chance for organization and adaptation, a better basis for securing greater income shares than was possible for the newly "immigrant" population coming from the countryside or from abroad. The increasing efficiency of the older, established urban population should also be taken into account. Furthermore, in democratic societies the growing political power of the urban lower-income groups led to a variety of protective and supporting legislation, much of it aimed to counteract the worst effects of rapid industrialization and urbanization and to support the claims of the broad masses for more adequate shares of the growing income of the country. Space does not permit the discussion of demographic, political, and social considerations that could be brought to bear to explain the offsets to any declines in the shares of the lower groups. . . .

OTHER TRENDS RELATED TO THOSE IN INCOME INEQUALITY

One aspect of the conjectural conclusion just reached deserves emphasis because of its possible interrelation with other important elements in the process and theory of economic growth. The scanty empirical evidence suggests that the narrowing of income inequality in the developed countries is relatively recent and probably did not characterize the earlier stages of their growth. Likewise, the various factors that have been suggested above would explain stability and narrowing in income inequality in the later rather than in the earlier phases of industrialization and urbanization. Indeed, they would suggest widening inequality in these early phases of economic growth, especially in the older countries where the emergence of the new industrial system had shattering effects on long-established pre-industrial economic and social institutions. This timing characteristic is particularly applicable to factors bearing upon the lower-income groups: the dislocating effects of the agricultural and industrial revolutions, combined with the "swarming" of population incident upon a rapid decline in death rates and the maintenance or even rise of birth rates, would be unfavorable to the relative economic position of lower-income groups. Furthermore, there may also have been a preponderance in the earlier periods of factors favoring maintenance or increase in the shares of top-income groups: in so far as their position was bolstered by gains arising out of new industries, by an unusually rapid rate of creation of new fortunes, we would expect these forces to be relatively stronger in the early phases of industrialization than in the later when the pace of industrial growth slackens.

One might thus assume a long swing in the inequality characterizing the secular income structure: widening in the early phases of economic growth when the transition from the pre-industrial to the industrial civilization was most rapid; becoming stabilized for a while; and then narrowing in the later phases. This long secular swing would be most pronounced for older countries where the dislocation effects of the earlier phases of modern economic growth were most conspicuous; but it might be found also in the "younger" countries like the United States, if the period preceding marked industrialization could be compared with the early phases of industrialization, and if the latter could be compared with the subsequent phases of greater maturity.

If there is some evidence for assuming this long swing in relative inequality in the distribution of income before direct taxes and excluding free benefits from government, there is surely a stronger case for assuming a long swing in inequality of income net of direct taxes and including government benefits. Progressivity of income taxes and, indeed, their very importance characterize only the more recent phases of development of the presently developed countries; in narrowing income inequality they must have accentuated the downward phase of the long swing, contributing to the reversal of trend in the secular widening and narrowing of income inequality.

No adequate empirical evidence is available for checking this conjecture of a long secular swing in income inequality; nor can the phases be dated precisely. However, to make it more specific, I would place the early phase in which income inequality might have been widening, from about 1780 to 1850 in England; from about 1840 to 1890, and particularly from 1870 on in the United States; and, from the 1840s to the 1890s in Germany. I would put the phase of narrowing income inequality somewhat later in the United States and Germany than in England—perhaps beginning with the first world war in the former and in the last quarter of the nineteenth century in the latter.

Is there a possible relation between this secular swing in income inequality and the long swing in other important components of the growth process? For the older countries a long swing is observed in the rate of growth of population—the upward phase represented by acceleration in the rate of growth reflecting the early reduction in the death rate which was not offset by a decline in the birth rate (and in some cases was accompanied by a rise in the birth rate); and the downward phase represented by a shrinking in the rate of growth reflecting the more pronounced downward trend in the birth rate. Again, in the older countries, and also perhaps in the younger, there may have been a secular swing in the rate of urbanization, in the sense that the proportional additions to urban population and the measures of internal migration that produced this shift of population probably increased for a while—from the earlier much lower levels; but then tended to diminish as urban population came to dominate the country and as the rural reservoirs of migration became proportionally much smaller. For old, and perhaps for young countries also, there must have been a secular swing in the proportions of savings or capital formation to total economic product. Per capita product in pre-industrial times was not large enough to permit as high a nation-wide rate of saving or capital formation as was attained in the course of industrial development: this is suggested by present comparisons between net-capital-formation rates of 3 to 5 percent of national product in underdeveloped countries and rates of 10 to 15 percent in developed countries. If then, at least in the older countries, and perhaps even in the younger ones—prior to initiation of the process of modern development—we begin with low secular levels in the savings proportions, there would be a rise in the early phases to appreciably higher levels. We also know that during recent periods the net capital formation proportion and even the gross, failed to rise and perhaps even declined.

Other trends might be suggested that would possibly trace long swings similar to those for inequality in income structure, rate of growth of population, rate of urbanization and internal migration, and the proportion of savings or capital formation to national product. For example, such swings might be found in the ratio of foreign trade to domestic activities; in the aspects, if we could only measure them properly, of government activity that bear upon market forces (there must have been a phase of increasing freedom of market forces, giving way to greater intervention by government). But the suggestions already made suffice to indicate that the long swing in income inequality must be viewed as part of a wider process of economic growth, and interrelated with similar movements in other elements. The long alternation in the rate of growth of population can be seen partly as a cause, partly as an effect of the long swing in income inequality which was associated with a secular rise in real per capita income levels. The long swing in income inequality is also probably closely associated with the swing in capital-formation proportions—in so far as wider inequality makes for higher, and narrower inequality for lower, country-wide savings proportions.

COMPARISON OF DEVELOPED AND UNDERDEVELOPED COUNTRIES

What is the bearing of the experience of the developed countries upon the economic growth of underdeveloped countries? Let us examine briefly the data on income distribution in the latter, and speculate upon some of the implications.

As might have been expected, such data for underdeveloped countries are scanty. For the present purpose distributions of family income for India in 1949-1950, for Ceylon in 1950, and for Puerto Rico in 1948 were used. While the coverage is narrow and the margin of error wide, the data show that income distribution in these underdeveloped countries is somewhat *more* unequal than in the developed countries during the period after World War II. Thus the shares of the lower 3 quintiles are 28 percent in India, 30 percent in Ceylon, and 24 percent in Puerto Rico—compared with 34 percent in the United States and 36 percent in the United Kingdom. The shares of the top quintile are 55 percent in India, 50 percent in Ceylon, and 56 percent in Puerto Rico, compared with 44 percent in the United States and 45 percent in the United Kingdom.[4]

This comparison is for income before direct taxes and excluding free benefits from governments. Since the burden and progressivity of direct taxes are much greater in developed countries, and since it is in the latter that substantial volumes of free economic assistance are extended to the lower-income groups, a comparison in terms of income net of direct taxes and including government benefits would only accentuate the wider inequality of income distributions in the underdeveloped countries. Is this difference a reliable reflection of wider inequality also in the distribution of *secular* income levels in underdeveloped countries? Even disregarding the margins of error in the data, the possibility raised earlier in this paper that transient disturbances in income levels may be more conspicuous under conditions of primitive material and economic technology would affect the comparison just made.

---

[4] For sources of these data see "Regional Economic Trends and Levels of Living," submitted at the Norman Waite Harris Foundation Institute of the University of Chicago in November 1954 (in press in the volume of proceedings). This paper, and an earlier one, "Underdeveloped Countries and the Pre-industrial Phases in the Advanced Countries: An Attempt at Comparison," prepared for the World Population Meetings in Rome held in September 1954 (in press) discuss issues raised in this section.

Since the distributions cited reflect the annual income levels, a greater allowance should perhaps be made for transient disturbances in the distributions for the underdeveloped than in those for the developed countries. Whether such a correction would obliterate the difference is a matter on which I have no relevant evidence.

Another consideration might tend to support this qualification. Underdeveloped countries are characterized by low average levels of income per capita, low enough to raise the question how the populations manage to survive. Let us assume that these countries represent fairly unified population groups, and exclude, for the moment, areas that combine large native populations with small enclaves of nonnative, privileged minorities, *e.g.,* Kenya and Rhodesia, where income inequality, because of the excessively high income shares of the privileged minority, is appreciably wider than even in the underdeveloped countries cited above.[5] On this assumption, one may infer that in countries with low average income, the secular level of income in the lower brackets could not be below a fairly sizable proportion of average income—otherwise, the groups could not survive. This means, to use a purely hypothetical figure, that the secular level of the share of the lowest decile could not fall far short of 6 or 7 percent, *i.e.,* the lowest decile could not have a per capita income less than six or seven tenths of the country-wide average. In more advanced countries, with higher average per capita incomes, even the *secular* share of the lowest bracket could easily be a smaller fraction of the countrywide average, say as small as 2 or 3 percent for the lowest decile, *i.e.,* from a fifth to a third of the country-wide average—without implying a materially impossible economic position for that group. To be sure, there is in all countries continuous pressure to raise the relative position of the bottom-income groups; but the fact remains that the lower limit of the proportional share in the secular income structure is higher when the real country-wide per capita income is low than when it is high.

If the long-term share of the lower-income groups is larger in the underdeveloped than in the average countries, income inequality in the former should be narrower, not wider as we have found. However, if the lower brackets receive larger shares, and at the same time the very top brackets also receive larger shares—which would mean that the intermediate income classes would not show as great a progression from the bottom—the net effect may well be wider inequality. To illustrate, let us compare the distributions for India and the United States. The first quintile in India receives 8 percent of total income, more than the 6-percent share of the first quintile in the United States. But the second quintile in India receives only 9 percent, the third 11, and the fourth 16; whereas in the United States, the shares of these quintiles

---

[5] In one year since World War II, the non-African group in Southern Rhodesia, which accounted for only 5 percent of total population, received 57 percent of total income; in Kenya, the minority of only 2.9 percent of total population, received 51 percent of total income; in Northern Rhodesia, the minority of only 1.4 percent of total population, received 45 percent of total income. See United Nations, *National Income and Its Distribution in Underdeveloped Countries,* Statistical Paper, Ser. E, no. 3, 1951, Table 12, p. 19.

are 12, 16, and 22 respectively. This is a rough statistical reflection of a fairly common observation relating to income distributions in underdeveloped compared with developed countries. The former have no "middle" classes: there is a sharp contrast between the preponderant proportion of population whose average income is well below the generally low country-wide average, and a small top group with a very large relative income excess. The developed countries, on the other hand, are characterized by a much more gradual rise from low to high shares, with substantial groups receiving more than the high country-wide income average, and the top groups securing smaller shares than the comparable ordinal groups in underdeveloped countries.

It is, therefore, possible that even the distributions of secular income levels would be more unequal in underdeveloped than in developed countries —not in the sense that the shares of the lower brackets would be lower in the former than in the latter, but in the sense that the shares of the very top groups would be higher and that those of the groups below the top would all be significantly lower than a low country-wide income average. This is even more likely to be true of the distribution of income net of direct taxes and inclusive of free government benefits. But whether a high probability weight can be attached to this conjecture is a matter for further study.

In the absence of evidence to the contrary, I assume that it is true: that the secular income structure is somewhat more unequal in underdeveloped countries than in the more advanced—particularly in those of Western and Northern Europe and their economically developed descendants in the New World (the United States, Canada, Australia, and New Zealand). This conclusion has a variety of important implications and leads to some pregnant questions, of which only a few can be stated here.

In the first place, the wider inequality in the secular income structure of underdeveloped countries is associated with a much lower level of average income per capita. Two corollaries follow—and they would follow even if the income inequalities were of the same relative range in the two groups of countries. First, the impact is far sharper in the underdeveloped countries, where the failure to reach an already low countrywide average spells much greater material and psychological misery than similar proportional deviations from the average in the richer, more advanced countries. Second, positive savings are obviously possible only at much higher relative income levels in the underdeveloped countries: if in the more advanced countries some savings are possible in the fourth quintile, in the underdeveloped countries savings could be realized only at the very peak of the income pyramid, say by the top 5 or 3 percent. If so, the concentration of savings and of assets is even more pronounced than in the developed countries; and the effects of such concentration in the past may serve to explain the peculiar characteristics of the secular income structure in underdeveloped countries today.

The second implication is that this unequal income structure presumably coexisted with a low rate of growth of income per capita. The underdeveloped countries today have not always lagged behind the presently developed areas in level of economic performance; indeed, some of the former may have been the economic leaders of the world in the centuries preceding the last two. The countries of Latin America, Africa, and particularly those of Asia, are underdeveloped today because in the last two centuries, and even in recent decades, their rate of economic growth has been far lower than that in the Western world—and low indeed, if any growth there was, on a per capita basis. The underlying shifts in industrial structure, the opportunities for internal mobility and for economic improvement, were far more limited than in the more rapidly growing countries now in the developed category. There was no hope, within the lifetime of a generation, of a significantly perceptible rise in the level of real income, or even that the next generation might fare much better. It was this hope that served as an important and realistic compensation for the wide inequality in income distribution that characterized the presently developed countries during the earlier phases of their growth.

The third implication follows from the preceding two. It is quite possible that income inequality has not narrowed in the underdeveloped countries within recent decades. There is no empirical evidence to check this conjectural implication, but it is suggested by the absence, in these areas, of the dynamic forces associated with rapid growth that in the developed countries checked the upward trend of the upper-income shares that was due to the cumulative effect of continuous concentration of past savings; and it is also indicated by the failure of the political and social systems of underdeveloped countries to initiate the governmental or political practices that effectively bolster the weak positions of the lower-income classes. Indeed, there is a possibility that inequality in the secular income structure of underdeveloped countries may have widened in recent decades—the only qualification being that where there has been a recent shift from colonial to independent status, a privileged, *nonnative* minority may have been eliminated. But the implication, in terms of the income distribution among the *native* population proper, still remains plausible.

The somber picture just presented may be an oversimplified one. But I believe that it is sufficiently realistic to lend weight to the questions it poses—questions as to the bearing of the recent levels and trends in income inequality, and the factors that determine them, upon the future prospect of underdeveloped countries within the orbit of the free world.

The questions are difficult, but they must be faced unless we are willing completely to disregard past experience or to extrapolate mechanically oversimplified impressions of past development. The first question is: Is the pattern of the older developed countries likely to be repeated in the sense that in the early phases of industrialization in the underdeveloped countries income inequalities will tend to widen before the leveling forces become strong enough first to stabilize and then reduce income inequalities? While the future cannot be an exact repetition of the past, there are already certain elements in the present conditions of underdeveloped societies, *e.g.*, "swarming" of population due to sharp cuts in death rates unaccompanied by declines in birth rates— that threaten to widen inequality by depressing the relative position of lower-income groups even further. Furthermore, if and when industrialization begins, the dislocating effects on these societies, in which there is often an old hardened crust of economic and social institutions, are likely to be quite sharp—so sharp as to destroy the positions of some of the lower groups more rapidly than opportunities elsewhere in the economy may be created for them.

The next question follows from an affirmative answer to the first. Can the political framework of the underdeveloped societies withstand the strain which further widening of income inequality is likely to generate? This query is pertinent if it is realized that the real per capita income level of many underdeveloped societies today is lower than the per capita income level of the presently developed societies before *their* initial phases of industrialization. And yet the stresses of the dislocations incident to early phases of industrialization in the developed countries were sufficiently acute to strain the political and social fabric of society, force major political reforms, and sometimes result in civil war.

The answer to the second question may be negative, even granted that industrialization may be accompanied by a rise in real per capita product. If, for many groups in society, the rise is even partly offset by a decline in their proportional share in total product; if, consequently, it is accompanied by widening of income inequality, the resulting pressures and conflicts may necessitate drastic changes in social and political organization. This gives rise to the next and crucial question: How can either the institutional and political framework of the underdeveloped societies or the processes of economic growth and industrialization be modified to favor a sustained rise to higher levels of economic performance and yet avoid the fatally simple remedy of an authoritarian regime that would use the population as cannon-fodder in the fight for economic achievement? How to minimize the cost of transition and avoid paying the heavy price—in internal tensions, in long-run inefficiency in providing means for satisfying wants of human beings as individuals—which the inflation of political power represented by authoritarian regimes requires?

Facing these acute problems, one is cognizant of the dangers of taking an extreme position. One extreme—particularly tempting to us—is to favor repetition of past patterns of the now developed countries, patterns that, under the markedly different conditions of the presently underdeveloped countries, are almost bound to put a strain on the existing social and economic institutions and eventuate in revolutionary explosions and authoritarian regimes. There is danger in simple analogies; in arguing that because an unequal income distribution in Western Europe in the past led to accumulation of savings and financing of basic capital formation, the preservation or accentuation of present income inequalities in the underdeveloped countries is necessary to secure the same result. Even disregarding the implications for the lower-income groups, we may find that in at least some of these countries today the consumption propensities of upper-income groups are far higher and savings propensities far lower than were those of the more puritanical upper-income groups of the presently developed countries. Because they may have proved favorable in the past, it is dangerous to argue that completely free markets, lack of penalties implicit in progressive taxation, and the like are indispensable for the economic growth of the now underdeveloped countries. Under present conditions the results may be quite the opposite—withdrawal of accumulated assets to relatively "safe" channels, either by flight abroad or into real estate; and the inability of governments to serve as basic agents in the kind of capital formation that is indispensable to economic growth. It is dangerous to argue that, because in the past foreign investment provided capital resources to spark satisfactory economic growth in some of the smaller European countries or in Europe's descendants across the seas, similar effects can be expected today if only the underdeveloped countries can be convinced of the need of a "favorable climate." Yet, it is equally dangerous to take the opposite position and claim that the present problems are entirely new and that we must devise solutions that are the product of imagination unrestrained by knowledge of the past, and therefore full of romantic violence. What we need, and I am afraid it is but a truism, is a clear perception of past trends and of conditions under which they occurred, as well as knowledge of the conditions that characterize the underdeveloped countries today. With this as a beginning, we can then attempt to translate the elements of a properly understood past into the conditions of an adequately understood present.

CONCLUDING REMARKS

In concluding this paper, I am acutely conscious of the meagerness of reliable information presented. The paper is perhaps 5 percent empirical information and 95 percent speculation, some of it possibly tainted by wishful thinking. The excuse for building an elaborate structure on such a shaky foundation is a deep interest in the subject and a wish to share it with members of the Association. The formal and no less genuine excuse is that the subject is central to much of economic analysis and thinking; that our knowledge of it is inadequate; that a more cogent view of the whole field may help channel our interests and work in intellectually profitable directions; that speculation is an effective way of presenting a broad view of the field; and that so long as it is recognized as a collection of hunches calling for further investigation rather than a set of fully tested conclusions, little harm and much good may result.

Let me add two final comments. The first bears upon the importance of additional knowledge and a better view of the secular structure of personal-income distribution. Since this distribution is a focal point at which the functioning of the economic system impinges upon the human beings who are the living members of society and for whom and through whom the society operates, it is an important datum for understanding the reactions and behavior patterns of human beings as producers, consumers, and savers. It follows that better knowledge and comprehension of the subject are indispensable, not only in and of itself but also as a step in learning more about the functioning of society—in both the long and short run. Without better knowledge of the trends in secular income structure and of the factors that determine them, our understanding of the whole process of economic growth is limited; and any insight we may derive from observing changes in country-wide aggregates over time will be defective if these changes are not translated into movements of shares of the various income groups.

But more than that, such knowledge will contribute to a better evaluation of past and present theorizing on the subject of economic growth. It was pointed out in the opening lines of this paper that the field is distinguished by looseness of concepts, extreme scarcity of relevant data, and, particularly, pressures of strongly held opinions. The distribution of national product among the various groups is a subject of acute interest to many and is discussed at length in any half-articulate society. When empirical data are scanty, as they are in this field, the natural tendency in such discussion is to generalize from what little experience is available—most often the short stretch of historical experience within the horizon of the interested scholar, which is brought to bear upon the particular policy problems in the forefront. It has repeatedly been observed that the grand dynamic economics of the classical school of the late eighteenth and early nineteenth centuries was a generalization, the main empirical contents of which were the observed developments during half to three quarters of a century in England, the mother country of that school; and that it bore many of the limitations which the brevity and exceptional character of that period and that place naturally imposed upon the theoretical structure. It is also possible that much of Marxian economics may be an overgeneralization of imperfectly understood trends in England during the first half of the nineteenth century when income inequality may have widened; and that extrapolations of these trends (*e.g.,* increasing misery of the working classes, polarization of society, etc.) proved wrong because due regard was not given to the possible effects upon the economic and social structure of technological changes, extension of the economic system to much of the then unoccupied world, and the very structure of human wants. Wider empirical foundations, observation of a greater variety of historical experience, and a recognition that any body of generalizations tends to reflect some limited stretch of historical experience must force us to evaluate any theory—past or present—in terms of its empirical contents and the consequent limits of its applicability—a precept which naturally should also be applied to the oversimplified generalizations contained in the present paper.

My final comment relates to the directions in which further exploration of the subject is likely to lead us. Even in this simple initial sketch, findings in the field of demography were used and references to political aspects of social life were made. Uncomfortable as are such ventures into unfamiliar and perhaps treacherous fields, they can not and should not be avoided. If we are to deal adequately with processes of economic growth, processes of long-term change in which the very technological, demographic, and social frameworks are also changing—and in ways that decidedly affect the operation of economic forces proper—it is inevitable that we venture into fields beyond those recognized in recent decades as the province of economics proper. For the study of the economic growth of nations, it is imperative that we become more familiar with findings in those related social disciplines that can help us understand population growth patterns, the nature and forces in technological change, the factors that determine the characteristics and trends in political institutions, and generally patterns of behavior of human beings— partly as a biological species, partly as social animals. Effective work in this field necessarily calls for a shift from market economics to political and social economy.

P. T. BAUER

and

B. S. YAMEY

||||||||||||||||||||||||||||||||||||||||||||||||||||||||||||||||||||||||||||||||||||||||||||||||||||||||||||||||||||||||||||||||||||||||||||||||||||||

Economic Progress and Occupational Distribution

The principal purpose of this article is to examine the validity and significance of the widely held view that economic progress is generally associated with certain distinct, necessary, and predictable changes in occupational distribution, in particular with a relative increase in the numbers engaged in tertiary activities.[1] Our method is largely analytical; but since a strong empirical basis is claimed for the generalization we are examining, we have found it necessary to make frequent descriptive reference to the composition of economic activity in economies at different stages of development. Most of the description is concentrated in the first section of the article, which de-

From *Economic Journal* (December 1951), pp. 741-755, with omissions. Reprinted by permission of the Royal Economic Society and the authors.

---

[1] "For convenience in international comparisons production may be defined as primary, secondary and tertiary. Under the former we include agricultural and pastoral production, fishing, forestry and hunting. Mining is more properly included with secondary production, covering manufacture, building construction and public works, gas and electricity supply. Tertiary production is defined by difference as consisting of all other economic activities, the principal of which are distribution, transport, public administration, domestic service and all other activities producing a non-material output." Colin Clark, *The Conditions of Economic Progress,* 1st ed., p. 182.

See also, Professor A. G. B. Fisher, *Economic Progress and Social Security,* pp. 5 and 6.

scribes and analyzes the volume and significance of trading activity in British West Africa. The remaining sections of the article examine the analytical and statistical foundations of the generalization and suggest that these are defective.

I

The few available occupational statistics of backward economies, especially in the colonies, purport to show that the great bulk of the population is occupied in agriculture. This impression is also often conveyed in official statements on economic activity in these territories. An example may be taken from *An African Survey:*

> In the Northern Province of Nigeria, at the census of 1931, about 84 percent of occupied males whose returns permitted them to be classified were shown as engaged in agriculture and fishing, about 9 percent in manufacture, and under 3 percent in commerce and finance. . . . For Southern Nigeria less detailed information is available. The returns, which are less reliable than those for Northern Nigeria, would suggest that the proportion of males engaged in agriculture is about 82 percent and that concerned with handicrafts about 4.7 percent.[2]

Trade and transport are not mentioned. No attempt is made to reconcile this with another statement (on the same page) that almost 30 percent of the population of Nigeria lived in towns of over 5000 inhabitants. In the same vein the official *Annual Report on Nigeria* states year after year that the great majority of the population is occupied in agriculture: trade is not among the other occupations listed.

In contrast to these statements and statistics a remarkable multitude of traders, especially of small-scale sellers of both local produce and of imported merchandise, is a most conspicuous feature of West Africa. This is so apparent that it has not escaped attention. It is freely said by responsible administrators that in the southern parts of Nigeria and the Gold Coast everybody is engaged in trade, and this is hardly an exaggeration.

For reasons to be explained it is not possible to give specific quantitative information about the volume of trade or of the numbers engaged in it. Certain sporadic but conservative data, relating, for example, to numbers of market stallholders and hawkers' licenses, indicate that the number of selling points, including children hawking very small quantities of goods, is very large in the principal markets. But the figures give an imperfect idea of the multitude of people engaged either part time or whole time in selling small quantities of goods or conveying them to dispersed points of sale. In the aggregate there is an enormous amount of activity the quantitative significance of which is obvious to the observer.

The seriously misleading impression created by official statistics and statements derives from the inappropriateness of classification by distinct occupational categories in an economy in which occupational specialization is

---

[2] *An African Survey,* 2d ed., pp. 1425-1426.

imperfect. The economic activity of a large proportion of the population of West Africa is better described as the performance of a number of different things rather than as the pursuit of a definite occupation. In many of the so-called agricultural households the head of the household trades part time even during the normally short farming season, and more actively outside the season, whilst members of the family trade intermittently throughout the year. Even if only main activities are considered, it is doubtful whether five-sixths of the population is engaged in agriculture; when it is realized that even the head of the family is likely to have part time economic activities and that many of his dependents (including children) are engaged at least periodically in trade, it becomes clear that the official statistics in their present form are apt to mislead.

The imperfect specialization of economic activity is not confined to the agricultural community. Many African doctors and lawyers and almost all the leading chiefs have extensive trading interests. Government employees and servants of the European population trade part time, either importing merchandise or dealing in merchandise and foodstuffs bought locally. The fluidity of activity extends to personal relations where they bear closely on economic life. A prominent African trader in Lagos whose children are being educated at expensive universities and schools in England includes his wife among his principal retailer customers. Similar commercial relations exist between other prominent Africans and their wives and children.

Even where the conceptual and statistical difficulties arising from imperfect occupational specialization are full appreciated[3] it is difficult to collect the required information on subsidiary activities of individuals, particularly on part-time trade. Africans frequently do not regard trade as an occupation, especially when carried on by dependents, and would not refer to it as such when questioned, because they regard it as part of existence and not as a distinct occupation. In many cases it may not be possible to draw the line between the social and commercial activities of, say, a group of women traders in the market. There is, however, no doubt that the commercial element is generally substantial.

Once the level of economic activity has risen from that of a subsistence economy to that of an emerging exchange economy—a process which is encouraged and promoted by the activities of traders—the task of distribution may require a substantial volume of resources. Much depends upon physical and climatic conditions. But the circumstances of West Africa are certainly not exceptional in requiring a large volume of distributive activity. The large number of dispersed farmers and holdings, poor natural communications and long distances and the difficulties of prolonged storage in the open, together postulate a substantial volume of resources in distribution and transport for raising and maintaining the economy above the subsistence level even at an early stage in economic development. In this type of economy the indispensable tasks of assembly, bulking, transport, breaking of bulk, and dispersal

---

[3] It is not suggested that those responsible for census work in the colonies are unaware of these difficulties. But they are not appreciated by many of those who publish and use the results of their work.

may require a large proportion of available resources. Moreover, in an economy which has recently emerged from the subsistence level, some transactions are still likely to be on a barter basis. Barter tends to use more resources, especially labor, than a fully developed money economy to transact a given volume of trade.

There is in West Africa widespread involuntary idleness of unskilled labor, resulting from lack of other cooperant resources, especially capital, to set it to work. This lack of employment is a major feature of comparatively undeveloped economies which in the aggregate comprise probably over half of the population of the world, including India, China, Java, large parts of Eastern and Southern Europe and much of Africa. The dependence of the volume of employment on the amount of the stock of capital used to be a major topic of political economy. The subject gradually receded from economic discussion as economists became preoccupied mainly with unemployment in advanced industrial economies, resulting not so much from lack of cooperant resources as from fluctuations in aggregate demand or various other influences discouraging investment and enterprise. Interest in the subject has revived with the growing realization of its importance. Very recently unemployment in the "empty economy"[4] has brought the problem nearer home.

The missing cooperant factor (or factors) of production can be capital, land, or technical and administrative skill. The type of scarcity or its incidence varies greatly in different regions and even districts in West Africa as elsewhere. But in many regions the low level of capital and of suitable administrative and technical skills constitutes the principal shortage.

Entry into small-scale trade is easy, as at this level no technical or administrative skill is required and only very little capital. Trade is attractive even for very low rewards in view of the absence of more profitable alternatives.[5] Women and children are also available for trade, partly for social reasons; for example, in some areas the wife is expected to make a contribution to the family's income; also there is little for women to do in the house and there are few schools for children.[6]

The type of resources to be found in trade and transport depends, given the state of technique, upon the relative terms at which different productive resources are available. In an economy such as West Africa, where capital is scarce and expensive and unskilled labor abundant and cheap, the large volume of resources in distribution and transport consists very largely of labor. As compared with more advanced economies there is a mass emphasis on labor rather than on capital. This tendency, which may proceed very far

---

[4] J. R. Hicks, "The Empty Economy," *Lloyds Bank Review* (July 1947).

[5] The relative increase in the numbers engaged in retail distribution in Great Britain and elsewhere during the depression of the early 1930s is a more familiar example which can be largely explained in terms of reduced supply price arising from the absence of suitable alternatives.

[6] It is possible that the numbers attracted into trade in West Africa are increased because of a largely institutional rigidity in money wages. But even if money wages were to fall to the equilibrium level, the number who would find trade attractive would still be very large as long as the underlying economic factors remained broadly unchanged.

and reveal unsuspected possibilities, permeates West African trading arrangements; a few examples will illustrate it.

In West Africa there is an extensive trade in empty containers such as kerosene, cigarette and soup tins, flour, salt, sugar and cement bags and beer bottles. Some types of container are turned into household articles or other commodities. Small oil-lamps are made from cigarette and soup tins, whilst salt bags are made into shirts or tunics. But more usually the containers are used again in the storage and movement of goods. Those who seek out, purchase, carry and distribute second-hand containers maintain the stock of capital. They prevent the destruction of the containers, usually improve their condition, distribute them to where they can best be used, and so extend their usefulness, the intensity of their use, and their effective life. The activities of the traders represent a substitution of labor for capital. Most of the entrepreneurs in the container trade are women or children. The substitution is economic as long as six or eight hours of their time are less valuable (in view of the lack of alternatives) than the small profit to be made from the sale of a few empty containers. So far from the system being wasteful it is highly economic in substituting superabundant for scarce resources; within the limits of available technical skill nothing is wasted in West Africa.

For various reasons, of which the low level of capital is one, the individual agriculturalist produces on a very small scale. Moreover, the same lack of capital is reflected in the absence of suitable storage facilities and of cash reserves. As a result each producer has to dispose of small quantities of produce at frequent intervals as they become available during and immediately after the harvesting season. This postulates a large number of intermediaries, who, because of the high cost of capital, employ methods of transportation using relatively little capital and much labor. Donkey and bicycle transport are examples, while in some cases there is still head loading and human porterage, especially in the short-distance movement of local crops. The available transport equipment is used continuously with the assistance of large quantities of labor (subject to frequent breakdowns owing to poor roads and low technical skill).

The same phenomenon of the more intensive use of capital, that is its more rapid turnover, can be observed in the breaking of bulk into the minute quantities in which imported merchandise is bought by the ultimate consumer. The purchase of a box of matches is often still a wholesale transaction as the buyer frequently breaks bulk and resells the contents to the final consumer in small bundles of ten to fifteen matches. Similarly, at the petty retail stage sugar is sold in lots of three cubes, trade perfume by the drop, salt by the cigarette tin and cheap biscuits by the small heap of three or six. The small purchases are the result of low incomes and low capital, and the activities of the numerous petty retailers represent a substitution of labor for capital.

In Nigeria the small number of telephones and the low rate of literacy render it necessary for the importing firms and the larger distributors to use the services of numerous intermediaries to keep contact with smaller traders and to distribute their goods to them at an economic rate of turnover. The intermediaries reduce the size of stocks which need to be held. This is of particular importance, since the low level of fixed capital tends to enhance the economy's requirements of working capital. The large accumulation of un-railed groundnuts in the producing region of Nigeria is a familiar instance of a general problem.

The narrowness of markets and the backwardness of communications are reflected in interregional price differences which provide profitable opportunities for successful arbitrage (particularly in locally produced goods), from region to region. This attracts traders and intermediaries, and also makes it profitable for nontrading travelers to take part in trade, which they frequently do on a casual basis.

The foregoing may be summarized as follows: in West Africa, as in other emerging economies, the indispensable task of commodity distribution is expensive relatively to available resources; of the available resources, capital is scarce and unskilled labor is abundant; the multiplicity of traders is the result of the mass use of unskilled labor instead of capital in the performance of the task of distribution. There is an extensive demand for the services of intermediaries, and there is a large section of the population available to perform these services at a low supply price in terms of daily earnings.

II

The description and analysis of Section I show that there are severe limitations and qualifications to the view that a high proportion of labor in tertiary production is both a consequence of and a pointer to a high standard of living. As is well known, this generally held view derives from the statistical investigations and analyses of Mr. Colin Clark and Professor A. G. B. Fisher. Thus according to Mr. Colin Clark:

> Studying economic progress in relation to the economic structure of different countries, we find a very firmly established generalization that a high average level of real income per head is always associated with a high proportion of the working population engaged in tertiary industries. . . . Low real income per head is always associated with a low proportion of the working population engaged in tertiary production and a high percentage in primary production, culminating in China, where 75-80 percent of the population are primary producers. High average real income per head compels a large proportion of producers to engage in tertiary production.[7]

Professor Fisher writes:

> We may say that in every progressive economy there has been a steady shift of employment and investment from the essential "primary" activities, without whose products life in even its most primitive forms would be impossible, to secondary activities of all kinds, and to a still greater extent into tertiary production. . . .
>
> The shifts of employment towards secondary and tertiary production revealed by the census are the inescapable reflection of economic progress.[8]

---

[7] *Op. cit.,* pp. 6-7.
[8] *Op. cit.,* pp. 6-7.

It would appear that the general proposition of Mr. Clark and Professor Fisher is based partly on analytical reasoning and partly on statistical evidence. Both types of verification appear to be defective.

The analytical reasoning purporting to sustain the generalization seems to be based on the view that tertiary production is less essential than primary or secondary production; and that its products are in the nature of luxuries which cannot be afforded in economies with low real incomes. In essence the argument is that the income elasticity of demand for tertiary products is higher than that for the products of primary and secondary activities; and that therefore the demand for tertiary products increases relatively more rapidly with economic progress. Moreover, it is argued that technical progress is relatively slower in tertiary production. For both reasons taken together the proportion of occupied labor in tertiary production is supposed to rise with economic progress. The next section calls into question the validity of this reasoning; in Section IV it is suggested that the statistical verification claimed for the generalization is inconclusive.

III

The analytical basis of the generalization of Mr. Clark and Professor Fisher is open to criticism on several independent grounds of which the following are the most important. First, a substantial proportion of tertiary products are not luxuries with a relatively high income elasticity of demand; conversely, some products of primary and secondary production, possibly on a large scale in their aggregate, are such luxuries. Secondly, there may be large-scale substitution of capital for labor in tertiary production in the course of economic progress. Thirdly, the concept of the income elasticity of demand applied to a whole economy raises problems of aggregation which render doubtful any universal proposition about changes in its average value in conditions of change and economic growth; and this is particularly doubtful when relative factor prices and the distribution of incomes change.

For reasons already mentioned in Section I the distributive task in the early stages of economic development is likely to be expensive in terms of *all* resources. A considerable volume of trading and transport is necessary to develop and sustain an exchange economy at an early stage of its development; it is an essential prerequisite for the development of specialization and thus to the raising of productivity in primary production. Thus the proportion of resources engaged in tertiary production, notably in trade and transport, is likely to be high. It is possible that this proportion may fall at certain stages because the distributive task becomes relatively easier and less expensive in resources as the economy develops. The task may become lighter with the growth of internal security, the development and improvement of communications, and the growth and stabilization of markets, all of which contribute toward more regular and continuous commercial contacts, more intensive use of available resources in distribution, and an increase in the size of trading units. These improvements are likely to have differential effects on productivity in various types of economic activity. It is not unlikely that trade and transport may be particularly favorably affected, and thus that the proportion of resources engaged in them may decline. This decline may continue until the fall is arrested by the possibly increasing volume of other kinds of tertiary products (including more elaborate distributive services) which may be called for at higher levels of real income.

Tertiary production, as it is usually understood, comprises a heterogeneous collection of different services. Some of these are qualitatively indispensable throughout economic development and quantitatively important at an early stage; others are not indispensable at all stages and are quantitatively important only in more advanced economies. The term "tertiary" carries the misleading suggestion that all these services belong to the latter category of luxuries.

There is no *a priori* reason to believe that as wealth increases a greater proportion of the luxuries consumed must be products of tertiary activities. The durable consumer goods of the North American economies provide numerous examples on a large scale of heavy expenditure on the products of secondary activities with growing wealth. Expensive motor cars, jewelery, works of art, mass-produced but high-grade textiles and handmade bespoke clothes and shoes are products of secondary activities.[9]

The proportion of all resources in tertiary production will not provide an index of economic progress. Moreover, even if it did it would not follow that the proportion of occupied labor engaged in tertiary production must rise with economic progress. This proposition would be valid only if additionally it were legitimate to assume that labor and other productive resources were employed in tertiary production in fixed proportions. This would be true only if substitution were not possible in the whole range of tertiary production, or if the relative terms upon which labor and other factors of production could be obtained remained unchanged throughout the whole course of economic progress. These assumptions are inadmissible. Technical possibilities of substitution between productive resources are obviously possible in tertiary production; and clearly the terms on which labor and capital are available are certain to change in a growing economy.

In Section I examples have been given to show the emphasis in the use of labor rather than capital in tertiary production in an underdeveloped economy. An example has also been given (the trade in used containers) to show how a tertiary activity expands with a lavish use of labor to make good a shortage in the products of secondary production. Conversely, examples abound in more advanced industrialized economies where capital replaces labor in tertiary activities and where secondary production expands to economize on labor-intensive tertiary activities. There are familiar examples on a large scale in domestic services, laundry and repair services, and restaurant and retailing services, where capital equipment is now used instead of labor. The purchase of precooked or prepared canned or processed food, or of paper cups and plates intended for one use only, represents an extension of

---

[9] Perhaps more fancifully purchases of fur coats, oysters, caviar, lobsters, pheasants, and orchids sustain hunting, fishing, and farming which are primary activities.

secondary production to replace the tertiary activities in the kitchen. The mass substitution of capital for labor in tertiary activity in North America is as striking as the reverse substitution in West Africa.[10]

The neglect of the "substitution effect" destroys the general validity of the quantitative law connecting society's real income and the proportion of occupied population in tertiary production. Technical progress may greatly affect the demand for labor in primary, secondary, and tertiary production, the possibilities of substitution between labor and other resources, and the relative supply prices of productive resources.

Changes in relative factor prices and differential rates of technical progress in different branches of production will also affect the relative prices at which different luxuries (that is, goods or services with relatively high income elasticities of demand whether the products of primary, secondary, or tertiary production) are available to consumers. This need not necessarily favor the luxuries which are the products of tertiary activities. If it were true, as is sometimes assumed, that productivity increases faster in secondary than in tertiary production, there would be a tendency for consumers to substitute luxuries which are produced by secondary production to those produced by tertiary production.[11]. . .

The foregoing analysis may now be summarized. Even if acceptable statistics were found which should show that the proportion of tertiary activities has increased in particular countries with economic progress, the findings would not be evidence of any necessary or predictable tendency. Tertiary production is an aggregation of many dissimilar activities, including domestic service, government service, transport, retail and wholesale distribution, entertainment, education, and others. There is no reason why the demand for every one of these should follow a common trend. The only feature common to all tertiary production is that the output is nonmaterial. This does not appear to provide a logical category of significance in the analysis of demand or of economic progress. Moreover, on the supply side the proportion of the labor force in tertiary production depends upon a number of different forces, the individual and total effect of which is in no way unambiguously determined by secular changes in the national income. Thus any observed correlation between economic progress and occupational distribution should be regarded as more in the nature of a statistical accident than as an indication or proof of a significant economic law.

IV

The empirical verification seems to be based upon occupational statistics which generally show both a high proportion of the occupied population in

---

[10] Of course, even in West Africa the time may come when eight hours of a woman's time may be more valuable than the profit margin on the sale of three beer bottles.

[11] There is no *a priori* reason why technical progress should always be relatively more rapid in primary and secondary production than in tertiary production. But even if it were, it would support Mr. Clark's generalization only if the possibility of substitution mentioned in the text is disregarded.

tertiary industries in advanced countries compared with underdeveloped countries and also an increasing proportion in time series for individual developing countries. These types of comparison seem to be vitiated principally on two counts. First, occupational statistics cannot take into account important difficulties arising out of imperfect economic specialization. Secondly, the comparability of these statistics is affected by shifts of labor between unpaid and paid activities. . . .

It would seem that the classification of economic activities into three types, while superficially convenient and clear, conceals large arbitrary elements which greatly reduce its value. The activities of the agricultural producer selling his crops can be regarded partly as primary and partly as tertiary; this is particularly evident where he sells to the final consumer. Yet until they are taken over by an intermediary, his activities will be regarded as primary. Where the intermediary is a member of the family, the activity may continue to be classed as primary. Its tertiary character is likely to be recognized only when the intermediary is an independent middleman. Since the emergence of an intermediary is likely to reduce the total effort in marketing a given volume of produce, tertiary activity may appear to be increasing at a time when it is actually decreasing. . . .

The substitution of unpaid labor, with or without capital, for paid labor (or vice versa) is a form of substitution which affects the proportion of occupied labor in tertiary production and which illustrates and emphasizes a conceptual difficulty present in a wide range of problems of economic statistics, particularly of indices of economic welfare. Such substitution takes place at all levels of economic progress, and not necessarily in the same direction at any given level. An obvious example in an advanced economy is the substitution of the activities of the household for those of the paid domestic servant; conversely, the household may frequently purchase the services of restaurants, laundries, and repair agencies. Economic progress provides no general indication of the direction in which the shift between paid and unpaid labor will take place. Retail trade provides examples. In a poor economy the poverty of consumers does not allow them to buy in advance of requirements and to store their purchases. The tasks of holding stocks and of breaking bulk into the small quantities required for almost daily consumption devolve upon the paid intermediary. In these instances the activities of middlemen arise in response to the needs of poor consumers, to whom they secure access to commodities which would otherwise be outside their reach. By contrast, in advanced economies today housewives may store substantial quantities of consumer goods, especially of food, and may actually break bulk themselves. This development has gone far in North America. The tertiary activity remains, but unpaid labor of consumers and their own capital are being substituted for the services of the intermediary.

The examples in the preceding paragraph underline the arbitrariness of certain distinctions which are fundamental to national income and employment statistics. The shifting lines of demarcation suggest the advisability of caution in the use of such statistics as indices of economic welfare or as the basis of extrapolation.

PART FIVE

Problems of Meaning and Measurement

BERNARD OKUN

and

RICHARD W. RICHARDSON

||||||||||||||||||||||||||||||||||||||||||||||||||||||||||||||||||||||||||||||||||||||||||||||||||||||||||||||||||||||||||||||||||||||||||||||||||||||||||||||

Economic Development: Concepts and Meaning

Despite the easy familiarity with which we speak of "economic development," the concept turns out, upon examination, to have rather complex and elusive meaning and implications. It seems wise, therefore, to devote some attention to its definition, as a prerequisite to clearer understanding of this field.

A TENTATIVE DEFINITION

What is "economic development"? We may first agree that the word "development" should in some sense be synonymous, or at least identified with, a long-run, sustained process involving improvement or progress. Furthermore, it is commonly agreed that "economic" refers to the material plane. Thus, at the most general level, "economic development" may be defined as a sustained, secular improvement in material well-being, which we may consider to be reflected in an increasing flow of goods and services. Perhaps, as an aside, it should be noted that while the *definition* of economic development is cast in material terms, the *study* of this subject is concerned with those changes—social, cultural, political, as well as economic—which contribute to or impede material progress.

ECONOMIC DEVELOPMENT AND SOCIAL WELFARE

Economists realize that it is a long step from material progress narrowly construed to improvements in social welfare in the broadest sense of the term. Generally, we expect economic progress to contribute positively to social well-being. But it is perfectly conceivable that social improvement may not always be coincident with economic progress; such progress may even occur at the expense of a deterioration of other, highly valued aspects of life.

Historians have illuminated some of these conflicts in connection with

230

the social changes associated with the Industrial Revolution in Europe. The enclosure movement, for example, was a prerequisite to improved agricultural productivity, but it created a large, landless class which of itself produced adverse social consequences. Similarly, some modern observers, particularly social anthropologists, are not a little fearful that the initiation of rapid economic change, especially when it is introduced from the outside, will prove to be, on balance, a disservice to traditional "underdeveloped" societies. Some countries, characterized by very poor economic performance, nevertheless have highly developed and very stable social and political structures which, though they may be, in and of themselves, important underlying sources of poor economic performance, are highly valued in terms of noneconomic criteria of human welfare. The extended family system, for example, may be high in the scale of social values; yet, to the degree that it inhibits individual economic initiative, as will be discussed in Part Seven, it tends to hamper economic development.

ECONOMIC DEVELOPMENT AND ECONOMIC WELFARE

Having decided to confine the concept of economic development to matters involving material well-being, we require some aggregate measure of the flow of goods and services, the stuff from which such material well-being is made. The index commonly used for measuring this flow is the Gross National Product (GNP), the value of all final goods and services produced with the components weighted at market prices.

One weakness of the GNP as a measure of economic progress and material well-being is that one of its major components—investment—is taken in gross terms: it includes the value of all machinery, plant, and other investment goods produced in the course of the year. But part of gross investment does not constitute a net addition to capital stock because some capital equipment previously produced has been subject to depreciation during the year. Mere replacement of worn-out investment goods does not lead to a net increase in economic capacity; it is only a means of maintaining the level of economic output previously attained. Therefore, there is ground for eliminating depreciation from the index; this leaves us with Net National Product (NNP), which is GNP minus depreciation.[1] (Professor Simon Kuznets, who has pioneered in the field of national income statistics, discusses some conceptual problems of measurement posed by these indices in the following selection.)

From what we have said earlier, it is clear that sustained growth in real national income does not inevitably imply an improvement in social welfare.[2]

---

[1] Some economists use the terms "net national product" and "national income" interchangeably, a practice we shall follow. Others choose to follow the United States Department of Commerce definition of "national income," which is net national product minus indirect business taxes.

[2] Real national income is defined as national income in constant prices; that is, a change in the price level does not itself affect the index.

What is worse, it cannot even be taken to mean an improvement in *economic* welfare.

Real national income is an aggregate measure of economic output. In order to relate this measure to individual economic welfare, we must find, as a first approximation, what on the average is available to each person. Therefore, it is necessary to distinguish between real national income and real per capita income, the latter being defined as real national income divided by total population. These two indices may move in opposite directions; for example, a *growth* in real national income may be accompanied by a more rapid growth of population; therefore per capita income would *decline*. It is also possible for the reverse situation to occur: because of a sharp drop in population, due to either a rise in the mortality rate or an increase in net emigration, a decline in real national income may accompany a rise in per capita income.

Which index is used as a measure of development depends, of course, upon whether one focuses upon the aggregate or upon the individual. For example, if one is concerned with the impact of development upon military power, then real national income is the more appropriate index; however, if one is interested in an improvement in individual economic welfare, then real per capita income (henceforth to be referred to simply as per capita income) is more appropriate. Perhaps the definition of economic development should most reasonably be taken as involving a rise *both* in real national income and in per capita income.

Even a rise in per capita income is not prima-facie evidence of an improvement in individual economic welfare. Per capita income, as a measure of economic welfare, may be misleading because it focuses on the fruits of economic activity while neglecting the sacrifice associated with the activity itself. It is generally assumed that work and effort constitute a disutility. If a greater output is attained only at the expense of a greater outlay of work and effort on the part of the population, the rise in per capita income may be accompanied by a fall (or a slower rise) in economic welfare. Historically, as the Western economies have developed, the work week has been shortened and the amount of leisure time has increased. This suggests that economic welfare has increased more rapidly than an index of per capita income would indicate, because leisure is a component of economic welfare but not of per capita income. In general, the more highly a society values leisure, the less direct is the relation between income per capita and economic welfare.

Because of the problem of allowing for leisure, an index of output per man-hour, rather than output (or income) per capita, might be a more suitable measure of economic welfare. Such an index measures not only output from economic activity (in the numerator) but also the input of human resources (in the denominator). The weakness of this type of index is that the average level of material well-being cannot be deduced from it with certainty. However, because output per man-hour significantly influences the average level of material well-being, it is not surprising that in fact there is a high positive correlation between the two.

Similar to the question of labor input is that of natural and irreproducible resources. One could argue that the depletion of such resources is not relevant to any measure of economic well-being or welfare if the present population of a country chooses to disregard the future entirely. If the population does place some value on the conservation of resources for future generations, however, the depletion of natural resources should perhaps be regarded as a negative factor in any assessment of economic welfare and the economy's performance.

Because the ultimate objective of economic activity is to increase the flow of goods and services to consumers, some economists argue that the concept of economic development should incorporate, as a prescriptive norm, some criterion of generally improved living standards. This raises a further question concerning the relevance of the per capita income index as a gauge of material well-being. National income and, of course, per capita income include not only present consumption goods but also investment goods destined to generate a future stream of consumption (and additional investment) goods. Thus, if in the extreme case one were to disregard the future entirely, no satisfaction would be derived from investment goods (because the present value of the future stream of consumption goods would then be zero), and economic welfare would derive only from present consumption. Hence, an index of consumption per capita would be a more meaningful measure of economic welfare than income per capita.

Because, in fact, people do not discount the future entirely, the problem is far more complex. An increase in investment, accomplished at the expense of a reduction of *present* consumption, will increase the stream of *future* consumption. For example, the Soviet Union is sacrificing present consumption partly for the purpose of enhancing future consumption. By contrast, the United States is devoting a relatively larger proportion of output to consumption goods, reflecting a shorter subjective time horizon. Therefore, an index of consumption per capita which purports to contrast differences in economic welfare between the Soviet Union and the United States is inadequate because it fails to allow for the different valuations of the future made by the public in the United States, on the one hand, and by the planners of the Soviet Union, on the other.

The concept of per capita income is obtained simply by dividing total income by population size; the *distribution* of income does not enter into the calculation. Therefore per capita income can be a misleading index of the state of development or the economic welfare of a country. A striking illustration of this is the case of Kuwait, which has an exceedingly high level of per capita income but which, by no stretch of the imagination, can be considered a developed country. Because of extensive royalties from oil, its aggregate income is very high relative to its small population; nevertheless, almost the entire population lives in poverty because the bulk of royalties accrue to the country's ruler. Clearly, the distribution of income is critical in assessing economic welfare, but attempts to specify some particular "satisfactory" distribution of income inevitably bog down in a morass of ethical complications, some of which involve interpersonal comparisons of utility. Still, even though value judgments are involved, the problem cannot be ignored. At least one writer, Professor Jacob Viner, adopts as one of his own criteria of economic progress the specification that it lead to an absolute reduction in the number of people living in conditions of "crushing poverty."[3]

Despite the serious shortcomings of per capita income as a measure of material well-being—its failure to take into account costs and sacrifice in terms of human effort and natural resources, its overly aggregative character in measuring total output rather than consumption or levels of living, and its disregard of the distributive aspects of personal income—it is nevertheless the most widely used measure of levels of, and changes in, national economic performance. Though the foregoing qualifications—as well as others to be discussed in the following selection by Kuznets—should be kept in mind when per capita income figures are used, such figures provide some indication of differences over time in the economic performance of a country, as well as differences among countries at a point in time.

SOME INTERNATIONAL COMPARISONS OF PER CAPITA INCOME

The following table presents data on population, net national product, and per capita income for 55 countries:

ESTIMATES OF POPULATION, NET NATIONAL PRODUCT, AND PER CAPITA PRODUCT OF 55 COUNTRIES

	Population, mid-year 1953 (thousands)	Net national product at factor cost (million US dollars)	Per capita product (US dollars)
			Average 1952-1954
Africa			
Uganda	5,343	270	50
Kenya	5,851	330	60
Belgian Congo	12,154	850	70
Rhodesia and Nyasaland	6,708	670	100
Egypt	22,062	2,650	120
Union of South Africa	13,153	3,950	300
America			
Peru	9,035	1,080	120
Paraguay	1,496	210	140
Ecuador	3,464	520	150
Honduras	1,564	230	150
Dominican Republic	2,291	360	160
Guatemala	3,049	490	160
Jamaica	1,457[a]	260[a]	180[a]
Mexico	28,056	6,170	220
Brazil	55,772	12,830	230
Colombia	12,111	3,030	250
Panama	863	220	250
Cuba	5,807	1,800	310

[3] Jacob Viner, *International Trade and Economic Development* (Glencoe, Ill.: The Free Press, 1952), pp. 126 ff.

ESTIMATES OF POPULATION, NET NATIONAL PRODUCT,
AND PER CAPITA PRODUCT OF 55 COUNTRIES—*Continued*

	Population, mid-year 1953 (thousands)	Net national product at factor cost (million US dollars)	Per capita product (US dollars)
		Average 1952-1954	
Chile	6,437	2,320	360
Puerto Rico	2,213	950	430
Argentina	18,393	8,460	460
Venezuela	5,440	2,940[b]	540[b]
Canada	14,781	19,360	1,310
United States	159,643	298,530	1,870
Asia			
Burma	19,045	950	50
India	372,000	22,320	60
Korea (South)	21,376	1,500	70
Pakistan	79,330	5,550	70
Thailand	19,556	1,560[b]	80[b]
Ceylon	8,155	890	110
Philippines	21,039	3,150	150
Japan	86,700	16,470	190
Turkey	22,461	4,720	210
Lebanon	1,353	350	260
Malaya	5,706	1,770[b]	310[b]
Israel	1,650	770	470
Europe			
Portugal	7,990	1,600	200
Greece	7,824	1,720	220
Italy	47,551	14,740	310
Austria	6,954	2,570	370
Ireland	2,945	1,210	410
Netherlands	10,493	5,250	500
Germany (Western)	48,994	24,990	510
Finland	4,141	2,770	670
France	42,860	31,720	740
Norway	3,359	2,490	740
Denmark	4,369	3,280	750
Iceland	151	120	780
United Kingdom	50,611	39,480	780
Belgium	8,778	7,020	800
Luxembourg	304	270	890
Sweden	7,171	6,810	950
Switzerland	4,877	4,930	1,010
Oceania			
Australia	8,815	8,400	950
New Zealand	2,047	2,050	1,000
Total of 55 countries	1,325,684	590,120	445

[a] 1952
[b] 1952 and 1953

Source: Per Capita National Product of Fifty-five Countries: 1952-1954 (New York: United Nations Statistical Papers, Series E, No. 4, 1957), pp. 8, 9.

A striking feature of the table is the enormous spread in income per capita, ranging from $1870 for the United States to $50 for Burma and Uganda. Equally striking is the extremely uneven distribution of population among the 55 countries: nine of them, or 16 percent, account for 75 percent of the total population. (Were the Soviet Union and Communist China included, the distribution would appear even more unequal.)

Conceptual difficulties in measurement and imperfections of available data caution against placing too much credence in the per capita income figures. They probably exaggerate the real differences among countries. For one thing, in poorer countries, relatively fewer economic activities are funneled through the market, and therefore are more likely to be overlooked in national income estimates. Nevertheless, the relative positions of the countries are probably fairly accurate, as is the broad picture of the wide inequality in the distribution of income per capita.

DEVELOPMENT, UNDERDEVELOPMENT, AND BACKWARDNESS

The size of per capita income is used by most writers as the criterion for differentiating between advanced and underdeveloped countries. But another concept distinguishes the two classes of country on the basis of the abundance or dearth of capital. A "lack of capital" does not refer to the absolute size of a country's capital stock but rather to the ratio of capital to some other factor of production or to the population. Economic theory suggests that where the ratio of capital to other factors is low, the marginal productivity of capital is high. This suggests that one could specify an underdeveloped country as one in which the marginal productivity of capital is high. It is not at all clear, however, that a scarcity of capital need imply that its marginal productivity is high, nor for that matter that a high marginal productivity of capital implies capital scarcity. In the first case, it has been pointed out that unfavorable influences, such as poor climate or bad government, may cause the marginal productivity of capital—and other factors of production as well—to be low, whatever its relative scarcity.[4] In the second case, it may be that in capital-rich countries like the United States the high marginal productivity of capital is the result of a complex of favorable conditions, such as the high quality of cooperating factors and large, accessible markets. But the major trouble with a definition of underdevelopment in such terms as capital per head is that it introduces a confusion between a causal and a definitional relationship. In fact, a low capital-per-head (or, for that matter, resources-per-head) ratio is in part a *cause* of underdevelopment. What is required is a concept, such as output per capita, which is a *reflection* of the state of development.

A final comment is in order concerning the use of the term "backward" to describe an underdeveloped country. "Backward" seems to connote some value judgments that were not intended by, nor were within the competence

---

[4] Cf. Viner, *op. cit.*, p. 123.

of, the economists using the term. It suggests that something more than the purely "economic" is involved. Because economists loathe to appear to be passing judgment on the religious, cultural, and social values of a country, the term "backward" has generally passed into disrepute. Whatever the merits of the abandonment of this term, it should serve to emphasize that economic development is not synonymous with social progress.

SIMON KUZNETS

||||||||||||||||||||||||||||||||||||||||||||||||||||||||||||||||||||||||||||||||||||||||||||||||||||||||||||||||||||||||||||||||||||||||||||||||||||||||||||

Some Conceptual Problems of Measurement

The problems of an acceptable definition of national product, discussed at length by generations of scholars in the field, can be grouped under three heads: (*a*) delimitation of scope, involving the distinction between economic activity and social life at large; (*b*) questions of valuation, involving the base to which economic activities are to be reduced; (*c*) and problems of netness and grossness, involving the distinction between costs and net returns of economic activity. Adequate discussion of these three complexes of problems is impossible here. We only indicate the major effects which their treatment has upon long-term estimates of national product. By so doing we hope to avoid two extreme impressions: that the conceptual difficulties are too great to yield useful estimates, and that the conceptual compromises are so negligible that the estimates represent a precise record.

A

In general, only activities whose results are channeled through the market place or through some other social institution extraneous to the family (*e.g.*, government) are easily recognized as economic and are likely to be fully reflected in measurement. Economic activities within the household tend to be mixed with others and one cannot tell whether housework is truly an economic activity or part of life in general. Even when such activities are recognized as economic and are measured in terms of persons engaged, hours spent, or products turned out, their proper evaluation is far from easy. Eco-

From *Economic Development and Cultural Change* (October 1956) pp. 6-9, with omissions. Reprinted by permission of the University of Chicago Press and the author. Copyright 1956 by the University of Chicago.

nomic growth is often accompanied by a shift in economic activities from the household into the market place; or by a more rapid rise in the volume of market- or society-bound activities than in the volume of those within the household. It follows that long-term product estimates tend to have an upward bias (*i.e.,* exaggerate the rate of growth): the omission of activities producing goods (whether consumer or capital goods) for internal consumption is likely to be relatively more important for the early part of any long period than for the later. This is particularly true if, for the country and period under observation, economic growth has been substantial: other conditions being equal, the greater the growth, the greater the shift from the household into markets (private or public) and the greater the possible upward bias arising from differential underestimation of nonmarket production.

B

The activities subsumed under national product, whether in terms of services of factors or in terms of products which they yield, are weighted by prices since prices are the only socially determined system of weights. Two aspects of this use of prices as weights in long-term records of national product should be noted. First, systems of price weights selected from different parts of a given long period may yield different rates of growth in national product in constant prices. In general, use of price relations for the early part of a period may yield a higher rate of growth since goods that are highly priced in the early years are likely, in response to these higher price levels, to grow more than other products, and their relative price position may be lower at the end of the period. Conversely, use of a more recent system of price relations is likely to yield a lower rate of growth in national product over the period. Such difficulties cannot be resolved by mixing the price weights, which only confuses the meaning of the resulting measures; or by using chain indexes, in which the shifts in weights become fractionalized in short links—only to be reassembled when the total long period is brought into focus.

It is misleading to speak of the upward bias resulting from the use of "early" price weights and of the downward bias resulting from the use of "late" price weights: these are not biases but reflections of different vantage points from which economic growth is seen. In the former case we look at them with the eyes of the contemporaries of the early period—say the 1860s; in the latter case with the eyes of contemporaries of the recent period—say the 1950s. And one may argue that, in general, economic growth should always be examined from the vantage point of the present, if only because this is a more complete view than that from the past looking forward. Whatever the argument, the usual practice is to employ recent-year weights— which means that every generation the indexes must be revised and history partially rewritten.

The other peculiarity of price series is a distinct defect—they lack sensitivity to aspects that should be reflected. Changes in quality, unless expressed through some overt product differentiation, are not usually recorded by prices. Many such changes, either deterioration or improvement, are not adequately measured in the available price indexes (which are often limited to standard commodities anyway). Since much of the adjustment for price changes takes the form of dividing current price totals by price indexes, and since we can assume that over the long run quality improvements far outweigh quality deterioration, the common practices mean a downward bias in national product in constant prices. Were such totals more sensitive to quality changes, the rates of growth might well be significantly higher than those now shown.

C

The distinction between costs and net returns of economic activity, or between intermediate (used in production) and final (for ultimate users) goods, turns essentially on what we recognize as the basic purposes of economic activity; and these may differ from one social order to another. But if we agree that in the economic societies of the last two centuries the basic purpose is satisfaction of wants of ultimate consumers, present and future, we can draw the main line of distinction and narrow the problem to institutional changes that shift that line perceptibly. Viewed in this fashion, the long-term records of national product suffer from a bias that reflects the increasing complexity of society in the process of economic growth, and the increasing use of resources that are on the borderline between business costs and ultimate consumption. In the private sector there are the increasing outlays on professional training, on union, association, banking, and other fees, etc.— the whole array of expenses undertaken largely or in good part for the sake of effective performance as an income earner in a complex urban civilization. In the public sector much of the increased governmental expenditures is not on services to ultimate consumers but on intermediate goods—whether services to business or for the maintenance of the fabric of society at large. Yet the customary estimates of national income include all these outlays as final products, suspect though they are of being at least in part costs of production. The resulting upward bias in the long-term series of national product is relative to a set of measures geared to stricter concepts of ultimate consumption and capital formation.

Even the brief statements above reveal that the complex problems in the definition and measurement of national product arise from the use by observers of one yardstick over long stretches of space and time, whereas different standards are in fact used in the real world. In the latter, institutional changes shift the line of distinction between what is *currently* recognized as economic activity and as human activity at large; the relative scales of valuation in different markets differ and change; increasing complexity of

life produces confusion between economic costs and net returns. The raw
facts would, therefore, be no help. In essence, the very concept of "economic," let alone of economic growth, is an abstraction; and is a distortion
of the observable flow of life since it exaggerates elements which are obscured
and beset by numerous changes and deviations.

And yet to abandon an attempt to study economic growth, to refuse to
introduce some comparability and continuity into changing historical reality,
would be even a greater distortion—for it would imply no similarity of purpose and organization between the society of today and yesterday, between
the United States in 1950 and in 1850, or for that matter between the United
States, the USSR, and India in 1950. Such an implication is clearly belied by
numerous chains of historical continuity within the development of any one
society, and by numerous links that bind various societies in the world to a
common heritage in which they all share. Even in individuals, whose life
spans are so much shorter than those of societies, memory, motivation, and
decisions cover long periods; and involve comparison of the present with the
past—denying that these are two different and separate worlds without continuity. This chain over time is all the more apparent in the ties that bind
successive generations. One is, therefore, compelled to distill a common set
of purposes, a common set of criteria that will provide the basis for comparability over time and space—a basis that should be acceptable, in one of
several variants, so long as there is no major break in historical continuity or
in the concert of societies with a common heritage.

Although there is agreement upon the relevance of and the need for
these common bases that transcend institutional shifts or differences over time
and space, there may be disputes as to precisely where to drawn the lines in
specific measurement for given countries and periods; and there may be
room for variant expressions or formulations of one set of common purposes
and criteria, which would be most illuminating in the quantitative differences
which the resulting variants would show. It is possible, and would be useful,
in estimating national product for a country over a long period, to attempt
approximations that yield at least the order of magnitudes of biases. An adequate attempt in this direction would, however, involve detailed monographic
studies since it is only through careful scrutiny of the changing institutional
structure of a country that useful estimates of such biases can be secured.
Such attempts would be welcome, and it is to be hoped that they will become
more numerous in years to come. But meanwhile we must operate with the
available long-term records, crude and subject to biases though they are, and
treating them as approximations, study them for the findings they may yield.

It is important to note that, on the basis of present evidence, the biases
of the type discussed above, while substantial, are not so dominant as to rob
the measures of meaning. Although it is impossible to present such evidence
in detail, we give one example relating to the biases that may result from
differential undercoverage of household activities. In the United States, the
share of agriculture in the labor force declined from about 50 percent in 1870
to about 13 percent in the late 1940s, and its share in net national product

(or income) declined from about 27 percent to about 8 percent.[1] Let us make the extreme assumption that underestimation of household activities was limited to the agricultural sector in 1870 and constituted 50 percent of agriculture's economic product included in the estimate. The initial national income figure for 1870 should, therefore, have been about 14 percent (*i.e.,* 0.27×0.51) higher, or 114 instead of 100. Yet, as measured, national income in constant prices rose from about $9.4 billion in the 1870s to about $109 billion in the 1940s, a rise from 1 to about 11.6.[2] Adjustment for the bias would reduce the growth to one from 1 to 10.2—still an impressive rise and still leaving the United States among the countries with high rates of long-term growth.

The illustration may be atypical in some respects, but . . . the rates of growth as recorded in the available series are large and the differences among them are substantial enough to dwarf the biases. Furthermore, the latter offset each other to some extent—some tend to exaggerate rates of growth, others to understate them. In short, the similarities and differences that are reflected in the measures of national product commonly used are quite real and generally accepted by those individuals who are aware of economic events and of differences in economic fortune among nations. The differences in power to satisfy wants expressed through disparities in rates of economic growth or in per capita income levels are not statistical illusions. They find their embodiment in flows of goods to consumers, in the stock of real capital over which they can dispose, and in the degree of their protection from material insecurities. Realization of the dependence of our measures on basic criteria and of the biases to which the estimates may be subject should not blind us to the fact that such biases are qualifications, not negations, of the significance of the measures.

---

[1] See *Income and Wealth of the United States,* Income and Wealth Series II (Bowes and Bowes, England, for the International Association for Research in Income and Wealth, 1952), Tables 17 and 19, pp. 102 and 107.

[2] *Ibid.,* Table 1, p. 30.

PART SIX

Land, Labor, Capital, and Entrepreneurship

Economists FREQUENTLY FIND IT CONVENIENT TO think of the economic forces governing growth and economic activity in general as factors of production, which are traditionally classified as "land," "labor," "capital," and (rather more recently) "entrepreneurship." The purpose of this section is to examine in some detail the nature and role of these factors of production in the process of economic development. The articles contained here do not develop formal theories; rather, they present a collection of ideas and propositions which may prove useful in the formulation of such theories.

The human factor, unlike any other in the productive process, is not only an instrument of economic activity and growth, but is itself the rationale for such activity in the first place. Thus, no discussion of labor as a factor of production can proceed far without an analysis of the population of which it is part. Because labor is the producing, "positive" force and population is the consuming, "negative" force, the ratio of labor force to total population would appear to be a significant variable. At any time, this ratio is affected by the age and sex composition of the population, which in turn is influenced by levels and trends of birth rates, mortality rates, and migration. The selection by the United Nations Population Division points out that in those countries where birth and death rates are high—characteristics jointly found only in some underdeveloped countries—the proportion of the population under fifteen years of age is high by comparison with other countries, and thus the proportion of the population of labor-force age is relatively low. With the onset of declining mortality rates among children, largely the result of the dissemination of medical knowledge, the labor-force percentage tends to rise, as more children survive to working age. But in some cases, economic and social factors—such as, for example, changing attitudes toward the employment of women—appear to be more prominent than demographic trends as determinants of the proportion of the population in the labor force; S. L. Wolfbein and A. J. Jaffe demonstrate this in the case of the United States for the period 1890-1930.

A classical factor affecting the potential growth of a country is the "land" available to it, where by "land" we mean not only the physical surface of the earth, but the total endowment of nonreproducible natural resources. To the extent that such resources are a fixed quantum, their progressive depletion may retard the development process by raising the real costs of industrial raw materials to excessively high levels. This problem, it will be recalled, concerned the classical economists; in the nature of the case, it must still be a matter of concern, as is made clear in the article by Edward S. Mason. Other things being equal, a country's growth potential will be greater, the higher is the ratio of natural resources to population.

Economic theory, as we have seen, attaches great importance to the accumulation of "capital" (the stock of physical, reproducible means of production) as a force in economic development. Moreover, what statistical information is available confirms the fact that growth of output per head is associated with growth in the ratio of capital to population (and to labor), presumably because within broad limits the productivity of labor is increased when each laborer has more (and therefore probably superior) capital equipment to work with.

Countries endeavoring to raise or even merely to maintain the ratio of capital to labor in the face of population growth encounter a dual problem. First, it is a matter of simple arithmetic that the net investment required to avoid a decline in the capital-labor ratio will be greater, the greater the rate of population growth. Secondly, it is generally true that when population is growing rapidly, it may be more difficult to elicit the savings necessary for undertaking the required investment. In advanced countries, where income and the propensity to save are already high, this obstacle is relatively easy to surmount. However, in underdeveloped countries, where income per capita and consequently the propensity to save is low, the problem is an acute one.

These and other problems related to the role of capital in underdeveloped countries are the prime concern of the selection by W. Arthur Lewis. His emphasis on capital follows from his assumption that the supply of labor is "unlimited," in the sense that in many underdeveloped countries population is so abundant relative to the stock of capital and natural resources that the marginal productivity of labor is effectively zero. Lewis recognizes, however, that these countries are usually short of high-level manpower (as distinguished from unskilled labor), which in many respects can be regarded as a shortage of "human capital." It might be noted that Lewis's article, unlike the others in this section, is a formal theory "written in the classical tradition"; it is included here rather than in the theory section because of its cogent discussion of the problem of capital formation in the process of growth.

"Entrepreneurship," the fourth factor of production, has been defined in several quite different ways. One definition equates entrepreneurship with management: in this sense, the function of the entrepreneur is to coordinate, administer, and control the activities of the firm. The critical importance of management is made clear in the selection by Frederick Harbison, where it is argued that shortages of managerial skills and consequent inefficient management serve to depress the productivity of labor (and therefore presumably retard economic growth). Egypt is cited as an example of a country where poor management keeps productivity exceedingly low, even in factories employing up-to-date technology.

The entrepreneur has also been viewed (by Frank Knight and others) as the decision maker who operates under conditions of risk and uncertainty. It is he who exercises judgment which is "liable to error," and it is he who bears responsibility for the correctness of those judgments. Of all the entrepreneur's economic decisions, it is the decision to invest which is most crucial in the context of economic growth. Any investment decision depends on a rational assessment of the size of the potential market, the supply of skilled labor, the availability of raw materials, and other factors that determine the profits or losses of the enterprise. Henry G. Aubrey contends that in underdeveloped countries information regarding these factors, particularly with respect to *industrial* investment, is notoriously lacking. Thus, the risk and uncertainty attached to such investments is increased, thereby creating a marked preference for investment in traditional areas of lower growth potential, such as real estate and money lending. Aubrey concludes that insufficient investment in industrial growth areas is explained, not (as is sometimes contended) by the absence of profit-motivated entrepreneurs, but rather by the low expected return, after discounting for risk, from industrial investment.

A third concept of entrepreneurship is an integral part of the theory of Joseph Schumpeter (see pp. 94-95). Here, the entrepreneur is an agent of innovation; indeed, as we have seen, Schumpeter's innovator is the driving force in the development process, acting to bring forth new products or new methods of production. The innovating entrepreneur is imbued with extraordinary personal attributes which make him a relative rarity in any society. Fortunately, as Aubrey notes, the underdeveloped countries do not at this time require *innovating,* as much as *imitating,* "entrepreneurs"—that is, individuals who can successfully import and apply productive techniques and methods already in use in the advanced countries.

The importance of technological change in the process of economic growth stands in marked contrast to the paucity of our knowledge in this area. An understanding of the process of technological change depends on our ability to trace and to explain the antecedents of such change, starting with basic discovery in the pure sciences, through the process of invention, and culminating in the application of invention to economic production. The further back in this chain one goes, the less is known about the determinants of its links. W. Rupert Maclaurin attempts to spell out in finer detail the elements in the sequence leading to technological change.

While relatively little is known about its *causes,* more can be said about the *effects* of technological change. Fundamentally, the impact of changing technology is manifested in increases in the productivity of labor and capital. But none of the "factors of production" is immune from its impact. For example, the efficiency of management is continually being enhanced by developments in communication, transportation, and data processing.

Even the traditional concept of "land" as a fixed quantum loses its precision. The earth's "stock" of raw materials is itself a concept dependent on the state of technology. As Mason observes, technological improvement (1) may facilitate discoveries of presently unknown resources, (2) may make economical the extraction of raw materials that formerly were too costly to mine, and (3) may decrease the cost of processing raw materials formerly considered to be of uneconomically low grade. Even more fundamentally, the very definition of "raw materials" depends on the state of technology. Thus, for example, uranium is a substance which assumed the status of a critical raw material only with the advent of the atomic age.

There is need for thought and research on the interrelationships between the advance of knowledge, technological progress, and economic growth.

Historically, the notion has long existed that there is a close link between technological advance and economic growth. But there also existed the belief, stemming from the analysis of the classical school, that technological progress would prove inadequate to overcome the obstacle to economic growth created by diminishing physical returns to "land." But with the passage of time, it has become obvious that advances in knowledge and resultant technological change make possible a continuation of economic growth at rates hitherto unimagined. It is therefore very likely that the upper limit of economic production is given, not by limitations of fixed resources, but by the advance of human knowledge. And who can contend that there is an upper limit to human knowledge?

UNITED NATIONS
POPULATION DIVISION

IIIIIIIIIIIIIIIIIIIIIIIIIIIIIIIIIIIIIIIIIIIIIIIIIIIIIIIIIIIIIIIIIIIIIIIIIIIIIIIIIIIIIIIIIIIIIIIIIIIIIIIIIIIIIIIIIIIIIIIIIIIIIIIIIIII

Population Growth and the Standard of Living in Underdeveloped Countries

The length of human life has been greatly extended in modern times, thanks to the progress of medicine and higher standards of living. Two hundred years ago, a newborn child could look forward, on the average, to no more than 30 or 35 years of life, even in the countries where conditions of health were most favorable. In many countries the average life expectancy has more than doubled since that time; and although premature mortality still takes a heavy toll in the regions where the level of living is lowest and medical and sanitary facilities are least developed, substantial progress is being made everywhere in the fight against disease and death. No one will deny that this is a great achievement, perhaps the greatest achievement of the modern age, but it also entails a major problem. As a consequence of the saving of lives, the growth of population has speeded up; and it is necessary to match the increase of numbers with an even greater expansion in production of the necessities and amenities of life, if the goal of a satisfactory living standard for all the world's peoples is to be attained.

About 2500 million men, women, and children inhabit the earth at

From *Proceedings of the World Population Conference* (1954), Vol. V, pp. 1095-1113. This is primarily a brief summary of relevant portions of the United Nations publication, *The Determinants and Consequences of Population Trends* (ST/SOA Series A, Population Studies, No. 17. New York, 1953, 404 pp.).

present. In 1750 the population was only about 700 million; in 1850 it was around 1200 million. The increase since 1850 has been greater than the growth in all the previous ages of man's existence on earth. At present, with about 30 million people being added each year through the excess of births over deaths, the population is increasing at a rate between 1 and $1\frac{1}{2}$ percent per annum, which is beyond any precedent in human history. It has been estimated that by 1980 the population will be at least 3000 million and perhaps as much as 3600 million. These figures imply an increase of 25 to 50 percent in a single generation.

Those who are concerned with planning for a better future must take the growth of population into account if they are to set realistic goals for employment, production, schools, and other needs of the coming generations. They also need to consider the effects of the increasing numbers of workers and consumers upon the productivity of labor and the level of living. If the policy-makers decide, as they have recently done in some countries, that it is advisable to restrain the growth of population, for example by encouraging emigration or family limitation, they need to know what results can be expected from specific measures for these purposes. So the study of population, the causes and consequences of its growth, takes more practical meaning in the modern world than ever before.

The United Nations Population Commission, when it met for the first time in 1947, foresaw that the councils of the United Nations as well as the member states would need information on this subject. The Commission requested the United Nations Secretariat to make a survey of existing scientific knowledge concerning the relationships between population growth and economic and social conditions, with special attention to the population problems of the economically underdeveloped countries. In the course of several years' work, the Secretariat surveyed hundreds of scientific writings relevant to the subject, published in many languages, and set down the principal findings in a voluminous report.

The present document is intended to present briefly the outstanding facts which were brought to light in that report, so far as they relate to the problem of economic and social development of underdeveloped countries.

CAN THE EARTH SUPPORT ITS PEOPLE?

Sometimes it is said that if population continues to multiply at the present rate, the limits of the earth's resources will soon be reached, and that starvation and strife must put an end to the increase unless men undertake to curb their reproduction. Scientific studies, however, do not give much support to this idea. The power of the earth to produce food and other necessities of life is very elastic, depending to a great extent on man's inventiveness. No one knows what increases of production may be made possible by future technological discoveries or new forms of economic organization. Even with present knowledge and with the existing forms of society, conservative estimates imply that it is technically possible to feed a much larger population than the earth now supports. If all potentially productive lands were cultivated and if modern agricultural science were fully applied everywhere, the production of food could be increased several times over. Studies of the reserves of coal, iron ore, and other sources of energy and industrial raw materials show that, with prudent use and conservation, they would be sufficient to meet the needs of a growing population for a long time to come. The possibilities of the use of solar and nuclear energy are only beginning to be realized.

Scientists have pointed out that in any case there is not much practical value in trying to calculate how many people the earth could eventually support if all its resources were fully utilized. It is the consequence of human frailty that what is technically possible is not always practically feasible. Ignorance, greed, strife, superstition, and blind adherence to tradition prevent men from accomplishing what is in their power, even though the alternative may be misery or starvation. A realistic view of the population problem must take these obstacles into account. The question is, whether or not, in the world as it is, increasing population hinders progress toward the twin goals of prosperity and peace which the founders of the United Nations wrote into the Charter.

THEORIES CONCERNING THE RELATIONS BETWEEN POPULATION AND THE STANDARD OF LIVING

Some 150 years ago the Reverend Malthus declared, in his famous essay on the "Principle of Population," that population growth was the principal cause of mass poverty. He laid down the rule that production of the means of subsistence could be increased only in arithmetic ratio, while population had a tendency to grow in geometric progression, being held within the limits of subsistence by the positive checks of war, pestilence, famine, and premature mortality. The consequent misery of the masses could not be relieved by social reforms, for any benefits from this source would shortly be consumed by new additions to the population. He held forth one hope for improving the standard of living in the long run: the practice of "moral restraint," by which he meant the prudential delay of marriage.

History has shown that Malthus oversimplified the laws of population and economic growth and the relations between them. Production is not necessarily limited to an arithmetical ratio of increase, nor does population necessarily grow in geometrical progression. The experience of countries like the United States and the Soviet Union has demonstrated that in favorable circumstances production may outstrip even a very rapid increase of population, and may continue to do so over long periods of time. Legislation improving the distribution of income and easing the condition of the poor has disproved the idea that the "principle of population" foredooms any effort to raise the living standards of the masses by means of social reform.

Marx and his followers emphatically opposed the teachings of Malthus. Considering that labor is the principal asset of society and the ultimate source of all value, they rejected the idea that population could be excessive in a well-organized system. In the Marxian view, the appearance of an excess population in capitalist countries is blamed on the imperfection of capitalism, which is thought to require a reserve of unused labor to guarantee its functioning. Socialism, on the other hand, is said to assure full utilization of available manpower and balanced development of natural resources so that increasing numbers of consumers are accommodated on a rising plane of living.

Modern scholars outside the socialist tradition also repudiate the oversimplified arguments of Malthus, but in general they agree that population increase in some circumstances may hinder economic and social progress. They generally recognize that the form of social organization is a relevant factor, but do not concede that social reform is necessarily sufficient to cure the ills which may come from excessive growth of numbers. They put more emphasis than the socialists do on obstacles to increasing production, such as shortage of land and other natural resources, of capital, and of trained and qualified manpower, which may make it difficult to balance rapid population increase with expanding production regardless of the type of social system. On the other hand, it is agreed that a large increase of population in some circumstances may be a positive advantage for economic development. It has certainly been so in the history of some countries that are in a position of economic leadership today; and it may now be so in some countries where large reserves of natural resources remain undeveloped for lack of sufficient manpower or sufficient markets for large-scale, low-cost industry.

The review of scientific studies points clearly to this conclusion: the question, how population growth affects the material welfare of the people, does not admit of any general answer that would be valid in all places and at all times. The answer depends on many cirmustances, all of which must be examined in order to understand the problem of population in any country. At present the relevant circumstances are very different in different parts of the world.

THE UNEVEN DISTRIBUTION OF WORLD POPULATION AND RESOURCES

The relation between the numbers of the people and the quantities of resources at their disposal is much less favorable in some parts of the world than in others. Asia (excluding the Soviet Union) has more than half of the world's population, but only about one-fifth of the land area. The average amount of land in crops per person is estimated at only one-half to eight-tenths of an acre in southern and eastern Asia, by comparison with four acres in the United States, Canada, Australia, and New Zealand, and two acres in the Soviet Union. Northern America and the USSR also have large areas of land suitable for agriculture which are not being cultivated, as well as valuable forest and mineral reserves. In proportion to its population, Asia has a much smaller share of such assets.

Many of the underdeveloped countries in Africa and Latin America have immense reserves of unused natural resources, but lack the capital and technically trained manpower to develop them. In fact, the distribution of man-made equipment and of manpower suitable for employment in an advanced modern economy is even more unequal than the distribution of natural resources. The world's great industrial plants are concentrated largely in a few countries of Europe and North America, while the least favored nations are handicapped by a lack of even simple tools such as iron plowshares and a shortage of personnel with even elementary education.

THE CHANGING BALANCE OF BIRTHS AND DEATHS

Present trends of population are such as to aggravate the existing inequality of numbers in relation to the means of production. Population is increasing most rapidly in the very regions which suffer the greatest economic handicaps, and in the future they will have to support a still larger share of the world's inhabitants. The reason for this trend is found in the events of the past two centuries, which led up to the present differences in the balance of births and deaths in various parts of the world.

Before the eighteenth century, every nation suffered a high death rate. In all parts of the world, a large number of each generation died in infancy, so that population grew only slowly in spite of the fact that birth rates were universally high. This uneasy balance of high fertility and heavy mortality was upset in Europe at the beginning of the modern era by an improvement in the living conditions of the masses due to the economic effects of the agricultural and industrial revolutions, which led to a substantial reduction of the death rate. The effect was a veritable mushroom growth of the European population. It has been estimated that between 1750 and 1900 the population of Europe with its emigrant offshoots overseas increased nearly fourfold.

The spurt of European population growth was finally checked by a drop in the birth rate. In some countries, notably France and the United States, this trend became evident early in the nineteenth century if not before, but it was only during the last part of that century that falling birth rates became generally characteristic of the leading industrial nations of Europe and "Europe overseas." During the early decades of the twentieth century, the growth of population in most European countries slackened in spite of the continuing decrease of death rates.

The causes of the falling birth rate were bound up with far-reaching changes in the conditions of life, brought about by the evolution of the urban-industrial society. Old traditions weakened; men began to shape their actions more in accordance with individual preferences and aspirations. They placed a lower value on the satisfaction of a numerous offspring, a higher value on the material comforts and personal independence which could be achieved by limiting the number of children. Efficient new contraceptives were among the technological inventions of the day; these were the means of putting the small-family idea into effect. The idea spread until, in the early 1930s, the birth rate in most of the western European countries was only slightly higher than the death rate, and many of them were no longer producing enough births to replace their population in the long run. The United States, Canada, Australia, and New Zealand were also rapidly approaching a state of constant or diminishing population.

The trend was interrupted by a revival of the birth rates in most of these countries during the late 1930s and again during World War II or its aftermath. In fifteen countries there was an increase of more than 30 percent in the birth rate from the minimum during the 1930s to the maximum during or shortly after the war. Some experts thought that these countries were entering a new era of rising birth rates and accelerating population growth, but in most cases, at least, the acceleration was temporary. The peak was passed in most of the countries within two or three years after the war ended, and the fall of the birth rate was resumed.

In 1947, while the "baby boom" was still going on, the average birth rate of Europe, Northern America, and Oceania was estimated at 2.4 births annually per 100 population, and the average death rate at 1.4 per 100, so that the population of these regions was increasing at about 1 percent per year. With declining birth rates, the rate of increase has fallen off since that time, and at present these regions—the most favored in the world from the economic point of view—have a rate of population growth distinctly below the world average.

Meanwhile the decline of the death rate has been spreading to other parts of the world where birth rates are still high. Especially during the years since World War II, remarkable gains have been recorded in the fight against premature mortality in the economically backward regions. In many countries of Latin America and in some parts of Asia and Africa, the death rates at present are only about one-half as high as they were just prior to the war. The birth rates of the underdeveloped countries, on the other hand, are generally as high as ever; in fact, they have increased in some cases at least, as a result of improved health conditions. The result is a spurt of population growth in these regions which surpasses what occurred in Europe, Northern America, and the British Dominions of Oceania during the nineteenth and early twentieth centuries.

In practically all the Asian, African, and Latin American countries where reasonably accurate vital statistics are available, the present birth rates exceed the death rates by a margin sufficient to increase the population at least 2 percent per annum. In Latin America as a whole, around 1947 the birth rate was around 4 and the death rate around 1.7 per 100 population, so that the population was multiplying at a rate of about 2.3 percent per annum. Since that time, with falling death rates and constant or rising birth rates, the rate of growth has risen higher. In some countries, both in Latin America and the other underdeveloped regions, death rates have been cut so sharply in the last few years that the natural growth of population now approximates or even exceeds 3 percent per annum. Examples are Mexico, Malaya, and Ceylon. At such a rate, the population will double in less than 25 years.

Accurate statistics of births and deaths are not available for some of the most important underdeveloped countries. This is the case of China, India, Indonesia, Pakistan, most of the Near Eastern countries, and all of Africa except Egypt. It is likely that the rate of growth in most of the countries for which data are lacking is somewhat slower than in the countries with good vital statistics—not because their birth rates are lower but because they have not yet made as much progress in cutting down their death rates.

The people of the regions which still suffer from high mortality will undoubtedly do what they can to reduce this waste of life in the future. They will take advantage of modern medical discoveries and of the assistance which the United Nations, the Specialized Agencies, and the more fortunate nations are prepared to offer. So there is every likelihood of lower death rates in the future throughout the underdeveloped regions of the world. Unless and until the scale is balanced by a similar reduction of birth rates, the population of these regions will continue to grow rapidly.

It is natural to assume that an increase of population due to a falling death rate is a symptom of economic as well as physical health in a nation; and in former times there was much truth in this idea. In eighteenth- and nineteenth-century Europe, the reduction of mortality and the consequent spurt of population growth were largely the effects of increasing wealth and better conditions of life for the masses. People lived longer because they were assured of a more ample food supply and because they could afford better housing and sanitary facilities, better medical care, and investments in the development of medical science.

In the underdeveloped countries today, the same relation between the trend of mortality and economic development no longer holds. Science has shown the way to cut down the death rate of an impoverished people quickly, with only modest investment of resources and without any major change in the material conditions of living. Spectacular results have been achieved by such devices as DDT spraying to control malarial mosquitoes and infection-spreading flies, mass inoculations against infectious diseases, and inexpensive improvements in sanitation and protection of water supplies. The results have been most remarkable in the case of infant mortality. In many countries where, until recently, one-fourth or one-fifth of all children born died within the first year, the rates of infant mortality have been reduced by one-half or more.

The fact that life expectancy has lengthened and that fewer children are dying in infancy does not mean that the population is now better fed, clothed, and housed than before. And what of the future? Will it be possible to increase the production of the necessities and amenities of life fast enough to outstrip the increase in the number of consumers which the saving of lives has brought about?

PRESSURE OF POPULATION AND SHORTAGE OF LAND

The economic difficulties which may be caused by rapid multiplication of the population are most easily seen in places like the Nile Valley, the river deltas of southern and eastern Asia, and such densely populated islands as Java, Jamaica, and Haiti, where a large farming population is trying to make a living on a limited area of cultivable land. In Egypt a population of more than 20 million, some two-thirds of them dependent on agriculture, is crowded into the narrow valley of the Nile. The density of population there is over 600 persons per square kilometer of inhabited area (1600 per square mile); that is, nearly twice as much as the density in the highly urbanized and industrialized Netherlands. Studies made in 1944 revealed that the average Egyptian fellah had only two or three acres of land to support himself and his family and to pay his rent and taxes. Any effort to make room for more people by extending irrigation into the surrounding desert involves enormous capital investments.

An excessively large agricultural population in relation to the area of cultivated land is an obstacle to the attainment of an adequate standard of living. The relative abundance of labor supply encourages the use of methods of cultivation which require much labor to produce a small return. It may not be economical to use even simple machinery or moderately advanced tools which save labor but which add little to the amount of the crops that can be grown on the limited area of land. The small size of farms hinders the application of those improved techniques which are of doubtful value unless they are used in operations on a certain scale. In some cases the workers, even practicing most laborious methods, are unable to keep themselves occupied on their little patches of land and spend a large part of each year in forced idleness. To make their plight worse, large landowners in many of the countries concerned take a major share of the product in the form of rents and profits. The excessive numbers of tenants and laborers weaken their position in dealing with the landlords.

Population pressure and shortage of land sometimes lead to overcropping and soil exhaustion or to the ultilization of lands which are not suitable for the production of crops and which deteriorate under the plow. A United Nations mission to Haiti found that the farmers on that island, constantly clearing new fields to accommodate their growing numbers, had stripped steep hillsides of their protective forest cover, with the result that the soil was washing into the valleys and the sea. In such cases the population is threatened by a shrinkage of the principal resource on which it depends for its livelihood, while its needs go on increasing with the numbers of the people.

Overcrowding of farm lands occurs not only in the regions where the density of population is high but also in underdeveloped countries which have a relatively low ratio of population to total land area. In Latin America, although vast regions of the interior remain almost uninhabited, the density of agricultural population in the cultivated areas is generally high. This is true particularly in Central America and in the western portion of South America. Latin America as a whole has about 75 or 80 persons dependent on agriculture per square kilometer of arable land (about 200 per square mile). Although this is less than one-third of the corresponding ratio for Asia, excluding the Soviet Union, it is five times as high as the average for the United States and Canada. Africa, which also ranks as one of the most sparsely settled continents, has a higher ratio of agricultural population to arable land than Latin America. For example, a survey of the United Nations Trust Territory of Tanganyika, in East Africa, showed that the density of population in nearly all the well-watered localities was over 150 persons per square kilometer in 1934, while two-thirds of the territory was uninhabited.

The mere existence of unoccupied land does not mean that there is no problem in making room for an increasing agricultural population. Much of the land which is not being cultivated is unsuitable for farming, and much of that which is technically usable is poor, remote, or inaccessible. To bring it under cultivation often requires large capital investments, and sometimes also a kind of technical knowledge and aptitude which the people of the region lack. Settlers from other regions may be discouraged by legal restrictions on migration if not by the cost of transporting themselves and their families and establishing new homes. The location may also be unattractive to settlers because of a poor climate, hazards to health, or an unsavory social and political environment. If the land is in the hands of private owners, they may prefer to hold it for speculative gains or put it to such uses as the grazing of livestock instead of opening it for settlement.

In the more densely populated regions at least, intensive development of agriculture on the lands already in use offers greater possibilities than extension of the cultivated area. Crop yields per unit of land could be greatly increased in all the underdeveloped countries if full advantage were taken of present technical knowledge. Much could be accomplished by even such simple improvements as composting, manuring, and crop rotation in areas where these arts are unknown; planting better varieties of crops and breeding better strains of livestock; taking steps to control plant and animal diseases; and applying chemical fertilizers. But here, too, there are difficulties, especially where the people are illiterate, superstitious, wedded to tradition and suspicious of new or foreign techniques, and where adequate means of communication are lacking.

So the agricultural population may continue to grow in areas which are already overcrowded, although there is unused land; and as the density of population rises the standard of living may fall, although the means of greatly increasing production are known. These results are not inevitable. Even in the poorest regions where the ratio of population to land resources is highest, the average product per agricultural worker could be maintained and increased in the face of a considerable growth of population, given a reasonable amount of capital and an energetic attack on the human and technical problems involved. It is difficult to escape the conclusion that the chances of success would be better, in most of the underdeveloped countries, if the numbers of workers engaged in agriculture did not increase so rapidly.

CAN INDUSTRIALIZATION SOLVE THE POPULATION PROBLEM?

One means of slowing the growth of the agricultural population and relieving the pressure of numbers upon the land is to transfer workers from agriculture into other fields of employment. In fact, it is generally agreed that enlargement of the industrial and commercial sectors of the economy is essential for successful economic development of most of the underdeveloped countries. The importance of industrialization and the development of foreign trade is most evident in countries where shortage of land seriously impedes agricultural development. By producing manufactured goods and trading them abroad for food, labor, which is plentiful, in effect is traded for land, which is scarce. Japan's economic development since the beginning of the twentieth century is a striking example. Without a great expansion of manufactures and foreign trade, Japan could hardly have managed to feed her growing population on her slender agricultural resources.

In favorable circumstances, industrialization may turn the growth of population to a valuable aid in attaining a higher standard of living. No one can deny that the increase of population has played such a positive role in the past development of some countries which are now highly industrialized. An example is the United States, where massive immigration, falling death rates, and a moderately high fertility increased the population from about 5 million in 1800 to 150 million in 1950. If the population had remained at its 1800 level, it could never have supplied the labor force to exploit the country's vast natural resources and to build and man its present industrial plant, nor could it have provided the markets to absorb the products of its large-scale, low-cost industries. In the future, if some of the underdeveloped countries with great reserves of unused resources and a relatively small population can launch a successful program of industrialization on a major scale, they also may be able to benefit from a large increase of numbers.

However important the benefits of industrialization might be, it would be a mistake to dismiss the population problems of the underdeveloped countries on the easy assumption that they will soon be solved in this way. It is a formidable task to develop large-scale industries in a predominantly agricultural country with a low level of income and little capital, even if the country is amply endowed with such resources as coal, oil, iron ore, or other sources of energy and industrial raw material. It is difficult enough to get the capital required for developing these resources and building the factories, railroads, and other facilities of an industrial economy. But there are also other difficulties which would hinder any rapid industrialization of most of the underdeveloped countries even if capital also were available in abundance.

In all the underdeveloped countries there is a scarcity of workers who possess the skills and abilities required for efficient operation and maintenance of machinery and for technical, clerical, and managerial occupations. It is not even easy to find suitable trainees for such jobs among a population composed mainly of peasant farmers and a few artisans using simple tools and little or no machinery. The formation of an efficient labor force depends not only on the abilities and aptitudes of the people but also on their willingness to learn and to do the kinds of work in question. The change of occupations often means a complete readjustment of the workers' way of living, and perhaps moving from the homes of their forefathers to new and strange communities. It is not surprising that the material comforts that can be purchased with the wages of new employments are not always sufficient to attract a large number of workers, or to hold them permanently.

The deficiency in education that is typical of most underdeveloped countries hampers their efforts to overcome these difficulties. To quote a few examples, 73 percent of the population in El Salvador, 79 percent in Turkey, 85 percent in Egypt, and 90 percent in India are unable to read or write. The lack of education not only hinders training of the workers needed for industrial development but also makes it the more difficult for them to adapt themselves to the conditions of life in an industrial and commercial society. Although every nation recognizes the need of a certain minimum education for all its people, it takes time to achieve this goal.

If the underdeveloped countries wish to sell manufactured goods abroad, they must find a way to produce these goods efficiently and cheaply in spite of their handicaps. They must compete with other nations that already possess a highly developed industrial plant, a skilled and efficient labor force, and an established position in the world markets. On the other hand, if they wish to industrialize by producing for the home market, they are handicapped by the limited size of the market which results from the inadequacy of income and purchasing power.

THE SHORTAGE OF CAPITAL IN UNDERDEVELOPED COUNTRIES

What has been said up to this point implies that the regions of retarded economic development could not be made into prosperous centers of industry within a short time, no matter how well they might be supplied with the physical equipment required. But in fact these regions are marked by a conspicuous lack of factories, machinery and tools, railroads, locomotives, warehouses, power plants, and other installations that are required for the development of manufacturing industries. The lack of equipment hinders not only industrialization but also the extension and improvement of agriculture.

Huge investments would be required to provide the underdeveloped countries with enough equipment to permit a satisfactory level of output per worker in both agriculture and industry. For example, to fit out all Asia with a modest average of $2000 worth of machinery and tools per worker would cost an amount equal to three times the national income of the United States.

It has been estimated that $540,000,000,000 worth of equipment would be needed to raise the average output per worker in the major part of Asia to the level that Japan had reached before World War II.

Heavy investments in working equipment are beyond the means of the underdeveloped countries, for the great majority of their small income necessarily goes for food and other day-to-day necessities. And by no means all of what they do manage to save is actually invested in income-producing improvements. For example, it has been estimated that net savings in Brazil in 1947 amounted to $13 per capita, but only $6 of this went into productive investments.

Within limits, the underdeveloped countries can increase their savings and investments by following appropriate fiscal, customs, and financial policies. Japan's experience over a period of 70 years shows how a country starting with a low per capita income can save and invest in such a way as to build up a powerful industrial plant in the course of time. But this cannot be accomplished overnight. The hoe cannot be asked to produce enough both to feed its owner today and purchase a tractor tomorrow.

Some of the needed equipment can be purchased abroad with the help of foreign loans. In fact, large loans from the richer nations have been called an essential condition for satisfactory progress in economic development of the retarded regions. But the underdeveloped countries cannot rely on foreign capital alone, if only because many kinds of equipment cannot economically be transported in foreign trade. A hydroelectric turbine, for example, may be imported, but not the power plant itself, nor the dam. And whatever is purchased on loans must be paid for within a reasonable time out of savings if the borrowing nation is to avoid an excessive burden of debt and maintain a good credit standing. So in the long run the underdeveloped countries must depend mainly on investments out of their own savings in order to work out a sound, balanced program of economic development.

HOW POPULATION GROWTH INTENSIFIES THE SHORTAGE OF CAPITAL

The faster the population grows, the more investments are necessary to keep up a given level of per capita production. In a country with a constant population, it is necessary only to replace the equipment which is worn out or becomes obsolete, in order to see that each generation is as well provided with the tools of production as the preceding one. Where the population is growing, an additional investment is required to maintain the same average amount of equipment per worker. An improvement of equipment which would permit a larger average product per worker and a higher standard of living can only be obtained by a further investment, over and above what is required by the growth of population. The size of this further investment, which an underdeveloped country can afford to spare from its annual income, is smaller if the population is growing rapidly than if it is growing slowly. Se the speeding-up of population growth in the underdeveloped countries makes it the more difficult for them to save and invest enough.

It has been estimated that an underdeveloped country with its population increasing at one percent per year must invest from 2 to 5 percent of its national income in order to keep a constant average amount of working equipment per worker. If the population increases at $2\frac{1}{2}$ percent per year, from 5 to $12\frac{1}{2}$ percent of the national income will be absorbed in such investments. It is not easy for any poor country to save such a large proportion of its income; but those where population is now growing most rapidly must save and invest still more if they are to reach a higher living standard. The difficulty is not confined to densely populated, resource-poor countries. It exists also where there is an abundance of land and other natural resources not being used for lack of the necessary capital or working equipment.

THE BURDEN OF DEPENDENT CHILDREN

It can be said that a nation is called upon to make investments in human capital as well as physical equipment. In other words, what is spent in rearing and educating the next generation is also an investment, which may pay handsomely in terms of future production and prosperity. The responsibility for this kind of investment is carried by the elder generation, and the weight of the burden which it represents for the average adult worker depends partly on the relative numbers of children and adults in the population. In the underdeveloped countries the ratio of children to adults is typically very high because of their high birth rates—and this aspect of their population situation further complicates their problem of savings and investments.

The age group from 15 to 60 years can be taken roughly to represent the adult population which has the responsibility of supporting the nation's children. In the underdeveloped regions of Asia, Africa, and Latin America, there are generally about 7 children under 15 to every 10 persons between 15 and 60 years old. On the other hand, the ratio in the economically most advanced countries of Europe, North America, and Oceania is typically around 4 or $4\frac{1}{2}$ children to 10 adults of the ages mentioned.

The people of the underdeveloped countries lighten their load of childhood dependency by putting the children to work at an early age. It is common practice in the rural areas of such countries for children to begin working more or less long hours in the fields or at various farm chores by the age of 10 or 12 years, if not earlier. In Turkey, for example, the 1945 census showed 49 percent of the boys 10 to 14 years old engaged in gainful occupations, whereas the corresponding figure for Sweden in 1940 was only 2 percent. But the employment of children at this age is not compatible with a high standard of education and therefore cannot be regarded as a satisfactory solution of the economic problem which a high ratio of children in the population creates.

Whatever is invested in rearing and educating a child is lost if the child dies before he reaches the age at which he can contribute to production. So it seems that the reduction of death rates in underdeveloped countries, permitting more children to survive, means a corresponding saving of material resources. Is this not a possible source of the additional investments which these countries need, both to improve the capacities of the coming generation of workers and to give them better physical equipment?

Unfortunately, it is not so. Although it seems at first thought that an increase in the proportion of children who survive should improve the ratio of adult to child population, this is a delusion. So long as the birth rates are not changed, any addition to the adult population implies a proportionate increase in the number of births. If death rates fall while birth rates remain constant, the size of each successive generation will be larger but the average number of dependent children per adult will be practically unchanged. This is the present situation of the underdeveloped countries generally, and they will continue to suffer the economic handicap of heavy childhood dependency as long as their present high birth rates continue.

THE THREE POPULATION PROBLEMS OF THE UNDERDEVELOPED COUNTRIES SUMMARIZED

To sum up, population enters into the problem of achieving satisfactory standards of living in the underdeveloped countries, in three principal ways.

First, their high birth rates create a heavy load of dependent children per adult. This makes it difficult to save enough, over and above what is required for the support of the workers and their dependents, for needed investments in equipment for economic development. It also seriously complicates the problem of providing the children with the education that is essential for social and economic progress in the long run. This aspect of the population problem is common to all the underdeveloped countries.

Second, falling death rates with high birth rates bring about a rapid increase of population. Large investments must be made to keep the growing numbers of workers equipped even with the same inadequate amounts of working equipment per man as they have had in the past. So the possibilities for investments which would improve the equipment and raise productivity per worker are diminished. This speeding up of population growth, aggravating the shortage of capital, is now taking place in very many underdeveloped countries, wherever successful public health campaigns have greatly reduced death rates.

Third, many of the underdeveloped countries have an excessive density of agricultural population in relation to the area of cultivated land. The average farmer has too little land to make a satisfactory living for himself and his family. Not all underdeveloped countries face this difficulty, but it exists in some which have large amounts of unused land, as well as in those where nearly all the cultivable land is fully occupied. At least some of the countries now suffering from acute agricultural overpopulation might be able to employ all their numbers to good advantage, and benefit in the long run from a substantially larger population, if they were better equipped to utilize the land resources which they possess, or if they could industrialize. But neither the necessary improvements of agriculture nor the development of industry can easily be accomplished, and the difficulties are increased by high birth rates and rapid population growth.

It appears that even in a country where population growth would be economically advantageous in the long run, economic progress will be hindered if the birth rate is so high and if the population grows so rapidly as to put an excessive strain on the economy.

WILL THE HIGH BIRTH RATES OF THE UNDERDEVELOPED COUNTRIES CONTINUE?

There are some reasons for expecting that the birth rates of the economically retarded nations would fall in the future, if they could industrialize and improve their standards of living to some extent. This expectation is based on the history of economically more advanced countries which, at an earlier stage of their economic development, had nearly as high birth rates as the underdeveloped countries generally do today.

The theory is that nations generally pass through a typical cycle of changing birth and death rates as they make the transition from a low-income agricultural to a high-income industrial economy. During the first phase of the cycle, the changes in economic conditions are not sufficient to have much effect on traditional attitudes and customs relating to marriage, the family, and the production of children. So the birth rate remains high, and as the death rate falls the population grows rapidly. But sooner or later the change from rural to city life, from the family farm to wage-earning industrial employment, with higher income, better education, and constantly increasing material wants, begins to affect people's ideas about the number of children they desire and the possibility of limiting the size of the family. Lower death rates also may affect these ideas, as parents come to realize that they no longer need to produce so many children to assure the survival of the number they want. Eventually the birth rate falls, balancing the lower death rate, and the growth of population slackens.

This theory fits reasonably well with the past trends of population and economic development in most countries of Europe and the industrialized countries of North America and Oceania. As a basis for predicting the future course of events in other parts of the world, it is subject to a certain weakness. The repercussions of industrialization and increasing wealth upon the birth rate may not be the same in different cultures. For example, the Bantu herdsmen of the African prairies, the Buddhist peasants of Ceylon, and the ancestor-worshipping farmers of Communist China may not react to these changes in the same way as the Europeans and their colonists overseas reacted.

Nevertheless, most experts presume that economic development of the now underdeveloped countries would ultimately lead, at least in most cases, to lower birth rates. If this is taken for granted, the question remains, what types and what degree of change in economic conditions would be required, and how much time would have to elapse before the birth rate would fall low enough to nearly balance the death rate?

The history of the European peoples does not give a very good basis for predictions in this matter. In Poland and Czechoslovakia, before World War II, the birth rate fell as much in about 12 years as it had fallen in France during a period of 70 years in the nineteenth and early twentieth century. It has been suggested that the tempo of such social changes has been quickened by improved means of communication, for example the invention of the radio, bringing the people of different countries into closer contact. But it is possible, in spite of these changes in the circumstances, that conditions favoring a low birth rate may develop more slowly in other parts of the world than they did in Europe, Northern America, and the British Dominions of Oceania.

Another question that may be even more important is whether or not the birth rates of the underdeveloped countries may fall before they have reached a much higher standard of living. It has been said that such an event is unlikely because people living in deep poverty and ignorance generally lack both the means and the will to control the size of their families. But some recent studies in low-income agricultural regions where birth rates are very high have shown a remarkably widespread desire to avoid having too many children and an interest in learning how to prevent it. Research on suitable methods of family planning for use in such countries and government programs of public education in this field may have an important effect on the future birth-rate trends.

CAN EMIGRATION SOLVE THE POPULATION PROBLEMS OF UNDERDEVELOPED COUNTRIES?

Overseas emigration helped European countries during the nineteenth and early twentieth centuries to escape some of the economic difficulties to which the rapid growth of their population might otherwise have led, before the birth rates were adjusted to falling death rates. According to one estimate, the population of Europe in 1910 was 88 million less than it would have been if there had been no emigration after 1800. The case of Ireland is remarkable. Beginning at the time of the potato famines in the 1840s, emigrants left Ireland at such a rate that the population decreased from more than 8 million in 1841 to less than 3 million in 1946. Without emigration the density of population on Irish farms would no doubt have mounted steadily, aggravating the constant problem of rural poverty in that country.

Countries like Great Britain and Germany benefited from emigration, not only as a relief from population pressure on the land, but also in other ways. The emigrants built up markets abroad for the products of the home countries' industries, supplying raw materials and food in exchange. The development of agriculture and industry in the areas of immigration overseas also furnished a profitable field for investment of European capital.

Today the densely populated underdeveloped countries have much less opportunity to ease their difficulties in this manner. There are no longer any great "new worlds" with vast areas of good farm land to be had for the labor of clearing and plowing it. Some lands are still available to immigrants in certain parts of the world—South America and Australia, for instance—but they are generally less productive and more costly to develop than the lands which the European emigrants took up earlier. Even where the land itself can be acquired cheaply, a substantial investment is generally required to cover the cost of transporting the migrants, outfitting them on their new farms with stock and equipment, maintaining them until they reap their first harvests, building their new homes and roads, schools, etc., for their new communities. Sometimes there is a need for further investments in irrigation, drainage, elimination of pests, etc., to make the land productive and habitable. The people of the underdeveloped countries can ill afford to bear these costs. On the other hand, the countries of immigration prefer to encourage settlers from more wealthy countries, who can generally bring more capital, a superior education and better knowledge of modern agricultural techniques with them.

While the opportunities for new agricultural settlements have diminished, the demand for workers in manufacturing, trade, service, and related occupations has greatly increased in many of the countries of immigration. In fact, a large and growing proportion of all international migrants since the end of the nineteenth century have found employment in the latter kinds of occupations. But migrants from the underdeveloped countries, for the most part, are not very well qualified for any but a fairly narrow range of relatively unskilled jobs outside of agriculture. Here again they are at a disadvantage in competition, not only with migrants from the more developed countries but also with the workers resident in the countries of immigration.

For these reasons it is unlikely that the underdeveloped countries would be able to send out emigrants in nearly such numbers as Europe did half a century ago, even if there were no legal barriers to exclude them from the countries of immigration. Actually there are now severe restrictions in all these countries both on the right of immigrants to enter and on the types of employment in which they may engage within the country. These restrictions are generally such as to make immigration particularly difficult for the nationals of underdeveloped countries, especially in Asia. In effect, they are virtually excluded from some of the most important immigration countries.

On the other hand, if emigration were to have any great effect on the trend of population in some of the largest, most densely populated underdeveloped countries, like India, China, and Java, they would not only have to equal but to surpass by a wide margin the highest emigration rates ever experienced in European countries during the era of the great trans-Atlantic movement. Such a feat appears to be entirely out of the question under the conditions that exist in the world today.

Within the limits of what is possible, emigration may nevertheless be of some help in relieving the economic pressures due to excessive density of agricultural population and too rapid growth of numbers, particularly in the smaller underdeveloped countries. Its possible effectiveness in favorable circumstances, at least in the short run, is shown by the recent experience of Puerto Rico. Puerto Rico, of course, is a special case, since its citizens have unrestricted access to the United States and the cost of their transportation and relocation in that country is minimal.

For the underdeveloped countries in general, and particularly for the larger and more populous ones, it is almost inevitable that the balance of births and deaths will continue in the future to be the major determinant of population trends. This being so, economic development within the underdeveloped countries themselves must be made to overbalance the natural growth of population, if the better standards of life desired for the future are to become a reality.

S. L. WOLFBEIN
and
A. J. JAFFE

||||||||||||||||||||||||||||||||||||||||||||||||||||||||||||||||||||||||||||||||||||||||||||||||||||||||||||||||||||||||

Demographic Factors in Labor Force Growth

INTRODUCTION

The period of time covering the National Defense Program and our active participation in the war witnessed not only a considerable change in the demographic characteristics of our population, but also served to reveal the great flexibility in the labor supply of the United States. Moreover, at no

From *American Sociological Review* (August 1956), pp. 392-396, with omissions. Reprinted by permission of the American Sociological Association and the authors.

other time was it so important to understand the connection between population characteristics and the labor supply. Thus, the elementary problems of obtaining the manpower needed for the military as well as for producing the goods for winning the war focused attention on the potential labor supply among women. No analysis of this potential was possible without knowledge and appreciation of the facts relative to the age, marital, and dependency status of the female population and their bearing upon labor market participation.

That these and many other demographic factors are major determinants of both the size and composition of the labor force at any given time is well known. Only a cursory examination of the relevant census volume for any decade will make apparent the crucial importance of the age and sex composition of the population, the marital and dependency status of women, or the proportion of colored or foreign-born in determining the size and composition of our working population.

In this paper the attempt will be made to assess the relative importance of demographic factors in the changing size and composition of the labor force over a *span of time*. More specifically, how important have changes in age, sex, marital status, color, and nativity been with relation to changes in the rate of labor force participation between 1890 and 1930? Indeed, what has been their importance in comparison with other social and economic factors which also have a bearing upon the size of the labor force? A similar set of questions will be asked for the war period. And finally, an analysis of the results and their bearing upon estimates of future population and labor force growth will be noted.

THE PERIOD 1890 TO 1930[1]

Practically all of the changes in demographic factors during the forty-year period from 1890 to 1930 operated in the direction of decreasing the worker rate. Thus, women have a much smaller worker rate than men: The sex ratio (for the population 15 years of age and over) dropped from 106.0 in 1890 to 102.4 in 1930. Married women are in the labor force in much smaller proportion: The proportion of married women to total went up from 56.8 to 61.1 during the same period. High worker rates are also characteristic of the foreign-born white: Their ratio in the total population fell from 23.3 percent to 16.9 percent. The colored population has always had a higher

---

[1] The choice of the period 1890 and 1930 for studying the effects of long-term demographic changes was dictated largely by considerations of available data. The 1890 Decennial Census contained very detailed tabulations of the gainfully occupied population by age, sex, marital status, color, nativity, etc.—more detail than in any ensuing census until 1940. The 1930 Decennial Census, of course, was the latest with comparable gainful worker data. Finally, the forty-year period was sufficiently long to allow for significant changes in the demographic factors under consideration.

TABLE 1. EFFECT OF DEMOGRAPHIC AND OTHER SOCIOECONOMIC
CHANGES ON PROPORTION OF POPULATION, 15 YEARS OF AGE
AND OVER, GAINFULLY OCCUPIED, 1890 AND 1930,
BY SEX AND MARITAL STATUS

	Total	Male	Female Total	Female Unmarried[a]	Female Married
1. 1890 gainful worker rates as enumerated (Decennial Census)	54.8	88.7	18.9	37.7	4.6
2. 1930 gainful worker rates as enumerated (Decennial Census)	55.9	86.2	24.8	45.4	11.7
3. 1930 gainful worker rates expected on basis of changing demographic factors[b]	52.6	88.3	16.0	34.9	4.0
4. Influence of demographic factors (line 3 minus line 1)	—2.2	—0.4	—2.9	—2.8	—0.6
5. Influence of other social-economic forces (line 2 minus line 3)	3.3	—2.1	8.8	10.5	7.7
Percentage change 1890 to 1930 due to:					
Changing social-economic factors	+6.0	—2.4	+46.6	+27.8	+167.4
Changing demographic factors	—4.0	—0.5[c]	—15.3	—7.4	—13.0
Both socioeconomic and demographic factors	+2.0	—2.9	+31.3	+20.4	+154.4

     [a] Includes single, widowed, and divorced.
     [b] Estimated by applying 1890 gainful worker rates by age, sex, color, nativity, and for female marital status, to the 1930 population similarly classified. 1890 gainful worker rates, classified by the various characteristics from Department of Interior: *Special Census Report of the Population of the United States at the Eleventh Census, 1890* (Washington, D. C. 1896), pp. 21 *et. seq.,* and *Report on Population of the United States at the Eleventh Census, 1890,* Pt. II (Washington, D. C. 1897), Tables 119 and 120. All figures adjusted for under-enumeration of gainful workers in younger age groups, *cf.* Department of Commerce and Labor, Bureau of the Census, Twelfth Census of U.S. (1900). Report on Occupation, pp. lxvi to lxxiii.
     [c] When applying 1930 specific gainful worker rates to the 1890 population classified as in note *b,* above, a practically identical percentage change was obtained.

rate of labor market participation than the whites: The proportion of colored, however, has decreased only from 11.0 to 10.7 over the forty-year period. Even the aging of the population served to operate in the same direction among women, since their worker rates begin to fall after the 20-24 age group. Among the men, a large part of the effect of the aging process was a shift within the middle-age group in which worker rates are close to 100 per cent anyway.

One demographic factor which undoubtedly operated in the direction of a higher worker rate was the decrease in fertility. Just how important the decreasing birth rate was in freeing women from the home is difficult to determine, although it may have been fairly important. (Data on dependency status are not available for this period.) If a woman has no children, she generally is free to take a job away from the home; if she has even one small child, she is tied to the home almost as much as if she had several.[2] The decrease in fertility resulted in large part from a decrease in the proportion of women who had large families (4 or more children ever born), and secondarily from an increase in the proportion of childless women.[3]

Table 1 summarizes the expected effects of demographic changes, assuming 1890 specific gainful worker rates had remained unchanged by 1930, and contrasts them with what actually happened between 1890 and 1930. For example, among all women aged 15 years and over the gainful worker rate *increased* by almost one-third, instead of decreasing by several percentage points as might have been expected on the basis of the demographic factors enumerated above. The contrast is especially marked for the married women among whom the gainful worker rate almost tripled between 1890 and 1930 instead of experiencing the small decline indicated on the basis of the demographic factors. Among the males, these demographic factors should have caused no change in the gainful worker rate between 1890 and 1930; actually, of course, the proportion of males gainfully occupied decreased somewhat.

It is quite clear, then, that the observed changes in the proportion of the population listed as gainful workers in 1890 as compared with 1930 were determined more by various social and economic factors than by the demographic aspects as such.[4] Perhaps most important was the social acceptance of women in employment outside the home—a reflection of a variety of forces including the growing importance of white-collar jobs, changes in technology and in industrial organization resulting in factory jobs in which women can perform adequately, the transfer of many activities from the home to the commercial sphere (food preparation, laundry, making of clothes, etc.), the

---

[2] The relationship of labor force participation to number of small children in the family is known for 1940. Among all women in the United States, married, husband present, aged 18 to 44 years, we find the following labor force participation rates:

Without children under 10 years of age	25.7%
With 1 child under 10 years of age	9.9%
With 2 or more children under 10 years of age	5.9%

(See 16th Census of the U.S., 1940, *Population, The Labor Force, Employment and Family Characteristics of Women,* Table II, p. 3.)

From these data it would appear that labor force participation for married women drops markedly—15.8 percentage points—with the advent of one young child (under 10 years of age), and then drops much less—4 percentage points—with the advent of subsequent young children.

[3] *Cf.* 16th Census of the United States, 1940. Population, *Differential Fertility, 1940 and 1910,* Women by Number of Children Ever Born, Tables 1 and 4.

[4] It might be argued that the aging of the entire population (all ages) between 1890 and 1930 should have resulted in an increase in the proportion of the total population who were classified as gainful workers. Thus, the median ages were:

	Males	*Females*
1890	21.2	20.7
1930	26.7	26.2

This aging of the population should have resulted in an increase in the proportion of all male gainful workers from 60.2 to 65.6; for females there should have been a decrease from 13.1 to 12.8 (standardizing on the basis of the 1890 age-sex, specific rates). Actually, the proportion of male gainful workers increased, by 1930, to only 61.3, and females to 17.7. Here again, the importance of the socioeconomic factors is emphasized.

changing role of women as evidenced by their gaining the vote and holding public offices, etc. Among males the decrease in worker rates over the forty-year period is essentially a product of later entrance into the labor force (and, conversely, more years of schooling) and earlier retirement.

Reference to Table 1 will indicate the relative importance of these social and economic factors and the demographic forces.[5]. . .

PREDICTING FUTURE LABOR-FORCE GROWTH

The major thesis of this paper—that other social and economic forces are much more important than measurable demographic factors in accounting for changes in the proportion of the population in the labor force—is significant for the problem of forecasting changes in the size of the labor force.

Demographic factors are only of secondary importance. The age and sex distribution of the population can be estimated for 1980, 1990, or even the year 2000. Similarly, 1940 or 1945 age-sex specific labor market participation rates could be applied to the extrapolated population. But how far off are we likely to be? What are the long-term trends in the nondemographic factors affecting the proportions of women who will be in the labor force at some future date? How are these socioeconomic factors determining the ages at which men and women first enter and leave the labor force? What would be the effect of a deep depression? Of a level approaching full employment? Of a considerably higher plane of living? Of wholesale technological change? Of a much shorter work week? Some of these factors will play a pivotal role even in an estimate of the size of the labor force for so close a year as 1950. It would seem, then, that much more fruitful fields of research would center about these nondemographic factors and their effects upon labor market participation.[6]

During the last half century (or longer) the proportion of women in the

---

[5] An extremely informative analysis not reflected in any of the tables can be made of the effects of increasing longevity, per se. As specific mortality rates decrease, the life-table population becomes older, increasing the over-all rate of labor market participation. One hundred thousand white males born in 1900 and subject to the age specific mortality rates of that year would have worked 3 million years by age 65, at 1890 worker rates. If these white males had been subject to mortality rates of 1929-1931, they would have worked some 3,700,000 years—24 percent more. In other words, if the only demographic change that had occurred had been in mortality, 24 percent additional jobs would have had to be found for the increased number of survivors. Should mortality continue to increase to, say, the level of New Zealand females in 1934-1938, the additional number of jobs required would increase to almost 40 percent. The same situation holds for white females.

[6] One of the few pieces of research which resulted in a projected labor force taking into account more than the usual demographic factors was that of Durand and Wood in their "Normal Growth of the Labor Force in the United States," Census release P-44 No. 12, June 12, 1944. Working with actual Census age-sex specific worker rates since 1920, they automatically concerned themselves with the sum total of all factors bearing upon labor-market participation, in extrapolating trends to 1950.

labor force has steadily increased.[7] Among men the proportion decreased somewhat up to the time of the beginning of World War II, after which it increased during the war years. What does the future hold? Will this wartime expansion of the male labor force continue for an indefinite period ahead? Will labor force participation among women continue to increase? Only analysis of the basic underlying socioeconomic forces can answer these questions.

EDWARD S. MASON

IIIIIIIIIIIIIIIIIIIIIIIIIIIIIIIIIIIIIIIIIIIIIIIIIIIIIIIIIIIIIIIIIIIIIIIIIIIIIIIIIIIIIIIIIIIIIIIIIIIIIIIIIIIIIIIIIIIIIIIIIIIIIIIIIIIIIIIIIIIIIIIIIIIII

Raw Materials and Economic Development

THE LONG-RUN OUTLOOK

. . . The principal question with which this paper is concerned is whether economic growth in the United States and the Free World is likely to be handicapped over the next few decades by rising real costs of industrial materials. . . .

If we accept the current Bureau of the Census median estimate for population growth in the United States, and if we assume that the per capita productivity of the labor force increases at the slightly less than 2 percent per annum that has been maintained over the last few decades, the Gross National Product of this country would approximately double over the next twenty-five years. Since the current activity of the durable goods industries, which are heavily material consuming, is abnormally high and since there may be a long-term trend toward tertiary production which is less heavily material consuming, the material requirements of the American economy may somewhat less than double over the same period. The rates of growth in the other principal industrial areas of the Free World, mainly Western Europe and Japan, will probably be somewhat less than this. On the other hand, materials consumption in other areas that are ripe for industrialization, notably Latin America and Southern Asia, may increase at a much more rapid rate. How-

From *Quarterly Journal of Economics* (August 1952), pp. 327-341, with omissions. Reprinted by permission of Harvard University Press and the author. Copyright 1952 by The President and Fellows of Harvard College.

---

[7] Professor Jaffe asked us to note that in another article he presents evidence casting serious doubt as to how large an increase there has really been in the labor force participation rate of women. See A. J. Jaffe, "Trends in the Participation of Women in the Working Force," *Monthly Labor Review* (May 1956), pp. 559-565.—EDS.

ever, it should be noted that since the United States consumes about one-half the raw materials of the Free World and, with Western Europe and Japan, accounts for well over 80 percent, even very high rates of industrialization in the rest of the Free World would not change the total rate of increase by very much. Perhaps, for the purpose of assigning some reasonable order of magnitude to the raw materials problem, we might assume that by some time in the decade of the 1970s Free-world requirements are, in the absence of war, likely to double.

This presents us with a formidable problem. In real terms the U.S. consumption of minerals, including oil, increased by five times between 1900 and 1950. We are now projecting for 1975 a rate of consumption roughly ten times the rate for 1900. Can these requirements be satisfied and, if so, without a substantial increase in real costs?

If we turn our attention to the United States and concentrate on so-called exhaustible materials, the picture, though undeniably obscure, presents certain potentially disturbing features. What we should like to know, of course, for every one of the important minerals used by industry, is the total amount of the material in the United States recoverable at various levels of cost. What is available in fact is information concerning the proved reserves of commercial grade plus geological estimates of the percentage of the earth's crust constituted by the mineral in question. In between these estimated magnitudes there exists a vast gulf of uncertainty. For certain minerals it is clear that the so-called proved reserves are not much more than the mining industry's working inventory which can be expanded whenever the industry sees fit to do so. For others there may be reason to suspect that the present estimate of proved reserves represents about all of the mineral that is likely to be obtainable in the United States at current costs and with presently available techniques of discovery.

Despite this uncertainty, however, there are various facts that help to indicate the probable trend in the relationship between U.S. output of and requirements for exhaustible materials. For certain important materials the country was, before [World War II], either self-sufficient or on a net export basis. It is now a net importer of these materials which include oil, copper, lead, zinc, iron ore, and other less important items. The available evidence concerning oil and various other minerals, moreover, indicates pretty clearly a rising real cost of discovery. In addition we know that with respect to copper, lead, and zinc, the trend has for decades been toward the extraction of lower and lower grade ores. Finally it should be mentioned that there has not been a really important new discovery of some of our most important metals for at least three decades. When these facts are added to scattered evidence concerning the potential availability of minerals of lower grades in the United States, it appears highly probable that in the absence of increasing imports or improved techniques of discovery, the relative price of many mineral products in this country is apt to increase sharply.

What has been said about the United States has, of course, been true of Western Europe for a long period of time. Not only will an increasing percentage of Western Europe's materials requirements have to be imported but for certain important items, with respect to which the area has been relatively self-sufficient, the prospect is for increasing dependence on foreign sources. In the field of energy resources, despite the maximum development of hydroelectric power, it seems probable that Western Europe will become a net importer of coal on a sizable scale and, barring war, it is plausible that the area's requirements for petroleum will triple during the next quarter century.

If, then, we consider how the rapidly growing materials requirements of the industrial areas of the world are to be met, it is clear that without a large expansion of output for export in the so-called underdeveloped areas of the world or large technological improvements in the discovery, extraction, or processing of materials, or both, the material requirements of the industrial areas will be met either not at all or only at sharply rising real costs. Before proceeding to a consideration of the conditions of expansion of raw material output in underdeveloped areas it is necessary to consider briefly the potential impact on the raw materials problem of technological development. The existing level of technological knowledge of synthetics and of other possibilities of materials substitution is sufficient to set very real limits to the dependence of this country on imports of raw materials and to the rise in real costs that a lack of availability of imports would otherwise entail. There are, furthermore, technological developments just over the horizon that will still further reduce these limits. It is important that the current and potential impact of the state of technology on the raw materials problem be recognized not only in this country but throughout the underdeveloped areas of the world.

It was mentioned above that the cost of finding oil in this country is probably—and rather sharply—on the increase. In the absence of substitutes this would mean an increase in the price of crude oil mitigated by an increasing flow of imports. However, with presently available technical knowledge, it is estimated by the National Petroleum Council[1] that petroleum products can be produced from shale at no more than 25 to 30 percent above the present price of these products; the Bureau of Mines says that shale oil is currently competitive. There are 125 billion barrels of oil in high-grade shales in this country and other hundreds of billions in lower grades. Furthermore, the hydrogenation and synthesis of coal, although at present more expensive than the production of oil from shale, give promise of further substantial technological development. Consequently the extent to which the cost and price of natural crude oil will rise in this country seems strictly limited.

Or, to take another example, consider the iron-ore situation in the United States. The approaching exhaustion of the high-grade Mesabi ores has already driven American companies to search for, and to find, large and rich deposits in Venezuela, Labrador, Liberia, and elsewhere. At existing price levels we may expect to see over the next few decades a large expansion in the share of our domestic requirements met from imports. If, however, the conditions

---

[1] Report of the National Petroleum Council's Committee on Synthetic Liquid Fuels Production Costs, October 31, 1951.

affecting the exploitation of foreign reserves should worsen in such fashion as substantially to raise the cost of imported ores, our practically unlimited caconite ores would come into production on a large scale. The existence of these reserves, which developing technology will make available at prices not much higher than current iron-ore prices, sets a very real limit to the future increase in the price of ores from other sources.

So it is with synthetic wool and other textiles, synthetic rubber, and a number of other synthetic materials the production of which is indefinitely expansible in the United States. The current and potential availability of these materials at prices somewhat higher than the current world-market prices for the natural materials will continue to set ceilings beyond which the prices of these natural materials cannot rise for long without curtailing imports into the United States.

The effect of developing technology upon materials availability is by no means limited to the exploitation of lower-grade ores and the production of synthetic substitutes. As the history of the last fifty years will show, the "mix" of the materials flow into American fabricating facilities is highly flexible. Over the next few decades we may expect to see a rapid substitution of aluminum, magnesium, titanium, and other expanding materials for materials whose output can increase only at rising costs. We shall continue that process of "engineering out of" tin and other scarce or vulnerable materials in which we have been engaged for some time past.

The principal relevance of current and potential technological development to the materials problem here under discussion is that it holds real possibilities for sharply restraining the increase in real costs of materials input to which the American economy would be subject if we should not be able to look toward an expansion of foreign sources of supply. At something like pre-Korean price relationships, however, we should, in fact, expect to see expanding American materials requirements increasingly satisfied from foreign sources. This has been the trend of the last few decades and there is no reason, except a sharp increase in the relative cost from foreign sources, why this trend should not continue. In other industrial areas of the world where the possibilities of substitution from domestic materials sources are not as real as in this country, an expansion of imports from foreign sources is likely to persist despite a substantial increase in relative prices. It appears, therefore, that the cost conditions under which expansion of materials production may occur in the underdeveloped areas of the world have an important bearing on the prospects for continued economic growth in Western Europe, Japan, and, to a smaller extent, in the United States.

FOREIGN SOURCES OF SUPPLY

The areas of the world to which we must principally look for expansion of minerals output for export are the Near East, South and Southeast Asia, Africa, and Latin America. As potential producers and exporters of mineral products, excluding oil, Africa comes first and Latin America second. The Near East is, of course, the prospective supplier of nearly the whole of Western Europe's oil requirements and may well become an important exporter to the United States. If we fasten our attention on minerals and look, in particular, at the high tonnage materials including oil, iron ore, copper, lead, zinc, manganese, and bauxite, it can be said with fair confidence that the known and inferred reserves of these minerals in the underdeveloped areas of the world are large enough and of sufficiently high grade to meet the Free-world requirements for at least the next twenty-five years at little or no increase in real costs. In fact we can extend this range of materials very considerably and still say that if resources were relatively free to flow to lowest-cost sources it is unlikely that economic growth in the free world would be handicapped over the next few decades by rising real costs of mineral materials. In fact, however, there may be serious governmentally imposed impediments and the result may well be a substantial worsening of the terms of trade for manufactured products. The current and potential technological possibilities of substitution could moderate this shift but could hardly prevent it. What happens therefore to the conditions under which materials will continue to be produced for export in the underdeveloped areas of the world is an important aspect of the problem.

The major part of the production for export of mineral products in these areas has been carried on by Western European and American capital under the ownership and control of a relatively small number of large companies. Oil-company investment abroad has accounted for three-quarters of the total American private investment abroad since the war and, if prospective Free-world requirements for oil are going to be met through the same channels in the future as they have been in the past, the private foreign investment for petroleum expansion in the Near East, Venezuela, and elsewhere will continue to be very large. Although private U.S. capital invested in foreign mining enterprises increased by not much more than $100 million between 1930 and 1950, current expansion of iron-ore properties and the increase in other mining facilities that would have to be undertaken if Free-world requirements for minerals are to be met largely by private production in underdeveloped areas presages a much higher rate of increase over the next quarter century. Are we going to witness such an expansion and, if so, is it going to take place through the medium of foreign private investment?

If the areas in question were all colonial possessions of Western powers, there is little doubt that both questions would be answered in the affirmative. Furthermore, it would be argued, at least in the West, via the doctrines of geographical specialization and comparative cost, that the well-being of the underdeveloped areas would advance more rapidly through expansion of raw material output than by large-scale diversion of resources into industrial production. And, within limits, it is by no means clear that this is not so.

We may take it for granted, however, that, with the possible exception of the African colonies of European powers, things are not going to work out in this fashion. In South and Southeast Asia many of the important raw-materials countries have recently thrown off colonial status and have taken their economic development in their own hands. In the Near East a fanatical nationalism has cast its shadow over any future expansion of foreign investment. In Latin America independent and sensitive governments increasingly resent the stigma of economic colonialism that frequently is attached to economies oriented heavily towards raw-materials exports. The political and economic differences among the areas in question and among the countries making up each area are great but, by and large, all these countries share the ambition to develop economically, and almost invariably economic development is interpreted to mean industrialization.

Industrialization may not be the road to economic salvation indicated by the sign post of comparative costs but it is widely suspected in the underdeveloped areas that this signpost is heavily warped in a westerly direction. For one thing the doctrine takes no account of what happens during cyclical depression to an economy which is strongly oriented toward the production for export of one, or a few, price-sensitive raw materials; for another, comparative cost is a static doctrine that does not reckon with a technological dynamism associated with industrialization that may affect conditions of production throughout the economy. The proper allocation of resources of today may, under the impact of industrialization, become the improper allocation of tomorrow. While there is merit in both of these contentions it is easy to exaggerate their importance and to appraise falsely their significance for raw materials development.

The experience of the 1930s indicated what *could* happen to the foreign-exchange earnings, government revenues, and the whole prosperity of an economy producing a few raw materials for the world market. Furthermore the 1930s followed upon a decade which, for agricultural raw materials, was also one of surplus. It is now fairly clear, however, that the change in the terms of trade unfavorable to raw materials during the interwar period marked the culmination of a trend that, by the end of the period, was already beginning to be reversed. And although the 1930s indicated what *could* happen to industrial demands for raw materials there are sound reasons for believing that it is not going to happen again. Raw-material-producing countries—at least in international conferences—seem excessively preoccupied with the experience of the 1930s and unwilling to turn their attention to long-term historical and prospective growth rates in raw material requirements. Certainly recessions of the 1949 variety and worse can and will happen; certainly, also, the percentage decline in the exports of raw materials will be a multiple of the decline in national income of the industrial countries importing raw materials. This constitutes a serious problem and merits attention to policies both national and international for mitigating the effects of the instability of the foreign exchange earnings of materials exporting countries. But the problem to be attacked appears to be one, henceforth, of evening out relatively small variations from a pronounced upward trend of materials requirements.

The more important *caveat* to the implications for economic development of the doctrine of comparative costs has to do with what Marshall would have called the external economies connected with expansion of output of industrial products and services. These "economies," so-called, are not only external to the firm but also to the industry. In an economy on the verge of industrialization one thing very much leads to another. In fact it is misleading to give the name "economies" to the creation of what are really new production functions facilitated, it is true, by the expansion of output of particular products, but in no proper sense "induced" by this expansion. At a certain stage of industrialization, as the example of Japan shows, the whole economic environment may be changed with effects that permeate through every form of economic activity.

While recognizing these possibilities there are, however, certain limits to the rate at which this process can proceed even under the most favorable circumstances and it does not follow that the attainment of a satisfactory or an optimum rate means industrialization à outrance. Clearly the possibilities of capital formation either from domestic savings or foreign investment set some sort of limit. Equally clearly, if industrialization means diversion of labor away from agriculture, the possibilities of releasing labor for industrial employment may require a substantial increase in agricultural productivity. In considering the advantages of industrialization in backward areas what is frequently encountered is a comparison of the very low productivity of labor in primitive agriculture with the very high productivity of the same or similar labor in industry working with Western techniques and machines. In all the industrial countries of the world, and particularly in the United States, statistical increases in per capita productivity are in part the result of a mere shift in employment from low-productivity agriculture to high-productivity industry. But a comparison of these relative productivities in underdeveloped areas stacks the cards much too heavily in favor of industrialization. Productivity in agriculture in most of these areas is as susceptible to improvement by the use of Western methods as is productivity in industry.

The application of Western methods requires capital not only for industry but for agriculture and, if economic development is to mean growth in national income and national wealth, and not merely industrialization, some sort of balance has to be struck between the expansion of agricultural and the expansion of industrial output. One of the considerations affecting this balance is the availability of foreign capital for certain uses but not for others. Another consideration has to do with quantities of domestic resources that are likely to be diverted from other uses and into the employments favored by foreign capital. If foreign capital can make a large contribution to the area's well-being with a relatively small diversion of local resources, it would appear desirable to encourage investment whether for raw material or industrial expansion. If, however, foreign investment heavily influences the allocation of local resources it may fasten on the area a specialization which though satisfying the current comparative cost conditions is not conducive to economic growth.

It is the contention of this paper that the expansion of mineral production is, in general, not only compatible with the economic growth of under-developed areas but may greatly facilitate industrialization in these areas. Mineral development has been to date largely undertaken by foreign capital and, given proper encouragement, additional capital is available in quantity for expansion of output. Such development can rarely take place without the expansion of auxiliary facilities—railroads, roads, port development, electric power, and the like—which have a contribution to make to general economic development. Mineral production requires the development of technical skills on the part of the local employees of foreign mining and petroleum companies that are readily usable in other types of industrial development. The yield to the source countries in government revenue and foreign exchange earnings tends to be a high percentage of the value of mineral output and can provide the financial basis for a domestic development program. Finally, the diversion of domestic resources away from other objectives tends to be rela-tively small.

Venezuela is, of course, a particularly striking example of a favorable juxtaposition of mineral and general economic development but the argument has wider validity. Petroleum royalties account for 97 percent of Venezuela's exchange earnings and 60 percent of government revenue. The oil industry, on the other hand, employs less than 5 percent of the labor force. The gov-ernment has in its hands the means to finance a large program of general economic development and has, in fact, undertaken important steps in this direction. Since the oil industry can look forward confidently to a very large expansion and since to oil has been added the prospects of large royalties from iron-ore development, together with a great auxiliary expansion of trans-portation and other public utility facilities, the potentialities of general eco-nomic development in Venezuela seem most promising.

The same complementarity between minerals production for export and the possibilities of general economic development exists elsewhere. One may lament the fact that the Bolivan balance of trade is too heavily dominated by tin exports and the Chilean balance by copper exports. But the most effective answer to this is a better use of the governmental revenues and foreign ex-change receipts of an expanding minerals export for general economic development.

OBSTACLES TO THE EXPANSION OF FOREIGN SOURCES OF SUPPLY

It has been the argument of the preceding paragraphs that, granted a relative freedom to develop low-cost resources, the minerals requirements of the Free World could be met for at least the next twenty to thirty years with little or no increase in real costs, and that the general economic development of source countries could be greatly stimulated by this expansion of mineral production for export. The argument is not here extended to agricultural materials and foodstuffs produced for export for two reasons. First, with currently used techniques, expansion of agricultural output may well encounter rising real costs. Second, the labor requirements for an expanded agricultural output could certainly conflict with an economically justifiable degree of industrialization. How these considerations would be affected by the spread of superior agricultural techniques is difficult to estimate. It is possible that improved methods in agriculture might release labor for industrialization at a rapid rate while still permitting the satisfaction of Free-world requirements for foodstuffs and agricultural raw materials at existing terms of trade. An examination of these possibilities, however, lies outside the limits of this paper.

Granted that mineral production could be expanded with no substantial change in the relative prices of materials and fabricated products and that the general development of underdeveloped areas could be greatly facilitated by this expansion, does it follow that events will take this course? To answer this question easily in the affirmative would be to ignore the evidence of increasing difficulties confronting foreign investment in resource development and of an increasing reluctance on the part of private capital to risk these difficulties.

The difficulties do not lie primarily in the obvious conflict of interest between foreign investors and the governments of source countries over the division of profits of minerals development. No doubt these governments are showing themselves to be increasingly hard bargainers and no doubt occasionally the terms offered are such as to discourage investment. But the principal difficulties are concerned with doubts whether bargains once made will be kept and with limitations that source countries seek to impose on the control and management of foreign enterprises within their borders. Oil companies can live with a "50-50" division of earnings; it is questionable whether they can live—or at least expand—under the threat of overt or "creeping" expropriation.

Space is lacking for an adequate discussion of the principal obstacles to private foreign investment. There should be mentioned, however, the legal uncertainties concerning the status of foreign ownership such as those that have deterred investment in Brazil since the end of the war; the requirements in many areas for extensive local participation in management; limitations on the scope and direction of operations; excessive requirements concerning numbers to be employed and continuity of operations; the administration of import and export controls; limitations on conversion of profits into dollars; and others. Perhaps more important than any of these is the growing uncertainty whether the conditions of operation which are bad today may not become much worse tomorrow.

It is not the purpose of this paper to examine the question of what steps the United States might take to lessen or to avoid the effects of these obstacles on the cost of our materials supplies. One route obviously lies in the direction of attempting to improve through negotiation with foreign governments, tax concessions and other measures, the conditions under which U.S. producers can operate abroad. Another opens up the possibility of the assumption by government of some of the increasing risks of foreign operations through insurance, long-term contracts, price guarantees, financing, etc. We may be sure that the greater the extent to which this route becomes available the less will investors and producers be willing to proceed without help. A third line of attack would be the provision of capital and technical assistance to foreign governments to develop their own resources. It is obvious that if this path is followed very far, other sources of capital will dry up fast. Finally we could increasingly direct resources into technical research for synthetics and other substitute materials to lessen our dependence on foreign sources of supply.

It would be interesting to speculate on what combination of policies would permit us to satisfy our materials requirements at least cost. To do so, however, would divert attention away from our main argument. Reasons have been advanced for believing that although mineral resources exist in the underdeveloped areas of the world in quantities and grades such as to permit a meeting of Free-world requirements over the next quarter century at no increase in real costs, governmental policies in these areas may well prevent this from happening. If so, it seems likely that economic growth both in the industrialized and the underdeveloped areas of the Free World may be hampered.

A substantial rise in the real price of imported minerals would not be a very serious problem for the United States. It would be a much more serious matter for industrial areas more dependent on foreign sources. And if, to rising costs of minerals, is added worsening terms of exchange of manufactured products for agricultural materials and foodstuffs, there emerges for Western Europe and Japan a balance-of-payments problem of great difficulty. It becomes, then, important to distinguish those segments of the problem that might economically be solved to the advantage of all concerned from those that involve a real divergence of interest. . . .

CONCLUSION

If consideration is limited to the mineral requirements of the United States, there is reason to believe that security interests will increase the cost of meeting these requirements and that obstacles to the expansion of output in underdeveloped areas may also do so. Although no attention has been given to the question here, it may be stated as the author's opinion that U.S. requirements for agricultural materials are likely to be satisfied over the next two or three decades at little or no increase in real costs. Taking materials as a whole the American economy may, then, face a slight increase in the unit cost of meeting its requirements. Increases in the real costs of particular materials will, in most cases, be strictly limited by substitution possibilities. When account is taken of the fact that the value of raw material production—excluding foodstuffs—is not over 10 percent of the total value of U.S. output, it must be concluded that the increases in real costs of materials production here contemplated are not likely to handicap economic growth over the next few decades. Although it has been impossible, for lack of space, to consider the situation faced by other industrial areas of the Free World, a warning must be given that, particularly when foodstuffs are included, the raw-materials prospect for these areas looks rather different.

W. ARTHUR LEWIS

||||||||||||||||||||||||||||||||||||||||||||||||||||||||||||||||||||||||||||||||||||||||||||||||||||||||||||||||||||||||

Economic Development with Unlimited Supplies of Labor

This essay is written in the classical tradition, making the classical assumption, and asking the classical question. The classics, from Smith to Marx, all assumed, or argued, that an unlimited supply of labor was available at subsistence wages. They then enquired how production grows through time. They found the answer in capital accumulation, which they explained in terms of their analysis of the distribution of income. Classical systems thus determined simultaneously income distribution and income growth, with the relative prices of commodities as a minor by-product.

Interest in prices and in income distribution survived into the neo-classical era, but labor ceased to be unlimited in supply, and the formal model of economic analysis was no longer expected to explain the expansion of the system through time. These changes of assumption and of interest served well enough in the European parts of the world, where labor was indeed limited in supply, and where for the next half century it looked as if economic expansion could indeed be assumed to be automatic. On the other hand over the greater part of Asia labor is unlimited in supply, and economic expansion certainly cannot be taken for granted. Asia's problems, however, attracted very few economists during the neo-classical era (even the Asian economists themselves absorbed the assumptions and preoccupations of European economics) and hardly any progress has been made for nearly a century with the kind of economics which would throw light upon the problems of countries with surplus populations.

When Keynes's *General Theory* appeared, it was thought at first that this was the book which would illuminate the problems of countries with surplus labor, since it assumed an unlimited supply of labor at the current price, and also, in its final pages, made a few remarks on secular economic expansion.

From *The Manchester School of Economic and Social Studies* (May 1954), pp. 139-191, with omissions. Reprinted by permission of *The Manchester School* and the author.

Further reflection, however, revealed that Keynes's book assumed not only that labor is unlimited in supply, but also, and more fundamentally, that land and capital are unlimited in supply—more fundamentally both in the short-run sense that once the monetary tap is turned the real limit to expansion is not physical resources but the limited supply of labor, and also in the long-run sense that secular expansion is embarrassed not by a shortage but by a super-fluity of saving. Given the Keynesian remedies the neo-classical system comes into its own again. Hence, from the point of view of countries with surplus labor, Keynesianism is only a footnote to neo-classicism—albeit a long, important, and fascinating footnote. The student of such economies has there-fore to work right back to the classical economists before he finds an analytical framework into which he can relevantly fit his problems.

The purpose of this essay is thus to see what can be made of the classical framework in solving problems of distribution, accumulation, and growth, first in a closed and then in an open economy. It is not primarily an essay in the history of economic doctrine, and will not therefore spend time on indi-vidual writers, inquiring what they meant, or assessing its validity or truth. Our purpose is rather to bring their framework up-to-date, in the light of modern knowledge, and to see how far it then helps us to understand the contemporary problems of large areas of the earth.

THE CLOSED ECONOMY

We have to begin by elaborating the assumption of an unlimited supply of labor and by establishing that it is a useful assumption. We are not arguing, let it be repeated, that this assumption should be made for all areas of the world. It is obviously not true of the United Kingdom, or of Northwest Europe. It is not true either of some of the countries usually now lumped together as underdeveloped; for example there is an acute shortage of male labor in some parts of Africa and of Latin America. On the other hand it is obviously the relevant assumption for the economies of Egypt, of India, or of Jamaica. Our present task is not to supersede neo-classical economics but merely to elaborate a different framework for those countries which the neo-classical (and Keynesian) assumptions do not fit.

In the first place, an unlimited supply of labor may be said to exist in those countries where population is so large relatively to capital and natural resources, that there are large sectors of the economy where the marginal productivity of labor is negligible, zero, or even negative. Several writers have drawn attention to the existence of such "disguised" unemployment in the agricultural sector, demonstrating in each case that the family holding is so small that if some members of the family obtained other employment the remaining members could cultivate the holding just as well (of course they would have to work harder: the argument includes the proposition that they would be willing to work harder in these circumstances). The phenomenon is not, however, by any means confined to the countryside. Another large sector to which it applies is the whole range of casual jobs—the workers on the docks, the young men who rush forward asking to carry your bag as you appear, the jobbing gardener, and the like. These occupations usually have a multiple of the number they need, each of them earning very small sums from occasional employment; frequently their number could be halved without reducing output in this sector. Petty retail trading is also exactly of this type; it is enormously expanded in overpopulated economies; each trader makes only a few sales; markets are crowded with stalls, and if the number of stalls were greatly reduced the consumers would be no whit worse off—they might even be better off, since retail margins might fall. Twenty years ago one could not write these sentences without having to stop and explain why in these circumstances the casual laborers do not bid their earnings down to zero, or why the farmers' product is not similarly all eaten up in rent, but these propositions present no terrors to contemporary economists.

A little more explanation has to be given of those cases where the workers are not self-employed, but are working for wages, since it is harder to believe that employers will pay wages exceeding marginal productivity. The most important of these sectors is domestic service, which is usually even more inflated in overpopulated countries than is petty trading (in Barbados 16 percent of the population is in domestic service). The reason is that in overpopulated countries the code of ethical behavior so shapes itself that it becomes good form for each person to offer as much employment as he can. The line between employees and dependents is very thinly drawn. Social prestige requires people to have servants, and the grandseigneur may have to keep a whole army of retainers who are really little more than a burden upon his purse. This is found not only in domestic service but in every sector of employment. Most businesses in underdeveloped countries employ a large number of "messengers," whose contribution is almost negligible; you see them sitting outside office doors or hanging around in the courtyard. And even in the severest slump the agricultural or commercial employer is expected to keep his labor force somehow or other—it would be immoral to turn them out, for how would they eat, in countries where the only form of unemployment assistance is the charity of relatives? So it comes about that even in the sectors where people are working for wages, and above all the domestic sector, marginal productivity may be negligible or even zero.

Whether marginal productivity is zero or negligible is not, however, of fundamental importance to our analysis. The price of labor, in these economies, is a wage at the subsistence level (we define this later). The supply of labor is therefore "unlimited" so long as the supply of labor at this price exceeds the demand. In this situation, new industries can be created, or old industries expanded without limit at the existing wage; or, to put it more exactly, shortage of labor is no limit to the creation of new sources of employment. . . .

. . . it is clear enough that there can be in an overpopulated economy an enormous expansion of new industries or new employment opportunities without any shortage of unskilled labor becoming apparent in the labor market. From the point of view of the effect of economic development on wages, the supply of labor is practically unlimited.

This applies only to unskilled labor. There may at any time be a shortage of skilled workers of any grade—ranging from masons, electricians, or welders to engineers, biologists, or administrators. Skilled labor may be the bottleneck in expansion, just like capital or land. Skilled labor, however, is only what Marshall might have called a "quasi-bottleneck," if he had not had so nice a sense of elegant language. For it is only a very temporary bottleneck, in the sense that if the capital is available for development, the capitalists or their government will soon provide the facilities for training more skilled people. The real bottlenecks to expansion are therefore capital and natural resources, and we can proceed on the assumption that so long as these are available the necessary skills will be provided as well, though perhaps with some time lag.

If unlimited labor is available, while capital is scarce, we know from the Law of Variable Proportions that the capital should not be spread thinly over all the labor. Only so much labor should be used with capital as will reduce the marginal productivity of labor to zero. In practice, however, labor is not available at a zero wage. Capital will therefore be applied only up to the point where the marginal productivity of labor equals the current wage. This is illustrated in Figure 1. The horizontal axis measures the quantity of labor,

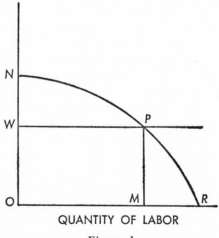

QUANTITY OF LABOR

Figure 1

and the vertical axis its marginal product. There is a fixed amount of capital. OW is the current wage. If the marginal product of labor were zero outside the capitalist sector, OR ought to be employed. But it will pay to employ only OM in the capitalist sector. WNP is the capitalists' surplus. $OWPM$ goes in wages to workers in the capitalist sector, while workers outside this sector (*i.e.,* beyond M) earn what they can in the subsistence sector of the economy.

The analysis requires further elaboration. In the first place, after what we have said earlier on about some employers in these economies keeping retainers, it may seem strange to be arguing now that labor will be employed up to the point where the wage equals the marginal productivity. Nevertheless, this is probably the right assumption to make when we are set upon analysing the expansion of the capitalist sector of the economy. For the type of capitalist who brings about economic expansion is not the same as the type of employer who treats his employees like retainers. He is more commercially minded, and more conscious of efficiency, cost, and profitability. Hence, if our interest is in an expanding capitalist sector, the assumption of profit maximization is probably a fair approximation to the truth.

Next, we note the use of the terms "capitalist" sector and "subsistence" sector. The capitalist sector is that part of the economy which uses reproducible capital and pays capitalists for the use thereof. (This coincides with Smith's definition of the productive workers, who are those who work with capital and whose product can therefore be sold at a price above their wages.) We can think, if we like, of capitalists hiring out their capital to peasants; in which case, there being by definition an unlimited number of peasants, only some will get capital, and these will have to pay for its use a price which leaves them only subsistence earnings. More usually, however, the use of capital is controlled by capitalists, who hire the services of labor. The classical analysis was therefore conducted on the assumption that capital was used for hiring people. It does not make any difference to the argument, and for convenience we will follow this usage. The subsistence sector is by difference all that part of the economy which is not using reproducible capital. Output per head is lower in this sector than in the capitalist sector, because it is not fructified by capital (this is why it was called "unproductive"; the distinction between productive and unproductive had nothing to do with whether the work yielded utility, as some neo-classicists have scornfully but erroneously asserted). As more capital becomes available more workers can be drawn into the capitalist from the subsistence sector, and their output per head rises as they move from the one sector to the other.

Thirdly we take account of the fact that the capitalist sector, like the subsistence sector, can also be subdivided. What we have is not one island of expanding capitalist employment, surrounded by a vast sea of subsistence workers, but rather a number of such tiny islands. This is very typical of countries in their early stages of development. We find a few industries highly capitalized, such as mining or electric power, side by side with the most primitive techniques; a few high-class shops, surrounded by masses of old-style traders; a few highly capitalized plantations, surrounded by a sea of peasants. But we find the same contrasts also outside their economic life. There are one or two modern towns, with the finest architecture, water supplies, communications and the like, into which people drift from other towns and villages which might almost belong to another planet. There is the same contrast even between people; between the few highly Westernized, trousered, natives, educated in Western universities, speaking Western languages, and glorying in Beethoven, Mill, Marx, or Einstein, and the great mass of their countrymen who live in quite other worlds. Capital and new ideas are not thinly diffused throughout the economy; they are highly concentrated at a number of points, from which they spread outwards.

Though the capitalized sector can be subdivided into islands, it remains a single sector because of the effect of competition in tending to equalize the earnings on capital. The competitive principle does not demand that the same amount of capital per person be employed on each "island," or that average profit per unit of capital be the same, but only that the marginal profit be the same. Thus, even if marginal profits were the same all round, islands which yield diminishing returns may be more profitable than others, the earliest capitalists having cornered the vantage points. But in any case marginal profits are not the same all round. In backward economies knowledge is one of the scarcest goods. Capitalists have experience of certain types of investment, say of trading or plantation agriculture, and not of other types, say of manufacturing, and they stick to what they know. So the economy is frequently lopsided in the sense that there is excessive investment in some parts and underinvestment in others. Also, financial institutions are more highly developed for some purposes than for others—capital can be got cheaply for trade, but not for house building or for peasant agriculture, for instance. Even in a very highly developed economy the tendency for capital to flow evenly through the economy is very weak; in a backward economy it hardly exists. Inevitably what one gets are very heavily developed patches of the economy, surrounded by economic darkness.

Next we must say something about the wage level. The wage which the expanding capitalist sector has to pay is determined by what people can earn outside that sector. The classical economists used to think of the wage as being determined by what is required for subsistence consumption, and this may be the right solution in some cases. However, in economies where the majority of the people are peasant farmers, working on their own land, we have a more objective index, for the minimum at which labor can be had is now set by the average product of the farmer; men will not leave the family farm to seek employment if the wage is worth less than they would be able to consume if they remained at home. This objective standard, alas, disappears again if the farmers have to pay rent, for their net earnings will then depend upon the amount of rent they have to pay, and in overpopulated countries the rent will probably be adjusted so as to leave them just enough for a conventional level of subsistence. It is not, however, of great importance to the argument whether earnings in the subsistence sector are determined objectively by the level of peasant productivity, or subjectively in terms of a conventional standard of living. Whatever the mechanism, the result is an unlimited supply of labor for which this is the minimum level of earnings.

The fact that the wage level in the capitalist sector depends upon earnings in the subsistence sector is sometimes of immense political importance, since its effect is that capitalists have a direct interest in holding down the productivity of the subsistence workers. Thus, the owners of plantations have no interest in seeing knowledge of new techniques or new seeds conveyed to the peasants, and if they are influential in the government, they will not be found using their influence to expand the facilities for agricultural extension. They will not support proposals for land settlement, and are often instead to be found engaged in turning the peasants off their lands. (*Cf.* Marx on "Primary Accumulation.") This is one of the worst features of imperialism, for instance. The imperialists invest capital and hire workers; it is to their advantage to keep wages low, and even in those cases where they do not actually go out of their way to impoverish the subsistence economy, they will at least very seldom be found doing anything to make it more productive. In actual fact the record of every imperial power in Africa in modern times is one of impoverishing the subsistence economy, either by taking away the people's land, or by demanding forced labor in the capitalist sector, or by imposing taxes to drive people to work for capitalist employers. Compared with what they have spent on providing facilities for European agriculture or mining, their expenditure on the improvement of African agriculture has been negligible. The failure of imperialism to raise living standards is not wholly to be attributed to self-interest, but there are many places where it can be traced directly to the effects of having imperial capital invested in agriculture or in mining.

Earnings in the subsistence sector set a floor to wages in the capitalist sector, but in practice wages have to be higher than this, and there is usually a gap of 30 percent or more between capitalist wages and subsistence earnings. This gap may be explained in several ways. Part of the difference is illusory, because of the higher cost of living in the capitalist sector. This may be due to the capitalist sector being concentrated in congested towns, so that rents and transport costs are higher. All the same, there is also usually a substantial difference in real wages. This may be required because of the psychological cost of transferring from the easygoing way of life of the subsistence sector to the more regimented and urbanized environment of the capitalist sector. Or it may be a recognition of the fact that even the unskilled worker is of more use to the capitalist sector after he has been there for some time than is the raw recruit from the country. Or it may itself represent a difference in conventional standards, workers in the capitalist sector acquiring tastes and a social prestige which have conventionally to be recognized by higher real wages. That this last may be the explanation is suggested by cases where the capitalist workers organize themselves into trade unions and strive to protect or increase their differential. But the differential exists even where there are no unions. . . .

So far we have merely been setting the stage. Now the play begins. For we can now begin to trace the process of economic expansion.

The key to the process is the use which is made of the capitalist surplus. In so far as this is reinvested in creating new capital, the capitalist sector expands, taking more people into capitalist employment out of the subsistence sector. The surplus is then larger still, capital formation is still greater, and so the process continues until the labor surplus disappears.

OS is as before average subsistence earnings, and OW the capitalist wage. WN_1Q_1 represents the surplus in the initial stage. Since some of this is reinvested, the amount of fixed capital increases. Hence the schedule of the marginal productivity of labor is now raised throughout, to the level of N_2Q_2. Both the surplus and capitalist employment are now larger. Further reinvestment raises the schedule of the marginal productivity of labor to N_3Q_3. And the process continues so long as there is surplus labor.

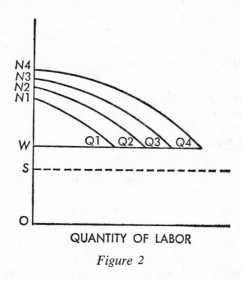

Figure 2

Various comments are needed in elaboration. First, as to the relationship between capital, technical progress, and productivity. In theory it should be possible to distinguish between the growth of capital and the growth of technical knowledge, but in practice it is neither possible nor necessary for this analysis. As a matter of statistical analysis, differentiating the effects of capital and of knowledge in any industry is straightforward if the product is homogeneous through time, if the physical inputs are also unchanged (in kind) and if the relative prices of the inputs have remained constant. But when we try to do it for any industry in practice we usually find that the product has changed, the inputs have changed and relative prices have changed, so that we get any number of indices of technical progress from the same data, according to the assumptions and the type of index number which we use. In any case, for the purpose of this analysis it is unnecessary to distinguish between capital formation and the growth of knowledge within the capitalist sector. Growth of technical knowledge outside the capitalist sector would be fundamentally important, since it would raise the level of wages, and so reduce the capitalist surplus. But inside the capitalist sector knowledge and capital work in the same direction, to raise the surplus and to increase employment. They also work together. The application of new technical knowledge usually requires new investment, and whether the new knowledge is capital-saving (and thus equivalent to an increase in capital) or labor-saving (and thus equivalent to an increase in the marginal productivity of labor) makes no difference to our diagram. Capital and technical knowledge also work together in the sense that in economies where techniques are stagnant savings are not so readily applied to increasing productive capital; in such economies it is more usual to use savings for building pyramids, churches, and other such durable consumer goods. Accordingly, in this analysis the growth of productive capital and the growth of technical knowledge are treated as a single phenomenon (just as we earlier decided that we could treat the growth of the supply of skilled labor and the growth of capital as a single phenomenon in long-run analysis).

Next we must consider more closely the capitalist surplus. Malthus wanted to know what the capitalists would do with this ever-growing surplus; surely this would be an embarrassing glut of commodities? Ricardo replied that there would be no glut; what the capitalists did not consume themselves, they would use for paying the wages of workers to create more fixed capital (this is a free interpretation, since the classical economists associated the expansion of employment with an increase of circulating rather than of fixed capital). This new fixed capital would then in the next stage make possible the employment of more people in the capitalist sector. Malthus persisted; why should the capitalists produce more capital to produce a larger surplus which could only be used for producing still more capital and so *ad infinitum*? To this Marx supplied one answer: capitalists have a passion for accumulating capital. Ricardo supplied another: if they don't want to accumulate, they will consume instead of saving; provided there is no propensity to hoard, there will be no glut. Employment in the next stage will not be as big as it would have been if they had created more fixed capital and so brought more workers into the capitalist sector, but so long as there is no hoarding it makes no difference to the current level of employment whether capitalists decide to consume or to save. Malthus then raised another question; suppose that the capitalists do save and invest without hoarding, surely the fact that capital is growing more rapidly than consumption must so lower the rate of profit on capital that there comes a point when they decide that it is not worthwhile to invest? This Ricardo replied, is impossible; since the supply of labor is unlimited, you can always find employment for any amount of capital. This is absolutely correct, for his model; in the neoclassical model capital grows faster than labor, and so one has to ask whether the rate of profit will not fall, but in the classical model the unlimited supply of labor means that the capital/labor ratio, and therefore the rate of surplus, can be held constant for any quantity of capital (*i.e.,* unlimited "widening" is possible). The only fly in the ointment is that there may develop a shortage of natural resources, so that though the capitalists get any amount of labor at a constant wage, they have to pay ever rising rents to landlords. This was what worried Ricardo; it was important to him to distinguish that part of the surplus which goes to landlords from that part which goes to capitalists, since he believed that economic development inevitably increases the relative scarcity of land. We are not so certain of this as he was. Certainly development increases the rent of urban sites fantastically, but its effect on rural rents depends on the rate of technical progress in agriculture, which Malthus and Ricardo both gravely underestimated. If we assume technical progress in agriculture, no hoarding, and unlimited labor at a constant wage, the rate of profit on capital cannot fall. On the contrary it must increase, since all the benefit of technical progress in the capitalist sector accrues to the capitalists.

Marx's interest in the surplus was ethical as well as scientific. He regarded it as robbery of the workers. His descendants are less certain of this. The surplus, after all, is only partly consumed; the other part is used for capital formation. As for the part which is consumed, some of it is a genuine payment for service rendered—for managerial or entrepreneurial services, as well as for the services of public administrators, whether these are paid salaries out of taxes, or whether they live off their rents or *rentes* while performing unpaid public duties as magistrates, lord-lieutenants, or the like. Even in the USSR all these functionaries are paid out of the surplus, and handsomely paid too. It is arguable that these services are overpaid; this is why we have progressive taxation, and it is also one of the more dubious arguments for nationalization (more dubious because the functionaries of public corporations have to be paid the market rate if the economy is only partially nationalized). But it is not arguable that all this part of the surplus (*i.e.,* the part consumed) morally belongs to the workers, in any sense. As for the part which is used for capital formation, the experience of the USSR is that this is increased, and not reduced, by transforming the ownership of capital. Expropriation deprives the capitalists of control over this part of the surplus, and of the right to consume this part at some later date, but it does nothing whatever to transfer this part of the surplus to the workers. Marx's emotional approach was a natural reaction to the classical writers, who sometimes in unguarded moments wrote as if the capitalist surplus and its increase were all that counted in the national income (*cf.* Ricardo, who called it "the net revenue" of production). All this, however, is by the way; for our present interest is not in ethical questions, but in how the model works.

The central problem in the theory of economic development is to understand the process by which a community which was previously saving and investing 4 or 5 percent of its national income or less converts itself into an economy where voluntary saving is running at about 12 to 15 percent of national income or more. This is the central problem because the central fact of economic development is rapid capital accumulation (including knowledge and skills with capital). We cannot explain any "industrial" revolution (as the economic historians pretend to do) until we can explain why saving increased relatively to national income.

It is possible that the explanation is simply that some psychological change occurs which causes people to be more thrifty. This, however, is not a plausible explanation. We are interested not in the people in general, but only say in the 10 percent of them with the largest incomes, who in countries with surplus labor receive up to 40 percent of the national income (nearer 30 percent in more developed countries). The remaining 90 percent of the people never manage to save a significant fraction of their incomes. The important question is why does the top 10 percent save more? The reason may be because they decide to consume less, but this reason does not square with the facts. There is no evidence of a fall in personal consumption by the top 10 percent at a time when industrial revolutions are occurring. It is also possible that, though they do not save any more, the top 10 percent spend less of their income on durable consumer goods (tombs, country houses, temples) and more on productive capital. Certainly, if one compares different civilizations this is a striking difference in the disposition of income. Civilizations in which there is a rapid growth of technical knowledge or expansion of other opportunities present more profitable outlets for investment than do technologically stagnant civilizations, and tempt capital into productive channels rather than into the building of monuments. But if one takes a country only over the course of the hundred years during which it undergoes a revolution in the rate of capital formation, there is no noticeable change in this regard. Certainly, judging by the novels, the top 10 percent in England were not spending noticeably less on durable consumer goods in 1800 than they were in 1700.

Much the most plausible explanation is that people save more because they have more to save. This is not to say merely that the national income per head is larger, since there is no clear evidence that the proportion of the national income saved increases with national income per head—at any rate our fragmentary evidence for the United Kingdom and for the United States suggests that this is not so. The explanation is much more likely to be that saving increases relatively to the national income because the incomes of the savers increase relatively to the national income. The central fact of economic development is that the distribution of incomes is altered in favor of the saving class.

Practically all saving is done by people who receive profits or rents. Workers' savings are very small. The middle classes save a little, but in practically every community the savings of the middle classes out of their salaries are of little consequence for productive investment. Most members of the middle class are engaged in the perpetual struggle to keep up with the Jones's; if they manage to save enough to buy the house in which they live, they are doing well. They may save to educate their children, or to subsist in their old age, but this saving is virtually offset by the savings being used up for the same purposes. Insurance is the middle class's favorite form of saving in modern societies, yet in the U.K., where the habit is extremely well developed, the annual net increase in insurance funds from all classes, rich, middle, and poor is less than 1½ percent of the national income. It is doubtful if the wage and salary classes ever anywhere save as much as 3 percent of the national income, net (possible exception: Japan). If we are interested in savings, we must concentrate attention upon profits and rents.

For our purpose it does not matter whether profits are distributed or undistributed; the major source of savings is profits, and if we find that savings are increasing as a proportion of the national income, we may take it for granted that this is because the share of profits in the national income is increasing. (As a refinement, for highly taxed communities, we should say profits net of taxes upon profits, whether personal income or corporate taxes.) Our problem then becomes what are the circumstances in which the share of profits in the national income increases?

The modified classical model which we are using here has the virtue of answering the question. In the beginning, the national income consists almost entirely of subsistence income. Abstracting from population growth and assuming that the marginal product of labor is zero, this subsistence income remains constant throughout the expansion, since by definition labor can be yielded up to the expanding capitalist sector without reducing subsistence output. The process therefore increases the capitalist surplus and the income of capitalist employees, taken together, as a proportion of the national income. It is possible to imagine conditions in which the surplus nevertheless does not increase relatively to national income. This requires that capitalist employment should expand relatively much faster than the surplus, so that within the capitalist sector gross margins or profit plus rent are falling sharply relatively to wages. We know that this does not happen. Even if gross margins were constant, profits in our model would be increasing relatively to national income. But gross margins are not likely to be constant in our model, which assumes that practically the whole benefit of capital accumulation and of technical progress goes into the surplus; because real wages are constant, all that the workers get out of the expansion is that more of them are employed at a wage above the subsistence earnings. The model says, in effect, that if unlimited supplies of labor are available at a constant real wage, and if any part of profits is reinvested in productive capacity, profits will grow continuously relatively to the national income, and capital formation will also grow relatively to the national income.

The model also covers the case of a technical revolution. Some historians have suggested that the capital for the British Industrial Revolution came out of profits made possible by a spate of inventions occurring together. This is extremely hard to fit into the neo-classical model, since it involves the assumption that these inventions raised the marginal productivity of capital more than they raised the marginal productivity of labor, a proposition which it is hard to establish in any economy where labor is scarce. (If we do not make this assumption, other incomes rise just as fast as profits, and investment does not increase relatively to national income.) On the other hand the suggestion fits beautifully into the modified classical model, since in this model practically the whole benefit of inventions goes into the surplus, and becomes available for further capital accumulation.

This model also helps us to face squarely the nature of the economic problem of backward countries. If we ask, "Why do they save so little?" the truthful answer is not "Because they are so poor," as we might be tempted to conclude from the path-breaking and praiseworthy correlations of Mr. Colin

Clark. The truthful answer is "Because their capitalist sector is so small" (remembering that "capitalist" here does not mean private capitalist, but would apply equally to state capitalist). If they had a larger capitalist sector, profits would be a greater part of their national income, and saving and investment would also be relatively larger. (The state capitalist can accumulate capital even faster than the private capitalist, since he can use for the purpose not only the profits of the capitalist sector, but also what he can force or tax out of the subsistence sector.)

Another point which we must note is that though the increase of the capitalist sector involves an increase in the inequality of incomes, as between capitalists and the rest, mere inequality of income is not enough to ensure a high level of saving. In point of fact the inequality of income is *greater* in overpopulated underdeveloped countries than it is in advanced industrial nations, for the simple reason that agricultural rents are so high in the former. Eighteenth-century British economists took it for granted that the landlord class is given to prodigal consumption rather than to productive investment, and this is certainly true of landlords in underdeveloped countries. Hence, given two countries of equal incomes, in which distribution is more unequal in one than in the other, savings may be greater where distribution is more equal if profits are higher relatively to rents. It is the inequality which goes with profits that favors capital formation, and not the inequality which goes with rents. Correspondingly, it is very hard to argue that these countries cannot afford to save more, when 40 percent or so of the national income is going to the top 10 percent, and so much of rent incomes is squandered.

Behind this analysis also lies the sociological problem of the emergence of a capitalist class, that is to say of a group of men who think in terms of investing capital productively. The dominant classes in backward economies— landlords, traders, moneylenders, priests, soldiers, princes—do not normally think in these terms. What causes a society to grow a capitalist class is a very difficult question, to which probably, there is no general answer. Most countries seem to begin by importing their capitalists from abroad; and in these days many (*e.g.,* USSR, India) are growing a class of state capitalists who, for political reasons of one sort or another, are determined to create capital rapidly on public account. As for indigenous private capitalists, their emergence is probably bound up with the emergence of new opportunities, especially something that widens the market, associated with some new technique which greatly increases the productivity of labor if labor and capital are used together. Once a capitalist sector has emerged, it is only a matter of time before it becomes sizable. If very little technical progress is occurring, the surplus will grow only slowly. But if for one reason or another the opportunities for using capital productively increase rapidly, the surplus will also grow rapidly, and the capitalist class with it.

In our model so far capital is created only out of profits earned. In the real world, however, capitalists also create capital as a result of a net increase in the supply of money—especially bank credit. We have now also to take account of this.

In the neo-classical model capital can be created only by withdrawing resources from producing consumer goods. In our model, however, there is surplus labor, and if (as we shall assume) its marginal productivity is zero, and if, also, capital can be created by labor without withdrawing scarce land and capital from other uses, then capital can be created without reducing the output of consumer goods. This second proviso is important, since if we need capital or land to make capital the results in our model are the same as the results in the neo-classical model, despite the fact that there is surplus labor. However, in practice the proviso is often fulfilled. Food cannot be grown without land, but roads, viaducts, irrigation channels, and buildings can be created by human labor with hardly any capital to speak of—witness the Pyramids, or the marvelous railway tunnels built in the mid-nineteenth century almost with bare hands. Even in modern industrial countries constructional activity, which lends itself to hand labor, is as much as 50 or 60 percent of gross fixed investment, so it is not difficult to think of labor creating capital without using any but the simplest tools. The classical economists were not wrong in thinking of lack of circulating capital as being a more serious obstacle to expansion in their world than lack of fixed capital. In the analysis which follows in this section we assume that surplus labor cannot be used to make consumer goods without using up more land or capital, but can be used to make capital goods without using any scarce factors.

If a community is short of capital, and has idle resources which can be set to creating capital, it seems very desirable on the face of the matter that this should be done, even if it means creating extra money to finance the extra employment. There is no loss of other output while the new capital is being made, and when it comes into use, it will raise output and employment in just the same way as would capital financed not by credit creation but out of profits. The difference between profit-financed and credit-financed capital is not in the ultimate effects on output, but in the immediate effects on prices and on the distribution of income.

Before we come to the effects on prices, however, we should pause a moment to notice what happens to the output of consumer goods in this model and the others while credit-financed capital is being created, but before it begins to be used. In the neo-classical model an increase in capital formation has to be accompanied by a corresponding fall in the output of consumer goods, since scarce resources can do one or the other. In the Keynesian model an increase in capital formation also increases the output of consumer goods, and if the multiplier exceeds 2, the output of consumer goods increases even more than capital formation. In our model capital formation goes up, but the output of consumer goods is not immediately affected. This is one of those crucial cases where it is important to be certain that one is using the right model when it comes to giving advice on economic policy.

In our model, if surplus labor is put to capital formation and paid out of new money, prices rise, because the stream of money purchases is swollen while the output of consumer goods is for the time being constant. What is happening is that the fixed amount of consumer goods is being redistributed, toward the workers newly employed, away from the rest of the community (this is where the lack of circulating capital comes into the picture). This process is not "forced saving" in the useful sense of that term. In the neo-classical model the output of consumer goods is reduced, forcing the community as a whole to save. In our model, however, consumer-goods output is not at any time reduced; there is a forced redistribution of consumption, but not forced saving. And, of course, as soon as the capital goods begin to yield output, consumption begins to rise.

This inflationary process does not go on forever; it comes to an end when voluntary savings increase to a level where they are equal to the inflated level of investment. Since savings are a function of profits, this means that the inflation continues until profits increase so much relatively to the national income that capitalists can now finance the higher rate of investment out of their profits without any further recourse to monetary expansion. Essentially equilibrium is secured by raising the ratio of profits to the national income. The equilibrator need not however be profits; it might equally be government receipts, if there is a structure of taxes such that the ratio of government receipts to the national income rises automatically as the national income rises. This seems to be just about what happened in the USSR. In the crucial years when the economy was being transformed from a 5 percent to a (probably) 20 percent net saver, there was a tremendous inflation of prices (apparently prices rose about 700 percent in a decade), but the inflationary profits largely went to the government in the form of turnover tax, and by the end of the decade a new equilibrium was in sight.

It is not, however, always a simple matter to raise profits relatively to national income simply by turning on the monetary tap. The simplest and most extreme model of an inflation would be to assume that when the capital-ists finance capital formation by creating credit, the money all comes back to them in the very next round in the form of an increase in their profits. In such a model profits, voluntary savings and capital formation can be raised to any desired level in a very short time, with only a small increase in prices. Something like this may well apply in the USSR. In real terms, however, this implies that there has been a fall in the share of the national income received by other people, including a fall in their real consumption, since they have had to release consumer goods for the previously unemployed who are now engaged in capital formation. It may be the farmers who are worse off, this showing itself in the prices of manufactures rising relatively to farm prices. Or it may be the workers in the capitalist sector who are worse off, because farm prices and the prices of manufactures rise faster than their wages. Or the blow may be falling upon salaried workers, pensioners, landlords, or creditors. Now in the real world none of these classes will take this lying down. In the USSR, where the intention was that the capital formation should be at the expense of the farmers, it led in the end to organized violence on both sides. In our model it is hard to get away with it at the expense of the workers, since the wage in the capitalist sector must stand at a certain minimum level above subsistence earnings if labor is to be available. Generally, what happens as prices rise is that new contracts have to be made to take account of rising price levels. Some classes get caught, but only temporarily.

Now, if one pursued this argument logically, it would lead to the conclusion that equilibrium could never be reached—at any rate, so long as the banking system is content to supply all "legitimate" demands for money. If none of the other classes can be soaked, it seems impossible for profits to rise relatively to the national income for more than a temporary space, and it therefore seems impossible to reach an equilibrium level of savings equal to the new level of investment. The inflation, once begun, goes on for ever. This, however, is not possible for another reason, namely the fact that the real national income is not fixed, but rising, as a result of the capital formation. Therefore all that is required is that capitalists' real incomes rise faster than other people's. Beyond the first year or two, when the additional consumer goods begin to appear, it is not necessary for any class to reduce its consumption. By the time the process of recontracting has begun, output has also begun to rise, and it is therefore possible to reach a *modus vivendi*.

We can give an exact description of this equilibrium in our modified classical model. In this model the average subsistence real income is given, and so also therefore is the real wage in the capitalist sector. It is not possible, by inflation or otherwise, to reach a new equilibrium in which the capitalist surplus has increased at the expense of either of these. If, therefore, the capitalists begin to finance capital formation out of credit, they lower the real incomes of the others only temporarily. Wages would then be chasing prices continuously but for the fact that, since output is growing all the time, profits are growing all the time. Hence the part of the investment which is financed out of credit is diminishing all the time, until equilibrium is reached. For example, suppose that an investment of £100 a year yields £20 a year profit, of which £10 a year is saved. Then, if capitalists invest an extra £100 a year, all of which in the first year is financed out of credit, by the eleventh year profits will be £200 a year greater, savings will be £100 a year greater and there will be no further monetary pressure on prices. All that will remain from the episode is that there will be £1,000 more useful productive capital at work than there would have if the credit creation had not taken place.

Thus we have two simple models marking the extreme cases. In the first, all the credit created comes back to the capitalists at once as profits (or to the state capitalist as taxes). Equilibrium is then reached easily, with the capitalists gaining at the expense of all others. In the other model the capitalists can only gain temporarily; equilibrium then takes much longer to reach, but it is reached eventually. In the first case we need only an expansion of money income; but in the second case it is the expansion of real income which eventually brings the capitalists the required proportion of the national income.

The fact that capital formation increases real output must also be borne in mind in the analysis of the effects of credit creation upon prices. The inflations which loom most in our minds are those which occur in wartime, when resources are being withdrawn from producing consumer goods. If the supply of money is increasing while the output of goods is falling, anything can happen to prices. Inflation for the purpose of capital formation, however, is a very different kettle of fish. For it results in increasing consumer-goods output, and this results in falling prices if the quantity of money is held constant. . . .

We may now sum up this section. Capital formation is financed not only out of profits but also out of an expansion of credit. This speeds up the growth of capital, and the growth of real income. It also results in some redistribution of the national income, either temporarily or permanently, according to the assumptions one makes—in the model we are using, the redistribution is only temporary. It also prevents prices from falling, as they otherwise would (if money is constant and output rising), and it may drive prices up substantially if (as in our model) the distribution of income cannot be altered permanently by monetary measures, since prices will then continue to rise until real output has risen enough to effect the required redistribution. Thereafter prices fall further, since inflation raises prices while capital is being created, but the increased output which then results brings them down again.

One point remains. We have seen that if new money is used to finance capital formation the rise of prices eventually peters out, as savings grow into equilibrium with investment; and reverses itself, as the output of consumer goods begins to pour out. The new equilibrium, however, may take a long time to reach, and if also the flow of new money is substantial the resulting rise of prices may strike fear into the hearts of the public. People do not panic if prices rise for two or three years; but after that they may begin to lose confidence in money, and it may become necessary to call a drastic halt. This is the most important practical limitation on the extent to which capital formation can be financed in this way. This is why the banking authorities have always tended to alternate short periods of easy credit with sharp periods of restriction. Bank credit moves three steps up and one step down instead of moving up continuously. This also brings us to the threshold of the trade cycle. If capital were financed exclusively out of profits, and if there were also no hoarding, capital formation would proceed steadily. It is mainly the existence of an elastic credit system which makes the trade cycle an integral part of the mechanism of economic development in an unplanned economy. It is not necessary, however, for us to enter into analysis of the cycle since in this respect the model we are using does not yield results different from those of other models.

We have said very little so far about the activities of government, since our basic model uses only capitalists, their employees, and subsistence producers. Governments affect the process of capital accumulation in many ways, however, and not least by the inflations into which they run. Many governments in backward countries are also currently anxious to use surplus manpower for capital formation, and as there is a great deal that can be done with labor and a few tools (roads, irrigation, river walls, schools and so on), it is useful to say something on the subject. We shall therefore in this section analyse the effect of inflation-financed government formation of capital, and thereby also give ourselves the chance to recapitulate the analysis of the previous section.

The results, it will be remembered, lie within two extremes. At one extreme all the money spent by the government comes back to it in taxes, and this is accepted by all classes. In this case, prices rise very little. At the other extreme, all classes refuse to accept a redistribution between themselves and the government. In this case prices tend to rise continuously, except that rising output (as a result of the capital formed) sooner or later catches up with prices and brings them down again. Rising output will also increase the government's "normal" share of the national income, and all monetary pressure will cease when the "normal" share has risen to the level of the inflated share which it was trying to get.

These results give us the questions we must ask. (1) What part of marginal income returns automatically to the government? (2) What effect does inflation have upon the various classes? And, (3) what effect has government capital formation upon output?

(One other point must be remembered. In all this analysis so far we have assumed a closed economy. In an open economy inflation plays havoc with the balance of payments. We have therefore to assume that the government has strict control over foreign transactions. This assumption holds for some backward economies; others would get into an awful mess if they launched upon inflationary finance.)

It is not possible that all the money spent by the government should come back to it in the first round, since this would presume that the government took 100 percent of marginal income. If the government takes any part of marginal income, some of the money will come back to it; but even the Keynesian multiplier will not bring it all back unless taxation is the only leakage (*i.e.,* there is no saving). The larger the government's share of marginal incomes, the more it will get back, the quicker it will get it, and the smaller will be the effect on prices.

Since World War II a number of governments of modern industrial states seem to be taking around 40 to 50 percent of marginal incomes in taxation, and this is one of the major reasons why their price levels have not risen more, despite heavy pressure on resources for capital formation, defense, etc. In backward countries, however, governments take only a very small part of marginal incomes. The best placed governments from this point of view are those in countries where output is concentrated in a few large units (mines, plantations) and therefore easily taxed, or where foreign trade is a large part of the national income, and is thus easily reached by import and export duties. One of the worst off is India, with a large part of its output produced by subsistence producers and small scale units, hard to reach, and with less than 10 percent of national income passing in foreign trade. In many cases, marginal taxation is less than average taxation, for when money incomes rise, the government continues to charge the same prices for railway travel or for stamps, and hesitates to raise land taxes on the peasants, with the result that money incomes rise faster than government receipts. No government should consider deficit financing without assuring itself that a large part of increases in money income will automatically come back to itself. By contrast, the USSR, with its very high rate of turnover tax, automatically mops up surplus funds injected into the system, before they are able to generate much demand inflation *via* the multiplier process.

The next question is the effect of inflation upon the distribution of income. The surplus money raises prices, some more than others. The government will probably try to prevent prices from rising, but will succeed better with some than with others. It is easy to apply price control to large-scale enterprises, but very hard to prevent the farmers from raising food prices or the petty traders from making big margins. From the point of view of capital formation, the best thing that can happen is for the surplus money to roll into the pockets of people who will reinvest it productively. The merchant classes would probably use it mainly for speculation in those commodities that are getting scarce. The middle classes would mainly buy big American cars with it, or go on trips to Europe, wangling the foreign exchange somehow. The peasants ought to use it to improve their farms, but probably most would use it only to pay off debt, or to buy more land. There is really only one class that is pretty certain to reinvest its profits productively, and that is the class of industrialists. The effects of an inflation on secondary capital formation therefore depend first on how large the industrial class is, and secondly on whether the benefit goes largely to this class. In countries which have only a small industrial class, inflation leads mainly to speculation in commodities and in land, and to the hoarding of foreign exchange. But in any country which has a substantial industrialist class, with the passion this class has for ruling over bigger and better factories, even the most frightening inflations (*e.g.*, Germany from 1919) leave behind a substantial increase in capital formation. (Have we hit here upon some deep psychological instinct which drives the industrialist to use his wealth more creatively than others? Probably not. It is just that his job is of the kind where passion for success results in capital formation. The peasant farmer wants to have more land, not more capital on his land [unless he is a modern capitalist farmer] so his passion is dissipated merely in changes in the price and distribution of land. The merchant wants to have a wider margin, or a quicker turnover, neither of which increases fixed capital. The banker wants more deposits. Only the industrialist's passion drives towards using profits to create a bigger empire of bricks and steel.) It follows that it is in industrial communities that inflations are most helpful to capital formation; whereas in countries where the industrial class is negligible, there is nothing to show for the inflation when it is over, except the original investment which started it off. We should also note that many governments do not like the fact that inflation enables industrialists to earn the extra profits with which they create fixed capital, since this results in an increase of private fortunes. They therefore do all they can to prevent the inflation from increasing the profits of industrialists. More especially, they clamp down on industrial prices, which are also from the administrative point of view the easiest prices to control. Since it is the industrialist class which saves most, the result is to exacerbate the inflation. It would be much sounder to pursue policies which would result in the profits of industrialists rising more rapidly than other incomes, and then to tax these profits away, either immediately or at death.

Inflation continues to be generated so long as the community is not willing to hold an amount equal to the increased investment expenditure. It is not therefore enough that savings should increase to this extent, for if these savings are used for additional investment the initial gap still remains. The gap is closed only if the savings are hoarded, or used to buy government bonds, so that the government can now finance its investments by borrowing, instead of by creating new money. Hence in practice, if the government wishes the inflation to be ended without reducing its investment, it must find means of bringing into its coffers as much in taxes or in loans as it is spending. If it is failing to do this, the inflation will continue; it is then better that it should continue because capitalists are spending their profits on further capital formation than because other classes are chasing a limited output of consumer goods; but if it is desired to end inflation as soon as possible, all classes should be encouraged to invest in government bonds rather than to spend in other ways.

Finally we come to the relation between capital and output. If the intention is to finance capital formation by creating credit, the best objects for such a policy are those which yield a large income quickly. To finance school building by creating credit is asking for trouble. On the other hand, there are a lot of agricultural programs (water supplies, fertilizers, seed farms, extension) where quick and substantial results may be expected from modest expenditure. If there are idle resources available for capital formation, it is foolish not to use them simply because of technical or political difficulties in raising taxes. But it would be equally foolish to use them on programs which take a long time to give a small result, when there are others which could give a large result quickly.

We may sum up as follows. If labor is abundant and physical resources scarce, the primary effect on output is exactly the same whether the government creates capital out of taxation or out of credit creation: the output of consumer goods is unchanged but is redistributed. Hence credit creation must be seen primarily as an alternative to taxation, which is worth the troubles it brings only if trying to raise taxes would bring even more troubles. Credit creation has however one further lead upon taxation in that if it also redistributes income toward the industrial class (if there is an industrial class), it will speed up capital formation out of profits. If it is impossible to increase taxation, and the alternative is between creating capital out of credit, and not creating it at all, the choice one has then to make is between stable prices or rising output. There is no simple formula for making this choice. In some communities any further inflation of prices would ruin their fragile social or political equilibrium; in others this equilibrium will be destroyed if there is not a sharp increase in output in the near future; and in still others the equilibrium will be ruined either way.

We may now resume our analysis. We have seen that if unlimited labor is available at a constant real wage, the capitalist surplus will rise continuously, and annual investment will be a rising proportion of the national income. Needless to say, this cannot go on forever.

The process must stop when capital accumulation has caught up with population, so that there is no longer surplus labor. But it may stop before that. It may stop of course for any number of reasons which are outside our system of analysis, ranging from earthquake or bubonic plague to social revolution. But it may also stop for the economic reason that, although there is a labor surplus, real wages may nevertheless rise so high as to reduce capitalists' profits to the level at which profits are all consumed and there is no net investment.

This may happen for one of four reasons. First, if capital accumulation is proceeding faster than population growth, and is therefore reducing absolutely the number of people in the subsistence sector, the average product per man in that sector rises automatically, not because production alters, but because there are fewer mouths to share the product. After a while the change actually becomes noticeable, and the capitalist wage begins to be forced up. Secondly, the increase in the size of the capitalist sector relatively to the subsistence sector may turn the terms of trade against the capitalist sector (if they are producing different things) and so force the capitalists to pay workers a higher percentage of their product, in order to keep their real income constant. Thirdly, the subsistence sector may also become more productive in the technical sense. For example, it may begin to imitate the techniques of the capitalist sector; the peasants may get hold of some of the new seeds, or hear about the new fertilizers or rotations. They may also benefit directly from some of the capitalist investments, *e.g.,* in irrigation works, in transport facilities, or in electricity. Anything which raises the productivity of the subsistence sector (average person) will raise real wages in the capitalist sector, and will therefore reduce the capitalist surplus and the rate of capital accumulation, unless it at the same time more than correspondingly moves the terms of trade against the subsistence sector. Alternatively, even if the productivity of the capitalist sector is unchanged, the workers in the capitalist sector may imitate the capitalist way of life, and may thus need more to live on. The subsistence level is only a conventional idea, and conventions change. The effect of this would be to widen the gap between earnings in the subsistence sector, and wages in the capitalist sector. This is hard to do, if labor is abundant, but it may be achieved by a combination of trade union pressure and capitalist conscience. If it is achieved, it will reduce the capitalist surplus, and also the rate of capital accumulation.

The most interesting of these possibilities is that the terms of trade may move against the capitalist sector. This assumes that the capitalist and subsistence sectors are producing different things. In practice this is a question of the relationship between industry and agriculture. If the capitalists are investing in plantation agriculture side by side with their investment in industry, we can think of the capitalist sector as self-contained. The expansion of this sector does not then generate any demand for anything produced in the subsistence sector, and there are therefore no terms of trade to upset the picture we have drawn. To bring the terms of trade in, the simplest assumption to make is that the subsistence sector consists of peasants producing food, while the capitalist sector produces everything else.

Now if the capitalist sector produces no food, its expansion increases the demand for food, raises the price of food in terms of capitalist products, and so reduces profits. This is one of the senses in which industrialization is dependent upon agricultural improvement; it is not profitable to produce a growing volume of manufactures unless agricultural production is growing simultaneously. This is also why industrial and agrarian revolutions always go together, and why economies in which agriculture is stagnant do not show industrial development. Hence, if we postulate that the capitalist sector is not producing food, we must either postulate that the subsistence sector is increasing its output, or else conclude that the expansion of the capitalist sector will be brought to an end through adverse terms of trade eating into profits. (Ricardo's problem of increasing rents is first cousin to this conclusion; he worried about rents increasing *inside* the capitalist sector, whereas we are dealing with rents *outside* the sector.)

On the other hand, if we assume that the subsistence sector is producing more food, while we escape the Scylla of adverse terms of trade we may be caught by the Charybdis of real wages rising because the subsistence sector is more productive. We escape both Scylla and Charybdis if rising productivity in the subsistence sector is more than offset by improving terms of trade. However, if the subsistence sector is producing food, the elasticity of demand for which is less than unity, increases in productivity will be more than offset by reductions in price. A rise in the productivity of the subsistence sector hurts the capitalist sector if there is no trade between the two, or if the demand of the capitalist sector for the subsistence sector's product is elastic. On the assumptions we have made, a rise in food productivity benefits the capitalist sector. Nevertheless, when we take rising demand into account, it is not at all unlikely that the price of food will not fall as fast as productivity increases, and this will force the capitalists to pay out a larger part of their product as wages.

If there is no hope of prices falling as fast as productivity increases (because demand is increasing), the capitalists' next best move is to prevent the farmer from getting all his extra production. In Japan this was achieved by raising rents against the farmers, and by taxing them more heavily, so that a large part of the rapid increase in productivity which occurred (between 1880 and 1910 it doubled) was taken away from the farmers and used for capital formation; at the same time the holding down of the farmers' income itself held down wages, to the advantage of profits in the capitalist sector.

Much the same happened in the USSR, where farm incomes per head were held down, in spite of farm mechanization and the considerable release of labor to the towns; this was done jointly by raising the prices of manufactures relatively to farm products and also by levying heavy taxes upon the collective farms.

This also defines for us the case in which it is true to say that it is agriculture which finances industrialization. If the capitalist sector is self-contained, its expansion is in no way dependent upon the peasants. The surplus is wholly "at the expense" of the workers in the capitalist sector. But if the capitalist sector depends upon the peasants for food, it is essential to get the peasants to produce more, while if at the same time they can be prevented from enjoying the full fruit of their extra production, wages can be reduced relatively to the capitalist surplus. By contrast a state which is ruled by peasants may be happy and prosperous, but it is not likely to show such a rapid accumulation of capital. (*E.g.,* will China and the USSR diverge in this respect?)

We conclude, therefore, that the expansion of the capitalist sector may be stopped because the price of subsistence goods rises, or because the price is not falling as fast as subsistence productivity per head is rising, or because capitalist workers raise their standard of what they need for subsistence. Any of these would raise wages relatively to the surplus. If none of these processes is enough to stop capital accumulation, the capitalist sector will continue to expand until there is no surplus labor left. This can happen even if population is growing. For example, if it takes 3 percent of annual income invested to employ 1 percent more people, an annual net investment of 12 percent can cope with as much as a 4-percent increase in population. But population in Western Europe at the relevant times grew only by 1 percent or so per annum (which is also the present rate of growth in India), and rates of growth exceeding 2½ percent per annum are even now rather rare. We cannot say that capital will always grow faster than labor (it obviously has not done so in Asia), but we can say that if conditions are favorable for the capitalist surplus to grow more rapidly than population, there must come a day when capital accumulation has caught up with labor supply. Ricardo and Malthus did not provide for this in their models, because they overestimated the rate of growth of population. Marx did not provide for it either, because he had persuaded himself that capital accumulation increases unemployment instead of reducing it. (He has a curious model in which the short-run effect of accumulation is to reduce unemployment, raise wages and thus provoke a crisis, while the long-run effect is to increase the reserve army of unemployed.) Of the classical economists only Adam Smith saw clearly that capital accumulation would eventually create a shortage of labor and raise wages above the subsistence level.

When the labor surplus disappears, our model of the closed economy no longer holds. Wages are no longer tied to a subsistence level. Adam Smith thought they would then depend upon the degree of monopoly (a doctrine which was represented in the 1930s as one of the novelties of modern economic analysis). The neo-classicists invented the doctrine of marginal productivity. The problem is not yet solved to anyone's satisfaction, except in static models which take no account of capital accumulation and of technical progress. It is, however, outside the terms of reference of this essay and we will not pursue it here.

Our task is not, however, finished. In the classical world all countries have surplus labor. In the neo-classical world labor is scarce in all countries. In the real world, however, countries which achieve labor scarcity continue to be surrounded by others which have abundant labor. Instead of concentrating on one country, and examining the expansion of its capitalist sector, we . . . have to see this country as part of the expanding capitalist sector of the world economy as a whole, and to enquire how the distribution of income inside the country and its rate of capital accumulation, are affected by the fact that there is abundant labor available elsewhere at a subsistence wage. . . .

SUMMARY

We may summarize this article as follows:

1. In many economies an unlimited supply of labor is available at a subsistence wage. This was the classical model. The neo-classical model (including the Keynesian) when applied to such economies gives erroneous results.

2. The main sources from which workers come as economic development proceeds are subsistence agriculture, casual labor, petty trade, domestic service, wives and daughters in the household, and the increase of population. In most but not all of these sectors, if the country is overpopulated relatively to its natural resources, the marginal productivity of labor is negligible, zero, or even negative.

3. The subsistence wage at which this surplus labor is available for employment may be determined by a conventional view of the minimum required for subsistence; or it may be equal to the average product per man in subsistence agriculture, plus a margin.

4. In such an economy employment expands in a capitalist sector as capital formation occurs.

5. Capital formation and technical progress result not in raising wages, but in raising the share of profits in the national income.

6. The reason why savings are low in an undeveloped economy relatively to national income is not that the people are poor, but that capitalist profits are low relatively to national income. As the capitalist sector expands, profits grow relatively, and an increasing proportion of national income is re-invested.

7. Capital is formed not only out of profits but also out of credit creation. The real cost of capital created by inflation is zero in this model, and this capital is just as useful as what is created in more respectable fashion (*i.e.,* out of profits).

8. Inflation for the purpose of getting hold of resources for war may be

cumulative; but inflation for the purpose of creating productive capital is self-destructive. Prices rise as the capital is created, and fall again as its output reaches the market.

9. The capitalist sector cannot expand in these ways indefinitely, since capital accumulation can proceed faster than population can grow. When the surplus is exhausted, wages begin to rise above the subsistence level. . . .

HENRY G. AUBREY

Industrial Investment Decisions: A Comparative Analysis

I

. . . One of the most important growth relationships is that which links an increase of output with a rise of investment or an increase of productivity, or both. The flow of investment, domestic and foreign, has therefore become the focus of a significant part of our development literature. It also constitutes the topic of this paper. A great deal of discussion has proceeded on a general level. A high propensity to invest in Western countries was associated with "rationality," with social, religious, or other cultural traits, and thereby, it seemed, moved beyond the boundaries of economic argument. Whether intended or not, this approach seems to imply that non-Western people lack the prerequisites for massive investment, unless and until they somehow acquire similar characteristics.

I cannot help sensing something faintly sanctimonious in the presumption that "rationality" goes with our Western attitudes, while less advanced people mostly obey tradition and sentiment. I would certainly not deny the strength of such noneconomic factors. Yet, as an economist I refuse to believe that, in less developed countries, businessmen who prove to have a very shrewd perception of profit opportunities, are swayed by noneconomic factors to quite the extent that has come to be accepted by many economists and historians. Could it be that we misinterpret their motives?

In order to experiment in this direction I am proposing a slight change of approach. I shall assume that investment preferences, including those termed "traditional," are rational and can therefore be explained in terms of

From *Journal of Economic History* (December 1955), pp. 335-351, with omissions. Reprinted by permission of the Economic History Association and the author.

the two chief considerations that enter into all investment decisions: profit and risk. Undoubtedly there are other factors, but I should prefer to assign them a residual role; in other words, I would first search for economic motivations of investment behavior before I concede that the limits of economic analysis have been reached, as they eventually must be.

This slight, and by no means revolutionary, change of emphasis makes for a more detailed scrutiny of the component elements of investment decisions. We have first to determine the individual factors a businessman wants to explore. Then only can we comprehend why the economic conditions in underdeveloped countries make for decisions that frequently seem undesirable from the developmental point of view. The method of comparison, historical, institutional, and perhaps also sociocultural, becomes again meaningful if we thus attempt to dissect the process of decision-making. While it is difficult to understand, describe, and compare general patterns, it is feasible to deal in this manner with concrete factors and magnitudes, and hence with the considerations and expectations to which they give rise in the prospective investor's mind. The present paper is an attempt to apply this method, first generally, and then specifically to industrial investment in the subcontinent of India and Pakistan. It is hoped that the discussants will be willing to bring their varied experiences in other regions to bear on this problem.

II

The literature on economic development is replete with references to lack of entrepreneurial initiative in underdeveloped countries. Individuals and institutions alike, observers say, prefer traditional activities to new ventures. Since industry is, by definition, rather new in these countries, the preferences run strongly to commerce, real estate, and money transactions. These activities, it is argued, are not "productive" like industry. Moreover, speculative types of transactions, for example, in real estate or commodities, are usually favored over "solid" long-term enterprise, like manufacturing.

These observers perhaps describe the symptoms of the trouble correctly, but their diagnosis is erroneous. True, businessmen in underdeveloped countries are not sufficiently guided by growth considerations in their investment decisions. It is, however, hardly constructive to assume that they are blind or act irrationally. On the contrary, they are shrewd followers of the profit motive. The relevant question therefore appears to be: Why do these businessmen consider it more profitable to invest in the so-called traditional pursuits, in preference to industry? What are the factors that shape their investment preferences? How could these preferences be made to conform to the investment requirements of growing economies?

The last item deserves scrutiny before we enter into the analysis of prevailing entrepreneurial motivations. We might first inquire what the role of entrepreneurship ought to be under contemporary conditions, a normative, not an analytical, question. At this point, it is customary to take recourse to Schumpeter, but in discussing development today this may be misleading.[1]

The less developed countries are not in need of "innovators" as much as of "imitators," people who apply the techniques already developed elsewhere. This does not seem to require the exceptional personal qualities of the "Schumpeterian" entrepreneur. Nor is it, perhaps, essential that the entire cultural-intellectual climate of the country be first reoriented in a direction that reproduces some favorable historic constellation in the West—if there really ever was without question anything so definite.

I do not mean to make light of the relevance of what is somewhat vaguely termed the "climate of entrepreneurship." Probably its most effective ingredient is the example set by a significant number of businessmen success-fully engaged in certain activities, particularly in manufacturing industry. But are these the Schumpeterian pioneers or their imitators? It is a peculiar twist of the Schumpeterian concept that the glory belongs to the pioneer; yet it is the imitation on a massive scale by his lowly followers that transforms the pioneer's forward step into a magnitude of economic relevance.[2]

To imitate what was initiated elsewhere requires knowledge of a very specific sort. Under backward conditions the absence of essential elements of information, skill, and experience is, however, quite pronounced. It is there-fore desirable to concentrate on such specifics in preference to the elusive concept of "climate." This will be done in the following section.

III

Since I have dealt with this topic before, an apology is due to readers of another paper[3] for using my earlier findings for a working hypothesis. It rests on the assumption that among businessmen, or prospective businessmen, profit motivation is the most forceful determinant. True, considerations of status, prestige, etc. may also be important but the pool of chiefly profit-oriented businessmen is large enough even in underdeveloped countries to invite investigation of their investment preferences without attempting to ex-plain why other persons stay away from business altogether.

Before a businessman invests in a new venture, he will attempt to weigh his profit prospects against the risk of incurring losses. To do so requires information in many specific directions. The factors that determine his future profit are the size of the market for his product and the share of the market

---

[1] See also H. W. Singer, "Obstacles to Economic Development," *Social Research,* XX (Spring 1953), pp. 19ff.

[2] In underdeveloped countries, moreover, the imitation and adaptation of foreign techniques is, in a way, also a pioneering step, as daring as innovation under more advanced conditions.

[3] "Investment Decisions in Underdeveloped Countries," in *Capital Formation and Economic Growth,* a conference volume of the National Bureau of Economic Research (Princeton, N. J., 1955). Since that paper was drafted there appeared an article on the subject by Martin Shubik: "Information, Risk, Ignorance and Indeterminacy," *Quarterly Journal of Economics,* LXVIII (November 1954). See also B. S. Keirstead, *An Essay in the Theory of Profits and Income Distribution* (Oxford, 1953), and W. T. Easter-brook, "Uncertainty and Economic Change," *The Journal of Economic History,* XIV, No. 4 (1954), pp. 346-360.

he can conquer, the selling price, his cost of production, including the cost of capital, selling expenses, and other overhead expenditure, and not overlooking reserves for bad debts and other contingencies.

The extent of information available on these items, to be discussed shortly, will shape the prospective investor's profit expectations. However, even if objectively complete information were available, this would not make for a state of subjective certainty because the investor will also have to weigh the possibility that all or some of the information cannot be safely projected into the future. The degree of such "predictability" of profits and risks, in turn, depends on objective and subjective factors related to the time horizon.

Rather than continue this discussion in general terms, I propose to take up a few of the items that enter into rational profit and loss appraisals in order to demonstrate the low state of information in underdeveloped countries compared with intelligence available elsewhere. One of the most crucial items is the *volume of sales* as determined by the size of the market and the competitive situation. To appraise the market for specific commodities is quite difficult because detailed statistics are usually lacking. In industrial countries, moreover, a prospective investor has other reference material, such as trade literature and market surveys; he can obtain the advice of trade associations or hire the services of skilled and experienced advisers. Such facilities are lacking in most underdeveloped countries and the prospective investor has to make the best guess he can about the magnitude of demand. To estimate future trends, cyclical, or growth of demand, may well exceed the ability of most traders, no matter how experienced.

Where the prospective market is very limited, the investor is apt to consider the entry too risky unless he is given some assurances that he will not have to share it with uncertain numbers of competitors. He attempts therefore to obtain, and often is granted by governments, security against the entry by others. At the least, he is customarily accorded protection against competitive foreign products through tariffs, import restrictions, and other devices. This, incidentally, reassures the prospective industrialists not only about the volume of future sales, but also regarding the *sales price,* another important determinant of his venture's profitability. Such measures will lessen his uncertainty and this, it will be recalled, is the relevant aspect for our purpose.

As a next step, a decision has to be taken about the *size of plant* and the *suitable technology.* In this respect smallness of the market may keep the plant from reaching the most economical size. The size of plants tends to be smaller in underdeveloped countries. Moreover, reversed factor costs, cheap labor, and high cost of capital may call for a technology that differs from that employed in industrial countries. Recognition of such an ambiguity introduces an additional element of uncertainty into investment decisions: if it is not safe to imitate advanced industrial techniques, what is the alternative? Where else can a more appropriate technology be found? Will the prospective investor have to become a "pioneer" after all?[4] His dilemma is intensified

---

[4] This corresponds to Schumpeter's "adaptive innovation."

by the fact that he lacks the advanced technical services that are locally available in industrial countries. If he has to secure experts from abroad, the difficulty of selection also makes for uncertainty, and the high cost adds to the risk.

Investors in underdeveloped countries are also at a comparative disadvantage in estimating their *capital requirements*. Since most equipment has to be imported, capital needs are inflated by the cost of transportation over great distances. Moreover, the absence of basic facilities often compels new industries to build their own power plant, transportation links, and repair shops; they also have to keep larger stocks of repair parts and raw materials than would be required in a more highly developed industrial and commercial framework. Furthermore, the correct estimation of all these requirements calls in turn for more technical knowledge and familiarity with sources of supply than is usually available locally. Underestimation is dangerous because additional capital is hard to secure owing to the wariness of commercial banks toward new ventures. Overcapitalization, however, is expensive because the cost of capital is very high in most underdeveloped countries. Either way, uncertainty results and the risk is increased on that score.

The *supply of labor* is another critical factor. As a rule, there is no shortage of unskilled labor but a very crucial one of skills on all levels. In contrast to advanced countries, there is no pool to draw on and most new enterprises have to train their workers, foremen, and even technicians and managers from scratch. This is expensive and, what is more, the actual cost is difficult to estimate in advance. Worse yet, productivity cannot be estimated with any degree of confidence. Many factors, including social and cultural characteristics, make for generally low productivity of labor, and this inevitably lowers the productivity of capital as well. Hence, advanced types of equipment often produce in underdeveloped countries less per unit of investment than anticipated. The risk of overestimation is very real in this field.

Cost calculations are also affected by uncertainties regarding the availability and cost of raw materials and all kinds of supplies that have to be brought in over great distances. Even where it seems possible to calculate the cost within tolerable limits, the degree of certainty diminishes rapidly as one looks into the future, since supply and international prices are beyond the control of any individual developing country.

The *time horizon* is of particular interest in this respect. As we have seen, it is difficult enough to obtain currently relevant information in many respects—and there are more items than I have discussed here. Moreover, the future significance of such limited information diminishes rapidly as we envisage longer time spans. In part, this is due to objective factors because the economic and political stability of underdeveloped countries is often in doubt. Their prosperity suffers from cyclical fluctuations abroad; this affects the size of the market and the price level. The foreign exchange position of such countries is usually extremely vulnerable; this affects the availability of imported raw materials and other supplies and, in the case of devaluation, also prices and markets. Furthermore, governments are often unstable, administrative arbitrariness is rife, and investors consequently lack a healthy sense of continuity and security.

This deficiency of confidence in the future might help explain the "flightiness" of *investment preferences* in underdeveloped countries. If investors shun long-term involvement and prefer rapid turnover, it may well be because a "quick dollar" is also a safe dollar. Commercial transactions are wound up in short order; if necessary, they can be liquidated in time to "get out from under," or at least rapidly adapted to changing conditions. One might object that preference for real-estate investment does not fit this explanation. However, real estate finds a ready market among individuals who seek a stable store of wealth in times of trouble, a hedge against inflation or rapid appreciation of value. This type of investment thus also offers the safety that is found in liquidity. Industrial capital, by contrast, is invariably tied down for unpredictably long periods, and this illiquidity breeds risks.

Hence, what is considered safe investment in Western countries may not necessarily appear secure under different conditions. Knowledge and information, as we saw, offer only a slim foundation for investors' expectations. The extent to which we can supplement such scant information by intuitive judgment resting on familiarity depends on the breadth of our *experience*. Ability to appraise the degree of uncertainty that is inherent in the time element comes more easily to a person who is familiar with past developments of comparable relevance. Traditional pursuits which rest on a broad base of experience therefore appear safer than new ventures.

New industries by definition lack a comparable background of experience. Therefore they are viewed as even more hazardous than objective factors of uncertainty make them appear. From this point of view one understands why industrial investment, especially in untried directions, should be regarded as a gamble—much more so than what we consider speculative activities; for the professional speculator makes his investment decisions not once, but many times over, and he can fall back on a vast background of experience in comparable transactions. Industrial ventures, by contrast, are started infrequently during an individual's lifetime, or only a single time.

To sum up our working hypothesis: investment preferences reflect the expectations of investors regarding probable profits and possible losses. These expectations will be partly shaped by the amount of information that can be secured about various components of cost calculations. In addition, the degree of certainty that such current calculations can safely be projected into the future will have to be taken into consideration. A foreshortened time horizon causes expected profits to be discounted, and the possibility of losses to be overrated. The state of information in the industrial field is low in underdeveloped countries. The extent to which it can be at least partially supplemented by intuitive judgment depends on the individual entrepreneur's background of experience. If his past activities can be related to essential characteristics of the proposed industrial venture, he will more easily discount the risks and do justice to the opportunities. . . .

IV

The preceding review suggests that the limits of economic analysis in the discussion of entrepreneurial behavior have not been reached. While I do not deny the strength of noneconomically motivated attitudes, I feel that the economist ought to give precedence to the search for underlying *economic* determinants of such apparently noneconomic motivation. This cannot be done unless suitable hypotheses are first developed. In the field of investment preferences I have suggested the breaking-down of the rationale of investment decisions into its component elements; in other words, to analyze the factual information available to a prospective investor, its relevance for the future, and the profit-and-loss expectations that arise from such considerations.

A cursory review intimates that we ought not to be content with explaining the strength of traditional preferences in underdeveloped countries in terms of their conservative, static character alone. We can find economic reasons for this attitude that are related to the greater degree of certainty with which the prospects of traditional ventures can be appraised, compared with long-term industrial investment. If my analysis of these factors in this and in my earlier paper is found sufficiently suggestive to warrant further investigation, it seems to open a rather wide field for comparative analysis. Historical material regarding the origin of industrial enterprises might be reviewed and special research undertaken to investigate the information on which investment decisions might be based. If intuition is substituted for imperfect information, the rationale of such judgments is equally interesting, since seemingly irrational thinking still rests on a verifiable image of reality.

For the economist the purpose of such research is not psychological insight but the formulation of policy. Persons interested in greater investment activity ought to know the obstacles, not in vague terms of "investment climates" but in specific directions that are amenable to remedial action. If concrete information is lacking, we can outline the requirements and suggest how the data can be secured and made available to investors. If lack of confidence is at fault, we can attempt to formulate realistic policies designed to restore it. Insecurity can be attacked by legal and institutional measures, even though the political and administrative shortcomings may be beyond immediate redress. The time horizon can be lengthened by safeguards and guaranties that promise to lessen the most intractable risks. Such policies, however, depend on a prior factual analysis of the relative weight of the various factors. In the past we have had to rely on a generalized conception of what the investor's needs were supposed to be. Moreover, the investor's case was all too frequently presented in a manner that was colored by the writers' own idiosyncrasies and that abounded in clichés and stereotypes. No matter how difficult the task, it is time for historical and comparative analysis to tackle the problem in a more thoughtful and judicious manner.

FREDERICK HARBISON

IIIIIIIIIIIIIIIIIIIIIIIIIIIIIIIIIIIIIIIIIIIIIIIIIIIIIIIIIIIIIIIIIIIIIIIIIIIIIIIIIIIIIIIIIIIIIIIIIIIIIIIIIIIIIIIIIIIIIIIIIIIIIIIIIIIIIIIIIIIIIIIIIIIIIIIIIII

Entrepreneurial Organization as a Factor in Economic Development

I

Most economists would agree that any well-rounded analysis of economic development should include some appraisal of the role of entrepreneurship. On the other hand, they have differed in their concepts of the functions of entrepreneurship. In economic literature, consequently, there are many different answers to the question: Who is the entrepreneur and what functions is he supposed to perform?

In general economists have stressed three functions: (1) the bearing of risk and uncertainty, (2) innovation, and (3) the organization and management of a business enterprise. Frank H. Knight is perhaps the best-known proponent of the notion that entrepreneurs are a specialized group of people who bear risks and deal with uncertainty.[1] Schumpeter argued that innovation is the primary function of entrepreneurship and that one is an entrepreneur only when he carries out new combinations of factors of production and distribution.[2] Some of the classical economists, however, had broader concepts of entrepreneurship. To Adam Smith the entrepreneur was a proprietary capitalist—a supplier of capital and at the same time a manager who intervenes between the laborer and the consumer, while Alfred Marshall assigned to the entrepreneur all three functions: risk-bearing, innovation, and management. Writing in 1890 Marshall described the functions of entrepreneurs in this way:

> The task of directing production so that a given effort may be most effective in supplying wants is so difficult under the complex conditions of

From the *Quarterly Journal of Economics* (August 1956), pp. 364-379, with omissions. Reprinted by permission of Harvard University Press and the author. Copyright 1956 by The President and Fellows of Harvard College.

---

[1] Frank H. Knight, *Risk, Uncertainty and Profit* (Boston: Houghton Mifflin Co., 1921).
[2] Joseph A. Schumpeter, *The Theory of Economic Development* (Cambridge, Mass.: Harvard University Press, 1934).

modern life, that it has to be broken up and given into the hands of a specialized body of employers, or to use a more general term, of businessmen; who
"adventure" or "undertake" its risks; who bring together the capital and the
labour required for the work; who arrange or "engineer" its general plan, and
who superintend its minor details.[3]

Marshall's concept, because of its comprehensiveness, is probably the
most realistic in explaining the activities of present-day complex business
enterprises. Its principal weakness is the implicit assumption that the entrepreneur is an individual person, for, only in a very small firm can a single
individual perform all of Marshall's entrepreneurial functions. In most enterprises, a hierarchy of individuals is required to perform them. Thus, the
entrepreneur is in essence *an organization* which comprises all of the people
required to perform entrepreneurial functions. Entrepreneurship should be
treated as a resource which has both qualitative attributes and quantitative
dimensions. It should be possible to make empirical studies of such entrepreneurial resources as they are related to other factors of production. The
objective of this paper is to suggest a framework for research along these lines.

II

The functions of the modern entrepreneurial organization, whether it be
privately or publicly owned and operated, may be categorized as follows:
(1) the undertaking or managing of risk and the handling of economic uncertainty; (2) planning and innovation; (3) coordination, administration,
and control; and (4) routine supervision. In the very small enterprise, of
course, these functions may all be performed by a single person—the propri-
etor. In larger establishments, there may be a division of functions among a
complex hierarchy of individuals. Ownership may be separated from management, and management itself may be subdivided into top, middle, and first-
line supervisory management, and into line and staff management. Obviously,
the large organization requires more managerial functionaries—and perhaps
different types and combinations of people—than the small or medium-sized
firm. Organizations can be quite simple or very complex depending upon the
nature of the business activity, the size of the firm, and the technology
employed.

In this paper, I shall use the term *organization* as a shorthand expression
for the integrated aggregation of those persons who are primarily involved
in managing risk and uncertainty-bearing, planning and innovation, coordination, administration and control, and routine supervision of an enterprise. I
shall refer to the persons who perform these functions as *managerial resources*.

---

[3] Marshall, *Principles,* 1st ed. (London: Macmillan and Co., 1890), I, pp. 334-335.
Essentially the same statement appears in the 8th ed., p. 293.

The other people employed in the enterprise, who do not perform these functions, will be referred to as labor resources.[4]. . .

Organizations of similar size may vary quite widely in their efficiency. They may have good or poor managerial resources; they may be well integrated or improperly integrated. They can be dynamic or static, rigid or flexible, modern or archaic. It is true that the effectiveness of business organizations, especially as they grow larger, is dependent upon innovators in the Schumpeterian sense. A dynamic organization needs its idea men, its creative thinkers, its people who can plan and initiate changes. I would suggest, however, that *organization-building ability* is probably the most critical skill needed for industrial development on a large scale. The organization-builder must be able to harness the new ideas of different innovators to the rest of the organization. He must be able at the same time to select and develop persons who can properly manage and control a labor force. His task is to stimulate initiative and enthusiasm in the accomplishment of the objectives of the organization. He must be able to "multiply himself" by effectively delegating responsibility to others. Indeed, the ability to build an organization is perhaps the most precious of all entrepreneurial skills, and thus those who can achieve success in this very critical area may be the ones who most nearly fulfill the role of the true entrepreneur. Such persons, however, do not always have new ideas nor do they necessarily carry out new combinations. They may be simply good leaders and excellent administrators.

This concept of organization certainly does not minimize the role of individual innovators as factors in industrial development. It suggests, however, that organization is more than a summation of the particular abilities of certain individuals. It is more than the statistical aggregate of managerial personnel. Organization connotes a constellation of functions, the persons and the abilities necessary to perform these functions, plus the integration of persons and functions in a common undertaking.

Organization may be treated as any other resource such as capital, labor, or natural resources. For example, one can conceive of "investment in organization" in the same terms as investment in machinery or equipment, and he may think of "accumulation of managerial resources" as a concept parallel to

---

[4] Persons who simply purchase or hold stock in a corporation, though risk-bearers in a sense, are not part of the entrepreneurial organization and are not here considered as managerial resources. The officers of the company, who represent the interests of the stockholders along with other interests, are part of the organization. They undertake to manage the bearing of risk and uncertainty and in many cases, of course, are themselves large stockholders.

Engineers, highly trained technicians, scientists, and staff experts, though they may not always manage or supervise the activities of others, are considered managerial resources because they are involved in research, planning, or control activities and are almost without exception on a par with other managerial personnel as far as pay and status in the organization are involved.

In supervision we include only those persons who spend their entire time supervising the work of others—usually clerical or manual labor resources. The so-called straw boss or working foreman, who spends part of his time actually performing tasks and part in supervising others performing similar tasks, is not here included in managerial resources.

capital formation and accumulation. Industries requiring large investments in machinery and processes—capital intensive industries—may also be industries requiring great "depth" in organization, and thus might be called "organization intensive industries."

III

This concept of organization is perhaps most useful in analyzing the prerequisites for economic growth in underdeveloped countries and the reasons for accelerated or retarded growth in more advanced countries. It provides a framework for tangible comparative studies of the role of entrepreneurship in industrial development. In this connection, let us now consider a few tentative propositions which may be of particular interest to those making empirical analyses of economic development.

These propositions are based upon some acquaintanceship over the past two years with approximately seventy-five business enterprises in the following countries: England, France, Germany, Italy, Belgium, Holland, Egypt, Saudi Arabia, Peru, and the United States. This acquaintanceship consists of a visit of a day or two in about three-fifths of the cases and more intensive studies of the managerial organization and labor policies, averaging about two weeks per enterprise, in the other two-fifths. Admittedly, the evidence at this stage of the research is more impressionistic than definitive. For this reason, the observations which follow are set forth as tentative propositions worthy of more exhaustive study rather than as final conclusions resulting from systematic research.

ORGANIZATION AND CAPITAL

Industries requiring large capital investment appear to require a correspondingly heavy investment in organization. Or, put in a different way, large expenditures for equipment and machinery are likely to be quite unproductive unless there is a corresponding investment in organization.

This proposition can be argued on logical grounds. Large investments in machinery and processes are usually associated with relatively large enterprises. A large enterprise, being more complex than a small one, naturally requires more and better trained managerial resources. Also, if the machinery and processes themselves are complicated, engineers, chemists, or other technical staff specialists are required. To the extent that machinery may displace unskilled or skilled labor, it usually requires greater investment in personnel who specialize in planning, production scheduling, engineering, and "control" of all kinds. Thus an additional cost involved in investment in modern processes or labor-saving machinery is that of procuring and developing the managerial resources necessary to utilize and to control it. If a business organization must employ a battery of technicians to supervise and control more complicated processes, there is also need for more experienced and expensive top management to coordinate their activities and to plan for future development.

On empirical grounds, this relationship can be illustrated by a rough comparison which we have made of steel mills in Germany, the United Kingdom, and the United States. The first comparison was made between a German and an American company, each producing a roughly comparable range of products and employing approximately the same total personnel (between 17,000 and 18,000 men). In comparison with the American company, the German enterprise had quite old machinery and processes which were in most respects inferior to that in the American company. Largely for this reason, the total annual production of the German company was only half that of its American counterpart.

The contrast in investment in managerial resources between the two companies was quite evident. In comparable steel-making and rolling departments, the American company used three foremen to every one in the German mill, and the educational level of the American foremen was in practically all cases much superior to that of the German foremen. In the German plant a greater burden of supervision was placed upon the group leader, an experienced skilled workman, whereas in the American company the supervisory functions were performed by full-time salaried foremen who were members of management. Some of the American foremen had Master's degrees and 15 percent had college degrees, but none of the German foremen had any equivalent higher education. In the States, moreover, foremen quite frequently advance into the upper ranks of management; in Germany, the position of foreman is generally the highest step in the ladder of promotion for workers; only on rare occasions do the German foremen become members of middle or upper management. An even more striking contrast existed with respect to the senior technical staff which comprises persons such as process engineers, chemists, specialists in industrial engineering, personnel, production control, and quality control. Here the American company employed 430 persons as compared with only 43 in the German enterprise. It was obvious that the top managers and the superintendents in the States had a great many highly trained assistants actually to perform technical work. In Germany, the members of top and middle management did most of the technical work themselves. For this reason, a much higher proportion of the managers and superintendents in the German company were themselves highly trained engineers, whereas many of their counterparts in the American company had either no formal technical training or perhaps merely a liberal arts college education. . . .

This steel-mill comparison, though it is admittedly suggestive rather than conclusive, indicates that there may be a direct and positive relationship between investment in technology and investment in organization. It also shows that where technology is comparable, labor productivity may be related positively to investment in managerial resources. We have noticed the same general relationships in the other companies with which we are acquainted. A thin managerial organization is usually associated with relatively extensive utilization of nonmanagerial labor forces and relatively primitive production methods, whereas a relatively deep managerial organization is almost always found in enterprises which have the largest investment in technology, particularly in labor-saving machinery. . . .

ORGANIZATION AND LABOR RESOURCES

A second proposition is that organization is probably the principal factor determining the productivity of labor, assuming that capital and natural resources are constant. A labor force is recruited, trained, developed, and managed by the organization, and the skills and qualities of manpower probably depend more on what the organization does than on any natural or innate characteristics of labor itself. This proposition, like the previous one, seems to be plausible on both logical and empirical grounds.

An essential management function is the selection, training, and development of the persons comprising the labor force. Most, though not all, skills of manual labor and even clerical employees are acquired on the job. Another management function is to provide the incentives for work. To these functions we can add many more which directly affect the productivity of labor: proper lay-out of machinery and processes, work study, breakdown of jobs in order to economize on use of critical skills, safety programs, systems for appraising performance and discovering talent, and many other related techniques. Such techniques of "scientific management," however, are expensive. They require the employment of specialized personnel and investment of time on the part of members of the line organization. Even more important, they require relatively high levels of education, experience and training among the members of the managerial organization. The development of such high-level talent in management would be too expensive, if not virtually impossible, in many present-day underdeveloped economies.

In some respects, of course, the efficiency of labor resources may be independent from organization. The more important factors here may be levels of education, conditions of health, nutrition, and general experience with and attitudes toward work. The organization, however, is able to influence these factors at least in part. Attitudes toward work can be molded by management; companies can provide medical services and adequate diets for employees; and some firms in underdeveloped countries even provide facilities for general education of members of the labor force. In the industrially advanced countries, of course, the laboring population may be generally more efficient because of long tradition and previous experience with industrial enterprises, and the development of high labor productivity in a primitive society may thus require a much higher investment in organization than in countries with a long industrial tradition. In short, I do not deny that some innate factors have influence on the quality of labor resources; my contention is simply that *the organization which employs labor* is probably the principal factor—the dominant force—in determining labor productivity with constant technology.

This contention has been fortified by observations of the utilization of labor resources in different enterprises. For example, in Egypt the productivity of labor is very low, even in factories which technologically may be among the most modern in the world. In the best Egyptian factories four to six workers are usually employed for every one in comparable establishments in the United States. But, managerial resources are scarce and managerial methods are quite primitive. Although there is an impressive awakening to the need for improvement of management on the part of progressive Egyptian enterprises, systematic procedures of selection and training operatives are not yet used. Programs for training and development of supervisors or middle management in the skills of handling people are almost nonexistent. Time and motion study, job evaluation, and other techniques for the systematic combination of labor with processes are still quite rare. The explanation for this "thinness of management" is obvious. First, labor is plentiful and cheap, so that there is no pressure to make a large investment in organization in order to economize in the utilization of labor; second, specialists in techniques of scientific management are scarce if they exist at all; and finally, the general level of existing managerial resources is not yet sufficiently high to utilize effectively modern techniques of manpower utilization.

Another convincing bit of evidence showing the relationship of labor productivity to organization is the "spotty" work performance which is evident in most factories, and particularly in those in the less developed countries. One frequently observes a very slow pace of work in most departments of a factory, whereas in one or two departments the work pace may be very high. In this connection, I have observed some teams of Egyptian workers on packaging operations whose rhythm and speed of work was equal to that in the best American factories, this being all the more remarkable because they were employed in factories with unusually poor labor productivity as a whole. The explanation for these spotty examples of labor efficiency lies in the peculiar or rare skills of the individuals planning or supervising these particular departments. The same spottiness also is apparent when one compares different factories in the same labor market. Again in Egypt, I visited two petroleum refineries located less than one-half mile apart. The labor productivity in one had been nearly double that in the other for many years. But recently under completely new management, the inefficient refinery was beginning to make quite spectacular improvements in efficiency with the same labor force. All of this evidence, of course, is suggestive rather than conclusive. Nevertheless, it leads to a strong presumption that the productivity of labor may be primarily a function of organization.

ORGANIZATIONAL "INEFFICIENCY"

Unlike land and capital, organization is a human resource. Business organizations are composed of animate human beings who are motivated by drives, hopes, desires, fears, and frustrations. The actions of human beings and hence also the actions of organizations are not determined exclusively by economic forces. From the standpoint of economic analysis, organizational behavior as all other human behavior is not always "rational." Indeed, the economist who studies any form of management soon finds out that business organizations are surprisingly "inefficient." The decision-making processes in the modern enterprise are not so precise or so rational as the economic theorist might presume, and a great deal of energy within the organization is absorbed in clearly noneconomic activities. Thus the economist may have good grounds for assuming that all business organizations are inefficient in terms of economic theory, the distinction between them being only that some are more inefficient than others. . . .

First of all, there is no reason to believe that the heads of typical or representative business organizations are always or even primarily striving to maximize profits. As Reder has pointed out, an entrepreneur may at times strive to retain control over the organization rather than to maximize profits.[5] He may be interested in prestige and power rather than sheer financial reward. Many French businessmen, for example, are as much interested in using the firm as a means of maintaining or building the family name as in amassing a large fortune. Landes has said that to the French entrepreneur, "the business is not an end in itself, nor is its purpose to be found in any such independent ideal as production or service. It exists by and for the family, and the honor, the reputation and wealth of the one are the honor, wealth and reputation of the other."[6] Thus, the risk-taker, the innovator, or the administrator may be as much concerned with getting his friends or his relatives into a business as he is with maximizing profits. In managing the enterprise, he may seek to maximize his social position or even his political power. He may be much more concerned with preserving his security than in seeking new opportunity. To the extent that he is concerned with such "extraneous" or noneconomic goals, the firm may be "inefficient" from an economic standpoint.

Another factor explaining the inherent inefficiency of the firm is that of the imperfect knowledge upon which decisions must be made. The risk-takers, planners, or administrators in any organization have at best imperfect facts concerning such things as the demand for their product, the marginal revenue productivities of capital or labor, the effects upon consumer demand of changes in either the price or the quality of articles produced, the future trend of costs of raw materials, and so forth. The business must operate on best guesses, hunches, and artificially constructed assumptions. Thus, the fact that business judgments must frequently be based upon imperfect knowledge makes completely logical and rational decision-making quite difficult. . . .

The third major source of organizational friction lies in the structure of the business organization itself. Specialization and division of labor increase the problems of integration, coordination, and control. This raises the very knotty question of the "span of control"—*i.e.,* the number of persons who can be properly directed and supervised by each boss. The appropriate span of control varies, of course, with the nature of the business operations, but it is also dependent upon more intangible factors such as individual personalities,

---

[5] M. W. Reder, "A Reconsideration of the Marginal Productivity Theory," *Journal of Political Economy,* LV (1947), p. 452.

[6] David Landes, "Business and the Businessman in France," in E. M. Earle (ed.), *Modern France* (Princeton, N. J.: Princeton University Press, 1951).

the communication process, authoritarian or democratic executive leadership, and the motivational patterns of working groups. Specialists in organizational planning are working vigorously on this thorny problem, and, as everyone familiar with business administration will agree, they have as yet arrived at no really definitive measures for eliminating the frictions generated by imperfections in this area. Another related problem is the proper integration of the functions of the specialist-expert and the general administrator—in administrative jargon, the relationships between staff and line. Modern business organizations require the services of specialists such as engineers, lawyers, industrial relations experts, and designers. Yet ideas coming from such advisors, particularly if they call for substantial innovation, are quite often resented and resisted by those in charge of operations. Consequently, a tremendous amount of energy must be devoted to "selling" the line management on new ideas and getting acceptance of necessary changes throughout the organization. These and many other similar organizational frictions are large consumers of energy within most business organizations. The consumption of this energy may be lowered by improvements in design of the organization and also by the use of appropriate human relations lubricants, but it can never be completely eliminated.

If the above analysis is correct, one cannot conceive of organization in purely quantitative terms. Thus it would be misleading to say that greater financial investment in managerial resources will automatically increase the efficiency of the firm. There is as yet no exact science or technology of organization-building. But in a rough way it may be possible to distinguish between a relatively good organization and a bad one, a complex one or a simple one, and an expensive one or a cheap one. The typical business organization in the United States is probably relatively more efficient and much more expensive than that, for example, in France, Italy, or Belgium. And, within the United States it is possible for informed observers to detect the difference between a reasonably progressive and efficient organization and one which is very poorly designed and obviously using organizational energy in an excessively wasteful manner.

IV

The argument presented can now be summarized. Organization may be looked upon as a resource, and in significant though not in all respects it is similar to other resources such as labor, capital, and natural resources. Organization is a broader concept than entrepreneurship. It connotes a constellation of functions including specifically the management of risk and uncertainty, planning and innovation, coordination, administration and control, and routine supervision of the enterprise; it connotes also the integrated hierarchy of the persons who are primarily concerned with exercise of these functions—the managerial resources.

In considering organization as related to other resources, three tentative propositions were advanced: (1) industries requiring large capital investment probably require a correspondingly large investment in organization; (2) organization is the principal factor determining the productivity of labor, assuming capital and natural resources to be constant; and (3) because of non-economic factors which determine in part the behavior of human beings as managerial resources, all organizations are probably "inefficient" in effecting the optimum combination of economic resources which is theoretically possible.

In analyzing problems of economic development, organization is a more precise and meaningful concept than entrepreneurship in its traditional sense. Organization denotes a concrete institution which describes realistic relationships between functions and functionaries, whereas entrepreneurship is often a rather vague abstraction which is subject to varying interpretations. To some extent at least, organization is subject to quantitative measurement, which permits one to set forth a series of possible relationships between quantities of capital or labor and quantities of managerial resources (depth of organization). For example, if it is possible to determine the quantity of capital investment necessary for a country to increase its production by a certain percentage, it may be possible also to estimate the extent and nature of investment required in managerial resources needed to make such capital investment effective. The idea of substitutability of labor and organization (as well as labor and capital) is also a useful concept in studying the processes of economic growth and development. The traditional notions about entrepreneurship were not designed for such kinds of analysis. . . .

W. RUPERT MACLAURIN

The Sequence from Invention to Innovation and Its Relation to Economic Growth

Professor Schumpeter, far more than anyone else, had the insight ahead of his time to see the structural outlines of a theory of economic development in which technology and innovation played a central role. I wish that he had

From the *Quarterly Journal of Economics* (February 1953), pp. 97-111. Reprinted by permission of the Harvard University Press. Copyright 1953 by The President and Fellows of Harvard College.

had the opportunity to carry it further. Yet in the preface to *Business Cycles* he wrote:

> The younger generation of economists should look upon this book as something to shoot at and to start from—as a moderated program for further research. Nothing, at any rate, could please me more.[1]

Schumpeter regarded the process of innovation as central to an understanding of economic growth. The innovator as such, rather than the investor or the inventor, represented the most sensitive individual figure in the economy. But perhaps because Schumpeter's principal work was done before the spectacular growth of organized science, he did not devote much attention to the role of science as a pacemaker of change.

Encouraged by Schumpeter,[2] I have tried elsewhere to break down the process of technological advance into elements that may eventually be more measurable.[3] My analysis suggests that in studying the determinants of investment in any advanced economy, it will be significant to assess the variations in the following factors[4]:

1. The propensity to develop pure science.
2. The propensity to invent.
3. The propensity to innovate.
4. The propensity to finance innovation.
5. The propensity to accept innovation.

Among advanced economies there are important differences in the relative strength of these propensities. For example, from 1900 to 1930 there is considerable evidence that England had a stronger propensity to develop pure science than did the United States, while the propensity to *innovate* was more pronounced here. One indication in science was the greater number of Nobel prize winners in England, and in innovation the much higher proportion of new firms established each year in America.

More recently there has been a heightened interest in pure science in America. As a young and rapidly growing country, with a strong urge to innovate, the United States was content for many years to borrow its pure science from Europe. But it was also logical that our talent for applied science and invention—an extension of "Yankee ingenuity"—should lead us to produce more pure science of our own, stimulated originally by Europeans emigrating to this country and gradually developing an important indigenous

---

[1] *Business Cycles* (New York: McGraw-Hill, 1939), Preface, p. v.

[2] It was one of Professor Schumpeter's striking qualities that he took such a lively and encouraging interest in the explorations of younger men who, like myself, had never been his students and frequently had no connection with his university.

[3] *Invention and Innovation in the Radio Industry* (New York: The Macmillan Company, 1949).

[4] For a discussion of economic growth in relation to these and other elements such as population growth in a broader historical context, see W. W. Rostow, *The Process of Economic Growth* (New York: W. W. Norton, 1952). I am much indebted to Professor Rostow for helping me to sharpen up my thinking on the elements on which I have focused attention in this paper.

contribution. Yet still today our principal forte is in the application of science rather than in pioneering speculative thought.

The important point for economic development is that careful study is needed of the institutional arrangements which are most conducive to the flourishing of all the major elements of dynamic growth.

Perhaps, therefore, we can make headway by discussing the propensities we have isolated and considering ways in which each of them can be measured.

THE PROPENSITY TO DEVELOP PURE SCIENCE

"'Pure science" is difficult to describe in a satisfactory manner, partly because the term suggests that applied science is somehow "impure" and therefore not of equal significance. Moreover, it cannot be assumed that pure science is undertaken without *any thought* of material ends. Since modern science began to emerge in the seventeenth century in Western Europe, it seems highly unlikely that the principal contributors have not been influenced by practical objectives; the doctrine of material progress has been too strong an element in our culture. In fact, exclusive personal dedication to "science for science's sake" does not apparently lead to the most fructifying concepts. The important point is that some scientists have been willing to speculate deeply and widely without *immediate* practical objectives in mind.

The significance of pure science to economic development depends on the capacity of the scientist to ask original and important questions which have far-reaching practical implications, and to find answers to them. By and large, it has been the great universities that have provided the environment, the freedom, and the incentives for pure science. Such institutions have attracted and encouraged the more unconventional scientific minds, permitting the best of them to explore the unknown with a minimum of direction and control.

In recent years, however, some of our large established industrial corporations have become increasingly interested in supporting pure science in their own laboratories. At first glance this might seem difficult to justify. If the research worker is given complete freedom of choice as to the type of problem he will work on, what is the probability that his speculations will bear any fruit that could be justified to a group of stockholders?

And yet this type of inquiry has tended to pay off in industrial terms. Most able people like to be regarded as useful members of the institution supporting them. So long as a company has broad interests, the chances are that at least part of the speculative work of its pure scientists will have some practical applications. To illustrate: the physicist Davisson won the Nobel prize for work conducted in the Bell Telephone Laboratories on electron diffraction. This had no immediate application to telephone communications; but Davisson's later work came much closer to the interests of the company. And the only other Nobel prize winner in American industry—Irving Langmuir—started work for General Electric on high vacuum with no thought of immediate applications. His line of inquiry led to some exceedingly important discoveries which enabled GE to dominate the incandescent-lamp and radio-tube industries for many years.[5]

Pure science rarely leads *directly* to a patentable invention or to immediate technological change. Our patent laws state that a process of *nature* cannot be patented; and, if a discovery is of such a high general level as to represent a fundamental contribution to knowledge, the courts have tended to refuse a patent to any one company claiming it.

Thus, in the Langmuir case the Supreme Court argued that the work on high vacuum was the discovery of a fundamental natural law and not patentable. The courts did, however, sustain Langmuir's patent on the gas-filled lamp—a by-product of the high-vacuum research giving GE undisputed patent control of the lamp industry from 1913 to 1930.

The scientist who makes an important discovery of wide generalization "may" be interested in its commercial applications. But frequently he is not. Most of the senior physicists of today—Einstein, Niels Bohr, Fermi, for example—have been motivated by the creative intellectual urge to widen our understanding of natural phenomena. The application of these advances, except under the special pressure of wartime service, they have left entirely to others.

It does not follow from this reference to Einstein that important contributions to pure science *must* be highly complicated and abstract.[6] New concepts may be very simple, as for example the Darwinian theory of evolution. The difficulty in such cases is to overcome the mental block resulting from long-established habits of thinking and teaching.

Can we measure the propensity to develop pure science in a particular country at a particular time? I think we could, though it has not been done.[7] Any efforts at measurement would have to be undertaken by fields of learning. In an age of specialization, few men are intimately conversant with more than one or two branches of their subject. But within the Western world there is enough intellectual interchange so that it should be possible to reach tolerable agreement on the major speculative contributions to the advancement of science. And these could be classified by fields, by countries, and over time. Such an appraisal would concentrate on the beacons. What we are looking for is the fruitful new hypotheses which led to a significant fresh approach to the subject.[8] Admittedly, science advances not only by discontinuities, but

---

[5] See Arthur A. Bright, Jr., *The Electric-Lamp Industry: Technological Change and Economic Development from 1800 to 1947* (New York: The Macmillan Company, 1949).

[6] I recall Ernest Rutherford once saying, "You know, I'm really no physicist." Yet he received the Nobel prize for his original contributions to the understanding of the atomic nucleus. He meant that he was not a mathematical physicist.

[7] In V. Bush, *Science: The Endless Frontier* (Washington, D. C.: U.S. Government Printing Office, 1945), the conclusion was reached that the United States lagged behind Europe in pure science and that positive steps should be taken to remedy this. But there were few supporting data assembled to prove the point.

[8] See J. B. Conant, *On Understanding Science* (New Haven, Conn.: Yale University Press, 1947).

by the much steadier flow of minor contributions. And yet concentration on the great contributors[9] should provide some more satisfactory evidence than we have today as to the environment in which the most useful speculative thought flourishes. It should also bring out more sharply basic differences between countries in this exceedingly important aspect of economic development.

The budget of science is also significant to examine. Great contributions are rarely made today in a garret, and the funds devoted to pure science are likely to have some effect on accomplishments.[10]

Finally, we might seek to measure the impact of major scientific breakthroughs and make a forecast of the probable time-scale involved in their commercial introduction. We have reached a sufficiently sophisticated stage in science and engineering so that something might be made of these predictions. There is considerable evidence, for example, that it would not have been too difficult to predict, say, in 1890, the probable impact of the electrical revolution on American industry in the next forty years. And by 1910 a similar forecast could have been made for the automobile. So today, with aviation, atomic power, and mass-production housing, a carefully selected group of well-informed individuals with diverse backgrounds *could* make a shrewd and reasonably accurate guess as to the general course of development over the next thirty years. This might be done in two stages—a probable rate of development based on past evidence and the current propensities of the country to invent, innovate, and accept innovations. The other stage would be to suggest an optimum rate, based on an evolutionary improvement in the institutions affecting the various propensities. We should at least attempt such guesses and spell out the factors influencing the prediction, if economics is to maximize its usefulness to the process of economic development.[11]

THE PROPENSITY TO INVENT

The economic growth or stagnation of a particular country or region is more *immediately* affected by the propensity to invent and to innovate than by the propensity to develop pure science. It is possible, as in the case of the United States until very recently, to have vigorous technological growth while relying on Europe for the principal path-breaking concepts. And, where the

---

[9] These are currently assessed in many ways that should be helpful as guides—by prizes, awards, medals, etc. Usually careful reviews are made by competent committees established to administer the major honors.

[10] The National Science Foundation was established by act of Congress in 1950 with one of the primary objectives to give financial assistance to pure science. The scientists who recommended the legislation believed that there was a real risk in the United States that the stream of radical inventions and innovations would dwindle under the weight of applied research.

[11] For a discussion of the problem of predicting inventions, see S. Collum Gilfillan, "The Lag between Inventions and Application, with Emphasis on Prediction of Technical Change," unpublished paper delivered at Princeton Conference, April 1951. See also W. F. Ogburn, *Social Effects of Aviation* (Boston: Riverside Press, 1946).

pace of change was slower, the great economic development of the Roman Empire was based on scientific and philosophical ideas which had flourished several centuries earlier in Greece. We could also conceive of China under the Manchus developing pure science as a branch of scholarly learning without any outlet in industry. Yet, as our technology becomes increasing complex, pure science is likely to become the father, if not actually the mother, of invention.

The significant feature of an invention is that it discloses an *operational* method of creating something new. Within the field of technology there are patentable and nonpatentable inventions—as a matter of law. For example, in the United States patents can no longer be obtained in most aspects of atomic energy—a very significant change in law, since during the electrical revolution of the last half of the nineteenth century practically all the new work in electric lighting, electric power, and electrical communications was blanketed with patents.

To obtain a United States patent today in the fields where patents are permissible (and this is still most fields), the inventor must disclose what he has done and prove that it has not been anticipated by someone else's patent or in the prior art. Over 2,500,000 patents have been issued in the United States, 750,000 in Germany, and 650,000 in England. There are patent offices today in almost all industrialized countries in the world, with total patents in the many millions.

And because no patent can be issued in any country if it has been anticipated in that country, each patent office is forced to develop a vast system of records. Perhaps because the data are so overwhelming in magnitude, but more probably because of the scant interest that economists have given to the sources of technological change, most of these data have remained untapped.[12] There has been no rapport between the economic statistician and the Patent Office comparable to that which has developed with the Census Bureau or the Bureau of Labor Statistics.

Could one obtain a satisfactory measure of the propensity to invent through the records of the Patent Office? I believe that something can be done with these records, but they have to be used with care. To begin with, a distinction ought to be made where possible between basic patents and improvement patents. For example, in the incandescent lamp, the early patents of Edison and Swan on different types of electrodes represented a major advance. So also did Langmuir's patent on the gas-filled lamp. But such minor later improvements as the "tipless" lamp, "inside frosting," and other comparable advances gave rise to a greater number of patents.

Two different companies in the same industry may vary in the emphasis which they give to patents, even though they have approximately the same policy on encouraging research and invention. A company anxious to develop

---

[12] See, however, two recent doctoral dissertations—*Technical Change and Patent Statistics,* submitted by Jacob Schmookler at the University of Pennsylvania, and *An Appraisal of Patent Statistics* by Alfred B. Stafford, College of Engineering, University of Wyoming, accepted by the University of Chicago in 1950.

licensing revenues is more likely to spend substantial sums on patent development; and while it is not possible to produce patents out of thin air, the presence of an able group of attorneys constantly on the alert for possible new inventions is much more likely to result in an "impressive" list of patents.

International comparisons are particularly tricky because patent laws and patenting procedures differ considerably from country to country. Germany requires an annual fee to maintain a patent, which is discouraging to individual as opposed to corporate inventors. Yet basically there are far more similarities than differences in the patent practices of most countries.

Still another consideration is that patents are obviously more important as a measure of the propensity to invent in some segments of the economy than in others. In government-sponsored research, which has become of greatly enhanced significance in such fields as agriculture, jet-propelled aircraft and guided missiles, there are very few patents taken out. This important trend, plus the fact that the individual inventor is now far less important in the American economy than he was fifty years ago, having been absorbed into the corporate research laboratory, has led some students of invention, such as Professor Gilfillan,[13] to reject patent statistics altogether as an effective measure of the propensity to invent.

This seems an extreme view: in every branch of engineering, some experts can be found in a position to give a reasonably objective evaluation and to offer advice on the use and abuse of patent statistics. In addition, the patent offices themselves have informed officials who are anxious to be helpful; and I have no doubt that, if their cooperation were enlisted properly, they would be able to supply more effective statistics on patent trends.

Patents, therefore, have the convenience of being carefully recorded, but they also have the weakness of representing only a segment of the total field of modern invention. Another type of measurement is to compute numbers of research workers and total expenditures for research.[14] We have now reached a stage in many fields where inventions are almost made to order, and where there *can* be a definite correlation between the numbers of applied scientists employed (and the funds at their disposal) and the inventive results. But one really gifted inventor is likely to be more productive than half a dozen men of lesser stature.[15] Typically, also, many industrial concerns[16] do not make adequate distinctions in their records between professional research

---

[13] Gilfillan makes the point that only about one-seventh of all technical inventions in the United States today are in fields in which patents play a significant role. Yet these remain very important fields—electrical manufacturing, the chemical industries, machinery and equipment.

[14] See figures in Bush, *Science: The Endless Frontier, op. cit.*

[15] See, for example, the extraordinary record of inventions by the men whom Taussig discusses in *Inventors and Money Makers* (New York: The Macmillan Company, 1915).

[16] Corporate, as opposed to individually held, patents have been steadily increasing in importance with the development of the industrial research laboratory and the decline of the lone inventor. In the United States in 1885, according to Stafford, all corporations produced 12 percent of the total number of patents issued. By 1945 they accounted for two-thirds of the total. Alfred B. Stafford, *op. cit.*

workers, engineers working primarily on service problems, and laboratory assistants who have no advanced professional training. The large companies with centralized research laboratories have such breakdowns, but it is very difficult to compare them with less formalized companies. There have been, too, a number of cases in which "impressive" research laboratories have been built up as a matter of top-management policy, but where the leadership of the laboratory, or the basic attitude of the company toward research, has not evoked notable results.[17] Granting these limitations, some useful over-all comparisons can be based on the number of professional research workers engaged in a particular task.

Also of significance is a chronological record of inventions by firms. This shows, more than anything else perhaps, the seriousness of purpose that a company may have in pursuing creative research and invention. Curiously enough, despite the use that advertising departments make of such terms as "The House of Magic" for General Electric, etc., most companies keep a very inadequate record of their own inventions. They have, of course, a list of their patents, which can most productively be scrutinized apart from the company's claims in respect to it. The student can be helped, however, by the testimony before the courts in patent litigation and by the reviews of the professional engineering societies which grant such annual awards as the Edison Medal for inventive achievement.

THE PROPENSITY TO INNOVATE

When an invention is introduced commercially as a new or improved product or process, it becomes an *innovation*. This important step is *by no means automatic*. Almost always today, different individuals, and frequently different institutions, are involved in the two stages of invention and innovation. Innovations cover a much wider area of possible new developments than inventions.[18] A new use of an old product may prove a more important turning point in the evolution of an industry than the commercialization of a new invention. Thus, there were experiments in wireless telephony which showed considerable promise as early as 1907; but it was not until the 1920s that radio broadcasting emerged as an innovation, undreamed of by such wireless inventors as Marconi.

Since the principal social obstacles to change occur at the outset, the innovator as an individual takes his place along with the pure scientist and the inventor as a key figure in material progress. To succeed, his imagination

---

[17] Sometimes this may stem from an error of management; in other cases from the use of research in part as window dressing.

[18] See Schumpeter, *Business Cycles, op. cit.,* p. 84: "It is entirely immaterial whether an innovation implies scientific novelty or not. Although most innovations can be traced to some conquest in the realm of either theoretical or practical knowledge that has occurred in the immediate or the remote past, there are many which cannot. Innovation is possible without anything we should identify as invention.

must be keen, though tempered with "business judgment." He must have the steady persistence to overcome obstructions, fear, and possible disaster. He must also have the capacity to pick able associates, to retain control, and yet to delegate authority (a rare gift), and to inspire loyalty. And he must be bold, yet capable of instilling confidence in his financial supporters. Innovations, in fact, may be becoming inherently more difficult. The current trend toward emphasizing smooth human relationships as the principal qualification for administrative responsibility tends to militate against the rise of innovators to top positions. Executive committees of enterprises are often afraid to choose a "strong man" for fear of his disruptive force.[19]

Many concerns are far less aware of the distinction between what are essentially minor improvements in standard products, such as have taken place in the automobile since 1927, and radically new innovations, such as nylon. It was this type of mental block that led Schumpeter to reason in *Business Cycles* that important innovations were characteristically "embodied in a new firm provided for the purpose"; and as a corollary that they were associated with "the rise to leadership of new men."[20]

When Schumpeter wrote *Business Cycles* in the mid-1930s, he believed that great firms did not "dominate the picture in any country"[21] as innovators. But in *Capitalism, Socialism and Democracy,* he modified this position and took up the defense of the great corporation for "largely creating what it exploited" through industrial research. And clearly today, the measurement of the propensity to innovate in an advanced technological country like America would be distorted if we concentrated on new firms. The growth of the industrial research laboratory has given rise to a tremendous concentration of inventions in the large enterprise.[22] In trying to understand the process of innovation, we must start, therefore, by recognizing the implications of modern industrial-research practices.

For the last 150 years, at least, there have almost always been possibilities of application of scientific discoveries to the practical arts which have far exceeded any current efforts to apply them. Until quite recently, the principal discoveries of science were announced in media which were not widely read or even understood by industrial practitioners. On the other hand, from the side of industry there has long been a vital creative force of innovation, with a life of its own, which has in turn had great possibilities for contributing to the stream of scientific discovery; but the reverse communication has been equally poor. The rise of the industrial research laboratory,

---

[19] See Joseph Spengler, "Theories of Socio-Economic Growth," *Problems in the Study of Economic Growth* (New York: National Bureau of Economic Research, 1949), p. 78: "Appraisal of the behavior and prospective growth of a social system must take into account how innovators are chosen, how they in turn choose among the potentialities accessible at any time, and how they respond to the prevailing value system."

[20] *Op. cit.,* Vol. I, p. 96.

[21] *Ibid.,* p. 97.

[22] The 450 largest corporations in the United States which held patents in 1938 accounted for 24.5 percent of all unexpired patents. (I have no doubt also that the concentration has increased further since then.)

fostered by large-scale enterprise, has made it possible to bring these two sources of ideas much closer together.

At the same time, advances in science and engineering have become so complex that the typical competitive unit of "Adam Smith capitalism" simply does not have the resources to support them. Television is a good case in point. It was nearly twenty years from their first appropriation for television research before the Telephone Company, Westinghouse, General Electric, and RCA obtained any financial returns; and during this period these companies spent millions on television research and engineering development.[23]

With the emergence of what Schumpeter called "trustified capitalism," an increasing proportion of large corporations are seeking to perpetuate themselves by developing their own fundamental research, their own inventions, and their own innovations. This does not mean, however, that we can ignore the new firm in assessing the propensity to innovate.

Even assuming the large monopolistic concern to behave as Schumpeter felt that it should, in "creating what it exploits," it frequently does not exploit everything it is capable of creating. Totally apart from any Veblenian retardation of innovation stemming from the character of entrepreneurial leadership in such companies, a large company cannot do everything with equal vigor. Top managements of enterprises develop fields of special interest, and it is not surprising therefore to find large concerns having certain lines in which they make every effort to be prominent and other lines which they tend to neglect, even though the latter show great possibilities for economic gain.

Here, then, is where the new firm is needed: to open up new lines which are neglected by the large established corporation, either because they are preoccupied, asleep, or slow.[24] And no matter how wide-awake the old company may be, the new risk-taking approach will often be neglected.

To measure the propensity to innovate, we must look, therefore, at both new firms and established firms. The most satisfactory procedure is to analyze innovations over time, industry by industry, through intimate inquiry.[25]

There is frequently widespread agreement as to which *new products* represent a significant innovation; and data are usually available on the annual sales volume of most products. *Process changes* can be studied through productivity figures on which there is a great deal of recorded information.

---

[23] For details see W. R. Maclaurin, "Patents and Technical Progress—A Study of Television," *Journal of Political Economy* (April 1950).

[24] For example, why did Eastman Kodak not invent the "picture-in-a-minute" camera? Why was Western Union oblivious to the potential impact, first of the telephone and then of wireless; and why did General Electric need the spur of Sylvania to speed its introduction of the fluorescent lamp (see "Economic Factors Influencing the Development and Introduction of the Fluorescent Lamp," by Arthur A. Bright, Jr., and W. Rupert Maclaurin, *Journal of Political Economy,* October 1943).

[25] Some preliminary work has already been done on the radio, electric-lamp, glass, and paper industries. See Maclaurin, *Invention and Innovation in The Radio Industry, op. cit.;* Bright, *The Electric-Lamp Industry, op. cit.;* Warren C. Scoville, *Revolution in Glassmaking* (Cambridge, Mass.: Harvard University Press, 1948); Robert L. Bishop, *The Mechanization of the Glass-Container Industry: A Study in the Economics of Technical Change* (Harvard University doctoral dissertation, 1950); and D. C. Vandermeulen, *Technological Change in the Paper Industry; Introduction of the Sulphate Process* (Harvard University doctoral dissertation, 1947).

Where the physical characteristics of the product have remained reasonably homogeneous for a period of years—such as in the case of the incandescent lamp—one can readily identify from the productivity figures the impact of the major types of new high-speed machinery. *New services* can be measured in part through data collected by the *Census of Business,* or, as in the aviation industry, through the statistics of the Civil Aeronautics Board.

A special effort must be made to estimate the magnitude of the investment involved in each innovation, not only in the direct but in the secondary effects.[26] The very process of doing this and publishing the measurements should lead to their refinement through criticism, and to a wider understanding of "innovation policy and practice." It should also enable us to see whether any general agreement could be reached on the dates when particular innovations have run their course. Could we agree, for example, that by about 1926 the principal innovating changes had occurred in the automobile industry, and that the next twenty-five years were comparatively stagnant; or in radio broadcasting, that the major early innovations had been worked out by 1928, with no very significant changes until frequency modulation and television came ten years later? And, if so, why?

THE PROPENSITY TO FINANCE INNOVATION

So far we have been discussing the economic forces leading to invention and innovation without assessing the obstacles to their introduction and acceptance. Yet a nation could contribute significantly to pure science and to invention but remain stagnant if too small a proportion of the capital supply in the country were channeled into new developments. This appears to have been true of England in the 1920s and 1930s. Certainly, this was a period in which the British made very important contributions to pure science; and that their potential inventive capacity was high is witnessed by their contributions to radar and jet engines at the beginning of World War II.[27]

Keynes attributed the failure of the British to finance new developments to "the professional investment classes," who had become more concerned with manipulating highly liquid investments than concentrating on long-term growth.[28] He believed that the remedy lay in state-financed capital works. However, for America, at least, experience may prove that there is a greater opportunity both for creative satisfaction[29] and for raising the long-term level of investment through developing private investment institutions to supply

[26] For such an attempt in the fluorescent-lamp industry, see Arthur A. Bright, Jr., "Some Broad Economic Implications of Hot-Cathode Fluorescent Lighting," *Transactions of the Electrochemical Society,* Vol. 87 (1945).

[27] See also R. S. Sayers, "The Springs of Technical Progress in Britain, 1919-39," *Economic Journal* (June 1950).

[28] See J. M. Keynes, *General Theory of Employment, Interest, and Money* (New York: Harcourt, Brace and World, 1936), pp. 153-161.

[29] See Bertrand Russell, "The Springs of Human Action," *Atlantic Monthly* (March 1952), p. 29: "Nothing in the world is more exciting than a moment of sudden discovery or invention, and many more people are capable of experiencing such moments than is sometimes thought."

intermediate term credit for new and growing ventures. Many professional investors today believe that large gains are available to them if they make a "cold calculation" of the possibilities. Current taxation also favors capital gains rather than dividend income. And the underlying inflationary forces, which are strong but not explosive, encourage investors to take risks to create capital rather than conserve existing assets.

To measure the propensity to finance innovation at any given time, we might begin by studying the number of new firms launched each year and the capital investment of such firms. Comprehensive *payroll statistics* on new firms by products and by states are now assembled by the Bureau of Old Age and Survivors' Insurance. New firms are usually privately financed and do not appear as new security issues. But some statistics are available on the magnitude of this type of private financing. And with the emergence of a few specialized institutions designed to provide venture capital for new enterprises, such as the Whitney Foundation and the American Research and Development Corporation, the statistical information should become more satisfactory.[30]

Some index also of the propensity of established firms to obtain financial support for innovations can be had from the figures on new plants constructed. We cannot assume that new plants always involve innovations. But in many American enterprises, it is customary to build extensions to existing plants for old products and save the new plant for the new product. And since it is increasingly difficult for corporations to finance new plants from earnings, a high rate of new plant construction is a strong indication that new capital is being made available for innovation.

THE PROPENSITY TO ACCEPT INNOVATIONS

There are marked variations between regions and between cultural groups in the propensity to accept innovations. And, if our analysis is to be adequately comprehensive, we must seek some means, first of measuring and then of explaining and predicting these differences.

In the United States acceptance of innovations has usually been rapid, if the innovation meets a real need and if the product or service has advanced to the stage where the principal early defects have been eliminated. But how much of a guide can the past provide for the future, and in what areas?

The more advanced the economy, the more major innovations tend to enter the public domain, requiring joint action by industry and government. The conquest of the air is an interesting illustration. Further advances in both commercial and private flying require a major new program of airport construction. It is *technically* possible today for the private airplane to begin

---

[30] It would also be interesting to study what happens to the capital applications rejected by the venture capital corporations. Since its formation in 1946, American Research and Development has received about 2,200 more or less formal applications. of which only 27 have been acted on favorably.

to compete with the automobile, both for commuting and for vacation use. Either helicopters or small planes that will land in a short space *could* be produced on a mass-production basis at moderate prices. A radar set in the plane would make it possible to fly safely in most weather conditions (or at least about as safely as driving an automobile). To make this possible, a great number of small landing fields would have to be constructed both in the cities and in the outlying suburbs. But, since the principal metropolitan centers in the United States are now largely built up, this would require the large-scale acquisition of privately developed property by eminent domain. Does this mean that such major innovations will require a longer time span to win acceptance than, for example, the railroads which were built with governmental assistance when we still had an open frontier?

If we measure the propensity to accept innovations, we must assemble growth curves for a wide variety of different types of products and services under different types of conditions and see what generalizations can be reached concerning the length of time required for mass acceptance and the reasons for the difference in particular cases. Such an appraisal could provide a guide for public and private investment policy both in the United States and in the less advanced regions of the world. And in the process of setting such goals, and in assessing the achievement, a much clearer picture would emerge of the sequence from invention to innovation and its basic relationship to economic development.

PART SEVEN

Values and Institutions

THE SIGNIFICANCE OF INSTITUTIONS AND SOCIAL VALUES has been more clearly recognized in the field of economic development than in any other area of economic thought. It may well be that the economic factors determining growth (discussed in Part Six) are shaped and affected by the formal social, political, and economic organizations prevailing in a particular country. These elements, which we here call institutions, are considered in the first part of this section. Also influencing the economic factors affecting growth are such basic forces as customs, values, modes of thought, attitudes, and motivations; these value elements are considered in the second part. Although one should recognize that institutions are closely related to values and attitudes—indeed, some writers choose to include all of these elements under the heading of "institutions"—we make a separation here in order to emphasize certain salient differences between the two categories.

Economic theory has been criticized by some noneconomists, as well as by adherents of the historical school of economics, on the ground that some of its central propositions, axioms, and conclusions lay claim to a universality of application which is unwarranted. It is unwarranted, they contend, because the theorist usually develops his analysis on the basis of the institutional and value setting of his own society. But this setting varies with respect to time and place. It has been argued, for example, that the theories of the classical school are relevant mainly to the England of the late eighteenth and early nineteenth centuries. But how relevant, these critics ask, is classical and other Western theory to the problems, for example, of contemporary underdeveloped countries, where institutions and values differ so markedly from those of Western society?

Perhaps a more important reason for the inapplicability of Western growth theory to underdeveloped countries lies in the fact that it does not treat *change* in institutions and values as a dynamic independent variable in the growth process. Because they form part of the social landscape which we tend to take for granted, it may be difficult to realize that in underdeveloped countries there are institutions and values which are inimical to growth, and which may have to undergo revolutionary change as a prerequisite for growth. What is required, perhaps, is not a new theory that merely alters its institutional and value premises to conform to a different, *given* setting, but a theory that treats the "setting" itself as a *variable* subject to change.

Because agricultural production weighs so heavily in the economies of many underdeveloped countries, it may well be that the initial thrust of economic development must occur in the agricultural sector. But the progress of this sector will be conditioned by the nature of its institutional structure. The selection from the United Nations study of land reform demonstrates that in many underdeveloped countries the agrarian structure is a serious obstacle to progress. Concentration of land ownership in large estates which are inadequately farmed, uneconomically small farm holdings, and other factors including "an unsatisfactory set of incentives for a rising and sustained agricultural production" are cited as impediments, the elimination of which may be a prerequisite of significant agricultural advance. In the history of many of the advanced countries, it is certainly clear that institutional change—in particular, the dissolution of the feudal agrarian system—was a precondition of the agricultural revolution.

The transition from a traditional agricultural society to a modern industrial economy must involve a radical transformation of existing institutions, social attitudes, and motivations. Economic growth is generally accompanied by pronounced shifts in the relative importance of different industries, occupations, and, sometimes, geographic locations. Such structural change requires that the factors of production be responsive to present as well as to changing economic opportunities and incentives, reflected by changing wages, profits, and other economic returns. But by comparison with advanced countries, such responsiveness seems to be lacking in some underdeveloped countries.

Some aspects of this problem in connection with labor are discussed by Wilbert E. Moore. Of particular interest as a barrier to mobility is the joint or extended family system prevalent in some underdeveloped countries, under which familial ties, rights, and obligations, normally confined in advanced countries to immediate relationships of parents and the young, are extended over a much wider range to encompass distant kin, sometimes numbering in the scores. Under this kinship system, all family members, however distant, claim the right of support from the group, as well as the right to advise and pass judgment on each other's activities, regardless of their individual contributions. The advantage of such a system lies in the economic security it provides to individuals living at or near subsistence levels. But to the extent that individual effort is motivated by personal economic reward, the extended family system offsets market incentives to labor mobility, and to increased effort more generally, because of the obligation of the individual to share his rewards with the family.

Even in the absence of such institutions as the extended family system, in some societies labor may not respond to new economic rewards and incentives, simply because material wants may not be sufficiently strong to elicit greater human effort. For one thing, ascetic attitudes, which involve the subordination of material wants, may prevail; these wants are usually replaced by goals of a religious or "philosophic" nature. The implications of ascetecism for economic growth are discussed in the selection by Karl F. Helleiner.

But wants are probably limited, not so much in an absolute sense as in relation to the effort required to satisfy them. In traditional rural areas of underdeveloped countries, there is a particularly strong reluctance to transfer into industrial occupations when, as Moore points out, the transfer involves a devaluation in the social status of the worker, a loss of his "freedom," and a severe problem of adaptation to a new way of life. What is more, in a society with a rigid class structure where, for example, social status is determined at birth, it may be exceedingly difficult or impossible to raise one's income, if a given income level is traditionally associated with a given social status. Thus, even if the worker were willing to make the sacrifices required to raise his income, he may be restrained from doing so by his social status.

Like labor and land, capital formation is also conditioned by prevailing institutions and values. The role of capital formation in the growth process has previously been demonstrated. Capital formation involves both the creation of savings and credit and their transformation into investment in new physical capital. In any country, this process is facilitated by the existence of financial institutions, either public or private, designed to collect savings and to create credit, and to channel them into their most productive uses. Therefore, the number and efficiency of such institutions, which include savings banks, bond and stock exchanges, investment banks, and the complex of dealers, brokers, and commercial banks that comprise the "money market," are of vital importance to the process of growth. The development of such institutions and the implications of their presence or absence are discussed in the selection by Bert F. Hoselitz.

The extended family system, already discussed in connection with the supply of labor, also affects the investment process. Charles Wolf, Jr., observes that under this system, although the costs and risks of investment are borne by the individual, the entire family has a lien on the potential returns, and thus the incentive to invest is reduced.

Differences in the level of investment between advanced and under-developed countries, as well as between different stages in the growth of a single country, depend in a critical way, as we have already seen, on the existence of an entrepreneurial class. But to explain adequately the determinants of the scope and effectiveness of entrepreneurship, one must consider a broad array of psychological and sociocultural phenomena not easily specified or evaluated. For one thing, the entrepreneur must be a highly motivated personality type, possessing a relatively rare combination of attributes, such as boldness, energy, and a willingness to undertake ventures of a novel and uncertain character. Such a type, Hoselitz and others have observed, tends to appear more frequently among socially marginal groups which tend to contain relatively more "social deviants" than nonmarginal groups. But personal motivation, though necessary, does not suffice to explain the existence of a large and vital entrepreneurial class, for as Hoselitz notes, the highly motivated may be found in the military, the priesthood, and the academy. An effective supply of entrepreneurs will be forthcoming only in a society that places the accumulation of material wealth well up in its hierarchy of social values and confers ample monetary rewards upon successful entrepreneurs.

It is the "pecuniary culture" which smoothes the path of the entrepreneur, channeling his energy and motivation in commercial, financial and industrial directions, and which accords him social status directly related to his material success. However, a more fundamental question is what determines the emergence and development of a pecuniary culture. Among the factors that condition such a culture, religion has received much attention. It would seem apparent that in a society where religious institutions and values are so important that the bulk of men's energy is diverted from the secular to the spiritual domain, economic growth will be blocked. It has been contended, however, that what is important here is not the degree of religious fervor but the content and interpretation of religious doctrine. There is, for example,

the well-known thesis advanced by Max Weber that the advent of Protestantism, especially in its Calvinist version, was a significant positive influence in
the rise of Western capitalism. This thesis is discussed in the selection by
Ephraim Fischoff.

What emerges from the above discussion is the critical role that values
and institutions exercise in the process of economic development. S. H.
Frankel demonstrates that it is hazardous, particularly with reference to underdeveloped countries, to analyze and to formulate policies and programs for
economic growth outside the context of social forces which condition growth,
and which in turn must be affected by it. As we have seen, there are values
and institutions, many of which prevail in underdeveloped countries, that offer
resistance to economic growth; their alteration or elimination, often a painful
process, constitutes a "social cost" which a country must bear as part of the
"price" of development.

BERT F. HOSELITZ

Noneconomic Factors in Economic Development

An adequate treatment of the varied ways in which economic and noneconomic factors interact in a process of economic growth or development
would require an entire book. In order to remain within the short space at
my disposal, I shall therefore discuss a special problem and hope that this
discussion will convey in a rough way the general flavor of the manner in
which we might proceed with a consideration of noneconomic factors in economic devlopment. I should like to select the question of the change which
occurs in an economy as it leaves a state of relatively slow growth or stagnation and starts a process of rapid growth. This apparently discontinuous
break with the past, which is usually associated with rapid industrialization,
has often been described. Students of the different industrial revolutions have
pointed to the rapid pace with which an economy broke out of a previous
condition of relative immobility and attained within one or at most two generations a level of performance on which self-sustained growth was possible.
Much of this evidence has recently been collected in an interesting paper by
W. W. Rostow on "The Take-off into Self-sustaining Growth" (*Economic*

From *American Economic Review* (May 1957), pp. 28-41. Reprinted by permission of the American Economic Association and the author.

Journal, 1956).[1] Apart from a detailed discussion of the take-off period, Rostow's essay also contains a discussion of three stages with the take-off as center. The first stage or period is one of preparation in which the preconditions of the take-off are established. This period may last a century or more. The second stage is the take-off itself, and the third period is the stage of self-sustained growth, when the further development of the economy occurs as a more or less normal and self-generating process.[2]

If we view the development process as following roughly such a tripartite schema, we are confronted with the problem of how to account for this explosive change which has so aptly been called an industrial revolution. Its inception is, as has often been observed, rather striking and sudden, and it usually ends almost as suddenly as it began. It has been accompanied in most cases by a concomitant population "explosion" which has obscured somewhat the rapidity and suddenness of economic growth during the discontinuous take-off period if measured in terms of per capita income. What is perhaps most important about the structural changes taking place during the take-off period is the adaptation of previously existing institutions for new ends, especially for capital formation. In fact, Rostow makes the difference in the rate of investment (*i.e.,* the ratio of net capital formation to net national product) the criterion of whether an economy is in a pre-take-off stage or is entering the phase of industrial revolution. Now why should an economy suddenly be capable of saving and investing a larger proportion of its net income, especially if it has apparently been unable to alter the rate of net investment for a very long period previous to the take-off? The answer may be found if we ask whether or not general environmental conditions have been created in the pre-take-off phase which make an increase in net capital formation attractive and achievable.

These "environmental conditions" must be sought chiefly in noneconomic aspects of the society. In other words, apart from the build-up of economic overhead capital, such as a communications and transport system and investment in harbor facilities, some warehouses, and similar installations favoring especially foreign trade, most of the innovations introduced during the preparatory period are based upon changes in the institutional arrangements in the legal, educational, familial, or motivational orders. Once these new institutions have been created, they operate as "gifts from the past," contributing freely to the vigorous spurt of economic activity in the period of take-off. We may then consider that from the point of view of providing an explanation of the process of economic growth, the main functions of the preparatory stage

---

[1] See the article by Rostow in this volume, pp. 183-199, for a further discussion of the stages of growth.—EDS.

[2] Rostow was, of course, not the first to have discovered the sudden incidence of industrial revolutions, nor to have stipulated a tripartite periodization. A similar scheme was presented by G. Célestine, "Dynamique des niveaux de production et de productivité," *Économie et Humanisme* (July-August 1952), pp. 60-67; and in one of my articles, "Algunos aspectos de las relaciones entre el cambio social y el desarollo económico," *De Economía* (July-August 1954), pp. 611-624. Further references to this process are cited in that article.

are the changes in the institutional order, especially in areas other than economic activity, which transform the society from one in which capital formation and the introduction of modern economic organization is difficult or impossible, to one in which the accumulation of capital and the introduction of new production processes appear as "natural" concomitants of general social progress.

Let us examine a few cases more in detail in order to see what role some noneconomic institutions have played in bringing about the explosive situation of an industrial revolution and in particular how they have affected the supply of productive factors. For although it has often been asserted that the chief bottleneck experienced by underdeveloped countries is the shortage of capital, there are other factors which are relatively scarce—above all, certain types of skilled labor (including the services of entrepreneurial personnel). For this reason there is special interest in institutional changes during the preparatory period which tend to affect the supply of capital or of such services as administrative and entrepreneurial activity and technical and scientific skills.

The need for capital on a relatively large scale requires the availability of institutions through which savings can be collected and channeled into projects employing productive capital. Hence a banking system or its equivalent in the form of a state agency collecting revenue and spending it on developmental projects is required. What is also required in a society in which investment decisions are made by private individuals is a legal institution, such as the corporation, which allows the combination of capitals of various individuals in order to support enterprises which, for technological reasons, can be undertaken economically only on a large scale. In Britain all these institutions were in existence at the time its industrial revolution began. It is granted that joint-stock companies required a special charter for their formation, and up to the early nineteenth century such charters were granted only for overseas commercial enterprises or for large-scale transportation enterprises. But as capital requirements in industry increased, the corporate form of enterprise came to be more and more widely applied to industry also. By the third decade of the nineteenth century, corporate charters for industrial firms were not uncommon and within the next fifteen years they became the rule in all but small enterprises.

It is also true that bank credit did not play an overwhelming role in the early phases of the industrial revolution in Britain. In fact, in contrast to France and Germany, a relatively large amount of capital employed in the early cotton and iron industry was supplied by merchants and even landowners. But here again, as the requirements of capital supply grew in dimension, the banks began to play a more and more important role.

Institutions providing for the collective use of capital also had been established in other European countries long before they entered the take-off phase. In France, the Napoleonic codes provided for joint-stock companies of two kinds (*sociétés en actions* and *sociétés en commandite*), and both these types of corporate enterprise were adopted by other European countries. The German legal reform lagged behind that of France, but it is significant that a

Prussian commercial code, embodying much of the French type of company legislation, was introduced at a very early stage in the industrial upsurge of Germany, whereas the general civil code did not become law until the turn of the twentieth century.

In Japan, because of the absence of traditions of corporate bodies similar to the medieval European company and because of the strong governmentally induced impetus to industrialization in its early phase, the supply of capital had to be channeled through institutions which differed from those of the West. Although Japan adopted in due course the institution of the Western corporation, the immediate post-restoration process of capital formation relied upon governmental capital creation and, more importantly, upon a change in the structure and hierarchy of Japanese society. In the new social order inaugurated with the Meiji restoration there developed an association of *samurai* and large-scale capitalist merchants and farmers. This association, which later also aided in the development of the monopolistic *zaibatsu,* had antecedents which reach far back into the pre-Meiji period. All through the nineteenth century, the economic basis of Tokugawa society had begun to crumble. Although political power remained officially in the hands of the *shogun,* it began slowly to pass into the hands of some of the more powerful clans; at the same time the economic basis of a predominantly agrarian quasi-feudal society had ceased to function. There were masses of impoverished *samurai* who, in order to make a livelihood, were forced into a life of business or farm administration. Moreover, there was a simultaneously rising class of mechants and large farmers and farmer-moneylenders, whose presence disturbed the officially imposed rough equality among the members of the non-noble classes. The gradual acquisition of power by these elements and their association with disgruntled *samurai* was a phenomenon whose beginning must be looked for in the period when, on the surface, the rule of the *shogun* appeared unimpaired. But this association was an important factor leading to a reinterpretation on the part of Japan's political elite of the over-all systemic objectives of the society. Whereas before the Japanese government had been concerned only with power, it was now clearly recognized that within this concern the development of the economy was an important, and perhaps the most important, feature. In this way an institutional framework, supported by an ideology, was created which became an efficient and powerful support of capital formation.

It is within a framework of this kind that a comparative institutional analysis of patterns of capital formation in economic development might be undertaken. Given the social and political forces at play, one could appraise by means of such an analysis the role which might be played by development corporations and investment banks or fiscal bodies in the collection of savings and the channeling of these savings into productive investment. One could appraise in this latter case the alternative function of a policy of forced savings either by inflation or by taxation and could relate the potential efficacy of each of these alternative policies to existing social and political institutions.

At the same time, one would find that the lack of suitable institutions or the presence of institutions which may lead to dissipation of accumulated savings will tend to prevent a society from arriving at a stage in which a take-off is likely or even possible. For example, nineteenth-century China had a series of institutional arrangements which facilitated the accumulation of capital. One was the institution of licensed merchants, such as the *hong* merchants at Canton who were supported by the government in their monopolistic control of foreign trade; another was the institution of imperially licensed salt merchants who enjoyed regional monopolies in the production and sale of salt. There were other groups of privileged traders, and even a large number of not specially privileged ones, who achieved considerable success in the amassing of large fortunes. But within the Chinese system the merchants operated upon the sufferance and with the support of the bureaucracy, and thus any profits made in trade or industry had to be shared with officials. The officials invested their share in land or spent it on luxury consumption, with the result that large accumulations of liquid funds tended to become sporadically dissipated rather than channeled into productive investment. Moreover, even in the few instances in which, with the aid and support of officials, capital was invested in productive enterprises, profits, instead of being reinvested, were distributed among a large number of claimants among the officialdom; the demands on trading, shipping, or industrial firms for the distribution of earnings among officials on all levels of the administrative scale were so strong that it was often difficult to maintain the initial capital intact. Thus the institutional tie-up between the merchant class and officialdom in China, superimposed upon the heavy tax system, contributed in Ch'ing China to the unavailability of capital accumulations of sufficient magnitude to form a foundation for rapid industrial development.

Let us now turn to the second problem of supply: the availability of skilled labor of various kinds, chiefly entrepreneurial services and the services of skilled administrators, engineers, scientists, and managerial personnel. These rather than manual skills are the types of labor normally in short supply in nonindustrialized countries, and it is the overcoming of bottlenecks in the supply of these kinds of services that a major developmental effort usually needs to be made. Since entrepreneurship and administrative talent on the one hand and scientific and engineering services on the other usually are associated with different institutions, it will be convenient to separate the discussion of the institutions within which these skills and inclinations to the pursuit of these occupations are fashioned. We shall first turn to the problem of the diffusion of science and technology.

As in the case of institutions designed to aid in the accumulation of capital, technological and scientific investigations had become institutionalized in Western Europe long before the countries which experienced a period of take-off actually entered the phase of industrialization on a rapid scale. For Britain this fact is well documented and has often been noted. The Royal Society was officially formed in 1662, although by 1645 there had been already in existence a small club of "divers worthy persons, inquisitive into natural philosophy, and particularly of what was called the New Philosophy, or Experimental Philosophy." Although its early extensive interest in technology was not fully maintained throughout the early eighteenth century, it was revived by the middle of the century and strengthened by the establishment in 1754 of the Society for the Encouragement of Arts, Manufactures, and Commerce. It is superfluous to describe in this place the institutionalization of scientific and technical progress in Britain during the seventeenth and eighteenth centuries more specifically, since a perusal of Robert K. Merton's *Science, Technology and Society in Seventeenth Century England* (Bruges, 1938) and G. N. Clark's *Science and Social Welfare in the Age of Newton* (Oxford, 1937) will yield exhaustive descriptions of this process. By the onset of the industrial revolution, technological research was widespread and had spilled over from being practiced in the laboratories of "experimental philosophers" to being carried on also in workshops, mines, and manufactories. In France and also in Germany, academies similar to the Royal Society were established in imitation of this organization, soon after it had started to operate, and in France especially technological training was given a tremendous impetus by the foundation of the École Polytechnique in 1794. This school became the pet of Napoleon, and it was through its influence more than any other that by the beginning of the nineteenth century France was in the forefront of scientific achievement. By 1825, Justus Liebig, who had studied under Gay-Lussac in Paris and had there convinced himself of the superiority of the French method, introduced laboratory science into Germany, and from that time on experimental and applied research in mechanics, chemistry, metallurgy, and other fields became common in German universities and technological institutes.

Thus in the various European countries there existed firmly entrenched institutions for scientific and technological research and training well before the onset of rapid industrialization. Similarly in Japan there had been considerable interest in "Dutch studies" under the Tokugawa. Many Japanese were engaged in learning Dutch and by means of this language became acquainted with Western science and technology. Schools for Dutch studies were established, not only by the *shogun* himself, but also by some of the more important clans, notably the Saga in whose territory Nagasaki was located. These schools taught not only languages but also such subjects as Western mathematics, astronomy, geography, physics, and metallurgy. The result was that before Perry's arrival there had been founded a number of iron smelting plants and foundries built by native engineers on the Western model, and by 1853 the Saga foundry cast the first satisfactory iron gun. In the same year a reverberatory furnace was built by Japanese engineers of the Satsuma clan, and shortly thereafter two more furnaces and supporting fabricating works by the Satsuma clan and the Mito clan.[3] It would be false to exaggerate the influence of these institutions and technical attainments. They are symptoms rather than results of a change in institutional arrangements

---

[3] *Cf.* Thomas C. Smith, *Political Change and Industrial Development in Japan: Government Enterprise, 1868-1880* (Stanford, Calif.: Stanford University Press, 1955), pp. 4-7.

affecting scientific research and technological achievement in Japan. But the practice of Dutch studies and the adoption of Western techniques before the fall of the shogunate set a stage which made possible the rapid adoption of Western educational and research facilities in science and technology once the new order had set in.

Again the picture was different in nineteenth-century China. Rather than enter in a lengthy elaboration of the role of Western science and technology in Ch'ing China, I should like to cite a passage from Hsiao-Tung Fei, who is an accurate and imaginative interpreter of Chinese "traditional" society. Fei says:

> In Chinese traditional society the intelligentsia have been a class without technical knowledge. They monopolized authority based on the wisdom of the past, spent time on literature, and tried to express themselves through art. Chinese literary language is very inapt to express scientific or technical knowledge. This indicates that, in the traditional scheme, the vested interests had no wish to improve production but thought only of privilege. Their main task was the perpetuation of established norms in order to set up a guide for conventional behavior. A man who sees the world only through human relations is inclined to be conservative, because in human relations the end is always mutual adjustment. And an adjusted equilibrium can only be founded on a stable and unchanging relation between man and nature. On the other hand, from the purely technical point of view, there are hardly any limits to man's control of nature. In emphasizing technical progress, one plunges into a struggle in which man's control over nature becomes ever changing, ever more efficient. Yet these technical changes may lead to conflict between man and man. The Chinese intelligentsia viewed the world humanistically. Lacking technical knowledge, they could not appreciate technical progress. And they saw no reason to wish to change man's relation to man.[4]

If we turn to institutions regulating the supply of entrepreneurial or managerial services, the picture is similar. But with reference to entrepreneurship in particular, there appears also to be involved not only an institutional but above all a motivational factor. Accumulation of capital and technical or scientific knowledge can be explained by pointing to the institutions through which practices of behavior leading to investment or the acquisition of technical knowledge may be furthered. Entrepreneurship is a more evasive thing. It is not so much a particular set of institutions through which it is brought to bear, but its presence or absence; its vigor or debility depends rather upon a whole series of environmental conditions and appropriate personal motivations. It has been shown—in my opinion successfully—that entrepreneurship is associated with a personality pattern in which achievement motivation is strong. But the presence of strong achievement motivation in a group of individuals does not necessarily produce an abundance of entrepreneurs unless certain other general conditions of social structure and culture strongly favor achievement-oriented individuals to enter economic pursuits. High-achieve-

---

[4] Hsiao-Tung Fei, *China's Gentry* (Chicago: University of Chicago Press, 1953), p. 74.

ment motivation has also been found among military leaders and may be found among scholars, priests, and bureaucrats. It is not too difficult to show that in a society in which the acquisition of wealth is regarded as a good thing in itself, persons with the appropriate motivational disposition will tend to enter an entrepreneurial career. But what about societies in which the accumulation of wealth in itself is frowned upon, or where it is considered to be a worthy object only if performed under certain restrictive conditions? What about a society in which the warrior, the priest, or the government official is rated vastly above the merchant or the industrialist?

Thus when we discuss the factor of entrepreneurship we must go beyond the mere analysis of social institutions in a limited sense and must include in our purview the entire social fabric in which this type of social behavior becomes predominant. But if we put the question in this form, we are immediately confronted with the further question of whether the same type of social constellation which provides a fruitful field for the development and exercise of entrepreneurial activity does not simultaneously further institutions designed to facilitate capital formation and scientific and technical progress. I believe, on the basis of my reading of the social and economic history of those peoples which have shown the capacity for rapid economic advance and those which have so far failed in this capacity, that the over-all social framework which favors entrepreneurship also favors scientific and technical progress and the development of institutions fostering the formation of capital.

In support of this proposition, one could show that the countries of Western Europe and Japan which have developed viable institutions for the accumulation of capital and its channeling in large lumps into productive investment and institutions enhancing the supply of persons capable of tackling the scientific and technological problems required for efficient production, also have developed vigorous entrepreneurial personalities, and that China, which in the nineteenth and early twentieth century has failed to produce these institutions, also has had a paucity of able entrepreneurs. The fact that Chinese emigrants in South Asia have, on the whole, succeeded in commerce and, at any rate, appear to have outdistanced in business acumen and entrepreneurial spirit members of their host peoples is rather a confirmation of this proposition. For I do not mean to argue that the Chinese have less inherent capacity for business leadership than other nations. The social fabric of imperial China was such that whenever potential motivations for entrepreneurial activity developed in aspiring young men, they were deflected into other career lines; and the men who in Western Europe or Japan would have taken on a business career tended to become officials or scholars in China. And once they had attained such positions their preoccupation was, as Professor Fei has argued, directed upon preservation of existing human relations rather than on innovations either in technology or in business enterprise.

Let me summarize the argument presented so far in a few sentences, in order to outline the conclusions at which we might arrive. Economic growth is a process which affects not only purely economic relations but the entire social, political, and cultural fabric of a society. The predominant problem of economic growth in our day is the overcoming of economic stagnation, which normally takes place through a process of industrialization. In most recorded cases in which industrialization took place and led to a level of self-sustaining growth, this phase of economic development was initiated by a rapidly "explosive" period which, in concordance with Rostow, we may call the take-off. The rapid structural and organizational changes affecting the productivity of a society which take place during the take-off phase are made possible because in a previous phase social institutions were created which allow the successful overcoming of supply bottlenecks, chiefly in the field of capital formation and the availability of a number of highly skilled and specialized services. The creation of these social institutions in turn, especially the "institutionalization" of entrepreneurship, *i.e.,* an innovating uncertainty-bearing activity, requires the establishment of a social framework within which these new institutions can exist and expand. In the last resort, we may thus have to answer the question of how such a social framework develops or is brought about by conscious design.

The answer to this question must be based on a general theoretical understanding of the nature of social and cultural change and, so far as I am aware, no general theory of social change which is universally accepted by sociologists exists as yet. It is clearly impossible for a nonspecialist to develop such a theory, but from the existing literature some general hints of what are some of the main points in this process of theorizing may be gleaned. Among these pieces of a theory of change, three concepts and their implications appear to be most significant for our problem. These are the appearance of behavioral deviance, the emergence of cultural or social marginality, and the process of redefinition of societal objectives by an elite. I have discussed these processes more extensively in another place and shall confine myself here, therefore, to presenting merely a sketch.[5]

Let us first turn to a brief consideration of social deviance. Although it may occur in many fields of social action, we are concerned here primarily with those forms of deviant behavior which are relevant for economic activity and organization. Now if the concept of deviance is to have operational meaning, it cannot be interpreted as signifying simply behavior which is new, but it must imply that this set of innovating acts is opposed in some way to existing social norms or approved forms of behavior. In other words, a deviant always engages in behavior which constitutes a breach of the existing order and which is either contrary to, or at least not positively weighted in, the hierarchy of existing social values. If we apply this concept to the behavior displayed by businessmen and merchants in the course of the economic development of Western Europe, we find that we can speak of genuine deviance in those periods and societies in which entrepreneurial behavior did not belong in the category of social actions which were considered as constituting

---

[5] *Cf.* my article "Sociological Approach to Economic Development," in Centro Nazionale di Prevenzione e Difesa Sociale, *Atti del Congresso Internazionale di Studio sul Problema delle Aree Arretrate* (Milan, 1955), pp. 755-778.

the "good life." As late as the fifteenth century this was true of financial entrepreneurship, which was always tainted by the official opposition against usury. And later, when financial entrepreneurship became fully respectable, industrial entrepreneurship came to be regarded with some disdain because it dirtied one's hands. These sentiments toward business or financial activity as not quite proper for a gentleman to carry on are familiar in many under-developed countries today. For this reason, deviant behavior is often exercised by persons who, in some sense, are marginal to society. In medieval Europe the earliest money lenders were often foreigners. In Italy at the time of the Gothic and Langobard rule, they were Syrians, Jews, and Byzantines. Later when Italians turned to financial entrepreneurship on a large scale, the Genoese and Pisans, Sienese and Florentines, who were all lumped together under the name of "Lombards," became the financial entrepreneurs north of the Alps.

The role of marginal individuals in various economic pursuits in many underdeveloped countries is eminently manifest today. One could cite the Chinese in various South Asian countries, the Indians in East Africa, and the widely scattered Lebanese who make their appearance as businessmen in West Africa, Latin America, and elsewhere in less advanced countries. We also should count a considerable number of American and other voluntary Western expatriates among this class of marginal individuals. Some who attempt to find an escape from their marginal position in the arts have tended to congregate on the Seine or the Arno, but those who find business more congenial are to be found all over Latin America and more recently also in many parts of Asia and Africa.

What is the mechanism which allows marginal individuals to perform the roles they apparently have so widely accepted? As Robert E. Park, the inventor of the concept and of the significance of social marginality, has stressed, marginal men are—precisely because of their ambiguous position from a cultural, ethnic, or social standpoint—very strongly motivated to make creative adjustments in situations of change, and, in the course of this adjustment process, to develop genuine innovations in social behavior. Although many of Park's very general propositions about marginality have been considerably refined by subsequent researchers, the theory of social marginality has not advanced enough to supply sufficiently convincing evidence for the role it may play in the explanation of episodes of social deviance wherever they occur. Even if it is admitted that marginal individuals tend to make creative adjustments more often than to relapse into new or old orthodoxies, the record is not at all clear, and there are some students who warn us that marginal individuals are more prone than others to experience *anomie* and thus to become carriers of trends leading toward social disorganization rather than to innovations of a creative type.

In circumstances in which a certain amount of deviant behavior has been displayed, the establishment of a new social institution is invaluable. E. H. Carr, writing in a different context, expressed the opinion that "the ideal, once it is embodied in an institution, ceases to be an ideal and becomes the expression of a selfish interest, which must be destroyed in the name of a new ideal."[6] Carr here expresses succinctly the interaction between social deviance and the growth of institutions. Once a form of deviant behavior can find the shelter of an institution, it becomes routinized, it ceases to be deviant, and it tends to become an accepted mode of social action. But the institution in which it is "laid down" forms an advance post, so to speak, from which further deviance is possible. Thus the institutions which arose in Western Europe before the industrial revolution and in Japan before the Meiji restoration were already the end products of a process of social change; but they, in turn, made possible, by their very existence, further social and economic change.

Whether or not deviant social behavior will lead to new social institutions and the routinization of new forms of behavior depends upon a number of factors which we cannot discuss here in detail. However, it is clear that one of the most important determinants of the relative success of deviance will be the system of sanctions which exist in a society. Such sanctions may be internalized, *i.e.,* they may reside ultimately in the values and beliefs of people; or they may be external sanctions, *i.e.,* they may be imposed by individuals in power, by the elite, against actual or would-be deviants. In imperial China, it appears that both types of sanctions were very strong. In pre-Meiji Japan, internal sanctions had broken down in some areas and the power of the *shogun* had decreased sufficiently so that many external sanctions were not adequate to prevent the formation of new institutions, or at least of their rudiments.

But it is clear from what has been said that the over-all strength and multiplicity of sanctions is an important determinant of the forms of deviance which are possible and successful, the kinds of persons (marginal or non-marginal individuals) who may engage in deviant action, and the speed with which deviance will result in new social institutions. Moreover, we should remember that sanctions rest with a different force upon different individuals in a society and that often the position in the social scale which a person occupies determines the degree to which he is subject to internal or external sanctions. We may then distinguish two cases in which change is slow because sanctions against deviance are strong. One is the case of an authoritarian regime in which external sanctions are strong and in which deviant behavior is often reserved for outsiders or marginal persons. The autocratic empires of antiquity and the medieval period roughly conformed to this picture, although in all these instances the force of external sanctions was buttressed by a vigorous system of widely accepted social values which constituted supporting internal sanctions.

The other case—which is of greater importance for us—is the country in which internal sanctions against social change among the masses of the people are quite strong and in which the members of the elite wish to employ this for whatever societal objectives they favor. As long as an elite is interested primarily in maintaining its own position of power and privilege, this may mean that the masses are degraded, that economic progress is slow, and that general poverty prevails. But in a few cases the members of the elite have

---

[6] Edward Hallet Carr, *The Twenty Years Crisis* (London, 1940), p. 92.

reinterpreted the social objectives to lie in the direction of economic progress. This, I believe, was one of the main changes in Japan after the Meiji restoration, and it appears to be paramount in many underdeveloped countries of today.

In general, the outward aspects of social transformation occurring under the impact of deviance, as against one taking place through a reorientation of social objectives on the part of an existing elite, will vary. The second type of social change may be more "orderly"; rather than developing entirely new institutions, new meaning may be given to existing old ones; and whereas in the former process industrialization will be preceded normally by a substantial alteration in relations between social classes, this will not take place, or only to a smaller extent, in the second case. For example, the basic social relations in Japan have changed singularly little from the time it was a quasi-feudal empire based primarily upon agriculture to the present when it is a predominantly industrial nation. Similarly, in some underdeveloped countries, where the development effort is spearheaded by the governmental elite, rigorous controls are often exercised to prevent social disorganization of various forms from setting in or taking on major proportions.

Since the development of new institutions by means of deviance has usually been outside the control and often even in opposition to the aims of the elite, it has been designated as an autonomous process. It also has involved conflict, and in Marxian theory it was described as a dialectic process called forth by the intrinsic historical forces of the class struggle. The alterations of social institutions by the elite, on the other hand, may be designated as a process of induced or planned change and, depending upon the distribution of power within a society, may proceed at a controlled rate. Moreover, in a system of induced change, some influence may be exerted on the timing with which new social institutions are created or old ones imbued with new meanings. Thus the clear distinction between a preparatory period for a take-off which could be relatively easily identified for countries with autonomous patterns of social and economic change becomes blurred in a country with induced change. Nevertheless, it appears that even in conditions in which social and economic change is controlled very tightly, the function of new institutions to influence changes in social behavior must not be overlooked with impunity. This seems to indicate that ultimately a theoretical system may have to be evolved in which the interrelations between the various processes determining institutions embodying social change are elucidated. We have more precise knowledge on the manner in which deviance leads to the establishment of new social institutions than on the process of how this is attained by methods of induced social change, because the former can be studied on the example of the social and economic history of Western countries. There, numerous sources exist, and the process has been going on for centuries. It would be an important step forward in our understanding of the noneconomic aspects of economic development if we could develop more certain knowledge of these processes as they occur presently in situations of induced economic growth.

CHARLES WOLF, JR.

‖‖

Institutions and Economic Development

The programming of economic development has been largely based on theories and assumptions which place primary stress on technological change and capital formation. Related to these approaches have been the practices of surveying existing methods of production in terms of yields and productivity, and the existing size and pattern of investment through an analysis of national income and expenditure accounts. The surveys provide a logical basis for program formulation, *i.e.*, for appraising the possibility of raising output by introducing new methods of production, and estimating the extent and kinds of new capital formation required and the increases in domestic savings or foreign capital needed to meet these capital requirements.

While, however, inadequacies of existing technology and investment invariably characterize underdeveloped economies, these characteristics are perhaps correlative rather than causal. The inadequacy of technology and capital formation may be due less to a shortage of information about techniques or of potential savings, than to shortages of the "right" kinds of institutions—"right" implying those kinds of institutions which permit or stimulate, rather than impede, the adoption of new techniques and the formation of productive capital.[1] In other words, institutions—as well as capital and technology—are productive; or, more accurately, different institutions have differentially productive consequences.[2] Growth-promoting institutions, without themselves adding resources to the economy—or at least by a process that is distinguishable from any resources which they directly add—may so restructure the environment in which factors of production meet that the rate at which combinations occur is accelerated.[3]

Hence, besides technological and investment surveys, as bases for programming technical assistance and capital projects, there is a need for institu-

From *American Economic Review* (December 1955), pp. 867-883. Reprinted by permission of the American Economic Association and the author.

---

[1] H. Belshaw, "Economic Development in Asia," *Economia Internazionale* (November 1952), V, 848-53.

[2] *Cf.* K. E. Boulding, *The Organizational Revolution* (New York, 1953), p. 168.

[3] The acceleration might involve *new* types of factor combinations (technological change), or an increase in those already known. In the latter case, the impact of growth-promoting institutions would result in mobilizing idle resources by overcoming the conditions of underemployment equilibrium typically characterizing underdeveloped economies.

tional surveys and institutional programming. An organized market for monetary capital, for example, may provide potential producers with an opportunity
both to maintain liquidity and realize an appreciation in their assets, and this
may fundamentally alter the pattern and quantity of investment in the economy. This is the kind of catalysis that institutional programming should appraise
and introduce into underdeveloped countries as a concomitant of direct
attempts to program investment and technical assistance. If this approach is
to be systematized, it is necessary to develop a framework for analyzing how
the social context influences economic behavior. The purpose of this paper is
to make some preliminary observations and suggestions concerning such a
framework, with reference to problems of development programming in the
economically underdeveloped areas.

In the discussion which follows, the term "institution" refers to *organizations* and *policies,* both governmental and private.[4] This limited definition is
used in order to select those elements in the existing or potential social context
which can be incorporated in institutional programs, accompanying and supplementing investment and technological programming.[5] Such programs are
conceived as groups of integrated and consciously planned institutional innovations designed to stimulate those kinds of behavior by management, farmers, labor, consumers, savers, investors, and innovators which can be expected
to initiate and sustain growth. The following discussion does not elaborate
these kinds of behavior in detail, but assumes they can be identified.

---

[4] *Cf.* B. Malinowski, *A Scientific Theory of Culture and Other Essays* (Chapel
Hill, N. C., 1944), pp. 52-54. Malinowski's concept of institution stresses and distinguishes the following components: (1) a charter, comprising the institution's objectives; (2) personnel, organized in terms of defined principles of authority and responsibility; (3) the norms or rules governing the conduct of personnel in accord with the
charter; and (4) the material apparatus or equipment which the institution's personnel
use. While the definition we are using adds the notion of policies to the Malinowski
concept of organization, it can be assumed that the effectiveness of policies, in the developmental context especially, depends on their embodiment in organizations. For some
of the many and widely variant uses of the term institution, see, among sociologists,
F. Znaniecki, "Social Organizations and Institutions," in *Twentieth Century Sociology,*
Gurvitch and Moore, editors (New York, 1945), pp. 172 ff.; R. B. Williams, *American
Society—A Sociological Interpretation* (New York, 1951), pp. 28-30; S. Winston, *Culture
and Human Behavior* (New York, 1933), pp. 130-132; C. M. Panunzio, *Major Social
Institutions* (New York, 1939), pp. 7-27; and among economists, see E. M. Burns, "Does
Institutionalism Complement or Compete with 'Orthodox Economics'?," *Am. Econ. Rev.*
(March 1931), XXI, p. 86; J. M. Clark, "Institutional Economics," *Am. Econ. Rev.—
Suppl.* (March 1932), XXII, p. 105, and K. E. Boulding, *op. cit.,* pp. 165, 169. 252.
It is not surprising that one writer divided institutional economists into two classes:
"those who refuse to define institutional economics and those whose definitions disagree,"
P. T. Homan, "An Appraisal of Institutional Economics," *Am. Econ. Rev.* (March
1932), XXII, p. 12.

[5] In a more extensive treatment, institutions might be regarded as sets or clusters
of organizations and policies, related to each other by a dominant common purpose.
Those organizations and policies which link the saver, the investor and the entrepreneur
(*e.g.,* securities markets, banks, insurance companies, loan and savings associations, credit
cooperatives, monetary policies, etc.) could be considered to comprise a society's
"capital-mobilizing" institution. A classification of institutions, relevant to the problems
of initiating and sustaining growth, might be useful but it is not attempted in this paper.
Consequently, the examples cited in the text generally refer to specific organizations and
policies rather than related clusters.

Institutions may stimulate or impede those kinds of behavior leading to economic growth by their effect on (1) the direct calculation of costs and benefits; (2) relationships between production and distribution (output and income); (3) the order, predictability, and probability of economic relationships; (4) knowledge of economic opportunities; and (5) motivations and values.[6] These categories may be briefly elaborated and exemplified:

1. *The Direct Calculation of Costs and Benefits.* The simplest and most rect influence which institutions can exert on economic behavior is through neir impact on costs and benefits entering into the calculations of entre-preneurs.[7]

In their effect on costs and benefits, institutions may directly change cost-price relationships to the advantage of particular enterprises. The initiation and enforcement of protectionist commercial policies, which raise domestic prices of imports through the imposition of tariffs or foreign exchange taxes, are a case in point. Adoption by the Philippines of a 17-percent foreign exchange tax in 1950 directly stimulated both domestic and foreign investment within the country.[8] The creation by Japan, after the Imperial Restoration, of institutions to subsidize and make low-interest loans to new industry also contributed to growth through their direct impact on cost-benefit calculations.[9]

A particular institutional innovation may simultaneously affect both entrepreneurial costs and benefits. The small-industries development program in Indonesia, for example, is based on the creation of local organizations, called *centrales* (or *induks*) whose purpose, aided by an initial government subsidy in personnel and equipment, is to service the needs of local entrepreneurs in specific, small industries. Services performed by the *centrales* involve both purchasing and processing of intermediate products for sale to local producers, and marketing finished output. The former service reduces entrepreneurial costs; the latter increases benefits by assuring a larger and more stable demand. While in this case the effects on costs and benefits are mutu-

---

[6] Clearly, the listed categories do not conform to traditional disciplinary lines; nor are they comparable as concerns their levels of generality or their precision. Nevertheless, they are believed to focus on significant, separable, and, at least potentially, measurable channels of influence on economic behavior which are of particular relevance to problems of economic growth.

[7] In this paper, the term "entrepreneur" is intended to denote those who make or directly affect the basic economic decisions concerning investment, employment, the scale and character of output, the adoption of new techniques, etc. This use embraces the various notions of "innovating" and "imitative" entrepreneurs which are differentiated in some of the literature. *Cf.* C. H. Danhof's classification in *Change and the Entrepreneur* (Cambridge, Mass., 1949), pp. 23-24. Contrary to Schumpeter's model, it may be that in underdeveloped countries there is a greater shortage of "imitators" than "innovators." Frequently, even the most retarded countries seem to have at least a sprinkling of the latter but an acute shortage of the former.

[8] The foreign exchange tax differed from a uniform ad valorem tariff in its economic effects in that the exchange tax applied to capital and invisible outpayments as well as imports. This may explain its important political advantage; *i.e.,* the Philippine tax was fairly easy to remove after five years.

[9] G. C. Allen and A. G. Donnithorne, *Western Enterprise in Far Eastern Economic Development: China and Japan* (London, 1954), p. 192.

ally reenforcing, it is also possible that particular institutional changes may have offsetting effects on costs and benefits.

Institutions may affect not only the *magnitude* of costs and benefits, but the *kinds* as well. By converting a share of fixed costs into variable costs, for example, institutional innovations may have a definite impact on entrepreneurial calculations and decisions. Typically in underdeveloped areas, the uncertainty associated with business ventures tends to be high.[10] Because lower fixed costs facilitate adjustment to the unexpected, they tend to increase willingness and ability to act under uncertainty conditions. Business opportunities which involve reduced fixed costs and higher operating costs are therefore likely to be more attractive to potential entrepreneurs in underdeveloped areas than those which possess the reverse characteristics, even if the present value of the anticipated increase in operating costs equals (and sometimes even if it exceeds) the reduction in fixed costs.

In British industrialization the important role usually assigned to institutional changes which converted labor from a fixed to a variable cost provides a case in point. Thus, economic historians have stressed the pressures increasingly exerted on the feudal serf by the manorial system in England and by the enclosure movement, as well as the attractions represented by the rise of towns, combining to stimulate a move to the towns and the creation of a wage labor force.[11] When the overhead costs of labor in the feudal manor became the "risk of existence" borne by the worker, the entrepreneur's calculations were fundamentally altered. With fixed costs lowered, and labor now a variable cost, urban investment grew rapidly. Current social legislation in underdeveloped countries may sometimes have a reverse impact. For example, Indian legislation which involves maintenance-of-employment requirements tends to make labor a fixed rather than variable cost with a corresponding influence on entrepreneurial calculations.

Institutional innovations which do not lower fixed costs may have a comparable effect on entrepreneurial calculations by making such costs easier to bear. Thus, establishment of a publicly supported market for equity capital may enable an entrepreneur to share fixed costs by sharing ownership. With this purpose in view, the government of Indonesia has recently helped to organize a stock market in Djakarta, though it is still too early to evaluate results.

Credit institutions may also facilitate the bearing of fixed costs by altering the share of initial investment requirements which can be met from the entrepreneur's future income rather than his current resources. Generally, in underdeveloped countries few institutions perform the normal function of extending long-term credit. Those which appear to do so often impose prohibitive collateral requirements and interest charges which in practice sharply

---

[10] See *infra*, p. 874 ff.
[11] M. Weber, *General Economic History* (London, 1927), pp. 128-130, and P. Mantoux, *The Industrial Revolution in the Eighteenth Century* (New York, 1927), pp. 156 ff.

restrict the access of entrepreneurs to loan funds.[12] Under such circumstances, alternative credit facilities and policies may be a pressing, though not readily apparent, requirement for accelerated growth.

2. *Relationships Between Production and Distribution.* Western technicians working in underdeveloped countries have frequently been struck by the apparently "irrational" character of individual responses to demonstrated economic opportunities. The marked and rapid impact on productivity of artificial fertilizer, row planting, double-cropping through irrigation, and other innovations in agricultural techniques may be demonstrated without producing any perceptible impetus toward an adoption of these improved methods. Assuming the obstacle is not a shortage of capital, this inertia is generally attributed to barriers of motivation and perception. Yet it is quite possible to hypothesize circumstances under which neither a shortage of capital nor motivational or perceptual barriers exist, and yet a marked reluctance to adopt widespread innovation persists. Indeed, cases of this kind may be considerably more common and significant in underdeveloped areas than those situations in which resistance to growth-producing behavior is due to motivational and perceptual obstacles.

By their effect on the structure of rewards in a society, institutions may differentiate between those *responsible* for adopting and financing innovations and those *benefiting* therefrom. Under such circumstances, a marked inertia to the adoption of improved methods will tend to persist despite growth-promoting motivational and perceptual patterns.[13] Where institutions operate to reduce the remuneration of a factor below its marginal productivity, individual factors with a high marginal productivity may remain unemployed, and opportunities promising a marked increase in output for new factor combinations may be neglected.

Consider the impact of land tenure institutions on incentives to innovate. One tenure arrangement typical of the Philippines, India, Pakistan, and other countries in South and Southeast Asia involves an organized relationship between landlord and tenant in which the tenant bears all the costs of land improvements, although he must share equally with the landlord any resulting increase in output. Before an improvement can be considered advantageous to the tenant, it must yield a gross return at least twice the improvement's cost to the tenant for the given accounting period. The effect of this situation, together with the complicating role played by credit institutions typical of this area, can be illustrated by a simple example.

---

[12] Normally this situation might be attributed simply to the risk involved. Frequently in underdeveloped countries there may be a considerable divergence between the "objective" risk and the lender's "subjective" calculations of risk. Where the yardstick of precedent is absent, subjective risk may tend to be unduly high. *Cf.* H. G. Aubrey, *Industrial Enterprise in Underdeveloped Countries* (New York, 1953), pp. 14-16.

[13] *Cf.* J. H. Boeke, *Economics and Economic Policy of Dual Societies* (Haarlem, 1953), pp. 33-35. See also B. H. Higgins, "Economic Development of Underdeveloped Areas: Past and Present," *Center for International Studies,* Massachusetts Institute of Technology (Cambridge, June 1954), pp. 18-19.

Assume a tenant is considering a particular capital improvement, *e.g.,* digging and equipping a shallow ground-well whose installed cost is 100 units. Assume further he can borrow for a period of two years at an interest rate of 25 percent per annum on the unpaid balance (a not unusual rate in Southeast Asia), and with amortization of principal divided equally between the two years. If the project is to be self-liquidating during the period of the loan, it must yield a minimum of 150 units of increased output in the first year and 125 units in the second year, because the tenant must pay half of the increased output to the landlord. Quite probably, tenure and credit institutions of this type have the effect of deterring a major share of the types of investment that, financially and technically, might otherwise be within the capacity of the cultivator.

The joint or extended family system provides another example of institutions deterring economic growth by creating discontinuities between production and distribution. The joint family, which generally characterizes the Asian area, involves a system of shared rights and obligations encompassing a large number of near and distant relatives. One characteristic of these relationships is that the individual family member receives the right of support and security from the group in return for the obligation to share his wealth to provide support and security for other members of the group. Where an individual member of the group contemplates a wealth-increasing activity, *e.g.,* through investment in a productive asset that will yield future returns, he must bear all of the costs associated therewith. Such costs are not a levy on the group since they are not essential to the individual's support or security. However, the fruits or returns from his investment *are* subject to sharing among the other members of the extended family. Because of the differentiation between responsible and benefiting economic units, what may appear objectively to be strong incentives to invest are not subjectively so regarded by the potential entrepreneur. Under these circumstances, shortages of capital, as well as motivational and perceptual barriers, may be removed without stimulating growth because the underlying institutional obstacle persists.

These examples have stressed the negative or deterrent role of adverse institutions which create discontinuities between responsible and benefiting economic units. Where institutional innovations remove such discontinuities, they tend to convert objectively existing, into subjectively recognized, opportunities. Altered land-tenure arrangements, which exempt from sharecropping the increments in physical productivity induced by a tenant's investment or his adoption of improved techniques, may be expected to have such a generative effect even if the crop-sharing arrangements applying to the normal or base output are not changed. Actually, recent land-reform proposals in the Southeast Asian countries, *e.g.,* the Philippines, have stressed the adjustment of average, rather than marginal, crop-sharing ratios in favor of tenants. While this stress has been amply justified on grounds of equity, the stimulus to productivity would be greater if adjustment were confined to the marginal ratio. Nevertheless, it is likely that any appreciable improvement in crop-sharing ratios—whether average or marginal—will have a significant influence on agricultural incentives, investment, and productivity.

In Western economic development, the channel of influence we have been describing was apparently of considerable significance. In some cases, a stimulus to growth was provided by a new institution acting to bridge the gap between the initiator and the beneficiary. A case in point is what Weber termed "the first rational patent law" in England in 1623. This law increased the incentive to invest by providing that an inventor receive a payment covering a fourteen-year period of initial use by an entrepreneur, and that subsequent utilization of the invention be made "conditional upon payment of an adequate royalty to the original inventor."[14] In other cases, the stimulus was provided by eliminating the kind of deterrent institutions we have referred to. The repeal of the British Corn Laws in 1846 is a case in point. By keeping food prices and wages down, and preventing a further channeling of the increasing output of British industry to landlords, repeal of the Corn Laws removed an important deterrent to further industrial investment in England. In each case the similarity of the causal nexus is apparent.

3. *Order, Predictability, and Probability.* Institutions may influence economic behavior by their effect on the amount of order in the economic environment. For our purposes, economic order may be divided into two components: (*a*) the predictability of the possible consequences of alternative economic actions; and (*b*) the probability of gain or loss associated with these consequences.

Probability refers to the *risk,* or odds on gain or loss, associated with particular actions on the assumption that their possible consequences can be foreseen. Predictability refers to the subjective confidence or certainty which the individual feels toward his risk estimates, or, more explicitly, the extent to which he feels he can make any reliable estimates at all.[15] Economic order may be said to increase when the consequences of economic action become more calculable or predictable, *i.e.,* when individuals feel more confidence in their ability to appraise the consequences of alternative action possibilities; or when probabilities are so altered that "growth-promoting" economic actions become more frequent or likely.

The above formulation assumes that "growth-promoting" actions can be objectively determined (or agreed upon) in a country's development planning, and ranked in order of priority or intensity of expected impact (*e.g.,* increasing investment at home rather than abroad, reducing underemployment, raising savings, etc.). Where increased economic order alters probabilities, the result will be to increase the likelihood that such actions will occur while reducing the likelihood of others.

---

[14] Weber, *op. cit.,* p. 312.

[15] For a more detailed treatment of the effect of these factors on economic decision-making, see Aubrey, *op. cit.,* pp. 12-18; F. H. Knight, *Risk, Uncertainty and Profit* (New York, 1921), pp. 216-232; A. G. Hart, *Anticipations, Uncertainty and Dynamic Planning* (Chicago, 1940), pp. 52 ff.; Jacob Marschak, "Lack of Confidence," *Social Research* (February 1941), VIII, pp. 52-53; and G. L. S. Shackle, *Expectation in Economics* (Cambridge, 1949), esp. pp. 10-19, 115-116.

The notion of probability, suggested above as a component of economic order, involves both the subjective estimation and the actuarial calculation of odds on gain or loss. *Cf.* Knight, *op. cit.,* pp. 223-226.

Institutions may affect one or both components of economic order. Where both are affected, the results may tend to be mutually reinforcing or offsetting. Institutions which insure against certain kinds of business risks will presumably increase the predictability of the consequences of specific economic acts. At the same time they may conceivably decrease or increase the probability of gain for any individual new investor depending, for example, on the character of competition and market structure resulting from the altered predictability conditions.

There is considerable evidence suggesting that changes in the degree of order in the economic environment have been among the most important historical influences exerted by those institutional innovations contributing to growth. Perhaps one of the basic prerequisites for accelerated growth in Western history lay in the proliferation at the end of the Middle Ages of a variety of associations, such as the *mercantile guild,* which lowered both uncertainty and risk from the standpoint of the individual entrepreneur. The guild negotiated commercial treaties to set up and regularize markets, and by arranging for docks, ports, and ships, made these contingencies more calculable for the entrepreneur. The ships of the guild sailed in convoys and were frequently armed, just as on land the merchants organized caravans and hired armed escorts. In the event of loss, the guild paid indemnities.[16]

In addition to associations like the guild and temporary partnerships among nonguild members, which operated through the pooling of risk and the sharing of facilities, predictabilities and probabilities were also altered by the appearance of institutions which permitted individuals or groups to specialize in the assumption of risk where maritime commerce was involved. Two of these, the *sea loan* and the *commenda,* may be briefly mentioned. In the operation of the sea loan, a merchant who borrowed in order to ship goods overseas was not required to repay his creditors in the event of loss of ship or cargo. If the shipment were successful, the lenders were entitled to a return of about 30 percent over and above the repayment of principal. Rates of profit and interest to the lender fluctuated up to 35 percent according to the risk.[17]

The *commenda* was an organization of merchants, some of whom provided capital and remained in the home port while others were traveling associates who marketed the goods abroad. The sedentary *socius* received 75 percent of the gain if he (or they) furnished all of the capital and assumed the entire risk, and a smaller share if the contribution was less. As was apparently typical of medieval partnerships, there was no permanency to a particular *commenda,* the accounts being closed after each expedition.[18] As it developed, the *commenda* performed the same function as the sea loan, differing from the latter primarily in form. The next step, assuming major

---

[16] See, for example, P. Boissonade, *Life and Work in Medieval Europe* (New York, 1927), p. 193, and H. Pirenne, *Economic and Social History of Medieval Europe* (New York, 1937), pp. 91-96.

[17] Weber, *op. cit.,* pp. 202-204.

[18] *Ibid.,* pp. 206-207.

importance in the sixteenth century, was a separation of the lending and insurance functions, as some capital owners began to write insurance contracts without loan features and gradually established premium scales in accordance with the risks involved.[19]

The same channel of influence seems to have played a significant role in Japanese development. A recent comparative study of Japanese and Chinese economic growth, for example, lays particular stress on the increased economic order created by Japanese policy and institutions as an explanation of the widely divergent patterns and rates of growth in Japan and China. While the Japanese government directly assisted the entrepreneur and stabilized the economic environment confronting him by creating institutions and facilities to provide credit, equipment, and foreign technical advice for new enterprise, the Chinese entrepreneur remained:

> . . . at the mercy of officialdom and subject to the arbitrary exactions of central and local authorities. Even when enlightened officials invited their cooperation in some enterprise, they hesitated because they had little confidence in the consistency of government policy.[20]

While economic order is closely related to the direct calculation of costs and benefits, the two categories are conceptually distinct. Changes in economic order either make the odds or estimates of gain or loss more calculable, or they alter the odds relating to particular actions. An owner of liquid capital in an underdeveloped country may decide to hold his assets abroad rather than to invest at home because of uncertainty concerning the possibilities of devaluation. This uncertainty may be removed by a government commitment to permit withdrawal of newly invested funds at a fixed rate of exchange. The investor, though now in a better position to predict, may continue to invest abroad because he expects a rate of return of, say, 6 percent with a .99 chance of gain compared to a rate of return from investing at home of perhaps 8 percent with a .66 chance of gain. A further increase in economic order might encourage domestic investment by raising the chance of gain to .90 (*i.e.,* altering probabilities) without affecting the rate of return. By contrast, an institutional change acting directly on costs and/or benefits might also encourage investment at home by raising the rate of return to say 15 percent without altering the chance of gain.

If one assumes the acceptance of a precise risk discount by the decision maker, the probability effect can readily be converted into a cost-benefit effect.[21] However, it is quite possible that the two effects will appeal differ-

---

[19] S. B. Clough and C. W. Cole, *Economic History of Europe* (Boston, 1946), pp. 306-307, 633.

[20] Allen and Donnithorne, *op. cit.,* pp. 192 ff. and p. 248. The arbitrary and unpredictable use of political power in France has also been stressed as a barrier to that country's early economic development. See, for example, G. Renard and G. Weulersse, *Life and Work in Modern Europe* (New York, 1926), p. 364.

[21] A particular decision maker may simply multiply the rate of return by the estimated probability coefficient in order to get a net rate of return to compare with other similarly discounted alternatives.

ently to different decision makers, and that under particular circumstances differing institutional innovations are needed to produce one or both effects if the desired pattern of behavior is to be encouraged.[22]

It is probable that increased economic order is a crucial and widespread need in the currently underdeveloped areas. One example of successful institutional innovation in this field has been the establishment of the State Agricultural Marketing Board in Burma. The SAMB, which functions as a government monopoly in the purchase and export of rice, was formed to assist economic recovery by stabilizing the internal rice market. In contrast to agricultural price supports in the United States, the SAMB has kept rice prices in Burma stable since 1950 at a level substantially *below* fluctuating world prices. Rice producers have thus paid a heavy tax which has provided the country's main source of development financing. At the same time, producers have been partially compensated by improved predictability conditions in what would otherwise have been a highly volatile market. Within limits, the parallel to an insurance premium is clear. While obviously it cannot be demonstrated that recovery of production has been expedited, it is at least suggestive that cultivated rice acreage in Burma increased by 11 percent and output by 10 percent between the crop years 1950-1951 and 1953-1954.

4. *Knowledge of Economic Opportunities.* Institutions may also affect growth by removing or reducing those imperfections, frictions, and rigidities in the market which are due to imperfect knowledge concerning purchasing, production, technical, or marketing opportunities. Overcoming imperfections of knowledge in underdeveloped countries is, however, a considerably more subtle process than simply the diffusion of information. A few of the complications involved may be briefly noted.

It is a commonly accepted law of perception that the perceiver systematically overlooks what he considers extraneous and irrelevant.[23] The problem of influencing perception thus extends to the question of how to alter what people regard as intrinsic and relevant; that is, how to alter what social psychologists call the perceiver's "cognitive structure"—the associations, recollections, and inferences with which the perceiver connects what he actually perceives.[24] Cultivators who typically produce for their own consumption and use, rather than for the market, may indeed value higher standards of personal welfare. However, they may not perceive the connection between using artificial fertilizer to raise yields of a commodity they *don't* need and obtaining a commodity or service (education, improved health, etc.) they *do* need. The

---

[22] *Cf.* G. Katona, *Psychological Analysis of Economic Behavior* (New York, 1951), pp. 248-250.

[23] R. B. MacLeod, "Social Psychology," in F. L. Marcuse (ed.), *Areas of Psychology* (New York, 1954), p. 201.

[24] D. Krech and R. S. Crutchfield, *Theory and Problems of Social Psychology* (New York, 1948), pp. 76-81. Morse has suggested that the social psychologist's distinction between cognition and perception has something in common with the economist's distinction between "stocks" and "flows." Thus, the "cognitive structure" may be considered to represent the "stock" of recollections and associations which gives significance to the "flow" of new perceptions. Cognition, as such, embraces the meaning and significance with which a perception is endowed, as well as the data or impression which the perception records.

availability of improved techniques may thus be overlooked as irrelevant to their "felt" needs. To influence perception, therefore, institutions frequently must not only disseminate information about techniques and opportunities, but must describe and facilitate the connection between such information and the realization of needs considered pressing by the perceiver.

For institutions to affect economic behavior by altering perception, they may have to act upon the perceiver as well as upon what is to be perceived. Even assuming that opportunities are preceived and that the probable consequences from exploiting such opportunities are valued, the economic agent may not perceive that it is his responsibility to initiate the action required to translate these opportunities into accomplishments. The problem may thus be one of altering the individual's perception of his own social role to embrace active response or "entrepreneurial" behavior, even if this only extends to the investment of his own labor.[25] This is a perhaps unnecessarily complicated formulation of the notion of "self-help" underlying technical assistance. To pursue the example previously cited, institutions must convey to the cultivator not only information concerning the techniques and results of improved fertilizer use, but the recognition that it is the cultivator's responsibility to take advantage of and apply the improved methods himself.

The problem of perception involves the arrangement and integration, as well as the dissemination, of information. Institutions which help to establish systematic methods of cost accounting, for example, may have the effect of so altering the arrangement of already-available information that perceptions and resulting behavioral patterns are markedly changed.

It is perhaps easier and more fruitful to exemplify than to define abstractly the kinds of institutions which may have the influence on perceptions and cognition we have been discussing. Boissonade, for example, refers to the importance of "journeymen's unions" in late medieval times in facilitating "the acquisition of technical instruction . . . [by] their members by organizing journeys from town to town and country to country which . . . sometimes lasted as long as five years."[26] In the nineteenth century and early part of the present century, Japan's intensive and deliberate efforts toward rapid industrialization, following the Meiji Restoration, adapted and elaborated this device. An organized and extensive program of foreign study for Japanese youth was consciously embarked upon to alter perceptions and accelerate the diffusion of information at home. This is a period and an experience in Japanese history that needs to be re-examined and evaluated in the light of current perceptual and motivational bottlenecks to growth in underdeveloped areas.[27] Knowles' emphasis on the importance, in nineteenth-century Germany's development, of institutions created and supported by the state for spreading technical education and for undertaking industrial research provides another example.[28]

---

[25] *Cf. ibid.*, pp. 72, 372-373 ff.

[26] *Op. cit.*, p. 305.

[27] W. W. Lockwood, *The Economic Development of Japan* (Princeton, 1954), pp. 510-512.

[28] L. C. A. Knowles, *Economic Development in the Nineteenth Century* (London, 1932), p. 173.

A recent example can be cited in the striking success of India's Community Development Program in raising agricultural productivity during the past three years. Though using the same tools of technical assistance (*e.g.*, demonstrations, free, or subsidized distribution of seed and fertilizer, etc.) as the earlier and unsuccessful "grow-more-food" program, Community Development altered the institutional setting by organizing and training extension workers to function as residents in the rural villages. As accepted members of the community, they are able to communicate improved techniques in terms meaningful to the cultivators, to explain the relationship between proximate returns and the village's "felt" needs, and to underscore the cultivator's responsibility for initiating improvements, thereby removing some of the perceptual barriers that had diminished the effectiveness of earlier technical assistance efforts at the village level.

Clearly, there is a close relationship between perception and cognition, and what we have referred to as economic order. The wider dissemination of coherent and integrated information, through extension services, market surveys, and similar institutions, may well affect the subjectively recognized predictabilities and probabilities of alternative economic choices, as well as the perception and cognition of opportunities. The distinction between the two is maintained because it suggests different channels of influence on economic behavior. In some cases, the failure to take advantage of an available opportunity may be due to the persistence of adverse predictability and probability conditions even though the opportunity may be perceived. In other cases, no predictability or probability estimates may be attempted because the opportunity is entirely overlooked by the individual as a result of its remoteness from his cognitive field.[29]

5. *Motivations and Values.* Values may be defined as individual and collective judgments (or assumptions) concerning what is desirable.[30] In "rational" human behavior, values provide the motivations which impel men to choose or avoid particular types of voluntary action.[31] Where motives differ among individuals or groups, differing action will result under otherwise identical circumstances. The backward sloping supply curve (of labor or commodities), frequently associated with "premodern" or "precapitalistic" societies,[32] is generally ascribed to the relatively high value placed on leisure by the worker or producer in these societies. Similarly, such growth-inhibiting phenomena as a highly inelastic supply of entrepreneurship, widely varying wage rates for comparable labor in "native" and "Western" enterprise, and

---

[29] Krech and Crutchfield, *op. cit.*, pp. 76-77.

[30] The term "value" as used here refers to norms and standards of judgment rather than the special meaning it is accorded in economics. *Cf.* J. J. Spengler, "Sociological Value Theory, Economic Analyses and Economic Policy," *American Economic Review, Proceedings* (May 1953), XLIII, pp. 342-343.

[31] Social psychologists frequently trace motivations to "needs" and "goals" rather than "values." But since values determine needs and goals, in "rational" as contrasted with "instinctive" behavior, the distinction does not appear fundamental, at least for our present purposes. *Cf.* MacLeod, "Social Psychology," *op. cit.*, pp. 193-197.

[32] See, for example, Boeke, *op. cit.*, p. 40.

varying marginal efficiencies of capital which show no tendency toward equalization may be explained in terms of the differing values motivating entrepreneurship, labor, and the owners of capital in underdeveloped societies.

Two points might be added to these general comments. The first concerns the ordering and weighting of values and motivations. The major difference in value and motivational patterns between developing and nondeveloping societies may lie not in the presence or absence of particular values, (*e.g.,* progress, wealth, economic security), but in the ranking and weighting of these values relative to others (*e.g.,* status, leisure, tradition). Achieving or shaping a "growth-promoting" pattern of values and motivations is thus frequently not so much a problem of transplanting unfamiliar values as it is of reordering existing values.

Second, values may be related to one another not only hierarchically (by ordering and weighting) but also instrumentally.[33] A value X may be regarded as a means to Z, as well as something to be desired in itself. Status and prestige may motivate action (or inaction) because they are valued in themselves, and also because they are a means to the achievement of economic security. To revert to a previous example, where the member of the joint family is not only accorded prestige and status but is also provided with a certain degree of economic security by the family, there will be a stronger motivation for him to remain within the established family unit than would be the case if the second valued consequence were not linked to the first. The separation of such "linked" values may be of significance in connection with the programming of growth-promoting institutions. If, for example, it becomes possible to realize economic security in underdeveloped countries through other means than those which depend on the established status and prestige structure, the character of economic choices (*e.g.,* career-choices, investment decisions, etc.) may be significantly affected. A further comment on this point will be made below.

What significance do these observations have with respect to the relationship between institutions and economic growth? By way of answer, it is suggested that institutions—if they are operative and effective—can modify and activate values and motivations.

In sociological literature discussing the relation between values and institutions, the causal sequence is generally presumed to be from changes in values and motivations to changes in institutions.[34] It is therefore presumed that significant changes in the institutional structure of a society must be preceded by a major shift in the society's value pattern. The familiar thesis attributing the growth of capitalist institutions in the West to the ethical innovations of the Protestant Reformation is an example of this view. The hypothesis we have suggested stresses the converse view that institutions can cause changes in values and motivations where these offer serious impedi-

---

[33] *Cf.* K. J. Arrow, *Social Choice and Individual Values* (New York, 1951), pp. 86-87, and H. A. Simon, *Administrative Behavior* (New York, 1947), pp. 49-50.

[34] *Cf.,* for example, Williams, *op. cit.,* pp. 373-374.

ments to growth.[35] In the case cited, it might therefore be argued that an innovation in religious institutions led to the ethical innovations which accelerated the rise of capitalism.

In many currently underdeveloped countries, the valuational pattern—or those aspects of the pattern which are most adverse to growth-promoting economic behavior—may be a rationalization of an institutional structure which inhibits growth. One way of adjusting to the fact that credit institutions charge excessive rates of interest, or that increased earnings may produce a flood of indigent relatives with whom the increase must be shared, is to adopt the view that, after all, increased output and earnings are not as important as leisure and salvation. What, therefore, appears to be a unique motivational characteristic of the "native" economy, may actually be an expedient accommodation to adverse institutions.[36] Under such circumstances, appropriate institutional innovations may produce a marked reordering in apparent values and motivations; that is, in the observed behavioral patterns from which values and motivations are inferred.[37]

Institutional innovation may have a similar effect on value reordering by separating "linked" values. As previously suggested, if status and prestige are valued not only in themselves but as necessary means to economic security, the provision of alternative means to the latter goal, *e.g.,* by insurance against unemployment or illness, may well diminish the relative value placed on status-oriented behavior.

Clearly, the inference of value reordering from behavioral changes, however pervasive they may be, is hazardous. In some cases, important changes in behavior may occur without any change in values. In India, for example, the point has frequently been made that there is a marked preference for careers in government and education rather than business enterprise or engineering. The indignity of manual labor and the relative prestige of civil service and education frequently constitute important motivations toward a

---

[35] Generally speaking, it is more accurate to describe the relationship between institutions and values as *interactive* rather than causal in one direction or the other. However, the position taken in the text derives from a conviction that most current writings on this problem in the underdeveloped areas have tended to overstress the causal primacy of values at all levels, and hence to overlook the equally important influence which institutional innovations can exert on values and motivations.

[36] Gerschenkron has expressed a somewhat similar point of view by observing that adverse values may not deter entrepreneurship (in "premodern" societies) unless these values or attitudes are allowed to become crystallized in adverse action. A. Gerschenkron, "Social Attitudes, Entrepreneurship and Economic Development," *Explorations in Entrepreneurial History* (October 1953), V, p. 15.

[37] Warren E. Miller, of the University of Michigan, in his helpful comments on the paper, has suggested that even though values originally evolved as a rationalization of an adverse institutional structure, they may be no less resistant to change. Though recognizing that my position implies a certain humanistic determinism, I would argue that an altered institutional structure can provide an opportunity for competing values to be perceived and adopted. In my judgment, human experience suggests that where there is an adequate opportunity for choosing "growth-promoting" values, the human species shows a marked propensity to make such a choice. Humans tend to value economic growth provided they have a reasonable chance to perceive it and to participate in it.

pattern of career choice adverse to the manpower requirements of accelerated growth. In this case, institutional changes (affecting, perhaps, the educational curricula in secondary schools or the degree of public recognition accorded the undermanned careers) might produce significant changes in attitudes and career choice without reordering values.

Institutions may also activate values that have been operationally dormant, without reordering them. The resulting behavioral changes may be so marked as to suggest a shift in the ordering of values. In fact, the changes in behavior may be due instead to the new opportunities provided by institutional innovations for the exercise of choice according to previously dormant values, even though no reordering of values occurs. Whether the observed behavioral pattern in such cases is due to a reordering of values, or to activation of dormant values as a result of the availability of new opportunities, may be impossible—and unnecessary—to ascertain. The operationally important question is whether growth-promoting behavior, which at least by inference can be associated with a modification of values and motivations, is evoked.

We have proposed and described several categories for analyzing and evaluating the influence of institutions on economic behavior. There are obvious limitations to the approach suggested. Even assuming effective institutional innovations function in the ways suggested, the basic questions of whether, to what extent, and under what conditions "alien" institutions are transmissible remain unanswered. Certainly the inference cannot be drawn that an institution which works effectively and in identifiable ways in one social context will operate similarly, or be accepted, in a different context. The process by which new institutions come into being, and the relationship between this process and the character of the existing social structure, are not dealt with in the preceding discussion.

More specifically, the preceding discussion has dealt with the influence of institutions in partial and static terms. Interrelationships among the categories have been alluded to rather than fully discussed. Yet, clearly, the functioning of effective institutions is likely to cut across many if not all of the categories suggested.[38]

Notwithstanding these limitations, certain results may follow from the taxonomic approach described. It may provide a framework for a more systematic discussion of the relationships between institutions and economic growth than has thus far taken place. An elaboration of the approach sug-

---

[38] An interesting case study illustrating this point is the recent study of the Philippine-American Life Insurance Company by the National Planning Association. The study describes the company's striking and rapid success in redirecting existing savings, apparently increasing the average savings propensities of many middle-class families, undertaking long-term productive investments itself and stimulating other enterprises as well. In the terminology we have been using, the company's generative influence in these fields, as described in the study, has involved an identifiable impact on motivations and perceptions, as well as on the amount of order in one segment of the economic environment, and on the benefits accruing to savers from using their income in an unaccustomed way. J. Lindeman, *A Case Study of the Philippine-American Life Insurance Company* (Washington, D. C., 1954).

gested may help in the classification and comparison of existing institutions in underdeveloped countries in terms of their influence on growth. Finally, it may assist program analysts in uncovering institutional obstacles to growth and in appraising the needs of developing countries for particular programs of institutional innovation.

UNITED NATIONS DEPARTMENT
OF ECONOMIC AFFAIRS

‖‖‖

Problems of Agrarian Structure
in Underdeveloped Countries

To a very large extent, the problem of the underdeveloped countries of the world is the problem of the poverty of their farm populations. Unduly low standards of living in rural areas are not confined to the underdeveloped countries; they can be found also in countries which have reached a high level of economic development. But in the underdeveloped countries the problem is of a different dimension, because the economy of these countries is mainly agricultural. Table 1 shows the proportion of agricultural population to total population in Asia, Africa, Central and South America as compared with the proportion in North America and Europe.

TABLE 1. PROPORTION OF WORLD POPULATION IN AGRICULTURE, 1949

Area	Total population (millions)	Agricultural population (millions)	Agricultural population as percentage of total
North America[a]	163	33	20
Europe	391	129	33
Oceania	12	4	33
South America	107	64	60
Central America[b]	50	33	67
Asia	1,255	878	70
Africa	198	146	74
World total	2,177	1,285	59

[a] Canada and the United States.
[b] Including Mexico.

Source: Food and Agriculture Organization of the United Nations, *Yearbook of Food and Agriculture,* 1950, p. 15.

From United Nations, Department of Economic Affairs, *Land Reform, Defects in Agrarian Structure as Obstacles to Economic Development* (New York: United Nations, 1951), pp. 3-49 and 89-93, with omissions.

Of the total population of the world, some 60 percent, or almost 1,300 million people, are dependent upon agriculture. Of these, over 1,000 million live in Asia, Africa, Central and South America, and only 162 million in Europe and North America. Whereas in Europe only one person out of three, and in North America only one person in five, is dependent on agriculture, in Asia and Africa three out of every four obtain their living from the land.

In the predominantly agricultural countries, the level of output per acre is generally lower than it is in the predominantly industrial countries; the level of output per person in agriculture is very much lower, because, generally speaking, the density of the farm population per acre is much greater, while the average yield per acre is less. As a long-term trend, these differences in productivity tend to become greater. The following table shows comparative levels of productivity in the agricultural and industrialized areas, by continents, before and after World War II.

TABLE 2. PRODUCTIVITY OF THE AGRICULTURAL POPULATION BY CONTINENTS AND FOR THE WORLD,[a] PREWAR AND 1947-1948

Continent	Yield per hectare			Yield per person in agriculture		
	Prewar (metric tons)	1947/48	1947/48 as percent of prewar	Prewar (metric tons)	1947/48	1947/48 as percent of prewar
World average	1.24	1.30	105	0.42	0.42	100
North and Central America	1.07	1.50	140	1.80	2.57	143
South America	1.28	1.39	109	0.58	0.48	83
Europe	1.51	1.34	89	1.04	0.88	85
Oceania	1.06	1.20	113	1.94	2.38	123
Asia	1.26	1.20	95	0.24	0.22	92
Africa	0.77	0.73	95	0.12	0.12	100

[a] Excluding the Union of Soviet Socialist Republics.
Source: Food and Agriculture Organization of the United Nations, *Monthly Bulletin of Food and Agricultural Statistics,* vol. 2, No. 9 (September 1949); arranged in order of yield per hectare in 1947-1948.

The differences in productivity per person in agriculture give some indication of the range of difference in rural living standards. Where the output per person in agriculture averages approximately 2½ tons, as it does in North America, the standard of living of the farm population will clearly be higher than where it is less than one quarter of a ton, as in Asia, or one eighth of a ton, as in Africa.

The causes of low productivity in agriculture and of low standards of living of the farm population are many: poor soils and unfavorable climates; backward techniques and inadequate equipment; excessively high densities of rural population; low prices received by the farmer. All these are important in varying degrees.

Among the most important factors which affect rural living standards is the agrarian structure. This term is here used to mean the institutional framework of agricultural production. It includes, in the first place, land tenure, the legal or customary system under which land is owned; the distribution of ownership of farm property between large estates and peasant farms or among peasant farms of various size; land tenancy, the system under which land is operated and its product divided between operator and owner; the organization of credit, production, and marketing; the mechanism through which agriculture is financed; the burdens imposed on rural populations by governments in the form of taxation; and the services supplied by governments to rural populations, such as technical advice and educational facilities, health services, water supply, and communications.

The different forms of agrarian structure and different systems of land tenure which exist in the underdeveloped countries of the world are the result in part of different forms of society and in part of the influence of foreign institutions. In many of the underdeveloped regions of the world, tribal or feudal institutions still form the social framework, even though under European influence the economic and political basis of tribal and feudal society has changed.

Since this report is concerned primarily with the effects of different forms of agrarian structure on the economic development of the societies in which they occur, neither the historical origins nor the legal forms are touched on, except where these relate to one of the many ways in which agrarian structure may be an obstacle to economic development and economic welfare. The agrarian structure may reduce the standard of living of the peasant by imposing on him exorbitant rents or high interest rates; it may deny him the incentive or opportunity to advance and it may check investment because it offers him no security; it may lead to the prevalence of farms which are too small to be efficient units of production or too large to cultivate intensively. The influence of the land-tenure system varies greatly from region to region and there are no defects which are present to the same degree in all the underdeveloped countries, though certain ones are very widespread.

In the following sections of this chapter some of the outstanding features of the land systems in the underdeveloped countries are considered; no attempt has been made to deal with every aspect of the subject as defined above. Only the more important features have been selected, for the purpose of indicating their effects in broad outline; those selected are common to more than one country and more than one continent. Examples have been chosen from different countries where the problems of development arise in an acute form, and where unsatisfactory agrarian structures have particularly noticeable effects. The instances which are given are examples only; they could be greatly multiplied. Nor are the countries selected to illustrate different aspects of agrarian problems necessarily the ones in which these problems are most acute, since lack of data strictly limits the number of examples in any particular case. In many countries the necessary data for analysis of the agrarian structure—statistics of farm population, agricultural income, land ownership, or size of farms, for example—are lacking. Wherever possible, official sources have been used, but since for some countries such material is not available, estimates made by independent observers have necessarily been used in some cases.

FARM SIZE AND LAYOUT

The outstanding feature of the agrarian structure in many underdeveloped countries is the extremely small size of the average farm holding. The definition of what acreage constitutes a small farm varies greatly from country to country. In most parts of the United States and in England a farm of 30 hectares (75 acres) would be considered a small farm, while in Eastern Europe, where the average size of farm holdings is 5 hectares (12½ acres), or in some Asian countries, where it is one hectare (2½ acres), such a farm would be considered very large indeed. Nor is it possible to establish a general criterion of what size farm constitutes a minimum size for economic operation, since this standard must necessarily vary with the type of cultivation and land utilization in different countries. Clearly the minimum size for economic operation will be smaller if the plough is drawn by bullocks than if it is drawn by a tractor.

UNECONOMIC HOLDINGS

In many underdeveloped countries, however, the question of what acreage constitutes a minimum economic holding, in the sense of what acreage will permit full utilization of the farmer's equipment, is less important than the question of what acreage provides a subsistence minimum, either directly by growing food or indirectly by providing an income from commercial crops. The standard is measured not in terms of a necessary scale of operation, but of a minimum standard of food consumption. Even on this basis, acreage alone is not a sufficient criterion, since there are great differences in the intensity of cultivation, and differences in cropping rates: an acre of land in an irrigated double-cropped river valley in India may produce six times as much as an acre of nonirrigated single-cropped land.

None the less, even when allowance is made for differences in intensity of cultivation, it is possible to state that there are many countries in which large numbers of farms are too small to provide a subsistence minimum for the cultivator and his family, or to provide them with full employment; and too small also to permit of any improvement in methods of cultivation. This feature of the agrarian structure may be the result either of the extreme subdivision of farms resulting from the pressure of population on the land, or of inequality in the distribution of land ownership; or it may result from the operation of both these factors together. Extreme subdivision of farm units tends to promote concentration of ownership and increase inequality in the distribution of property, because the small owners are generally unable to gain a subsistence from their farms, and in consequence become indebted to landowners and moneylenders who thereby acquire possession of the land.[1]

Where the density of the agricultural population is extremely high, the average farm holding is as a rule extremely small. The relation of farm population to the cultivated area varies greatly between different countries, and between different continents. . . . it appears that the countries where density of total population in relation to the area of arable land is highest are, in order of highest density, Japan, Egypt, Haiti, Korea, Indonesia, Lebanon, Indochina, Ceylon, China, and India.[2] In all these countries there is less than one third of a hectare (less than one acre) per head of total population. The significance of these figures is clear if the relationship between rural population and land resources is considered on the basis of estimates of the rural population. Japan has a farm population of 34.5 million on 5.9 million hectares of arable land.[3] Egypt has a rural population of between 14 and 15 million on 2.5 million hectares; in Indonesia, Java and Madura have a rural population of between 45 and 50 million on 10 million hectares of cultivated land; the average size of holdings in 1938 was 0.86 hectare. India has a rural population of 285 million [4] living on 98 million hectares or arable land. Though the density of the rural population per hectare in India is lower than in the three countries mentioned above, the effects of a high density on the living standard are more acute, in that the level of productivity per hectare is far lower; crop yields are much smaller, and double-cropping is only practiced on a small proportion of the land, whereas in Egypt, Japan, and Java, yields are very high and double-cropping is general. In China, the density of the rural population is extremely high in many regions: surveys of 17,000 farms in twelve provinces reveal a farm population of some 1,500 persons per square mile, or half an acre of land for each person on farms.[5] Thus the average density in these regions is twice as high as in India, but average crop yields are also twice as high. . . .

In these overcrowded conditions, the average farm holding would be small, even if all the land were equally distributed. Where the average holding is small, the greater the degree of inequality in the size of farm holdings, the larger will be the number of farm units below average size, and the larger therefore the number of holdings below the subsistence minimum.

---

[1] See section on credit and agricultural indebtedness.

[2] Three Latin American countries, Bolivia, Colombia, and Peru, show a similar relationship. But here the area of arable land per person is not a sufficient indication of excessive density of farm population as it is in Asia, because pasture farming plays a much larger part in the economy, and also because much cultivable land is not classified as arable.

[3] This figure is somewhat larger than that given for the cultivated area on pages 54 and 55 [in this report] because it includes the whole of Japan. Supreme Command, Allied Powers, *Japanese Agricultural Land Statistics,* Natural Resources Report 101 (Tokyo, 1948), p. 11.

[4] Estimated as 80 percent of total population, as reported in the census of 1951.

[5] J. Lossing Buck, "Fact and Theory about China's Land," *Foreign Affairs* (New York, October 1949).

In Japan, for example, the average size of farm is one hectare, or 2½ acres; the recent reform has made farm sizes much more equal, yet 41 percent of farm holdings are still under 1.2 acres . . . . [6]

In greater or less degree, the problem of large numbers of extremely small farms affects India, parts of China, and all Southeast Asia except Burma. It is present also in the Caribbean countries, and in Egypt and Japan in an extreme degree. In so far as it results from an excessively high density of rural population, it is not a problem which can be dealt with by change in the agrarian structure alone.

Though it is in the rurally overpopulated countries that this problem assumes its most serious dimensions, farms of noneconomic size can also be found in countries which do not suffer from great congestion on the land. In the Philippines, for example, the average size of farm holdings is four hectares (10 acres) but more than half the farms are under two hectares, because of extremely unequal distribution of ownership and because of the concentration of population in Luzon and the Visayan islands.

Even in countries of very extensive cultivation with large reserves of land, overcultivated small holdings exist. Their part in the economy is a different one, in that the small holding may not be the sole source of the cultivator's income as it is in some parts of Asia, but a subsistence holding to supplement wages. Where such holdings are the sole source of the cultivator's income, they are usually overcultivated. A recent report of the international Bank for Reconstruction and Development has drawn attention to the ill effects of *minifundia*.[7]

In the sparsely populated countries of South America, there would appear good reason to believe that many holdings are uneconomically large. In Argentina, 85 percent of the privately held agricultural land is in estates larger than 500 hectares (1,250 acres), while 80 percent of the farm population own no land.[8] . . . A characteristic feature of the agrarian structure in Latin America is the large area of grazing land on the large estates, shown . . . by the large share of the total agricultural area (as distinct from the cultivated area) held by establishments of more than 1,000 hectares. The ownership of land on this scale tends to prevent more intensive cultivation and better forms of land utilization.[9]

FRAGMENTATION OF HOLDINGS

The splitting up of a farm holding into numerous different plots scattered over a wide area is a feature of the field layout in countries at all levels of economic development. It is not associated with any particular form of land tenure. It may be seen in countries as highly developed as Switzerland,

---

[6] Supreme Command, Allied Powers, *Japanese Land Reform Program,* Natural Resources Report 127 (Tokyo, 1950), p. 86. Prior to the reform, 34 percent of Japanese farms were under 1.2 acres.

[7] Excessive and uneconomic subdivision of land.—EDS.

[8] Wendell C. Gordon, *The Economy of Latin America* (New York, 1950), p. 35.

[9] See pp. 25 and 26 [in this report].

France, and southern Germany.[10] In Eastern Europe, notably in Poland and in the Balkan countries, the process has gone to extreme lengths; a farm of twelve acres, in Yugoslavia, for instance, may be divided into thirty separate plots. It is a widespread condition in Asia, particularly in India and China, and in the Middle Eastern countries.

Fragmentation has several causes. It originated in remote times from the traditional field layout in which holdings were divided into several strips located in different parts of a village. In the course of time these original strips have been divided and subdivided, as a result of the increase of the farm population and of inheritance laws which encourage the subdivision of land among many heirs. In Western Europe, where pressure of rural population is not acute, the principle of succession established in the Code Napoléon exercises a major influence, while in Eastern Europe and in Asia, the pressure of population would appear to be the predominant cause, though laws of succession reinforce an inevitable trend.

The evils of fragmentation need no emphasis: waste of time and effort, the impossibility of rational cultivation are obvious effects. None the less, the consolidation of holdings is not an easy reform to carry through. The conservatism of the peasant is one obstacle, the high cost per acre of surveying and exchanging many small plots is another. Even in a country so advanced as Switzerland the process of consolidation has been slow. . . .

TENANCY

Tenancy is a feature of the land-tenure system in many underdeveloped countries. The proportion of tenants to the number of farmers varies widely from one country to another. In Asia, the proportion as a rule is very high. As a broad generalization, it would appear that in Burma, China, India, and Japan, prior to the recent changes, about half the land was worked by tenants cultivating small holdings leased to them by landowners and that the majority of the cultivators were either tenants or part owners and part tenants. In Southeast Asia, tenancy is an important feature of the land system in Burma, Cochin China [South Vietnam], the Philippines, and central Thailand.

For the countries of the Middle East no estimate of the proportion of tenants to owners can be made owing to the lack of statistical data. There are some regions where peasant proprietorship is established. In Cyprus, Egypt, Lebanon, and Turkey most of the farmers own land. Apart from these countries, tenancy is widely prevalent. In Syria, it is estimated that about half the land is owned by large landowners and cultivated by small share tenants; in southern Iraq, large landowners own most of the land, letting it to share tenants through a series of intermediary lessees. In Iran, also, tenancy is the prevalent form. It is estimated that only 15 percent of the claimed

---

[10] Food and Agriculture Organization of the United Nations, *Consolidation of Fragmented Agricultural Holdings.* Agricultural Studies No. 11, prepared by B. O. Binns (Washington, D. C., September 1950).

land[11] belongs to small holders, as against about half to some 100,000 large landowners, the balance consisting of state domain or religious endowments. A sample survey conducted in 1949 showed that 60 percent of rural families owned no land at all, 25 percent owned less than one hectare, and 10 percent between one and three hectares.[12]

Tenancy is also a prevalent form of tenure in several South American countries, notably in Argentina, where some 60 percent of the land is leased to tenants. In Brazil, tenancy is not common, though sharecropping is increasing in the cotton and rice districts.

Tenancy is, of course, not in itself an unsatisfactory form of tenure, where rents are not excessive and where security of tenure is safeguarded by legislation. But these conditions, generally speaking, are lacking in underdeveloped countries, where tenancy systems are characterized by exorbitant rent charges and lack of security of tenure.

RENTS

Rents are payable in various forms: in money, in produce, and in labor. A common form in Asia is the proportionate produce or share rent, by which the landowner takes a proportion of the gross crop. This proportion is fixed sometimes by custom, sometimes by legal agreement. It varies according to whether the landlord provides the land only or whether he provides seed (or part of the seed), water, and ploughing livestock. It varies also according to local conditions, being higher where population pressure is greater.

Although there is much variation in practice, some examples of the level of rents may be given. The most commonly practiced division of the crop in India (before the recent changes) was half to the landlord and half to the peasant cultivator, who provided his own labor and that of his bullocks, while the landlord provided the land, and in some cases, half the seed.[13] In Indonesia, the Philippines, and Thailand, equal sharing of the crop between tenant and landlord seems to be a common practice. Rents in Ceylon vary from one-sixth to one-half of the crop, depending on the region and the type of crop. . . .

In those countries of Latin America where land is plentiful and labor scarce, share rents are considerably lower than they are in Asia and in the Middle East. Little statistical information on the subject is available, but from the 1948 legislation in Argentina for the compulsory reduction of rents to 20 percent of the gross crop, it appears that before the introduction of the law the customary share of the gross crop payable as rent was 38 percent for corn and 36 percent for wheat. In the countries of Latin America where land is less plentiful, rents are higher, and in some countries reach levels comparable with those prevailing in Asia.

The payment of rent in the form of fixed amounts of produce, or pay-

---

[11] Large areas are not claimed, and the ownership of many plots is in dispute.

[12] Gideon Hadary, "The Agrarian Reform Problem in Iran," *Middle East Journal* (spring issue, 1951).

[13] *Report of the Indian Famine Commission,* Vol. II, part IV, pp. 25-26.

ment in fixed sums of money, are less common forms of tenancy in under-developed countries. From the standpoint of the tenant, these forms are clearly preferable, since with a fixed rental he has an incentive to increase production and he gains the full benefit of any improvement on the land in so far as his tenancy is secure. Fixed produce rents were until recently the customary form of payment in Burma[14] and in Japan; they are still prevalent in many parts of India. In Japan, rents were assessed each year in advance of the harvest, and varied from 50 percent to 70 percent of the gross product.[15]

Where payment of rent is made on a fixed cash basis, the entire burden of risk is passed on to the cultivator. Cash rents are not, however, a general feature of tenancy systems in underdeveloped countries, and, as a rule, are found only in certain regions and for special crops. Such rents are extremely high. An investigation in Madras, for example, showed that in the districts of Guntur and West Godavari rents of 300 to 350 rupees per acre were charged on lands growing tobacco, and rents of 400 to 500 rupees per acre on lands growing sugar cane.[16]. . .

Labor rents are not a usual form of tenancy except in some countries of Latin America, in parts of India, and in Iran. In Latin America, this form is common in Bolivia, Chile, Colombia, Ecuador, Peru, and Venezuela, among estate laborers who receive a small piece of land from the estate owner in return for which they must work unpaid for a certain number of days per week. In remote regions of Iran, the feudal obligation of labor service on land cultivated by the landlord can still be exacted from villagers. In India, this form of payment is rare; it may be noted that the recent Bombay tenancy act prohibits it.

SECURITY OF TENURE

Cultivators who hold land under these forms of tenancy as a rule hold it on a customary basis, with no legal agreement to define their obligations. In India, the rights and obligations of tenants with occupancy rights are defined by legislation, but the actual cultivators, in many cases sharecroppers, enjoy no such legal protection. Where customary rights are not recognized, there is great insecurity and great poverty among the sharecroppers. In Burma, where holdings are generally larger than in India, and tenants are better off, there is also great insecurity; investigations in different parts of the country in the nineteen thirties showed that the number of tenants who had cultivated the same plot of land for more than three years represented, in most cases, only a quarter to a third of the total, while the number of those whose tenancy did not go back more than one year ranged between a sixth and a half.[17] In some countries of the Middle East, the peasant does

---

[14] B. O. Binns, *Agricultural Economy in Burma* (Rangoon, 1948), p. 17.

[15] Supreme Command, Allied Powers, *The Japanese Village in Transition,* Natural Resources Report 136, prepared by A. F. Raper (Tokyo, 1950), p. 249.

[16] A. V. Sayana. *Agrarian Problems of Madras Province* (Madras, 1949).

[17] J. Russell Andrus, *Burmese Economic Life* (Stanford, Calif.: Stanford University Press, 1947), p. 72.

not even cultivate the same plot of land from year to year; the landlord or his agent frequently gives the most fertile plots to favored tenants who please him in one way or another. The peasant therefore has usually one aim, to get the best out of his land during his short tenancy, regardless of the effect on the fertility of the soil. . . .

It is evident that the tenancy system in the conditions described above is a powerful obstacle to economic development, in three ways. In the first place, the tenant has little incentive to increase his output, since a large share in any such increase will accrue to the landowner, who has incurred no part of its cost. In the second place, the high share of the produce taken by the landowner may leave the peasant with a bare subsistence minimum, with no margin for investment; in a bad year, he gets more heavily in debt; in a good year, he can reduce his indebtedness. Thirdly, it means that wealth is held in the form of land, and that the accumulation of capital does not lead to productive investment. In Asia, the landowner is also a moneylender, and in this capacity depends more on interest on loans to small cultivators than on increased income from the improvement of land.

In such conditions it is important to emphasize that the existence of large-scale property ownership does not secure any of the advantages of large-scale operation or investment. The tenants secure no benefit of working with better equipment, or with better seed; their methods of work are the same as those of the small owner. Landowners are less interested in maintaining the fertility of the soil, or in increasing agricultural production, than in holding wealth in a secure form. Even in irrigated regions where the land-owner in theory provides water, the actual maintenance of ditches or channels must be undertaken by the tenants themselves, under the supervision of sublandlords or landowners' officials. In some countries, the landowners' share in the gross crop may not represent the sum total of the peasant's obligations: he may also have to surrender a further share to sublandlords, or to undertake the transportation of the landowner's share in the crop.

ESTATES AND PLANTATIONS

In the Caribbean, throughout South America, in Southeast Asia, in Ceylon, and in parts of East Africa, the agrarian structure is dominated by large estates. Unlike the large landholdings of Asia and the Middle East, referred to in the preceding section, these estates are large centrally managed and operated units of production, employing paid labor. This type of farm organization exists in widely differing conditions: in regions with much unused land and sparse population, and in regions where there is a great shortage of land and an excess of labor. In the former setting, the large estate may be a cattle ranch, covering great areas of grazing land. In the second setting, it is a plantation, with highly intensive cultivation, a large investment of capital and large labor requirements per acre. In their social effects both types of estate have a common feature: they offer the farm population unsatisfactory conditions of employment, and no degree of responsibility or initiative in management. In their economic effects they differ widely and must be considered separately.

LARGE ESTATES WITH EXTENSIVE AGRICULTURE

This type of farm organization, the *latifundia,* is a special feature of the agrarian structure of Latin America. With the exception of parts of Costa Rica, El Salvador, Haiti, and Mexico, large estates take up the greater part of the cultivable land area throughout the continent. In Latin America as a whole, about one and one half percent of the individual landholdings exceed 15,000 acres. The total of these holdings constitutes about 50 percent of all agricultural land. While much of the land is not suitable for crop production, a substantial proportion consists of idle lands that have been held for generations. Large plantations are also included in these great landholdings, but do not account for the greater part of the land so held. At the other extreme are the small landowners who practice subsistence farming on a few over-cultivated or unproductive acres. While there are also farmers with medium-sized holdings, the bulk of the remaining rural population consists of small tenants and landless laborers.

A peculiarity of the agrarian structure in Latin America is the absence of a clear line of division between the last two categories. In the more advanced countries, a proportion of the land is leased to tenant farmers on fixed rentals. But elsewhere tenancy arrangements are less systematized. When labor is scarce, squatters settle temporarily on the borders of an estate, cultivating a small area for their own requirements, and working on the estate without paying rent. A characteristic feature in many countries, notably in Bolivia, Chile, Guatemala, and Peru, is the patron-tenant relationship, under which the tenants *(colonos)* receive a piece of land for cultivation in return for a specified number of days' work per week on the estate. This relationship is associated with a low social status and an extremely low living standard for the farm workers.

Clearly, high levels of productive efficiency and rising standards of living are not likely to be achieved in an agrarian structure of this kind. Some of the effects of the tenancy system on farm productivity have already been considered in the preceding section. Here attention may be drawn to the broad effects of this form of agrarian structure on the utilization of land.

One obvious effect of this type of structure is that agricultural production is not adjusted to the demand for food, particularly foods of high nutritional value. The prevalence of large estates devoted to extensive grazing prevents an expansion of food production to meet the needs of the urban population, as well as the needs of the rural population itself. Throughout Latin America there is a shortage of dairy produce, which could be overcome by the introduction of better breeding stock, more attention to soil conditions, and better pasture management. Several South American countries, with a predominantly agricultural population and large land resources, import food for their urban population, part of which could be supplied by more intensive cultivation of the land, or by bringing idle land into cultivation. In Venezuela, for example, within easy reach of the capital now there are fertile regions utilized for extensive grazing which, with a different system of land tenure, could become a market garden area for Caracas. In other regions, all the produce from the areas of intensive cultivation on less fertile and steeply sloping hillsides has to be transported by human beings or pack animals across less intensively cultivated fertile areas to the town.[18]

The pattern of land utilization is thus the reverse of that which market conditions and natural resources require. The hillside land, which is best suited for pasture and woodland, is intensively cultivated for subsistence crops by hoe culture which destroys the top soil, while the valley floors, more suited for arable cultivation, are used for grazing. . . .

If the medium-sized farms played a larger part in the economy, there is reason to believe that the volume of agricultural production would rise, and that standards of living, both urban and rural, could be raised also. Provided that such farms could be established in the grazing lands, methods of land utilization could also be improved. In Brazil, the pattern of agricultural production would appear to be changing in favor of the small and medium-sized farms, of which the numbers are increasing, chiefly as a result of the tendency to sell off land from the older coffee plantations. Market conditions also favor this change. The one limiting factor to a further expansion of small and medium-sized holdings is everywhere the shortage of capital, which prevents the small tenant or subsistence cultivator from increasing the size of his holding. At present, however, the provision of capital to the small farmer is not adequately organized. Cooperative credit societies play very little part in the credit system. If this obstacle were removed, the conditions for the development of family farms in many regions would be highly favorable. Shortage of land is not a limiting factor in most Latin American countries, and, given adequate credit facilities, farms in the more advanced countries should be able to attain an economic size. In the less advanced countries, and in noncultivated areas, the provision of educational and technical assistance by the government and the extension of health services would be a necessary accompaniment of any change in the agrarian structure.

PLANTATIONS

Large estates which practice intensive farming cannot generally be said to impede economic development; on the contrary, large increases in land productivity and high yields per acre are usually a feature of the plantation system. The demand for a reform of the estate system in plantation economies is motivated by social considerations: the need for more equal distribution of income and greater possibilities of social advance.[19] In many regions today this type of agrarian structure gives rise to acute social tension.

The sugar plantation economy of the West Indies is one example among many which might be given of the conflicts which now center on this type of

---

[18] Raymond E. Crist, "Land Tenure Problems in Venezuela," *American Journal of Economics and Sociology* (New York, January 1942).

[19] International Labor Organization, Committee on Work on Plantations, *Basic Problems of Plantation Labour* (Geneva, 1950).

agrarian structure. In this region the disproportion between population and natural resouces is very great. The density of the farm population in the islands is among the highest in the world, ranging from thirty to fifty persons in agriculture for every hundred acres of cultivated land. The cultivated land is owned predominantly by large estates, either centrally operated or leased to tenants on small holdings. Such holdings are fragmented and occupy only a minor part of the total area. The sugar industry has been subject to long periods of depression, in which estates have gone out of cultivation and unemployment has increased.

In this situation the demand for land reform has taken the form of a demand for land settlement, as a means of relieving unemployment, and as a means of improving the conditions of employment. That there is possible scope for increasing employment by the division of the sugar-cane plantations seems unlikely since the cultivation of sugar cane requires an intensive use of labor to the acre. With the existing density of farm population it would appear that no reorganization of the agrarian structure is likely to increase the employment possibilities. None the less, from the social point of view, the plantation system is everywhere unpopular.

> The sugar industry in the West Indies has reached a political impasse. It cannot continue on its present basis because that basis gives too much political offence. This offence shows itself not only in a general atmosphere of hostility, but also in strikes, riots, the burning of canes, and in some colonies even in uncertainty from year to year whether the state of labour relations will permit the whole crop to be taken off. This state of tension is a luxury which the West Indies cannot afford. New forms of organization must be tried, and must be tried urgently.[20]

. . . In the Caribbean region, the main objections to the plantation system are social. In other regions of the world, however, the plantation system, in addition to similar social consequences, has had serious economic disadvantages. The sugar plantations of Java, for example, though successful in that they produced a high return on private capital, dominated the whole economy of the districts in which they were situated, and had adverse effects on crop rotation by facilitating the cultivation of sugar at the expense of rice. They also had unfavorable effects on food production for local needs and on the volume and conditions of employment. As a result, the area of sugar production in Java has long been a "classical stage for social unrest"[21] as it has been in the Caribbean. . . .

CREDIT AND AGRICULTURAL INDEBTEDNESS

High rates of interest and a high burden of farm debt are characteristic features of the agrarian structure in many underdeveloped agricultural coun-

---

[20] W. Arthur Lewis, *Issues in Land Settlement Policy,* a report to the Caribbean Commission West Indian Conference, 1950.

[21] For a full treatment of these effects, see E. H. Jacoby, *Agrarian Unrest in Southeast Asia* (Columbia University Press, New York, 1949), p. 56.

tries. Shortage of credit may be both cause and effect of poverty. It may be a cause, in that lack of ready money in the hands of the farmer prevents investment in the farm. But it may also be the effect or symptom of poverty, in that high interest rates and a high burden of debt may reflect a chronic insufficiency of the farmers' income, and a permanent tendency for consumption to outrun production. In the first case, the shortage of credit arises from the fact that the structure of the banking system is not adapted to the needs of the small farmer; to the extent that shortage of credit is due to such structural deficiencies, it can be remedied by the creation of special agencies to provide agricultural credit in appropriate forms. In the second case, where shortage of credit reflects a retrogressive condition in agricultural production, the provision of a better form of organization, though it may have useful results, is not likely to go to the roots of the problem of credit shortage.

There can be little doubt that in many agricultural countries the unsuitability of existing credit agencies is a major obstacle to the expansion of output on small farms.[22] The banking system is adjusted to meet the credit needs of large industrial concerns and commercial enterprises, and of agricultural production in so far as it is organized in large estates or plantations. The greater part of agricultural production, however, is in the hands of individuals or families conducting relatively small independent enterprises with very limited capital. "The huge number of producing units, the limited capital resources of the average producer, and the personal nature of each enterprise cause many of the difficulties inherent in the provision of agricultural credit."[22] The long production period in agriculture also tends to eliminate the ordinary commercial banks as direct sources of credit to farmers. "The financing of land purchase and other forms of long-term mortgage business are highly specialized forms of banking, but even medium-term loans of from three to five years' duration, which constitute the type of loan usually required by the small farmer for the purchase of cattle or machinery or for the execution of minor improvements, are outside the usual scope of most commercial banks."[22]

Consequently, the financing of small-scale agricultural production requires the provision of credit through special agencies. How great this need is can be seen from the sources of credit which are normally available to the peasant cultivator in the absence of special credit facilities. In Asia and in the Middle East he must obtain credit from one of three sources. One is the village shopkeeper who gives credit on day-to-day purchases at rates of 100 percent to 250 percent per annum; the second is the landlord who himself borrows from government agencies or moneylenders to lend to tenant cultivators against the security of the crop; the third is the middleman or moneylender. Moneylenders may be large commercial firms or small local lenders; according to a report of the Food and Agriculture Organization, "the degree of harshness and avarice displayed by a moneylender in his transac-

---

[22] Food and Agriculture Organization of the United Nations, *Agricultural Credit for Small Farmers* (Rome, 1951).

tions tends to vary inversely with the volume of his business."[23] In dealing with moneylenders small farmers are at a disadvantage as compared with the large landowners. In India,

> the large landowners can raise loans, due to approved security, at rates varying from 9 percent to 12 percent in most provinces. But in the case of small cultivators, who constitute the bulk of the debtors, rates charged are materially different. On secured loans, rates vary from 12 to 50 percent but on unsecured loans the rates may be up to 300 percent. The rate of interest charged per annum on grain loans is generally 50 percent, but rises up to 100 percent in several cases.[24]

. . . Apart from its effects on the farm population, the existence of high interest rates for short-term lending has far-reaching effects on the economy as a whole. Such rates are an obstacle to general economic development since clearly no ordinary investment in agricultural production or industrial enterprise can compete with the rate which the moneylender or landlord can get by short-term lending to cultivators. The habit of investment in land and the possibility of charging high interest rates because of the cultivators' need is "one of the key problems for increased mobilization of resources."[25]

The high burden of indebtedness, itself in part a result of unsatisfactory forms of land tenure, tends to increase the concentration of land property in the hands of large landowners and moneylenders. Since money is borrowed at high interest rates predominantly for consumption, farmers are usually unable to pay their debts and have no choice but to transfer the whole or part of their land to the moneylender and to become landless laborers or tenants. This process of growing concentration of ownership is particularly noticeable in Southeast Asia, where it was greatly accelerated by the price fall of the nineteen thirties. The classical example is Burma, where foreign moneylenders, the Chettiyar community and others, financed the expansion of rice cultivation in Lower Burma during the late nineteenth and early twentieth centuries. During the agricultural depression, the proportion of the total cultivated area owned by the Chettiyars in thirteen principal rice-growing districts of Lower Burma increased from 6 percent in 1930 to 25 percent in 1937; and the proportion of land owned by moneylending non-agriculturists increased from 19 percent in 1930 to 50 percent in 1937.[26] In India the same trend has long been apparent, and in the Middle Eastern countries also many large landholdings have been accumulated through the indebtedness of the fellaheen.[27]. . .

---

[23] Food and Agriculture Organization of the United Nations, *Agricultural Credit for Small Farmers.*

[24] International Labor Organization Preparatory Asian Regional Conference, *The Economic Background of Social Policy* (New Delhi, 1947), p. 46.

[25] United Nations Economic Commission for Asia and the Far East, *Mobilization of Domestic Capital through Financial Institutions of the ECAFE Region* (Lahore, United Nations, 1951), p. 8.

[26] J. Russell Andrus, *op. cit.,* p. 70.

[27] In Moslem countries, the tendency to accumulate land in this way is strengthened by a form of mortgage which is used to overcome the prohibition contained in the Koran against lending money or usury, the usufructuary mortgage, under which the mortgagor surrenders possession of the mortgaged land until the debt is liquidated.

The foregoing analysis shows that for many countries the agrarian structure, and in particular systems of land tenure, prevent a rise in the standard of living of small farmers and agricultural laborers and impede economic development, both by preventing the expansion of the food supply and by causing agriculture—usually the major economic activity of the country—to stagnate. Among the features of the agrarian structure which have most serious effects are the uneconomic size of farms; the maldistribution of land ownership with concentration of large estates insufficiently utilized and the landlessness of a large part of the rural population; the fragmentation of holdings; the high rents and insecurity of tenure characteristic of many tenancy systems; indebtedness and lack of adequate credit facilities for the small farmer; absence of settled title to land and water; plantation economies which offer low wages and no share in management to the cultivators; taxation policies which impose undue burdens on the small farmers and farm laborers; and in general an unsatisfactory set of incentives for a rising and sustained agricultural production. . . .

In countries where the relationship between population and land is unfavorable and where the density of the farm population is increasing, large estates generally take the form, not of owner-operated farms, but of large concentrations of small units of land leased to tenants. In these conditions the redistribution of land ownership involves a change in status which may lead to an improvement in the cultivator's income, and so raise his standard of living: it may also increase farm production by increasing both the cultivator's ability and his willingness to invest. But under such circumstances the redistribution of ownership will not be likely to enlarge the smaller holdings: the average farm size will still be very small, and large numbers of uneconomic holdings will still remain. Thus, land reform in these conditions will not in itself remove one of the most serious defects of the agrarian structure, the large number of excessively small farms, nor is it likely to offer land or fuller employment to most of the landless laborers. Such agrarian reform, though it may improve the condition of the farm population and may be a necessary stage in the improvement of the state of agriculture, cannot itself overcome the disparity between land and population.

To secure economic development in such circumstances will require a broader range of measures with specific emphasis on greater intensification and greater diversification of production to absorb the excess population. Intensification of agricultural production will require the provision of more capital to agriculture, since the labor-intensity of cultivation is already very high. In addition, some countries confronted with this situation have developed small-scale rural industries for the purpose of providing more employment in the rural community. Properly equipped and guided, such industries can fulfill a useful function, chiefly because they provide the basis for the development of industry on a wide scale. It is particularly at this point, however, that proposals for land reform may need to be integrated with economic development plans as a whole, for the correction of the disparity between land and population in such conditions requires action of a much broader character. It is beyond the scope of this report to explore the appropriate relationship between changes in agrarian structure on the one hand and plans for the general economic development of underdeveloped countries on the other. Clearly there will be, and indeed should be, interaction between the policies adopted in these two fields of action.[28]. . .

So far as generalization . . . is possible, it would appear that changes in the land tenure system are more likely to lead to a rise in the standard of living of the farmers and farm workers when they form part of a general program for the improvement of agricultural organization than when they are undertaken in isolation. Many of the benefits which might be expected to result from reform of the tenure system will be nullified if steps are not taken to provide appropriate services and facilities to the newly established small farmer, either individually or as a member of an association. It has been indicated that the provision of credit facilities, cooperative marketing, advisory technical and health services are among the major services and facilities needed. Where it is desired to enable small farmers to make use of better equipment, or to introduce new methods of farming, the organization of production in some form of producers' cooperatives has definite advantages. Tax policies designed to lighten the burden on the small farmer and on farm laborers should play an essential part in such general programs.

The conclusion may be drawn that in many countries conditions exist which could be improved by the adoption, with appropriate adjustments and safeguards, of general programs combining measures such as those described here. The extent to which measures for the reform of the agrarian structure, and in particular measures for the redistribution of land ownership, can be effective in promoting a general rise in the standard of living depends in great part on the relation between population, land, and other resources. Where there is no shortage of land, and where there are favorable market conditions, there is good reason to expect a change in the size of farms to be beneficial where it takes the form of redistributing land from large extensively cultivated estates to farm workers or tenants for more intensive operation in smaller (not necessarily very small) units. Where additional land can be brought under cultivation, surplus rural population can be absorbed and productive work can be provided for unemployed or underemployed members. The benefit derived from such a change would be influenced by the availability of such ancillary services and facilities as are noted above. Such change would be beneficial to the farm population in that the income of the farm workers would be raised and employment increased; it would be beneficial also to the economy as a whole in that better land utilization would increase the food supply and so raise the national income, thus enlarging the domestic market for industry. Where large owner-operated estates practice intensive farming, subdivision of large units might lead to a decline in production unless accompanied by further measures such as the establishment of cooperatives and the provision of credit, fertilizers, and machinery. In such a case new forms of organization would need to be considered.

[28] United Nations, *Measures for the Economic Development of Under-Developed Countries* (May 1951); see especially Ch. VIII, section on industry and agriculture. p. 58.

WILBERT E. MOORE

IIIIIIIIIIIIIIIIIIIIIIIIIIIIIIIIIIIIIIIIIIIIIIIIIIIIIIIIIIIIIIIIIIIIIIIIIIIIIIIIIIIIIIIIIIIIIIIIIIIIIIIIIIIIIIIIIIIIIIIIIIIIIIIIIIIIIIIIIIIIIIIIIIIIIIIIIIIIIIIIII

Labor Attitudes toward Industrialization in Underdeveloped Countries

In the literature on economic development a certain notable division between optimists and pessimists is apparent. This division is highly predictive of disciplinary origin. Economists—representatives of the "dismal science"—are customarily optimistic about economic growth and its social consequences. Anthropologists and sociologists are customarily pessimistic about the possibilities of economic growth and particularly about its consequences. Although possibly these fields attract different personality types— the manic and the depressed—it seems more likely that conventional theory and habits of thought explain the differences.

SOME CONTRASTING THEORY

THEORY OF MOTIVES AND CONSEQUENCES

Traditional economic theory has not been strongly concerned with attitudes and motives. Human attitudes and motives are simply assumed to be appropriate to rational choice of means effective for maximizing satisfactions as economically defined and measured. Human wants are thought to be essentially unlimited and human nature pretty much the same wherever encountered. A monetary market system coordinates the factors of production and allocates rewards, and financial incentives are assumed to be effective in allocating labor. The movement of labor between sectors of the economy is regarded as a function of its differential marginal productivity, which is principally determined by relative states of capitalization, technique, and, possibly, enterprise.

Given these assumptions, such hints of pessimism that economists have about economic growth in undeveloped areas could be expected to center on questions of capital, market organization, and entrepreneurial activity, but not on the willingness of potential workers to work. And since the economist has a normal prejudice toward the view that improvements in levels of pro-

From *American Economic Review* (May 1955), pp. 156-165. Reprinted by permission of the American Economic Association and the author.

duction and consumption are consistent with universal human aspirations, he is certainly inclined to optimism about the consequences of economic growth.

Anthropological and sociological theory stands in sharp contrast to this set of views. Attitudes and motives are of more central concern as variables, related to differential positions within any social system. The person is viewed as having been socialized in ways appropriate to differential social roles, to hold values appropriate to group activity and its survival, and to behave in ways that are "irrational" and "nonrational" as judged on economic grounds. Wants are thus viewed as limited and relative to social position. The social system is viewed as strongly resistant to change, in part because of secondary and tertiary consequences of changes in a complex functional network. If these considerations are important within societies, they are even more marked between them. To contrast with the economist's "similarity of human nature" assumption, the anthropologist or sociologist offers "cultural relativity." He is likely to emphasize differences in values and aspirations in space and time, and to be extremely reluctant to assume that Western experience can be used as a guide to behavior in Dahomey, Nepal, or even Peru.

Given these assumptions, such hints of optimism that anthropologists or sociologists have about economic growth in undeveloped areas could be expected to center on the adaptability of economic incentives and organization to traditional attitudes and patterns, and especially on the willingness of potential workers to work. And since the anthropologist-sociologist has a normal prejudice toward the view that bread or all purchasable goods and services are not enough to satisfy human values, he is certainly inclined to pessimism about the consequences of economic change.

These contrasts are, of course, moderately unfair to both professional groups. Many economists, and especially those who have studied labor mobility, the operation of labor markets, and worker behavior, have expressed strong misgivings about the assumptions of traditional theory. Many anthropologists and sociologists, and especially those who have studied the actual impact of modern economic forms in undeveloped areas, have noted the stresses and tensions in traditional systems and the considerable success of the new employment alternatives in recruiting labor.

THEORY OF ORGANIZED COOPERATION

The literature on economic development has included very little material on another aspect of theory, on which our two professional groups tend to disagree. There are differing views on the nature of business and industrial organization as related to the attitudes or motives of participants.

Traditional economic theory has little to say on this subject, since labor is viewed as allocated by market mechanisms and the relation between employer and employee the same in principle as any other economic contract. The productive efficiency of the division of labor has received consistent attention, but the problems associated with the authoritative coordination of labor implicit in factory organization remain relatively unexplored. Only in

Marxist economic theory and, more recently, in attempts to construct alternative theories of the labor movement and management-union relations have variables such as power and group loyalties been considered.

Traditional anthropological and sociological theory also has little to say on business or industrial organization, partly because of a concentration on the structure of society generally, partly because economic organization was thought to be the proper province of economists. Only in Weberian sociological theory and, more recently, in attempts to treat "the factory as a social system" have variables such as the authority of office, communication systems, and "informal organization" been considered.

Despite the recent and still somewhat peripheral attention given industrial organization in the disciplines we have been comparing, some differences between the disciplines can be detected. There is a notable tendency for the economist to emphasize—and exaggerate—individual, competitive aspirations, and an equally notable tendency for the anthropologist or sociologist to emphasize—and exaggerate—group, cooperative aspirations. If the economist's model of behavior tends to be the prize fight, the sociologist's model tends to be the quilting bee.

SOME EMPIRICAL EVIDENCE

Faced with such contrasting views of economic behavior and its motivational sources, the analyst may be forgiven some confusion and permitted to seek refuge in the data. Unfortunately, evidence has not been collected or analyzed in ways that permit a clear resolution of theoretical disputes. It is possible, however, to get some leverage on the issues by reference to the reported experience in the recruitment and utilization of labor in undeveloped areas.[1]

APATHY AND OPPOSITION

A considerable body of evidence runs contrary to the notions that human wants are unlimited, that financial incentives will transfer labor from nonindustrial to industrial pursuits, and thus that the potential worker may be viewed as welcoming release from traditional restraints. Some of this evidence can be interpreted in terms of "rational conduct," but not in terms of economic maximization. The potential worker in undeveloped areas is typically required to give up traditional forms of organization and reciprocal obligations that have combined to afford him security—both material and affective. The kinship system in any nonindustrial society is likely to provide a major barrier to individual mobility, because it is a social security system, because it is the focus of positive values and advantages, and because extended kin obligations are likely to reduce the effective appeal of individual

---

[1] This section represents a selective summary of a rather extensive discussion, with citations to the literature, in Wilbert E. Moore, *Industrialization and Labor* (Ithaca, N. Y.: Cornell University Press, 1951).

rewards. With an extended kinship system, if the individual faces adversity, his kinsmen are obliged to come to his aid. If he prospers, he is obliged to share his good fortune with great uncles and second cousins once removed. Industrialization breaks up such units, by geographical separation and more importantly by social separation.

The other side of the coin (an inappropriate metaphor in its connotations) is the lack of appreciation of the new status system. This may take the form of a relatively low and highly particular appeal of wages, often commented on with reference to "native" laborers, but also commented on by preclassical writers in economic theory with reference to workers in the early stages of the Industrial Revolution. The principle bears extension, however. New occupations simply do not fit traditional standards of prestige, or are valued negatively because they involve manual labor and merit placement irrespective of age, kinship position, caste, or other forms of "ascribed" status. To the extent that the potential worker operates as an independent producer, the change to wage labor involves some loss of "freedom," even if it offers higher rewards. To the extent that the potential worker operates as the equivalent of a craftsman, the change to factory employment is likely to involve a loss of socially recognized skills, of "workmanship," in the division of labor and its subordination to machine processes.

It would be hard to deny that a considerable part of this apathy and opposition is "reasonable," but equally hard to deny that its explanation lies partly in social standards and values that are badly served by wage incentives and by industrial forms of labor allocation.

THE FORCE OF CIRCUMSTANCES

If wages have a limited appeal to nonindustrial populations and new employments are negatively valued, it is not surprising that workers are more commonly "pushed" than "pulled" into modern forms of economic activity. Much of the "push" is in fact the largely unintentional consequence of external intervention. The successful attempt to reduce mortality has the effect of deteriorating man-land ratios, thus increasing agricultural underemployment and causing the landless and impoverished rural dweller to seek and accept other means of livelihood. The introduction of cheap manufactured goods may well displace the handicraft worker and make available an additional pool of workers, either directly or through increased dependency on agriculture. Even the trader may be displaced by large-scale distribution, or simply by more efficient organization of established markets.

The coercion of hunger does not exhaust the available pressures. Direct political coercion also has an extensive record, ranging from forced labor to the indirect coercion of taxation—a system which has been widely used as a device in colonial Africa.

Not all of the sources of pressure on the potential worker are so clearly external in origin. Any society exhibits some degree of tension and strain, some evidence of dissatisfaction. The presence of new alternatives may allow the deviant who seeks to evade the sanctions of the traditional order to escape from unwanted and oppressive controls.

Again it would be hard to deny that the attitudes implicit in these types of behavior are reasonable and again equally hard to deny that they do not correspond to notions of high sensitivity to slight differences in incentives and opportunity.

THE EFFICACY OF POSITIVE INDUCEMENTS

Not all of the empirical evidence involves such negative attitudes toward industrial labor. Wages do have an appeal, particularly if they can be used for goods and services that form part of traditional patterns of consumption and traditional modes of relationship. The transitional forms are many, and often oddly at variance with Western conceptions of market operation. The African from the native reserve who works long enough in the mines to pay his hut tax is presumably not highly integrated into a market system. He becomes slightly more integrated when he uses wages to buy cattle for use as a bride price, but this still has a distinctly exotic flavor. His behavior fits our standard conceptions better when he proves interested in all sorts of commercialized goods and services, but of course by then he is likely to have little in common with the values of the preindustrial community.

In some places other inducements to work seem to have operated, although not necessarily in the absence of financial incentives or contrary to their economically expected effect. Patriotic motives and other collective goals have formed the basis of appeals to workers in most industrial societies, with what effect it is difficult to say precisely. Certainly it is likely that a sense of voluntary participation in a worthwhile common enterprise offers some source of satisfaction to workers, although the standard forms of productive organization are not well adapted to making the use of such appeals very convincing. Here, it may be noted, is a possible positive role for union-type organization. Certainly the Communists have attempted to involve workers in undeveloped areas in the organized building of the new as well as the destroying of the old forms of social allegiance and power.

TOWARD A TENABLE THEORY

The discussion to this point implies the rejection of two extreme theoretical positions, both of which constitute alternatives available in the literature. The one extreme may be attributed to economics, although by no means all economists would subscribe. To traditional economists, labor attitudes are simply unproblematical, as they are adequately subsumed under assumptions of maximizing want satisfactions. The other extreme may be attributed to anthropology, in the same unrepresentative sense. To the anthropologist labor attitudes are so problematical, because they are so conditioned by variable cultures, that no other general statement about them is possible.

The attempt to formulate here the elements of a low-order theory rests upon the assumption that it is possible to give a general characterization to the undeveloped areas, to specify some of the crucial characteristics of modern economic organization, and to indicate some of the labor attitudes which are significant for transition from one to the other.

THE NATURE OF UNDEVELOPED AREAS

Although it is true that cultures differ, and in many ways, it is possible at a higher level of generalization to detect common and essential functions in the organization of society. Every society has provisions and rules for reproduction, socialization of the young, production and allocation of goods and services, adjustment to the nonhuman environment, maintenance of order. It is also possible to detect some common bases in cognitive orientations and values. All societies encourage some material aspirations (although not necessarily expanding and competitive), some rational, technical orientation to the use of the environment (although not necessarily innovative), and some positive value on health and length of life.

There are internal sources of tension and strain in all societies. The model of the perfectly integrated society is a useful analytical fiction for many purposes but ought not to be confused with primitive or agrarian societies. The sources of strain include, at least, uncertainties in socialization from generation to generation, chance innovations, and competing role demands given scarcities of time, treasure, and energy (or affective loyalty).

All undeveloped areas have already been disrupted in some form and degree by the "external" influence of Western patterns. The consequences of this interference may or may not be favorable to continuous economic development, but this will depend in some measure on the strategy adopted in view of the situation, as well as on the probable effects of influences so far.

One negative generalization is also negative in its implications for labor attitudes toward industrialization. Mobility on the basis of individual performance is generally not markedly present in undeveloped areas and does not generally form a part of the positive value system. Whether for the individual or for the system as a whole, continuity and not change is likely to be the major value.

THE NATURE OF MODERN ECONOMIC ORGANIZATION

It is now commonly recognized that modern economic enterprise depends upon a complex institutional structure. For purposes of simplification this may be partially summarized as a monetary-market mechanism for allocation of the factors of production and for achieving distribution of goods and services. For the nonhuman factors of production this involves at least transferable property rights and rational cost accounting. For the human factors of production this involves a wage system for putting into the hands of the specialized worker a medium for commanding the necessary and appropriate goods and services for himself and his dependents.

Although part of the division of labor will be coordinated by impersonal market mechanisms, the fixed capital and economies of scale in the productive unit characteristic of industrial organization imply also administrative coordination and the development of scales of authority.

If labor is to be rationally allocated and optimally utilized, it appears essential to select on the basis of technical competence, to coordinate on the basis of relationships specific to the interdependent tasks, and to tie rewards to types of activities. These rewards need not be exclusively financial and indeed rarely will be. All of the rewards imply a system of social ranking closely related to position in the productive system.

THE NATURE OF THE TRANSITION

Whether one looks at undeveloped areas or the most highly industrialized ones, a fundamental theoretical point is evident. That point is the great complexity of human motivation. Men will work for as many reasons as there are values to be served by such activity and will refuse to work where that serves his values. The fact that industrial systems emphasize values that are commanded in a market and incentives that provide monetary claims on a market should not blind us to the diversity of ends or the diversity of means for their satisfaction.

The effectiveness of wage incentives is relative to the availability of goods and services in the market that form part of the effective wants of workers. This is essentially a common-sense static principle. But it is quite limiting, and failure to recognize it accounts for some of the exasperation of observers of "irrational" natives. The worker in an undeveloped area is typically not accustomed to expect, or even to aspire to, any considerable raising of ceilings on his consumption and social position. And there are many wants typically not satisfiable by market mechanisms. So we have both limited demand and limited supply.

To translate this principle into dynamic terms, the available evidence indicates that we should expect an increase in demand through knowledge, education, and the development of new values, and in supply through the addition of goods newly available because of industrialization and the movement of services into the market.

This view of market-oriented attitudes can be broadened, with considerable benefit to its theoretical importance.

The effectiveness of the appeal of new employment alternatives is relative to the availability of need-satisfying rewards. This principle will still apply if material or even financial well-being is held constant. The potential rewards include prestige and esteem within an acceptable system of social valuation. This also is a common-sense static principle and is also limiting. The traditional system of social valuation will not typically include the new activities, and the latter compete or conflict with the former. Both change and choice tend to be devalued. If some relationship between wages and markets has been established, higher wage levels can be used as a principal lever on conservative traditions, and this has been their historic role. The private employer is unlikely to act "correctly" in this matter, and this may be a major area for governmental policy in economic development.

Over time, we should expect an increase in aspiration and the addition of values associated with status mobility, merit evaluation, and a realistic sense of choice and initiative. We should also expect new systems of social organization and stratification to which these aspirations and values are appropriate.

Economic growth, in so far as it is affected by labor attitudes, is likely to be radically retarded or contained by any one of several vicious circles. There is considerable evidence of a reciprocal relationship between low wages and low productivity, whether the connection works through mere physical energy or through more subtle frustration and apathy. The failure to detect and utilize convertible craft skills, the assumption that initially un- skilled local labor is incapable of training, and the adoption of the "color bar" as an extreme and open manifestation of these practices constitute waste in the short run and possible failure of continued development in the long run.

It appears evident that neither the available skills nor the appropriate attitudes can be assumed to be adequate among the potential workers in undeveloped areas. Growth seems to have been most rapid and most prob- ably continuous in the future where considerable resources have been devoted to formal education and where education and in-service training have been most closely geared to the skill demands of an industrial economy. Now, clearly, education in many colonial areas has encouraged anything but the development of mechanical and technical skills, and the opportunities for use of any such skills have not been made available to natives. That the new native leaders tend to be political agitators rather than economic administra- tors is scarcely surprising in view of colonial political and economic policies.

The development of positive labor attitudes toward industrialization would probably be enhanced by the fostering of a sense of social participa- tion as well as by the expansion of individual opportunity and the provision of amenities and security at least equivalent to those available in traditional organization. A sense of social participation has been consistently neglected even in advanced industrial societies. We do not know how flexible industrial organization may be made. But if economic development entails a revolu- tionary change in the organization of society, as it does, there is at least some theoretical reason for supposing that workers as well as managers or government officials might welcome positive participation in partial com- pensation for their uprooting.

In view of the complex richness of human motivation, the idea that economic and noneconomic incentives are necessarily competitive for a limited supply is untenable. Both may be increased simultaneously and con- tinuously within very high limits.

A METHODOLOGICAL NOTE

The reason for our interest in attitudes toward industrialization is clear and simple: we want to predict behavior relevant to the industrial mode of production. In stable situations the best predictor of behavior is previous behavior, and attitudes become "intervening variables" in the strict sense.

That is, attitudes are necessary but inferential phenomena required to explain the mechanism of action to answer the motivational "Why?"

To predict behavior in novel situations we are likely to want to attach greater significance to attitudes as prime variables. Attitudes may be defined as those psychological attributes of the individual which determine his tendencies to act in specified ways in specified situations. Such tendencies to act involve both a cognitive "definition of the situation" and an affective "evaluation of the situation." Any behavior we are likely to be interested in necessarily involves affective or evaluative components—at the very least, ends and criteria of choice.

Since attitudes are not directly observable phenomena, but some such variable is theoretically required, we are faced with some nasty methodological problems. We infer attitudes from behavior, including verbal behavior but not excluding other behavior. It is not necessarily true that verbal statements of attitudes are more reliable predictors than are previous relevant actions, if known. The reliability of attitude measures in forecasting subsequent behavior is rather low. But since representative samples of action are often difficult to observe, considerations of convenience lead many social scientists to rely on interview data. If the behavior to be predicted is itself novel, such as reactions to new modes of employment, we are likely to want several indexes of attitudes in the hope of increasing our probabilities. Given a population with some relevant knowledge and experience, personal or vicarious, it is possible that attitudes can be uncovered by techniques ranging from direct questions to projective tests. At best, we are relying on the human characteristics of generalization, transfer of learning, and transfer of values as ways of indicating probable reactions to new situations.

Asking direct questions is, of course, not the only recourse, but it is one appropriate partial procedure. The alternatives, which underlie most of the allegations in this paper, include extrapolation from "comparable" situations at other times and places, and "pure" functional analysis for locating types and degrees of vested interests, sources of tension and strain, and opportunistic and disgruntled elements in the preindustrial situation. Any prediction from any available procedure is somewhat hazardous, for experience is still the best teacher of social scientists, as it is of men.

KARL F. HELLEINER

||||||||||||||||||||||||||||||||||||||||||||||||||||||||||||||||||||||||||||||||||||||||||||||||||||||||||||||||

Moral Conditions of Economic Growth

. . . Man's capacity to satisfy his wants has grown from paleolithic times to the present, and more rapidly during the past few hundred years in

From *Journal of Economic History* (spring 1951), pp. 97-116, with omissions. Reprinted by permission of the Economic History Association and the author.

Western society than at any other time. Whether this increase in the means of want satisfaction has resulted in greater welfare would depend on at least two conditions, neither of which can be shown conclusively to be fulfilled. It would depend, first of all, on the beneficial character of man's wants. If his preponderant wants be injurious or destructive, a greater ability to satisfy them would, of course, be conducive to misery rather than well-being. But who is to pass judgment on the wisdom of our wants? Whether happiness has grown as a result of man's increased capacity to satisfy his wants would depend, secondly, on the rate at which the intensity and number of his desires have changed. If the intensity and number of man's desires had grown at a faster rate than his capacity to satisfy them, his greater opulence would avail him little: he would still be worse off than before. But, then, we have no means of measuring aggregate intensity of desire. These, of course, are old and familiar arguments. The decision to repeat them here was motivated by the belief that one of them, at any rate, will serve as a convenient starting point for the following exposition.

We suggested that wealth—defined as the capacity to satisfy one's wants—must be balanced against the number and intensity of one's desires. It follows that, if the objective of wealth-getting is the reduction of marginal utility of all consumers' goods and services, this aim can be accomplished by an alternative method; namely, by reducing the intensity of some or all of our desires. (A sufficiently drastic reduction would, of course, lead to the complete elimination of some wants.) The limiting case would be one in which the marginal utilities of all goods and services were reduced to zero. This "state of bliss," once more, can be approached along two different roads: by seeking control of *things,* or by gaining mastery of one's *self.* The first alternative consists in trying to make the means of want satisfaction so abundant that all our wants, even though their number and intensity be high and growing, could be completely satisfied. If all goods and services could be made available in unlimited quantities (if they could be made "free goods," like air and water), no desire would need to be left unsatisfied. The other alternative would be so to reduce the intensity of all our wants that they could be satiated with very limited means.

This second alternative calls for the development of spiritual powers and involves perfecting ascetic techniques. The practitioner of asceticism learns how to govern his soul (or, as he himself would probably put it, his "flesh"). He attempts to subdue his carnal desires: his sexual appetites, his craving for food and drink and sleep, as well as his subtler, but perhaps even more potent, wishes—his craving for distinction and power.

Of course, the ascetic cannot succeed in an absolute sense, short of committing suicide. He may deaden his conscious desires, but he cannot expect to escape his biological limitations. There exist physiological minima—probably variable between rather wide limits—that must be available to man as an organism, if he is to survive: a minimum of sleep and rest, a minimum of food and drink, a minimum of warmth. But to the extent that the ascetic deliberately reduces all his wants to these minimum requirements, his practice of renunciation is not only an alternative to wealth-getting but actually militates against economic progress. For, if man concentrates his efforts on the control of his self, he is not likely to pay much attention to making additions to, and improving, the means of want satisfaction. You cannot renounce "the kingdoms of the world and the glory of them" and yet retain an interest in their aggrandizement. A civilization that succumbs to the fascination of asceticism and embraces religious or philosophical gospels of self-denial is not likely to increase its wealth very much. A society that is dominated by ascetic ideals will, generally, be less interested in accumulation and innovation than one whose members give free rein to their appetites.

Conversely, any community that permits and encourages the intensity of desires to increase among its members will be stimulated into an intensification of efforts to achieve greater control of things. The creation of new wants as well as the intensification of existing ones will, under certain conditions, have the effect of promoting economic exertions.

Intensification and multiplication of wants can be promoted by various techniques and institutions. In modern society, advertising in all its forms ranks high among the forces that act as stimuli to man's intensity of desire. A more fundamental factor, however—and one that operates more or less in all civilized societies—is the existence of class divisions, and its concomitant, the awareness, that is, of differences in the standards of consumption. What Thorstein Veblen has termed "conspicuous consumption," the wish to equal and, if possible, to outdo one's neighbors, would tend to strengthen any existing intensity of wants. A society that encourages such a spirit of social emulation and the practice of "showing off" will not be one in which asceticism can thrive. Intensification rather than repression of desires will prevail, and people will rely on increments of the means of want satisfaction rather than on self-denial.

A further intensification of desires may be achieved by political propaganda. Anything that aims at promoting invidious comparisons and discontent among the underprivileged, be it the mild gospel of social reformers or the incendiary propaganda of revolutionary parties, is intrinsically opposed to the development of ascetic attitudes. Once man begins to question his "station in life" and the justice of the existing distribution of property and income, his desire "to do something about it" awakens. Remedial action, as will be seen presently, may consist in a resort to violence, that is, to revolutionary or criminal action, or to war; or else it may involve the nonviolent exercise of political power, leading to transfer of income and property by legislation, to the acquisition of monopoly positions through graft and "pull," and so on. However, the effect of social envy and discontent may also lead to increased economic efforts, a fixed determination to succeed through hard work, saving, or innovation.

Before developing the argument any further it becomes necessary to introduce an important qualification. Ascetic attitudes may, but need not, be inspired by religious feelings and beliefs: they can also be produced by certain forms of hedonist philosophy. If happiness be defined as freedom from pain, the most promising method of achieving it is to raise the psychical "threshold"; by so doing the ascetic hedonist expects to become independent of the outside world. He attempts to subdue his desires, because he yearns for the bliss which freedom from want promises to give. In other words, mastery over one's passions and appetites need not be, as it is in Christianity, a *prerequisite* of salvation: freedom from the pangs of desire can be equated with salvation *itself*. This, in a certain sense, is the attitude of the great Hindu religions;[1] and it was the attitude underlying some of the most influential philosophical schools of later antiquity. Both the Epicurean and the Stoic—not to mention the Cynic—strove to attain happiness by so disciplining the soul that it should become impervious to the influences of the external world. . . .

However, this attitude of prudent restraint and serene detachment gradually shaded off into something much cruder and fiercer. The mildly ascetic tenets which had been developed in a spirit of aristocratic rationalism by the Stoic and Epicurean philosophers of Hellenistic times were embraced eagerly by coarser minds in the late Roman period. That is to say, those ancient doctrines of philosophical resignation tended to form a compound with heterogeneous elements which betray their origin from among the downtrodden and frustrated proletariat of the Near East. In this process, renunciation came to be regarded as meritorious in a metaphysical and religious sense. Once it becomes endowed with sacrificial significance, however, self-denial acquires a much higher degree of intensity. Thus a vulgarized asceticism finally blossomed forth in the fantastic and—to us—absurd practices of Eastern monasticism, described by Edward Gibbon in his celebrated thirty-seventh chapter of the *Decline and Fall of the Roman Empire.* Self-control became "mortification of the flesh." The ascetic virtuoso, if his feats of devotion and self-denial could not be imitated by the multitude, was nevertheless regarded as the religious ideal. Sexual continence, severe fasts, self-inflicted punishments of the body, and other acts of fanatical self-chastisement came to be admired. Asceticism became a means of seeking the social distinction and esteem which in other societies could be secured by conspicuous consumption, and it was accepted as the surest road to salvation.

Whether and how seriously this intensification of the ascetic spirit and practice in late Roman times militated against economic growth is a question that cannot easily be answered on a priori grounds. For even if he leaves aside the most intractable question of fact—namely, to what extent the behavior of the broad masses was influenced by the spread of fanatical asceticism[2]—the historian finds himself confronted with a curious sociological

---

[1] See Albert Schweitzer, *Indian Thought and Its Development,* trans. Mrs. Charles E. B. Russell, 2d ed. (London: Hodder & Stoughton, 1936).

[2] The statement of a Christian writer of the second half of the fourth century, Tyrannius Rufinus, that in Egypt the number of monks was nearly equal to the remainder of the people (Edward Gibbon, *The Decline and Fall of the Roman Empire* [Modern Library; New York: Random House], II, p. 4, n. 15) was undoubtedly a gross exaggeration. But we may give some credence to other contemporary authors (quoted by Gibbon), all of whom testify to the multitude of anchorites and monasteries in various regions of the Hellenistic world

paradox. On the one hand, there can be little doubt that the prevalence of ascetic ideals and practices did sap the economic energies of late Roman society. The withdrawal from production of a sizable number of men and women—even though these monks and nuns were very modest consumers—must have made some difference to the size of the disposable surplus of society. Had it been only the idle rich exchanging one life of leisure for another, the loss of labor would not have been very serious to the economy. But no less a person than St. Augustine testifies to the fact that the monastic communities recruited themselves from all ranks of society, and more especially from the working classes: *"ex vita rusticana, et ex opificum exercitatione, et plebeio labore."*[3] Peasants, skilled artisans, and common laborers asked for, and secured, admission to monasteries.[4] Of even greater economic importance than the loss of labor was the fact referred to previously, that under the influence of ascetic ideas man's interest in wealth-getting must have generally been weakened very seriously.

On the other hand, these negative factors may have been offset by positive elements whose influence on man's economic behavior seems to have been rather powerful in the long run. Ascetic self-denial may, but need not, be connected with expectations of an existence beyond the grave. In Christianity, the renunciation of earthly happiness was indeed the price paid by the faithful for a life of future bliss in heaven—a life not seldom conceived in grossly material terms. To the extent that the Christian religion thus held out to its followers the prospect of greater returns in time to come for a temporary abstinence from enjoyment, it may be supposed to have acted as a strong agent not only of spiritual but of economic discipline. "Waiting," "postponement of satisfaction" for the sake of greater returns at a later date, is the essential prerequisite of accumulation. By cultivating this ability to wait, ascetic Christianity provided an excellent moral training ground for its adherents. Accustomed to balance future benefits against present sacrifices, the Christian ascetic developed the very mental traits which, if transferred to the economic field, enabled him to save and accumulate. In this sense, Christianity—and not only its later Puritan variety—must be classified among the positive factors of economic growth.

The paradox that man, through the practice of self-denial, should have increased his capacity to produce the very satisfactions which he was so eager to renounce becomes even more glaring when one considers the attitude of the religiously inspired ascetic toward leisure. As indicated above, the hedonist ascetic, while imposing upon himself restraints and controls of various kinds for the sake of spiritual freedom, yet saw no reason for denying himself enjoyment of leisure. However, as soon as renunciation assumed the positive character of a religious sacrifice, the range of ascetic practices tended

---

[3] St. Augustine, *De opere monachorum,* Ch. 22, quoted by Gibbon, II, p. 7, n. 30.

[4] To many of these people the attractions of monastic life may not have been purely spiritual. The economic and social security of the cloister must often have appeared preferable to the hardships and dangers of worldly life. To oppressed tenant farmers and poor mechanics the ascetic discipline to which they had to submit may have seemed sweet and lenient, compared with the toil and misery of their previous existence.

to broaden. In his search for ever new and more exacting methods of self-chastisement, the religious perfectionist was bound to discover the ascetic possibilties of work. Looked upon as a curse by Greeks and Jews alike, manual labor came to be regarded as yet another powerful means of mortification. . . .

That the combination of Puritan frugality and industry was productive of that high rate of accumulation which was one of the main prerequisites of nascent capitalism is a thesis too well known to require further elaboration.[5] But we would urge that the "inner-worldly asceticism" of the Protestant sects and churches was rooted in much more ancient habits and beliefs. At what point the purely passive "asceticism of renunciation" acquired that high intensity which finally gave birth to an "asceticism of work" cannot be ascertained. It is known that the manufacture of wooden sandals and the weaving of mats and baskets from the fibers of palm leaves were practiced among the monks of Egypt. But whether work of this sort was regarded as intrinsically meritorious, or whether it merely served the purpose of maintaining the monastic community, must remain doubtful. It is quite certain, however, that in Western monasticism, among the Benedictines and their offshoots, manual and mental labor assumed the character of a holy duty, just like prayers, fasts, or vigils. To quote from the *Rule of St. Benedict of Nursia* (ca. 480-ca. 553). "Idleness is the enemy of the soul. And therefore, at fixed times, the brothers ought to be occupied in manual labour; and again, at fixed times, in sacred reading. . . . But, if the exigency of poverty of the place demands that they be occupied . . . in picking fruits, they shall not be dismayed: for then they are truly monks if they live by the labours of their hands; as did also our fathers and the apostles."[6]

From the viewpoint of economic growth it was of supreme importance that in Western society religion should have provided a strong incentive for that form of self-denial which we have termed "asceticism of work." For it is highly doubtful whether man's desire to gain control of "things" would have been strong enough to produce any great and sustained exertions. It was no less a social scientist than Malthus who observed that "an efficient taste for luxuries and conveniences, that is, such a taste as will properly stimulate industry, . . . is a plant of slow growth."[7] In other words, an attitude of resignation, involving underconsumption of goods and services combined with overconsumption of leisure, so far from requiring spiritual motives, seems to have been the "natural" attitude of man in most societies over long stretches of history. What Malthus calls "indolence" is much more prevalent than is assumed by the modern economist, who is too prone to accept uncritically the premise of the insatiability of wants. (Of this "precapitalist" attitude Max Weber has given some striking illustrations.) It is

---

[5] See, for instance, Max Weber, *The Protestant Ethic and the Spirit of Capitalism* (London: G. Allen & Unwin, 1930), and R. H. Tawney, *Religion and the Rise of Capitalism* (Harmondsworth, Eng.: Pelican Books, 1938).

[6] *Introduction to Contemporary Civilization: A Source Book* (New York: Columbia University Press, 1946), I, pp. 139 f.

[7] Thomas Robert Malthus, *Principles of Political Economy*, 2d. ed. (London School of Economics Reprints), p. 321.

only when religious inspiration furnishes incentives for both forms of self-denial—restriction of consumption *and* of leisure—that asceticism results in accumulation.

Adam Smith's confident reference to people's "universal, continual, and uninterrupted effort to better their own condition, . . . which has maintained . . . progress . . . towards opulence and improvement"[8] would seem to be a correct appraisal of man's attitude in modern economic society. But the principle is not of universal validity. What Adam Smith treats as a powerful natural urge, comparable to man's desire to propagate his species, namely, people's willingness to exert themselves for the sake of increasing their means of want satisfaction, is by no means an invariant force.[9] As has been shown, active pursuit of wealth may appear so hopeless that man has recourse to the alternative of resignation.

But even when he did not altogether refuse to entertain hopes of achieving control of things through efforts of his own, it would seem that it rarely occurred to man in preindustrial society that there was any road to great opulence and power, except the one described in legends and fairy tales: riches are gained by means of magic. Aladdin's lamp, which guides its bearer to treasures beyond the dreams of avarice; the secret knowledge, revealed by a kobold, of how to spin straw into gold; gifts bestowed by a fairy godmother; or a pact with the devil—these are some of the sources of wealth; and as if the narrator wished to emphasize the futility of all rational efforts, he often represents the laziest and stupidest fellow as the recipient of such supernatural favors. . . .

The economic historian cannot but pronounce the attempt to control things by means of magic futile. As far as we can judge, incantations, spells, and other such magic performances are ineffectual as such, though it must be admitted that the confidence which the practitioner of magic derives from his activities can be an important psychological element of success in other lines of endeavor. It should also be pointed out that magic practices have, as a matter of fact, yielded positive results on more than one occasion—accidentally, as it were. The domestication of animals and the growing of cereals may have originated in what were, in the beginning, magic rites.[10] The alchemist, if he did not find the philosophers' stone, nor the elixir of life, yet made significant contributions to industrial chemistry. However, when all is said it still remains true that magic and rational technics are, to some extent, alternatives, and that reliance on the former militates against the development of the latter. If you are confident that you can dominate and direct supernatural forces, you will, *ceteris paribus,* pay less attention and devote less effort to the perfection of your material and intellectual equipment. A community that has recourse to magical incantations for the cure of an illness is not likely to develop great medical or surgical skill. A

---

[8] Adam Smith, *An Inquiry into the Nature and Causes of the Wealth of Nations,* ed. Edwin Cannan (Modern Library; New York: Random House), p. 329.

[9] See James S. Duesenberry, "Some Aspects of the Theory of Economic Development," *Explorations in Entrepreneurial History,* III (1950), p. 72.

[10] See Fritz Heichelheim, *Wirtschaftsgeschichte des Altertums* (Leiden: A. W. Siithoff. 1938). I, pp. 38 ff. and 45 ff.

society that believes in the efficacy of the rain maker's rites will tend to neglect such means of environmental control as water wheels and irrigation ditches. The conjurer who hopes to discover hidden hoards of gold with the help of ghosts will hardly waste his time in the mine and the smelting house.

If the foregoing premise be accepted as valid, the unique success of Western civilization in matters economic would seem to be attributable, among other things, to the fact that recourse to magic, while it was never blocked completely, was nevertheless rendered increasingly difficult to European man. It cannot be the purpose of this paper to trace in any detail the long and complex process that led to this relative repression of magical beliefs and practices in Western society. Suffice it to point to two main factors.

It has often been remarked that ordinarily no evidence of past failures is likely to discourage the practitioner of magic. "If heaven and earth do not answer him, the rite is simply unconsummated; it was not therefore a 'mistake.' Its failure can be redeemed by finding some extenuating circumstance, some 'counter-charm' that explains the miscarriage."[11] However, members of a society whose intellectual heritage comprised some elements, at least, of Greek rationalism, with its notion of an orderly universe, were bound sooner or later to develop fundamental doubts about the efficacy of magical technics. The belief that human acts should be capable of deflecting the course of events could hardly be reconciled with the idea of a cosmos governed throughout by Divine Providence. The mere attempt to interfere with God's immutable decrees must have appeared wanton and wicked.

At this point the rationalist legacy of Greece readily combined with the religious traditions of monotheistic Judaism to produce a strong antimagical bias in Christianity. To coerce the deity apparently did not seem impossible to the Jewish believer; but it was regarded as an abomination. Hence the strict prohibition against "graven images," which might be used to conjure with, as well as against pronouncing the name of Yahweh, the sounding of which might give the mortal power over the godhead.[12] This Jewish abhorrence of magic was passed on to Christianity.

To be sure, neither rational doubts about the efficacy of magical practices nor religious scruples about their propriety were strong enough to cause their complete disappearance in Western civilization. Impatient of the slow and scanty returns of ordinary efforts, man was always tempted to seek a short cut to wealth, power, and knowledge, but perhaps never more passionately than in the age of the Renaissance.

> Philosophy is odious and obscure;
> Both law and physic are for petty wits;
> Divinity is basest of the three. . . .
> 'Tis magic, magic, that hath ravished me.

---

[11] Suzanne K. Langer, *Philosophy in a New Key* (Cambridge, Mass.: Harvard University Press, 1957), p. 129.

[12] On this point see Max Weber, *Gesammelte Aufsätze zur Religionssoziologie* (Tübingen: Mohr, 1921), III, pp. 233 ff.

However, when Christopher Marlowe put these words into the mouth of Doctor Faustus, the days of magic as a serious competitor to rational methods of controlling things were already numbered. On the one hand, as *magia naturalis,* the secret arts were shading off into the new Science of Nature, or else were paling into innocuous philosophical speculations. In sixteenth-century Cracow, magic was even made a subject of instruction at the university. On the other hand, the sinister features of magic became ever more pronounced. At this end of the scale, the quest for wealth and power degenerated into "black magic," the secret lore of the underworld of vagrants, gypsies, hangmen, and criminals.[13] As such, magical practices finally became subject to ruthless suppression by public authority. The trials for witchcraft, which are so characteristic a feature of the sixteenth and seventeenth centuries, were not entirely the product of mass delusion. They were attempts— albeit with inappropriate means—to stamp out the cankerous growth of fiendish and sacrilegious practices. For the rest, belief in magic of any sort had only scant chances of survival in an age whose thought and action came to be governed more and more by the principles of experimental science.[14] (What looks like a curious recrudescence of magic in the Age of Reason— its pretended use by such notorious eighteenth-century impostors as the Count of St. Germain and Cagliostro—belongs in a different category altogether.)

When Western man finally recognized the futility of the magical arts, or at any rate, like Prospero, renounced their exercise—

> .... this rough magic
> I here abjure: ....
> .... I'll break my staff,
> Bury it certain fathoms in the earth,
> And, deeper than did ever plummet sound,
> I'll drown my book.

—pursuit of gain became a rational affair, as far as methods were concerned. But wealth-getting by rational means is not limited to those forms of behavior that are commonly classified as "productive," such as work, real investment, resource allocation, and the like. Alternative modes of action, alluded to once or twice previously, are force and fraud.

It should hardly be necessary to emphasize that the employment of violence, actual or potential, as a means of enrichment must be distinguished from the "feudal" interest in power for power's sake. The exercise of power has a strong fascination for man, quite apart from the greater ability to

---

[13] See Otto Brunner, *Adeliges Landleben und europäischer Geist. Leben und Werk Wolf Helmhards von Hohberg, 1612-1688* (Salzburg: O. Müller, 1949), pp. 72 f.

[14] Enlightened opinion on the subject was summarized by Daniel Defoe in the preface to his *A System of Magick or a History of the Black Art* (London, 1727) in these words: "I see no great Harm in our present Pretenders to Magick, if the poor People could but keep their Money in their Pockets; and that they should have their Pockets pick'd by such an unperforming, unmeaning, ignorant Crew as these are, is the only Magick that I can find in the whole Science."

satisfy his wants which its possession entails. In the actual mechanism of motivation these two aspects cannot easily be separated; but, theoretically, the instrumental character of force can and must be considered by itself.

It goes without saying that economic history records innumerable instances of transfer of wealth by means other than voluntary exchange of goods and services. War, piracy, robbery, and similar acts of violence have always been resorted to by individuals and groups with the object of increasing their means of want satisfaction.[15] By despoiling conquered foes of their land or their movable possessions, by imposing tributes and war indemnities on the vanquished, or by exacting from them monopolistic trading privileges, men have often gained more wealth than they could have obtained had they applied themselves and their capital resources to peaceful pursuits. Likewise with treachery and fraud: cheating can be used quite successfully to *"corriger la fortune."*

Nor would it be correct to argue that violence and fraud have served merely to bring about a redistribution of *existing* means of want satisfaction. Increments of total wealth can be created by means of coercion. For instance, by reducing human beings to slavery it is possible to make them perform labor services for their masters, not only exceeding in value the outlay for their keep, but also in excess of what they might have produced in the absence of compulsion. Power can also be used to bring about a higher rate of accumulation than could be achieved voluntarily. Compulsory saving—whether it be induced directly, by confiscatory taxation, or indirectly, by maintaining a grossly unequal distribution of property and income—is in the last analysis a consequence of the exercise of political power.

At this point it should be recalled once more that peaceful and "honest" means of wealth-getting on the one hand and the acquisition of property or income by violence and fraud on the other are alternatives. To the extent that acquisition of wealth by violent or dishonest means becomes difficult in practice and morally objectionable, the range of acts conducive to wealth-getting narrows down to "economic" behavior, that is, to productive labor, saving, and innovation. In other words, the ease with which an individual or a group can possess themselves of the means of want satisfaction by "non-economic" methods is likely to stand in inverse ratio to the effort bestowed on "productive" pursuits.

The gradual reduction and partial elimination of violence in Western society—or rather the monopolizing of *legitimate* violence in the hands of the State—as well as the growing subtlety in the legal and moral distinctions between "honest" and "dishonest" acts, these are processes much too complex to be traced in any detail within the scope of this paper. Suffice it to say that violent forms of acquisition met with only scant moral disapproval in early societies. If directed against a member of the in-group, transfer of

---

[15] This badly neglected "plutological" aspect of war has been made the subject of a highly stimulating study by Frederic C. Lane, "The Economic Meaning of War and Protection," *Journal of Social Philosophy and Jurisprudence*, VII (1942), pp. 254 ff.

wealth by means of force would be resisted, no doubt. But the alien aggressor—the pirate, the robber, the slave raider—did not "lose face" on account of his activities. He would be an object of hatred and fear: a foe, but not a criminal. The naivete and lack of moral concern with which strangers inquired of Ulysses and his companions whether they were merchants or pirates has often been commented upon.

But even as recently as the European Middle Ages, the scope accorded to lawful violence within society was so broad that modern students of feudal institutions long failed to grasp their essential meaning. Oligopolistic dispersion of coercive power, so far from being accepted as a primary datum of medieval society, was liable to be interpreted as the result of a degenerative process. Historians and lawyers whose notions of sovereignty were derived from observations of modern bodies politic could not but regard feudal lordship as usurpation of "public" rights, and feudal warfare as lawlessness, made possible by the deplorable "weakness" of the Crown. This anachronistic interpretation of medieval history has now been decisively refuted.[16] We have come to realize that the medieval world was indeed pervaded by violence: yet not because the Middle Ages were times of "feudal anarchy," but for the reason that particles of sovereignty, entailing the right to exercise force, were vested in a very large number of individuals and corporations.

Since then, the lawful exercise of violence by persons other than agents of the State has been all but eliminated. Only the strictly limited right of using force in self-defense has survived.[17] What Friedrich von Wieser once called the "law of diminishing force" in history[18] has been operative in Western society with remarkable vigor; and its most significant manifestation was the rise of the modern State. Its emergence created conditions uniquely favorable to economic growth. In the first place, the suppression of violence within society helped to establish security, factual as well as psychological, an element that is essential to accumulation and risk taking.[19] The concentration of lawful force in the hands of the national government, secondly, must have tended to channel man's acquisitive energies more and more into "productive" pursuits. When all forms of "private" violence became not only increasingly risky but downright criminal acts, man had to fall back on what remained the only licit means of wealth getting, namely, industry, thrift, and enterprise.

This tendency to concentrate on "economic" methods of acquisition must have been strengthened by sustained and increasingly successful efforts

---

[16] See Otto Brunner, *Land und Herrschaft,* 3d ed. (Brünn, Munich, Vienna: R. M. Rohrer, 1943).

[17] In recent times, however, an increasingly broad interpretation of labor's right to "peaceful" picketing threatens to introduce an element of neofeudalism—nor can it be said to be the only one—into modern society.

[18] Friedrich von Wieser, *Das Gesetz der Macht* (Vienna: J. Springer, 1926), pp. 254 ff.

[19] See W. T. Easterbrook, "The Climate of Enterprise," *American Economic Review, Papers and Proceedings,* XXXIX (1949), pp. 322 ff.

on the part of the State, and more especially the Church, to block off still another "nonproductive" source of gain, namely, fraud in all its forms. The medieval Church has often received praise or blame (depending on the political and social predilections of the writers) for having retarded the growth of modern economic institutions by its conservative doctrines on price and interest. However, before friends and foes of capitalism have it out, they would do well to re-examine the question of fact. For it is at least arguable that the teachings of the Church did as much and more to promote genuine enterprise than they did to obstruct it. As far as the practical application of the usury laws in the confessional and the courts Christian was concerned, that was demonstrably the case. The prohibition of interest may have interfered with the business of petty pawnbrokers and people of that ilk; it did little to hamper the dealings of the great merchant bankers.[20] Indeed, since the Church objected to lending at a profit only if the creditor's gain was certain, but did not disapprove of putting money "in adventure,"[21] the usury laws, while preventing the concentration of capital in the hands of a class of passive *rentiers,* must have encouraged the practice of risk taking and stimulated the spirit of enterprise.

The ecclesiastical doctrines on *pretium justum,* aimed as they were, first and foremost, against monopolistic malpractices, must have helped materially to strengthen the competitive elements in the economy. But they did more than that. The subtle disquisitions of theologians and canon lawyers on questions of right and wrong in buying and selling undoubtedly did much to sharpen the moral sense of confessors and popular preachers, and, through them, to arouse the dormant conscience of their penitents or listeners. At the same time, the labored efforts of medieval writers on business ethics to prove that certain obviously crooked practices are morally objectionable are a source of constant wonderment to the modern reader. Should it really have been necessary for St. Thomas Aquinas to demonstrate with the help of Holy Writ that "if anyone knowingly make use of a faulty measure in selling, he is guilty of fraud"?[22] However, all those long-winded arguments merely show that the moralists deemed it advisable to be as explicit as possible, because people's sense of right and wrong in matters of business was deplorably deficient. Desiderius Erasmus, the famous Dutch humanist—a mild-mannered man—has this to say of the low moral caliber of the merchants at the beginning of the sixteenth century: "The most foolish and sordid of all are your merchants, in that they carry on the most sordid business of all, and this by the most sordid methods; for on occasion they lie, they steal, they

---

[20] See Benjamin N. Nelson, "The Usurer and the Merchant Prince: Italian Businessmen and the Ecclesiastical Law of Restitution," *The Tasks of Economic History* (Supplemental Issue of *The Journal of Economic History*), VII (1947), pp. 104 ff.

[21] See Raymond de Roover, *Money, Banking and Credit in Mediaeval Bruges* (Cambridge: The Mediaeval Academy of America, 1948), pp. 54 and 305 ff.

[22] *The "Summa Theologica" of St. Thomas Aquinas,* literally translated by fathers of the English Dominican province, Part II² (London: Burns Oates & Washbourne, 1918), p. 321 (quaestio LXXVII, art. 2).

cheat, they impose on the public. Yet they make themselves men of importance—because they have gold rings on their fingers."[23]

Need we assert that such an atmosphere of deceit and trickery—the moral climate of an Oriental bazaar—would have been anything but favorable to the growth of an industrial civilization? The businessman who unscrupulously and with impunity exploits the ignorance of his trading partners is no more likely to pay much attention to technical or managerial improvements than the feudal noble who enriches himself by means of violence and extortion. However, the work of moral education which was carried on indefatigably from the pulpit and in the confessional began gradually to bear fruit. The Church's insistence on honesty in business deals made it imperative to play the economic game according to more subtle rules. It would seem that a new type of businessman was emerging, men who relied for their gain on superior technology and managerial efficiency rather than on their powers of deceitful persuasion and unscrupulous misrepresentation. Daniel Defoe distinguished the new type from the old in the following memorable sentences: "Masters of more cunning than their neighbours turn their thoughts to private methods of trick and cheat. . . . Others turn their thoughts to honest invention, founded upon the platform of ingenuity and integrity. . . . A mere projector, then, is a contemptible thing. . . . But the honest projector is he who, having by fair and plain principles of sense, honesty and ingenuity brought any contrivance to a suitable perfection, . . . turns his project into execution, and contents himself with the real produce of his invention."[24] Here we have, it would seem, one of the first definitions of the genuine "entrepreneur," as distinguished from the adventurer and trickster.

It has been the purpose of this paper to isolate a number of factors whose operation in Western society has tended to transform, repress, or eliminate certain modes of behavior that are altogether inimical to wealth-getting, or else are less effective alternatives to "productive" pursuits. It has been shown that passive renunciation, under the impact of ascetic Christianity, assumed the character of religiously meritorious self-denial, thus leading to underconsumption not only of goods and services but also of leisure. It has also been made apparent that magical, violent, and fraudulent forms of acquisition not only met growing opposition from secular as well as ecclesiastical authorities but encountered strong moral inhibitions. This gradual elimination of practices that were largely futile or misguided as methods of increasing total wealth deserves to be considered an important agent of secular economic growth. Their elimination channeled man's endeavor "to better himself" toward more promising lines of conduct, and was instrumental in creating the kind of world we live in: a world full of new perils, to be sure, but one that has at least a chance to do away with dire poverty.

---

[23] Desiderius Erasmus, *The Praise of Folly,* trans. Hoyt Hopewell Hudson (Princeton, N. J.: Princeton University Press, 1941), p. 69.

[24] Daniel Defoe, *An Essay upon Projects* (London, 1702), reprinted in *The Works of Daniel Defoe,* ed. William Hazlitt (London, 1843), III, 11.

EPHRAIM FISCHOFF

||||||||||||||||||||||||||||||||||||||||||||||||||||||||||||||||||||||||||||||||||||||||||||||||||||||||||||||||||||||||||||||||||||||||||||||||||||||||

The Protestant Ethic
and the Spirit of Capitalism

The History of a Controversy

I

The whole question of the effects of the Reformation upon subsequent economic development, and particularly of the intimate relation held to subsist between Protestantism, especially in its Calvinistic forms, and the rise of modern capitalism, has evoked a great literature of controversy ever since the publication at the beginning of this century of Max Weber's provocative essay on Protestantism. This continues to be the versatile German pundit's best known work, perhaps the more so because its intent was largely misunderstood. For over a quarter of a century it has occasioned much debate among social and economic historians on what has been termed the most interesting single question in the field of economic history.[1]. . .

II

Weber's original intention in *The Protestant Ethic* must be seen against the background of his time. An heir of the historical school (he regarded himself as one of the epigoni of Schmoller) and of the Marxist tradition, both of which had combated the isolative treatment of the economic process and the *homo economicus* by abstract classical economics, he probed the history of culture to determine the decisive interconnections of economics with the totality of culture. The whole historical work of Weber has ultimately one primary object, the understanding of contemporary European culture, especially modern capitalism. It presses forward to the underlying morale (*Geist*) of capitalism and its pervasive attitudes to life; and beyond this to

From *Social Research* (February 1944), pp. 53-77, with omissions. Reprinted by permission of *Social Research* and the author.

[1] F. L. Nussbaum, "The Economic History of Renaissance Europe," *Journal of Modern History*, Vol. 13 (1941), p. 537.

modern Occidental rationalism as such, which he came to regard as the crucial characteristic of the modern world.

The discussion of problems raised by Marx, who gave the subject of capitalism its large importance in modern social theory, resulted in a great literature on this theme. Certain German scholars had already begun to assimilate Marx's theoretical work into the conceptual framework developed by the German historical school, among them some of the *Kathedersozialisten,* principally Toennies and Sombart. These bourgeois economists and social theorists were much concerned with the problem of the psychological foundations of capitalism, and suggested certain corrections of the Marxist hypotheses under the general rubric of "the spirit of capitalism." Weber paid the highest tribute to Marx's genius and recognized the enormous usefulness of the materialistic method as a heuristic device,[2] but he resisted all efforts to absolutize it into the sole method of social science, much less into a *Weltanschauung.* The truth value of this method, as indeed of all intellectual schemata, he regarded as only "ideal-typical." As against the Marxian doctrine of the economic determinism of social change, Weber propounded a pluralistic interactional theory.

It is necessary to be clear as to the limited character of Weber's goal and the cautious manner of his procedure in this essay. In this first work inquiring into the influence of religious doctrines on economic behavior, he had not the slightest intention of producing a complete theory of capitalism, a social theory of religion, or even a complete treatment of the relation between religion and the rise of capitalism. The essay was intended as a tentative effort at understanding one of the basic and distinctive aspects of the modern ethos, its professional, specialized character and its sense of calling or vocation. Already he was impressed by the dominantly rational character of modern life; and he was concerned to demonstrate that there were various types of rationalization, a fact generally overlooked by technological theories of history.

Defining capitalism from his historistic view as a unique system[3] characterized by the general trends of antitraditionalism, dynamism, rationalism, and calculated long-range industrial production, he was principally concerned to analyze and trace the genesis of the character-structure adequate to and congruent with it. In his view, modern capitalism was not the automatic product of technological development but of many objective factors, including

---

[2] . . . Weber indicated an interest in reestablishing the value of the method of historical materialism, but only in the functional sense. Yet he adds significantly that to derive capitalism from religious ideas would be quite inadequate.

[3] It was Weber's contention that in the economic history of the world there was a whole scale of capitalisms, adventurous, piratical, usurious, speculative, financial, etc., and that modern rational industrial capitalism, idiosyncratic of our Occidental culture complex, was distinctively different from these earlier forms. The nub of Weber's argument is that for the emergence of our type of capitalism there was required a combination of factors: the full development of certain economic tendencies, the beginnings of which had been apparent in the culture area but which had been impeded for various historical reasons; and the emergence of a "capitalistic spirit," a morale or set of attitudes growing out of the various great historical forces which crystallized our distinctive *Lebensform.*

climate—which influences the conduct of life and labor costs—and many social-political factors, such as the character of the medieval inland city and its citizenry. But he insisted that there was one factor which could not be ignored: the emergence of a rational, antitraditional spirit in the human agents involved. The two main aspects of this are the evolution of modern science and its comparatively modern relationship to economics, and the growth of the modern organization of individual life (*Lebensführung*), particularly in its practical consequences for economic activity. Weber's limited thesis was merely that in the formation of this pattern of rationally ordered life, with its energetic and unremitting pursuit of a goal and eschewal of all magical escapes, the religious component must be considered as an important factor. How important he was unable to say, and indeed he felt that in historical imputation such quantification is impossible. Consequently his view was that no one can tell how the capitalist economic system would have evolved had the specifically modern elements of the capitalistic spirit been lacking.

In tracing the affinity between the bourgeois life pattern and certain components of the religious stylization of life, as shown most consistently by ascetic Protestantism, Weber emphasized the gradual genesis of a psychological habit which enabled men to meet the requirements of early modern capitalism. That is, instead of the entrepreneur feeling that his gaining of wealth was at best tolerated by God, or that his *usuraria pravitas* had to be atoned for (as did the native Hindu trader), he went about his business with sturdy confidence that Providence purposely enabled him to prosper for God's glory, that this success was construable as a visible sign of God and, when achieved by legal means, as a measure of his value before God as well as man. On the other hand, the handworker or laborer, with his willingness to work, derived his sense of a religious state of grace from his conscientiousness in his calling. Finally, because of the abomination of the generic sin of idolatry or apotheosis of created things (*Kreaturvergötterung*), as manifested in hoarding possessions, indulgence, and frivolous consumption, the money accumulated in the exercise of a calling was turned back into the business enterprise, or saved.

Weber strongly emphasized the importance to bourgeois accumulation of planned this-worldly asceticism (*innerweltliche Askese*), as distinguished from other-worldly asceticism, and of the emotional type of pietism. He insisted that Protestant sects, especially the Quakers and Baptists, engendered a methodical regulation of life, in striking contrast to Catholicism, Lutheranism, and Anglicanism. His crucial point was that ascetic Protestantism created for capitalism the appropriate spirit, so that the vocational man (*Berufsmenschen*) in his acquisition of wealth no longer suffered from the deep inner lesions characteristic of the more earnest individuals of an earlier day, no matter what their apparent solidity and exemplary power. One example of this inner uncertainty regarding economic activity was the practice of restoring at death goods obtained by usury; another was the establishment of religious institutions to atone for financial success. There were innumerable theoretical and practical compromises between conscience and economic activity, between the ideal of *Deo placere non potest,* accepted even by Luther, and the acquisitive careers entered into by many earnest Catholics. In Weber's view the noteworthy degree of congruence or affinity between the modern capitalistic system and the set of attitudes toward it made for a high inner integration, which was of great importance for the subsequent development of capitalism. It was this integration which was the central concern of his essay (*Archiv,* vol. 30, p. 200). . . .

The Protestant essay was not regarded by Weber as a final or dogmatic formulation of a theory of the genesis or evolution of the Reformation, but as a preliminary investigation of the influence of certain religious ideas on the development of an economic spirit or the ethos of an economic system. He was not producing an idealistic (or as he preferred to term it, a spiritual) interpretation of capitalism, deriving it from religious factors. Much nonsense has been written on this point because of his alleged rejection of Marxism. Actually, he was an admirer of the Marxian hypothesis, only objecting that it should not be made absolute and universal, a summary philosophy; but then he rejected all absolutes and all monisms. Hence he rejected at least as forcibly any idealistic monism, and in the essay and its supplements he explicitly disavowed the foolish attribution to him of any spiritualistic hypothesis.

He sought no "psychological determination of economic events," but rather emphasized the "fundamental importance of the economic factor." He recognized clearly that economic changes arise in response to economic needs, and are conditioned by a wide variety of factors, including the demogogic, geographic, technological, and monetary. He recognized that capitalism would have arisen without Protestantism, in fact that it had done so in many culture complexes; and that it would not and did not come about where the objective conditions were not ripe for it. He admitted that several other systems of religious ethics had developed approaches to the religious ethic of Reformed Protestantism, but he insisted that the psychological motivations involved were necessarily different; what was decisive was the ethos engendered, not preachments or theological compendia, and this, he argued, was unique in Reformed Protestantism for a variety of reasons. He recognized that there are constant functional interactions between the realms of religion and economics, but in this study he concentrated on the influences emanating from the side of religion. He not only indicated his awareness of the other side, but demonstrated how by an irony of fate the very fulfillment of religious injunctions had induced changes in the economic structure, which in turn engendered the massive irreligion of a capitalist order. He admitted that the religious ethic itself is not determined exclusively by religion, and he clearly urged the necessity of investigating the influence of the social milieu, especially economic conditions, upon the character and development of religious attitudes. . . .

Most animadversions on his thesis, even in works composed during the last decade, spring from a misunderstanding or oversimplification of his theory, for which he is only slightly to blame. Surely Weber, one of the foremost historians of jurisprudence and economics in his generation, needed no reminder that the origins of capitalism are complex and diverse, and are due to changes in economic process as well as in spiritual outlook.[4] By and large most of his critics have simply not perceived the direction of his interest, the moderation of his purpose and the caution of his procedure. . . .

His employment of the ideal-type method leads to various distortions, as in his overemphasis of the concepts of vocation and predestination. Here a bias in the choice of the historical atom to be interpreted and in the definition of its character and influence makes itself strongly felt. The oversimplification induced by the method also extends to his construction of the Protestant ethic as a component of Calvinism, Puritanism, Pietism, Methodism, and the Anabaptist sects, and to his treatment of Puritanism. Another instance is his definition of modern capitalism, accentuating its novelty, rationality, and ascetic character. Once he had so defined it he did not have much difficulty in discovering elements of congruity with the schematic construction of the Protestant ethic slanted in the same direction. To the empirical historian the whole procedure necessarily appears suffused by a tendency to idealization, with a comparative neglect of secular factors, economic, political, and technological.

Weber's method of atomistic isolation necessarily leads to oversimplification of a complex historical entity through the accentuation and isolation of a particular component factor regarded as significant from a certain point of view; its tracing of alleged influences on the further course of historical evolution; and its tendency toward reifying the particular component factors of a given historical entity. In the nature of the case this method cannot serve for the illumination of a total historical problem, or the interpretation of a whole epoch or movement. . . .

For the historian concerned with determining the causes of a particular historical datum, the problem of timing historical phenomena and tracing temporal variations is one of the crucial difficulties arising out of the impossibility, inherent in Weber's method, of determining the degree of influence to be assigned to the various factors involved. The ideal-type method neglects the time coefficient, or at any rate impairs the possibility of establishing time sequences, because it involves a telescoping of data. Granted, for instance,

---

[4] Thus, in accounting for the nonappearance of a positive dynamic attitude toward capitalism in antiquity, despite the presence of "capitalist" activities, Weber remarks that the causes are essentially political, the requirements of *Staatsräson* and the autarchy of the polis. He held that the bias of ancient political theory against the gaining of wealth was not primarily ethical, at least was far less so than that of the mediaeval church, which was antipathetic to purely commercial relations because of their impersonal character. But he insisted that one could not leave out of consideration the psychological factor of the antipathy to work and productive activity in general, including business, which was the dominant attitude of the ruling class. There was no ethical idealization of vocational activity (*Erwerbsarbeit*); and only among the cynics and Hellenistic-Oriental petty *bourgeoisie* are there even slight traces of such activity. Thus the "economic man" of antiquity lacked the support for the rationalization of economic life which his counterpart found at the beginning of the modern period in the vocational ethic, largely a product of religious motivation. The lack of integration in men's attitudes to economic activity must therefore be accounted as one of the reasons for the nonappearance in antiquity of the modern type of capitalism. See "Agrarverhältnisse im Altertum," *Handwörterbuch der Staatswissenschaften,* 3d ed., Vol. 1 (1909), pp. 66 ff.; *Archiv,* Vol. 31, p. 593, n. 25.

that Weber's interpretation of Calvinist theology is correct and that it was of the type that would result in activism, dynamism, industry, etc., the question still remains whether these influences did not begin to exert a significant effect only after capitalism had already reached a dominant position.

Consequently, while there is readiness enough to accept the congruity between Calvinism and capitalism, it has been suggested that a consideration of the crucial question of timing will show that Calvinism emerged later than capitalism where the latter became decisively powerful. Hence the conclusion that Calvinism could not have causally influenced capitalism, and that its subsequent favorable disposition to capitalist practice and ethics is rather to be construed as an adaptation.

The development of the Weberian thesis by Troeltsch, and his American disciple, Reinhold Niebuhr, meets this criticism by tracing the modifications induced in later Calvinism by the various social factors impinging upon it after the first appearance of the original doctrine, such as religious wars, political pressures, and the exigencies of acquisitive life. His rich analysis reveals how the social ethic was the net result of the particular religious and ethical peculiarities of Calvinism, which showed a marked individuality in its doctrine of predestination, its activism and its ethic, aiming at achieving what was possible and practical. On the other hand, Troeltsch emphasizes the importance in the evolution of the ethic of the republican tendency in politics, the capitalistic tendency in economics and the diplomatic and militaristic tendencies in international affairs. All these tendencies radiated from Geneva, at first in a very limited way; then they united with similar elements within the Calvinist religion and ethic, and in this union they became stronger and stronger, until in connection with the political, social, and ecclesiastical history of individual countries they received that particular character of the religious morality of the middle classes (or bourgeois world) which differs from the early Calvinism of Geneva and France.

In the light of all this, Weber's thesis must be construed not according to the usual interpretation, as an effort to trace the causative influence of the Protestant ethic upon the emergence of capitalism, but as an exposition of the rich congruency of such diverse aspects of a culture as religion and economics. The essay should be considered as a stimulating project of hermeneutics, a demonstration of interesting correlations between diverse cultural factors. Although at the time of the republication of the essay Weber insisted that he had not changed his views on this matter at all, the whole intent of his later work does show an implicit shift of view, or at any rate of emphasis. No longer laying the basic stress on the causal factors in the economic ethic of radical Protestantism as related to the capitalist spirit, his later researches, culminating in the systematic sociology of religion, accepted rather the congruency of these diverse aspects of our culture, and their subsumption under the comprehensive process of rationalization. It is important to emphasize that some of the distortions involved in Weber's ideal-type method are neutralized in his later sociological studies of the non-Christian religions, to which all too little attention has been paid. In these mighty studies, which are cultural sociologies of the *Weltreligionen*, Weber traces the influence of material, geographic, and economic circumstances on the religious and ethical ideas of different cultures. Yet though he treated religious norms, institutions, and practices with cold detachment, he never denied the historical reality and power of the religious complex. His general view remained that human affairs are infinitely complicated, with numerous elements interacting; and it was his unshakable conviction that to attribute causal primacy is to be guilty of oversimplification.

In view of Weber's limited intention and the cautious demarcation of his task (including the frequently expressed indication of its incompleteness), his idiosyncratic method which would not permit statistical proof or disproof, and his later supplementation of the original effort by systematic studies in the sociology of religion, it must be concluded that his task was justified by its results. Although the discussion of his problem has not in itself promoted our knowledge of past economic life in proportion to the considerable effort it has evoked, it has greatly sharpened our appreciation of Catholic and Protestant doctrinal history; and it has also paved the way for the formulation of an adequate social theory of religion. Weber's essay on *The Protestant Ethic* is also in a peculiar sense an introduction to his massive system of sociology and his philosophy of history, and exemplifies in striking fashion the anfractuosities of his intellect and temper. As an illuminating tentative[5] approach to a great problem, as an introduction to the domain of the sociology of religion which it served to stake out, as the stimulus to a generation of researchers in this new discipline, and finally, as the precursor of functional analysis in culture history, Weber's essay deserves a better fate than it has thus far enjoyed.

S. H. FRANKEL

||||||||||||||||||||||||||||||||||||||||||||||||||||||||||||||||||||||||||||||||||||||||||||||||||||||||||||||||||||||||||||||

Some Aspects of Technical Change

DEFINITIONS

When I was privileged to receive an invitation to contribute this article to a symposium on "Social Implications of Technical Change," I hesitated for

From *International Social Science Bulletin,* Vol. IV, No. 2 (1952), pp. 263-269. This article also appeared in S. H. Frankel, The *Economic Impact on Underdeveloped Countries* (Oxford: Basil Blackwell, 1953), pp. 18-28. Reprinted by permission of UNESCO and the author.

[5] A poignant expression of Weber's feeling concerning the tentativeness of science and the fateful transiency of the achievements of the scientist, who must none the less accept this tragic fact as his destiny and persevere in his calling, is his eloquent essay, "Wissenschaft als Beruf," now in *Gesammelte Aufsätze zur Wissenschaftslehre.*

some time before accepting it. I wanted to try to define more clearly in my own mind the problem involved, and the contribution which an economist might make to a discussion of it at the present time.

I came to the conclusion that perhaps the most useful approach would be to examine some of the conceptual ideas which, consciously or unconsciously, provide the framework of controversy in this field of study. In doing so, I shall not confine myself to any particular stage of economic development, or any particular region, except for purposes of illustration.

As a starting-point it may be useful to draw attention to certain semantic peculiarities which, I think, are in themselves indicative both of the present climate of opinion and of some confusions which seem worthy of further examination.

The first of these semantic, or definitional, peculiarities is the fact that we so readily tend to speak of "the social consequences of technical change," and not of "technical change as a social consequence." This is very significant. It shows that we have formed the habit of regarding technical change in mechanistic terms—as an independent force, which, by impinging on society, sets in motion certain desirable, or undesirable, reactions. These reactions, since they are regarded as the inevitable consequence of the external force, are then presumed to require study in the same fatalistic spirit in which one might try to cope with the destruction left in the wake of a battle or of an earthquake.

A parallel can be drawn between the use of the term "the Industrial Revolution," with its undertones of cataclysmic suddenness and consequences, and the frequent implication that technical change necessarily takes a similar form, and shatters all around it. But, as an eminent contemporary economic historian[1] has reminded us: "the changes . . . spoken of as the Industrial Revolution . . . were not merely 'industrial' but also social and intellectual. . . . The word 'revolution' implies a suddenness of change that is not in fact characteristic of economic processes." He remarks that "the phrase Industrial Revolution has . . . become so firmly embedded in common speech that it would be pedantic to offer a substitute." Let us hope that the term technical change is not yet as inseparable from its present narrow mechanistic connotation.

The Oxford Dictionary defines technique as the "manner of artistic execution or performance" and the word technical as "belonging or relating to an art or arts." None of these (or other available) definitions indicates the presence of any exogenous forces affecting the work of individuals concerned with changing techniques. On the contrary, they refer to the ways in which certain activities are conducted. But as Professor Oakeshott has emphasized in his Inaugural Lecture on Political Education to "understand an activity *is to know it as a concrete whole; it is to recognize the activity as having the source of its movement within itself* [italics not in the original]. An understanding which leaves the activity in debt to something outside itself is, for that reason,

---

[1] Professor T. S. Ashton, *Industrial Revolution, 1760-1830* (Oxford: Oxford University Press, 1948).

an inadequate understanding. And if political activity is impossible without a certain kind of knowledge and a certain sort of education, then this knowledge and education are not mere appendages to the activity but are part of the activity itself and must be incorporated in our understanding of it."[2]

KNOWING AND DOING

In the same way, I submit, it is important to recognize that an activity (or performance) which, for convenience, we describe as technical, does not consist as it were of two parts, namely of (a) knowing how to do a thing and of (b) doing it. It consists essentially of one process as a whole: the conducting of the activity itself. This can be illustrated by the arrestingly simple example which Professor Oakeshott has used in support of his thesis that "political activity comes first and a political ideology follows after." He takes the example of cookery:

> It might be supposed that an ignorant man, some edible materials, and a cookery book compose together the necessities of a self-moved activity called cooking. But nothing is further from the truth. The cookery book is not an independently generated beginning from which cooking can spring; it is nothing more than an abstract of somebody's knowledge of how to cook: it is the stepchild, not the parent of the activity. The book, in its turn, may help to set a man on to dressing a dinner, but if it were his sole guide he could never, in fact, begin: the book speaks only to those who know already the kind of thing to expect from it and consequently how to interpret it.
>
> Now, just as a cookery book presupposes somebody who knows how to cook, and its use presupposes somebody who already knows how to use it, and just as a scientific hypothesis springs from a knowledge of how to conduct a scientific investigation, and separated from that knowledge is powerless to set empiricism to work, so a political ideology must be understood, not as an independently premeditated beginning for political activity, but as knowledge (in an abstracted and generalized form) of a traditional manner of attending to the arrangements of a society. The catechism which sets out the purposes to be pursued merely abridges a concrete manner of behaviour in which those purposes are already hidden.

Similarly, if we are to speak meaningfully of the effects of technical change we must, I suggest, be very careful to avoid falling into the common, and facile, error of thinking that changes in knowing how to do a certain thing can be separated from changes in the actual doing of it. This is the type of error which is frequently introduced when we speak of making available to a backward society the "know-how" of a new technical process: we are not making available two processes, namely, a mental process of abstract technical knowledge on the one hand, and of the actual performance on the other. We

---

[2] *Political Education*, An Inaugural Lecture by Professor Michael Oakeshott (Cambridge, Eng.: Bowes and Bowes, 1951).

are speaking only of the one process—the performance itself. The idea that technical change is somehow an exogenous force altering the established day-to-day activities of society springs, I suggest, from this erroneous way of speaking and thinking. It consists in the fallacious belief that a society's activities proceed in two separate compartments: the first containing the process of abstract willing or knowing, the other containing the application of such willing or knowing. It is on the basis of a similarly erroneous conception of the nature of economic activity that we so readily conclude that technical change is a kind of abstract force which has certain social consequences, and fail to see that what we describe as the consequences of this imaginary force is simply part and parcel of the activity itself. When, for example, there is a change from farming to coal mining, this will involve the development of new aptitudes and new habits of work over a wide range of new economic and social activities. The change will not be completed until it has resulted in a community all of whose activities (and not only those directly related to the production of coal) have been rearranged or have grown into a new pattern of life and work. If now we regard the introduction of coal mining as a purely mechanical process, which will have certain social consequences, we fail to see that what we regard as the result or consequence, is but the continuous, and necessarily uneven, process of change itself. Thus, if the workers in the coal mine are inadequately housed, or suffer deficiencies in the standard of nutrition, education, or recreation now necessary in their new environment, these are not the consequence of the process of change to coal mining, but rather of a failure to complete it. Even the direct activity of extracting coal cannot be brought to optimum efficiency unless all the other economic and social activities to which that task must be related, and with which it must be integrated, have been developed. Indeed, coal mining cannot even begin until some change in the previous aptitudes, habits, and patterns of social organization have taken place.

Let us examine, for the sake of illustration, a highly simplified example of what, presumably, would nowadays be regarded merely as a technical change. Let us assume that it is desired to increase the productivity of a sub-sistence cattle-owning African community which has never engaged in the production of butter or cheese, either for sale or for its own consumption. It is hoped not only to get this community to consume these products itself, but also to market some of them so as to enable the society to increase its income by selling the surplus dairy produce, and buying other goods with the money so obtained.

PREREQUISITES OF TECHNICAL CHANGE

At first sight the problem might appear to be merely one of introducing new methods of production, and the instruments, tools, or machines appro-priate thereto. But what is really involved is a vast change in social beliefs and practices—if, that is, it be assumed that the society in question is to remain intact as a society—an assumption which, as we shall see, raises questions of quite another kind. Here, for the moment, let us consider only what far-reaching social changes will have to be made to enable technical change— which we nowadays so readily tend to abstract as the prime mover—to be introduced at all. The utilization of cattle as a source of income in a monetary and accounting sense presupposes a basic alteration in the economic structure of the society. It presupposes not only the introduction of money, but a complete re-casting of the traditional values of the community. Thus it presupposes a change in the system of land ownership and use; in the laws and conventions governing access to land, and in the traditional beliefs as to how, and by whom, it is to be cultivated—whether by men or by women, by individuals working for themselves or for others. Moreover it presupposes an aptitude, ability, and willingness to tolerate, recognize, and provide for the emergence and training of groups in the community which are not attached to the land at all. This, in turn, presupposes the growth of new aptitudes and patterns of behavior which will regulate their social and mutual relations not in accordance with the customs suited to shifting subsistence cultivation, roaming cattle herds, and the thrill of the chase, but to those of a settled agricultural and urban population. There is presupposed, therefore, the parallel emergence of a group of persons concerned not only with dairy production itself but with the transport, distribution, marketing, and finance of all that the new producers have to buy and all they have to sell. These, however, necessitate a political structure—local, provincial, national, and trans-national—suited to the establishment of these complementary economic, scientific, and financial activities; they presuppose therefore the willingness, aptitude, and ability of the community to permit, and, indeed, to promote the growth of all the legal, political, and administrative institutions necessary to harmonize the rights and duties of the persons engaged in this new complex interdependent economy.

The purpose of this long list of social adjustments is to show that whatever it be that we may care to designate as technical change, it is but one aspect of mutually determined, and determining, processes of growth on many fronts of the social structure as a whole. It is idle to endeavor to ascertain which change is the innovation or cause, and which is the effect. For when we designate one change as cause and another as effect, we are but examining the process of change itself from different points of observation.

The attempt to establish particular absolute causes of change is misleading, for it misconceives the very nature of the process of change or growth itself.

Let me revert again to that commonplace view of technical change which regards it as resulting from the application of new knowledge—of technical "know-how." Such a view presupposes a kind of mental certainty as to the change which is required in order to bring about a particular consequence in the near or distant future. Basic to this way of thinking is the implicit assumption that the "know-how" exists, as it were, as a stock of techniques—like a stock of raw materials—which can be drawn upon at will, and applied to any situation, in order to produce the desired, and therefore foreseeable, end. It is because we tend to think in such abstract terms that we are led to imagine that somehow economic development, or the lack of it, can be explained in terms of the presence or absence of adequate quantities of factors of production; as when it is suggested that all that is required to assist the development of backward societies is to give to or lend to them part of the world's accumulated technical knowledge and capital—just as one might give an injection to a patient to cure him.

This way of speaking is based on a profound misconception: technical knowledge, the machine, and capital goods in general never exist in the abstract but always only in the relatively fleeting form suited to the momentary situation, and to that complex of unique problems to which they have been adapted. They have no power independent of the performance of which they are capable. They are the expression of man's response to the changing problems set by the environment and by his fellow men. When the problems which constitute man's framework of reference change, they become useless. That is why they cannot be readily transferred from one situation to another. For meeting any new situation, new thoughts, new aptitudes, new action will be required. But knowledge has to grow; capital has to be created afresh on the basis of continuous experiment; and new hopes and beliefs have to evolve to urge men and women forward—for in the last resort they alone are the carriers alike of past experience, and of new endeavor. It is because all these new activities are not independent of the existing institutions into which they have to be fitted, and which have in turn to be adjusted to them, that the process of change is so complex and—if it is to proceed harmoniously—necessarily so slow.

DISCONTINUOUS CHANGES

It is the attempt to simplify that process, to avoid the gradualness of change in order to pluck the quick fruits of endeavor in one direction—at the expense of inactivity in others—which accounts for social maladjustments. In a society in which all changes were to take place at rates so well adjusted to each other as not to disturb the basic harmony and integration of its constitutent parts, there would be no social consequences of change but only harmonious change itself. When, however, rates of change are very discontinuous, it may well happen that one sector of the society cannot be meaningfully integrated into the social life of the community at all—so that, as far as that sector is concerned, society as a whole no longer exists.

The most extreme case of failure to achieve a balanced rate of change is that of slavery. It illustrates in its most terrible form the deliberate disintegration of established patterns of social and human values in order to pursue an immediate objective. Slavery not only detaches men and women by force from an established pattern of social relationships but, by using them as chattels for the ends of others, denies them both the opportunity to reconstruct a new society for themselves, and the right to become an integrated meaningful part of the society of their masters. In a society based on slavery the uneasy and unstable rule of force takes the place of that social harmony necessary for the full development of each part of the disrupted whole.

Slavery is an extreme case of the establishment of new structural patterns which by their very nature prevent further economic and social growth. But there have been, and continue to be, many less extreme, yet parallel, situations.

The large movements of indentured labor during the nineteenth century —like the migration of some recruited labor in Africa today—illustrate the consequences of attempts to use labor in pursuance of an immediate objective without considering the need to integrate the individuals concerned into a new meaningful social pattern.

In South Africa, for example, the need to obtain Indian labor for the Natal sugar industry arose because it was not possible to detach Africans for that purpose from their own indigenous society. The structure of the sugar industry was thus established on the basis of Indian unskilled labor, and the Indians were forced to remain separated from both the European and the African social structures. This not only inhibited the evolution of a meaningful society for Indians in South Africa, but also froze the economic pattern of the sugar industry itself. The whole economic evolution of Natal was retarded by the failure to establish the Indian immigrant as a creative part of South African society.

I suggest that when we view the problems of change in the light of these considerations we shall accustom ourselves to focus our studies, to a greater extent than heretofore, on the historical evolution of the structural patterns of developing societies. By so doing we shall, I believe, be able to place the emphasis in studies of change where it belongs: on the need to discover to what extent rates of change in different parts of the society are moving towards, or diverging from, that minimum degree of social and psychological harmony necessary for its maintenance or evolution.

In using these terms I am aware of the fact that I am begging many questions. However, what I have in mind is something far simpler than the necessarily vague terminology I have used may at first sight indicate.

To illustrate this let me again refer to the lessons of the Industrial Revolution and quote again from Professor Ashton's valuable judgment: "Experience has taught us," he writes,

> that an industrial society needs a framework of public services if it is to operate without social discomfort. . . . With the best will in the world, the transition from farms and cottages to factories and cities could never have been smooth. If the legislative machine had turned out statutes with the same speed as the mules turned out yarn, there would still have been social disorder. For much of the overcrowding and squalor was the result of the fact that progress in science was then, as today, more rapid than in admin-

istration. "The remote influence of arrangements has been somewhat neglected," wrote Dr. Kay in 1832, adding to this meiosis that the neglect arose "not from the want of humanity, but from the pressure of occupation and the deficiency of time." Not until the whole apparatus of government had been drastically reformed and a body of qualified public servants had been called into being could life in urban areas be other than squalid. If the Industrial Revolution was not able to bring its rewards in full measure to the ordinary man and woman it is to the effects of administrative, and not of economic processes, that the failure must be ascribed.

CONCLUSION

What, I suggest, is most required now, in relation to the thought and practice of our predecessors, is a new awareness, not only of the need to adapt administrative and social arrangements to the pressure of economic and political events, but also of the fact that the political and economic pressures themselves so largely depend on those arrangements. Thus we should envisage neither the pressure of technical, nor those of political happenings as accidental, in the sense that they are independent causes of our problems. Instead we should accustom ourselves to see them as mutually interdependent processes. For that reason we must discipline ourselves to examine them everywhere in sufficient detail to lay bare their mutual relations. By so doing we may perhaps hope to quicken that sense of social inventiveness and responsibility which makes change not a burden, but an adventure in the art of government and mutual adaptation in free societies. For the sting of change lies not in change itself but in change which is devoid of social meaning.

Let me conclude with a final example. All over Africa, and, indeed, in many parts of the underdeveloped world, erstwhile members of simple rural economies find themselves drawn into urban centers of industry. For many of these men and women these centers are only the places in which they work; their social self remains located with their families, which are still eking out a precarious livelihood in rural conditions as yet unadapted to modern forms of production, or to the basic needs of health, education, and the like. Even when these families come to the towns they find themselves psychologically and socially ill-equipped to establish satisfactory patterns of living there. Yet we know little so far about the administrative arrangements which must be evolved to cope with the changing activities of these wanderers in the twilight of newly emerging social structures. Very few detailed studies of their thinking and their needs exist; fewer still of their psychological reactions, and least of all of the ways and means of emancipating them to grapple with their problems by that most basic form of all political education—the conscious sharing in the governance of affairs by trial and error.

We know little of the processes involved in the vast change of aptitudes which these developments require, of the time they take, and the obstacles they encounter. There is need of carefully documented comparative studies of them in different regions. Moreover, only experience, and a knowledge which exhibits clearly the full burden of change, can prevent needlessly hasty development in this or that direction. All too often a socially uneconomic development is embarked upon because those who initiate it are unaware of its cost, or not responsible for its unavoidable accompanying economic and social changes. But change which is not in harmony with the social resources and needs of a community may well prove to be not a blessing but a curse.

It is here that the economist can be of help in examining the relative individual and social costs and benefits of alternative choices, and in disentangling the real from the apparent expected effects of the fiscal and economic burdens involved.

PART EIGHT

||||||||||||||||||||||||||||||||||||||||||||||||||||||||||||||||||||||||||||||||||||||||||||||||||||||||||||

Policies and Plans for Development

ONE OF THE IMPORTANT FUNCTIONS OF A NATIONAL state is to set the conditions for economic growth. Historically, the emergence of sovereign national states in Europe beginning in the fifteenth century may well have been a critical precondition of subsequent economic growth. The development of national states led to the establishment of uniform laws, efforts to create a uniform currency, the breakdown of internal trade barriers, the encouragement of private domestic industry, the growth of transportation networks, and a wide variety of other activities and institutions, all of which were to influence significantly the rate of economic growth. The responsibility for certain decisions which were inevitably to affect economic growth necessarily devolved upon government as the ultimate authority in resolving secular issues. For example, the United States government has had to deal with questions of slavery, immigration, foreign trade, internal improvements, corporate structure, and the banking system; decisions in these areas surely had a profound effect upon American economic development.

Clearly, then, certain key decisions affecting economic development must be made by government. Whatever form the government may take, it must possess the strength and stability to reach and to enforce decisions that will not be subject to recurrent drastic alteration or reversal. These characteristics are lacking in the governments of some underdeveloped countries today. For one thing, many of these countries have only recently emerged from colonial status and have not yet acquired much experience in self-government. In addition, tribal elements in some underdeveloped countries create a divisive influence that tends to undermine the effectiveness of national government. Offsetting such factors to a greater or lesser extent is the phenomenon of nationalism, which fosters a spirit of patriotic identification with the state, and instills in people a willingness to accept centrally made decisions, as well as the adjustments and sacrifices required by such decisions.

Even with strong and stable government, the question of how prominent its role is to be in economic development remains unanswered. Two major aspects of the role of government should be distinguished. The first concerns the *scope* of governmental activity, relating to what objectives of control are to be considered within the legitimate province of government. The second concerns the *means* of control—that is, given the objectives of control, what are the proper avenues for achieving them? These broad questions lie at the root of specific and highly controversial issues. Should, for example, governmental activity with respect to capital formation extend to the housing industry? If so, should government depend mainly upon direct planning, or upon more indirect techniques, such as monetary and fiscal policy? Both at the practical and philosophic levels, it is clear that different countries have solved these questions differently.

The Rockefeller Report presents a program of policy objectives that it believes will promote more rapid growth in the United States. Recognizing the influence of such factors as capital formation, foreign trade, scientific advance, the development of natural resources, and the existence of an appropriate economic "climate," the report recommends governmental policies that will, in its opinion, have a favorable impact on these variables. These recommendations, it should be noted, are geared to a free-enterprise society, in the sense that little or no reliance is placed upon direct government intervention. Rather, much weight is placed upon monetary, fiscal, and other policy weapons such as "balanced" and "flexible" enforcement of antitrust legislation.

The Rockefeller Report, concerned with the growth problems of the United States, takes for granted the enduring desirability of the free-enterprise system and gears its policy recommendations to this value judgment. Many underdeveloped countries seriously question the efficacy of relying entirely on this type of approach in meeting their own peculiar needs. The remaining selections of this section are concerned with the role of government in promoting growth in the underdeveloped countries, and consider a wider range of alternative economic philosophies and policies.

Governments of underdeveloped countries, in attempting to attain higher rates of growth through productive investment, have frequently incurred large budgetary deficits. Because of the low level of savings generally characteristic of these countries, these deficits have been largely financed through the expansion of bank credit, the result being a continuous process of inflation. Despite its undesirable side effects, the apparent ease of financing investment through inflation has persuaded some governments to follow this course. Inflation tends to raise profits disproportionately, thus providing higher incomes to a group that normally has a higher propensity to save. Moreover, it has been argued that inflationary expansion of bank credit allocated to investors creates "forced savings," because certain scarce resources are bid away from consumer to investment-goods industries, causing a decline in the quantity of consumer goods produced. Thus consumer-goods prices must rise, and real consumption must fall. However, as E. M. Bernstein and I. G. Patel note, higher consumer-goods prices result in lower real wages. If, as is likely, labor is aware of this loss and offsets it by demanding and obtaining higher money wages, the favorable effect upon investment of the initial inflationary redistribution of income will tend to be cancelled. Thus, a continuing process of inflation may not lead to higher levels of investment. What is more, Bernstein and Patel point to the unfavorable effects of inflation upon the composition of investment, which tends to be diverted to areas of low economic-growth potential, such as real estate, luxury goods, and foreign assets.

The inflationary potential inherent in underdeveloped countries striving for growth focuses attention on the key role of the central bank because of its responsibility for controlling the supply of money and credit. While it is true that the central bank is the instrument through which the money supply is determined, it may often be the case that the monetary authority lacks the independence to pursue an anti-inflationary policy which is in apparent conflict with other governmental objectives. Strenuous government efforts toward rapid economic development, combined with inelastic supplies of real savings and resources, place heavy political pressure upon the central bank to accommodate a government policy of deficit finance by permitting excessive and inflationary credit expansion.

But the role of the monetary authority should be more than one of passive accommodation. The central bank must inevitably be concerned with economic growth, and it can make a positive contribution by supporting the development of securities markets, by imposing selective controls designed to promote or discourage certain types of investment, by encouraging the development of savings and financial institutions, and by other measures. The scope of central banking in underdeveloped countries may thus have to be broader than is typical in the advanced countries.

The essentially accommodating role which, as we have noted, is assigned to monetary policy is a result of the heavy reliance that many governments place upon fiscal policy in fostering growth. The selection by Walter Heller[1] first examines the potentialities of government taxation and expenditure policies in encouraging capital formation. Tax policy for development in advanced countries is largely confined, Heller suggests, to the collection of revenue with a minimum of interference with the processes of savings and investment. In the underdeveloped countries, where savings levels are inadequate for developmental needs, tax policy is confronted with the more immediate problem of generating higher levels of savings. But the savings process need not depend on private initiative. Taxation derived at the expense of private consumption and used for government investment purposes could effectively increase the aggregate level of real "savings" and investment. Very low income levels make it difficult for governments in underdeveloped countries to increase taxes by amounts which in advanced countries would be considered tolerable, but even a modest percentage increase of tax revenue, Heller points out, may have a significant effect upon the government's contribution to development expenditures.

As we have noted earlier, not only the level but also the composition of investment is of critical importance. Inflation-financed investment tends to flow into comparatively unproductive areas such as land, construction, and inventories. Tax-supported investment, however, can be directed toward more productive areas, particularly if the tax structure is such that investment in relatively unproductive areas is penalized—for example, by heavy levies on idle land.

Heller devotes much attention to fiscal policies designed to ameliorate the problems confronting the "exposed economy"—i.e., the underdeveloped country which is heavily dependent for income upon foreign markets and vulnerable to fluctuations in price and volume in those markets. He contends that, despite some objectionable features, there are circumstances under which the imposition of such measures as import and export taxes and multiple exchange rates is justified, in order to mitigate the instability generated in "exposed economies" through the balance of payments.

A discussion confined to monetary, fiscal, and other policy weapons leaves open the more basic question of the underlying philosophy of the rela-

---

[1] The ideas expressed in the selection by Professor Heller assume somewhat greater practical significance because of his appointment, in 1961 as head of the Council of Economic Advisors.

tion of government to the economy. This question, needless to remark, has occupied political economists and philosophers for centuries. It was Adam Smith who first posited the principle of the "invisible hand," symbolizing the notion that inherent order, harmony, and maximum good would endure in a freely competitive economic society in which each individual pursues his own self-interest. It followed, in Smith's mind, that there should be a minimum of government intervention in economic life.

Whatever its social and economic philosophy, every society has in fact recognized certain legitimate grounds for government intervention. Indeed, Smith himself acknowledged the right and obligation of government to provide for defense, the administration of justice, and even the construction of certain categories of public works. In general, several grounds for government intervention in the economy may be distinguished. One that is virtually self-evident is the function of government in maintaining and supporting the basic institutions of the society: for example, in a competitive free-enterprise system, government would normally provide police protection of private property, and in some cases combat monopolistic practices through the enactment and enforcement of antitrust legislation.

Equity considerations provide a second ground for government intervention. An example of this is the provision of free education, whereby equal educational opportunity is made available to all, regardless of income. If education had to be purchased in the free market, educational opportunity would be related to income, thus violating the principle of equality of opportunity.

Interestingly enough, public support of education can be justified on another ground. An individual is economically motivated to purchase education because he expects that this will enhance his future income stream. However, the benefits of education extend beyond the individual to society as a whole—to take a dramatic example, the social benefits of the education of Einstein far exceeded his personal monetary gain. It would therefore seem socially beneficial for government to hold the price of education below what would prevail in the free market, in order to induce people to acquire more education than they otherwise would. Such a case, where the "social marginal product" exceeds the "private marginal product," provides a ground for government intervention in the free market.

Akin to the question of education is that of "social overhead capital." Every society needs a certain minimum of "basic facilities," such as transportation and communication networks, sources of power, school buildings, and hospitals. The general characteristic common to such facilities is that their benefits are widespread, but that in some cases it is difficult to apportion their cost equitably among the direct users. Even were it possible to apportion costs equitably, private enterprise may be discouraged from undertaking investments, returns on which extend further into the future than is within the calculable time horizon of the private investor. Because profits are the chief incentive to private investment, such investments will not be undertaken; they will appear unprofitable due to the limitations in the investor's time horizon. Moreover, investments that require very large initial capital outlays may also discourage potential investors, particularly in underdeveloped countries in which there are severe limitations upon capital availability. It is then clear that where the private sector is unable or unwilling to provide essential capital facilities, the government may have to bear the responsibility for filling this gap.

It must be recognized that however justifiable the need for government intervention on the grounds to which we have alluded, other principles may exist which tend to limit the extent of such intervention. Consider the case of a society in which a philosophy of "economic freedom" looms large in the scheme of social values. Thus, for example, equity considerations might suggest the imposition of a progressive tax structure to reduce income inequality, but considerations of "economic freedom" might militate against governmental measures which alter the distribution of income as determined by the free market. Moreover, even where there is general agreement on the desirability of a goal such as the reduction of income inequality, a more difficult problem remains. This is to ascertain the degree by which such inequality should be reduced; in other words, how progressive should the tax structure be?

One is confronted with a similar problem with respect to social overhead capital. In some underdeveloped countries, it may well be that in order to maximize economic growth, a large proportion of total investment should be in the form of additions to social overhead capital. In principle, the responsibility for such additions falls upon government because, as we have noted, this function has generally been abdicated by the free market. But at the same time, a society may wish to restrict the influence of government in the total investment process. Hence, the share of total investment represented by net additions to social overhead capital may be below that which would maximize economic growth.

To the extent that government intervention replaces reliance upon the free market, some degree of government planning is implied: the "invisible hand" is joined by a visible one. Let us assume that an investment plan has been devised. The thorny problem of implementation now arises. One method of implementation involves the assumption by government of outright ownership, as is generally the case in the Soviet Union. An alternative to this would be to allow ownership to remain in private hands, but for government to influence investment by interfering with the structure of prices, costs, and profits. In the United States, for example, the federal government fostered the development of railroads and state universities by generous land grants which materially reduced costs. While most would agree that this policy contributed to the development of the United States, a subsidization policy is subject to misuse in some contexts. State-sponsored enterprises which are subsidized through artificially reduced factor costs will appear relatively profitable in comparison to strictly private projects which are constrained by realistic factor costs. Consequently, resources tend to be diverted to state-sponsored enterprises in greater quantity than would occur if the free-market costs and profit structure were not subjected to government interference. A misallocation of resources therefore results. It should be emphasized, however, that government may have deliberately altered the cost and profit structure in recognition of the failure of the free market effectively to allocate investment, for the reasons mentioned earlier in this section.

The concluding article of this section, by Albert O. Hirschman, discusses some strategic political and economic aspects of planning. The underdeveloped countries exhibit a marked propensity to experiment with new economic programs and policies. There is a danger, Hirschman suggests, that this propensity may lead to erratic policy behavior which will retard economic progress. But the other extreme, rigid "straitjacket" programing, is politically and socially intolerable. Hirschman therefore calls for a middle ground: a flexible approach, allowing for revisions and modifications of programs and policies, but within limits that will not produce a public image of unstable and chaotic government.

THE ROCKEFELLER BROTHERS FUND

The Encouragement of Growth

It is the essence of an economy of growth that its frontiers are constantly changing. The frontiers of today become the familiar territory of tomorrow.

The full harvest of a growth economy can be reaped only in an environment that affords incentives. Initiative and enterprise, the willingness to save and invest capital, and confidence in the future are essential ingredients of a growth economy and flourish where constructive effort carries the expectancy of satisfying reward.

The basic factor that will determine this country's future rate of economic progress is the degree to which we keep alive the incentives upon which growth depends. Profit and competition are the mainsprings of business initiative and imagination, as well as the weighing-scale of business competence. The expectancy of progressively increasing income, the raises that go with promotions in an expanding economy, and the prospect of achieving ownership status through an investment stake or even through independent proprietorship have been a vital part of our tradition.

The policies, private and public, to encourage long-term growth are the concern of this section.

From *The Challenge to America: Its Economic and Social Aspects* (The Rockefeller Report) (New York: Doubleday & Company, 1958), pp. 18-36, with omissions. Copyright © 1958 Rockefeller Brothers Fund, Inc. Reprinted by permission of Doubleday & Company, Inc.

GOVERNMENT RESPONSIBILITY FOR A CLIMATE OF GROWTH

Government policy and action influence the economic climate in a host of indirect ways quite apart from its direct purchases of goods and services and its fiscal operations.

The incidence of its tax stuctures can encourage or blight incentives. The same is true of its regulations governing domestic and foreign trade, its patent laws, the intricate fabric of its legislative and administrative dealings with business, agriculture, and labor. The way in which it administers its stock-piling programs, disposes of its surpluses, the management of its procurement policies, the extent and manner of its direct competition with private enter-prise—all of these build or undermine an environment conducive to growth.

The matter of government attitude is scarcely less important than the letter of its laws. We are quick to recognize the presence or absence of a favorable or unfavorable economic climate in foreign countries, but less aware of the limitations in the climate at home. Since the health of our private economy will determine our growth progress, it is incumbent upon us to see that our government provides a climate in which private incentives flourish.

Throughout most of this nation's history, the government's direct role in economic life was of relatively minor weight. In 1929 government expendi-tures for goods and services—federal, state, and local—absorbed only 8 per-cent of the country's total output. The federal government's outlays, including expenditures for national defense, were outweighed by state and local govern-ment expenditures by a ratio of almost six to one.

The heavy burden of national security requirements combined with a variety of additional responsibilities with which government has been charged have increased the relative weight of government purchases in our economy to two and one half times what they were in 1929. And within the govern-ment sector, federal expenditures are now over 40 percent larger than state and local combined.

Today government, through its spending and taxing measures, exercises an important influence upon the demand side of the national economy's ledger. But its role in contributing to the supply of goods and services produced is of relatively modest weight. The private sector of the economy produces most of what government buys as well as almost all of the much larger purchases of private consumers and investors. Hence our ability to service the expanding demands of our economy as a whole depends primarily upon the growth trend of private business and industry.

STRENGTHEN COMPETITION AND REMOVE RIGIDITIES
THAT IMPEDE GROWTH

If we genuinely believe in the competitive system, we should be willing to abide by its rules. Chief among these, is the requirement that businesses should compete. Each should stand on its own feet, justify its existence by its offerings in the marketplace, and sell on a price-quality basis against all competition. It similarly should be incumbent upon both business and labor to adjust to changes that promote the progressive improvement in productivity upon which increased living standards importantly depend.

The natural adaptation of a free economy is not always quick or complete. There is a tendency to seek protection against pressure for change. When this resistance takes deep-rooted forms, or when it acquires legislative sanction, rigidities impede and distort the over-all advance.

The protective tariff is a leading example of a policy aimed at protecting industries against the forces of change. Our tariffs were originally intended to help new American industries take root. However, at present, our tariffs often serve to impede rather than to encourage the achievement of a higher national product and lower costs for the consumer. Since the economic health and rising living standards of the other nations of the free world depend importantly on their ability to trade with us, considerations of foreign policy are added to those of economic efficiency in urging tariff reduction.

This does not mean the wholesale reduction or elimination of tariffs. Grave damage could be wrought by tariff cuts indiscriminately applied. But there is a need for a tariff policy which moves steadily toward our goal of lower trade barriers. This could be coupled with provision to help redirect the resources and efforts of those industries and workers seriously affected by tariff reduction. . . .

A second group of rigidities that impede economic growth are those caused by the formation of monopolies or collusive practices that reduce the invigorating stimulus of a genuine competition. Government must be alert at all times to maintain and strengthen competition throughout our economy. This was and remains the purpose of our antitrust laws. Yet in the enforcement of the antitrust laws a balanced flexibility must be attained. Their administration must be sufficiently flexible to adapt to the realities of change in business structures and operations, yet not so volatile as to risk a paralysis of responsible business activity because of uncertainty.

A third area in which a greater degree of flexibility is needed relates to the remaining instances of resistance to modernization and efficiency in production. Rules that require more labor than is needed for given jobs, the retention of outmoded equipment or processes or any restrictions that interfere with the goal of expanding production with due regard to the welfare of workers are inconsistent with our national growth.

TAX REFORM TO PROMOTE INCENTIVES FOR GROWTH

In 1957, government—federal, state, and local combined—collected in taxes the equivalent of 25 percent of the nation's total output. About two-fifths of this covered federal government expenditures for national security purposes.

One-fifth (the so-called transfer payments) was collected by government from one group of citizens and paid out to others, as welfare payments, payments under the several social insurance programs, and as interest on government debt. The remainder went for the purchase of goods and services on government accounts including payrolls of public servants. Thus, government at all levels collected in taxes 25 percent of the national product and purchased 20 percent of all goods and services produced by the economy on direct government account.

Clearly, government institutions determine the direction of a formidably large portion of total economic activity in the United States, and their tax takings are even larger. Before World War II, their tax takings were proportionately less than half as large. Yet our tax structure has grown haphazardly, with numerous changes in rates, but without a serious consideration of how the incidence and rate structure were affecting the incentives that determine growth upon which ability to pay taxes depends. Systematic tax reform, at federal, state, and local levels, is long overdue. The prospect of a substantial future increase in over-all government expenditures, and hence of tax collections, in the years ahead make this an even more urgent requirement.

As presently constituted, our tax system presents a series of important impediments to growth. The very high graduated rates in the personal income tax structure reduce the incentive and the ability to accumulate capital and put it to productive use. The failure to develop averaging devices presents an impediment to certain groups. The very high corporate tax rates and present depreciation provisions slow the growth of corporate enterprise. . . .

THE PROBLEM OF CAPITAL ACCUMULATION

Without private capital for investment, we would, as we know, lack one of the essential ingredients for our growth. But the special vitality of the American economy is based on more than the mere availability of private capital—it finds its wellsprings of vigor in the very possibility and the actual process of capital accumulation. It is this expectation and the process of realizing it which has given our society much of its uniquely buoyant thrust.

As our tax structure has developed it has steadily become more difficult for those who start without capital to accumulate it. This is especially true of those who are dependent on salaries or those who elect to do business as sole proprietors or partners. For it is on individuals in these categories that our high tax rates—and particularly the high graduated rates on any increases in incomes—fall with devastating effect. At the same time, it is the able and energetic individuals in these groups that we must particularly encourage for the drive and imagination essential to growth.

The largest source of taxation in this country is the tax on individual incomes. Our strong reliance on income taxation reflects our belief that personal incomes are the best index of ability to pay, and we graduate our personal income tax because we believe that those with higher incomes have a greater relative ability to pay than those in lower income classes.

But experience strongly suggests that the nation would be better served by an income tax with somewhat lower rates that would apply more equally among persons with the same income. With personal incomes in excess of $340 billion we now levy rates starting at 20 percent and rising to as high as 91 percent in order to collect $37 billion.

At all income levels, there are entirely legal opportunities for people to avoid the stated rates. The reason these opportunities exist is that Congress has legislated special relief provisions believed to be in the national interest and designed either to soften the impact of the high rates on particular groups or to encourage particular activities. In some cases, the relief provisions were enacted many years ago when their revenue consequences were small. In most cases there has been no careful modern review of these exemptions, exclusions, credits, and preferential provisions to balance the loss of revenue they involve against the contribution they now make to growth in the economy as a whole.

There should, we believe, be a fundamental review of our income tax structure to determine its effectiveness in achieving its fundamental purposes of revenue collection and promotion of growth. Without such a comprehensive review, and the revisions in our tax laws which it establishes as necessary, the next decades will not see the fruitful economic growth which is possible and which the well-being of the people in America and the free world will require.

If our tax structure is equitable and promotes healthy growth, we will not find individuals spending disproportionate time and effort on earning incomes in ways that receive preferential tax treatment but which may no longer fully contribute to national growth and well-being. A distortion in incentives to work, save, and invest is tolerable and warranted only if it promotes a better allocation of resources and thus insures an even greater rate of economic growth for the nation as a whole.

INCOME TAX AVERAGING

All taxpayers, individual and corporate, experience variations in income. Some, however, by the nature of their occupation are more subject to such variations. This is true of creative artists and many professional people whose incomes have sharp peaks and valleys. It is also true of athletes and others who may crowd peak earnings into a relatively short span of years. The problem is compounded for self-employed persons who cannot set aside a part of their earnings free of tax under retirement plans to provide income in their older, less productive years.

Small business, too, is vulnerable to sharp variations in earnings. Small businesses tend to be less stable, to be frequently associated with more risks, and to have less depth and variety of resources to cushion and spread the normal risks of free enterprise.

Our present tax system unduly penalizes the taxpayer whose income is not evenly spread, but concentrated in a relatively few years of high earnings. Greater equity and more incentive would, therefore, be achieved by a system which permitted the averaging of income over a period of years.

Provisions for income averaging are familiar in our tax system and they take many forms—including, for example, tax loss carry backs and carry forwards, and provisions for spreading back certain types of income earned over a period of more than three years. The difficulty is that such equitable principles are not always consistently applied throughout the tax laws and frequently they are not available to all taxpayers. The present situation should be corrected. It is discriminatory in its impact and tends to distort the form and manner of our economic growth.

DEPRECIATION ALLOWANCES

Depreciation allowances under the tax law greatly influence the extent and timing of capital investments by business. All capital outlays involve risk and uncertainty. The sooner a capital outlay can be expected to be recovered, the greater will be the willingness to invest in depreciable property and the greater will be the opportunity to secure funds for such investments. . . .

MODERATION OF CORPORATE INCOME TAXES

The present corporation tax rate of 52 percent is the highest corporation tax rate in our history with the exception of wartime periods, when excess profits taxes were levied. High corporate tax rates encourage wasteful expenditures, and promote tax considerations to a dominant place in business decisions. Excessive rates discriminate against equity financing and encourage debt financing, thus making business more vulnerable to decline in business activity. In short the high corporate tax rate tends to distort and inhibit the vital contribution which business through the use and investment of its capital must make to our natural growth. Some moderation of the general corporate rate is long overdue.

Even with reforms, the impact of our basic tax structure will remain great. If our needs or our desires for public expenditure increase faster than our total economic growth, then our tax burden will be the heavier. Economic growth alone can keep that burden from becoming excessive. In any case, taxes will be a constant burden on the foreseeable future. It is the cost we pay for freedom, and for the ends we choose to pursue under freedom.

We have identified four areas in which there is ground for believing that reform is needed and, where intelligently applied, it should promote higher national product and income to offset the effect of lowered rates. But we are fully conscious that a responsible position in this field requires a careful weighing of the effect of any changes on revenue requirements as a whole. We believe that no time should be lost in setting out upon this task.

PUBLIC EXPENDITURES IN SUPPORT OF GROWTH

Public expenditures in support of growth are a traditional and an essential part of our economy. Far from being a hindrance to progress, they provide the environment within which our economy moves forward.

As set forth in other sections of this report, we shall need, in the next decade, a greatly expanded school system to broaden and improve education. We shall need urban redevelopment on a vast scale to lift the living standards and the social and cultural content of metropolitan life. We shall need more and better highways and improved modes of transportation to spur commerce, communication, and travel. We shall need better water supply and pollution control systems to meet domestic, industrial, and agricultural requirements. We shall need more health and hospital facilities, more basic and applied research, more recreation areas. The list is extensive, and as the final section of this report sets forth, estimates indicate an increase of almost 50 percent in government purchases of goods and services by 1967.

If total national output grows at a comparable rate, then government's share in the total would stay at approximately the present level. Without such growth, however, these "social capital" investments will either have to be curtailed, or they will take a larger share of the national output, leaving a smaller share to the private economy. Since most of the dynamic thrust of our growth comes from private activities, there is danger that too large and too rapid a diversion of funds to public expenditure will react adversely on the entire economy.

Therefore, the very magnitude of prospective claims for publicly directed expenditures imposes upon us the obligation to exercise wise and vigilant discipline. We must see that wasteful government expenditures are eliminated, and that less important public purposes are subordinated to those with higher priority. This poses a challenge to our political system as much as to our economic one. It raises questions of leadership, of government information policy, of the relevance of established institutions of government to new and difficult tasks. . . .

Unwarranted public demands on government must be checked. Notable among these are numerous subsidies which have no place in a growing and prosperous economy.

Many of these subsidies have their roots in the 1930s or World War II and no longer serve the public interest. For example, the stockpile programs have been used to support the prices of some industrial raw materials, rather than to store materials that may be needed in the event of war. Pensions to some veterans for nonservice-connected disabilities, as well as subsidies in other fields also warrant re-examination. And the agriculture program should be redirected along the lines discussed elsewhere in this report in order to bring supply and demand into better balance.

GOVERNMENT MONETARY AND FISCAL POLICIES CONTRIBUTING TO GROWTH

Since we have set forth our ideas on the responsible use of monetary and fiscal powers as stabilization instruments earlier in this section, it would be redundant to discuss here procedures already described.

It is appropriate, however, to point out that the moderation of the fluctuations in either direction not only serves to prevent serious hardships but contributes constructively to the growth process itself. The fear of inflation or deflation inhibits alike business and consumer decisions that make for growth, causes distortions in our economy that are not quickly remedied.

The lost ground incident to a serious decline may take years to make good. Even the current relatively moderate recession has cut gross national output by an annual rate of $25 billion, from the $450 billion level that we might by now have achieved on a steady growth trend to the $425 billion actual rate of the first quarter of 1958. Since government has been taxing at an over-all 25-percent rate, this in itself means a $6 billion annual loss rate in government revenues if production for all of 1958 does not average above current levels. If a tax cut could importantly influence a prompt recovery that might not otherwise take place, it would be a good bargain for the economy as a whole, and for the fiscal position of the federal government as well.

Quite apart from their specialized use as stabilization instruments, sound monetary and fiscal policies play a continuing role in supporting a growth economy. The flow of money and credit has to be geared to expanding demand, and its availability is a condition of expansion. Government expenditures, when budgets are generally in balance, contribute to over-all demand, as do private expenditures, without exerting an influence in the direction of either inflation or deflation.

THE ENCOURAGEMENT OF SMALL BUSINESS

Basic to much of our past economic achievement has been our ability to encourage men with new ideas and new products to establish their own enterprises. Our great industries began as small-scale operations, and the majority of them are still less than 50 years old.

We still possess a very great reservoir of such economic initiative in the 4.2 million nonfarm businesses of our nation. This is the largest total in our history. Although there is a rapid turnover of some 300,000 to 400,000 of the smallest of these businesses—the figures indicate that there is no shortage of the spirit of enterprise in the business population. They may also indicate that managerial experience and competence is the most important factor in growth.

There is, however, a growing body of evidence that smaller and medium-sized businesses, and particularly manufacturing firms—even those that have successfully established themselves in their industries and have solid prospects for growth—have difficulty in obtaining financing for the expansion of their operations. There is also a probability that inadequate financing reduces the rate at which new firms are established.

The need is primarily for long-term equity or loan funds. As a result of the inability to obtain capital funds, the opportunity for establishing a new firm, or for expanding an established firm, is too often lost. Often the established firm merges with a larger enterprise that can command the necessary resources. The past few years have seen a wave of such mergers. Such a condition is neither conducive to vigorous competition nor to economic growth. . . .

NATURAL RESOURCES

Any serious effort to project our growth potential for the future must take account of our supply of natural resources. These are the bone and sinew of our economy, upon which all else—domestic and international—depends.

The drain on our traditional supplies of raw materials is prodigious. In 1900 our production of all raw materials exceeded our consumption by 15 percent. By 1950 our consumption exceeded our production by 9 percent. By 1975 our consumption will exceed our production by 20 percent. It is estimated that our reserves of good U.S. iron ores—those containing more than 50-percent iron—will have vanished in the next two decades. Only our reserves of poorer ores are still substantial and it is to these lower-grade ores that we will have to resort through the development of new technologies, new plants, more efficient extraction processes, and more efficient use.

Here, the challenge to innovation and inventive thinking is immense. New technologies, more efficient extraction processes, new uses may open up new worlds. Even now we can discern the outlines of a future in which, through the use of the split atom, our resources both of power and raw materials will be limitless. But the theoretically possible is not yet within our grasp. Pending the necessary scientific and technological breakthroughs, we must face the fact that our supplies are not inexhaustible. . . .

AN EXPANDING WORLD ECONOMY

An expanding volume of trade can make a most significant contribution to our general economic growth. The essence of trade is that both parties gain from the process—we exchange things we can produce most efficiently for products which can be produced most efficiently someplace else. In this manner we enlarge the supplies of goods and services available in our economy by enlarging trade.

Our growing dependence on raw-material imports highlights the importance to the future growth of our country of an expanding world economy. In the long run, the economic growth of the world will be best served if each country develops those resources which it can produce most economically. Where foreign oil and other mineral deposits can be discovered and developed more cheaply than those in the United States, both we and the rest of the world stand to benefit by their use.

At the same time, we can through our international trade and investment make an expanding contribution to the development of the world economy.

Our imports provide dollars to other nations and these dollars can be used to purchase from us the machinery and equipment needed to support economic development. Our private foreign investment not only provides funds for the purchase of capital goods but also provides technical assistance to producers in other nations. Our programs of technical assistance and mutual aid contribute to the development of a vigorous world economy. . . .

THE ENCOURAGEMENT OF SCIENTIFIC ADVANCE

The greatest single active force toward economic growth is scientific advance. It was the scientific and technological revolution of the seventeenth century which paved the way for the Industrial Revolution; the subsequent expansive history of capitalism has been stimulated by its successful incorporation of the brilliant and steady scientific discoveries of the eighteenth and nineteenth centuries; and in the twentieth century the unprecedented acceleration of scientific advance promises that we are only on the threshold of a new age of science.

The world may well be on the verge of a major revolution in available energy. Already the proven reserves of uranium and thorium, in terms of energy equivalent, are at least 1,000 times the world resources of coal, gas, and oil. Our own needs for energy from nuclear power are not immediately pressing, thanks to the availability of plentiful low-cost power from coal, oil, natural gas, and water power. By the 1970s, however the significance of nuclear power will not reside alone in achieving costs competitive with fossil fuels, but in the utilization of such power in stationary installations in order to conserve the known supplies of oil for other uses. In some tasks, such as earth removal jobs and mining, nuclear explosions may soon assume major significance. This could relieve some of our important shortages of raw materials.

Nuclear energy is not the only frontier at which we are now pioneering. Research in the physical chemistry of the cell opens new vistas not alone for health and for the extension of life, but for the control of agriculture on a totally new scale. New advances in solid-state physics, in polymer chemistry, in the design of electronic equipment have resulted in astonishing extension of our boundaries of control over nature. We have begun to consider realistically problems—such as weather control and the exploration of space—which were unimaginable only a decade ago.

The translation of scientific advance into economic growth and advancement of human welfare is a task to which our system has in the past shown itself marvelously well adapted. But the encouragement of science itself is not a task which we have hitherto taken upon ourselves consciously to perform. Clearly our economic growth will reflect to an important and perhaps critical degree the effectiveness with which we stimulate free inquiry, the incentives by which we induce our potential young scientific talents to devote themselves to this field, and the quality we obtain in the whole of our education program. . . .

Here we must stress their importance, and set forth three basic guides to national policy in this area:

a. The nation should put primary emphasis on the broad potentials for economic and social growth inherent in scientific developments. The nation should not permit the pace, direction, or nature of its scientific effort to be limited either by possible military applications, important as they are, or by the fortuitous availability of shorter-run economic incentives to developmental activity by private industry.

b. Restraints on the free flow of basic scientific information, always a temptation where military applications are in any way involved, should be resisted since it is through the free flow of such information that both scientific progress and economic and social growth are, in the long run, made possible.

c. When normal economic incentives are insufficient to bring about a high rate of scientific development, the government should be alert and resourceful to foster the desired activity by any one of the numerous devices, including grants, tax incentives, and long-term loans, which we have found in the past can be successful in enlisting private initiative and resources to meet a public need. In some cases, the necessary scope of scientific development is beyond the means of private enterprise or of institutions which depend on endowment and support from private funds. In these cases, the government should generously support the needed scientific development. Areas which might qualify for such support include atomic energy, space exploration, meteorology, oceanography, agriculture, and health.

E. M. BERNSTEIN

and

I. G. PATEL

||||||||||||||||||||||||||||||||||||||||||||||||||||||||||||||||||||||||||||||||||||||||||||||||||||||||||||||||||

Inflation in Relation to Economic Development

The process of economic development is exceptionally complex. It involves much more than the provision of mechanical equipment. It requires an attitude receptive to new fields and new methods of production, institutional arrangements that encourage enterprise and investment, and technical and

From *International Monetary Fund Staff Papers* (November 1952), pp. 363-398, with omissions. Reprinted by permission of the International Monetary Fund and the authors.

managerial skills that make new methods of production effective. And it requires a healthy and well-trained labor force that can adapt itself to new methods of production. Such an environment cannot be created at once. It is more likely to appear gradually in a few sectors of the economy. Opportunities for development will thus be opened up, and they will be broadened as the country responds to development in particular fields.

CRITERIA OF UNDERDEVELOPMENT

From the economic point of view, the most rational basis for defining an underdeveloped country is not the degree of its industrialization. Countries may have very low incomes from industrial production, but very high incomes from agricultural production. The best test of an underdeveloped country is its level of real income and the rate at which per capita real income is increasing. In short, an underdeveloped country is one in which output per capita is relatively low and in which productive efficiency is increasing very slowly, if at all.[1] Data on real income must, however, be interpreted with great caution. For one thing, money-price comparisons of real income have a large margin of error, as the relative prices of home goods and export-import goods vary greatly among countries. On changes in real income, it should also be noted that an improvement in the terms of trade will be reflected in a rise in real income. Such an increase in real income, however, does not mean an increase in productive efficiency but a better market situation.

Not every measure for economic progress requires large investment. In some sectors of the economy a quite moderate capital outlay can give favorable results in production. This is most notable in agriculture, where better selection of seed, larger use of fertilizer, greater efforts at pest control, and proper rotation of crops may bring a startling increase in production. Improvements in production along these lines depend largely on practical education through agricultural extension services and to a much lesser extent on the availability of finance. The basic concept of the Point IV program is that such opportunities for increasing productive efficiency do exist. There are large and important sectors of the economy, including agriculture, where economic development, however, will involve considerable investment in construction and equipment. In particular, large investment in transportation, communications and power, and where necessary irrigation works, may be essential before any widespread investment can be undertaken in agriculture and industry.

It is characteristic of the underdeveloped countries that the resources they put into investment are generally a smaller proportion of their very much

---

[1] In the United States and Canada, per capita real income increased by approximately 50 percent during the decade 1938-1948, and in the Union of South Africa by nearly 25 percent. But in Egypt and India, for example, per capita real consumption in the postwar years has been somewhat lower than in 1938, and per capita real income has probably not increased since 1938.

smaller national product than is true for the more highly developed countries. Whereas about 15 to 18 percent of the national income has been used in the United States and Canada for net private investment in recent years, less than half of this proportion is used in most underdeveloped countries. In India, "total home-financed investment is now about 2½ percent of the national income."[2] Investment on such a scale is barely sufficient to provide the growing population with the minimum shelter and equipment they require. There is very little left for investment in projects that raise the productive efficiency of the country. . . .

AVAILABILITY OF SAVINGS

The proportionally low level of investment in underdeveloped countries may be due to various factors. Frequently, though not universally, the cause of inadequate investment is the unavailability of savings. In many under-developed countries there are opportunities for profitable and productive investment that cannot be exploited because savings or finance cannot be obtained. The inadequacy of investment is prima facie evidence that there is a deficiency of savings. This would ordinarily be expected in low-income countries, although the great inequalities in wealth found in some of them make possible considerable savings by the wealthy class.

In the United States and Canada, personal savings under more or less noninflationary conditions may amount to about 4 to 6 percent of national income, although they may amount to a considerably larger proportion of disposable personal incomes. Of equal or greater magnitude are the business savings of corporate enterprises, which may amount to 5 to 8 percent of the national income. Net private savings at present levels of real income and taxes amount in round figures to about 15 percent of the national income in the United States and Canada. To this should be added the surplus (or from this should be subtracted the deficit) in the governmental accounts and the increase in the social security reserves and other governmental trust funds. The aggregate is the net savings of the country. The component parts of net savings vary considerably from year to year, but aggregate net savings normally form a considerable proportion of the national income in such high-income countries as the United States and Canada.

Detailed and complete information about savings is not available for most underdeveloped countries, but scattered data indicate that personal savings of the nonbusiness class through savings institutions are generally very low. For example, in the Philippines, the average annual increase in time and savings deposits in the Postal Savings Bank and in other banks amounted to only ₱18 million from 1948 to 1951 (₱1=US$0.50). The average annual increase in the legal reserves of insurance companies amounted to only ₱16 million from 1949 to 1951. No doubt, personal savings of the nonbusiness

[2] *The Columbo Plan* (Report of the Commonwealth Consultations Committee, 1950, Cmd 8080).

class took other forms, probably the hoarding of notes and coin. In the same period, however, there were very large savings by the business class (including foreign companies), as indicated by investment in reconstruction and by transfers of profits abroad.

The amount of personal savings through savings institutions in underdeveloped countries with a level of income somewhat higher than in the Philippines may be illustrated by reference to Brazil. The steady inflation in that country probably tends to inhibit personal savings through financial institutions, currency and demand deposits aside. Nevertheless, considerable sums seem to have been saved by persons of low and moderate income. In 1949, for example, when national income was probably just under 200 billion cruzeiros, the addition to accounts in the Federal and State Savings Banks and in "popular" deposits and time and term deposits in commercial banks amounted to 4.3 billion cruzeiros (Table 1), although this includes some

TABLE 1. PERSONAL SAVINGS THROUGH SAVINGS INSTITUTIONS
IN RELATION TO NATIONAL INCOME, BRAZIL, 1946-1949

| | National income[a] | Personal Savings | | | | | Personal savings as percent of national income |
		Savings deposits[b]	Capitaliza-tion banks	Insurance reserves	Social security[c]	Total	
		(million cruzeiros)					
1946	128,610	2,828	210	393	2,144	5,575	4.34
1947	148,050	2,994	253	393	2,407	6,047	4.08
1948	169,160	2,135	322	391	2,643	5,491	3.25
1949	193,710	4,291	244	368	3,572	8,475	4.38

[a] 85 percent of gross national product.
[b] Federal Savings Banks, State Savings Banks of São Paulo and Minas Geraes (except 1949, only São Paulo), and time, term, and "popular" deposits in other banks.
[c] Excludes IPASE (Government Employees Fund).

Source: International Monetary Fund compilations.

increase in such deposits by business firms (Cr\$1=US\$0.054). The increase in the technical reserves of the capitalization banks was 244 million cruzeiros, and the increase in the technical reserves of the insurance companies was 368 million. In addition, about 3.6 billion was added to the assets of social security funds and institutes, except the Institute for Government Employees.

These figures for Brazil are by no means typical. For savings deposits, they may exaggerate the increase in true savings, because time and term deposits include to some extent business deposits. But even with allowance for this factor, the relation of personal savings through savings institutions is unusually high for a low-income country. . . .

Obviously, these data on personal savings do not show the total amount of savings in the country. They exclude personal savings invested in new securities, loans on mortgage and in the erection of buildings, etc.; and they do not include the vastly greater sums saved and invested by business firms. But even when allowance is made for personal savings in other forms and for business savings, the fact remains that aggregate savings are very small in most underdeveloped countries. . . .

Not only are total savings low, but personal savings are not easily directed into agricultural and industrial investment. New security issues sold to the public are of negligible importance. A considerable amount of savings is diverted into holding precious metals (particularly in the Far East) and dollar currency, deposits, and securities (particularly in Latin America). Deep-seated institutional causes hold down personal savings and divert them from productive investment. One important aspect of the problem of encouraging development is dealing with these institutional factors.

ECONOMIC PROCESS OF INFLATION

Because of the inadequacy of savings and the difficulty of directing them into productive investment, there is a strong temptation to raise the level of investment by expanding bank credit—that is, by inflation. The rationale of such a policy is that inflation acts on each of the elements essential to an increase in investment. By raising profits, inflation raises materially the return from investment and induces enterprises to expand the scale of their operations. The expansion of bank credit to businessmen provides them directly with the means of acquiring the initial resources for investment. At the same time, inflation transfers real income to a "saving" group, and the savings out of profits enable businessmen to maintain indefinitely a higher level of investment. These claims for the beneficial effects of inflation on development are far-reaching. They must be analyzed to see whether the expectations on which they are based are justified. And they must be tested by actual experience in underdeveloped countries to see the extent to which the expectations are, in practice, realized.

INITIATING INFLATION

The ordinary functioning of an economy should result in distributing and using income in such a manner that aggregate demand for output is equivalent to the cost of producing total output, including profits and taxes. At times, however, the government, businessmen, or labor may attempt to secure a larger part of the output than would thus accrue to them. If other sectors are not prepared to acquiesce in this increase in the share of output used by any one sector, all of the sectors together will be trying to get more of the national output than production has provided. This is the basic framework for the inflation process, when aggregate demand for all purposes—consumption, investment, and government—exceeds the supply of goods at current prices.

Assume, for example, that the government wants to use more of the national output than the ordinary functioning of the economy provides through taxes and loans from the public. If the government is insistent on securing additional resources, it will get them in one way or another, e.g., by issuing currency or by borrowing from the central bank and commercial banks. If other economic sectors—particularly the active sectors, business and labor—are unwilling to contract their investment or their consumption by the amount of these additional resources used by the government, an inflationary process will be initiated.

Similarly, if businessmen wish to use more of the national output than the ordinary functioning of the economy provides through savings out of profits and savings lent or invested by the public, the additional funds for financing a higher level of investment may then come from bank loans; in this way businessmen will secure the means to acquire more resources for investment. If other sectors of the economy—and in effect this means labor—are unwilling to contract consumption by the amount of these additional resources, an inflationary process will be initiated.

Consider, on the other hand, what would happen if labor were to acquiesce in a reduction of consumption and allow a shift in the share of total output going into investment. The initial impact toward inflation (that is, the expansion of investment) would then result in a rise of prices. With wages and other nonprofit incomes unchanged, the consumption of wage earners and other nonprofits receivers would decline. Prices would rise and total consumption would decline to the extent necessary to provide the additional resources that businessmen are using for investment. With a higher level of prices and an unchanged level of wages, the national income would be distributed in a manner that would enable businessmen to maintain, thereafter, the expanded scale of investment without any further rise in prices.

If this should happen, the economy would have established a tenuous stability that might or might not be easily upset—depending very much on the rigidity of wages. The expansion of investment will have made profits high relative to what businessmen ordinarily expect. They may then compete with each other to expand their scale of operations by bidding up the rate of wages. If this happens, wages may rise, investment may subside, and the distribution of real income revert approximately to its previous pattern. The inflation will have resulted in a once-for-all expansion of investment. On the other hand, wages may be quite rigid, remaining relatively fixed despite the high profits. In the Philippines, for example, profits were exceptionally high in the period 1947-1950 without apparently affecting customary wage rates. The index of money wages for skilled labor in Manila was 101 in 1947, 100 in 1948, and 102 in 1949 and 1950. Prices fell gradually, however, as the initial cause of the expansion in investment (reconstruction) began to lose its force and ultimately subsided.

Several diverse results may follow an initial expansion in investment. One may be an initial rise in prices, relatively stable wages, an increase in profits and savings, and a larger scale of investment with stability in prices at a higher level. A second result may be an initial rise in prices, a later rise in wages, a decline in investment to the pre-expansion level, and stability in prices at a higher level. A third may be an initial rise in prices, a subsequent decline in investment to the pre-expansion level, and a fall in prices to the previous level. A fourth result may be an initial rise in prices, a subsequent rise in wages, a new expansion of credit to sustain investment, and a spiral of rising prices and wages.

PRICE-WAGE SPIRAL

Only the continuous inflation of a price-wage spiral is so striking as to be regarded unequivocally as a manifest inflation. A price-wage spiral is actually far less common in underdeveloped countries than is commonly supposed. One reason, of course, is that relatively few underdeveloped countries have tried to increase investment to a significant extent by a large expansion of bank credit. And in some of the countries where investment has been financed by expanding bank credit, the inflation manifests itself in a distorted distribution of income (*i.e.,* high profits and rents relative to wages), some spill-over of the low-grade inflation into a balance of payments deficit, and moderate stability in prices relative to the prices of the United States and the United Kingdom. Even when prices have risen considerably in some underdeveloped countries, a considerable part of the rise has been a consequence of higher export and import prices, the rise in domestic prices and wages being an essential means of distributing throughout the economy the real benefits of an improvement in the terms of trade.

As pointed out above, the process of continuous inflation depends on the resistance of one sector in the economy to a reduction in its share of the national output and the insistence of another sector on an increase in its share of the national output. Thus, when prices rise, real wages fall. If labor recognizes and resists this change in real wages, it will insist on an equivalent rise in wage rates. Businessmen will be in a position to meet the wage demands because profits are higher. But the rise in wages will necessitate a reduction in investment, unless businessmen find a way to meet the higher wage demands and still maintain investment. If they have easy access to bank credit, they may persist in maintaining the larger scale of investment. There will then be an unresolved struggle for the distribution of the national output, each rise in prices being followed by a rise in wages, and each rise in wages being followed by a new rise in prices.

Although this paper is concerned particularly with the relation of inflation to development, it is necessary to recognize that inflation may be initiated by the effort of any sector of the economy to secure a share of the national output which is larger than would be provided by the ordinary functioning of the economy. This is obvious where the government acquires additional resources by the issue of currency or by credit from the central bank or commercial banks. It is equally true where labor is insistent on real wages higher than the economy can provide. While labor is not in the same position as business or government to take the initiative in securing the additional resources through bank credit, it may be able to exert pressure on businessmen and the government to yield to its wage demands. . . .

Labor occupies a key role in the inflation process, for it is labor's insistence on a certain level of real wages that is an essential part of the continuous rise in prices. This does not in any sense imply that labor's excessive expectations of real wages and social security benefits are always or even often the cause of the price-wage spiral. It may very well be that the steady demand for higher wages which businessmen have steadily met—and also steadily offset—by higher prices is no more than an attempt by labor to defend its interest in an equitable distribution of the national output. In considering the possibility of directing more real resources into development, one point to be kept in mind is that the acquiescence of labor is required. Otherwise, the stimulation of development will initiate a continuous inflation through a price-wage spiral.

ROLE OF THE MONETARY SYSTEM

A continuous rise in prices could not occur unless some means were found to finance the prevailing scale of production at the higher level of prices and costs. At any given time, the public holds an amount of money (currency plus deposits) that is in general adequate to finance production, consumption, and investment. A rise in prices and wages reduces the liquidity of the public and for this reason tends to bring the inflation process to a halt. That is not to say, of course, that prices and wages cannot rise at all unless the amount of money is expanded. Clearly, there is some flexibility in the capacity of the public to adjust itself to variations in liquidity; but this flexibility is limited and the limit can ordinarily be quickly approached if prices and wages rise while the money supply is unchanged.

Labor could, of course, press for higher wages even if the money supply did not expand, and might actually secure higher wages under such conditions. But businessmen might have difficulty in financing the same level of employment and production at higher costs. And even it if were possible to finance the same level of employment, production, and investment with a moderate rise in prices and wages, it would be quite impossible to do so with a substantial and continuous rise in prices and wages. Under such conditions, the rise in wages would soon compel some curtailment of employment, production, and investment. Prices would rise less than costs. The inflation process would come to an end. It is only the steady expansion of the money supply that permits the price-wage spiral to continue.

The money supply is seldom expanded through the simple procedure of issuing currency, even when the government is itself the initiating factor in inflation. With modern budgetary procedures, the process is likely to be different in form if not in substance. The budget authorizes spending in excess of tax revenues. The deficit must be covered by borrowing. As the public is unwilling or unable to provide loans equivalent to the deficit, the government must have recourse to the banks. The banks themselves are limited in their capacity to lend to the government, even if they are willing, for the loans to the government will increase deposits which will be partly withdrawn in the form of currency. In any case, the larger volume of deposits will compel the banks to hold larger reserves, either to meet legal requirements or to meet their legitimate needs for vault cash and clearing funds. The banks, therefore, can lend only limited amounts to the government (and then only by holding down their loans to business) unless they can obtain additional resources.

The central bank is in a position either to facilitate or to halt this expansion. Unless it provides reserves for the banking system, the loans to the government must stop. It can facilitate the expansion, however, by lending directly to the government, which will have some effect in strengthening the free reserves of the banks, or by lending to the banks through rediscounts or advances (or by purchase of their holdings of government obligations), which will strengthen the free reserves of the banks to the full extent of these operations. As the banks secure free reserves, they are able to acquire currency and to meet their needs for cash withdrawals, clearings, and legal reserve requirements, if any. . . .

In the end, the monetary authorities are the ones that bear the responsibility for a continuous inflation. They alone have the power to limit credit expansion. In a very real sense, they make credit policy, even if the policy is one of indifference to the manner in which the inflation is fed by a steady expansion of credit. This expansion of credit is the key to the price-wage spiral. Without a steady addition to the money supply the spiral would come to a halt. The parallel movements of an expanding money supply and rising prices, wherever there has been a large and continuous inflation, are evidence of the important role of credit in this process.

EFFECTS OF INFLATION ON SAVING AND INVESTMENT

It is generally agreed that inflation causes certain social injustices and gives rise to various economic evils. There are many persons, however, not only businessmen but economists, who argue that in an underdeveloped country inflation is necessary, and even indispensable, for providing the saving and investment which allows the economy to progress. The social and economic costs of an inflation (which are discussed in the next section) are alleged to be a small price to pay for economic progress. This is a question that can be resolved only by seeing in particular cases what is accomplished by an investment inflation and what its consequences are.

The ideal case of credit expansion to finance investment is a modification of the case presented by the industrial countries during the depression of the 1930s. When unemployment is severe, investment in public works permits the use of labor and productive capacity that would otherwise be idle. The increase in investment involves no reduction in aggregate consumption, although there may be some small shift of consumption from those who were previously employed to those who are newly employed, if the expansion of production of consumer goods lags and prices rise.

In underdeveloped countries, labor is not, strictly speaking, unemployed, but it may be engaged in low output work. This is likely in countries where work opportunities are limited and inefficient agricultural production is carried on by excessive application of labor. A shift of labor from such ineffective employment into investment fields would presumably reduce the supply of consumer goods very little. The incomes of the new workers in the investment sector would be higher than formerly. Prices would rise primarily because of the increase in incomes, and secondarily because of the reduction in the supply of consumer goods. Real income would be shifted from other workers to the new workers in the investment sector.

Every rise in prices involves a shift in real income from consumers generally to recipients of profits. In the ideal case given above, the transfer of relatively ineffective labor to the investment sector would improve the market for labor in all fields by creating new work opportunities, and this might moderate the shift in real income. The effort to retain the working force in other fields might lead to a general rise in wages at the expense of profits and rents. Even in the short run, it is possible, although not likely, that aggregate consumption of workers might be maintained despite a slight reduction of output of consumer goods. In a longer period, after investment has begun to affect output, there would be a larger supply of consumer goods and a rise in real income. By raising productivity, the new investment would affect the trend of real wages, quite apart from the temporary impact on the relation of incomes to available supplies, which might for a time keep real wages below the trend.

This is the ideal case. It canot be regarded as the universal or even the general case. The ideal case is most likely to be approximated where new investment starts from an exceptionally low level, where it involves a very moderate amount of investment, and where it is directed toward increasing production of consumer goods (preferably those used by wage earners). Investment will then have the greatest impact on the trend of real wages and the least impact on shifting income. Investment in irrigation projects, which would open new land to cultivation and increase output of food, or investment in textile mills, which would provide new work opportunities and increase output of cloth, will have a much more favorable effect on the trend of real wages than investment in the construction of luxury apartments or the accumulation of inventories.

It cannot be assumed that, when large credits are extended by banks to businessmen, the volume of investment is increased by a corresponding amount. The investment financed through bank credit is always offset somewhat by a decrease in the investment financed out of the savings of the non-profits receiving group. When prices rise and the real incomes of some groups fall, those groups attempt to maintain their consumption by reducing their current savings. If the pressure on the real incomes of part of the saving groups becomes very great, as it may after prolonged inflation, such groups may even draw on previous savings to protect their standard of living.

It is sometimes said that inflation will not have an adverse effect on the total savings of the nonprofits receiving group because it will compel some saving by the public to restore or maintain the real value of the cash balances they hold to finance consumption. This may not be large, in real terms, if the public lets the real value of cash balances decline, as it may, in response to the inflation. In an environment of monetary stability, the public will ordinarily do some saving in the form of additions to cash balances; and in an underdeveloped country which is expanding, this may not be inconsiderable. The growth in national output will necessitate larger cash holdings of the public, and this need will be greater as the money sector of the economy tends to grow relative to the subsistence sector.

Nevertheless, savings in the form of additions to cash balances, in real terms, will be greater under inflationary than under stable conditions. This is certain to be offset, however, by a reduction in other forms of savings of the nonprofits receiving group. Furthermore, the liquidation of some types of previous savings by this group provides profits receivers with a means of using their savings without undertaking new investment. The net effect of inflation on saving and investment may be quite small. Whereas under fairly stable monetary conditions, the savings and net investment in an underdeveloped country might amount to, say, 6 percent of the national income, under inflationary conditions, even with the increased savings out of profits, savings and net investment are not likely to exceed, say, 8 percent of the national income. . . .

There is evidence that credit expansion is more likely to stimulate investment in the early than in the late stages of a continuous inflation. The tendency for wage adjustment to keep pace with price increases is much more marked as the continuous rise in prices makes workers more alert to protect their interests. In fact, wage increases may exceed and begin to anticipate the expected price increases. In countries where prices have been rising steadily for many years, it is common to find businessmen complain that profits in real terms are not unusually high. This in itself would indicate that investment is not much more than it might have been with reasonably stable prices, since the level of real profits under continuous inflation is closely related to the volume of investment.

Despite the effort of labor to protect real wages, it would always be possible for businessmen to maintain a high level of investment, if investment seemed profitable and the banking system were prepared to provide whatever finance was necessary for continuing the high investment level. This would probably cause hyper-inflation, but it could be done. The fact that investment does not remain unusually high can probably be explained in terms of the nature of the investment encouraged by inflation and the paradoxical resistance of the monetary system to hyper-inflation, even while it is financing a continuous inflation. . . .

There is no assurance that after inflation has continued for a number of years businessmen could finance a large volume of investment. The social unrest that accompanies inflation and the repugnance to the absolute destruction of the monetary system make the monetary authorities resist hyper-inflation even as they yield to continuous inflation. The price-wage spiral may be difficult to break, once it has begun. The expansion of credit to finance production and employment at a rising level of prices and costs may be regarded as an evil that must be tolerated to avoid strikes and unemployment and widespread bankruptcies from excessive commitments by business in anticipation of steadily rising prices. The expansion of credit to maintain a high level of investment at the risk of hyper-inflation is never accepted as a justifiable policy. It is amazing how much attention the monetary authorities give to selective credit controls and to limiting credit to the "legitimate needs of business" after inflation has continued for some time. . . .

The overpowering strength of the forces let loose by inflation to achieve what in fact is likely to be only a moderate increase in investment (which could have been achieved, in large part if not entirely, by less aggressive means) ultimately converts continuous inflation into a destructive policy. A large part of any increase in investment will take forms that are of negligible importance in increasing agricultural and industrial production. The economy is distorted by the inflation so that its use of productive resources is less effective than it would otherwise be. And the effects of the inflation on the distribution of income and wealth are unhealthy and may be dangerous in countries with low incomes.

ECONOMIC AND SOCIAL COSTS OF INVESTMENT INFLATION

The effects of a large and continuous inflation are so pervasive that a complete analysis of the innumerable ways in which it acts on the economy cannot be made in this paper. It is enough to note that every aspect of economic behavior is adjusted to take account of the expected rise in prices, to avoid the losses it entails, and to share in the windfalls it brings. The economic and social costs of continuous inflation can best be appreciated by considering the shifts of income and wealth and the distortion of investment, both of which reflect the uneconomic use of productive resources.

SHIFT OF INCOME AND WEALTH

In order to increase investment under conditions of full employment, businessmen must bid up the prices of materials and labor needed for investment, using for this purpose the credit made available to them by banks. By offering higher prices and higher wages, they attract productive resources away from the consumption field into the investment field. Prices must rise, in turn, in the consumption sector, partly because incomes will be higher and partly because the supply of consumer goods will be diminished. The effects on the supply of such goods will depend on the productivity of the labor drawn away from producing them and on the scale of the expanded investment.

The rise in prices and the lag in wages, particularly in the consumer-goods industries, will increase profits and shift real income to the recipients of profits. It is out of these increased profits that the additional saving will take place, which is equivalent to the increase in investment that businessmen have undertaken on the basis of bank credit. It must not be assumed, of course, that businessmen will save all of the increase in their profits (in real terms), and that the shift in real income to profits will be precisely equal to the increase in investment. On the contrary, some of the increase in profits will be paid in taxes, some will be used to increase consumption, some will be used to transfer funds abroad, and some will be used to acquire other assets at home; only the remainder will provide the net addition to savings that is the necessary concomitant of the increase in investment. The proportion of the increase in profits that remains as savings for the increase in investment will determine how large a shift in real income is necessary to induce a given increase in investment. . . .

An inflation that is successful in increasing the volume of investment not only reduces aggregate consumption by the amount of the additional investment, but also reduces the consumption of the public other than the profits receivers by a much larger amount. The additional reduction of the consumption of the nonprofits receivers makes possible the increased consumption of the profits receivers. Nor is the reduction in consumption among nonprofits receivers likely to be distributed evenly. Apart from the fact that those living on savings and pensions are less able to protect their consumption standard, the incidence of the reduction in consumption is quite unequal even among workers. Labor in the inflation-favored industries may be able to secure a rise in wages that maintains or raises its standard of consumption. Labor in the inflation-penalized industries may have no means of protecting its standard of consumption. For example, in Brazil, the rise in wages in the construction industry enabled the workers there to secure a substantial improvement in their economic position relative to that of other workers.

As pointed out above, the savings that businessmen are induced to undertake out of their inflated profits do not represent in their entirety a net increase in real savings. In the absence of inflation, there would have been some voluntary savings, however small. With inflation, some voluntary savings will cease because it no longer pays to hold savings in the form of money assets and because the real income of some savers will be reduced. To the extent that businessmen provide savings out of profits equivalent to the reduction in savings by other sectors of the economy, there is no net increase in investment. There is simply a shift in the ownership of such investment from the general public to the profits receivers. The ownership of wealth becomes more concentrated.

This concentration is not confined to the newly created wealth. While new savings in the form of money assets is discouraged by the depreciation of purchasing power, other savers may even attempt to protect their standard of consumption by liquidating past savings. The public as a whole cannot succeed in getting more consumption in this way. Those who liquidate past savings will succeed in protecting their standard of consumption only at the expense of other consumers who are not profit receivers. As far as profit receivers are concerned, this process of dis-saving merely assures them that the ownership of both new and old wealth will come to them in larger part.

The public thus pays an extremely high price for investment financed by inflation. The net increase in investment is bound to be less than the investment financed by [non-] inflationary devices. The general public gives up consumption to the extent of some multiple—say, for example, three times—of the amount of the investment financed in this way. Of the shift of income to businessmen, two-thirds has no other economic function than to be large enough to induce them to save one-third of the increase in their profits. Beyond this increase in the consumption of the profits receivers at the cost of the general public, businessmen become the proprietors of the investment goods that emerge and of some of the old wealth as well.

FORM OF INVESTMENT

. . . Not all investment contributes in equal degree to the attainment of increased production and higher standards of living. Continuous inflation, in fact, usually induces the wrong kind of investment. When the investment is of a type that increases the demand for labor, and increases the supply of goods for consumption by the lower income groups, its use (social) benefits are high. Such investment tends to raise wages relative to other incomes and to hold down the cost of living relative to other prices. Investment in industry and in agriculture is notably of this type. On the other hand, when the investment is of a type that offers large profits, including capital gains, its ownership (private) benefits are high. Investment in holding foreign assets is of this type. In fact, any investment in holding wealth rather than using it is likely to involve a high degree of ownership benefits and a low degree of use benefits.

The businessman is concerned primarily with the ownership benefits— profits and capital gains—rather than the use benefits. Under stable conditions, this distinction is of small consequence, because the field of profitable investment where the use benefits are relatively low and the ownership benefits are relatively high is quite circumscribed. However, the windfall profits and capital gains of inflation broaden very considerably the scope of profitable investment where the use benefits are low and the ownership benefits are high. Three such fields of investment are inventories, some types of construction, and foreign assets.

One characteristic of inflation is that cash accumulations and fixed money assets depreciate in real value, and therefore the holding of such forms of wealth is avoided. It takes foresight and enterprise to undertake and manage well-conceived investment in agriculture and industry. A businessman who is accumulating cash from inflation profits may find that the opportunity for expansion in his own business is limited, and he may have neither the facilities nor the inclination for investment in other business. For such businessmen, and particularly for merchants, the accumulation of inventories is an attractive investment. Prices are bound to rise, supplies are likely to be more difficult to get, especially import goods, and inventories, within limits, can always be liquidated if necessary or used as collateral for bank credit. They are, for this reason, a favored type of investment.

Another form of investment likely to be abnormally expanded under the impact of inflation is real estate investment, particularly in the form of high-priced apartments and elaborate commercial buildings. In some underdeveloped countries, great prestige is attached to the ownership of real estate. There is, further, the mistaken view that no special capacity is needed to manage real estate investment. Professional people and beneficiaries of inflation profits, with limited opportunity for investment in an operating enterprise, are likely to be attracted by real estate investment with its sure appreciation of the money value of investment. The fact that lending institutions regard real estate as very secure collateral adds materially to the attractiveness of this form of investment. In the Philippines, a secured bank loan almost invariably means a loan with real estate collateral.

Finally, the ownership of foreign assets (including gold) is a form of holding wealth which may become extremely profitable. Where continuous inflation leads to an expectation of exchange depreciation, there is a strong temptation to hold some assets in the form of foreign funds. The inducement to hold some investment in this form is much greater when inflation involves rapid adjustment in wages, so that the real level of profits may be little higher than it would be under conditions of monetary stability. Funds transferred abroad prior to devaluation may yield enormous ownership benefits. The use benefits of such investment are zero.

It is not, however, merely through the incentive given to forms of investment which approach the pure holding of wealth that the pattern of investment encouraged by continuous inflation is unsatisfactory. The fields in which investment is most likely to be best suited to the economies of underdeveloped countries are the consumer-goods industries and the export industries. Yet the low-income consumer-goods industries are the ones that are penalized by the inflation which shifts income to profits receivers. Furthermore, the illusion that inflation can be held down by price control often leads to the maintenance of unprofitably low prices on home-produced foodstuffs and the import of foodstuffs at exchange rates which are in effect subsidies. Similarly, the export industries in which the country has special advantages may be held down by an overvalued currency—the inevitable concomitant of continuous inflation. Thus, investment is discouraged in the fields which have the highest use benefits. And even where investment in production is encouraged by inflation, it is likely to be excessively concentrated in the field of luxury consumer goods, the imports of which are sharply curtailed by import and exchange controls, and which the economy is not well suited to produce.

PROCESS OF STABILIZATION

A socially and economically sound program of development requires a much more efficient means of building up productive capital than is provided by continuous inflation. The first step in securing such a program is to restore economic stability—that is, to end the inflation. . . .

The process of stabilization following an inflation involves much more than merely preventing a further expansion in the money supply and a further rise in prices. Inflation will have distorted the relative prices of different sectors of the economy and the relative incomes of the different factors of production. It will have brought about major changes in the use of productive resources by different sectors of the economy. The process of stabilization must involve correction of these price and income distortions, for otherwise the continued imbalance will generate new elements of instability. The new pattern of relative prices and the new distribution of income must induce such use of productive resources by different sectors of the economy as will be consistent with the maintenance of stability. . . .

ROLE OF POLICY

It would, of course, be possible to take the view that the inflation will be halted—say, by stopping the expansion of bank credit—and the economy will then be allowed to adjust itself to a stable position. . . .

[But] the policy in such a situation is not exclusively the better control of credit. The continuous inflation will have brought about an undesirable use of resources and an unfair distribution of incomes which must be corrected. The price and wage adjustments are two facets of the same process of shifting real income and productive resources until they approximate a pattern suited to a stable economy. The authorities are more likely to be successful in restoring stability if their policies comprise the whole field of credit, budget, wages, investment, and international payments than if they are confined entirely to the limitation of credit.

PROGRESS WITH STABILITY

Despite the great social and economic costs of inflation, countries will inevitably be driven to dependence on credit expansion to finance investment unless other means can be found to provide the real resources they need. Monetary stability has little attraction as a policy if it is presented as an alternative to economic development; it may, however, be accepted as a desirable policy if it can be shown that it will assist in the more effective achievement of that objective. . . .

WALTER HELLER

IIIIIIIIIIIIIIIIIIIIIIIIIIIIIIIIIIIIIIIIIIIIIIIIIIIIIIIIIIIIIIIIIIIIIIIIIIIIIIIIIIIIIIIIIIIIIIIIIIIIIIIIIIIIIIIIIIIIIIIIIIIIIIIIIIIIIIIIIIIII

Fiscal Policies for Underdeveloped Economies

THE APPROACH TO DEVELOPMENTAL FISCAL POLICY

Fiscal policy, like other governmental policy, derives its meaning and direction from the aspirations and goals of the society within which it operates,

From United Nations, *Taxes and Fiscal Policy in Underdeveloped Countries* (New York: United Nations, 1954), pp. 1-22, with omissions. Reprinted by permission of the author.

of the people whom it serves. The aspirations of the peoples of the under-developed countries are clear: economic betterment and stability to provide the material soil within which human dignity and political freedom can grow. These aspirations are reflected in the objectives of the Charter of the United Nations "to promote social progress and better standards of life in larger freedom."[1] Pursuit of this end, in turn, involves acceptance of the following as economic objectives of tax and budgetary policy: (1) to make available for economic development the maximum flow of human and material resources consistent with minimum current consumption requirements; (2) to maintain reasonable economic stability in the face of long-run inflationary pressure and short-run international price movements; (3) to reduce, where they exist, the extreme inequalities in wealth, income, and consumption standards which undermine productive efficiency, offend justice, and endanger political stability.

These objectives are not basically different from the economic goals of allocative efficiency, economic growth, stability, and optimum income distribution which guide fiscal policy in advanced countries on a free-enterprise basis. Similarities in goals should not, however, be permitted to conceal the vast differences in economic conditions, in the cultural, legal, and political environment within which economic policy must operate, and, indeed, in the state of development of the art of taxation and the science of government. Failure to comprehend the nature and significance of these differences could result—in fact, in the past sometimes has resulted—in mistaken and costly transplanting of inapplicable experience to the economies of underdeveloped countries.

Before examining these differences more closely, it may be useful to sound a note of caution. Inevitably, to classify national economies into "developed" and "underdeveloped" and treat them as two more or less homogeneous groups, does violence to individual countries in each group. The under-developed countries represent a wide band rather than a single color on the economic and fiscal spectrum—perhaps too wide to justify some of the generalizations that will be made in this report. Nonetheless, there are significant differences between the *bulk* of the underdeveloped economies and the *bulk* of the developed economies. In spite of individual variations, it is not only possible to identify these differences but essential to the success of technical assistance efforts that they be given full weight in diagnosing and seeking cures for the economic and fiscal ills of underdeveloped economies.

FISCAL POLICY AND CAPITAL FORMATION

Many of the factors which give the tax and fiscal problem of the under-developed economies its distinctive character come to light in a consideration of the central problem of capital formation, the main key to economic development. In a highly developed economy like that of the United States, high average income almost automatically generates a large flow of business and personal savings. Fiscal policy for investment therefore consists largely in

---

[1] Preamble of the Charter, paragraph 4.

minimizing the interference of taxation with the incentives to absorb those savings in productive investment. Together with public expenditure policy, tax policy seeks also to reduce or offset the fluctuations in the volume of capital formation and the consequent destabilizing influence on the economy as a whole. Finally, tax policy concerns itself with the composition of investment, as for example, in the granting of preferential tax treatment to defense-oriented investment in foreign areas.

In the underdeveloped economies, taxation is increasingly assigned a far more positive role in the process of capital formation and technological change. The reason for this is implicit in the extremely low levels of income and saving which serve as the source of capital formation. Annual per capita incomes in the Middle East, in Asia, and in Latin America are typically under 200 U.S. dollars, or less than one-seventh of the United States level and one-fourth of the Canadian level.[2] Propensities to consume out of these incomes are understandably high. Little remains for saving after meeting the pressing demands of sheer subsistence in the lower income strata and of traditionally lavish living, reinforced by the "demonstration effect" of American consumption standards, in the higher income strata. The ratio of net private savings to national income falls far short of the 10 to 15 percent or even higher levels experienced in advanced countries under noninflationary conditions. Even worse, a considerable part of the meager savings is diverted into real estate and inventory speculation and the holding of precious metals, currency, and foreign exchange.

In contrast with the 15 to 18 percent of national income used for net private investment in the United States and Canada in recent years, it appears that less than half of this proportion commonly prevails in the underdeveloped countries. Total home-financed investment in India was recently estimated to be only about 2½ percent of the national income.[3] As a consequence, investment barely suffices to provide minimum shelter and equipment for the growing population. In contrast with increases in per capita real income from 1938 to 1948 of nearly 50 percent in the United States and Canada and nearly 25 percent in the Union of South Africa, per capita real income in Egypt and India did not appear to have increased at all; in fact per capita real consumption was somewhat lower than in 1938.[4]

These countries are caught in the vicious circle of extreme poverty, a circle proceeding from low incomes to high consumption propensities to low savings to low rates of capital formation to a continuation of low levels of

---

[2] For detailed estimates and a discussion of the limitations of their use, see United Nations Statistical Papers, Series E, No. 1, *National and Per Capita Incomes in Seventy Countries - 1949* (ST/STAT/SER. E/1, 20 September 1950) and *National Income and its Distribution in Under-developed Countries* (ST/STAT/SER. E/3, 9 October 1951).

[3] Figures cited in E. M. Bernstein and I. G. Patel "Inflation in Relation to Economic Development," *International Monetary Fund Staff Papers*, Vol. II, No. 3 (Washington, November 1952), p. 364. [See this volume, p. 435.—EDS.]

[4] *Ibid.*

income. To break out of this circle, apart from foreign aid, calls for vigorous taxation and government development programs; on this point, expert opinion is nearing a consensus.[5] Fiscal policy is assigned the central task of wresting from the pitifully low output of these countries sufficient savings to finance economic development programs and to set the stage for more vigorous private investment activity.

The problem of capital formation in the underdeveloped economies, as it confronts public finance, breaks down into three main parts. The first concerns the financing of social overhead investment which must be undertaken directly by government. The second deals with an intermediate zone in which the actual investment projects are in private hands but the funds are made available through government finance. The third deals with the necessary incentives to private investment, both domestic and foreign, as they are influenced by taxation and other fiscal measures. In all three categories, government effort is directed toward maximizing savings, mobilizing them for productive investment, and canalizing them so as to serve the purposes of a balanced development program. . . .

FINANCING GOVERNMENT'S SHARE IN
ECONOMIC DEVELOPMENT

The Role of Government Perhaps the most striking feature of the capital formation process in the underdeveloped economy is the large and inescapable role that government must play in providing "social overhead capital" both as a direct instrument of economic development and as a prerequisite to increased participation of private capital in the development process. In economies at all stages of development, there are investment projects which are not inherently attractive to private investment, yet promise large social gains. The unwillingness of private investors to offer their resources in spite of the large social gains involved may be based on any one of several grounds. (1) There may be a sharp divergence between the opportunity for private gain and social gain; the benefits conferred upon the direct recipient of the service, which are the basis for market pricing and private profits, may be strongly supplemented by benefits to third parties, *i.e.,* to society as a whole. Education, health, and sanitation measures clearly fall in this category. Such investment in the formation of human capital may pay rich social and economic dividends, yet provide no opportunity for private investors to exact charges commensurate with the benefits or the costs. Devel-

---

[5] See, for example, the discussions by Ragnar Nurkse of Columbia University and John H. Adler of the International Bank for Reconstruction and Development in the *American Economic Review* (May 1952), especially pp. 583 and 592-596; Ragnar Nurkse, *Problems of Capital Formation in Underdeveloped Countries* (Oxford, 1953); the discussion by Bernstein and Patel, *op. cit.,* pp. 393-395; various United Nations studies, *e.g., Domestic Financing of Economic Development,* United Nations Publications, Sales No.: 1951.II.B.1, and *Economic Development in Selected Countries,* Vols. I and II, United Nations Publications, Sales Nos.: 1948.II.B.1 and 1950.II.B.1. . . .

opment of transport, soil improvement, and river development are examples of physical investment which also fall at least partially in this category. (2) Returns from the investment may be too remote, too slow to materialize, to attract private investors. (3) The amount of investment involved in the project in question may be too large to be handled by private investors. Examples of the second and third categories are power installations, river development, and various conservation projects.

A brief consideration of the relationship of these types of investment to the development process will make clear why governments of underdeveloped countries have to play such a central role in the capital formation process and why, in turn, the strengthening of the tax system to yield adequate revenues is of such primary concern. Apart from its direct contribution to human well-being, the social overhead investment of government makes two essential contributions to economic development. First, large-scale improvements in health, education, and training expand productive capacity by increasing the stamina and strength of the workers on one hand and enlarging their fund of knowledge and skills on the other; this represents fully as much of an increase in the resources at the disposal of the economy as do investments which increase the fund of physical capital. Second, the foregoing increases in human capacity, combined with investments in highways, power projects, irrigation, and the like, provide the necessary economic environment—the external economies—needed to make private investments more attractive. Unlike investors in advanced countries, those in the underdeveloped economies cannot take for granted a supply of skilled and healthy labor, easy transport and communications, availability of power and water, and readily available supplies of raw materials. The apparent profitability of many investments in such countries is therefore cut down by the large costs that have to be incurred either to develop these prerequisites to the productive process or to operate without some of them. By utilizing their fiscal power to produce these services, governments can provide many of the external economies needed to raise rates of return to levels which will attract private investors.

Implications for Budgetary Management   The foregoing consideration of the relation of government outlays to the development process illustrates some of the difficulties involved in proper analysis and classification in governmental budget accounting. For example, outlays on teachers' and doctors' salaries, insect sprays, and medicines result in additions to the stock of human capital. Yet, they do not result in the creation of the depreciable assets which are admissible to government capital accounts. Related to this budgeting dilemma is the tendency to assign priorities to government projects on the basis of their financial return rather than their real return. From the discussion above, it is clear that the greatest real returns may be realizable in precisely those areas where there are no direct financial returns. Balanced economic development depends on assigning priorities to projects according to their contribution to the productivity of the economy rather than to their chances of being self-liquidating. Only where the financial returns add to the *total*

resources available for developmental investment should the financial over-
tones affect the scale of priorities.[6]. . .

Capacity for tax increases   The pressing need for large government outlays for economic development strongly influences the approach to the
problem of determining the appropriate level of taxation in an underdeveloped
country. In a highly developed economy, tax policy tends to accept the level
of expenditures as its revenue goal (modified, of course, by considerations
relating to the levels of employment, prices, and economic activity). The
sequence of decision tends to run from expenditures to taxes. But in underdeveloped countries the level of expenditures depends much more heavily on
the ability of the tax system to place the required revenues at the disposal of
the government. By the same token, the size of the government's development
program depends in large part on the economic and administrative capacity of
its tax system to marshal the necessary resources. In this sense, the sequence
of decision tends to run from taxation to expenditures.

Recognizing the strategic importance of an adequate flow of tax revenues
—and the inadequacy of their own revenues—the governments of many developing countries have sought to increase the proportion of national income
collected in taxes. Much of the increased demand for technical assistance in
fiscal matters since World War II apparently grows out of this desire for a
more productive tax system. Underdeveloped countries are under no illusion
that they can—or should—push their tax ratios of 10 to 15 percent of national
income to the 30- to 40-percent levels reached in such advanced countries as
Austria, Belgium, France, Germany, the Netherlands, Norway, the United
Kingdom, and the United States. But they are aware that even a modest
increase in taxation may be able to finance a large percentage increase in a
government's contribution to the development program. A country in which
the share of the government sector in the gross national product is 12 percent
may be taken as fairly typical of low-income countries.[7] If one assumes that
not more than one-third of the government's share is devoted to economic
development, an increase of only 2 percentage points in the ratio of taxes to
national income (to 14 percent) would enable the government to increase its
contribution to development expenditures by 50 percent.

Does experience or informed judgment provide any reliable guide as to

---

[6] Extensive discussions of the principles which govern the planning of development
programs and the participation of the government in them are contained in various
United Nations studies, *e.g., Methods of Financing Economic Development in Underdeveloped Countries,* United Nations Publications, Sales No.: 1949.II.B.4, *Domestic
Financing of Economic Development, op. cit., Measures for the Economic Development
of Under-developed Countries,* United Nations Publications, Sales No.: 1951.II.B.2 and
Formulation and Economic Appraisal of Development Projects, United Nations Publications, Sales No.: 1951.II.B.4, Vols. I and II.

[7] See the recent article by John H. Adler, "Fiscal Problems in Economic Development" in *Rapports pour le Congrès de Londres de l'Institut international de finances
publiques* (Paris, 1951). In it, he concludes that for a number of underdeveloped countries, particularly in Latin America, "The share of the government sector in the gross
national product, varies between 10 and 16 percent and is in most countries not higher
than 12 percent."

what level of taxation is appropriate for an underdeveloped economy? Experience shows, first, that the less advanced the economy of a country, generally, the lower the ratio of tax payments to national income. It shows, second, that through intensive administrative and legislative efforts (and in some cases, aided by favorable international market conditions or by foreign aid), quite a few less advanced countries have considerably increased their ratios in postwar years. For example, the Commonwealth Government of the Philippines increased its tax revenues by 80 percent from 1950 to 1951.

The judgment of technical assistance experts in public finance, as reflected in their mission reports and other writings, appears to be that most underdeveloped countries could increase the proportion of their national income taken by taxation without unduly disturbing the economy and perhaps even with positive gains in the face of inflationary pressures.[8] Yet where the optimum level lies permits of no doctrinaire answer. It will differ from country to country depending on the preferences of citizens, the administrative competence in government, the relative importance of existing tax levels on one hand and undeveloped external economies on the other as barriers to private investment, and many other factors. As regards taxation, one of the key factors is whether additional taxes can be so levied as to tap funds that otherwise would have gone into such channels as luxury consumption or socially unproductive investment or foreign exchange hoarding, or whether they would simply displace private productive investment and essential consumption. No categorical answer can be given, then, to this question: How far and how fast can taxes be raised? Only through a careful enquiry into economic characteristics, social and cultural institutions, and prevailing standards of tax administration and compliance can an intelligent approximation be provided for any given country.

TAXATION AND PRIVATE INVESTMENT

The foregoing discussion revolves around the use of taxation to mobilize the resources required by the government to carry out its share of the development program. The discussion now turns to the impact of taxation on the flow and pattern of resources devoted to private capital formation. Even though the government may take a large hand in the financing of some of the projects, they are basically private investments undertaken for private profit.

Publicly Financed Private Investment   In view of the lack of developed capital markets in many countries, and the additional fact that controls may be necessary to divert funds from lavish consumption or speculation into productive investment in agriculture and industry, an increasing number of the less developed countries are using taxes to raise funds to be loaned to private investors. For example, *Institutos de Fomento* and specialized corporations or commissions for industrial or agricultural development have been established in Bolivia, Brazil, Chile, Colombia, India, Mexico, and Peru.[9] Some countries

---

[8] Bernstein and Patel, *op. cit.*, p. 395.

[9] See *Economic Development in Selected Countries, op. cit.*, Vols. I and II.

have also provided financial assistance to private enterprises like airlines and shipping companies whose requirements for capital are large and not easily obtainable from private sources.[10] Alternatively, governments can place tax-generated savings at the disposal of private entrepreneurs through the private banking system, *e.g.,* by retiring bank-held debt. Such action makes room for noninflationary extension of credit for the support of private investment projects.[11]

Privately Financed Private Investment   The final category of investment, namely, private investment undertaken without the use of government funds, involves the most difficult and delicate problems of tax composition and structure. As is brought out elsewhere in this paper, such private investment is also influenced very substantially by other aspects of governmental fiscal policy. Section 1 has already brought out the role of government in developing transport, power, technical training, and similar facilities to create external economies for private investment.

Section 4 suggests that where deficient domestic markets are blocking the flow of private funds into desired domestic industries, governments may wish to orient their taxing and spending policies toward strengthening such markets. In addition, fiscal policy influences the level and direction of investment through its impact on inflation and economic stability; some of the possibilities and limitations of fiscal policy in this regard are examined in Section 3.

The position is sometimes taken that governments should not go too far in trying to prevent inflation in an underdeveloped economy because (*a*) this may require unduly high taxes and (*b*) within bounds, inflation is itself an acceptable pragmatic instrument of a developmental policy. While the pros and cons of this position cannot be fully aired here, the implications for tax policy of this pro-inflationary position are so far-reaching that it cannot be dismissed without comment.

With respect to "unduly high taxes," a point may somewhere be reached where inflation is preferable to higher taxes, but given a reasonably well-structured tax system, this point seems rather remote at levels of taxation approximating 15 percent of national income. Moreover, a government which is aggressively participating in the development process will have other (though related) reasons for levying higher taxes. In a developmental setting, then, higher taxes are seen not as a positive good but as the lesser of evils.

On behalf of inflation, it can be noted that where it is the only available alternative to persistent stagnation, it may be attractive as a last resort in spite of its risks. One may even contend, somewhat more positively, that inflation has an invigorating effect by loosening economic and social relationships and giving the more ingenious and enterprising elements in the population a chance to come to the fore. But even without examining the pitfalls in these positions, one is entitled to the gravest doubts, on both economic and social

---

[10] See "Domestic Financing of Economic Development," *op. cit.,* p. 44.

[11] Nurkse, *op. cit.,* p. 151. A similar point is made in reference to the economies of Western Europe since World War II in Howard S. Ellis, *The Economics of Freedom* (New York, 1950), p. 40.

justice grounds, about accepting inflation as an instrument for economic development.

The process by which credit-induced inflation generates capital investment is sympathetically described in terms of three steps: (*a*) the credit expansion provides the initial means of diverting resources from the remainder of the community; (*b*) profits generated in this process yield additional savings to perpetuate the capital-forming process; (*c*) profits thus generated also serve as the inducement to undertake the investment. But this is a costly and inequitable way of transferring resources from consumption to capital formation. First, enlarged profits to investors combined with dis-saving by consumers trying to maintain previous levels of consumption will increase rather than decrease inequalities of income and wealth. Second, inflation channels much of the resulting investment into real estate, inventories, foreign exchange, and other "riskless" holdings designed to reap capital gains from socially unproductive undertakings. Third, even where investment flows into industrial production, inflation tends to elicit investment in luxury industries rather than those producing necessities. Finally, inflation is eventually self-defeating if it discourages the voluntary savings which provide the solid foundation for economic development.[12]

Turning from the level to the structure of taxation, one finds much disagreement on what constitutes the most effective policy for maximizing private investment and guiding it into the most useful channels. On some points, of course, fairly extensive agreement has been reached among experts in public finance. It is fairly widely agreed, for example, that full use should be made of tax measures which can seek out and impound income that would otherwise be squandered on lavish living and luxury imports. Commodity taxes in the form of high import duties and excises on luxury items are widely advocated as instruments of such policy in underdeveloped countries. Also, personal income taxes with steeply progressive rates in the upper brackets are often favored as instruments for tapping such income.

There is also considerable agreement that taxes should, if possible, penalize the diversion of savings into land, buildings, inventories, and similar investments held for speculative gain or prestige purposes rather than productive use. Among the tax instruments recommended for use to this end are land value increment taxes, taxes on idle land, progressive taxes on either net worth or real estate holdings, and either special capital gains taxes or inclusion of capital gains in part or in full as taxable income. At the present time, many countries—especially those following the British tax pattern—exempt capital gains on casual transactions. While some experts defend this as necessary to implement a traditional definition of income, others condemn it because it provides an incentive for speculative investments which draw savings away from the development program.

The foregoing is not meant to say that there is a complete consensus among experts on the desirability of these measures. A few would contend,

---

[12] For a fuller development of this analysis, see Bernstein and Patel, *op. cit.*

for example, that exorbitant profits, luxury living, and the implicit inequalities of income and wealth are necessary as stimulants to investment and human effort, objectionable as they may be in terms of distributive justice. Others who might not go quite this far would nonetheless prefer tax concessions for desirable investment activities to penalty taxes on undesirable activities. Another point of view is that the tax administrations of many of the underdeveloped countries are too inefficient and unreliable to practice the finer arts of taxation; where this situation prevails, only simple taxes levied at relatively low rates are said to be capable of tolerable enforcement.

Even apart from the question of administrative feasibility, there is a wide diversity of opinions concerning the desirability and effectiveness of special tax concessions for private domestic and foreign investment. One point of view is that they are relatively ineffective either because levels of taxation in the underdeveloped countries are not generally high enough to inhibit investment seriously or because barriers like political instability and restrictions on foreign exchange conversion loom so much larger than the tax barrier.[13]

A very different view of the matter is reflected in the tax policies of India. Very extensive income tax concessions are granted with respect to returns from certain types of economic activity. For example, new industrial undertakings are exempt from income tax for five years up to 6 percent of their invested capital and accelerated depreciation is allowed on new buildings, plant, and machinery.[14]

Although preferential tax treatment does not enter into the government's budget at any point, it is nonetheless a disguised government expenditure. The use of revenues raised by taxation to grant subsidies to private investment differs in form but not in substance from subsidies granted in terms of reduced tax liabilities. The danger also exists that tax concessions will be converted into tax loopholes. Taxpayers are ever watchful to gain tax benefits by meeting the formal requirements of the concession provisions without carrying out the underlying intent. In spite of these and other defects, a considerable number of persons concerned with the formation of tax policy in underdeveloped countries warmly defend tax concessions as an incentive to investment. Moreover, the line between questionable tax concessions and desirable improvements in tax structure is not always easy to draw.

Among the structural improvements and incentive devices most widely supported in the field of business income taxation are the following: (1) The allowance of extensive carry-overs of net business losses in one year as offsets against net business gains in other years; this reduces or removes the deterrent

---

[13] "There is no evidence that taxation in Colombia has tended to reduce the overall level of investment either by cutting the supply of savings or by reducing investment returns and hence the willingness to invest." (International Bank for Reconstruction and Development, *The Basis of a Development Programme for Colombia*, Washington, 1950, IBRD Special Publication, Sales No.: IBRD.1950.2, p. 264.)

[14] See *Foreign Investment Laws and Regulations of the countries of Asia and the Far East*, United Nations Publications, Sales No.: 1951.II.F.1, p. 27, and *The Use of Taxation Techniques as Incentive to Private Investment in Far Eastern Countries*, United Nations document ECAFE/I and T/FED/19, 8 September 1953.

to investment that otherwise results from the lack of opportunity to deduct business outlays in full from income subject to taxation. (2) Accelerated depreciation, permitting the more rapid recapture of productive investment; this device has the effect of giving the investor an interest-free loan from the government. (3) Preferential rates for reinvested business profits or, alternatively, additional taxes on profits declared as dividends; this measure recognizes such profits as a prime source of investment funds and seeks to discourage their dissipation in consumption or their "loss" by transfer abroad.

From the foregoing discussion, it is apparent that tax policy faces a basic dilemma in its role as an instrument of capital formation for economic development. On one hand, high levels of taxation are necessary to finance that part of the developmental process which falls in the government sphere and to mobilize for investment the private resources that might otherwise be dissipated. On the other hand, the lower the taxes the greater will be the inducement to private investors, per unit of net income, to take the risks associated with investment in agricultural and industrial development. The dilemma is worsened by the fact that those taxes which are most effective in capturing a large share of the gains from economic development for further capital formation are the ones most likely to affect the returns from private investment. For it is the taxes which vary directly and rise progressively with the size of income that are most effective in absorbing the gains from development (and are generally preferred on equity grounds); yet these are precisely the ones which are likely to affect marginal effort and risk-taking.

One way out of the dilemma may be to combine high rates of taxation in general with preferential treatment for categories of desired developmental activity (and penalty taxes or rates on undesirable economic activities). To implement such a policy requires careful economic analysis and planning, skillful structuring of taxes, ruling out of political favoritism, and competent tax administration. An important function of technical assistance in public finance is to ascertain for the country in question not only what combination of tax policies might best serve the interests of economic development (in the light, always, of the country's ethical preferences) but also how those policies have to be modified in translating them into tax measures which are operational in terms of the country's capacity for tax administration and conditions of tax compliance.

FISCAL POLICY FOR THE "EXPOSED ECONOMY"

Another factor which strongly conditions the role of fiscal policy in many underdeveloped countries is the vulnerability of their economies to world-market developments lying outside of their control. Their exposed position grows mainly out of their heavy dependence on the exports of one or two agricultural or mineral products both as a source of national income and as a source of foreign exchange. Their exposure is increased by their dependence on foreign sources for manufactured products and often for foodstuffs as well.

Finally, they often find that their attempts to maintain domestic economic stability are complicated by the dominant position of foreign investment in their primary industries combined with a tendency of both foreign and domestic investors to seek safe haven for their profits abroad. Increasingly, underdeveloped countries have sought to protect their "exposed economies" from the buffetings of fluctuating world-market demand and prices by the use of flexible fiscal and foreign exchange measures in the short run and diversification of their economies in the long run.

Examples of countries whose productive patterns and dependence on exports put them in the category of "exposed economies" are: Bolivia where, between 1938 and 1948, exports of mineral products averaged nearly 95 percent of the total value of exports[15]; Chile, where copper in 1950 accounted for 50 percent and nitrates for 25 percent of total exports[16]; Cuba, where the sugar sector contributed directly between 24 percent (1945) and 37 percent (1947) of the national income and where exports of sugar and sugar products account for nearly 90 percent of total exports (1949).[17] Similar examples can be found in the Central American countries: in El Salvador, for example, coffee accounts for 12 percent of the gross national product (1946)[18] and for 89 percent of total exports (1950).[19] In Guatemala bananas and coffee contributed 13 percent of the gross national product (1947-1948) and more than 80 percent of total exports (coffee: 72 percent in 1949).[20] In the last two countries, moreover, the largest part of the active population is engaged in the production of the one or two export commodities. Further examples are provided by the oil-producing countries, such as Iran, Iraq, and Venezuela, where oil exports accounted respectively for 90 percent (1949), 51 percent (1950), and 97 percent (1950) of the total value of exports.[21] In the Far Eastern countries the following countries may be mentioned: Ceylon (1951: tea 42 percent, rubber 31 percent of the total value of exports); Indonesia (1951: rubber 42 percent, oil 20 percent); Thailand (1949: rice 63 percent).[22] In the Federation of Malaya rubber in 1948 accounted for nearly 20 percent of the net national product.[23]

Although all of these countries depend heavily on one or two primary

---

[15] *Report of the United Nations Mission of Technical Assistance to Bolivia,* United Nations Publications, Sales No.: 1951.II.B.5.

[16] *International Financial Statistics,* International Monetary Fund (October 1952), p. 140.

[17] *Report on Cuba, Findings and Recommendations by a Mission of the International Bank for Reconstruction and Development* (Washington, 1951), IBRD Special Publication, Sales No.: IBRD.1951.3, Ch. 40.

[18] H. D. Wallich and J. H. Adler, *Public Finance in a Developing Country, El Salvador, a Case Study* (Cambridge, Mass.: Harvard University Press, 1951), p. 25.

[19] See *International Financial Statistics* (October 1952), p. 46.

[20] *The Economic Development of Guatemala, Report of a Mission by the International Bank for Reconstruction and Development* (Washington, 1951), IBRD Special Publication, Sales No.: IBRD.1951.2, pp. 10 and 12.

[21] *International Financial Statistics* (October 1952), pp. 66, 68, and 134.

[22] *Ibid.,* pp. 139, 151, and 161.

[23] See Frederick Benham, *The National Income of Malaya, 1947-1949* (Singapore: Government Printing Office, 1951).

commodities sold in world markets, they differ both in the price they pay for such dependence—in the degree of instability to which they are exposed—and in the benefits they derive—in the degree of comparative advantage they enjoy. To take an extreme example, a one-commodity country whose main export is uranium seems assured of a strong market, favorable terms of trade, and a steady supply of dollar exchange. A less extreme example of a favored mono-cultural economy is that of Cuba, whose peculiar relation to the United States market reduces the risks involved in its reliance on sugar. Moreover, the low-income, undiversified economy is not the only one to suffer from external destabilizing influences. Any export-oriented economy runs this risk. Yet, other things being equal, a country whose economic fate depends on world markets for one or two primary products risks greater instability and finds conventional fiscal policy less effective in dealing with it than a country which is industrially more diversified. Economic exposure characterizes so many of the world's underdeveloped economies that it requires special consideration in an analysis of their fiscal policies.

FISCAL MEASURES FOR ECONOMIC STABILIZATION

To the extent that instability is the product of external movements of prices and demand for the export products which dominate the local economy, the applicability of generalized expansionary and contractionary fiscal policy is correspondingly limited. It does not follow that the nonindustrialized country has no fiscal weapons to use in defending the domestic economy against the vicissitudes of world-market fluctuations. Such specific instruments as export taxes may lend themselves more readily to this kind of stabilization activity than more general measures like sales and income taxation.

Increases in export taxes and manipulation of exchange rates were used by many primary producing countries to take advantage of the sudden shift in the terms of trade in the post-Korean spurt of world-market prices. These measures were used to siphon off some of the windfall gains of the export sector and to impound a large amount of precious foreign exchange. In some cases, the proceeds were used to good advantage (a) in shielding the economy from the inflationary impact of rising world-market prices and (b) in financing capital imports for the development program. Where export levies are used to build up foreign-exchange reserves or perhaps even a formal "foreign-exchange stabilization fund," the effects of a subsequent worsening of the terms of trade can be cushioned by adjusting such levies downward and by drawing on exchange reserves.

The advantages to be gained in reducing the exposure of primary producers to the ebbs and flows of world markets by skillful manipulation of export and import taxes or multiple exchange rates do not, of course, wipe out the traditional objections to these fiscal devices: namely, (a) that they may interfere with the optimum pattern of world trade; (b) that they are inferior in equity terms to a progressive income tax; (c) that they may lead to uneconomic productive practices, particularly in the extractive industries; and (d) that especially in the case of multiple exchange rates they may seriously inhibit foreign investment by interfering with the free flow of returns on such investment.[24] Moreover, the potential contribution to internal economic stability and development can be realized only through an uncommon fusion of political will and economic skill: (*a*) will, for example, to resist a high propensity to import consumer goods, especially luxuries; and (*b*) skill not only in managing tax and exchange rates but also in so timing the changes and channeling the proceeds as to promote stable and balanced economic development.

Without gainsaying the objectionable features of these devices, especially in their interference with international monetary flows, one may acknowledge their attractions as tax measures under certain circumstances in which underdeveloped countries may find themselves. First, these devices can be adjusted up or down more easily than, for example, the income tax. Second, they are better suited than general taxes like the income tax to single out the export-import sector of the economy and counteract destabilizing influences that arise from it. Finally, they are relatively simple to administer and difficult to evade. In a setting of weak administration and low taxpaying morale, this can be a decisive advantage for export and import levies as instruments for economic stabilization.[25]

The application of fiscal policy for economic stabilization in underdeveloped primary producing countries is also complicated by the internal characteristics of their economies. Especially in predominantly agricultural economies, supply is likely to be relatively inelastic. Moreover, the organization of production is characterized by many institutional rigidities. Custom, tradition, systems of land tenure, and the like tend to block or impede the free flow of resources, both human and material, from one use into another. Nor is economic motivation such that opportunities for profit are as quickly recognized and exploited as in industrial nations. Consequently, a cautious and segmental rather than bold and aggregative approach must be taken to the use of compensatory fiscal policy.

Economically developed countries find themselves in a very different position in this respect. They generally enjoy a considerably greater degree of insulation against external destabilizing influences and a correspondingly greater opportunity to regulate their own economies. Further, since their economies are usually diversified, industrialized, and elastic, the effects of compensatory finance transmit themselves relatively smoothly and evenly throughout the economy. In this setting, for example, reductions and increases in public works or transfer payments translate themselves rather readily into higher levels of employment and income. In the underdeveloped economy, in contrast, injections of purchasing power may in considerable part run off into

---

[24] For a development of some of these points see E. M. Bernstein, "Some Economic Aspects of Multiple Exchange Rates," *International Monetary Fund Staff Papers,* Vol. I, No. 3 (Washington, September 1950), and the section on taxation and public finance in the *Report of the United Nations Mission of Technical Assistance to Bolivia, op. cit.*

[25] See E. R. Schlesinger, *Multiple Exchange Rates and Economic Development* (Princeton, N. J., 1952), p. 20.

higher prices of the inelastic domestic supplies on one hand and into larger imports on the other. Much of the multiplier effect is thus thwarted or transmitted abroad. Since deficit financing may aggravate the external trade deficit, the virtues of unbalancing the governmental accounts may have to be set off against the vices of unbalancing the external trade accounts.

One of the major attractions of industrialization in underdeveloped countries is apparent in the foregoing discussion. In the absence of effective international measures for economic stabilization, these countries are striving to reduce the exposure of their economies by diversification.[26] In doing so, they are also motivated by a number of other considerations which suggest that the law of comparative advantage can be pursued too far: (1) Often the mono-cultural economy is characterized by disguised unemployment in the form of redundant labor in agricultural pursuits or seasonal unemployment in those pursuits; through diversification, it is hoped that a productive outlet for this labor can be provided. (2) Where exports are the only or main outlet for increased production, the pursuit of comparative advantage may be thwarted by relatively stationary or inelastic demands on the world market. (3) Without an attempt at diversification, a country may not in fact be aware of the pursuits in which its greatest comparative economic advantage lies. (4) An economy's advantage in producing a particular good may be acquired rather than inherent, in which case the shifting of resources may result in acquiring advantages in the production of goods previously imported, thereby saving transport costs and the like. (5) Agrarian societies are often economically and sometimes culturally backward; industrialization not only releases men's skills and provides new fields for expression but tends to make the social structure more fluid.

In exploring some of the reasons why countries with exposed economies so often seek to industrialize and diversify, the foregoing discussion does not mean to suggest that economic development is synonymous with industrialization. The primary purpose of economic development is, of course, the raising of per capita income and living standards rather than the promotion of economic stability. Where investment in the agricultural and other primary producing sectors clearly offers the greatest returns, it would retard economic development to make a fetish of industrialization. New Zealand and Denmark serve as examples of economic advancement primarily through agriculture.

At the same time, it is essential to count *all* the costs as well as *all* the benefits in allocating developmental resources between industry and agriculture. Where industrialization absorbs manpower that would otherwise run to waste in agricultural unemployment, where it releases latent skills, and

---

[26] This view is reflected, for example, in the study, *Theoretical and Practical Problems of Economic Growth*, by the United Nations Economic Commission for Latin America (document E/CN.12/221 of 18 May 1951). It states (p. 43): "Certain productive activities, in which the level of productivity is lower than in others, may nevertheless be eminently advantageous, owing to the fact that they diminish a country's vulnerability to foreign fluctuations and contingencies." See also *The Economic Development of Latin America and its Principal Problems*, United Nations Publications, Sales No.: 1950,II.G.2, Ch. VII.

where it reduces economic instability and its heavy attendant costs, the real balance of advantages may be tipped toward investment in industry even though the apparent balance of direct increase in productivity favors agriculture. Under these circumstances, a fiscal policy that facilitates capital formation and technological progress in industry serves the ends of both economic stability and fuller use of resources. . . .

OTHER FISCAL PROBLEMS OF THE "EXPOSED ECONOMY"

A somewhat different aspect of the exposure of many underdeveloped economies to external economic influence is the extensive participation of foreign investment in certain segments of the economy, especially the extractive industries. It has been estimated, for example, that local participation in the form of wages, royalties, and taxes in the Bolivian tin industry amounted to only about 20 percent of the value of minerals exported during the 1920s and perhaps 45 percent in recent years. While this may have the questionable virtue of transmitting more of the instability of the minerals industry abroad, it has the offsetting vice from the standpoint of the underdeveloped country of drawing off income and foreign exchange out of which consumption levels could be raised or investment for economic development could be expanded. This is not to say, of course, that the country is worse off than if the foreign capital had not come in at all. It merely re-emphasizes that the country seeking development faces an uncomfortable dilemma in tax policy. On one hand, it wishes to maximize total output by attracting foreign capital into the country, an objective which in appropriate cases may be advanced by low taxes or special tax incentives. On the other hand, it wishes to maximize its share of any given output, presumably by levying high taxes and royalties. It is not easy to strike the proper balance.

Foreign investment exposes the tax system of the underdeveloped country to other elements beyond its immediate control. For example, the credits allowed by some of the major capital exporting countries, *e.g.,* the United States and England to their individual and corporate investors in foreign countries specify rather closely what types of foreign taxes shall be eligible under the crediting provisions. This may influence the country seeking investment from abroad to adjust its tax system so as to draw full advantage from the credit provisions both for its own revenue and for the foreign investor.

Another factor is the complication of tax administration and structure. Where profits accrue to foreign owners or where the business unit in the taxing country is integrated with one in another country, it is administratively hard to determine the base for income taxes and even in some cases for ad valorem export taxes. Moreover, opportunities for evasion are significantly increased. Finally, the relationship between the domestic and foreign arms of many undertakings make it more difficult to integrate corporate with individual income taxes so as to prevent both (*a*) discriminatory double taxation of distributed earnings and (*b*) avoidance of personal income tax either through unreasonable corporate accumulations or through distribution of earnings to nonresident shareholders. Such difficulties as the foregoing have undoubtedly decreased the attractiveness of income taxes relative to export and import duties in the less advanced economies.

REDISTRIBUTIVE ASPECTS OF FISCAL POLICY

In advanced economies, the function of fiscal policy as it affects income and wealth distribution is largely one of attempting to attain that degree of redistribution through taxation and government spending which most neatly balances (a) the humanitarian interest in sharing economic well-being more equally, against (b) the efficiency interest in maintaining sufficient inequalities of reward to serve as an incentive to the exercise of special economic effort and ingenuity. Inequalities of wealth and income, while still substantial, have been narrowed in most developed economies by a combination of increases in productivity and various redistributive policies of government. The magnitudes involved in the inequalities which remain are generally large enough to offer fertile ground for progressive taxation and redistributive expenditure. In most advanced countries, the machinery of progressive income and wealth taxation is sufficiently well developed to carry out its share of a redistributive fiscal policy.

Contrast the setting, role, and magnitudes of redistributive finance in the less advanced economies. Many are characterized by extremes of wealth and poverty which, in terms of the equalitarian ethic as accepted throughout the free world, constitute a compelling case for redistributive government finance.[27] Not only is the humanitarian interest often more intense than in advanced countries, but the efficiency interest may differ sharply in both nature and emphasis, as brought out below. However extreme the existing inequalities may be, the impact of distributive considerations on fiscal policy in less advanced countries must in practice be tempered by the limits they encounter in varying degrees with respect to (a) the absolute size of existing concentrations of income and wealth and (b) the ability of their tax systems to tap these concentrations.

Within these limits, what role does redistributive finance play as an instrument of economic policy in the country seeking development? Qualitatively, the answer goes to the very root of the problem of economic productivity. Investments in human beings are an integral part of government programs for improving productivity and technology. Improvements in sanitation, health, and nutrition build up working capacity and thus increase the quantity of manpower available for economic development. Education and training programs reduce illiteracy and increase skill and thus increase the quality of manpower. To the extent that taxation finances this process of human capital formation at the expense of lavish consumption, speculation, and foreign-

---

[27] Some statistical evidence on the commonly accepted conclusion that the inequalities are marked is provided in "National Income and its Distribution in Underdeveloped Countries," *United Nations Statistical Papers, op. cit.*

exchange hoarding rather than at the expense of productive private investment, it increases productivity and accelerates development.

Countries seeking to establish home industries in the interests of balanced economic growth often find that domestic markets are too limited to support such undertakings.[28] In so far as redistributive government finance increases the productivity and real income of the bulk of the population, it tends to broaden the base of the domestic market. It may also contribute to this end by shifting demand from luxury items ordinarily imported from abroad to more needed items which can be produced domestically. How much of the purchasing power diverted from luxury consumption or created by increased productivity should be siphoned off for further capital formation and how much should be permitted to express itself in higher levels of mass consumption will depend on the stage of economic development and the preferences of the society in question. One country may wish to mobilize every available source of saving for a program of social overhead investment. Another may put more emphasis on increases in consumption as (a) a source of human capital formation; (b) an incentive to harder work; and (c) a method of widening markets and thereby increasing the private inducement to invest. Although redistributive government finance can be oriented toward either policy, the latter necessarily implies a combination of taxes and expenditures that will reduce economic inequalities.

In the less advanced as in the more advanced economies, adverse incentive effects on initiative, risk-taking, and managerial efforts place limits on progressive taxation. Yet, high incomes in underdeveloped countries may, comparatively speaking, be derived from such sources and devoted to such uses that the disincentive effects are less damaging than in developed countries. The greatest damage occurs where high marginal rates bear oppressively on incomes whose source is largely in entrepreneurial effort and whose use is largely in further investment. But where land rents and interest charges are a dominant or very important source of large income and where luxury spending, speculation, and hoarding dominate the use of such funds—a combination which describes many economically underdeveloped societies—the danger of discouraging private contributions to economic development by redistributive fiscal measures is considerably lessened.[29]

Redistributive finance, then, appears to offer greater gains and involve

---

[28] For a thorough discussion of this point, see Nurkse, *op. cit.*, Ch. I, "The Size of the Market and the Inducement to Invest."

[29] Progressive taxation has, in fact, been put forward for several positive incentive uses in less advanced economies, *e.g.*, in stimulating changes in land use and land tenure. Thus, where large landholdings are held idle or are undercultivated, steeply graduated taxes on net wealth or property or land values may serve as an important stimulus to full utilization of the land. Progressive taxes on land value increments, or on capital gains, or on net income including capital gains have been used or recommended to discourage the holding of land for speculative purposes. Countries seeking to discourage accumulation or encourage subdivision of large landholdings may find graduated wealth or income taxes more attractive on this account. Steeply progressive death duties can have this effect by forcing disposal of parts of large holdings in order to meet tax liabilities at death.

less costs to underdeveloped than to developed economies. Accepting this qualitative appraisal as valid does not, of course, resolve doubts concerning the quantities involved. The contribution to economic progress through human capital formation and enlarged markets depends less on the degree of economic inequality than on the absolute amounts concentrated at or near the top of the income scale. The conspicuously large fortunes in many underdeveloped countries may offer only a limited field for redistributive finance, both because the aggregate resources they represent may be small relative to the huge numbers at the other end of the income scale and because tax administration may not be equal to its share of the task. This hardly vitiates the economic argument, but cautions against letting it carry more weight in shaping fiscal policy than the quantities involved may justify.

Turning from economic to ethical and political interests in reduced inequality, the situation is reversed: the total sums involved are much less significant than the degree of inequality. The contribution to a sense of justice depends far more on how much the gap between the top and bottom incomes is narrowed than on how much income or wealth is transferred in the process.

Similar considerations govern the contribution of redistributive finance to political stability. Development of the backward economies does little to advance the cause of freedom and stable self-government if the benefits are concentrated in the hands of the few. Instead, such concentration polarizes interests by widening and deepening the gulf between the wealthy and powerful at one extreme, the poor and the weak at the other. Fiscal policies which reduce this gap reduce the accompanying threat to political stability.

As a country's economy develops, as the lot of its people improves through a wide sharing of benefits, and as economies of scale and adequate markets are provided to improve the climate for private investment, redistributive finance offers less benefits and higher costs per unit of income redistribution. For example, the marginal productivity of investments in human beings may gradually diminish. At the same time, as social overhead investment and widening markets remove basic economic barriers to private investment, the adverse incentive effects of progressive taxes may be felt more keenly. As an instrument of economic growth and political stability, redistributive finance will become less attractive. But in the earlier stages of development, it forms an integral part of a developmental program which seeks to achieve its goals of technical progress and economic advancement without disrupting upheavals in political and social structure.

FISCAL INSTRUMENTS AND INSTITUTIONS

The emphasis in the preceding sections of this chapter has been on the distinguishing features of the economic setting and aspirations of the underdeveloped countries as they affect the tasks which their tax systems (in combination, of course, with government spending) are called upon to perform. This section inquires whether these tax systems are equal to the modern tasks of fiscal policy as they stand or can be made equal to them by transfer of techniques from the advanced countries. Again, because of the wide diversity in the tax structures and administrations of the less developed countries, each generalization in this area is subject to significant exceptions.

The tax systems of the underdeveloped economies differ most noticeably from the pattern in advanced countries in their heavy emphasis on commodity taxation and the taxation of exports and imports. The dominance of *in rem* as against personal taxes is particularly marked in Latin American countries. Reflecting in part their Spanish origins, the tax systems of these countries have traditionally relied on stamp taxes and commodity taxes. They also stressed the schedular rather than the global approach to income taxation (though several countries have in recent years superimposed a global income tax or even substituted it for the schedular tax). The net impact of this influence has been toward regressivity and retarded growth of progressive instruments of taxation. In those underdeveloped countries to which the British system has in part or in whole been exported, the tendency is to rely somewhat more heavily on income taxation as, for example, in India and Israel.

In analyses of the tax problems of underdeveloped economies, the traditional objectives of progressivity and equity in taxation, reinforced by the modern economic objectives of taxation, have pointed strongly to more aggressive use of net income and wealth taxation. Particularly before World War II, public finance missions seldom failed to urge the adoption of fuller use of net income taxes. Frequently, these recommendations seemed to reflect the ideological precepts of the technical advisers rather than an appreciation of the institutional setting of the country in which the recommendations were to be put into practice.

Fortunately, in recent years, there has been a growing sensitivity to the institutional framework within which technical assistance efforts are to be applied. There is a growing realization that conditions within which the most modern, equitable, and flexible instruments of taxation thrive do not yet prevail in many of the underdeveloped countries and that substantial modifications of the fiscal techniques applicable in developed countries are necessary to adapt them to the underdeveloped economy. To translate this point into specific terms, Richard Goode, a member of the United Nations Technical Assistance Mission to Bolivia, set forth the conditions for successful use of income taxation side by side with the conditions actually found in underdeveloped countries. Problems involved in modernizing the tax systems of underdeveloped countries are brought out so effectively in his analysis that it is quoted here at some length.[30]

1. The first condition is the existence of a predominantly money economy. The subsistence farmer cannot be satisfactorily reached by an income tax, not so much because he does not have money to pay—that may mean that

---

[30] This is an excerpt from an address by Dr. Richard Goode before the Forty-Fourth Annual Conference of the National Tax Association, 1951, and is published in the *Proceedings* of that conference, pp. 212-222.

he cannot pay a tax of any kind—as because the greater part of his real income cannot be satisfactorily assessed. Even highly skilled administrators have made little progress toward including the value of home-produced and consumed foods in the taxable income of farmers. In many underdeveloped countries these products and others obtained by barter make up a major fraction of the total real income of large segments of the population. Admittedly these groups are usually the poorest in the society, and failure to subject them to direct taxation may not be seriously objectionable from the equity point of view. It does, however, encourage use of other taxes.

2. Another condition that may not be strictly necessary but is very helpful is a high standard of literacy among taxpayers. In many underdeveloped countries the majority of the population is illiterate. For example, among the eleven Latin American republics for which data are readily available, seven have illiteracy ratios higher than 50 percent.[31] In many regions of Asia and Africa the figure is higher, as it probably also is for several Latin American countries for which data are not available. Illiteracy, like exclusion from the money economy, is most characteristic of the poorest farmers, but often wage earners, independent craftsmen, and small shopkeepers cannot read and write well enough to fill out the simplest income tax return with the guidance of printed instructions. Wage earners may be covered by withholding, but in any refined system they must be able to file claims for exemptions and refunds.

3. Prevalence of accounting records honestly and reliably maintained is another prosaic but important condition for satisfactory income taxation. In most underdeveloped countries many businessmen keep no books at all; others maintain two or more sets. Vigorous tax administration can do much to improve accounting standards if combined with an educational campaign, but more trained personnel and office equipment are essential.

4. A fourth requirement for satisfactory income taxation is a large degree of voluntary compliance on the part of taxpayers. The best administrative organization cannot satisfactorily collect income taxes from the self-employed when, as in many countries, evasion is generally attempted and incurs little or no moral disapproval from the public. The roots of a tradition of voluntary compliance with tax laws are not easy to trace, but it is fairly clear that such a spirit does not grow up over night. Although something can be done in the short run, a long period of popular education and efficient and equitable administration of those taxes that can actually be enforced seems necessary to establish firmly the habit of general voluntary acceptance of the fiscal responsibilities of citizenship. Adoption of elaborate measures that will not be uniformly applied delays improvement in taxpayer morale.

5. The political conditions for development of income taxes into a major revenue source, like the spirit of voluntary compliance, are intangible and hard to explain. The environment most favorable to progressive taxation seems to be one of free political democracy. In many underdeveloped coun-

---

[31] United Nations *Statistical Yearbook, 1949-50,* pp. 486-494. The figures are for various dates between 1930 and 1945 and refer to the population 7-10 years of age and over.

tries wealth groups have enough political power to block tax measures that they consider threats to their position. Until the popular will is stronger and more united or until the rich are ready to accept the ability-to-pay principle— whether from altruism or a sense of guilt or fear—steeply progressive taxes will not be collected.

6. Honest and efficient administration is needed for any tax, but minimum acceptable standards appear to be higher for income taxes than for many other levies. Difficult as the task of establishing a satisfactory administration may be, it is probably the condition for successful income taxation that can be met most quickly. The expert, nevertheless, must guard against the assumption that a tidy organization chart and nonpolitical staffing assure good administration. Nor can he be confident that the best obtainable administration will eliminate obstacles to heavy reliance on income taxes. . . .

ALBERT O. HIRSCHMAN

||||||||||||||||||||||||||||||||||||||||||||||||||||||||||||||||||||||||||||||||||||||||||||||||||||||||||||||||||||||||||||||||||||||||

Economic Policy in Underdeveloped Countries

Little attention appears to have been given by economists and other social scientists to any analysis, systematic or casual, of the behavior of governments of underdeveloped countries as revealed by their economic policy decisions over a period of time. Nevertheless, in view of the considerable role played today by governments in the development process, it is clear that governmental behavior should be subjected to just as close scrutiny as is being given to the motivations and conduct of entrepreneurs.

In fact, in the absence of more knowledge about probably actions and reactions of governments, our best-intentioned technical assistance efforts are liable to fail. This conclusion is inescapable to anyone who has been watching the economists and other social science "experts" who are sent on foreign assignments. At the outset of their mission, they are likely to think that the principal problem they are going to be confronted with will be that of determining what *ought* to be done, *e.g.,* in what sector the principal investment effort should be undertaken, and what monetary, fiscal, and foreign-exchange policies should be adopted. But soon they realize that they have little trouble in deciding *what* to do or rather what to advise to do, while by far the largest

From *Economic Development and Cultural Change* (July 1957), pp. 362-370, with omissions. Reprinted by permission of the University of Chicago Press and the author.

portion of their time is devoted to energy-consuming and often frustrating efforts to put their ideas and proposals across.

Let me say that my remarks apply primarily to the important group of underdeveloped countries whose economies have already registered important advances. In such countries, a few obviously useful investment projects are always at hand; some monetary and fiscal reforms usually cry out to be taken; certain changes in the institutional and administrative structure would no doubt further stimulate development. The story of a technical assistance mission is then the story of its successes and failures in having these projects, reforms, and changes firmly adopted. The huge difficulties of this task are not always properly appreciated, partly, I suspect, because, in order to do so, one must catch the experts themselves during their unguarded moments rather than rely on their reports to headquarters; and partly, because the whole tale here is in terms of personalities and of human passions, frailties, and frustrations which the experts, once they are "back home," are liable to forget as easily and completely as physical pain. And if they reminisce, it seems to them that they were facing fortuitous circumstances which do not lend themselves to any kind of generalized analysis.

Here they could be mistaken. After all, underdeveloped countries and their governments may find themselves typically in situations which make likely the adoption of seemingly irrational economic policies. It is also conceivable that the emergence of oscillations and even of inconsistencies in such policies could be predicted with a fair degree of accuracy from a knowledge of their economic structure and problems.

An analysis that would deal with these probabilities would permit the economic adviser to gain some understanding of the economic policies—good or bad—and of the resistance that he and his proposals are likely to encounter. Not only would it thereby contribute to his mental health—by saving him from unnecessary exasperation—but it might make him into a more effective operator. Indeed, the governments may also profit from knowing more about themselves. In the following I shall attempt to give some examples of this kind of analysis from selected areas of economic policy making.

ATTITUDES TOWARD NATIONAL DEVELOPMENT PROGRAMING

There is no field of economic policy in underdeveloped countries that stands as much in the limelight as the programing of economic development. To have a five-year plan for economic development has become a matter of prestige, second only to the importance of having a first-class international airport near the capital. In this, as in many other respects, governments are more powerfully subject to the "demonstration effect" than individuals for the simple reason that communications between governments are far more developed than between citizens of different countries.

The reasons for which the adoption of development plans has proven so attractive, are well-known: the plan or program is a concrete expression of the universal aspiration toward better living standards and the elaboration and adoption of such a program is a source of considerable popularity for any government; on various occasions, countries have found that the possession of a development program was an essential condition for being considered eligible for foreign assistance, or at least was helpful in connection with the application for such assistance; similarly, the existence of a program makes it easier for a government to secure additional *domestic* financing through taxation or other measures which by themselves would encounter considerable opposition; finally, a development program is a convenient device for the national government in dealing with the many requests for financial aid to which it is constantly subjected from its own agencies. It seems so much more convincing to tell the visiting mayor of a provincial town who comes to lobby for an aqueduct that no provision for this project is made in this year's portion of the five-year plan than simply to plead old-fashioned lack of funds, which in any event is an unsatisfactory explanation when aqueducts are being built at the same time for several other towns.

The development program is therefore a convenient restraint on the central government which permits it to push through high-priority projects without being side-tracked. This function of a development program is usually not the principal motive for adopting it in the first place, but the realization of its usefulness becomes often a major reason for continuing the experience. On the other hand, this very freedom-of-choice-limiting property of development programs can be felt as excessive and then results in the frequently observed spectacle of a government acting in contradiction to the course of action which it had laid down for itself.

Sometimes such behavior reflects nothing but the inherent impatience of most governments of underdeveloped countries with any kind of limitation of their powers, whether such limitation is inflicted from the outside or is self-imposed, and whether or not it is rational. But often the violation by the country of its own development program is due to the unreasonable and excessive character of the constraints laid down in the program. Governments of underdeveloped countries appear to have a tendency to subject themselves to overly rigid rules of conduct which, later on, they find themselves inevitably unable to follow. From this viewpoint, one may discern a genuine, though unexpected similarity between the orthodox and rigid monetary and banking legislations adopted in many Latin American countries in the twenties and the "integrated," long-term development programs of today. These programs often pretend to commit governments firmly to an all-embracing investment pattern in spite of the avowed weakness of our knowledge about appropriate investment criteria and even though the character and reality content of the estimates which make up the program differ widely from one economic sector to another.[1] If, in some sectors, the proposed spending is based only on the vaguest kind of criteria and extrapolations, then there is a good chance that

---

[1] On this point, see my "Economics and Investment Criteria—Reflections Based on Experience in Colombia," in Max F. Millikan, ed., *Investment Criteria and Economic Growth* (Cambridge, Mass., 1955; planographed).

the program figures should be radically revised once detailed engineering and economic studies have been undertaken. If it were made perfectly clear upon the publication and acceptance of a development program, which are the sectors where proposed spending results from careful screening of individual projects that are ready to be undertaken, and which are the ones where no such detailed planning has as yet been possible, then governments could change their minds about parts of the program without feeling that they are toppling the whole laboriously erected structure.

It should be added that provision for possible changes in the program should be made even with respect to those parts which have received careful attention and study as even here it is unlikely that all the alternatives have been fully considered. The distinction which we have made between sectors where planning has been sufficiently thorough to warrant full commitment by the government to the program and those where the planning is of so general a nature that the government should retain considerable freedom of action to modify the tentatively set goals as better knowledge becomes available is clearly overdrawn. The plan will ordinarily consist of a series of sectoral programs and projects which can be ranked according to the quantity and quality of expert planning that has gone into them and which should then command correspondingly decreasing degrees of allegiance on the part of the national government.

After the many experiences with national economic planning which have not been wholly successful, it might be time to recognize that governments of underdeveloped countries exhibit side by side with a "propensity to plan" a "propensity to experiment and to improvise." If this is so, is it really wise to identify the former propensity with everything that is sensible and virtuous and the latter with all that is unreasonable and sinful? Would it not be far better to proceed in accordance with the prescriptions of any elementary textbook in psychology and provide healthy and constructive outlets for both propensities? Admittedly, there is nothing more exasperating and demoralizing than the spectacle, frequently on display in underdeveloped countries, of half-finished structures in reinforced concrete which were intended to become government buildings, hospitals, stadiums, etc. While the lack of planning and the arbitrary reversal of previously taken investment decisions that are responsible for these unsightly "modern ruins" are deplorable, improvisation and experimentation must be recognized not only as irrepressible urges of governments, but also as a force which, properly directed, can be made to play a beneficial role in the development process.

For instance, even with the best of plans, governments of underdeveloped countries certainly cannot and should not give up the permanent search for new and better ways of using the country's natural resources. If the search is successful, the investment pattern laid down in any previously adopted program *ought* to be disturbed. In our planning for certain average rates of growth, we are apt to forget that these average rates were realized in the industrial countries only because some very much higher rates were achieved in some sectors, often as a result of experimentation and improvisation. In underdeveloped countries, many dynamic growth sectors remain to be discovered; many patterns of social organization conducive to economic progress remain to be identified; and much flexibility in programing economic development must be preserved to enable governments and investors to take advantage of changing trends in world markets and of the changing whims of international development capital. Here, then, is a wide area where governments can and should make the utmost use of their urge to be imaginative, unpredictable, and uncoercible. . . .

CYCLES IN FOREIGN-EXCHANGE AND FISCAL POLICY

Let us next consider briefly a closely allied area of economic policy, namely foreign-exchange rates and controls. Here a characteristic cycle may often be observed: a country with an impossibly complex multiple-rate and exchange-control structure adopts one day an excellent reform which sweeps away all the complications and sets up a unitary exchange rate, possibly incorporating into revised customs duties the protection previously resulting from some features of the abolished multiple rates. As time goes on, however, differential exchange rates and controls infiltrate again here and there. This goes on for some time until the situation is once more so chaotic that the country is ripe for another thorough exchange-rate reform.

A similar cycle can be observed with respect to fiscal policy. A common feature of the revenue structure of many underdeveloped countries is the excessive earmarking of taxes for specific expenditures, in other words the violation of the principle of budgetary unity. Every once in a while, the situation becomes so intricate and the general budget so anemic that a law is passed eliminating all earmarkings—but here also one may be sure that soon there will be backsliding into the old ways.

These gyrations in economic policy are precisely what seems so discouraging to observers or advising experts who do not realize that there is some "method in this madness," but see only the flouting of their advice and the total inability on the part of the authorities to adhere to a once elected course of action. Since the kind of policy-making we have described requires frequent disregard for principles that were just recently proclaimed as inviolate, it attracts persons who do not have any qualms about such disregard. In this way, the optical illusion is created that the frequent turn-abouts in economic policy are due to the fact that a capricious minister is in power when in actual fact the more pertinent causation may work the other way around. Unsavory jobs are usually handled by unsavory individuals. But if society wants these jobs to be done, it is surely wrong to focus on the individuals and to hold them uniquely responsible.

The tendencies that are disruptive of unitary exchange-rate systems and of the unity principle in budgeting are directly related to the economic structure and problems of underdeveloped countries. For instance, special incentive export rates are bound to be tried from time to time in countries which feel that they rely too heavily on one or two commodities for their export earnings. Earlier in this paper, we have already presented one argument favoring special import prohibitions, or special exchange rates designed to deter certain imports. In case domestic inflationary pressures dictate a devaluation, it may also become necessary to grant temporary privileged status to some imports. Consider, for instance, equipment imports on the part of public utilities which are undertaking important expansion projects. Privileged exchange-rate treatment for such imports may become a desirable offset to the handicap resulting for public utilities from the usual lag of their rates behind rises in the general price level.

In public finance the special earmarking of tax revenues is usually associated with the expansion of the government's activities. As a new field for governmental responsibility, say low-cost housing, is recognized, a new source of revenue must be discovered. It is only natural that at first the expenditure and the revenue which finances it, are coupled together. In this way the new fiscal device becomes far more acceptable to public opinion which always suspects "waste" in the expenditure of general treasury funds.

The conclusion I draw from this is not that to understand everything is to forgive everything. But I do think that to understand some of these real problems under which policy makers of underdeveloped countries labor will help in making our technical assistance more constructive. For instance, the preceding reasoning would seem to indicate that we should avoid those Fundamental Reforms accompanied by solemn declarations of principle and resounding commitments "never to do it again." In any reform, it would seem far wiser to circumscribe and to regulate such practices as multiple exchange rates and earmarking of fiscal revenues than to prohibit them outright.

CYCLES IN THE ADMINISTRATION OF ECONOMIC DEVELOPMENT

Cycles in economic policy such as the ones we have just described with regard to exchange rates and fiscal policy are paralleled in the administration of economic development. They are particularly disturbing as, under the best of circumstances, public administration presents many deficiencies in underdeveloped countries. On the other hand, policy changes in this area are perhaps more easily condoned by the foreign observer, as all governments seem to experience considerable difficulties in creating a workable and durable administrative structure for the exercise of new functions in the economic field. For here lies the origin of the trouble: a government decides that it should undertake a new function or carry on an existing one much more effectively than heretofore. It finds that for this purpose administrative procedures prevailing within the government itself are too cumbersome and slow; that salaries are too low to attract the kind of talent one wants to secure; and, most important usually, that political pressure ought to be removed from the scene. As a result of all these cogent reasons, a new Institute, Corporation, Bank, or Agency, with semi-autonomous status, is created and starts on its career accompanied by many high hopes on the part of its founders and the general public.

One trouble with this solution is that the government of a developing country is liable to encounter one economic function after the other that ought to be newly undertaken or that must be carried out more efficiently. Thus the semi-autonomous Institutes soon begin to mushroom until one day a new Cabinet comes in, the economic ministers find that the existence of these Institutes—to which many important taxes are assigned—make budgetary and economic planning practically impossible, and that it sharply curtails their own power to the full exercise of which they were hopefully looking forward. The result is that a thorough reorganization is decided upon which places all the new agencies right back into the government and under the ministries.

The likelihood of such a development is enhanced by the fact that the presidents, directors, or managers of the Institutes are usually quite high-powered individuals at the start, but are soon replaced by others of lower standing, whereas no such process of progressive downgrading applies to the holders of ministerial jobs. Moreover, the autonomous Institutes do not fare so well if the governments take too seriously their autonomous status, for then they lack the political and financial support which they vitally need for their success. Finally, there exists a well-known and time-honored propensity in many underdeveloped countries to "solve" serious economic problems by means of legislation alone. This practice has often blocked real progress. Today many governments are apparently under the similar and similarly dangerous illusion that they actually solve a problem by setting up an Institute to which they delegate the task of solving the problem.

The preceding remarks are not meant to deny that the new tasks which governments need to undertake will often require institutional innovations. But they may be taken as a warning against advocating too freely the "autonomous institute free of political interference" as *the* solution. What is needed, besides a very few institutes of this kind, is primarily a reorganization of the economic ministries which would enable them to carry out some of the new functions efficiently through their own subdivisions, or through institutes closely integrated with them.

CONCLUSION

We have noted here some salient examples of the apparently inherent instability of economic policy in underdeveloped countries. While the specific causes of this kind of instability are different in each case, a few general remarks may be in order by way of conclusion.

In the first place, we must understand this instability as the reflection of some very general characteristics of underdeveloped countries. After all, their political structures themselves are unstable and ill-defined, the legitimacy of their governments is often in doubt, and in general the powers of the state fail to be clearly bounded by custom or observed constitutional law.

Secondly, there is the desire to experiment and to manipulate. Anxious to use their newly won sovereignty to the full, confident that the basic potential of their economies leaves them some latitude for making mistakes, governments of underdeveloped countries are powerfully attracted by new gadgets in economic policy making. Just as they have made the transition from mule to airplane in one generation, so they pass easily from the complete absence of monetary controls to the imposition of complicated differential reserve requirements. In economic policy, however, the meaning of progress is not nearly as clear as in technology. There are many more possibilities of going too far and too fast and, unlike technical progress, policy is typically reversible. If it is reversed too often, demoralization results, not only among the foreign advisers, but—and this is far more serious—among the country's policy-makers and the general public. An impression of unpredictability and of lack of purpose is created which may even be damaging to economic progress itself. A rift develops between the business community which acquires the feeling that it is the only real creator of wealth in the country and the government with its bungling and erratic policies.

Much is therefore to be said for trying to make governmental policies more stable. Our analysis has shown that this aim cannot be achieved by once-and-for-all Reforms or Programs. Underdeveloped countries will not tolerate any straitjackets. The money doctor who prescribes a uniform financial diet or the economic advisor who lays down a rigid investment pattern may be obeyed for a while, but soon he becomes a father image that must be destroyed. Account must be taken of the propensity to change and to experiment so that, when it is indulged in, it does not come as a revolt against intolerable restraints but as an action that is foreseen as well as regulated. Economic policy in underdeveloped countries will then continue to fluctuate, but the limits of these fluctuations should gradually become narrower and the oscillation between those limits slower, as experiences with diverse policies are assimilated.

For economic policy in underdeveloped countries to become more stable, two conditions must therefore be fulfilled: first the institutional framework must be elastic and must regulate change rather than proscribe it; and second, home-grown experience must be accumulated, and made to yield a body of home-tested principles. As economists we can contribute importantly to this process: we can help underdeveloped countries to understand themselves and their experiences.

Conclusion

III

Is Economic Growth Desirable?

Like everything else, economic growth has its costs. If economic growth could be achieved without any disadvantages, everybody would be wholly in its favor. But since growth has real disadvantages, people differ in their attitude to growth according to the different assessment which they give to its advantages and disadvantages. They may dislike the kind of society which is associated with economic growth, preferring the attitudes and institutions which prevail in stable societies. Or, even if they are reconciled to the institutions of growing societies, they may dislike the transitional processes in the course of which stable societies are converted into growing societies; they may therefore conclude either that the benefits of growth are not worth the cost of the disturbance it involves, or also that growth should be introduced slowly, so that the society may have as long as possible to adjust itself to the changes which economic growth requires. We shall begin with the advantages of growth, and then consider the costs of growth in terms of the attitudes it requires, and in terms of the disturbances involved in the process of transition.

THE BENEFITS OF ECONOMIC GROWTH

The advantage of economic growth is not that wealth increases happiness, but that it increases the range of human choice. It is very hard to correlate wealth and happiness. Happiness results from the way one looks at life, taking it as it comes, dwelling on the pleasant rather than the unpleasant, and living without fear of what the future may bring. Wealth would increase happiness if it increased resources more than it increased wants, but it does not necessarily do this, and there is no evidence that the rich are happier than the poor, or that individuals grow happier as their incomes increase. Wealth decreases happiness if in the acquisition of wealth one ceases to take life as it comes, and worries more about resources and the future. There is, indeed, some evidence that this is the case; in so far as economic growth results from alertness in seeking out and seizing economic opportunities, it is only to be expected that it should be associated with less happiness than we find in societies where people are not so concerned with growth. There is evidence of much greater

From *The Theory of Economic Growth* (Homewood, Ill.: Richard D. Irwin, Inc., 1955), pp. 420-435. Reprinted by permission of the publisher and the author.

mental disturbance in the United States of America than there is in other countries, and, even when allowance is made for differences in statistical reporting, it is at least plausible that the higher suicide rate is causally connected with the drive for greater success in an already rich community. We certainly cannot say that an increase in wealth makes people happier. We cannot say, either, that an increase in wealth makes people less happy, and even if we could say this, it would not be a decisive argument against economic growth, since happiness is not the only good thing in life. We do not know what the purpose of life is, but if it were happiness, then evolution could just as well have stopped a long time ago, since there is no reason to believe that men are happier than pigs, or than fishes. What distinguishes men from pigs is that men have greater control over their environment; not that they are more happy. And on this test, economic growth is greatly to be desired.

The case for economic growth is that it gives man greater control over his environment, and thereby increases his freedom.

We can see this first in man's relations with nature. At primitive levels, man has to struggle for subsistence. With great drudgery he succeeds in wresting from the soil barely enough to keep himself alive. Every year he passes through a starvation period for several months, because the year's crop barely lasts out until the next harvest. Regularly he is visited by famine, plague, or pestilence. Half his children die before reaching the age of ten, and at forty his wife is wrinkled and old. Economic growth enables him to escape from this servitude. Improved techniques yield more abundant and more varied food for less labor. Famine is banished, the infant mortality rate falls from 300 to 30 per thousand; the death rate from 40 to 10 per thousand. Cholera, smallpox, malaria, hookworm, yellow fever, plague, leprosy, and tuberculosis disappear altogether. Thus life itself is freed from some of nature's menaces. Not everybody considers this a gain. If you think that it is better to die than to live, and best not to be born, you are not impressed by the fact that economic growth permits a reduction of death rates. But most of us are still primitive enough to take it as axiomatic that life is better than death.

Economic growth also gives us freedom to choose greater leisure. In the primitive state we have to work extremely hard merely to keep alive. With economic growth we can choose to have more leisure or more goods, and we do indeed choose to have more of both. The opposite impression is created if a comparison is made between impoverished agricultural countries and rich industrial countries, since in the former labor is idle through much of the year, when the weather is unfavorable to agriculture, whereas in the latter men work regularly throughout the year; but this is a false comparison. If we compare not industry with agriculture, but the industrial sector in rich with the industrial sector in poor countries, and similarly the agricultural sector in both countries, we shall find almost invariably shorter hours of work in each sector, as income grows; and also less drudgery, with increased use of mechanical power.

Also, it is economic growth which permits us to have more services, as well as more goods or leisure. In the poorest communities 60 or 70 percent of the people are needed in agriculture to procure food; whereas in the richest countries 12 to 15 percent suffice to give a standard of nutrition twice as good. The richer countries can therefore spare more people for other activities—to be doctors, nurses, and dentists; to be teachers; to be actors and entertainers; to be artists or musicians. Many of the "higher" activities which philosophers value—art, music, the study of philosophy itself—are in a sense a luxury which society can afford to develop only as economic growth permits it to spare increasing numbers from the basic task of growing food. It is true that only a relatively small surplus is needed to support the arts, and that some of the highest artistic achievements date back to societies where the masses of the people were very poor. The raising of living standards over the past century has widened the opportunity to appreciate and practice the arts, without necessarily affecting the quality or quantity of the best art one way or the other. However, leaving aside the highest art, there has without doubt been an enormous increase in popular leisure and the popular opportunities for enjoying what were previously the luxuries open to very few. Relatively far more people hear the work of the best composers today than heard the work of Mozart or of Bach in their own times, or saw the work of Rembrandt or of El Greco.

Women benefit from these changes even more than men. In most under-developed countries woman is a drudge, doing in the household tasks which in more advanced societies are done by mechanical power—grinding grain for hours, walking miles to fetch pails of water, and so on. Economic growth transfers these and many other tasks—spinning and weaving, teaching children, minding the sick—to external establishments, where they are done with greater specialization and greater capital, and with all the advantages of large-scale production. In the process woman gains freedom from drudgery, is emancipated from the seclusion of the household, and gains at last the chance to be a full human being, exercising her mind and her talents in the same way as men. It is open to men to debate whether economic progress is good for men or not, but for women to debate the desirability of economic growth is to debate whether women should have the chance to cease to be beasts of burden, and to join the human race.

Economic growth also permits mankind to indulge in the luxury of greater humanitarianism. For instance, at the lowest levels of subsistence there is little to spare for those who cannot help themselves, and the weakest must go to the wall. It is only as the surplus increases that men take increasing care of the leper, the mentally deranged, the crippled, the blind, and other victims of chance. The desire to care for the sick, the incompetent, the unlucky, the widow, and the orphan is not necessarily greater in civilized than in primitive societies, but the former have more means to spare for the purpose, and therefore do in fact display greater humanitarianism. Some people are disturbed by this; they think that it is against the eugenic interest of society to maintain persons who are not able to keep up in a competitive struggle, and they consider that the long-run effect will be to reduce biological vigor unless such persons are sterilized. But these are as yet in a minority.

Economic growth may be particularly important to societies where political aspirations are currently in excess of resources, since growth may forestall what might otherwise prove to be unbearable social tension. For example, in some countries, such as Great Britain, the working classes or their spokesmen are demanding ever larger wage-packets, and ever increasing expenditure on housing, education, health, and other amenities. If in such societies income per head is stable, the desires of one group can be met only at the expense of other groups, and this is bound to lead to civil strife. In these democratic days, most countries of the world are passing through a phase where bitter civil strife is inevitable unless there is a rapid increase in production per head, so that resources are brought nearer to aspirations. This is the aspect of economic growth which impresses itself most upon statesmen, so it is not surprising that democratic statesmen are everywhere very much convinced of the urgency of stimulating rapid economic growth. At the same time it must be admitted that economic growth does not always diminish strife. It may on the contrary have the effect of disturbing relatively stable social relationships, of stimulating envy and desire, and of precipitating class, racial, or religious conflict. This is related to the proposition that economic growth does not necessarily increase happiness. Neither does it necessarily increase political freedom. It increases the opportunity for dictators to control men's minds, through mass communication, and men's bodies, through highly organized police services. So it is not possible to argue that economic growth necessarily improves political relations.

Another aspect of the disproportion between aspirations and resources is to be seen in the political attitudes of countries of low international status. Peoples now in colonial status are anxious to become independent. Independent nations, numerous in population but poor in income, are anxious to have a higher status in the counsels of the nations. Rightly or wrongly such peoples think that if they were richer, and especially if they were rich enough to have powerful armed forces, they would count for more in international affairs, and there would be more respect for their nationals and for their way of life. There are some nationalists whose reaction to the modern world is to turn away from it, and to urge their people to return to the old ways of life. But most of the nationalists who have acquired power believe that it is necessary to have rapid economic growth. Many people believe that great differences between countries in wealth or economic development provoke war, and that the world would be nearer to peace if there were not wide disparities in standards of living. This is a very doubtful proposition, since societies which are undergoing rapid economic growth are often tempted to fall upon their neighbors. In any case, the causes of war are so numerous, and so indirectly related to economic considerations that it hardly helps to discuss the case for economic growth in terms of possible effects on peace or war.

It is sometimes argued that any expectation that all the nations of the world can raise their standards of living continuously must be illusory, since the effect would be only to exhaust rapidly the world's accumulated stocks of minerals and of fuel. This argument rests upon two uncertain assumptions. First it presumes that human ingenuity must in due course fail to find new substitutes for what is used up, an assumption which is rendered increasingly doubtful by what we are learning about the nature of the atom, and about the transformation of one element into another. And secondly it assumes that future generations have an equal claim to the world's resources. Why should we stay poor so that the life of the human race may in some centuries to come be extended for a further century or so? Is there not as good a case for the present generations to make the best of the resources they find, and to leave the distant centuries to look after themselves? Even if these questions are answered negatively, there remains the further point that it is not the poorest nations of the world who are using up the minerals and fuel rapidly, but the richest. If the argument has validity it may be taken as a counsel to Europe and to North America to stop raising their standards of living any further, but it is much less forceful as counsel to Asians and Africans, whose current draft on accumulated reserves is so small, to continue in their present poverty.

THE ACQUISITIVE SOCIETY

If the benefits listed above were available without cost, nearly everyone would favor them. Many people, however, consider that the attitudes and institutions which are necessary for economic growth are undesirable in themselves; they prefer the attitudes and institutions which belong to stable societies.

In the first place, they dislike the economizing spirit, which is one of the conditions of economic growth. If other things are equal, growth is most rapid in those societies where people give their minds to seeking out and seizing opportunities of economic gain, whether by means of increasing earnings, or by means of reducing costs. And this propensity to economize, though it might equally well spring solely from a desire to reduce drudgery and increase the leisure available for enjoyment or for spiritual pursuits, seems in practice not to be well developed except when it is associated with a desire for wealth, either for its own sake, or for the social prestige or the power over people which it brings. It is arguable that economy is a virtue, in the sense that there is the same sacred duty imposed upon man to abhor waste and to make the best use of his resources as there is to abhor murder and to look after the widows and orphans—in fact the parable of the talents says that this is so. Not everyone agrees that we have a sacred duty to fuss and bother about resources, or about fleeting time; these would say that economy costs too much in nervous energy and human happiness, and is rather a vice than a virtue. They might admit a duty to economize or work enough to reach some minimum standard of living, necessary for health and comfort (a dubious concept) but would argue that economy beyond this level is not worth the effort. Moreover, even those who accept economy to be a virtue may nevertheless deplore the fact (if it is a fact) that this virtue is found only in association with the vice (if it is a vice) of materialism. It is possible to desire that children should be taught to make the best use of the resources and opportunities available to them (the virtue of economy), and at the same time not to want more than they already have (to avoid the vice of cupidity). If this were done, and if the teaching were effective, there would still be economic growth; only, instead of its showing itself in ever-rising material standards of living, it would show itself in ever increasing leisure at constant material standards; and if this leisure were not to result also in the ever-increasing vice of idleness (if this is a vice), children would have also to be taught to use their leisure in ways which resulted neither in idleness nor in the production of economic goods and services. We cannot, in practice, get very far by pursuing lines of enquiry which depend on assuming human nature to be other than it is. Man likes to have more wealth, likes to economize, and likes to be idle. None of these desires seems to be intrinsically either virtuous or vicious, but any one of them pursued to its extreme, in disregard of other duties, obligations, or rights results in unbalanced personalities and also in harm to other persons. It is just as much possible for a society to be "not materialistic enough," as it is for it to be "too materialistic." Or, to put the matter the other way round, economic growth is desirable, but we can certainly have too much of it (more than is good for spiritual or social health) just as well as we may have too little of it.

Exactly the same comment can be made in relation to individualism, which is the second score on which economic growth is attacked. It seems to be the case that economic growth is more likely if individuals attend primarily to their own interests and those of their more immediate relations than if they are bound by a much wider net of social obligations. This is why economic growth is associated, both as cause and as effect, with the disappearance of extended family and joint family systems; with the erosion of social systems based on status (slavery, serfdom, caste, age, family, race) and their substitution by systems based upon contract and upon equality of opportunity; with a high level of vertical social mobility; and with the decline of tribal bonds, and the reduced recognition generally of the claims of social groups. This is another problem which cannot be solved by making a virtue of one side of the argument and a vice of the other. There are some rights which all individuals ought to have, and which should be protected against all social claims; and at the same time every individual belongs to a group, or whole series of groups, whose existence is necessary to his own social health, and whose continuance depends upon his recognizing the claims of the group and loyally accepting its authority. The growth of individualism in the past five hundred years has had its evil side, but it has also been a valuable and liberating influence. Economic growth cannot therefore be attacked for being associated with individualism as if the only good things in human relations were tribalism, social status, extended family relations, and political authoritarianism.

A third line of attack upon economic growth derives from its association with reliance on reason. Economic growth depends upon improving technology, and this in turn is greatest where men have a reasoning attitude both toward nature and also toward social relations. Now the reasoning mind is suspect, either because it is believed to result in religious agnosticism or in atheism, or also because it is considered incompatible with the acceptance of authority. As for religious belief, it is an open question whether decline of belief in God or gods is to be blamed for the evils of our time, or even whether the evils of our time are greater than those of previous ages in which religious belief was commoner. But, in any case, it is not true that belief in the importance of reason is inconsistent with belief in God. The existence of God cannot be proved or disproved by rational means, so there is no reason whatsoever why the most rational of men should not also believe in the existence of God. Reason erodes not religion but authority, and it is only in so far as religion is based upon authority that the reasoning mind is hostile to religion. But in this sense the reasoning mind is just as hostile to science as it is to religion; for it is hostile to any attempt to claim that current doctrine is not open to re-examination from the roots upward, or that only the initiated have the right to question its validity. Here again, however, as with materialism and with individualism, so also with reason; truth is not to be found by identifying virtue with one only of two opposites. For, just as materialism and spirituality are both desirable, so also society needs to have both reason and authority. The good life is founded in weaving a pattern of opposite principles, not in rejecting some and using only the others.

A fourth line of attack is pursued by those who do not like the growth of scale which is associated with economic growth. The economies of scale show themselves in the first instance, in the division of labor and in the use of machinery. This is disliked by some who dislike machine-made goods and who prefer the products of the skilled handicraftsman. Economic growth destroys old handicraft skills, and though it creates even more new skills, machine skills and others (for specialization greatly increases the range of skills), there are many people who regret the passing of the old skills and the old craft products, and who find no consolation either in the growth of the new skills or in the multiplication and cheapening of output which mass production makes possible. The principle of specialization is itself attacked, for specialization results in people having to do the same thing over and over again and this, whether it be turning nuts on bolts, or packing chocolates into boxes, or repeating the same university lecture, or practicing musical scales, or taking out appendixes, is necessarily boring, until one gets so used to one's job that one can do it without giving the whole of one's mind to it.

The economies of scale show themselves also in the growth of the size of the administrative unit. Thus businesses, units of governments, and other organizations grow in scale. In the process, men are separated from the ownership of their tools, and are proletarianized. Large-scale organization brings with it also peculiar social tensions; such organizations have to be run on hierarchical lines, which means that a few command while the majority obey, however much one may seek to democratize the process; these organizations have also to find some means of distributing work and reward which is at the same time efficient and accepted as just. We have not yet succeeded in learning how to run large scale organizations without creating unrest, and many people therefore think that we would be better off without them.

Large-scale organizations are also disliked because of the discipline they impose; day after day men must rise at the same hour, arrive at their place of work at the same hour, do much the same things, and return home at the same time. Some think that this makes life drab and monotonous, and reduces human beings to the mechanical role of cogs in some vast wheel. They would prefer that men should not be tied to the clock, and should have greater free- dom of choice from day to day, though it is by no means clear either that the man who works in the one-man business is less a slave of the clock, or that having regular habits is something to be deplored.

The economies of large-scale organization also result in the growth of towns, especially when this is associated with growing real income per head, which increases the demand for manufactured products and for services rela- tively to the demand for agricultural products. In so far as the revolt against large towns is associated with a preference for agricultural occupations, it is really a revolt against technological progress. For it is technological progress which enables a country to produce with 15 percent of its population enough food to feed the whole, and if we are to return to the days when 70 percent of the people were needed upon the land either we must abandon all that agri- cultural science has taught us, or else we must reduce hours of work to about ten a week. It is technological progress in agriculture which results in the growth of urban occupations, but it is the economies of large-scale organiza- tion which result in these urban occupations being concentrated in ever larger towns. That this is undesirable is by no means clear. The majority of people, when given the chance of working in the town or in the village, choose the town—this is why towns grow at the expense of villages; only a minority prefer the village to the town, and many of those who denounce the town are in fact careful to avoid living in villages. If towns are thrown up in a great hurry, without proper planning or control, they can indeed be slummy, drab, ugly, and unhealthy; but in these days there is no reason why new towns (or even old ones for that matter) should not be as beautiful, gracious, healthy, and inspiring as any village, as well as providing far wider opportunities for exercising body, mind, and soul than any village could ever hope to offer.

Finally, economic growth may be deplored in so far as it is dependent upon inequality of income. That this dependence exists cannot be denied since growth would be small or negative if differential awards were not available for hard work, for conscientious work, for skill, for responsibility, and for initiative. It is arguable in any given situation whether the existing differentials are too great or too small, in the restricted sense of being greater or less than is required to achieve the desired rate of economic growth. But it is not arguable, as the rulers of the USSR soon discovered, that significant economic growth could be achieved even if there were no differentials at all. Now, part of the revolt against economic growth on this score is no more than an argu- ment that in some particular place or time the differentials existing are greater than are necessary for the achieved level of growth, and are due to faulty social organization. To this extent the argument simply becomes one of alter- ing social institutions (inheritance of property, ownership of land, taxation, educational opportunities, etc.) in ways which alter the distribution of income or of property without reducing the rate of economic growth. But there are also situations where the degree of differentiation which economic growth demands is not acceptable even when it is fully admitted that smaller differentiation would reduce growth—for example, situations where foreign teachers or technicians cannot be had except at salaries which are high by local standards, or where pioneering foreign or domestic entrepreneurs are unwilling to initiate developments unless they are allowed the chance to make and keep profits at a rate far in excess of what is locally thought to be "reasonable." The economic test in such matters is that of supply and demand: "reasonable" differentials are those salaries or profits which are objectively necessary in the situation to secure the required supply of skill or initiative. But what is "reasonable" on this test may well be "unreasonable" by some other standard of merit or social justice.

Three conclusions follow from this analysis. First, some of the alleged costs of economic growth are not necessary consequences of growth at all—the ugliness of towns or the impoverishment of the working classes, for instance. Secondly, some of the alleged evils are not in fact intrinsically evil—the growth of individualism, or of reasoning, or of towns, for example. As in all human life, such things can be taken to excess, but they are not intrinsically any less desirable than their opposites. From this it follows, however, thirdly, that the rate of economic growth can be too high for the health of society. Economic growth is only one good thing among many, and we can take it to excess. Excessive growth may result in, or be the result of, excessive materialism, excessive individualism, excessive mobility of population, excessive inequality of income, or the like. Societies are not necessarily wise to choose to speed up their rate of growth above its current level; if they do, they will enjoy substantial benefits but they may also incur substantial costs, in social or in spiritual terms, and whether the potential gains exceed the potential losses must be assessed separately in each situation as best we may. It is because economic growth has both its gains and its losses that we are all almost without exception ambivalent in our attitudes towards economic growth. We demand the abolition of poverty, illiteracy, and disease, but we cling desperately to the beliefs, habits, and social arrangements which we like, even when these are the very cause of the poverty which we deplore.

PROBLEMS OF TRANSITION

Special problems arise when it is a matter of introducing economic growth into societies which have existed for some centuries at low levels more or less of economic stagnation. For it is then necessary to transform beliefs, habits, and institutions, and though in due course when the new beliefs, habits, and institutions have been going for some time, and have become firmly rooted, a new dynamic equilibrium may be reached which is in every sense superior to the old static social equilibrium, nevertheless the transition may produce temporary but very painful situations.

One of the more obvious of these is changing peoples' habits of work. For example, suppose that copper is discovered in a very primitive country where all the people have land of their own which enables them to live to their own satisfaction, though at very low levels of health, of material standards, or of culture. These people do not want to work in copper mines, and it may be that they will not voluntarily accept employment at any wage which would make it remunerative to work the mines. On the other hand, it is also possible that if they were forced to work in the mines the wealth they could thereby produce would make it possible to give them very much higher standards of material well-being, of health, of education, and of culture. Suppose also that if initially forced they would after a while acquire such a taste for the new kind of work, such an appreciation of their high standards, and such contempt for their previous ways of life that in due course they would be glad to work in the mines after the force was removed. Is the temporary use of force justified in these circumstances? This abstract example is by no means a mere academic exercise, since it is not at all dissimilar to what has happened in some parts of Africa, where the people have been forced to work in mines or on plantations, whether by orders issued through their chiefs, or because this was the only way of earning money to pay the taxes imposed on them for this purpose, or because they were driven off their lands. What actually happened in these cases is more complicated than the facts given in our abstract example, because of the additional fact that those who exercised force in these circumstances did it primarily to enrich themselves, and not because they wished to benefit the Africans. In some of these cases there is also the further fact that the Africans have not even benefited materially; on the contrary, their former villages are ruined economically, their way of life has been destroyed, while they themselves live in barracks, slums and shanty towns in material no less than in spiritual impoverishment. We have always emphasized in this enquiry that it is possible to have economic growth, in the sense of increasing output per head, without the majority of the people being any better off, because the increased output enriches only a powerful few. Most people in the world would agree that such developments are immoral, and would condemn economic policies which benefit the few at the cost of the many no matter how great the increased output that would result. This, however, is quite different from the abstract case we are examining, since it is one of the presuppositions of this case that the effect will be greatly to increase both the material and the cultural standards of the people involved, and that they themselves will in due course prefer the new way of life to the old. Faced with this example people react in different ways. Some rest their case on opposition to compulsion: however good the ultimate effects, they say, no man should be coerced for his own good, or for the good of his descendants. Others rest their case on happiness; even if the people come to prefer the new way of life to the old, they say, they are not really any better off because they are not any happier; hence they have had a painful transition to no purpose, since they have gained nothing that matters—a questionable argument, as we have already seen, since it is doubtful whether happiness is an appropriate test of change. Still others react differently, and would justify coercion if it greatly benefited the coerced. Thus, Negroes in the New World condemn the act of slavery which took them there, but in truth not all of them regret that their forefathers were not left in the jungle villages of West Africa. So also there will always be politicians and statesmen, while the world lasts, who will not hesitate to coerce their subjects for the ultimate good of the coerced.

The question of the limits of permissible force is currently very acute since it has been demonstrated by the USSR that a ruthless government can raise real output very rapidly if it is willing to deal severely with those who oppose its plans. All underdeveloped countries are being invited, by Communist or other propaganda, to yield up their liberties in return for a promise of rapid economic growth. The invitation is somewhat misleading. They are told that the loss of liberty would be temporary; that the "dictatorship of the proletariat"—or the caudillo, or the army leader, or whoever it may be—is only a transitional phase, to be followed by the "withering away" of the state; but we may well doubt whether liberties once surrendered are ever so easily regained. Neither does the invitation guarantee a rising standard of living; output may rise rapidly, but the dictator may decide to use it for purposes other than raising the standard of living of ordinary people. In any case, it is quite clear that it is not necessary to have a dictatorship in order to have economic growth. One or two democratic governments of underdeveloped countries—Burma, the Gold Coast—have shown that they have the will and the courage to find the resources which are necessary for growth, and that this can be done within the democratic framework by leaders who enjoy widespread confidence and support. It is up to other democracies to show that they can do the same.

Another painful transition is that which has to be made in social relations. The opposition of reason to authority, the movement from status to contract, and the change from social stability to vertical social mobility all upset existing relationships, whether in the matter of class, religion, political obedience, or family ties. This is clearly enough the case if the transition comes to a head in violent revolution, but even without this the transition is painful because it frustrates existing expectations and rights in every sphere. Many people are opposed to economic growth on this account. Some take the view that the old relationships are as good as the new or even better—they dislike the new freedom of family relations, the alleged "rights" of the "common man," and the destruction of the old social harmonies. Others, who do not believe that the old relationships were particularly harmonious, and who prefer the new, nevertheless question whether the difference is worth the cost. This, clearly, is an issue which can be decided only in terms of the valuation which one sets upon such matters as increased knowledge, equality of opportunity, better health standards, longer life, and the other fruits of economic growth.

Then there is the transition which has to be made in moral values. In the old society children are brought up into a code of behavior, of duties, and of loyalties. The new society has a different code. Good behavior in one society may be bad behavior in the other. The duties and loyalties shift from one set of persons and institutions to another set—from the age group to the trade union, or from the chief to an employer, or from the family to impersonal customers. In due course the new code may be established, and may work as smoothly as its predecessor, but meanwhile the community may pass through a trying time, during which the old morality has been cast off before the new has taken hold. Such transitions have been particularly painful in the past because we have not understood what was taking place. The transition is made much easier if the morality of the old society and the morality of the new society are both well known, and if those who are responsible for setting or guarding the moral standards of the community (especially the priests, the teachers, and the legislators) deliberately set out to preach the new morality, right from the beginning of the change. But, in the first place, it is only recently that we have come to understand these matters, and to appreciate in particular the extent to which moral codes are bound up with and appropriate to particular social and economic patterns. In the second place, those who guard the moral standards of the community usually consider it to be their duty to guard the old code; they are hostile to the change, and regard the new code as immoral. And thirdly, even if they were won over to the new code, much of their authority disappears in the transitional phase, because of the growth of reliance on reason, and because of the public's loss of confidence in the institutions and practices with which these guardians have hitherto been identified. Thus the new code is not introduced systematically, or authoritatively. It is picked up only gradually, and in parts. New beliefs and old beliefs mix inconsistently. And there is much frustration and bewilderment when people do what they know to be the right thing to do, and find themselves ridiculed, scolded, or punished for behaving in that way.

Painful transitions are inherent in the transformation of a society from one way of life to another; they cannot be altogether avoided except by avoiding change itself. This no one can do. The propensity to change is inherent in the nature of man. For man is essentially curious, and therefore forever accumulates knowledge, which alters his way of life. He is also prone to dissatisfaction, wanting more than he has, or moving about, or coveting his neighbor's status or possessions. He has also a sense of adventure, which makes him take chances, and a sense of rebellion, which is a constant challenge to hierarchical relations. It is therefore a waste of time to think in terms of stopping social change, and a waste of sentiment to regret that all established institutions must pass away. For social change arises just out of those parts of our nature which distinguish us from the rest of the animal kingdom.

All the same, though we cannot prevent change we can accelerate it or retard it. We have already emphasized that the rate of change can be too high, as well as too low. In the present context our problem is not the appropriate rate of growth of output, but rather the appropriate length of the period of transition from one pattern of social attitudes and institutions to another. Here there is no easy generalization; there is as good a case for getting transitions over quickly as there is for allowing plenty of time for adjustment.

In practice, we have no opportunity to choose retardation. The leaven of economic change is already working in every society—even in Tibet—thanks to the linkage of the world which has been achieved in the past eighty years by steamships, by imperialism, by airplanes, by wireless, by migration, by Hollywood, and by the printed word. There have, in particular, been two developments which make it imperative not to retard but to accelerate further growth. One of these is the fact that aspirations have grown faster than production. And the other is the fact that death rates are falling faster than birth rates.

In all the underdeveloped world aspirations now greatly exceed production, and the gap is growing. The masses of the people are beginning to believe that their poverty is unnecessary, and that it could be ended by changing their allegiances. Some few believe that it could be changed by their own individual endeavor, but many more believe that the solution lies in repudiating their landlords, or their employers, their priests, or their present political rulers. Some politicians also have great aspirations, whether it be to raise the material and cultural standards of their people, or also to raise the standing of their country in international affairs. Now a large gap between aspirations and production can be very dangerous, since it produces frustrations from which almost anything may emerge. Many people fear that the result will be "communism" (a word which no longer has any precise meaning). Some fear the spread of native breeds of "fascism" (a word which has to be interpreted to include the traditional warlordism of many Eastern countries, as well as the Latin American "caudillo"). Others again see a strong likelihood that power will pass to religious fanatics (to mullahs, Mahasabas, rabbis, and the like). It is not therefore surprising that the leaders of many underdeveloped countries give a very high priority to measures for rapidly increasing production. Whether they will have the courage, and the necessary internal and external support, to raise the necessary resources may be doubted. And it is also doubtful whether in any case aspirations will not continue to outdistance production. But those who believe that it would be wrong to speed up production because of the effects on social relations, or on moral codes, usually forget both that these are already changing rapidly, and also that the results of frustrated aspirations may be even more dangerous to existing patterns than speeding up production would be.

The population dilemma is even less escapable. Underdeveloped countries untouched by external influences seem to have stable populations, with birth and death rates both very high by current standards. Once these countries are drawn into the modern world, with the consequent eradication of local famines and introduction of public health and medical care, the death rate begins to drop rapidly, and may fall from 40 to 10 per thousand in less than two generations. It then becomes necessary to begin to increase total production by rates of one or 2 or 3 percent per annum, to keep up with rising population. Also, unless there is plenty of land available, it also becomes necessary to take steps to reduce birth rates to the same spectacular degree as death rates. This seems, however, almost certainly to require that production should grow even faster than population, since most of the explanations of the reasons why people adopt family limitation ultimately turn upon rising standards of living. In such a situation we cannot really choose to retard the growth of production; on the contrary in practically every one of the countries usually called underdeveloped the situation is that the current rate of growth of production is not adequate to permit the population problem to be tackled seriously. Again those who argue for retardation have usually overlooked what is happening to population, and have forgotten that the consequences of a population explosion may be much more damaging to existing social structures and moral codes than the consequences of any likely increase in production would be.

Selected Bibliography

Selected Bibliography

Part One. Introduction

Bauer, P. T., and B. S. Yamey, *The Economics of Underdeveloped Countries.* Cambridge, Eng., Cambridge University Press, 1957.

Buchanan, N. S., and H. S. Ellis, *Approaches to Economic Development.* New York, Twentieth Century Fund, 1955.

Higgins, B., *Economic Development.* New York, W. W. Norton & Co., 1959.

Kindleberger, C. P., *Economic Development.* New York, McGraw-Hill Book Co., 1958.

Kuznets, S., *Economic Change.* New York, W. W. Norton & Co., 1953.

————, *Six Lectures on Economic Growth.* Glencoe, Ill., The Free Press, 1959.

Lewis, W. A., *The Theory of Economic Growth.* Homewood, Ill., Richard D. Irwin, 1955.

Meier, G. M., and R. E. Baldwin, *Economic Development.* New York, John Wiley & Sons, 1957.

Villard, H. H., *Economic Development.* New York, Holt, Rinehart and Winston, 1959.

Part Two. The Advanced Countries: Theories and Models of Growth

Domar, E. D., *Essays in the Theory of Economic Growth.* New York, Oxford University Press, 1957.

Harrod, R. F., *Towards a Dynamic Economics.* London, Macmillan & Co., 1948.

Kuznets, S., "Toward a Theory of Economic Growth." In R. Lekachman (ed.), *National Policy for Economic Welfare at Home and Abroad,* New York, Doubleday & Co., 1955, pp. 12-77.

Lewis, W. A., "Unlimited Labour: Further Notes." *The Manchester School of Economics and Social Studies,* Vol. XXVI, No. 1 (January 1958), pp. 1-32.

Lowe, A., "The Classical Theory of Economic Growth." *Social Research,* Vol. 21, No. 2 (Summer 1954), pp. 127-158.

McKinley, E., "The Problem of Underdevelopment in the English Classical School." *Quarterly Journal of Economics,* Vol. LXIX, No. 2 (May 1955), pp. 235-252.

Myrdal, G., *Economic Theory and Underdeveloped Regions.* London, Gerald Duckworth & Co., 1957.

Spiegel, H. W., "Theories of Economic Development: History and Classification." *Journal of the History of Ideas,* Vol. XVI, No. 4 (October 1955), pp. 518-539.

495

Part Three.   The Underdeveloped Countries: Modern Approaches to Development

Arndt, H. W., "External Economies in Economic Growth." *Economic Record,* Vol. XXXI, No. 61 (November 1955), pp. 192-214.

Hirschman, A. O., *The Strategy of Economic Development.* New Haven, Conn., Yale University Press, 1958.

Nurkse, R., *Problems of Capital Formation in Underdeveloped Countries.* Oxford, Basil Blackwell & Mott, 1953.

Scitovsky, T., "Two Concepts of External Economies." *Journal of Political Economy,* Vol. LXII, No. 2 (April 1954), pp. 143-151.

Viner, J., *International Trade and Economic Development.* Oxford, The Clarendon Press, 1953.

Young, A., "Increasing Returns and Economic Progress." *Economic Journal,* Vol. XXXVIII, No. 152 (December 1928), pp. 527-542.

Part Four.   Characteristics of Growing Economies

Giersch, H., "Stages and Spurts of Economic Development." *International Social Science Bulletin,* Vol. VI, No. 2 (1954), pp. 198-205.

Leibenstein, H., *Economic Backwardness and Economic Growth.* New York, John Wiley & Sons, 1957. Chaps. 3, 4.

Rostow, W. W., *The Stages of Economic Growth.* Cambridge, Eng., Cambridge University Press, 1960.

———, "Take-off into Self-Sustained Growth." *Economic Journal,* Vol. LXVI, No. 261 (March 1956), pp. 25-48.

Triantis, S. G., "Economic Progress, Occupational Redistribution, and International Terms of Trade." *Economic Journal,* Vol. LXIII, No. 251 (September 1953), pp. 627-637.

Part Five.   Problems of Meaning and Measurement

Kuznets, S., "National Income and Industrial Structure." In *Economic Change,* New York, W. W. Norton & Co., 1953, pp. 145-191.

Myint, H., "An Interpretation of Economic Backwardness." *Oxford Economic Papers,* Vol. VI, No. 2 (June 1954), pp. 132-163.

Niculescu, B. M., "Underdeveloped, Backward, or Low Income?" *Economic Journal,* Vol. LXV, No. 259 (September 1955), pp. 546-548.

Nutter, G. W., "On Measuring Economic Growth." *Journal of Political Economy,* Vol. LXV, No. 1 (February 1957), pp. 51-63.

Part Six.   Land, Labor, Capital, and Entrepreneurship

Bator, F. M., "On Capital Productivity, Input Allocation and Growth." *Quarterly Journal of Economics,* Vol. LXXI, No. 1 (February 1957), pp. 86-106.

Brozen, Y., "Technological Change in Underdeveloped Areas." *Explorations in Entrepreneurial History,* Vol. 3, No. 3 (February 1951), pp. 142-160.

Bruton, H. J., "Innovation and Equilibrium Growth." *Economic Journal,* Vol. LXVI, No. 263 (September 1956), pp. 455-466.

Cairncross, A. K., "Place of Capital in Economic Progress." *International Social Science Bulletin,* Vol. VI, No. 2 (1954), pp. 232-237.

Coale, A. J., and E. M. Hoover, *Population Growth and Economic Development in Low-Income Countries.* Princeton, N. J., Princeton University Press, 1958.

Hagen, E., "Population and Economic Growth." *American Economic Review,* Vol. XLIX, No. 3 (June 1959), pp. 310-327.

Penrose, E. F., "Malthus and the Underdeveloped Areas." *Economic Journal,* Vol. LXVII, No. 266 (June 1957), pp. 219-239.

Schultz, T. W., "The Supply of Food in Relation to Economic Development." *Economic Development and Cultural Change,* Vol. I, No. 4 (December 1952), pp. 244-249.

Spengler, J. J., "Economic Factors in Economic Development." *American Economic Review,* Vol. XLVII, No. 2 (May 1957), pp. 42-56.

Part Seven. Values and Institutions

Baran, P., "On the Political Economy of Backwardness." *Manchester School of Economics and Social Studies,* Vol. XX, No. 1 (January 1952), pp. 66-84.

Belshaw, J. P., "Social and Economic Revolution for the Development of Backward Countries." *Economic Record,* Vol. XXXII, No. 63 (November 1956), pp. 319-333.

Hoselitz, B. F. (ed.), *The Progress of Underdeveloped Areas,* Harris Foundation Lectures. Chicago, University of Chicago Press, 1952.

Hoyt, E., "Want Development in Underdeveloped Areas." *Journal of Political Economy,* Vol. LIX, No. 3 (June 1951), pp. 194-202.

Levy, M., "Contrasting Factors in the Modernization of China and Japan." *Economic Development and Cultural Change,* Vol. II, No. 3 (October 1953), pp. 161-197.

Moore, W. E., *Industrialization and Labor.* Ithaca, N. Y., Cornell University Press, 1951.

Spengler, J. J., "Theories of Socio-Economic Growth." In *Problems in the Study of Economic Growth,* New York, National Bureau of Economic Research, 1959.

Tawney, R. H., *Religion and the Rise of Capitalism,* 2d ed. London, John Murray, 1937. (New York, Harcourt, Brace & World, 1947.)

Wright, D. M., "Moral, Psychological, and Political Aspects of Economic Growth." *Ekonomisk Tidskrift,* Vol. LVI, No. 3 (October 1954), pp. 173-194.

Part Eight. Policies and Plans for Development

Bloomfield, A. I., "Some Problems of Central Banking in Underdeveloped Countries." *Journal of Finance,* Vol. XII, No. 2 (May 1957), pp. 190-204.

Chenery, H. B., "The Application of Investment Criteria." *Quarterly Journal of Economics,* Vol. LXVII, No. 1 (February 1953), pp. 76-96.

Ellis, H. S., "The Financing of Economic Development in Underdeveloped Areas." *Indian Economic Journal,* Vol. III, No. 3 (January 1956), pp. 256-268.

Galenson, W., and H. Leibenstein, "Investment Criteria, Productivity and Economic Development." *Quarterly Journal of Economics,* Vol. LXIX, No. 3 (August 1955), pp. 343-370.

Hicks, U. K., "Direct Taxation and Economic Growth." *Oxford Economic Papers,* Vol. 8, No. 3 (October 1956), pp. 302-317.

Higgins, B., "Development Planning and the Economic Calculus." *Social Research,* Vol. 23, No. 1 (Spring 1956), pp. 35-56.

Kahn, A. E., "Investment Criteria in Development." *Quarterly Journal of Economics,* Vol. LXV, No. 1 (February 1951), pp. 38-61.

Kapp, K. W., "Economic Development, National Planning and Public Administration." *Kyklos,* Vol. XIII, Fasc. 2 (1960), pp. 172-204.

Mark, L., Jr., "The Favored Status of the State Entrepreneur in Economic Development Programs." *Economic Development and Cultural Change,* Vol. VII, No. 4 (July 1959), pp. 422-430.

Rogge, B., "The Role of Government in Latin American Economic Development." *Inter-American Economic Affairs,* Vol. 9, No. 3 (Winter 1955), pp. 45-66.